CREATE YOUR OWN INTEGRATED MARKETING COMMUNICATION PLAN!

THE IMC PLANPRO HANDBOOK & YOU

- A comprehensive integrated marketing communications plan
- Software guided
- Examples of IMC Plans

The IMC PlanPro Handbook package consists of a booklet and disk. The IMC PlanPro disk provides an exercise that requires you to prepare an entire marketing communications program. The booklet provides step-by-step instructions on how to use the disk and gives brief explanations of the IMC concepts that are part of the program. A chapter-by-chapter outline guides you through the software and instructs on which portions of the communication plan should be completed with the goal of having a finished IMC Plan at the end of the semester.

Integrated Advertising, Promotion, and Marketing Communications

Integrated Advertising, Promotion, and Marketing Communications

FOURTH EDITION

Kenneth E. Clow

University of Louisiana at Monroe

Donald Baack

Pittsburg State University

Prentice Hall
Upper Saddle River, New Jersey 07458

Library of Congress Cataloging-in-Publication Data

Clow, Kenneth E.
  Integrated advertising, promotion, and marketing communications/Kenneth E. Clow,
Donald Baack.—4th ed.
    p.   cm.
Includes bibliographical references and index.
ISBN 978-0-13-607942-2 (pbk. : alk. paper)
1. Communication in marketing.   2. Advertising.   I. Baack, Donald.   II. Title.
HF5415.123.C58 2010
659.1—dc22

                                                                                2008043641

Acquisitions Editor: James Heine
Editorial Director: Sally Yagan
Product Development Manager: Ashley Santora
Editorial Assistant: Karin Williams
Senior Marketing Manager: Anne Fahlgren
Marketing Assistant: Susan Osterlitz
Permissions Project Manager: Charles Morris
Senior Managing Editor: Judy Leale
Production Project Manager: Kelly Warsak
Senior Operations Specialist: Arnold Vila
Assistant Editor, Media: Denise Vaughn
Art Director: Anthony Gemmellaro
Designer: Ilze Lemesis
Cover Designer: Ilze Lemesis
Director, Image Resource Center: Melinda Patelli
Manager, Rights and Permissions: Zina Arabia
Manager, Visual Research: Beth Brenzel
Image Permission Coordinator: Ang'John Ferreri
**Manager, Cover Visual Research &
    Permissions:** Karen Sanatar
Composition: Integra Software Services
Full-Service Project Management: BookMasters, Inc.
Printer/Binder: Courier/Kendallville
Cover Printer: Lehigh-Phoenix Color
Typeface: 10.5/12 Times New Roman

Credits and acknowledgments borrowed from other sources and reproduced, with permission, in this textbook
appear on appropriate page within text.

Pearson Education Ltd., London
Pearson Education Singapore, Pte. Ltd
Pearson Education, Canada, Inc.
Pearson Education–Japan
Pearson Education Australia PTY, Limited

Pearson Education North Asia, Ltd., Hong Kong
Pearson Educación de Mexico, S.A. de C.V.
Pearson Education Malaysia, Pte. Ltd
Pearson Education Upper Saddle River,
    New Jersey

Prentice Hall
is an imprint of

www.pearsonhighered.com

10 9 8 7 6 5 4 3 2
ISBN-13: 978-0-13-607942-2
ISBN-10:   0-13-607942-3

To my sons Dallas, Wes, Tim, and Roy, who provided encouragement, and especially to my wife, Susan, whose sacrifice and love made this textbook possible.

—Kenneth E. Clow

I would like to dedicate my efforts and contributions to the book to my wife Pam; children Jessica, Daniel, and David; and grandchildren Danielle, Rile, Andy, Emilee, Jason, Damon, and Tatum.

—Donald Baack

Brief Contents

Brief Contents

Contents

PART 4

IMC PROMOTIONAL TOOLS 295

Preface

Advertising, promotions, and marketing communications are integral components of marketing. If you are a marketing major, understanding how companies can effectively communicate with customers and potential customers is the foundation needed to develop effective marketing programs. This will help you succeed in your marketing career.

If you are not a marketing major, consider all of the marketing communications around you. Any company or organization you work for will be involved in marketing its products or services. It is important to understand how the communications component of marketing is developed and why. Not only will this knowledge provide you with a better understanding of those involved in marketing in the organization where you will work, it will also provide you with better information to function as a consumer.

We created *Integrated Advertising, Promotion, and Marketing Communications,* in part, to help students understand the importance of integrating all marketing communications (IMC) and how they are produced and transmitted. When our first edition was written, almost all marketing communication textbooks focused exclusively on advertising. As you know from your everyday experiences and the courses you have taken in college, marketing is much more than that. It includes promotions such as coupons, price discounts, and contests. Marketing has expanded to blogs on the Internet, customer reviews of products, messages delivered to cell phones, and newer programs such as buzz marketing. These venues are vital ingredients in effectively reaching consumers. They must also be carefully integrated in to one clear message and voice for customers to hear.

We prepared this textbook and all of the additional materials in a way that will best help you to understand integrated marketing communications. Students need opportunities to apply concepts to real life situations. This helps them clearly understand and retain the ideas. As a result, we have prepared a variety of end-of-chapter materials that are designed to help you practice using the concepts. These materials include integrated learning exercises, critical thinking exercises, creative exercises, and cases.

INTEGRATED LEARNING PACKAGE

We have created several devices that are designed to help you learn the materials in this text, if you take advantage of them. Let's be more positive here. Advertising is an interesting and enjoyable subject and the materials have been developed to make learning interactive and fun!

- **Lead-in vignettes.** Each chapter begins with a vignette related to the presented topic. The majority of the vignettes revolve around success stories in companies most will recognize, such as Google and Levi-Strauss. In this edition, new vignettes have been introduced, including stories about PETsMART, Apple's iPhone, Dove, and Red Bull. There is a vignette devoted to Harry Potter. True, it is old news, but the vignette challenges you to think and wonder why it was such a craze and how such phenomena occur.

- **Business-to-business marketing concepts.** Many marketing and business majors are likely to hold jobs that emphasize marketing to other businesses. We include business-to-business components in many of the discussions in the text. B-to-B examples, cases, text illustrations, and Internet exercises are woven into the materials. They show how marketing communications programs differ, depending on the nature of the customer.

- **International marketing discussions.** Some of you have traveled to other countries. Most of you interact with students from other countries. Global, international business is all around. This makes understanding international marketing issues important. This book features international concerns that match the presented materials. Also, a section called "International Implications" is found at the end of every chapter.

- **Critical thinking exercises and discussion questions.** To better appreciate the materials in the text, the end-of-chapter materials are a must. They include a variety of exercises designed to help you comprehend and apply the chapter concepts. They are not simple reviews. Each requires additional thought. These exercises are designed to challenge your thinking and encourage you to dig deeper. The best way to know that you have truly learned a concept or theory is when you can apply it to a different situation. These critical thinking and discussion exercises require you to apply knowledge to a wide array of marketing situations.

- **Integrated learning exercises.** The Internet is now a fact of life. Most people use it on a daily basis. At the end of each chapter, a set of questions guides you to the Internet to access information that ties into the subject matter covered. These exercises provide an opportunity to look up various companies and organizations to see how they utilize the concepts presented in the chapter.

- **Creative corner exercises.** A new feature has been added to this edition. Most students enjoy the opportunity to use their creative abilities. As a result, we feature a new exercise called the Creative Corner, which asks you to design advertisements and other marketing-related materials. We suggest you complete these, even when they are not assigned. They are designed to help you realize that you are more creative than you might think, and to be fun. Ken Clow has taught students who said they had zero creative ability. Yet these same students were able to produce ads that won ADDY awards in student competitions sponsored by the American Advertising Federation (AAF). If you don't know anything about the AAF student competition, go the organization's Web site at **www.aaf.org**. Entering the annual competition is exciting and participating looks great on a resume.

- **Cases.** Two cases are provided at the conclusion of each chapter. They were written to help you learn by providing plausible scenarios that require thought and review of chapter materials. The short cases should help you conceptually understand chapter components and the larger, more general marketing issues.

- **Companion Website:** By visiting **www.pearsonhigher.com/clow** you can take online quizzes to help you determine whether you understand the key concepts in the chapters. You can also link to Web sites mentioned in the book and access the Building an IMC Campaign Workbook.

ACKNOWLEDGMENTS

We would like to thank the following individuals who assisted in the development of the first four editions through their careful and thoughtful reviews:

We are grateful to these reviewers for portions of the fourth edition:

John Bennett, University of Missouri–Columbia

MaryEllen Campbell, University of Montana, Missoula

Donna Falgiatore, St. Joseph's University

Deanna Mulholland, Iowa Western Community College

Jim Munz, Illinois State University

Prema Nakra, Marist College

Allen Smith, Florida Atlantic University

Amanda Walton, Indiana Business College

We are grateful to these reviewers for the third edition:

Jeffrey C. Bauer, University of Cincinnati–Clermont

MaryElllen Campbell, University of Montana, Missoula

Sherry Cook, Missouri State University

Catherine Curran, University of Massachusetts–Dartmouth

Michael A. Dickerson, George Mason University

Donna Falgiatore, St. Joseph's University

Charles S. Gulas, Wright State University

Diana Haytko, Missouri State University

Al Mattison, Unversity of California–Berkeley

Deanna Mulholland, Iowa Western Community College

Jim Munz, Illinois State University

Charlie Schwepker, University of Central Missouri

Eugene Secunda, New York University

Allen E. Smith, Florida Atlantic University

Bonni Stachowiak, Vanguard University

Rod Warnick, University of Massachusetts–Amherst

Patti Williams, Wharton Business School

We are grateful to these reviewers for the second edition:

Robert W. Armstrong, University of North Alabama

Jerome Christa, Coastal Carolina University

Stefanie Garcia, University of Central Florida

Robert J. Gulovsen, Washington University–Saint Louis

Sreedhar Kavil, St. John's University

Franklin Krohn, SUNY–Buffalo

Tom Laughon, Florida State University

William C. Lesch, University of North Dakota

James M. Maskulka, Lehigh University

Darrel D. Muehling, Washington State University

Esther S. Page-Wood, Western Michigan University

Venkatesh Shankar, University of Maryland

Albert J. Taylor, Austin Peay State University

Jerald Weaver, SUNY—Brockport

We are grateful to these reviewers of the first edition:

Craig Andrews, Marquette University

Ronald Bauerly, Western Illinois University

Mary Ellen Campbell, University of Montana

Les Carlson, Clemson University

Newell Chiesl, Indiana State University

John Cragin, Oklahoma Baptist College

J. Charlene Davis, Trinity University

Steven Edwards, Michigan State University

P. Everett Fergenson, Iona College

James Finch, University of Wisconsin–La Crosse

Thomas Jensen, University of Arkansas

Russell W. Jones, University of Central Oklahoma

Dave Kurtz, University of Arkansas

Monle Lee, Indiana University–South Bend

Ron Lennon, Barry University

Charles L. Martin, Wichita State University

Robert D. Montgomery, University of Evansville

S. Scott Nadler, University of Alabama

Ben Oumlil, University of Dayton

Melodie R. Phillips, Middle Tennessee State University

Don Roy, Middle Tennessee State University

Elise Sautter, New Mexico State University

Janice E. Taylor, Miami University

Robert L. Underwood, Bradley University

Robert Welch, California State University–Long Beach

Although there were many individuals who helped us with advertising programs, we want to thank a few who were especially helpful. We appreciate the owners and employees of advertising agencies Newcomer, Morris, and Young, and Sartor Associates for providing us with a large number of advertisements. We also appreciate the staff at the *Joplin Globe* for providing many local advertisements.

On a personal note, we would like to thank Leah Johnson, who signed us for the first edition of the book. Thank you to Ashley Santora and Sally Yagan for helping with this edition as it moved forward and to Kelly Warsak for guiding the production process. We would also like to thank the entire Prentice Hall production group.

Kenneth Clow would like to thank the University of Louisiana at Monroe for providing a supportive environment to work on this text. He is thankful to his sons Dallas, Wes, Tim, and Roy, who always provided encouragement and support.

Donald Baack would like to thank Mimi Morrison for her continued assistance in all his work at Pittsburg State University. Eric Harris has been a great help in his role as department chairperson. He helped make the workload manageable during the preparation of the manuscript. Jami Sticklan, his graduate assistant, also contributed to this work.

We would like to especially thank our wives, Susan Clow and Pam Baack, for being patient and supportive during those times when we were swamped by the work involved in completing this edition. They have been enthusiastic and understanding throughout this entire journey.

Integrated Advertising, Promotion, and Marketing Communications

PART 1

The IMC Foundation

1

Integrated Marketing Communications

RON JON SURF SHOP

Chapter Objectives

After reading this chapter, you should be able to answer the following questions:

- **What** role does communication play in marketing programs?

- **What** is the nature of the communication process?

- **How** should the communications model be applied to marketing issues?

- **What** are the characteristics of a fully integrated advertising and marketing communications approach?

- **How** does the concept of integrated marketing communications pertain to international operations?

IMC and Brand Building Go to the Beach

If there is one common denominator among beachside communities, it would be that there are plenty of surfing and swimwear shops located nearby. Most people couldn't tell you the name of any one store, unless they have visited a Ron Jon Surf Shop. Ron Jon is a prime example of how to develop and build strong brand awareness and loyalty in an industry in which mostly small, single-owner stores are located along the shorelines of beaches and lake-towns across the United States.

In the 1960s, surfboard technology was changing. Homemade wooden boards were being replaced with mass-produced fiberglass models. A surfer-dude named Ron DiMenna was frustrated that he could not buy one of these new and improved rides. As a result, he founded the first Ron Jon Surf Shop in New Jersey. In the early days, DiMenna would buy three boards and sell two with a markup that gave him the third board for "free." As time passed, the company grew, and additional locations were opened on both the East and West Coast.

The center of the Ron Jon empire is located in Cocoa Beach, Florida. At the Ron Jon Surf Shop near the beach, surfer and beach-lover figures that look like sand sculptures greet customers as they approach. Huge billboards showing images of happy and relaxed swimmers and beautiful beach enthusiasts line the top of the building. The store itself covers more than 52,000 square feet. It is filled with an amazing variety of items. Swimsuits, sunglasses, toys, surfboards, towels, shirts, and even beach-themed home decorations are available. A refreshment stand with picnic tables is located outside the store for patrons to enjoy. This Ron Jon unit is open 24 hours per day, 365 days a year—just like the beach.

One of the most memorable Ron Jon images is its logo. The company's beach-themed, fun-loving image has led loyal customers to attach Ron Jon decals carrying the logo practically everywhere, including one near the top of the Eiffel Tower and another aboard the U.S. space station. Many of the products sold in the store also display the logo.

The Ron Jon marketing team effectively utilizes advertising by creating cooperative programs with other companies. When the Cocoa Beach store celebrated its 40th anniversary, Chrysler Corporation joined in and created a limited edition Ron Jon PT Cruiser. The autos were

customized to display Ron Jon decal art on the outside. Each car came with numerous novelty items, including a Ron Jon sports bag, blankets, license plates, bumper stickers, key chains, and a T-shirt that guaranteed the car owner special bragging rights. Only 1,000 Ron Jon cars were made. One was given away as the grand prize of a local surfing event.

The 40th anniversary celebration also featured a contest in which Ron Jon memorabilia were solicited. Entrants sent in old photos, news articles, postcards, and personal stories. Each item gave the person a chance at a gift certificate for Ron Jon merchandise.

Ron Jon sponsors events that tie in with the company's primary business. This includes a natural alliance with professional surfing contests and other beachwear manufacturers, such as Billabong. In 2007, Ron John hosted an autograph-signing event in Cocoa Beach featuring renowned surfer Bruce Irons.

Awareness of Ron Jon's presence has grown through innovative marketing programs. At one point, Ron Jon Surf Shop was featured in a MasterCard commercial. Now, Ron Jon is expanding its reach to international customers. The company has received in-store visits from people all around the world. Part of the reason, according to vice president for corporate development Bill Bieberbach, is that international customers prefer name-brand items. Ron Jon is a powerful brand that reaches beach lovers in other countries.

Ron Jon has also expanded into land-based sports. In the mid-2000s, the company sponsored an "End of Summer Skateboard Contest" in Florida. Skateboarders competed for cash prizes and merchandise. Pepsi was a cosponsor of the event. Later, the two companies held autograph sessions with Globe Pro Skateboarding. These events were aimed at new, young customers who enjoy skateboarding as much as they do surfing.

Ron Jon also has launched several public relations campaigns focused on community involvement. In 2007, these events included a drive for patrons to donate blood, a beach cleanup drive, and major donations to the United Way campaign.

The company established new licensing agreements and other extensions of the Ron Jon brand. Ron Jon Surf Shop opened new store locations in Orlando, Tampa, and Miami under these agreements. Ron Jon merchandise is offered at several international airports, including Newark International Airport and the airport at Cozumel, Mexico. The brand extensions also led to the surf-themed Ron Jon Cape Caribe Resort in Cape Canaveral, Florida, Ron Jon bottled water products, and the Ron Jon Surf School by Craig Carroll in Cocoa Beach.

Ron Jon Surf Shop's future remains bright. The overall theme of fun, relaxation, and enjoyment makes the Ron Jon brand a major force in what is often a no-name marketplace.[1]

OVERVIEW

The global marketplace consists of a complex set of competitors battling for customers in a rapidly changing environment. New companies are formed on a daily basis. Small businesses, Internet-based operations, and global conglomerates that have expanded through takeovers and mergers are all part of a worldwide marketing environment.

A wide variety of media are available to the leaders of these companies. Advertising and marketing methods range from simple stand-alone billboard advertisements to complex, multilingual global Web sites. The number of ways to reach potential customers continually increases as nontraditional methods expand and become more popular.

In the face of these sophisticated and cluttered market conditions, firms try to be heard. Marketing experts know that a company's communications must speak with a clear voice. Customers must understand the essence of a business and the benefits of the firm's goods and services. With the increasing variety of advertising and promotional venues, and so many companies bombarding potential customers with messages, the task is challenging.

Three trends have emerged in this turbulent new marketing communications context (Figure 1.1). First, *accountability* is a primary focus. Advertising agencies are expected to produce tangible results. Company leaders who hire advertising agencies cannot spend unlimited dollars on marketing programs. The funds must be spent wisely. A coupon promotion, a contest, a rebate program, or an advertising campaign must yield measurable gains in sales, market share, brand awareness, or customer loyalty to be considered successful.

The push for accountability is being driven by chief executive officers (CEOs), chief financial officers (CFOs), and boards of directors who seek visible, measurable results from marketing expenditures. According to Martyn Straw, chief strategy officer of the advertising agency BBDO Worldwide, corporate executives and business owners are tired of "funneling cash into TV commercials and glossy ads" that keep increasing in cost and seem to do less and less. As a result, a company such as PepsiCo is less likely to rely on 30-second television spots. Instead, alternative communication venues are combined with special events where names, profiles, and addresses of prospective Pepsi drinkers can be collected and tracked. Straw believes that marketing has gone from being a cost or expense to an investment. Promotional dollars must add value to generate new sales and higher profits.[2]

The second new trend in advertising is tied to the first. Major changes have emerged in the *tasks performed* by all of the players in an advertising program. The first person facing new job responsibilities is the *account executive*, the person in an advertising agency who directs and oversees advertising and promotional programs for client companies. The demand for accountability places the account manager on the hot seat. He or

FIGURE 1.1
Current Trends Affecting Marketing Communications

- ◆ Accountability for measurable results
- ◆ Changes in tasks performed by key players in advertising programs
- ◆ Increased use of alternative media

she must respond to the scrutiny directed at each marketing campaign. This increased responsibility has changed the account executive's day-to-day activities. In the past, an account executive mainly served as a liaison between the people who prepared commercials and client companies. Now, the account manager may be involved in developing overall strategic communication plans while, at the same time, trying to make sure each individual promotional activity achieves tangible results.

Another person facing greater accountability is the *brand* or *product manager*, the individual who manages a specific brand or line of products for the client company. When sales of a brand slow, the brand manager looks for ways to boost them. The brand manager works diligently with the advertising agency, the trade promotion specialist, the consumer promotion specialist, and any other individual or agency involved in conveying that brand image to customers. The brand manager must be a master at organizing the activities of many individuals while integrating each marketing campaign. Every promotional effort is coordinated to make each message speak with the same voice.

Johnson & Johnson has increased use of alternative media in marketing baby products.

The final group of individuals facing new responsibilities is *creatives*, the people who develop the actual advertisements and promotional materials. Most creatives are employed by advertising agencies. Some work for individual companies; others are freelancers. In this new era where attracting attention to a company, good, or service is difficult, creatives are being asked to perform additional functions. This includes contributing ideas about the strategic marketing direction of the firm while developing individual advertisements. Creatives are also being held accountable for the effectiveness of advertising campaigns.

As a result, a new partnership among account executives, brand managers, and creatives has emerged. Most advertising and marketing agencies do more than create ads. They help the client company develop a totally integrated communications program. This trend toward a more integrated approach to advertising and communication continues.

The third new trend is the explosive development of *alternative media*. The Internet has evolved from simple Web-based advertisements to include blogs, interactive sites, and popular sites such as MySpace, Facebook, YouTube, Napster, Morpheus, and Kazaa. New handheld technologies such as iPhones and text-messaging systems have created an entirely new landscape and, in some cases, nearly a new language. As a result, companies are cutting expenditures on traditional media commericals and are moving to nontraditional or alternative media. Johnson & Johnson shifted approximately 20 percent of its marketing budget to nontraditional media for many products, including Neutrogena, Aveeno, and the flagship Johnson & Johnson baby products.[3]

Younger consumers with considerable amounts of purchasing power are less inclined to watch television. They are more likely to engage in technologically based interactions with friends around the world. The challenge becomes finding ways to reach consumers who are increasingly sophisticated at blocking out traditional advertising messages but who can be reached through new technologies. Current thinking in marketing suggests that you cannot assume that the best approach is to capture someone's attention. Instead, marketing communication now means finding ways to engage with and interact with consumers.

This textbook is devoted to explaining marketing communications from the perspective of the decision makers both inside and outside the firm. Various topics are viewed from the vantage points of the key individuals involved, including account managers, brand managers, creatives, media buyers, and Webmasters.

This chapter explains the nature of an integrated advertising and marketing communications program. First, communication processes are described. Understanding how communication works builds the foundation for an integrated marketing program. Next, a totally integrated marketing communications program is described. Finally, the integrated marketing communications process is applied to global or international operations, generating the term *GIMC,* or *globally integrated marketing communications.*

COMMUNICATION AND IMC PROGRAMS

Communication can be defined as transmitting, receiving, and processing information. When a person, group, or organization attempts to transfer an idea or message, communication occurs when the receiver (another person or group) is able to comprehend the information. The model of communication shown in Figure 1.2 shows how communication takes place as the message that was sent reaches its destination in a form that is understood by the intended audience.[4]

The communication process is part of any advertising or marketing program. Consider a person planning to buy a pair of athletic shoes. Using the communications model (Figure 1.2), the **senders** are companies that manufacture and sell shoes. New Balance, ASICS, Reebok, and Skechers all try to gain the customer's attention. Most of these firms hire advertising agencies. Others utilize an in-house marketing group.

Encoding the message is the second step. A creative takes the idea and transforms it into attention-getting advertisements designed for various media (television, magazines, the Internet, and others). The athletic shoe advertisements shown in this section are examples of encoding.

Messages travel to audiences through various **transmission devices**. The third stage of the marketing communication process occurs when a channel or medium delivers the message. The channel may be a television carrying an advertisement, a Sunday paper with a coupon placed in it, a letter to the purchasing agent of a large retail store, or a blog on a company's Web site. The shoe ads in this section were transmitted through various magazines.

Decoding occurs when the message reaches one or more of the receiver's senses. Consumers both hear and see television ads. Others consumers handle (touch) and read (see) a coupon offer. It is even possible to "smell" a message. A well-placed perfume sample might entice a buyer to purchase both the magazine containing the sample and the perfume being advertised. People who are interested in purchasing athletic shoes pay closer attention to advertisements and other information about shoes. Consider the athletic shoe advertisements shown in this section and then answer the following questions:

1. Which advertisement most dramatically attracted your attention? Why?
2. Which advertisement is the least appealing? Why?
3. How important is the brand name in each ad? Why?
4. What is the major message of each individual advertisement?
5. What makes each advertisement effective or ineffective?
6. Discuss your thoughts about each advertisement with other students.

It is possible that the same advertisement will be interpreted differently by different people. In other words, the message may not be received. Quality marketing communication occurs when customers (the **receivers**) decode or understand the message as it was intended by the sender. In the case of the shoe ads, effective marketing communications depend on

FIGURE 1.2
The Communications Process

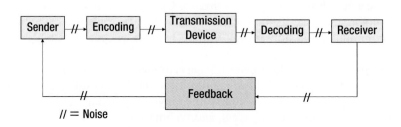

// = Noise

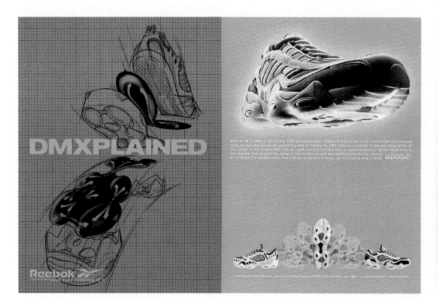

Various ads for shoes.

receivers getting the right message and responding in the desired fashion (such as shopping, buying, or telling their friends about the shoes).

Examine the Web sites of the four athletic shoe companies featured in the advertisements:

- Reebok (**www.rbk.com**)
- ASICS (**www.asics.com**)
- New Balance (**www.newbalance.com**)
- Skechers (**www.skechers.com**)

The sites provide additional insights about the messages these companies are trying to send. Compare the materials on the Web sites to the shoe advertisements. You should be able to see how the two messages go together. If they do not, the IMC program is not completely developed or fully integrated.

One obstacle that prevents marketing messages from being efficient and effective is noise. **Noise** is anything that distorts or disrupts a message. It can occur at any stage in the communication process, as shown in Figure 1.2. Examples of noise that affect television advertising are provided in Figure 1.3.

FIGURE 1.3
Communication Noise Affects Television Advertising

- The viewer is talking on the phone.
- The viewer is getting something to eat during the ad.
- The viewer of the ad dislikes or is offended by the nature of the ad.
- The ad is placed on a TV show that is seldom watched by the producer's target audience.
- The advertisement is placed next to an ad by a competitor.
- The creative designed an ad that the target audience did not get.
- The person in the ad overpowers the message.
- The producer of the ad changed the background of the ad from what the creative wanted.

Source: Courtesy of Summer Bradley.

The most common form of noise affecting marketing communications is **clutter**. Modern consumers are exposed to hundreds of marketing messages each day. Most are tuned out. Clutter includes:

- Eight minutes of commercials per half hour of television and radio programs
- A Sunday newspaper jammed with advertising supplements
- An endless barrage of billboards on a major street
- The inside of a bus or subway car papered with ads
- Web sites and servers loaded with commercials

The final component of the communication process is **feedback**. It takes the form of purchases, inquiries, complaints, questions, visits to the store, blogs, and Web site hits. Each indicates that the message has reached the receiver and that the receiver is responding.

Account managers, creatives, brand managers, and others involved in the marketing process pay attention to every part of the communications model. They make sure that the proper audiences receive the messages. They try to make sure the message cuts through noise and clutter. In the case of athletic shoes, increases in market share, sales, and brand loyalty are common outcomes the marketing team tries to achieve.

Remember, however, that communicating with consumers and other businesses requires more than simply creating attractive advertisements. In the next section, the nature of a fully developed integrated marketing communications program is described. An effective integrated marketing communications program integrates numerous marketing activities into a single package in order to effectively reach target markets and other audiences.

INTEGRATED MARKETING COMMUNICATIONS

An integrated marketing communications program can be built on the foundation provided by the communications model. Although IMC programs may be described in several ways, the consensus is to define them as follows: **Integrated marketing communications (IMC)** is the coordination and integration of all marketing communication tools, avenues, and sources within a company into a seamless program that maximizes the impact on customers and other stakeholders at a minimal cost. This integration affects all of a firm's business-to-business, marketing channel, customer-focused, and internally directed communications.[5]

Before further examining the IMC concept, consider the traditional framework of marketing. The **marketing mix** is the starting point. As shown in Figure 1.4, promotion is

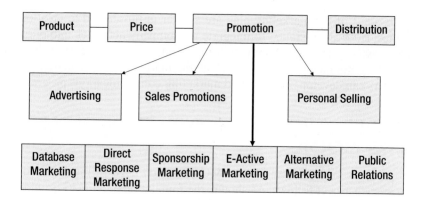

FIGURE 1.4
The Components of Promotion

one of the four components of the mix. For years, the traditional view was that promotional activities included advertising, sales promotions, and personal selling activities. Sales promotions include both sales and trade promotions, with sales promotions aimed at end users or consumers of goods and services and trade promotions directed toward distributors and retailers. This traditional view has changed somewhat due to the accountability issue discussed earlier. The drive to integrate all promotional efforts has expanded promotions beyond the three traditional elements of advertising, sales promotions, and personal selling. Now, it also includes activities such as database marketing, direct marketing, sponsorship marketing, e-active marketing, guerrilla marketing, alternative marketing, and public relations.

A complete IMC plan incorporates every element of the marketing mix: products, prices, distribution methods, and promotions. This textbook primarily deals with the promotions component. Keep in mind, however, that to present a unified message, the other elements of the marketing mix must be blended into the program.

AN INTEGRATED MARKETING COMMUNICATIONS PLAN

Integrated marketing is based on a strategic marketing plan. The plan coordinates efforts in all components of the marketing mix. The purpose is to achieve harmony in the messages sent to customers and others. The same plan integrates all promotional efforts to keep the company's total communications program in sync.

Figure 1.5 lists the steps required to complete a marketing plan. The first step is a *situational analysis*, which is the process of examining factors from the organization's internal and external environments. The analysis identifies marketing problems and opportunities present in the external environment as well as internal company strengths and weaknesses.

When the situation is fully understood, the second step is to define primary *marketing objectives*. These objectives include targets such as higher sales, an increase in market share, a new competitive position, or desired customer actions, such as visiting the store and making purchases.

Based on the marketing objectives, a *marketing budget* is prepared and *marketing strategies* are finalized. Marketing strategies apply to all the ingredients of the marketing mix, plus any positioning, differentiation, or branding strategies.

From these strategies, *marketing tactics* guide the day-by-day activities necessary to support marketing strategies. The final step in the marketing plan is stating how to *evaluate performance*.

◆ Situation analysis	◆ Marketing strategies
◆ Marketing objectives	◆ Marketing tactics
◆ Marketing budget	◆ Evaluation of performance

FIGURE 1.5
The Marketing Plan

These six steps of the marketing plan are similar to those used in creating management strategies. Both are designed to integrate all company activities into one consistent effort and to provide guidance to company leaders and marketing experts as they integrate the firm's total communications package. Once the marketing plan has been established, company leaders can develop an integrated marketing communications program.

IMC COMPONENTS AND THE DESIGN OF THIS BOOK

Figure 1.6 presents an overview of the IMC approach used in this textbook. A brief description of each aspect follows. As shown, the foundation of an IMC program consists of a careful review of the company's image, the buyers to be served, and the markets in which the buyers are located.

Advertising programs are built on this foundation, as are the other elements of the promotional mix. Finally, the integration tools located at the peak of the pyramid help the company's marketing team make certain that the elements of the plan are consistent and effective.

The IMC Foundation

The first section of this text builds the foundation for an IMC program. Chapter 2 describes the corporate image and brand management elements. Strengthening the firm's image and brands answers the question, "Who are we and what message are we trying to send?" From there it is possible to identify target markets.

Chapter 3 describes buyer behaviors. The steps of the consumer purchasing process explain how individuals make choices. Marketers identify the motives leading to purchases and factors affecting those decisions. Then, the IMC program can be designed to influence these consumer choices. Business-to-business buyer behaviors are also examined. Knowing how to reach purchasing managers and other decision makers within target businesses is another critical element in an integrated communications plan. Discovering viable business-to-business marketing opportunities plays a vital role in overall company success.

Chapter 4 describes the promotions opportunity analysis element of an IMC program. This includes identifying all target markets. Consumer market segments are identified using demographics, income, social class, and various psychographic variables. Business markets are segmented by understanding the demographics of the

FIGURE 1.6
Overview of Integrated Marketing Communications

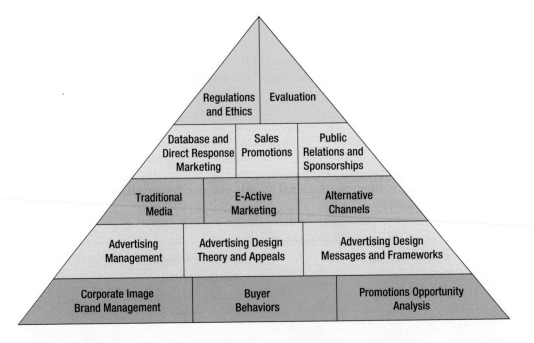

company's buying team, noting who the end users will be, and by determining the benefits other businesses expect to receive from the goods and services they buy.

Advertising Tools

The second section of this text is devoted to advertising issues. Advertising management, as described in Chapter 5, addresses the major functions of advertising, the general direction the company takes, and the selection of an advertising agency. The functions performed by an advertising agency's account manager as well as those provided by the advertising creative are also described.

Several advertising theories, which are explored in Chapter 6, are available to help the creative design advertisements. The various advertising appeals that can be used, including those oriented toward fear, humor, sex, music, and logic, are explained in the chapter.

Chapter 7 reveals the ingredients involved in creating effective message strategies. The messages are delivered via various executional frameworks, which are various ways to construct the actual commercial or advertisement. Creatives and other advertising professionals know that effective advertising includes the use of effective sources or spokespersons and following well-established principles of success.

IMC Media Tools

The third section of this book contains information regarding both traditional and new cutting-edge ideas about how to reach potential customers. First, the traditional media channels, including television, radio, magazines, newspapers, outdoor signs, and direct mail, are described in Chapter 8, along with the advantages and disadvantages of each medium. The roles provided by media planners and media buyers are also identified.

Advertising is a crucial component of a firm's IMC program.

Chapter 9 is devoted to issues associated with the Internet, with a new term, *e-active marketing,* used to summarize the various activities involved. E-active marketing integrates e-commerce programs with more recent trends that have evolved with Internet usage. These include social networks and blogs, among the other activities that consumers pursue online. Consumers play an active role in receiving and sending messages when the Internet is utilized. Consequently, the channel deserves special attention from the marketing department.

Many communication channels are available beyond both the traditional networks and the Internet. These methods are described in Chapter 10, titled "Alternative Marketing." The programs that are described include buzz marketing, guerilla marketing, product placements and branded entertainment, and lifestyle marketing. The concept of a brand community is also examined.

Promotional Tools

The next level of the IMC pyramid adds database and direct response marketing programs, trade promotions, consumer promotions, public relations efforts, and sponsorship programs. When marketing managers carefully design all of the steps taken up to this point, the firm is in a better position to integrate these activities. Messages presented in the advertising campaign can be reinforced with a variety of communication promotions.

Database and direct response marketing programs are outlined in Chapter 11. The chapter first describes effective data collection and analysis. Then, the information gained can be used to develop data-driven marketing programs, including permission marketing, frequency programs, and customer relationship management systems.

An ad for Celestial Seasonings Green Tea offering a 55 cents-off coupon.

Consumer and trade promotions are described in Chapter 12, which has the general title of "Sales Promotions." Trade promotions include trade incentives, cooperative advertising, slotting fees, and other promotions and discounts that help the manufacturer or channel member to push the product through the distribution channel. Consumer promotions are directed at end users and include coupons, contests, premiums, refunds, rebates, free samples, and price-off offers. The ad for Green Tea in this section includes a coupon for 55 cents off.

Chapter 13 focuses on public relations programs that connect with consumers in positive ways. This includes emphasizing positive events and dealing with negative publicity. In many cases the marketing team utilizes public relations efforts to help a sponsorship program achieve the greatest impact.

Integration Tools

The "top" level of the IMC program includes the integration tools needed to make sure all customers are effectively served. Chapter 14 begins with an examination of the many legal and regulatory issues that are part of the advertising and promotions environment. Further, ethical issues in marketing communications are discussed. Ethical systems go beyond simply meeting the letter of the law.

Chapter 15, the final chapter of this textbook, explains how to evaluate an integrated marketing program. It is crucial to evaluate communication programs. Evaluations can begin prior to any promotional campaign and continue during the campaign to postcampaign evaluations. These evaluations can provide valuable information to alter campaigns before they are commercially introduced, as well as providing input to modify programs that have already run. A promotions evaluation process holds everything together; it drives the entire IMC process. Fully integrated marketing requires a careful linkage between planning and evaluation processes; one cannot occur without the other.

Refining the IMC Program

IMC involves much more than writing a plan. It is also not limited to the company's marketing department. IMC is a company-wide activity. To be successful, every part of the organization's operation must be included. A study conducted by the American Productivity & Quality Center of Houston indicates that four stages are involved in designing an IMC system (see Figure 1.7).[6]

The first stage is to identify, coordinate, and manage all forms of marketing communication. The objective is to bring all of the company's communication elements together under one umbrella. This includes advertising, promotions, direct marketing, Internet and e-commerce programs, public relations, sponsorships, and other marketing activities.

FIGURE 1.7
Four Stages of an Effective Integrated Marketing Communications System

1. Identify, coordinate, and manage all forms of marketing communication.	3. Use information technology to better serve customers.
2. Analyze customer contact points.	4. Use information technology to assist corporate strategic planning.

In the second stage, communications are examined from the perspective of the customer. The marketing team analyzes every contact method that might influence customers. This means studying every internal and external group that might affect perceptions of the company and its products. Employees, distributors, retailers, dealers, product package designers, and others are part of the integrated marketing program.

Information technology comes to the forefront in the third stage. Company leaders find ways to use information technology to enhance IMC programs. With computer technology and abundance of information, the marketing team has the capability to develop data-driven programs to meet the needs of individual customers and allow for the customization of marketing messages.

The fourth and final stage of IMC development occurs when the organization uses customer data information and insights to assist corporate strategic planning. The information guides marketing decisions and the communication approaches aimed at individual customer segments. Firms reaching this stage, such as Dow Chemical, FedEx, and Hewlett-Packard, take databases and use them to calculate and establish a customer value for each buyer. All customers are not equally valuable. Dow Chemical, FedEx, and Hewlett-Packard allocate sales and marketing communication resources to those customers with the greatest potential for return, based on calculations of customer values. This helps company leaders understand each customer's worth and treat each one individually, resulting in the highest possible return on investment for marketing expenditures.

THE VALUE OF IMC PLANS

Advances in technology and communications are major new forces in integrated marketing communications. Consumers must be reached in a holistic fashion, which means companies cannot rely totally on traditional media and marketing methods. There is a strong movement toward nontraditional and alternative methods of reaching consumers. Figure 1.8 lists several trends linked to the increasing importance of integrated advertising and marketing communications programs.

Information Technology

Technology enables instant communications among business executives, employees, channel members, and others around the world. It also creates opportunities for marketing communications. For example, in the past, predictions of consumer purchasing behaviors were based on the results of test markets, attitudinal research, and intention-to-buy surveys. Although these are excellent means of obtaining information about consumers, they are slow, costly, and potentially unreliable.

Today, purchase-behavior predictions are more precise due to the development of the UPC (universal product code) bar-code system. The technology was originally used to manage inventories. Scanning every sale meant retailers were better able to develop efficient inventory-control systems.

At the same time, UPC codes combined with other technology programs allow large amounts of data and information about customers to be gathered. Advanced statistical software helps company leaders analyze these data. Connections between financial (e.g., credit card, banking) and business firms make it possible to collect purchasing data. Using this information, demographic and psychographic information about consumers can be correlated with the items they buy, as well as when and where they make

◆ Development of information technology	◆ Integration of information by consumers
◆ Changes in channel power	◆ Decline in effectiveness of television advertising
◆ Increase in competition	
◆ Brand parity	

FIGURE 1.8
Trends Impacting Integrated Advertising and Marketing Communications

This Visa advertisement
encourages consumers
to book vacations online.

purchases. Consequently, marketers can determine who is buying a company's products and the best communication channels to reach them.

Changes in Channel Power

A marketing channel consists of a producer or manufacturer vending goods to wholesalers or middlemen, who in turn sell items to retailers, where the same items are finally sold to consumers. Numerous technological developments have changed the levels of power held by members of the channel. Oftentimes retailers hold the most channel power, because they control shelf space and purchase data. Retailers are able to determine what products and brands will be placed on store shelves, and thus available to consumers. Through checkout scanners, retailers know what products and brands are selling. Many retailers share the data with suppliers and require them to ensure that store shelves remain well stocked. The size and power of mega-retailers means manufacturers and suppliers have no choice but to follow the dictates of these "big box" stores.

At the same time, the advancement of the World Wide Web and information technology has caused some channel power to shift to consumers.[7] Consumers can obtain information about goods and services and purchase almost anything using the Internet. For example, the Visa advertisement in this section encourages consumers to book hotel rooms, air travel, and car rentals online. Internet-driven sales have grown at a tremendous rate. In fact, in just one year, from 2006 to 2007, U.S. online retail sales grew by 18.3 percent. Total U.S. retail sales in the United States was $243.1 billion. Figure 1.9 highlights the major segments of U.S. online retail sales. It also displays the percentage each category represents of total U.S. online retail sales.[8]

To illustrate how technology is changing channel power, think about an individual in the market for a cell phone provider. First, she goes to the Internet and searches for information. She then identifies several possible brands and narrows them down to three. Next, she may travel to a local mall to investigate the carriers or visit with them by phone. Asking questions of the salespeople helps her gather additional product information.

FIGURE 1.9
U.S. Online Retail Sales

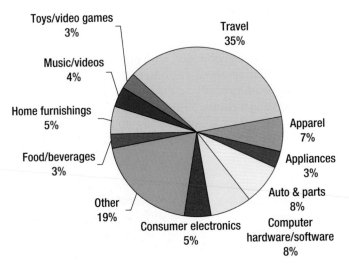

Going home, she then logs on to the Web sites of the three systems to learn about warranties; the type of phone being offered; company policies, such as how easy it is to change calling plans and about rollover minutes; and other details about the services. Having gathered sufficient information to make a decision, she can use Internet sources, the telephone, or a personal visit to the carrier's store to finalize the purchase. She may even play one carrier off against another to get a better price. Soon, she has a new phone along with the paperwork used to complete the transaction. The result is that the buyer is in charge of the entire process. Although many individuals still purchase the majority of products in brick-and-mortar stores, individuals are shifting to more integrated approaches to learning about products and to making purchases.

The same principles apply to business-to-business purchasing activities. Buyers who shop on behalf of organizations and other company members seeking business-to-business services are able to tap into the same resources (i.e., Web sites, databases). This means that the same kind of shift in channel power is taking place in the business-to-business sector.

Increases in Competition

Information technology and communication advances have dramatically changed the marketplace in other ways. Consumers can purchase goods and services from anywhere in the world. Competition no longer comes from the company just down the street—it can come from a firm 10,000 miles away that can supply a product faster and cheaper. Consumers want quality, but they also want a low price. The company that delivers on both quality and price gets the business, regardless of its location. Advancements in delivery systems make it possible for purchases to arrive almost anywhere in a matter of days.

In this competitive environment, it seems as if the only way one firm can gain sales is to take customers away from another. Consequently, integrating advertising and other marketing communications becomes extremely important. Advertising alone is not enough to maintain sales. This situation is further complicated for manufacturers when retailers hold stronger channel power and control the flow of merchandise to consumers. In that circumstance, manufacturers invest in trade promotions (e.g., dealer incentives, slotting allowances, discounts) to keep products in various retail outlets. Encouraging retailers to promote a manufacturer's brand or prominently display it for consumer viewing requires even greater promotional dollars. Manufacturers also invest in consumer promotions (e.g., coupons, contests, sweepstakes, bonus packs, and price-off deals) to keep customers. The goal is to keep a brand attractive to the retailer.

The U.S. running shoe market provides an excellent example of how growth for any given company comes at the expense of competing brands. Figure 1.10 displays market

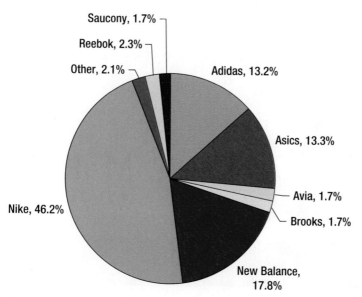

FIGURE 1.10
Market Share of Top Brands in the Running Shoe Industry

Saucony, 1.7%
Reebok, 2.3%
Other, 2.1%
Adidas, 13.2%
Asics, 13.3%
Avia, 1.7%
Brooks, 1.7%
Nike, 46.2%
New Balance, 17.8%

Source: Based on Matt Powell, "A Steady Stride," *SCB* 39, no. 11 (November 2006), p. 15.

shares for the top brands in the running shoe industry. Notice that Nike is the market leader, with 46.2 percent of the market, compared to the number two brand, New Balance, at 17.8 percent, and the number three brand, Adidas, at 13.2 percent. About the only way New Balance, Adidas, Reebok, and other brands can gain market share is to take it away from another brand.[9] Nike is the market leader. Consequently, it is often the target for such strategies.

At the same time that manufacturers fight for market share, retailers, equipped with scanner data, control product placement within a store and shelf-space allocation. To gain prominence for a particular brand at the retail level, the manufacturer's marketing team coordinates all advertising, trade promotions, and consumer promotions. The goal is to maximize marketing dollars by gaining maximum exposure to consumers and retailers. Retailers, in turn, focus on IMC efforts that are designed to maintain customer loyalty along with positive relationships with manufacturers. It is crucial for each company in the marketing chain to create a quality IMC program that reaches both customers and others in the distribution chain.

Brand Parity

The increase in national and global competition is due to the availability of multiple brands. Many of these products have nearly identical benefits. When consumers believe that most brands offer the same set of attributes, the result is **brand parity**. From the consumer's perspective, this means that shoppers will purchase from a *group* of accepted brands rather than one specific brand. When brand parity is present, quality is often not a major concern because consumers believe that only minor quality differences exist. Consumers routinely view quality levels of products as being nearly equal. As a result, they often base purchase decisions on other criteria, such as price, availability, or a specific promotional deal. The net effect is that brand loyalty has experienced a steady decline.[10] Brand loyalty has also been reduced because of a growing acceptance of private brands.

A recent survey conducted by Top Brands revealed that consumers are willing to switch brands in most product categories.[11] In response, the marketing team tries to create messages that express how the company's products are clearly different. The messages are designed to convince consumers that the company's brand is superior and is not the same as the competition's. A quality IMC program is, in part, designed to gain the benefits associated with a strong brand name.

Integration of Information

Today's consumers have a variety of choices regarding where they obtain information about a brand. If consumers are not satisfied with what they hear, they can seek additional information. They might go to the Internet and read about other brands and companies.

Source: Courtesy of Newcomer, Morris & Young, Inc.

Many businesses, such as the Marion State Bank, include a Web address on company advertisements.

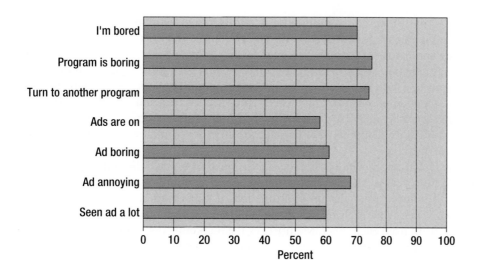

FIGURE 1.11
Reasons Viewers Do Not Watch Ads During a Commercial Break

As a result, most companies now list Internet addresses on advertisements. Web users can now discuss products and companies with other customers in chat rooms or in blogs. They may also travel to retail stores and discuss various options with the salesclerk. Others will consult independent sources of information such as *Consumer Reports.*

The marketing team should be concerned with the ways consumers integrate this information. Company leaders should make sure that every contact point projects the same message. **Contact points** are the places where customers interact with or acquire additional information from a company. These contacts may be direct or indirect, planned or unplanned. An effective IMC program sends a consistent message about the nature of the company, its products, and the benefits that result from making a purchase from the organization.

Decline in the Effectiveness of Television Advertising

The influence of mass-media television advertising has declined dramatically. VCRs and DVR systems allow consumers to watch programs without commercials. The rise in popularity of cable TV, DVR recorders, and satellite dishes means consumers have a wide variety of viewing choices. Using the remote while watching television means that it is likely that, during most commercials, the viewer is surfing other channels to see what else is on. Many television advertisements are not seen, even by those people watching a particular program. In a recent survey by conducted by *Brandweek* magazine, only 16 percent of viewers said that they watch commercials during a program.[12] Why do viewers switch channels or engage in other activities? Figure 1.11 provides some answers. In general, viewers find television ads to be boring, annoying, intrusive, and too repetitious.[13] To overcome this problem, it is vital to create new and innovative communications programs that can hold the viewer's attention, which is not an easy task.

Many firms employ advertising agencies to assist in marketing efforts. Until 1970, almost all advertising agencies focused only on the advertising aspect of the marketing plan. Now, however, many advertising agencies spend substantial amounts of time assisting clients in the development of IMC programs.[14] In addition to advertisements, these agencies design consumer promotion materials and direct-marketing programs, along with other marketing tactics.

INTERNATIONAL IMPLICATIONS

The same trend that exists among advertising agencies in the United States also occurs in the international arena. Instead of being called "IMC," however, it is known as *GIMC*, or a *globally integrated marketing communications program*.[15] The goal is still the same—to coordinate marketing efforts. The challenges are greater due to larger national and cultural differences in target markets.

In the past, marketers could employ two different strategies for global companies. The first approach was **standardization**, in which the idea was to standardize the product and message across countries. The goal of this approach was generating economies of scale in production while creating a global product using the same promotional theme. The language would be different, but the basic marketing message would be the same.

The second approach to global marketing was **adaptation**. Products and marketing messages were designed for and adapted to individual countries. Thus, the manner by which a product was marketed in France was different from how it was marketed in Italy, India, or Australia.

The GIMC approach is easier to apply when a company relies on the standardization method; however, GIMC can and should be used with either adaptation or standardization.[16] To reduce costs, careful coordination of marketing efforts should occur across countries. Even when a firm uses the adaptation strategy, marketers from various countries can learn from each other. Members of the marketing department should not feel like they have to reinvent the wheel. Synergy can occur between countries. More importantly, learning can occur. As telecommunications continue to expand, contacts between peoples of different countries are much more frequent.

Remember, a commercial targeted for customers in France may also be viewed by people in Spain using satellite technologies. Therefore, a company should try to transmit a consistent theme, even when there are differences in local messages. In terms of marketing, the philosophy many companies use is "market globally, but act locally." When marketers design or encode messages for local markets, they need to have the freedom to tailor or alter the message so that it fits the local culture and the target market. The final message conveyed in each country often varies. Development of a GIMC is the final extension to an IMC plan. With its completion, companies are able to compete more effectively both at home and abroad.

SUMMARY

A new era is unfolding in the fields of advertising, promotions, and marketing communications. Marketing departments and advertising agencies, as well as individual account managers, brand managers, and creatives, encounter strong pressures. They are being held accountable for expenditures of marketing communications dollars. Company leaders expect tangible results from promotional campaigns and other marketing programs. As a result, new partnerships are forming among account executives, creatives, and the companies that hire them. The duties of the account manager have expanded in the direction of a more strategically oriented approach to advertising and marketing communications. Those preparing to become advertising or promotions professionals must be aware of both accountability issues and the new aspects of these jobs, including accounting for all of the new forms of alternative media.

Communication is transmitting, receiving, and processing information. It is a two-way street in which a sender must establish a clear connection with a receiver. Effective communication is the glue holding the relationship between two entities together. When communication breaks down, conflicts, misunderstandings, and other problems can develop.

The components of the communication process include the sender, an encoding process, the transmission device, the decoding process, and the receiver. Noise is anything that distorts or disrupts the flow of information from the sender to the receiver.

In the marketing arena, senders are companies seeking to transmit ideas to consumers, employees, other companies, retail outlets, and others. Encoding devices are the means of transmitting information and include advertisements, public relations efforts, press releases, sales activities, promotions, and a wide variety of additional verbal and nonverbal cues sent to receivers. Transmission devices are the media and spokespersons who carry the message. Decoding occurs when the receivers (such as customers or retailers) encounter the message. Noise takes many forms in marketing, most notably the clutter of an overabundance of messages in every available channel.

Integrated marketing communications (IMC) takes advantage of the effective management of the communications channel. Within the marketing mix of products, prices, distribution systems, and promotions, firms that speak with one clear voice are able to coordinate and integrate all marketing tools. The goal is to have a strong and positive impact on consumers, businesses, and other end users.

IMC plans are vital to achieving success. The reasons for their importance begin with the explosion of information technologies. Channel power has shifted from manufacturers to retailers and is now shifting to consumers. Company leaders must adjust in order to maintain a strong market standing, and IMC programs can assist in this effort. New levels of competition drive marketers to better understand their customers and be certain that those end users are hearing a clear and consistent message from the firm. As consumers develop a stronger sense of brand parity, whereby no real differences in product or service quality are perceived, marketers must re-create a situation in which their brand holds a distinct advantage over others. This is difficult, because consumers can collect and integrate information about products from a wide variety of sources, including technological outlets (Web sites) and interpersonal (sales reps) sources. Quality IMC programs help maintain the strong voice a company needs to ensure that its messages is heard. An additional challenge is the decline in effectiveness of mass-media advertising. IMC helps company leaders find new ways to contact consumers with a unified message.

When a firm conducts business internationally, a GIMC, or globally integrated marketing communications system, can be of great value. By developing one strong theme and then adapting that theme to individual countries, the firm conveys a message that integrates international operations into a more coherent package.

This text explains the issues involved in establishing an effective IMC program. The importance of business-to-business marketing efforts is noted, because many firms market items as much to other companies as they do to consumers. Successful development of an IMC program should help firms remain profitable and vibrant, even when the complexities of the marketplace make these goals more difficult to reach.

KEY TERMS

communication Transmitting, receiving, and processing information.

senders The person(s) attempting to deliver a message or idea.

encoding The verbal (words, sounds) and nonverbal (gestures, facial expressions, posture) cues that the sender utilizes in dispatching a message.

transmission devices All of the items that carry a message from the sender to the receiver.

decoding When the receiver employs any of his or her senses (hearing, seeing, feeling) in an attempt to capture a message.

receivers The intended audience for a message.

noise Anything that distorts or disrupts a message.

clutter Exists when consumers are exposed to hundreds of marketing messages per day, and most are tuned out.

feedback Information the sender obtains from the receiver regarding the receiver's perception or interpretation of a message.

integrated marketing communications (IMC) The coordination and integration of all marketing communication tools, avenues, and sources within a company into a seamless program that maximizes the impact on customers and other end users at a minimal cost. This affects all of a firm's business-to-business, marketing channel, customer-focused, and internally oriented communications.

marketing mix Consists of products, prices, places (the distribution system), and promotions.

brand parity Occurs when there is the perception that most products and services are essentially the same.

contact points The places where customers interact with or acquire additional information about a firm.

standardization When a firm standardizes its products and market offerings across countries with the goal of generating economies of scale in production while using the same promotional theme.

adaptation Occurs when products and marketing messages are designed for and adapted to individual countries.

REVIEW QUESTIONS

1. How has the job of an advertising account executive changed? How has the job of a creative changed? How has the job of a brand manager changed? How do the three jobs interact in the new marketing environment?

2. Define communication. Why does it play such a crucial role in marketing and business?

3. What are the parts of an individual communications model?

4. Who are the typical senders in marketing communications? Who are the receivers?

5. Name the transmission devices, both human and nonhuman, that carry marketing messages. How can the human element become a problem?

6. Define clutter. Name some of the forms of clutter in marketing communications.

7. Define integrated marketing communications (IMC).

8. What are the four parts of the marketing mix?

9. What steps are required to write a marketing plan?

10. Describe firm and brand image.

11. What are the main components of advertising?

12. How has the growth of information technology made IMC programs vital to marketing efforts?

13. What reasons were given to explain the growth in importance of IMC plans in this chapter?

14. What is channel power? How has it changed in the past few decades?

15. What is brand parity? How is it related to successful marketing efforts?

16. What is a GIMC? Why is it important for multinational firms?

17. What is the difference between standardization and adaptation in GIMC programs?

CRITICAL THINKING EXERCISES

Discussion Questions

1. The marketing director for a furniture manufacturer is assigned the task of developing an integrated marketing communications program to emphasize the furniture's natural look. Discuss the problems the director might encounter in developing this message and in ensuring that consumers understand the message correctly. Refer to the communication process in Figure 1.2 for ideas. What kinds of noise interferes with the communication process?

2. Referring to Exercise 1, assume the director wants to develop an integrated marketing communications program emphasizing a theme focused on the furniture's natural look. This theme applies to all of the company's markets, that is, both retailers and consumers. Using Figure 1.6 as a guide, briefly discuss each element of the integrated marketing communications plan and how to incorporate it into an overall theme.

3. The marketing director for a manufacturer of automobile tires wants to integrate the company's marketing program internationally. Should the director use a standardization or adaptation approach? How could the company be certain that its marketing program will effectively be integrated among the different countries in which it sells tires?

4. What do you typically do during commercials on television? What percentage of the time do you watch commercials? What makes you watch? Ask these same questions of 10 other people. What type of activities do people engage in during commercials?

5. Nike's tagline is "Just do it." What meaning is conveyed by the tagline? Do you think this conveys a clear message about the company's operations?

6. Brand parity has become a major issue for companies. Identify three product categories where the brand you purchase is not very important. Why is the brand name not important? Identify three product categories where the brand is important. What brand or brands do you typically purchase in each category?

INTEGRATED LEARNING EXERCISES

1. Ron Jon Surf Shop is probably the best known retail store brand for ocean gear in Florida. In Hawaii, the dominant name is Hilo Hattie. Go to the Hilo Hattie Web site at **www.hilohattie.com.** Compare it to the Ron Jon site at **www.ronjons.com.** Do the two sites have relatively common themes? Which is the more attractive site? Why?

2. Find each of the following companies on the Internet. For each company, discuss how effective its Web site is in communicating an overall message. Also, discuss how well the marketing team integrates the material on the Web site. How well does the Web site integrate the company's advertising with other marketing communications?

   a. Revlon (**www.revlon.com**)

   b. J.B. Hunt (**www.jbhunt.com**)

   c. United Airlines (**www.united.com**)

   d. Steamboat Resorts (**www.steamboatresorts.com**)

3. Information is one key to developing a successful integrated marketing communications program. Access each of the following Web sites and examine the information and news available on each site. How would this information help in developing an integrated marketing campaign?

   a. *Brandweek* (**www.brandweek.com**)

   b. *Adweek* (**www.adweek.com**)

   c. *Mediaweek* (**www.mediaweek.com**)

   d. *Branding Asia* (**www.brandingasia.com**)

STUDENT PROJECT

Creative Corner

One of Procter & Gamble's fastest growing products is Febreze. It is aimed at individuals who do not like washing laundry and has been positioned by P&G as an alternative method of completing this chore. An ideal target market is the 18 million college students in the United States. With busy class schedules, work, and social events, who has time to do laundry? For jeans and other clothes that are not quite dirty yet, Febreze offers the chance to "refresh" the clothes and kill any possible odors. John Paquin, Executive Vice-President at the advertising agency WPP Grey Worldwide, which handles the Febreze product, states that "washing is not a convenient part of the lifestyle at college." He also recognizes that "mainstream media buys [such as television] are not effective for the 18- to 22-year-olds.[17] For more information about Febreze, access the Febreze Web site at **www.febreze.com.**

1. Identify alternative media you would use to reach 18- to 22-year-old college students.

2. Design an advertisement for Febreze aimed at the college demographic. Where would you place your ad? Why?

CASE 1 A NEW SALSA SENSATION

Hector Fernandez created a salsa that became legendary within just a few years. Hector operated a successful restaurant, *El Casa Grande*, in Taos, New Mexico, for many years. A new chapter in his life opened when he was approached by two of his best customers, who offered to help him produce and market his salsa throughout the state, with the goal of reaching regional distribution in 5 years.

As a first step, Hector located the home office of a major advertising agency in Albuquerque. The agency positioned itself as being a "full-service" organization. Hector wondered exactly what that meant. He was introduced to Matt Barnes, who was to serve as his marketing and promotions consultant.

Matt's first questions were about Hector's salsa: "What makes your salsa better?" and "Is there a way we can convince people of the difference?" Hector responded that his customers often commented about both the taste and the texture of the salsa. He had a secret formula that had a few unusual seasonings that made his salsa burst with flavor. Hector also believed that it was less "runny" than others.

The next item the two discussed was potential customers. Hector noted that Tex-Mex was a popular form of dining in New Mexico as well as across the country. He believed that his salsa would appeal to a wide variety of people who enjoy Tex-Mex cuisine.

Matt's next question was simple: "Who do you think are your major competitors?"

Hector responded, "That's easy, Pace and Old El Paso."

Matt then asked what Hector thought of the two companies and their products. He suggested an investigation on both a personal and competitive basis. For example, Matt asked, "What do you think of when you hear the name Pace? How about Old El Paso?" He noted that both brands were solid and that Hector's company would need a compelling brand in order to compete.

The next step was a visit to the Web site of each company (www.pacefoods.com and www.oldelpaso.com). They noticed that the two companies offered some products that were the same and others that were not.

Matt asked Hector what he thought about the advertising and promotions for each company and its products. Hector replied, "Well, to tell you the truth, I only remember one television ad. It said something about one of the two companies was located in New York City instead of near Mexico, but I can't remember which was which." They concluded that it was possible that neither company was involved in a great deal of traditional advertising or that Hector was simply too busy with his own company to notice. Hector noted that he used a DVR to watch television and that he listened to satellite radio in both his restaurant and his car.

Matt suggested that Hector should look in Sunday papers for the past several weeks to see if either company was offering price-off coupons or other promotions, such as a contest or sweepstakes. He told Hector it would be a good idea to attend events where salsa was being sampled or sold, such as at county fairs, Mexican heritage events, and at ball parks and other sports stadiums where nachos were on the menu.

Hector had a great salsa, but no brand name and no marketing communications plan.

The two then discussed a crucial issue: How could Hector's new company convince grocers and others to designate some shelf space for his salsa, thereby taking space away from some other product?

Finally, Matt handed Hector a package of materials (see Figure 1.12). He asked Hector to consider how to reach every possible type of customer for his product, including grocery stores, other restaurants, and individual consumers shopping for salsa. He suggested that Hector would need to think about what type of sales tactics to use, which promotional programs were most important, and how the company should look—from its logo, to its letterhead, to the business cards handed out by sales representatives. Remember, Matt stated, "Everything communicates."

1. Can you think of a brand name that could be used not only for salsa, but for any other product related to salsa that Hector's company might sell?

2. How can Hector's company compete with Pace and Old El Paso? Is there a market niche the company can locate?

3. What kinds of advertising and promotions tactics should the company use? Will the tactics be the same in 5 years?

FIGURE 1.12
Items to Be Included in an IMC Program

- Company logo
- Product brand name and company name
- Business cards
- Letterhead
- Carry home bags (paper or plastic)
- Wrapping paper
- Coupons
- Promotional giveaways (coffee mugs, pens, pencils, calendars)
- Design of booth for trade shows
- Advertisements (billboards, space used on cars and busses, television, radio, magazines, and newspapers)
- Toll-free 800 or 888 number
- Company database

- Cooperative advertising with other businesses
- Personal selling pitches
- Characteristics of target market buyers
- Characteristics of business buyers
- Sales incentives provided to salesforce (contests, prizes, bonuses, and commissions)
- Internal messages
- Company magazines and newspapers
- Statements to shareholders
- Speeches by company leaders
- Public relations releases
- Sponsorship programs
- Web site

 CASE 2   THE CABLE COMPANY

Rachel Peterson knew she faced several major challenges as she took the job of marketing director for CableNOW. The company was the sole cable provider for six communities in northeast Louisiana. All of the cities were essentially "licensed monopolies" in the sense that no other cable company could compete within the city limits. In spite of this edge, however, competition was becoming a major problem.

Satellite television was the primary competitor for CableNOW's customers. Both DirecTV and the Dish Network had set up operations in the six communities. The two providers were able to charge lower prices for basic services. They had also started to compete by offering price reductions on installations. This made switching from cable to satellite much easier for local residents.

CableNOW's primary selling point was in the delivery of programming during bad weather. Thunderstorms and snowstorms completely disrupt a satellite signal. Severe weather is common in that part of Louisiana; however, the weather events do not affect a cable picture. CableNOW also held a competitive advantage because the company offered local business and real estate listings to subscribers. The firm also was able to

provide local radar and weather forecasts during the "Local on the 8s" segments on the Weather Channel. The satellite companies could not provide these special options.

When Rachel took the job, she knew another issue was about to unfold. CableNOW had been able to transmit each city's local channels as part of the basic cable package. Until this year, the satellite companies could not. Dish Network was changing the mix. Dish Network had just signed a contract to provide the local stations to subscribers. DirecTV did not, but did offer a greater number of channels in the company's basic package. As a result, Rachel knew she had her work cut out as the marketing department struggled to maintain share in each city.

1. What image or theme should CableNOW portray to subscribers?

2. Can you think of a way to emphasize the advantages CableNOW has in an advertising campaign?

3. Do you believe CableNOW will survive these changes over the next 10 years? Why or why not?

ENDNOTES

1. Donald Baack, "Ron Jon's Surf Shop: Building a Brand in a No-name Marketplace," *IMC Communique* (Spring 2004), p. 5; **www.ronjon.com** accessed November 7, 2007.

2. Diane Brady, "Making Marketing Measure Up," *BusinessWeek* (December 13, 2004), pp. 112–13; "Top 10: Issues Facing Senior

Marketers in 2007," *Advertising Age* 78, no. 17 (April 23, 2007), p. 23.

3. Jack Neff, "J&J Jolts 'Old' Media with $250M Spend Shift," *Advertising Age* 78, no. 12 (March 19, 2007), pp. 1, 29.

4. Donald Baack, "Communication Processes," *Organizational Behavior*. Houston: Dame Publications, Inc. (1998), pp. 313–37.

5. James G. Hutton, "Integrated Marketing Communications and the Evolution of Marketing Thought," *Journal of Business Research* 37 (November 1996), pp. 155–62.

6. Don Schultz, "Invest in Integration," *Industry Week*, 247, no. 10 (May 18, 1998), p. 20; "Integrated Marketing Communications,"

Consortium Benchmarking Study, American Productivity & Quality Center (1999).

7. Lauren Keller Johnson, "Harnessing the Power of the Customer," *Harvard Management Update*, 9 (March 2004), pp. 3–5; Patricia Seybold, *The Customer Revolution*. London: Random House Business Books (2006).

8. "U.S. Online Retail Sales," *Digital Marketing & Media Fact Pack*, Advertising Age, Crain Communications, Inc. (2007), p. 34.

9. Matt Powell, "A Steady Stride," *SCB* 39, no. 11 (November 2006), p. 15.

10. Jean-Noel Kapferer, "The Roots of Brand Loyalty Decline: An International Comparison," *Ivey Business Journal* 69, no. 4 (March–April 2005), pp. 1–6.

11. Debbie Howell, "Today's Consumers More Open to Try New Brands," *DSN Retailing Today* 43, no. 20 (October 25, 2004), pp. 29–32.

12. Sandy Brown, "Study: DVR Users Skip Live Ads, Too," *Brandweek*, 45, no. 37 (October 18, 2004), p. 7; Jennifer Lach, "Commercial Overload," *American Demographics* 21, no. 9 (September 1999), p. 20.

13. "Commercial Breakdown," *Brand Strategy* (March 2004), pp. 46–47.

14. Don E. Schultz and Philip J. Kitchen, "Integrated Marketing Communications in U.S. Advertising Agencies: An Exploratory Study," *Journal of Advertising Research* (September–October 1997), pp. 7–18.

15. Stephen J. Gould, Dawn B. Lerman, and Andreas F. Grein, "Agency Perceptions and Practices on Global IMC," *Journal of Advertising Research* (January–February 1999), pp. 7–26.

16. Ibid.

17. Parekh Rupal, "Febreze Sniffs Out New Target: Dorm Dwellers," *Advertising Age* (April, 2004), pp. 34–35.

2

Corporate Image and Brand Management

Chapter Objectives

After reading this chapter, you should be able to answer the following questions:

- **Why** is a corporation's image vitally important?

- **What** kinds of tactics and plans can be used to build an effective corporate image?

- **What** are family brands, brand extensions, flanker brands, co-brands, private brands, brand equity, and brand recognition?

- **How** are logos, packages, and labels related to image and brand management?

- **Which** brand and product characteristics can be used to establish a positive position in the market?

GUCCI

One Strong Brand Works with Others

How many Gucci items do you own? Before answering, remember that Gucci stores also sell Yves Saint Laurent, Sergio Rossi, Alexander McQueen, Oscar de la Renta, and other brands. From its humble beginnings as a single-product firm, Gucci has grown and evolved into a dominant player in the fashion industry. The path was not always easy. Gucci started in Italy, took a detour through Bahrain, and has ended up in The Netherlands.

The House of Gucci was founded by Guccio Gucci in Florence, Italy, in 1921. Gucci was the son of a leather craftsman. While visiting Paris and London, he was impressed by the sophistication of the cultures he encountered. He returned to Italy to open his store, which sold small luggage and saddlery. Soon Gucci was a widely popular store, selling exclusive leather goods.

As the Gucci company grew, the product line continued to expand, as did the number of locations. Rome and Milan were two of the new sites. Guccio Gucci died in 1953, leaving his company to his brothers and family members. The Gucci heirs opened new stores in London, Paris, New York, and Palm Beach.

When the Gucci family sold the remainder of its interests in the company in the 1980s, the firm that purchased it was located in Bahrain. Unfortunately, the company had expanded so quickly that it had lost control over quality and distribution.

The newest owners are the Gucci Group NV, located in Amsterdam. The corporation fixed many problems by issuing shares of stock to finance growth. Currently the Gucci line includes watches, leather goods, perfumes, jewelry, and other items. Gucci Group NV now owns and operates 348 stores around the world.

In the United States, Gucci is marketed as a seductive, high-fashion brand. Visitors to the Gucci Web site can view the many products and stores that are all part of Gucci's image. High fashion is a major feature of the Gucci line. All of Gucci's products are advertised to enhance the same position.

Recently, Gucci appointed three new creative directors. One directs the women's ready-to-wear collection, the second leads the men's ready-to-wear collection, and the third manages the company's fashion accessories.

Gucci provides an excellent example of how the leaders of one company were able to take a single line of products and eventually build a powerful international presence featuring dozens of products and brand names. Maintaining a cutting-edge position and image drives the marketing team at Gucci to innovate and grow with each new fashion trend.[1]

"

OVERVIEW

One of the most critical ingredients in the successful development of an integrated marketing communications plan is effective management of an organization's image. A firm's **image** is based on the feelings consumers and businesses have about the overall organization and its individual brands. Advertising, consumer promotions, trade promotions, personal selling, the company's Web site, and other marketing activities all affect consumer perceptions of the firm. A strong brand creates a major advantage for any product or service. When the image of an organization or one of its brands is somehow tarnished, sales revenues and profits can plummet. Rebuilding or revitalizing an image is a difficult task.

Brand managers and advertising account executives are responsible for developing and maintaining a quality image. A company's image has a "bottom line" that can even be assigned a value on accounting statements. Advertising managers and other marketing experts are expected to create messages that (1) sell products in the short term and (2) build a firm's image over time. Advertising creatives must think about both goals as they design advertisements and promotional campaigns.

When the marketing team is able to clearly understand the firm's image and has knowledge about the strengths of individual brands, it is easier to make solid connections with consumers and business-to-business customers. A strong IMC foundation combines understanding of the firm's image and brands with assessments of consumer and business buyer behaviors. Then, the

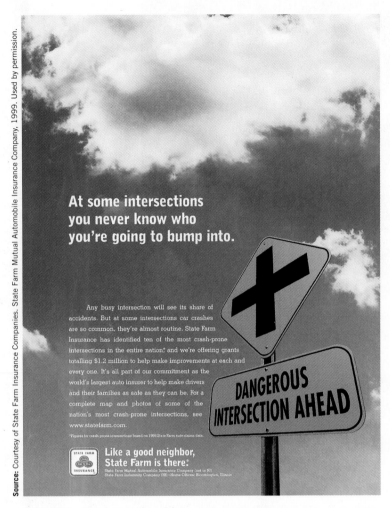

At some intersections you never know who you're going to bump into.

Any busy intersection will see its share of accidents. But at some intersections car crashes are so common, they're almost routine. State Farm Insurance has identified ten of the most crash-prone intersections in the entire nation,* and we're offering grants totalling $1.2 million to help make improvements at each and every one. It's all part of our commitment as the world's largest auto insurer to help make drivers and their families as safe as they can be. For a complete map and photos of some of the nation's most crash-prone intersections, see www.statefarm.com.

*Figures for crash-prone intersections based on 1998 State Farm auto claims data.

Like a good neighbor, State Farm is there.®

State Farm Mutual Automobile Insurance Company (not in NJ)
State Farm Indemnity Company (NJ)–Home Offices: Bloomington, Illinois

A State Farm ad stressing driver safety.

marketing team can prepare consistent messages designed to reach all of the individuals who might purchase a company's goods and services.

The first part of this chapter examines the activities involved in managing a corporation's image. The second part addresses ways to develop and promote the various forms of brand names. Brand equity and brand parity are also described. Brand names, company logos, packages, and labels are closely tied to a firm's image.

CORPORATE IMAGE

Effective marketing communication starts with a clearly defined corporate image. The image summarizes what the company stands for and the position the company has established. Whether it is the "good hands" of Allstate Insurance or the "good neighbors" at State Farm Insurance, the goal of image management is to create a specific impression in the minds of clients and customers. In the case of insurance companies, helpfulness, safety, and security are common and favorable elements of strong image.

Remember that what *consumers* believe about a firm is far more important than how company officials view the image. Corporate names such as Dell, Toyota, Nike, and ExxonMobile all conjure images in the minds of consumers. Although the specific version of the image varies from consumer to consumer or business buyer to business buyer, the overall image of a firm is determined by the combined views of all publics, which in turn can have a positive or a negative influence on customers.

Components of a Corporate Image

Consumers encounter many things as they interact with a company or an organization. One primary component of a corporate image is customer perceptions of the goods or services the organization offers. In a study conducted by Edelman Asia Pacific, the quality of a company's goods and services ranked as the most important component of corporate image. The willingness of a firm to stand behind its goods and services when something went wrong was a close second. Third on the list were perceptions of how the firm dealt with customers, such as by being pleasant, helpful, or professional.[2]

Every firm's image consists of a unique set of components. The corporate image of an automobile manufacturer such as Porsche, Mazda, Toyota, or General Motors might be based on the following: (1) evaluations of vehicles, (2) whether the company is foreign or domestic, (3) customer views of each company's advertisements, and (4) reactions to the local dealership. Further, the corporation's image might include consumer assessments of company employees. In fact, the mechanic trying to repair a vehicle at a local Mr. Goodwrench garage could become the dominant factor that shapes a customer's image of General Motors.

Recently, Subaru and Mazda created programs that were designed to emphasize the importance of the dealership as an influence on consumer assessments of an automobile company's corporate image. Both firms launched aggressive remodeling plans for local dealerships, with the goal of providing a more pleasant shopping environment. These new-look dealerships helped boost the images of both Subaru and Mazda, resulting in higher sales. Subaru dealers that remodeled using the new retail format sold 54 percent more vehicles in the following year. Mazda dealers that adopted the new retail design sold 30 percent more vehicles.[3] Toyota, recognizing that many women purchase automobiles, and that an even greater number have a significant influence on the purchase decision, launched "Image USA II." The program's recommendations suggested that every Toyota dealer provide a children's play area in the showroom, a coffee bar in the service area, and nicely decorated restrooms.[4] The idea was to make the dealership image more attractive to female customers to enhance the company's image.

A corporate image also contains invisible and intangible elements (see Figure 2.1). When consumers learn that a pharmaceutical or cosmetic company has a policy that prohibits product testing on animals, this information will be integrated into their attitudes toward the firm. Personnel policies and practices impact the firm's image. Strikes and labor disputes often have a negative impact on a firm's image. The business philosophies of Bill Gates at Microsoft and Rachel Ray (**www.rachelray.com**) affect the images consumers have of the two companies. The beliefs and attitudes consumers have about Japan might influence their views of companies such as Sony and Toyota.

Negative publicity has the potential to stain or damage consumer perceptions of a corporation's image. Powerful examples of these events took place at Enron, WorldCom, and Tyco. Some writers believe the problems at these companies have created distrust of all corporations.

The Role of a Corporate Image— Consumer Perspective

From a consumer's perspective, the corporate image serves several useful functions. These include:

Pity you have nothing left to wish for.

It's all come true. The endless horizon. The precise handling. And the way the sounds and sensations of the night resonate throughout the open cockpit. The 911 Turbo Cabriolet delivers the road in its most potent form. Perhaps it's time you followed your dreams. Porsche. There is no substitute.

The new 911 Turbo Cabriolet

Porsche maintains a strong and positive corporate image.

- Providing assurance regarding purchase decisions of familiar products in unfamiliar settings
- Giving assurance about the purchase when the buyer has little or no previous experience with the good or service
- Reducing search time in purchase decisions
- Providing psychological reinforcement and social acceptance of purchases

A well-known corporate image provides consumers with positive assurance about what to expect from a firm. A can of Coke or Pepsi purchased in Anchorage, Alaska, has

Tangible Elements	Intangible Elements
1. Goods and services sold	1. Corporate, personnel, and environmental policies
2. Retail outlets where the product is sold	2. Ideals and beliefs of corporate personnel
3. Factories where the product is produced	3. Culture of country and location of company
4. Advertising, promotions, and other forms of communications	4. Media reports
5. Corporate name and logo	
6. Packages and labels	
7. Employees	

FIGURE 2.1
Elements of a Corporate Image

a comparable taste to one purchased in Liverpool, England, or Kuala Lumpur, Malaysia. KFC serves the same or similar meals in San Francisco as the ones sold in Minneapolis or Paris. A consumer on vacation knows that if she makes a purchase from a Wal-Mart in Texas, a defective item can be returned to a local store in Toronto, Canada.

This assurance has even greater value when consumers seek to purchase goods or services with which they have little experience. Consider families on vacation. Many travelers look for names or logos of companies from their native areas. Purchasing from a familiar corporation is viewed as being a "safer" strategy than buying something from an unknown company. Taking a room at a hotel that the consumer has never heard of seems riskier than utilizing a familiar one. Thus, a family visiting Brazil might normally not stay at the Holiday Inn, but because it is a recognizable name they believe it is a lower-risk option than an unknown hotel.

Another significant role corporate image plays for the consumer is reducing search time. Purchasing a product from a familiar firm saves time and effort. An individual loyal to Ford spends fewer hours searching for a new car than does someone with no loyalty to any automobile manufacturer. The same holds in purchasing low-cost items such as groceries. Search time is saved when a consumer purchases items from the same organization, such as Campbell's or Nabisco.

For many individuals, purchasing from a highly recognized company provides psychological reinforcement and social acceptance. Psychological reinforcement comes from feeling that a wise choice was made and the belief that the good or service will perform well. Social acceptance is derived from knowing that many other individuals also have purchased from the same firm. More importantly, other people, such as family and friends, are likely to accept the choice.

Which are the most reputable firms? Intrabrand produced a list of the top 100 corporate brands. Companies, such as Procter & Gamble, that have a portfolio of products and brands, were not included in the evaluation. In addition, companies that are privately held, such as VISA, or companies that operate under different names in different countries, such as Wal-Mart, were not included. The list only notes corporations that provide products under one name. Using these criteria, Interbrand ranked Coca-Cola as the top global corporate brand. Microsoft was second. See Table 2.1 for a complete listing.

The Role of a Corporate Image—Business-to-Business Perspective

A strong corporate image creates a major competitive advantage in the business-to-business marketplace. Many of the processes that affect individual consumers also affect business buyers. This means that purchasing from a well-known company reduces the

TABLE 2.1 Top 10 Global Corporate Brands

Rank	Company	Brand Value (billions)	Country of Ownership
1	Coca-Cola	$65.3	United States
2	Microsoft	$58.7	United States
3	IBM	$57.1	United States
4	General Electric	$51.5	United States
5	Nokia	$33.7	Finland
6	Toyota	$32.1	Japan
7	Intel	$30.9	United States
8	McDonald's	$29.4	United States
9	Disney	$29.2	United States
10	Mercedes-Benz	$23.6	Germany

Source: Based on "The 100 Top Brands," *BusinessWeek* (August 6, 2007), pp. 59–64.

feelings of risk. A firm with a well-established image makes the choice easier for business customers seeking to reduce search time. Psychological reinforcement and social acceptance may also be present. Company buyers who make quality purchases might receive praise from organizational leaders and others involved in the process. Therefore, once again, a strong company image or brand name can make the difference in a choice between competitors.

Brand image is especially valuable to a company expanding internationally. Members of foreign businesses are likely to feel more comfortable making transactions with a firm that has a strong corporate image. Risk and uncertainty are reduced when the buyer knows something about the seller. Therefore, a company such as IBM can expand into a new country and more quickly gain the confidence of consumers and businesses.

The Role of a Corporate Image—Company Perspective

From the viewpoint of the firm itself, a highly reputable image generates many benefits:

- Extension of positive consumer feelings to new products
- The ability to charge a higher price or fee
- Consumer loyalty leading to more frequent purchases
- Positive word-of-mouth endorsements
- Higher level of channel power
- The ability to attract quality employees
- More favorable ratings by financial observers and analysts

A quality corporate image provides the basis for the development of new goods and services. When consumers are already familiar with the corporate name and image, the introduction of a new product becomes much easier, because long-term customers are willing to give something new a try. Customers normally transfer their trust in and beliefs about the corporation to a new product.

A strong corporate image allows a company to charge more for its goods and services. Most customers believe they "get what they pay for." Better quality is often associated with a higher price. This, in turn, can lead to greater markup margins and profits for the firm.

Further, firms with well-developed images have more loyal customers. Customer loyalty results in patrons purchasing more products over time. Loyal customers also are less likely to make substitution purchases when other companies offer discounts, sales, and other enticements to switch brands.

Heightened levels of customer loyalty are often associated with positive word-of-mouth endorsements. Favorable comments help generate additional sales and attract new customers. Most consumers have more faith in personal references than in any form of advertising or promotion.

Positive consumer attitudes create corporate equity, which provides greater channel power. Retailers offer brands that are viewed positively by customers. Retailers buy the brands that pull customers into stores. As a result, a company that has a high positive image has more control and power in the channel and with retailers.

Another advantage of a dominant corporate image is attracting quality employees. Just as consumers are drawn to strong firms, potential workers apply for jobs at companies with solid reputations. Consequently, recruiting and selection costs are reduced. There is less employee turnover, so long as employees are treated fairly.

A strong corporate reputation often results in a more favorable rating by Wall Street analysts and by other financial institutions. This is especially helpful when a company seeks to raise

The strong General Mills brand name makes the introduction of new products easier.

Source: Reprinted with the permission of General Mills, Inc.

FIGURE 2.2
Customer and Company Benefits of a Positive Corporate Image

Customer Benefits	Company Benefits
◆ Assurance of product quality	◆ Brand extensions are easier
◆ Assurance when not familiar with product category	◆ Can charge a higher price
◆ Reduces search time	◆ Higher customer loyalty
◆ Psychological and social acceptance	◆ More frequent purchases
	◆ Positive word-of-mouth communications
	◆ Ability to attract quality employees
	◆ More favorable view by financial analysts

capital. Further, legislators and governmental agencies tend to act in a more supportive manner toward companies with strong and positive reputations. Lawmakers are less inclined to pursue actions that might hurt the business. Members of regulatory agencies are less likely to believe rumors of wrongdoing.

Building a strong corporate image provides tangible and intangible benefits. Both customers and organizations benefit from a well-known firm with an established reputation. Figure 2.2 summarizes these benefits. Organizational leaders devote considerable amounts of time and energy to building and maintaining a positive organizational image. Client companies expect advertising account managers and creatives to help design marketing programs that take advantage of the benefits of a strong corporate image.

PROMOTING THE DESIRED IMAGE

The right image can be a major part of an organization's success. To promote the desired image, the marketing team should first try to understand the nature of the company's current image. Then future communications can be tailored to promote the right image. These communications reach every constituency, including customers, suppliers, and employees.

Company leaders study the firm's image during the promotions opportunity analysis (see Chapter 4) phase of the IMC program. Image is connected to a company's strengths and weaknesses. A strong image can be combined with an opportunity discovered in the external environment to create a major strategic advantage for the firm.

As the advertising team studies a company's image, other consumers, especially non-customers of the firm, should be approached to ascertain their views. Once those in the firm understand how others see the company, they can make decisions about how to correct any misperceptions and/or build on the image that customers currently hold. In making decisions about the image to be projected, marketers should remember four things:

1. The image being projected accurately portrays the firm and coincides with the goods and services offered.
2. Reinforcing or rejuvenating a current image that is consistent with the view of consumers is easier to accomplish than changing a well-established image.
3. It is difficult to change the images people hold about a given company. In some cases, modifying the current image or trying to create an entirely new image is not possible.
4. Any negative or bad press can quickly destroy an image that took years to build. Reestablishing or rebuilding the firm's image takes a great deal of time when the firm's reputation has been damaged.

Creating the Right Image

In each industry, the right image sends a clear message about the unique nature of an organization and its products. A strong image accurately portrays what the firm sells. In the BMW advertisement in this section, the goal is to reinforce the idea that BMW is a quality product and the top brand in the motorcycle industry. The message is that "BMW

Motorcycles are the indisputable mark of a real ride," according to BMW brand manager Kerri Martin.[5] When an image is well established, other promotions can be built around the reputation. This fuels long-term customer loyalty and future sales.

Creating the right image is often more challenging for a small business. Oftentimes no specific image exists. For example, Portillo's Hot Dogs had been operating in Chicago for 42 years. When owner Dick Portillo decided to open a new outlet, he was shocked to learn that 30 percent of the people in the area had never heard of Portillo's. With over 2,300 places in Chicago offering hot dogs, it was going to be difficult to attract the attention of potential buyers.

Portillo met with an advertising agency. Together they decided to create television and radio advertisements that would project an image in which Portillo's restaurants were "warm and fun." According to Portillo, the integrated image advertising program that was produced created a "warm and fun" image and put his chain of restaurants "on a roll."[6]

Let's just say tailgaters aren't a problem.

An image-building ad for BMW Motorcycles.

Source: Courtesy of BMW of North America, LLC. © 1999 BMW of North America, Inc. All Rights Reserved. The BMW trademark and logo are registered. This advertisement is reproduced with the permission of BMW of North America, Inc. for promotional purposes only.

Rejuvenating an Image

Rejuvenating an image helps a firm sell new products and can attract new customers. At the same time, reinforcing previous aspects of an image assists the company in retaining loyal patrons, who are comfortable with the firm's original image. The key to successful image reengineering is to remain consistent with a previous image while at the same time building to incorporate new elements to expand the firm's target audience.

Rejuvenating a firm's image can be difficult. It takes time and effort. McDonald's faced this problem when the company encountered negative publicity about health-related concerns and its menu. According to Wendy Cook, McDonald's vice president of U.S. menu innovations and marketing, the key to rejuvenating the company's image was to send the message that it is possible to buy healthy food at McDonald's. The main product leading the effort was a series of salads. Before launching the new salad line, McDonald's marketing team talked to women, the target market. The team learned that women notice details such as all-natural dressings with low-fat options and the 16 different kinds of lettuce. Using this information, new advertisements were developed using a "girl talk" approach where women discovered a great salad with a variety of options. This integrated marketing approach helped modify McDonald's image for working women who might stop there for lunch.[7]

Holiday Inn faced a similar situation. Consumers viewed the hotel chain as consisting of outdated hotels with old décor. To regain its image as a midlevel hotel, over $1 billion was spent on interior and exterior renovations and updates; 150 properties that did not meet the new standards were sold and the proceeds were invested in the remaining hotels. Helen Travers, a corporate travel planner, stated, "It's about time. My clients haven't stayed in Holiday Inns in years [because] the chain hasn't kept up." Holiday Inn's marketing team also created a new logo. The goal was to rejuvenate the brand and regain the business travelers it had lost.[8]

Changing an Image

It is difficult to completely change the image people have about a company. Changing an image becomes necessary, however, when target markets have begun to shrink or disappear, or the firm's image no longer matches industry trends and consumer expectations. At that point, company leaders must carefully consider what they wish to change, why they wish to make a change, and how they intend to accomplish the task.

One company that recognized the need to change its image while facing immense challenges is AT&T. Many consumers associate AT&T with the old-fashioned landline

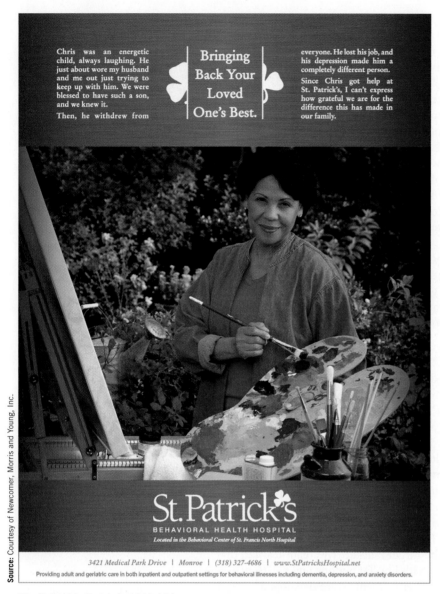

St. Patrick's Behavioral Health Hospital created this ad to help change the public's perception of mental health care.

phones and the huge yellow telephone directories. They do not see the company as a leader among high-speed digital networks and cell phones. With its purchase of Cingular, AT&T entered into the cell phone service and networking industries. At the time of the purchase, company executives decided to keep the AT&T name and convince consumers that the company was now new and could meet everyone's communication needs. Still, the image change did not occur.

Recognizing the need to modify consumer perceptions of AT&T, company officials incorporated Cingular's orange color into its branding scheme. Monthly billing statements added the orange color, as did retail stores and the company's Web site. To coincide with the addition of the orange color, AT&T launched a national advertising campaign featuring mobile professionals and young people from all over the world using AT&T wireless products. The company also partnered with Apple to launch the iPhone.[9]

The question remains as to whether these changes will be enough to refurbish AT&T's image from the old-fashioned landline phone company to something more modern. Some marketing experts think the image is too ingrained to change. Others feel it can be done. Time will tell. AT&T's management team recognizes it will not be easy to change an image that has developed over decades.

Changing an image requires more than one well-made ad or press release or adding color to a logo and retail store signage. It begins with internal company personnel and products and then moves outward to suppliers, other businesses, and especially to consumers.[10]

CORPORATE NAME

A corporate name is the overall banner under which all other operations occur. According to David Placek, president and founder of Lexicon, Inc., "The corporate name is really the cornerstone of a company's relationship with its customers. It sets an attitude and tone and is the first step toward a personality."[11] Corporate names can be divided into the following four categories based on their actual, implied, or visionary meaning (see Figure 2.3).[12]

Overt names include Midwest Airlines and BMW Motorcycles USA. *Implied names* include FedEx and IBM (International Business Machines). *Conceptual names*, such as Google and Krispy Kreme, take a different approach. The name "Google" evokes a vision of a place where an endless number of items can be found, and "Krispy

FIGURE 2.3
Categories of Corporate Names

- ◆ **Overt names.** Reveal what a company does.
- ◆ **Implied names.** Contain recognizable words or word parts that convey what a company does.
- ◆ **Conceptual names.** Capture the essence of what a company offers.
- ◆ **Iconoclastic names.** Represent something unique, different, and memorable.

Kreme" suggests confectionaries filled with tasty crème. Monster.com and Fathead.com are examples of *iconoclastic names.*

The first two categories (overt and implied) are easier to market. They make it easier for consumers to recall the good or service. The other two categories (conceptual and iconoclastic) require a greater marketing effort to ensure that consumers connect the corporate name with the goods and services that are being sold.

CORPORATE LOGOS

Another aspect of a corporation's image is its logo. A **corporate logo** is a symbol used to identify a company and its brands, helping to convey the overall corporate image. The logo should be carefully designed to be compatible with the corporation's name. Many organizations have spent millions of dollars selecting and promoting corporate names and logos. Consumers are flooded with numerous advertisements every day. A strong corporate name featuring a well-designed logo can be a powerful aid that helps consumers to remember specific brands and company advertisements. Search time might also be reduced as consumers look for specific corporate products that are easily identified by logos and names. Quality logos and corporate names should meet the four tests shown in Figure 2.4.[13]

Logos are especially important for in-store shopping. The mind processes visuals faster than it does words. A corporate logo might be more quickly recognized by shoppers. Logo recognition can occur at two levels. First, a consumer might remember seeing the logo in the past. It is stored in memory, and when it is seen at the store, that memory is jogged. Second, a logo may remind the consumer of the brand or corporate name. This reminder can elicit positive feelings regarding either the corporation or branded item.

Successful logos elicit shared meanings across consumers. When a logo elicits a consensual meaning among customers, the process is known as **stimulus codability**. Logos with high stimulus codability evoke consensual meanings within a culture or subculture (such as the Prudential Rock). Logos with a high degree of codability are more easily recognized, such as Apple, McDonald's, and Pepsi. Companies that have logos with a low degree of codability must spend more money on advertising. Recognition comes from familiarity rather than stimulus codability. For example, Nike spent a considerable amount of resources making the "swoosh" recognizable to those in various target markets. Early in its life, the swoosh, by itself, did not conjure any specific image of the firm.

Figure 2.5 provides insights about the creation of some famous logos. Notice that the Apple logo created by Rob Janoff of Regis McKenna Advertising in 1977 had a bite taken from the apple so consumers wouldn't mistake it for a tomato. The Nike swoosh logo was created in 1971 by Carolyn Davidson, a graphic-design student. She was only paid $35 for the design.

Haik Humble Eye Center is an overt corporate name.

Sartor Associates designed five different logos for Achievers, Inc.

- ◆ Recognizable
- ◆ Familiar
- ◆ Elicits a consensual meaning among those in the firm's target market
- ◆ Evokes positive feelings

FIGURE 2.4
Four Tests of Quality Logos and Corporate Names

FIGURE 2.5
How Were These Logos Developed?

+ **Apple**—Created by Rob Janoff of Regis McKenna Advertising in 1977. Some people think the bite represents Adam and Eve, but it was actually placed there so people wouldn't mistake it for a tomato.
+ **Coke**—One of the most preeminent logos in the world. It was created in 1886 by Frank Robinson, who was the bookkeeper for John Pemberton, creator of Coca-Cola. Robinson was selected to design the logo because he had good handwriting.
+ **FedEx**—Created by Landor Associates in 1994. The logo designers kept the orange and purple color but shortened the name to "FedEx" as a verb.
+ **McDonald's**—Before it was adopted by McDonald's, the arches represented military triumph. Now they represent the triumph of the cheeseburger. The arches were adopted in 1962 as the logo. Before the arches, McDonald's used the cartoon mascot Speedee.
+ **Nike**—The swoosh was designed in 1971 by Carolyn Davidson, a graphic-design student. She was paid $35 for the design by Phil Knight, founder of Nike. In 1983, she was rewarded with shares of Nike stock.
+ *Playboy*—Hugh Hefner originally planned on calling the magazine *Stag Party* and used a stag as the logo. Just before the first issue was published, his attorney advised against the name and logo. The bunny logo was created by art director Art Paul in just 30 minutes. It was placed on the second issue of the magazine.
+ **Starbucks**—The stylized mermaid logo was created in 1971. At the original store in Seattle, the mermaid is topless and her hair is different. The logo was based on work done by Hadank, a graphic designer in Germany.

Source: From "The Logo" by Gavin Edwards from *Rolling Stone*, May 15, 2003 © Rolling Stone LLC 2003 All Rights Reserved. Reprinted by Permission.

Later, however, Phil Knight, founder of Nike, decided that she should receive additional compensation.

BRANDING

Many of the benefits of a strong corporate image also apply to brands. The primary difference between the two is that of scope. **Brands** are names assigned to an individual good or service or to a group of complementary products. A corporation's image covers every aspect of the firm's operations. The Hormel corporation offers several brands, including Dinty Moore, Jennie-O, Chi-Chi's Mexican Products, Valley Fresh, Farmer John, and SPAM.

An effective brand name allows a company to charge more for products, which in turn increases gross margins. Strong brands provide customers with assurances of quality and reduction of search time in the purchasing process.

One primary feature that keeps a brand strong is that it contains something that is **salient** to customers. The salient attribute can come from several sources. One is that the product or brand has benefits consumers consider important and of higher quality than other brands. Another may come from the view that the brand is a good value. A third might be the belief that the brand is superior to other brands because if its image. Consumers recommend brands to their families and friends because of one or more salient properties.[14]

Developing a Strong Brand Name

Developing a strong brand begins with discovering why consumers buy a brand and why they rebuy the brand. Questions to be asked include:

- What are the brand's most compelling benefits?
- What emotions are elicited by the brand either during or after the purchase?
- What one word best describes the brand?
- What is important to consumers in the purchase of the brand?

Once the answers to these questions are known, a company's marketing team can cultivate a stronger brand position.

Two important processes help establish stronger brand prestige. First, the brand name must be prominently promoted through repetitious ads. The overwhelming numbers of brands and advertisements consumers see make repetition essential to capturing the buyer's attention. Repetition increases the odds that a brand and its accompanying message will be stored in long-term memory and recalled.

Second, the brand name should be associated with the product's most prominent characteristic. Many consumers associate Crest with "cavity prevention." Coca-Cola seeks to associate its name with a product that is "refreshing." For Volvo, the impression is "safety." For BMW, it is "performance driving."

Brands develop histories. They have personalities. They include strengths, weaknesses, and flaws. Many brands produce family trees. A **family brand** is one in which a company offers a series or group of products under one brand name. For example, the Black & Decker brand is present on numerous power tools. The advantage of a family brand is that consumers usually transfer the image associated with the brand name to any new products added to current lines. When Black & Decker offers a new power tool, the new item automatically assumes the reputation associated with the Black & Decker name. These transfer associations occur as long as the new product is within the same product category. When additional products are not related to the brand's core merchandise, the transfer of loyalty might not occur as easily.

The goal of branding is to set a product apart from its competitors. Market researchers must seek to identify the "one thing" the brand can stand for, that consumers recognize, and that is salient to consumers. When these tasks are successfully completed, more powerful brand recognition occurs. In the marketplace for automotive suspension systems, the Skyjacker brand is well-known to many consumers, distributors, and automobile manufacturers.

In the automotive suspension system marketplace, Skyjacker is a well-known brand.

After brand recognition has been achieved, the next step is to prolong its success. The secret to a long brand life is finding one unique selling point and staying with it. Crest has touted its cavity-fighting ability for years. Tide has been viewed as a powerful laundry detergent for decades. Remember that some brands experience decline. If a company waits too long to respond, the result might be the eventual death of the brand. If caught in time, a brand can be revived and given new life. The marketing team must pay careful attention to how each brand is perceived and how it is performing over time.[15]

BRAND EQUITY

One major problem many established companies encounter is *brand parity.* Brand parity occurs when there are few tangible distinctions between competing brands in mature markets. Brand parity means customers see only minor product differences. In many product categories, even minor variations are hard to find.

One major force that can help fight the problem of brand parity is brand equity. **Brand equity** is a set of characteristics that are unique to a brand. In essence, brand equity is the perception that a good or service with a given brand name is different and better.

Brand equity creates several benefits. First, brand equity allows the company to charge a higher price. The company will retain a greater market share than would otherwise be expected for an undifferentiated product. Brand equity is a source of channel power as

FIGURE 2.6
Benefits of Brand Equity

1. Allows manufacturers to charge more for products	4. Captures additional retail shelf space
2. Creates higher gross margins	5. Serves as a weapon against consumers switching due to sales promotions
3. Provides power with retailers and wholesalers	6. Prevents erosion of market share

the company deals with retailers. This power, in turn, leads to an improved position in terms of shelf space and displays. Brand equity also influences wholesalers by affecting what they stock and which brands they encourage their customers to purchase. Wholesalers often will stock several brands but place greater emphasis on high-equity brands.

In business-to-business markets, brand equity often allows a company to charge a higher price. Equity also influences selections in the buying decision-making process. Products with strong brand equity are often selected over products with low brand equity or brands that firms know little about. The same scenario is present in international markets. Brand equity opens doors of foreign firms, brokers, and retailers and provides privileges that products with low brand equity cannot obtain.

Brand equity is a strong weapon that might dissuade consumers from looking for a cheaper product or for special deals or incentives to purchase another brand. Brand equity prevents erosion of a product's market share, even when there is a proliferation of brands coupled with endless promotional maneuvers by competitors. Additional benefits of brand equity are displayed in Figure 2.6.

Steps to Building Brand Equity

Brand-name recognition and recall can be built through repetitious advertising. Building brand equity, however, requires the company to achieve more than brand recognition. Recognition is only the first phase of the marketing program. Building brand equity includes the steps outlined in Figure 2.7.

The first step to building brand equity is having a distinctive brand and deciding what unique selling point should be promoted. Part of this analysis involves the need to continually innovate. Many products compete in mature markets. Companies that do not innovate and move forward quickly fall behind. For example, it may be tempting for Procter & Gamble not to tinker with Tide. Doing so, however, might mean a steady erosion of market share to brands with new features. Instead, Procter & Gamble's management team widened the Tide family of detergents to include new products such as Tide Coldwater and Tide Kick. Tide Kick is a combination measuring cup and stain penetrator. The result of this continuous innovation was a 2.6 percent gain in sales when industry sales increased less than 1 percent.[16]

In today's society, customers want innovations and new products. They also want them *fast*. Handbag designer Coach used to introduce new products quarterly. Now new items are released monthly. Coach CEO Lew Frankfort states that "For brands to stay relevant, they have to stay on their toes. Complacency has no place in this market." In any given month, new products account for up to 30 percent of U.S. retail store sales.[17]

Another ingredient in building brand equity is to integrate new and old media. Consumers are bombarded with advertising messages from a multitude of sources. Therefore, the marketing team must try to integrate all messages while looking for new, nontraditional methods of communicating. Although television, radio, magazines, and newspapers remain as key media, newer alternative advertising methods can help strengthen a brand name. For instance, Pontiac has shifted a large portion of its television advertising from prime-time television time to the NCAA basketball tournament and

FIGURE 2.7
Steps in Building Brand Equity

1. Research and analyze what it would take to make the brand distinctive.	3. Move fast.
	4. Integrate new and old media.
2. Engage in continuous innovation.	5. Focus on domination.

other sports entertainment shows. In addition, the marketing team shifted significant dollars to online gaming, Internet ads, and branded music.[18]

Pepperidge Farm has gone even farther. The company has a new campaign theme, "Connecting through cookies." The primary component of the campaign is a Web site, **www.artofthecookie. com**, where women can keep in contact with each other. One quote on the site says "Our friendship with our girlfriends makes our lives much richer." In addition to allowing women to connect with each other, the site also displays video clips of Sally Horchow's cross-country trip from Las Vegas to Nantucket. During the trip, Ms. Horchow spoke to women about making and maintaining friendships. She serves as a co-host for the site and is the author of the book *The Art of Friendship: 70 Simple Rules for Making Meaningful Connections.*[19]

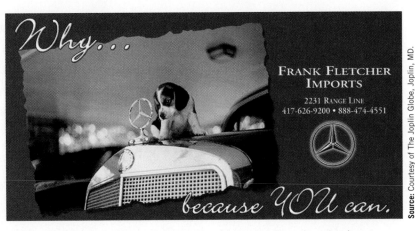

Mercedes Benz is a dominant brand in the luxury vehicle class.

The Web site has been supported by print ads as well as a public relations initiative that involved a survey of American women on the topic of friendship. The ads ran in magazines such as *Country Living, Good Housekeeping*, and *Redbook*. The headline for each was "Friendship. Is yours an art form or a lost art?" The goal of the Web site and the print ads is to forge an emotional connection with customers that is difficult to reach using broadcast advertising alone.

Pepperidge Farm is not alone in the move to social network marketing. A growing number of other companies, such as Blockbuster, Circuit City, Coca-Cola, Sony, and Microsoft now advertise on social networking Web sites such as Bebo, Buzznet, Facebook, and MySpace. According to eMarketer, a research firm, over $2 billion per year is spent on advertising on these types of Web sites.[20]

Brand equity involves domination. *Domination* is a strongly held view that the brand is number one in its product category. Domination can take place in a geographic region or in a smaller product category or market niche. To dominate, the brand must be viewed as number one in some way. Intel processors hold this status. For automobiles, the number-one car in terms of safety is Volvo. Domination means delivering on the promise. Customers must believe that the Intel processor is the best and that Volvo is the safest.

Developing brand equity in today's competitive global market requires cutting-edge innovation. Company leaders know they must offer state-of-the-art products and move faster than the competition in order to effectively reach the marketplace. The brand message must stand out. Brand equity grows when the same integrated message that was heard before reaches consumers in a new place, through a different medium.

Measuring Brand Equity

Trying to determine whether brand equity exists is difficult. One method marketing experts use is brand metrics. **Brand metrics** measure returns on branding investments. Attitudinal measures associated with branding can be used to track awareness, recall, and recognition. To increase their power, these factors can be tied with other variables (e.g., brand awareness coupled with intent to buy). Brand awareness can also be connected to use of either the product class (mustard) or the brand (Kraft, Grey Poupon). Remember that when measuring awareness, recall, and recognition, a brand can be recalled for negative as well as positive reasons.[21]

Recognizing that popular brands are not always powerful brands, AlixPartners developed a method for measuring a brand's strength based on its popularity, its level of trust, and its level of distrust. Figure 2.8 shows the top 10 most powerful brands, according to AlixPartners.[22] According to this firm, the best brands in the future will be those that have a high level of awareness, are trusted by consumers, and have low levels of distrust, resulting in higher brand power index scores (BPI).

FIGURE 2.8
Top 10 Most Powerful Brands

Brand	Trust Rate (%)	Distrust Rate (%)	BPI
Sony	9.2%	1.8%	75.1
Johnson & Johnson	5.7	0.5	55.3
Kraft	5.2	0.6	48.7
Procter & Gamble	5.8	1.1	48.2
Campbell's	3.5	0.4	32.9
Toyota	4.1	1.2	28.0
Tylenol	3.2	0.6	27.2
Dell	5.1	2.1	27.0
General Mills	2.7	0.2	25.9
Hewlett-Packard	4.0	1.5	23.5

Source: Based on Fred Crawford, "Branding Isn't Like High School," *Retail Merchandiser* 47, no. 6 (July–August 2007), pp. S4–S9.

DSN Retailing used a different method for measuring brand equity, asking consumers to identify their most preferred brand in a particular product category.[23] Figure 2.9 displays the complete list in each of the categories.

Although these methods of measuring brand equity can provide valid information, CEOs and other corporate leaders often want real, hard numbers. One such method for generating hard numbers is known as the *revenue premium* approach. The method compares a branded product to the same product without a brand name. To calculate a brand's revenue premium, the revenue generated by a particular brand is compared to a private-label brand. The difference is the revenue premium, or value, of that brand and would equate to the brand equity that has accrued.[24]

BRAND EXTENSIONS AND FLANKER BRANDS

One common approach a firm can use to enter a new market is a *brand extension strategy.* Figure 2.10 identifies several types of brand strategies. **Brand extension** is the use of an established brand name on goods or services. The extension might or might not be related to the core brand. For example, Nike has been successful in extending its brand name to a line of clothing. Black & Decker has been successful in extending its brand name to new types of power tools. It has not been as successful, however, in extending its line to small kitchen appliances.

FIGURE 2.9
Most Preferred Brands

Women's Apparel
1. Hanes (39%)
2. Levi's (10%)
3. Victoria's Secret (6%)
4. Liz Claiborne (4%)
5. Nike (4%)
6. Fruit-of-the-Loom (4%)

Snacks
1. Frito Lay/Lays (19%)
2. Doritos (10%)
3. Hershey's (6%)
4. Pringles (6%)
5. Oreos (5%)

Beverages
1. Coke (26%)
2. Pepsi (22%)
3. Dr. Pepper (6%)
4. Mountain Dew (5%)

Consumer Electronics
1. Sony (27%)
2. RCA (6%)
3. Panasonic (6%)
4. Dell (5%)
5. Duracell (4%)

Source: Based on Debbie Howell, "Top Brands," *DSN Retailing Today* 44, no. 20 (October 24, 2005), pp. 38–42.

FIGURE 2.10
Types of Brands

- **Family brands.** A group of related products sold under one name.
- **Brand extension.** The use of an established brand name on products or services not related to the core brand.
- **Flanker brand.** The development of a new brand sold in the same category as another product.
- **Co-branding.** The offering of two or more brands in a single marketing offer.
- **Ingredient branding.** The placement of one brand within another brand.
- **Cooperative branding.** The joint venture of two or more brands into a new product or service.
- **Complementary branding.** The marketing of two brands together for co-consumption.
- **Private brands.** Proprietary brands marketed by an organization and sold within the organization's outlets.

An alternative to a brand extension program is a flanker brand. A **flanker brand** is the development of a new brand by a company in a good or service category in which it currently has a brand offering. For example, Procter & Gamble's primary laundry detergents are Cheer and Tide. Over the years, P&G has introduced a number of additional brands, such as Ivory Snow. In total, P&G offers 11 different brands of detergents in North America; 16 in Latin America; 12 in Asia; and 17 in Europe, the Middle East, and Africa. Table 2.2 lists Procter & Gamble's various brands of laundry detergents,

TABLE 2.2 Brands Sold by Procter & Gamble

Product Category	North America	Latin America	Asia	Europe, Middle East, and Africa
Laundry and cleaning brands	Bold	Ace	Ariel	Ace
	Bounce	Ariel	Bonus	Alo
	Cheer	Bold	Bounce	Ariel
	Downy	Downy	Cheer	Azurit
	Dreft	Duplex	Doll	Bold
	Dryel	InExtra	Ezee	Bonux
	Era	Limay	Gaofuli	Bounce
	Gain	Magia Blanca	Lanxiang	Dash
	Ivory Snow	ODD Fases	Panda	Daz
	Oxydol	Pop	Perla	Dreft
	Tide	Quanto	Tide	Fairy
		Rapido	Trilo	Lenor
		Ridex		Maintax
		Romtensid		Myth
		Supermo		Rei
		Tide		Tide
				Tix
Cosmetics	Cover Girl	Cover Girl	Cover Girl	Cover Girl
	Max Factor	Max Factor	Max Factor	Max Factor
	Oil of Olay			Ellen Betrix
Hair Care	Head & Shoulders	Drene	Head & Shoulders	Head & Shoulders
	Mediker	Head & Shoulders	Mediker	Mediker
	Pantene Pro-V	Pantene Pro-V	Pantene Pro-V	Pantene Pro-V
	Physique	Pert Plus	Rejoy–Rejoice	Rejoy–Rejoice
	Rejoy–Rejoice		Pert Plus	Pert Plus
	Pert Plus		Vidal Sassoon	Vidal Sassoon
	Vidal Sassoon			

An example of cooperative branding.

cosmetics, and hair-care products. The company's marketing team introduced these flanker brands to appeal to target markets in which the main brand was not reaching customers. Thus, using a set of flanker brands can help a company offer a more complete line of products. This creates barriers to entry for competing firms.

Sometimes a flanker brand is introduced when company leaders think that offering the product under the current brand name might adversely affect the overall marketing program. Hallmark created a flanker brand known as Shoebox Greetings. These cards sell in discount stores as well as Hallmark outlets; however, the Hallmark brand is only sold in retail stores carrying the Hallmark name. Shoebox Greeting cards are lower priced and allow Hallmark to attract a larger percentage of the market. Firms operating in high-end markets often use this strategy when they compete in low-end markets. It also is used in international expansion. For example, Procter & Gamble sells Ariel laundry detergent in Latin America, Asia, Europe, the Middle East, and Africa, but not in North America. Offering different brands for specific markets is a common flanker brand strategy that helps a firm to expand into international markets using more than its current brands.

CO-BRANDING

In addition to flanker brands and brand extensions, other branding methods also are possible. **Co-branding** takes three forms: ingredient branding, cooperative branding, and complementary branding (see Figure 2.11). **Ingredient branding** is the placement of one brand within another brand, such as Intel microprocessors in HP computers. **Cooperative branding** is the joint venture of two or more brands into a new good or service. Study the advertisement featuring a cooperating branding venture by Citibank with American Airlines and MasterCard in this section. **Complementary branding** is the marketing of two brands together to encourage co-consumption or co-purchases, such as Seagram's 7 encouraging 7-Up as a compatible mixer or Oreo milkshakes sold in Dairy Queen stores. Locating Subway sandwich shops in convenience stores, Little Caesar's in Kmart outlets, and McDonald's in Wal-Mart stores is another type of co-branding trend.

Co-branding succeeds when it builds the brand equity of both brands. For example, when Monsanto created NutraSweet, consumer trust was built by placing the NutraSweet logo on venerable brands consumers trusted, such as Diet Coke, Wrigley's Chewing Gum (Wrigley's Extra), and Crystal Light. The strategy worked so well that NutraSweet is now the standard of quality in the sweetener industry.[25]

Conversely, co-branding is not without risk. If the relationship fails to do well in the marketplace, normally both brands suffer. To reduce the risk of failure, co-branding should be undertaken only with well-known brands. Co-branding of goods and services that are highly compatible generally will be less risky. Ingredient and cooperative

FIGURE 2.11
Forms of Co-Branding

branding tend to be less risky than complementary branding because both companies have more at stake and devote greater resources to ensure success.

For small companies and brands that are not as well known, co-branding is an excellent strategy. The difficult part is finding a well-known brand that is willing to take on a lesser-known product as a co-brand. Yet, if such an alliance can be made, the co-brand relationship often builds brand equity for the lesser-known brand, as in the case of NutraSweet. Co-branding also provides access to distribution channels that may be difficult to obtain either because of lack of size or dominance by the major brands.

PRIVATE BRANDS

Private brands (also known as *private labels* and *store brands*) are proprietary brands marketed by an organization and normally distributed exclusively within the organization's outlets. Private brands have experienced a rollercoaster ride in terms of popularity and sales. To many individuals, private brands carry the connotation of a lower price and inferior quality. Historically, the primary audiences for private labels were price-sensitive individuals and low-income families. This is no longer true; retailers now are investing marketing dollars to develop their private brands, which now account for approximately 15 percent of all retail sales and 19 percent of food items sold. According to ACNielsen, in the last 10 years store brand sales increased 64 percent compared to 30 percent for major manufacturers' brands.[26]

Over the past few years, several changes have occurred in the private brand arena, which are summarized in Figure 2.12.[27] Although private labels still tend to be priced between 15 and 30 percent lower than national brands, they also generate higher gross margins than national brands, because there are no middlemen. This higher margin enables retailers to earn higher profits on private brands, or, alternatively, to reduce the price of the private brands to make them more attractive to price-sensitive consumers. Retailers that maintain the higher markup on private labels have the opportunity to use some of the margin for advertising and promotions of the brands.

Another emerging trend in retailing is that loyalty toward retail stores has been gaining while loyalty toward individual brands has been declining. Rather than going to outlets that sell specific brands, many shoppers go to specific stores and are willing to buy from the brands offered by that store. This increase in loyalty to retailers has caused several department and specialty stores to expand the number of private-brand products that are offered. To do so, however, requires that the retailer develop a private brand that is congruent with a customer's image of the retailer.[28]

Savvy retailers recognize the value of private labels and how they can be used to differentiate the store from competing retailers and from national brands. These stores promote these labels as distinctive brands aimed toward specific market segments. Emphasis is on meeting needs of consumers with a quality product. It is not based on price.

JCPenney has been very successful with private branding in apparel lines. JCPenney offers more than 30 private labels, accounting for more than 40 percent of sales.[29] To better meet the needs of customers, the company launched a new private brand called a.n.a, which stands for "a new approach." The primary target is 30- to 50-year-old women who are modern and fashion conscious. A new line for men, called Solitude, was also launched. The line is aimed at 25- to 50-year-old males seeking a "relaxed, casual lifestyle."[30] Liz Sweeney of JCPenney stated, "We are dedicated to creating and managing winning private brands that develop customer loyalty. This means managing and marketing our key private brands as true brands versus labels."[31]

◆ Improved quality	◆ Used to differentiate retail outlets
◆ Perceived as a value purchase	◆ Increased advertising of private brands
◆ Higher loyalty toward retail outlets and lower loyalty toward specific brands	◆ Increased quality of in-store displays and packaging of private brands

FIGURE 2.12
Changes in Private Brands

Private labels are often displayed in retail store windows.

New trends in the use of private labels are emerging. Many retailers treat private brands more like national brands. Marketing dollars are spent on improving the actual label, on more noticeable in-store displays, and on packaging.[32] Retailers without large national ad budgets must rely more on displays and attractive packaging. A drab, cheap display does not convey the message that a private brand is as good as or better than a national brand. For many consumers, the two are indistinguishable. Unless they are familiar with the store's private brand labels, they might think they are purchasing a national brand.

Some retailers are taking this one step further by designing the advertising of their private brands apart from the store's regular advertising program. Recently, Sears launched a series of advertisements featuring its Kenmore and Craftsman brands. Sears was only mentioned in the context of being the place to purchase Kenmore and Craftsman products. Kmart promotes its private lines, including Martha Stewart Everyday, Chic, Jaclyn Smith, Kathy Ireland, Expressions, Route 66, and Sesame Street. Wal-Mart has 14 private labels of clothing, including labels such as Basic Image, Bobbie Brooks, Catalina, Jordache, and Kathy Lee. The purpose of this approach is to help establish the name as a bona fide brand competing head-to-head with national products and to divorce the brand from its retail parent.

How do manufacturers respond to the inroads made by private labels? Figure 2.13 lists some of the strategies.[33] Many manufacturers focus on a few core brands rather than split advertising dollars among a large number of brands. The core brands are advertised heavily. This helps the manufacturer maintain its brand name and reinforces the message that consumers are making the right decision when they purchase the manufacturer's national brand. The goal is to make an emotional connection with consumers both before and after the purchase.

Manufacturers may attempt to reduce the impact of private labels on sales by expanding product offerings. Private labels are normally copies of national brands. By aggressively introducing new products and new versions of current products, a manufacturer can maintain the loyalty of its current customers and be seen as an innovator. The Sara Lee Corporation owns a number of name brand apparel companies, such as Bali, Playtex, Champion, Ocean, and Hanes. The company expanded into the active wear market with the Hanes Sport casual collection. The surge in popularity of active lifestyle clothing created an increase in sales of other related products, such as the sports underwear featured in the Hanes ad in this section. Hanes Sport now manufactures products for women, men, and children.

Manufacturers must improve in-store displays and packaging to counter private labels. In displays and on packages, the manufacturer's brand must have a clear and compelling place. In some cases, it is the package that sells the product. Vendors of condiments, such as ketchup and mustard, know that the container has become extremely important to consumers.

FIGURE 2.13

Tactics Used by Manufacturers to Fight Gains Made by Private Labels

- ◆ Focus on core brands.
- ◆ Increase advertising.
- ◆ Introduce new products.
- ◆ Focus on in-store selling and packaging.
- ◆ Use alternative methods of marketing.

Source: Based on Vanessa L. Facenda, "A Swift Kick to the Privates," *Brandweek* 48, no. 31 (September 3, 2007), pp. 24–28.

In addition to advertising, many manufacturers have turned to alternative product promotion methods, including social networking and guerrilla marketing techniques (which are described in Chapter 10). Gillette's marketing team realized that to encourage young males to use company products they needed to place samples in their hands. Consequently, the Fusion razor is mailed to men within 1 month of their 18th birthdays. Both Huggies and Pampers have developed Web sites that furnish usable information for young mothers. The sites also allow young mothers to communicate with each other.

The success of private brands has influenced both manufacturers and retailers. Each must pay careful attention to where this trend leads in the next decade and be willing to move beyond traditional advertising methods. It will take new ideas and new strategies to be successful.

PACKAGING

In many large retail stores, most employees are either stockers or cashiers. Few know anything about the products that are on the shelves. Therefore, the product's package is the last opportunity to make an impression on a consumer. Marketing surveys have revealed that only 31 percent of purchases are planned prior to reaching a store. This means 69 percent of purchase decisions are made in the store. Other research indicates that when consumers walk within 10 to 15 feet of a product, the brand has 3 seconds to make contact with the consumer.[34]

A package design must stand out. It must tell consumers what is inside and why the brand should be purchased. Traditionally, the primary purposes of packaging were those shown in Figure 2.14. Now, however, packages and labels are increasingly viewed as a key part of a company's integrated marketing communications program. It makes little sense to spend millions of dollars on advertising only to lose the sale in the store because of a lackluster, dull package design that does not communicate to potential customers.

The Reynolds Company recognized the value of packaging tie-ins during the early 2000s. The entire wraps category was experiencing declining sales. The marketing team at Reynolds discovered that consumers enjoy using products that make them feel like experts. The firm created a new brand message that Reynolds was a "helper in the kitchen." This new brand message was extended and reinforced in ads showing how to use the product to prepare foods as well as by including recipes on the packaging. When tied to the perception that Reynolds was the premium brand in the marketplace, strong sales were continued.[35]

Most retail purchase decisions are made based on familiarity with a brand or product at a retail store. Consequently, a unique package that is attractive or that captures the buyer's attention increases the chances the product will be purchased, sometimes as an impulse buy. For many years, winemakers strongly resisted the use of marketing tactics for fear of being perceived as having questionable quality. Products such as Blue Nun, Ripple, and Boone's Farm were major marketing successes, but they did not enjoy reputations for high quality. Recently, however, some wineries have begun to accept the value

Introducing Hanes Sport™ Underwear
THE CLOTHES YOU'D RATHER BE IN

Hanes Sport Underwear for your active lifestyle
www.hanessport.com

Hanes Sport is one company that has introduced new products into the active lifestyle wear market.

◆ Protect the product inside.
◆ Provide for ease of shipping, moving, and handling.
◆ Provide for easy placement on store shelves.
◆ Prevent or reduce the possibility of theft.
◆ Prevent tampering (drugs and foods).

FIGURE 2.14
Primary Purposes of Packaging

FIGURE 2.15
New Trends in Packaging

- ◆ Meets consumer needs for speed, convenience, and portability
- ◆ Must be contemporary and striking
- ◆ Must be designed for ease of use

of a quality package. Many Australian wineries captured market share based on the knowledge that men (who are more likely to make the wine purchase) look at a wine's country of origin, followed by grape variety, and finally aesthetics. Australian wine is perceived as new, different, and of sufficient quality, especially in the Shiraz lines. As a result, attractive bottles featuring names such as Vale, Valley Hill, and Cloudy Bay with images of mountain peaks and vineyards receding in the distance have been designed. Bottle color is crucial; buyers prefer dark, warm, and intense colors (red and blue). These changes and the successes of the Australians have caused French and German wine-makers to change their packages and labels to compete.[36]

New Trends in Packaging

Some of the new trends in packaging are based on changes in the ways in which consumers use products (see Figure 2.15). In the foods market, foods that are fast, convenient, portable, and fresh are selling quickly. The package must accommodate these needs. Recent research by DuPont found that half of consumers surveyed said that taste and freshness were more important than price, convenience, and brand name. It is the packaging that determines if a food item maintains its freshness. Consumers who experienced inferior packaging were more likely to switch to another brand on their next purchases.[37]

The marketing team at Alcoa Rigid Packaging watched consumers as they bought groceries and stocked refrigerators. The team noticed that the standard 3-by-4-can (12-pack) beverage box was too large for the refrigerator. This meant that consumers took out only a few cans at a time to cool. It seemed logical that if more cans were cold, consumers might drink more. This observation led to the design of a box that was easier and more convenient to use, the 6-by-2-can box, which is longer and slimmer. This newly designed 12-pack fits into the refrigerator door or on a shelf. It is also self-dispensing. As a can is taken out, a new one automatically slides down to the front of the box. This innovation improved sales for both Alcoa and several soft-drink manufacturers, who loved the new package.[38]

Consumers tend to buy packages that are eye-catching and contemporary. When Nestlé created a new line of products called Nescafé Original, one primary consideration was the package. The goal was to create a package that would protect the contents but that would also stand out. The result was a container with a unique geometrical set of shapes designed to appeal to younger consumers. The approach was very successful.[39]

The trends in packaging in international markets are much the same as in the United States. Ease of use is a key feature. When shipping products overseas, however, one key issue is that the buyer must feel reassured the package will not break or become contaminated.

Smaller households have led to the creation of smaller packages.

LABELS

Labels on packages serve several functions. First, they must meet legal requirements. This includes identifying the product contained in the package and any other specific information about content, such as nutritional information on foods. The Food and Drug Administration (FDA) regulates food labels in the United States. Also, many times warranties and guarantees are printed on the label.

The label represents another marketing opportunity. Many times the only distinguishing feature of a product, such as a 12-ounce bottle of beer or a 1-gallon container of milk, is the label. The company's logo and the brand name must appear prominently. Labels often contain special offers and other tie-ins, such as a box of cereal with a toy contained inside. The consumer is notified of the offer on the label.

Labels often carry terms designed to build consumer interest and confidence in making the purchase. Word such as "gourmet," "natural," "premium," "adult formula," and "industrial strength" make the product seem like a better buy. At the same time, consumers are used to such puffery. A label on a private brand is often very plain. This matches the buyer's perception that the price is being held down by reducing the use of marketing tools. In general, a company's image, brand, logo, and theme should extend to the design of the package and label. Doing so allows the marketing team one more opportunity to make the sale when the consumer is in the store making a final purchasing decision.

To prevent cannibalism of its other teas, Celestial Seasonings positions each version for individual target markets.

POSITIONING

A final element in corporate and brand image management is product positioning. **Positioning** is the process of creating a perception in the consumer's mind regarding the nature of a company and its products relative to competitors. Positioning is created by variables such as the quality of products, prices charged, methods of distribution, packaging, image, and other factors. A product's position is based on two elements: (1) the product's standing relative to the competition and (2) how the product is perceived by consumers.

Consumers ultimately determine the position a product holds. Marketing programs are designed to position a product effectively. To do so, marketing communications must either reinforce what consumers already believe about a product and its brand name or shift consumer views toward a more desirable position. The first strategy is certainly easier to accomplish. The goal of positioning is to find that niche in a consumer's mind that a product can occupy.

Positioning is vital for companies such as Procter & Gamble, VF Corporation, Sara Lee Corporation, and Campbell's Soups, because it helps prevent cannibalism among various brands within a product category. Campbell's produces five different types of V8 juice. The one pictured in this section is being marketed to individuals who are concerned about calories and fat content. Campbell's offers a low-sodium version of V8 for individuals on a low-sodium diet, a spicy hot version for consumers who

RATHER THAN TALK ABOUT HOW HEALTHY OUR GREEN TEA IS **WE MAKE IT SO DELICIOUS YOU'LL WANT TO DRINK IT ANYWAY.**

Drinking a cup of Celestial Seasonings might be the easiest and most delicious way to stay healthy. Our green teas are packed with antioxidants and antioxidants have been shown to provide multiple health benefits. And with 14 tantalizing flavors of green tea to choose from, taking care of yourself has never tasted so wonderful.

celestialseasonings.com

FIGURE 2.16
Product Positioning Strategies

- ◆ Attributes
- ◆ Competitors
- ◆ Use or application
- ◆ Price–quality relationship

- ◆ Product user
- ◆ Product class
- ◆ Cultural symbol

want something with more taste or who need a mixer, and a calcium-enriched version for those who desire more calcium, potassium, or vitamins A and C.

Effective positioning can be achieved in seven different ways (see Figure 2.16). Although companies might try two or three approaches, such efforts generally only manage to confuse customers. The best method is to use one of these approaches consistently.

An *attribute* is a product trait or characteristic that sets it apart from other products. In the Toyota advertisement shown in this section, the Echo is positioned based on the attribute of gas mileage, because the car gets 41 miles per gallon. The Sony ad is aimed at business customers. The advertisement promotes the attribute of quality, because the projector provides stronger light. Both ads attempt to convey the message that the attribute featured by the brand outperforms the competition.

Another common tactic is using *competitors* to establish position. This is done by contrasting the company's product against others. For years, Avis ran advertisements comparing itself to Hertz. Avis admitted it was not number one, but turned that position into an advantage, because Avis was willing to "try harder" for business.

Use or *application* positioning involves creating a memorable set of uses for a product. Arm & Hammer has long utilized this approach in its attempt to convince consumers to use its baking soda as a deodorizer in the refrigerator. Arm & Hammer has also been featured as a co-brand in toothpaste, creating yet another use for the product.

An advertisement by Echo positioning the automobile on the basis of high gas mileage.

A business-to-business advertisement positioned based on the projector's attributes.

Businesses on the extremes of the price range often use the *price–quality relationship*. At the top end, businesses emphasize high quality, whereas at the bottom end, low prices are emphasized. Hallmark cards cost more but are for those who "only want to send the very best." Other firms seek to be a "low-price leader," with no corresponding statement about quality.

A *product user* positioning strategy distinguishes a brand or product by clearly specifying who might use it. Apple Computers originally positioned itself as the computer for educational institutions. Although this strategy helped the company to grow rapidly, Apple had a difficult time convincing businesses to use its computers. Apple's marketing team had done such a good job creating the company's original position strategy that changing peoples' minds was difficult.

Sometimes firms seek to position themselves in a particular *product class*. Orange juice was long considered part of the breakfast drink product class. Years ago, those in the industry decided to create advertisements designed to move orange juice into a new product class, with slogans such as "it's not just for breakfast anymore." This repositioning has been fairly successful. Many consumers drink orange juice at other times during the day. This result was due, in part, to the perception that orange juice is a healthy drink. Orange juice cannot compete with Pepsi or Coke. Instead, it must be viewed as an alternative to a sugary soft drink.

Identifying a product with a *cultural symbol* is difficult but, if done successfully, can become a strong competitive advantage for a firm. Chevrolet used this type of positioning strategy. For years, Chevrolet was advertised as being as American as baseball and apple pie during the summer. Playboy has evolved into an entertainment empire by becoming a cultural symbol, albeit a controversial one. In its advertisement shown in this section, Stetson cologne is tied to the American cowboy and the spirit of the West. The ad copy reads that "The attraction is legendary." The purpose of placing this ad in *Glamour* magazine was to entice women to purchase the product for the men in their lives.

Other Elements of Positioning

A brand's position is never completely fixed. It can be changed. Gillette is a brand that was traditionally firmly entrenched with men. Then the company launched a massive campaign to position itself in the women's market. New products, including the Sensor Excel razor and Satin Care Shave Gel, were offered by mail to consumer homes, and free samples were placed in homeroom bags for 14- and 15-year-old girls at school. Gillette's advertisements encouraged women to view the products as a key part of being physically and psychologically ready for anything. The ad copy asked "Are you ready?" and answered "Yes, I am!" This positioning matches with the position of Gillette's products for men, which are marketed using the "Best a man can get" slogan.[40]

Understanding how consumers view a product is important to successful positioning. Increasing and volatile gasoline prices, the war in Iraq, and the concern for the environment caused some marketing executives at General Motors to worry that the Hummer might become an icon for gas guzzling and waste. Consequently, GM hired an independent agency, Modernista Boston, to create ads that would position the Hummer as a force for good. A television and print campaign was developed called "Hummer Heroes." Hummer owners were encouraged to send stories with photos of how they used their Hummer for good. Based on real life stories and enacted scenes, ads were developed that showed Hummers being used to carry water to disaster victims and rescuing individuals in remote locations inaccessible by other types of vehicles.[41]

An advertisement by Stetson using the cultural symbolism of the cowboy as the positioning strategy.

THE ATTRACTION IS LEGENDARY

Brand positioning must also be applied to business-to-business marketing efforts. InterContinental Hotels Group, which owns InterContinental, Crowne Plaza, Holiday Inn, Holiday Inn Express, Staybridge Suites, and Candlewood Suites, understands the needs of business travelers and offers unique services that add value to the businessperson's stay. High-speed Internet access is available at all of the properties, and at the Crowne Plaza wireless connections are available at any location on the property. Understanding that time and convenience are important to business travelers, InterContinental Hotels offers an online wireless reservation system that allows business guests to review, cancel, or modify reservations online. To ensure that business guests have a good night's sleep, Crowne Plaza offers a guaranteed wake-up call, quiet floors, sleep amenities, sleep CDs, and relaxation tips.[42] These features all emphasize the attribute and product user–based positions associated with offering all of the conveniences and services a businessperson would want.

Effective positioning is vitally important in the international arena. Plans must be made to build an effective position when a firm expands into new countries. Often the positioning strategy used in one country will not work in another. Marketing experts carefully analyze the competition as well as the consumers or businesses that are potential customers. After this analysis, the marketing team is better able to choose a positioning strategy. Although the positioning strategy might need to be modified for each country, the company's overall theme and the brand image should be consistent.

Brand positioning is a critical part of image and brand-name management. Consumers have an extensive set of purchasing options. This means consumers can try products with specific advantages or attributes. Effective positioning, by whatever tactic chosen, increases sales and strengthens the long-term positions of both individual products and the total organization.

The 3M Post-it brand has become a generic term.

3M

Growth through reliability

Post-it® Flags make it easy to mark, flag and find important information for a wide range of applications. And thanks to our unique repositionable adhesive, Post-it® Flags stick securely and remove cleanly. 3M's reliable quality products deliver results that help drive the office supply industry. One more reason why Post-it® and Scotch® are among the world's most recognized brands.

ETHICAL ISSUES IN BRAND MANAGEMENT

There have always been ethical issues associated with brand management. For years, the most common problem was *brand infringement.* Brand infringement occurs when a company creates a brand name that closely resembles a popular or successful brand, such as when the Korrs beer company was formed. In that case, the courts deemed the brand an intentional infringement, and the name was abandoned. Another brand-infringing company that was forced by the courts to give up its name was Victor's Secret.

The brand infringement issue becomes more complex when a brand is so well established that it may be considered a generic term, such as a Kleenex tissue or a Xerox copy. Band-Aid encountered the problem in the 1970s, forcing the marketing team to make sure the product was identified as "Band-Aid Brand Strips" rather than simply "band aids," to keep the competition from being able to use the name. The most vulnerable new brand name might be Google, because the name has entered everyday conversation, as in "I Googled myself" or "I Googled it."

The newest form of unethical behavior, at least according to some sources, is *domain squatting,* or *cyber squatting*. This is the controversial practice of buying domain names (barnesandnoble.com, kohls.com, labronjames.com, etc.) that are valuable to specific people or businesses in the hopes of making a profit by reselling the name. At the extreme, whitehouse.com was a pornographic Web site. Any new company trying to build a presence in the marketplace might find itself stifled by domain squatters. Names matter, and cyber squatters are willing to take advantage of that to make profits at someone else's expense.

INTERNATIONAL IMPLICATIONS

In international markets, product development, branding, and maintaining an image are more complex. As discussed in Chapter 1, firms can either use an *adaptation* strategy or a *standardization* strategy in promotional programs. These two approaches can be applied to the products themselves as well as to brand names. With standardization, the same brand name and product are sold in all countries. With adaptation, the brand and/or the actual product may be different in each country or region. This can mean a product may be viewed as a local brand. Mr. Clean uses the adaptation brand approach for the same products. Items are sold under the names of "Mr. Proper" and "Maestro Limpio," as well as other names in various countries.

Using a standardized global brand reduces costs. Instead of advertising each local brand with a separate communication strategy, one standardized message can be sent. Standardized global brands also allow for the transference of best practices from one country to another. Further, purchasing a standardized global brand can be viewed as a better choice than buying a local brand. The global brand might have a higher perceived quality. The consumer's self-concept of being cosmopolitan, sophisticated, and modern can be enhanced when buying a global brand.[43] As the world continues to shrink through advances in telecommunications, consumers are becoming increasingly similar, displaying comparable consumer characteristics and purchase behaviors. This may lead to even greater use of standardized global brands.

Despite all of the advantages of global brands, some efforts to standardize brand names have met with resistance. A number of global brands that were introduced were not received with enthusiasm. Although consumer behavior might have converged somewhat throughout the world, there are still many local idiosyncrasies. Global brands enjoy the most success in high-profile, high-involvement products. Local brands have performed the best in low-involvement everyday products. Automobiles and computers have done well as global brands. Food, candy, and some soft drinks have done better using a local brand approach.[44] A common GIMC strategy is to "think globally, but act locally." This approach can also be applied to branding. Developing global brands might be the ultimate goal; still the marketing team should consider each local market's unique features and be sensitive to supporting and developing local brands.

Packaging and labeling issues are more complex for global firms. The label must meet the legal requirements of the country where the product is sold. Remember that an attractive label is an attention-getting device that can draw the consumer to the product. This feature is vitally important in the United States as well as in other countries. For example, many Asian purchases are, in part, driven by the appeal of the label.[45] At the same time, some culturally sensitive items, such as lingerie and other personal products, carry labels that basically disguise or hide the contents. Packages must also be able to withstand the rigors of being shipped longer distances, meet any legal restrictions, and be as cost-effective as possible.

Image and positioning issues become complicated in global markets. Part of the confusion might be that a particular country is held in low regard by other countries. Consequently, these negative feelings transfer to any products sold by companies from that country. Positioning might be harder to achieve due to differences in language, restrictions on advertising messages, additional taxes or tariffs that raise prices, and other less controllable factors.

SUMMARY

An effective integrated marketing communications plan must emphasize a strong and positive company or corporate image as part of the program. An image consists of consumer and business-to-business feelings toward the overall organization as well as evaluations of each individual brand the firm carries. An image has both tangible and intangible components. Tangible elements include products, advertisements, names, logos, and services provided. Intangible elements consist of policies and practices that change or enhance the company's image in the consumer's mind. A well-developed and well-established image benefits both customers and the company in many ways.

Creating an effective image is a difficult task. It is important to know how all publics view the firm before seeking to build or enhance an image. Rejuvenating the image involves reminding customers of their previous conceptions of the company while at the same time expanding into a closely related area of concern. Once an image is strongly pressed into the minds of customers, it becomes difficult, if not impossible, to change.

A corporate name is the overall banner under which all other operations occur. The corporate logo accompanying the name is the symbol used to identify a company and its brands, helping to convey the overall corporate image. The firm's name and image are important not only to general customers, but also to any firms that might purchase from or conduct business with a manufacturer or service provider.

Brands are names given to goods or services or groups of complementary products. Effective brands give the firm an advantage, especially in mature markets containing fewer actual products or where service differences exist. Strong brands convey the most compelling benefits of the product, elicit proper consumer emotions, and help create loyalty. There are many versions of brands, including family brands, flanker brands, and co-brands. In each, brand equity is built by domination or the recognition that the brand has one key advantage or characteristic.

Private brands, or private labels, have become an important component in the success of both producers and retailers. Consumers now view private brands as having quality equal to or close to that of more famous manufacturer brand names. At the same time, customers expect price advantages in private label products. Consequently, effective management of brands and products includes creating a mix of offerings that both end users and retailers recognize as a beneficial range of choices.

Positioning is the relative psychological location of the good or service as compared to its competitors' in the views of customers. Marketing managers must select a positioning strategy that highlights the best features of the company's products. Positioning is never fixed, because markets evolve over time. Positioning can be established with both the general public and business-to-business customers.

KEY TERMS

image   Overall consumer perceptions or end-user feelings toward a company along with its goods and services.

corporate logo   The symbol used to identify a company and its brands, helping to convey the overall corporate image.

stimulus codability   Items that easily evoke consensually held meanings within a culture or subculture.

brands   Names generally assigned to a good or service or a group of complementary products.

salient   When consumers are aware of the brand, have it in their consideration sets (things they consider when making purchases), regard the product and brand as a good value, buy it or use it on a regular basis, and recommend it to others.

family brand   When a company offers a series or group of products under one brand name.

brand equity   A set of brand assets that add to the value assigned to a product.

brand metrics   Measures of returns on brand investments.

brand extension   The use of an established brand name on goods or services not related to the core brand.

flanker brand   The development of a new brand by a company in a good or service category in which it currently has a brand offering.

co-branding   Offering two or more brands in a single marketing effort.

ingredient branding   A form of co-branding in which the name of one brand is placed within another brand.

cooperative branding   A form of co-branding in which two firms create a joint venture of two or more brands into a new good or service.

complementary branding   A form of co-branding in which the marketing of two brands together encourages co-consumption or co-purchases.

private brands   (also known as *private labels*) Proprietary brands marketed by an organization and normally distributed exclusively within the organization's outlets.

positioning   The process of creating a perception in the consumer's mind about the nature of a company and its products relative to the competition. It is created by the quality of products, prices charged, methods of distribution, image, and other factors.

REVIEW QUESTIONS

1. What is meant by the term corporate image? What are the tangible aspects of a corporate image?

2. How does a corporation's image help customers? How does it help the specific company?

3. How will company leaders know when they have created the "right" image for their firm?

4. What is a corporate logo? What are the characteristics of an effective corporate logo?

5. What is meant by the term stimulus codability?

6. What is the difference between a brand name and a corporation's overall image?

7. What are the characteristics of a strong and effective brand name?

8. What is the difference between brand equity and brand parity?

9. Why is brand equity important? How is it measured?

10. Describe the use of brand extension and flanker brand strategies.

11. Identify and describe three types of co-brands.

12. How has private branding, or private labeling, changed in the past decade?

13. What role does a product's package play in the marketing program?

14. How can a label support an IMC program or advertising campaign?

15. What is product–brand positioning? Give examples of various types of positioning strategies.

16. What ethical issues are associated with brand management?

17. How do the concepts of standardization and adaptation apply to products, brand names, and marketing strategies?

CRITICAL THINKING EXERCISES

Discussion Questions

1. Dalton Office Supply Company has been in operation for over 50 years and has been the predominant office supply company in its region during that time. Approximately 85 percent of Dalton's business is based on providing materials to other businesses. Only 15 percent comes from walk-in customers. Recently, low-cost providers such as Office Depot have cut into Dalton's market share. Surveys of consumers indicate that Dalton has an image of being outdated and pricey. Consumers did report that Dalton's customer service was above average. What image should Dalton project to regain its market share? Outline a plan to rejuvenate the company's image.

2. Henry and Becky Thompson plan to open a new floral and gift shop in Orlando, Florida. They want to project an image of being trendy, upscale, and fashionable. They are trying to decide on a name and a logo. What should be the name of their company? What kind of logo should they develop?

3. Go to a local retail store. Choose five packages that are effective. Describe why they are effective. Choose five labels that are effective at capturing attention. What are the attention-getting aspects of each label?

4. Suppose Terminix Pest Control wants to expand through co-branding. To gather more information about Terminix, access its Web site at **www.terminix.net**. What kind of co-branding would you suggest? Which companies should Terminix contact?

INTEGRATED LEARNING EXERCISES

1. Web sites are an important element of a company's image. Access the Web sites of the following companies to get a feel for the image each company tries to project. Is the image projected on the Web site consistent with the image portrayed in the company's advertisements?

   a. Bluenotes (**www.bluenotesjeans.com**)

   b. Portillo's Restaurants (**www.portillos.com**)

   c. BMW Motorcycles (**www.bmwmotorcycles.com**)

   d. McDonald's (**www.mcdonalds.com**)

   e. Hewlett-Packard (**www.hp.com**)

2. A major consulting firm that has been a leader in extending marketing knowledge and in the area of brand development is the Boston Consulting Group. Other companies that have actively been involved in brand development include Lexicon Branding and Corporate Branding. Access each firm's Web site. What kinds of services does each provide?

   a. Boston Consulting Group (**www.bcg.com**)

   b. Lexicon Branding, Inc. (**www.lexicon-branding.com**)

   c. Corporate Branding (**www.corebrand.com**)

3. Brand extension and flanker branding are common strategies for large corporations. Access the following Web sites. Identify the various brand extension strategies and flanker brands used by each company.

   a. Marriott Hotels (**www.marriott.com**)

   b. Procter & Gamble (**www.pg.com**)

   c. Sara Lee Corporation (**www.saralee.com**)

   d. VF Corporation (**www.vfc.com**)

4. Private labels are an important source of revenue for many retail stores and manufacturers. The Private Label Manufacturers' Association promotes manufacturers that produce private labels. From the Web site at **www.plma. com**, identify the press updates, store brands, and upcoming events that illustrate the importance of private labels for both retailers and manufactures.

5. Look up one of the following companies on the Internet. Discuss the image conveyed by each company's Web site. What positioning strategy does it use? What changes or improvements could it make?

   a. Scubaworld (**www.scubaworld.com**)

   b. Union Pacific Railroad (**www.uprr.com**)

   c. Bicycle Museum of America (**www.bicyclemuseum. com**)

   d. Metropolitan Transportation Commission (**www.mtc. ca.gov**)

   e. Canyon Beachwear (**www.canyonbeachwear.com**)

STUDENT PROJECT

Creative Corner

The brand name and positioning of a brand are two critical elements a marketing manager must consider when introducing a new product. Pick one of the products from the following list. Assume that you are the new product manager and that your company has introduced a new brand within the product category. Your first task is to decide how you will position your brand in the marketplace. Using the Internet, identify by name at least 3 competing brands. How are they positioned? How will your position be different? Part of this decision will be your target market. Who will you target your product to? Which of the seven positioning strategies will you use? Once you have made the positioning decision based on your target market, create a brand name for your product. Discuss why you chose the name.

Products

1. A new brand of ski boat used for recreational boating
2. A new optical store that sells eyeglasses and contacts
3. A new brand of chocolate candy bar
4. A new brand of jeans
5. A new energy drink
6. A new perfume or cologne

CASE 1 IS IMAGE EVERYTHING?

For many years, the soft drink Sprite's advertising featured the tag line, "Image is Everything," with various sports figures as spokespersons. In the world of sports, news about one negative incident travels much farther than a dozen feature stories about altruism. Recently, image once again came under attack in professional sports. During the final week of July in 2007, three major leagues were plagued by bad press.

One startling incident emerged when the FBI arrested NBA referee Tim Donaghy, who was accused of influencing the scores of games in order to win bets and pay off gambling debts to bookies connected with organized crime. Gambling casts a powerful shadow over sports. If fans cannot believe that the rules are fair and being enforced equally, the legitimacy of what is taking place cannot be restored. Each time a questionable call takes place, fans will wonder if the referee has a vested interest in the outcome of the contest.

NBA Commissioner David Stern quickly moved to assure the world that the one ref was a loner and that the overall integrity of the league remained solid. He was countering the many "conspiracy theories" that linger around the sport, and have for many years, dating back to what were once known as the "Jordan rules," whereby Michael Jordan was alleged to receive special treatment from officials, among other charges.

At the same time, NFL quarterback Michael Vick was arrested and charged with running a dog-fighting ring on his personal property. Dog lovers of all kinds, from the PETA to individual owners, were appalled. The brutality of dog-fighting, along with the unsavory characters associated with it, caused Vick to lose endorsement contracts for athletic shoes and clothes.

The Atlanta Falcons team owners struggled with the choice of suspending Vick for only four games, which clearly would have led to protests and more negative press, or to allow NFL officials to suspend him for the entire year. Suspending Vick for an entire year would have undoubtedly caused the team to lose games. One cynical reporter noted that Vick would have been better off as a rapist than as a dog-fighter. Members of several professional sports that had been charged with sexual assault or with spousal abuse continued their careers without a great deal of ongoing publicity or criticism.

Also during that troubling week, baseball's Barry Bonds was on the verge of breaking one of the most noteworthy records in Major League Baseball. Henry Aaron's all-time home run record was about to fall. At the time, Bonds was under investigation for not only using steroids, but also for lying to a grand jury about that use. Congressional and criminal investigations were underway, and Bonds eventually faced criminal charges.

Bond's personal demeanor contributed to the image problem. Aaron was a popular and heroic figure. Bonds was viewed as being difficult, sullen, and disagreeable to members of the media and the public. His credibility was injured by conflicting statements about unknowingly rubbing a steroid cream on his legs and arms, yet claiming he never used banned substances.

Doping and steroid use have clearly affected professional sports for many years. The *Tour de France* has identified several violations over the years. Professional football has been tainted as much as baseball. The harshest critics, including some associated with various sports, insist that all records that were broken by athletes using human growth hormone or steroids should be stricken.

The popularity of various sports had clearly started to diminish. Television ratings for the 2007 NBA Finals were down

Incidents involving sports figures often have a strong impact on young fans.

from previous years, as were ratings for baseball's World Series, where Game 1 had lower ratings than a pay-per-view event featuring mixed martial arts (extreme) fighting. Sports fans have more choices than ever. The NBA playoffs overlap with the playoffs in professional hockey. Baseball overlaps with the collegiate and professional football season. In such an environment, it becomes clear that those associated with each sport should probably consider the fact that "Image is Everything."

Sources: Sean Gregory, "Five Ways to Think about Barry Bonds," *Time* 170, no. 3 (July 16, 2007), pp. 40–41; Judy Battista, "NFL Faces Protests and Pressure over Vick," *New York Times* (July 21, 2007), p. D4; Jack McCallum, "Game-Fixing and Dogfighting Rock Pro Sports (and Barry Bonds Marches On)," *Sports Illustrated* 107, no. 4 (July 30, 2007), pp. 34–48; Tom Knott, "Donaghy Will Cause Paranoia," *The Washington Times* (August 17, 2007), section Sports, p. 1.

1. As a marketing professional, how should each league respond to its image problems?

2. What tools are available to help a team or league react to negative publicity?

3. Can you think of any other methods to help a professional sport build a positive image?

4. Go to the Web sites of the NBA, the NFL, and MLB. What types of image-building stories, activities, or involvements are present?

A HEALTHY IMAGE

Mary Wilson was both nervous and excited as she opened her first staff meeting in the marketing department of St. Margaret's General Hospital. Mary's new role was Director of Marketing and Communications. Her primary task was to increase the visibility of St. Margaret's Hospital in order to raise the image of the institution in the eyes of the many publics served. The long-term goal was to attract the best possible physicians while increasing use of the hospital's facilities and attracting more patients.

The world of health care has changed dramatically in the past decade. Government regulations and support, concerns about lawsuits, evolving and expensive technologies, and changes in health insurance provisions affect hospitals of all sizes. In addition, St. Margaret's faces strong competition. The hospital's primary location is in a major metropolitan area in Minnesota. Two other large hospitals also offer comparable services in the same city. Each seeks to sign physicians to exclusive contracts in which they will only provide care with one organization.

The other significant challenge to St. Margaret's is its proximity to the Mayo Clinic. Clearly, Mayo holds the highest level of prestige in the state, and even in the region. Most physicians are inclined to think of Mayo first when making referrals for patients with difficult medical problems. Mayo would be viewed by most publics as the "best" care possible.

The key issues in the image of any health organization are developing trust and a feeling of confidence in the quality of care that will be received. Beyond technological advantages, other, more subtle elements of an image could have an influence. Mary noted that to most patients the nurse plays a primary role in determining how the hospital is viewed. An uncaring and inattentive nurse is likely to drive away both the patient who encountered the nurse and all of the patient's family and friends. Negative word-of-mouth, Mary said, must be held to an absolute minimum.

Mary believed St. Margaret's needed to overcome two problems. First, the name "Margaret" is not commonly used anymore. Some publics may view it as an "old-fashioned" name. Second, there was nothing distinctive about the hospital's image. The overlap in services provided (heart care, cancer treatment) made it difficult to differentiate St. Margaret's from other providers.

If there was any advantage, Mary believed it was that St. Margaret's was affiliated with the Catholic Church. It was the only nonprofit hospital of the three major competitors. This attracted both Catholic patients and some Catholic physicians. Also, the hospital was able to utilize the services of a wide variety of volunteers.

As the marketing meeting opened, the agenda was to discuss all of the ways St. Margaret's could build its client base. The task would not be easy, but everyone in the room believed the hospital offered high-quality services in a caring atmosphere.

1. What are the image issues in this case?

2. What are the brand-name issues? Should the brand name be changed? If so, to what?

3. What types of advertisements should Mary develop for St. Margaret's General Hospital?

4. What other types of activities could St. Margaret's pursue to build a strong and positive corporate image?

ENDNOTES

1. Gucci (**www.gucci.com**, accessed February 28, 2005).

2. Arun Sudhaman, "Brand Quality Still Key to Corporate Reputation: Edelman," *Media Asia* (November 19, 2004), p. 8.

3. Kari Greenberg, "Mazda, Subaru Racing to Upgrade Dealerships," *Brandweek* 45, no. 39 (November 1, 2004), p. 10.

4. Joan Voight, "The Lady Means Business," *Adweek* 47, no. 15 (April 10, 2006), pp. 32–36.

5. Interview with Kerri L. Martin, brand manager for BMW Motorcycles USA (October 12, 2002).

6. Gregg Cebrzynski, "Low Brand Awareness Prompts Portillo's Image Ads," *Nation's Restaurant News* 38, no. 26 (June 28, 2004), p. 18.

7. Kate MacArthur, "Salad Days at McDonald's," *Advertising Age* 75, no. 50 (December 13, 2004), p. S-2.

8. David Kiley, "Holiday Inn's $1 Billion Revamp," *BusinessWeek Online* (October 39, 2007), p. 19.

9. Matt Vella, "AT&T Rebrands. Again," *BusinessWeek Online* (September 12, 2007), p. 20.

10. Jennifer McFarland, "Branding from the Inside Out, and from the Outside In," *Harvard Management Update* 7, no. 2 (February 2002), pp. 3–4.

11. Paul McNamara, "The Name Game," *Network World* (April 20, 1998), pp. 77–78.

12. Max Du Bois, "Making Your Company One in a Million," *Brand Strategy*, no. 153 (November 2001), pp. 10–11.

13. Pamela W. Henderson and Joseph A. Cote, "Guidelines for Selecting or Modifying Logos," *Journal of Marketing* (April 1998), pp. 14–30.

14. Andrew Ehrenberg, Neil Barnard, and John Scriven, "Differentiation or Salience," *Journal of Advertising Research* (November–December 1997), pp. 7–14.

15. Debra Semans, "The Brand You Save," *Marketing Management* 13, no. 3 (May–June 2004), pp. 29–32.

16. Nanette Byrnes, Robert Berner, Wendy Zellner, and William C. Symonds, "Branding: Five New Lessons," *BusinessWeek* (February 14, 2005), pp. 26–28.

17. Ibid.

18. Jean Halliday, "Don't Expect to See Pontiac Prime Time" (**www.adage.com/print?article_id=121923**, accessed November 12, 2007).

19. Stuart Elliott, "Making Social Connections and Selling Cookies" (**www.nytimes.com/2007/11/21/business/media/21adco.html**, accessed November 21, 2007).

20. Ibid.

21. Don E. Schultz, "Mastering Brand Metrics," *Marketing Management* 11, no. 3 (May–June 2002), pp. 8–9; Daniel Baack and Mark N. Hatala, "Predictors of Brand Rating and Brand Recall: An Empirical Investigation," *Regional Business Review* 17 (1998), pp. 17–34.

22. Fred Crawford, "Branding Isn't Like High School," *Retail Merchandiser* 47, no. 6 (July–August 2007), pp. S4–S9.

23. Debbie Howell, "Top Brands," *DSN Retailing Today* 33, no. 20 (October 24, 2005), pp. 38–42.

24. Kusum L. Ailawaldi, Scott A. Neslin, and Donald R. Lehman, "Revenue Premium As an Outcome Measure of Brand Equity," *Journal of Marketing* 67, no. 4 (October 2003), pp. 1–18.

25. Ibid.

26. Sonia Reyes, "Saving Private Labels," *Brandweek* 47, no. 19 (May 8, 2006), pp. 30–34.

27. Ibid.

28. Dongdae Lee, "Image Congruence and Attitude Toward Private Brands," *Advances in Consumer Research* 31 (2004), pp. 435–41.

29. Rusty Williamson, "Penney's Launching New Line," *Women's Wear Daily (WWD)* 191, no. 83 (April 19, 2006), p. 2.

30. Kelly Nolan, "Apparel & Accessories: A Label for Every Style at JCP," *Retailing Today* 45, no. 14 (August 7, 2006), pp. 27, 36.

31. Ibid.

32. Thomas J. Ryan, "Private Labels: Strong, Strategic & Growing," *Apparel Magazine* 44, no. 10 (June 2003), pp. 32–39; Reyes, "Saving Private Labels."

33. Vanessa L. Facenda, "A Swift Kick to the Privates," *Brandweek* 48, No. 31 (September 3, 2007), pp. 24–28.

34. Kris Perry, "Do You Help Your Customers Sell or Market?" *Paperboard Packaging* 89, no. 11 (November 2004), p. 8.

35. Ibid.

36. Victoria Moore and Frances Stonor Saunders, "Message on a Bottle," *New Statesman* 130, no. 4538 (May 21, 2001), pp. 49–53.

37. "Packaging Affects Brand Loyalty," *Supermarket News* 53, no. 45 (November 7, 2005), p. 36.

38. Andrea Zoe Aster, "Good Drinks Come in Smart Packaging," *Marketing Magazine* 109, no. 32 (October 4–11, 2004), pp. 13–15.

39. "A Sleek Look for Nescafe," *Food Manufacture* 76, no. 11 (November 2001), p. 21.

40. Pat Sloan, "Gillette Bets $80 Mil on Women," *Advertising Age* (May 4, 1998), p. 63.

41. Jean Halliday, "GM's New Spin: Buy a Hummer, Save Humanity" (**www.adage.com/print?article_id=121560**, accessed October 29, 2007).

42. "Intercontinental Hotels Group," *Business Travel News* 21, no. 6 (April 19, 2004), p. 67.

43. Johnny K. Johansson and Ilkka A. Ronkainen, "Consider Implications of Local Brands in a Global Arena," *Marketing News* 38 (May 15, 2004), pp. 46–48.

44. Ibid.

45. Ibid.

3

Buyer Behaviors

Chapter Objectives

After reading this chapter, you should be able to answer the following questions:

- **What** are the steps and issues associated with the consumer buying decision-making process?

- **How** do attitudes and values influence buyer behaviors?

- **How** can traditional factors and new trends affect consumer purchasing decisions?

- **When** does the marketing team know that it has effectively sent messages to business buyers?

- **How** can business and consumer markets be integrated into an effective dual channel marketing program?

APPLE'S IPHONE

Dialing Up New Customers

In late July 2007, Apple began selling the iPhone, a touch-screen-controlled cell phone device that plays music, supports Web browsing, and delivers voice and e-mail. The new and exciting device quickly generated a great deal of publicity and interest through the announcement of the iPhone's release by Apple CEO Steve Jobs, trade show appearances, and various contacts via the Internet and mainstream media. By the time the product had been placed on shelves, lines had formed in front of retail stores across the country, filled with those who wanted to be the "first on the block" to own the new $600 gadget.

Early evidence suggested that the first wave of marketing had been a grand success. Within the first 2 days, more than 270,000 units had been sold. Company leaders quickly repeated the goal of selling 1 million iPhones in the next quarter, 10 million by the end of 2008, and even more when the product became available in Europe.

To achieve these lofty sales goals, the marketing team was undoubtedly aware of the phases a new product introduction encounters. *Innovators* are those individuals who seek out new items. Clearly, Apple had effectively reached this group. The next set of buyers, the *early adopters*, are individuals of relatively high social status who rely on mass media and social contacts for guidance when making purchasing decisions. This group would be the one to sustain sales following the initial excitement of the release. The *early majority* consists of consumers who hold average social status, and, due to more limited resources, are more cautious about making purchases. The early majority would be one of Apple's major targets in the next year. The *late majority* is the last set of buyers. They are late to the party due to limited income, and they normally display greater caution and skepticism. Only strong social pressure by others will lead these individuals to buy items. Finally, *laggards* or *nonadopters* simply refuse to purchase new goods, even when there is overwhelming evidence that an item is a success.

Apple's challenges in selling the iPhone quickly emerged. During the first 2 days following the release, more than half of the people who had bought the phone had not activated it. Selling partner AT&T experienced a small technical glitch that delayed the activation process. Needless to say, neither company was pleased with this initial start-up problem; however, it was quickly resolved, and sales marched forward.

Not long after, stories surfaced that it was possible to hack into an iPhone system to see the user's files. Worries about security have plagued several new technologies and products. Consumer confidence is a must to sustain sales over the long term.

Then, social critics began to protest that users were being discourteous by playing iPhone music loudly in crowded settings and disturbing others. Another common complaint was that iPhone users would be distracted drivers and annoying travelers on airplanes and mass transit vehicles. After 3 months had passed, Apple dropped the price of the iPhone by nearly $200, leading to another wave of poor publicity, because early adopters felt they had been duped into paying more than the product should have cost.

It would take a sustained marketing effort to convince the early majority to buy the product. Advertisements and press releases were utilized to respond to the early technical problems and other issues.

One of the iPhone's major advantages was a strong name, based on the iPod and Apple brand. In fact, during the quarter in which the iPhone was released, Apple's profits soared, in part due to additional sales of iPods and the Mac line of personal computers. It seemed likely that the positive reactions to the iPhone had affected other parts of Apple's operations. At the same time, a new hurdle appeared. One of Apple's competitors, Cisco, filed a lawsuit claiming ownership of the name iPhone within days of the iPhone's release by Apple.

The partnership between Apple and AT&T benefited both companies. AT&T reported that sales of iPhones were greater in one weekend than they had been in over an entire month for every other phone the company had offered. Combined with the fees for the service itself, AT&T experienced strong financial returns as well.

Buyers are fickle, especially when a new product is launched. A successful IMC program accounts for skepticism, bad press, and attacks by competitors, while at the same time creating buzz, building the brand, and solving problems as they occur. Time will tell if the iPhone's sales will sustain Apple until the next technological breakthrough occurs.[1]

OVERVIEW

Developing effective methods to persuade people to buy goods and services is a primary goal of an integrated marketing communications program. Understanding how a buyer makes the decision to purchase from a specific vendor helps the marketing team reach this goal. Two types of buyer behaviors—consumer buyer behaviors and business-to-business buyer behaviors—receive attention in this chapter. When the steps followed in making purchasing decisions are more fully understood, it becomes possible to develop stronger marketing communications programs.

Consumer purchasing processes are examined in the first half of this chapter. Two stages in the process are the key to marketing communications. The first is the *information search* stage, in which the customer reviews previous memories and experiences looking for acceptable ways to meet a need by buying a product. The second stage is the *evaluation of alternatives* process, in which the individual compares various purchasing possibilities. An effective IMC program targets potential buyers involved in these processes. To help the marketing team, a review of the traditional factors affecting consumers, along with discussion of some of the newer trends present in the consumer buying environment, is provided.

Business-to-business buyer behaviors are the focus of the second part of this chapter. First, the five major roles played in business buying, from what is known as the *buying center*, are reviewed. Next, the types of purchases companies make are noted, along with the steps involved in the purchasing process. Finally, dual channel marketing, which involves selling the same product to both consumers and business buyers, is presented. Effective IMC programs identify potential customers from both markets. This leads to increased sales and helps a company maintain a strong presence in the marketplace.

CONSUMER PURCHASING PROCESS

Finding ways to influence the consumer purchasing process is a vital activity in marketing communications. Many marketers are held directly accountable for results of individual campaigns. Consequently, they try to carefully develop enticing messages that lead customers to buy products.

Figure 3.1 models the consumer buying decision-making process. Each step of the decision-making process is important; however, two of the components are the most directly related to developing quality integrated marketing communications:

- Information search
- Evaluation of alternatives

These two components are examined next. Discovering how customers seek out product information and then evaluate that information are keys to creating effective marketing communications programs.

FIGURE 3.1
Consumer Decision-Making Process

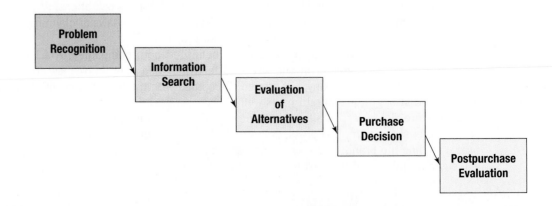

INFORMATION SEARCH

The first step of the buying decision-making process occurs when the consumer notices a need or want. The individual then conducts a search for information. Typically, a consumer begins with an internal search, mentally recalling products that might satisfy or meet the need. Often, the individual remembers how the need was met in the past. If a particular brand was chosen and the experience with that brand was positive, the consumer will likely make the same purchase decision. When this happens, the information search ends. If, however, the previous experience did not work out, the consumer conducts a more complete internal search. This includes memories of past experiences as well as the examination of other brands.

Internal Search

When conducting a more complete internal search, the consumer thinks about the brands he or she is willing to consider. This group does not normally contain every possible brand the consumer has experienced. The consumer removes brands that were tried but that did not result in a positive experience. The consumer also eliminates brands he or she knows little about. This means that during the information search process, the consumer quickly reduces the number of brands to a more manageable group.

Making sure a company's brand becomes part of the consumer's set of potential purchase alternatives is a key objective for creatives and brand managers. Achieving this goal greatly increases the chance that the brand will be purchased. A brand that has obtained a high level of brand equity is more likely to be included in the consumer's set of potential alternatives. High-quality, reasonably priced goods and services accompanied by attractive and powerful advertising messages usually become finalists in the purchasing decision. The Neutrogena advertisement shown in this section uses "#1" four times to persuade consumers that Neutrogena is the number-one antiwrinkle cream. The idea is to cause consumers who want an antiwrinkle cream to think about Neutrogena, hopefully as the first and best choice.

External Search

Following an internal search, the consumer makes a mental decision regarding an *external search*. If the customer has sufficient internal information, he or she moves to the next step of the decision-making process: evaluating the alternatives. When the consumer remains uncertain about the right brand to purchase, an external search takes place.

External information might be gathered from a variety of sources, including friends, relatives, experts, books, magazines, newspapers, advertisements, exposure to public relations activities, in-store displays, salespeople, and the Internet. The amount of time a consumer spends on an external search depends on three factors: (1) ability, (2) motivation, and (3) costs versus benefits (see Figure 3.2).[2]

The *ability to search* partially determines the extent of an information search. Ability consists of a person's educational level combined with the specific knowledge he or she has about a product and the brands in that product's category. Educated individuals are more likely to spend time searching for information. They are also more inclined to visit stores prior to making

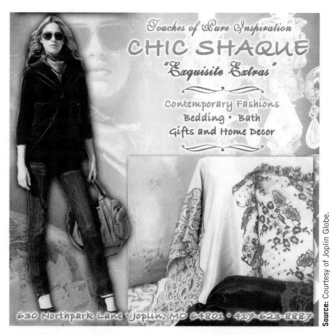

This advertisement for Chic Shaque may trigger a search for more information about contemporary fashions.

A Neutrogena ad designed to convince consumers that the product should be the first choice when selecting an antiwrinkle cream.

FIGURE 3.2
**Factors Impacting the Amount
of Time a Consumer Spends
Conducting an External Search**

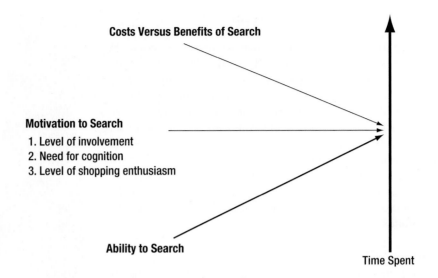

FIGURE 3.2
Factors Impacting the Amount of Time a Consumer Spends Conducting an External Search

decisions. Consumers possessing extensive knowledge about individual brands and product categories are better able to conduct a more involved external search. Thus, someone who knows a great deal about digital cameras has a more sophisticated ability to examine information than does someone who knows little about the technology. In addition, a person with more comprehensive knowledge of a product area often collects additional data, even when he or she is not in the market for the product.[3]

In terms of the amount of time an individual devotes to the external search process, a different phenomenon occurs. Although extensive product category knowledge provides individuals with a greater ability to search for external information, these consumers normally spend less time on the external search process. With knowledge already stored internally, there is no need to conduct an extensive external search for additional information. Consumers at the other end of the spectrum also spend less time in the external search process, but for the opposite reason. They do not have knowledge about the product category and do not know what type of information to ask for or what type of information is even needed, which means they lack the ability to search for information. Individuals in the middle, who have some knowledge of a product category but feel they need additional information to make intelligent decisions, typically spend the most time searching for external information.

The degree to which an external search takes place also depends on the customer's *level of motivation*. The greater the motivation is, the greater the extent of an external search. Motivation is determined by the consumer's:

- Level of involvement
- Need for cognition
- Level of shopping enthusiasm

Individuals are motivated to search for information when their involvement levels are high. **Involvement** means the extent to which a stimulus or task is relevant to a consumer's existing needs, wants, or values. When a consumer deems a product to be important, it becomes more likely he or she will engage in an external search. The amount of involvement is based on factors such as the *cost* of the product and its *importance*. The more a product costs, the more time an individual is willing to spend searching for information.

The same holds true for importance. Choosing clothes might not be an important decision to some young males, which suggests their clothing purchases typically have low involvement. Picking a tux for the high school prom, however, may spur greater involvement and a higher level of information search due to the social ramifications of dressing poorly at such an important event. The higher level of involvement emerges due to the addition of a new element—a major occasion in the person's life.

The **need for cognition** is a personality characteristic an individual displays when he or she engages in and enjoys mental activities. These mental exercises have a positive impact on the information search process. People with high needs for cognition gather more information and search more thoroughly than do individuals with a lower need for cognition.

The search also depends on a person's **enthusiasm for shopping**. Customers who like to shop will undertake a more in-depth search for goods and services. Involvement, need for cognition, and enthusiasm for shopping combine to determine an individual's motivation to search for information.[4]

The final factors that influence an information search are the *perceived costs* versus the *perceived benefits* of the search. Higher perceived benefits increase the tendency to search. One benefit that a consumer often seeks while examining external information is the ability to reduce purchase risk. By obtaining additional information, the customer lowers the chances of making a mistake in the purchase selection. The cost of the search consists of several items:

Enthusiasm for shopping has an impact on the amount of time spent on an external search.

- The actual cost of the good or service
- The subjective costs associated with the search, including time spent and anxiety experienced while making a decision
- The opportunity cost of foregoing other activities to search for information (e.g., going shopping instead of playing golf or watching a movie)

The greater the perceived subjective cost of the external information search, the less likely the consumer will conduct a search.[5]

The three factors that make up an external search (ability, motivation, costs versus benefits) are normally considered simultaneously. When the perceived cost of a search is low and the perceived benefit high, a consumer has a higher motivation to search for information. A consumer with a minimal amount of product knowledge and a low level of education is less likely to undertake an external search, because the consumer lacks the ability to find the right information.

From an integrated marketing communication perspective, the search process represents an important time to reach the consumer with information about a particular brand. The consumer's objective in making the effort to perform an external search is to acquire information leading to a better, more informed decision. The marketing team should try to provide information that leads consumers to choose the company's products. One ideal time to attempt to influence the decision-making process occurs when the consumer has not yet made up his or her mind. The key is to provide quality information at that time. Marketing experts can utilize three models of the information search process: (1) attitudes, (2) values, and (3) cognitive mapping.

Consumer Attitudes

Consumer attitudes can be influenced by effective marketing communications. An **attitude** is a mental position taken toward a topic, a person, or an event that influences the holder's feelings, perceptions, learning processes, and subsequent behaviors.[6] From a marketing communications perspective, attitudes can drive purchase decisions. If a consumer has a positive attitude toward a brand, the propensity to purchase the brand rises. If a consumer likes an advertisement, the probability of purchasing the product increases.

Attitudes consist of three components: (1) affective, (2) cognitive, and (3) conative.[7] The *affective* component consists of the feelings or emotions a person has about the

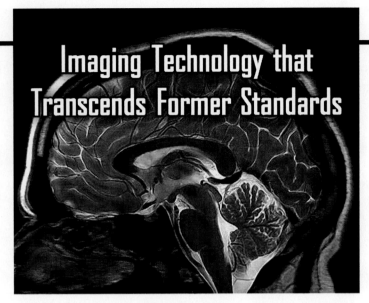

Imaging Technology that Transcends Former Standards

Providing brain imaging with uncompromised image quality, even with patient motion due to young age or uncontrollable tremors.

St. Francis North Hospital is pleased to announce that we now offer a state-of-the-art high definition magnetic resonance (HDMR) system, the Signa® EXCITE 1.5T. Similar to high definition television, HDMR provides physicians with highly detailed pictures to help them evaluate a wide range of patient conditions, including stroke, musculoskeletal, abdominal, breast and vascular disease. This system provides outstanding image quality for a confident diagnosis, and less likelihood of patient rescans, even in the most challenging circumstances.

Once again, St. Francis leads the way in our region with its continual effort to make the most advanced diagnostic equipment available to your doctor, and provide the best healthcare for you.

ST. FRANCIS NORTH HOSPITAL
An Affiliate of St. Francis Medical Center

3421 Medical Park Dr. • Monroe, LA • (318) 388-1946 • www.stfran.com

First in Technology.
Foremost in Care.

This advertisement for St. Francis North Hospital features a cognitive appeal.

object, topic, or idea. The *cognitive* component refers to a person's mental images, understanding, and interpretations of the person, object, or issue. The *conative* component is an individual's intentions, actions, or behavior. A common sequence of events that takes place as an attitude forms is:

Cognitive → Affective → Conative

Most of the time, a person first develops an understanding about an idea or object. In the case of marketing, these ideas center on the benefits of the good or service. Thoughts about the product emerge from watching or reading advertisements. Other thoughts may result from exposures to information from other sources, such as the Internet or a friend's referral. Eventually, these ideas become beliefs the consumer holds about a particular product. For instance, a consumer seeing the St. Francis North Hospital advertisement shown in this section might develop the impression that St. Francis offers high quality imaging technology to help detect brain disorders.

The affective part of the attitude is the general feeling or emotion a person attaches to the idea. In the case of goods and services, the product, its name, and other features can all generate emotions. For example, consider your emotional reactions to the following goods and services:

- Cough medicine
- Diaper wipes
- Motorcycles
- Children's toys made in China
- *Sports Illustrated*'s annual swimsuit issue
- Condoms

What emotions and thoughts did you associate with diaper wipes? The goal of the Pampers diaper wipe advertisement shown in this section is to influence your emotions. Does the picture in the ad change your feelings about Pampers or diaper wipes? As you consider the items listed here, some of your emotions or attitudes about them are relatively benign. Others are more strongly held. It is likely that cough medicine does not evoke much of an emotional response, but the swimsuit issue or condoms may generate a much stronger response.

Decision and action tendencies are the conative parts of attitudes. Therefore, if a person feels strongly enough about the swimsuit issue, he or she might cancel a subscription to *Sports Illustrated* or buy extra copies for friends. Oftentimes, attitudes are not held that strongly. Some people might feel favorably about a topic, such as green marketing, but not be moved to change their purchasing behaviors.

Attitudes can develop in other ways. An alternative process is:

$$\text{Affective} \rightarrow \text{Conative} \rightarrow \text{Cognitive}$$

In marketing, advertisements and other communications often appeal first to the emotions or feelings held by consumers. The idea is to move the consumer to "like" a product and then make the purchase (the conative component). Cognitive understanding of the product follows. For example, a young woman may be exposed to a perfume or skin product advertisement featuring soft, gentle images of nature; the ad might not even show the physical product. Still, the ad conjures favorable emotions. The woman eventually purchases the product and finally learns more about it by using it and reading directions, instructions, and other information on the package or label.

Some attitudes result from a third combination of the components, as follows:

$$\text{Conative} \rightarrow \text{Cognitive} \rightarrow \text{Affective}$$

Purchases that require little thought, that have a low price, or that do not demand a great deal of emotional involvement might follow this path. For instance, while shopping for groceries a customer may notice a new brand of cookies on sale. The person may have never seen the brand or flavor before but, because it is on sale, decides to give it a try. As the consumer eats the cookies, she develops a greater understanding of the product's taste, texture, and other qualities. Finally, the consumer reads the package to learn more about contents, including how many calories were devoured in each bite. Then the buyer finally develops feelings toward the cookies that will affect future cookie purchases.

No matter which path is taken to develop attitudes, each component is present to some extent. Some attitudes are relatively trivial (e.g., "I like table tennis, even though I hardly ever get to play"). Others are staunchly held, such as "I hate cigarette smoking!" Both are associated with feelings toward things, including products in the marketplace that may eventually result in behaviors (purchases).

Source: Courtesy of D'Arcy Masius Benton & Bowles Inc. © Procter & Gamble Productions, Inc. 1999. Photograph by Penny Gentieu.

What emotions does this ad for Pampers Wipes elicit? affective

Consumer Values

Attitudes are shaped, in part, by an individual's personal values. **Values** are strongly held beliefs about various topics or concepts. Values frame attitudes and lead to the judgments that guide personal behaviors. Values tend to be enduring. They normally form during childhood, although they can change as a person ages and experiences life.

Figure 3.3 lists some of the more common personal values. Individuals hold them to differing degrees. Factors that affect a person's values include the individual's personality,

◆ Comfortable life	◆ Pleasure
◆ Equality	◆ Salvation
◆ Excitement	◆ Security
◆ Freedom	◆ Self-fulfillment
◆ Fun, exciting life	◆ Self-respect
◆ Happiness	◆ Sense of belonging
◆ Inner peace	◆ Social acceptance
◆ Mature love	◆ Wisdom
◆ Personal accomplishment	

FIGURE 3.3
Personal Values

temperament, environment, and culture. By appealing to basic values, marketers hope to convince prospective customers to buy the company's products by acting on those values. At the same time, creatives know it is easier to change a person's attitude than an entire value structure.

In terms of consumer decision-making processes, both attitudes and values help marketing experts. If a good or service can be tied to a relatively universal *value,* such as patriotism, then the firm can take advantage of the linkage to present a positive image of the product. Following the September 11 tragedy, many firms attempted to tie into patriotism.

Attitudes can also be used in marketing communications. Most people consider being "put on hold" to be a nuisance. An advertising creative might be able to tap that attitude and use it to present a good or service in a more favorable light. Making the time pass pleasantly while on hold turns a negative attitude into a more positive experience.

Cognitive Mapping

The manner in which individuals store information further affects decisions, because it impacts what is recalled. Knowing how people store, retrieve, and evaluate information can help a company's marketing team develop advertisements and other marketing communications. The first step is to understand how various thought processes and memories work.

Cognitive maps are simulations of the knowledge structures and memories embedded in an individual's brain.[8] These structures contain a person's assumptions, beliefs, interpretation of facts, feelings, and attitudes about the larger world. People use these thought processes to interpret new information and to determine an appropriate response to fresh information or a novel situation. Figure 3.4 depicts a hypothetical cognitive map for an individual thinking about a Ruby Tuesday restaurant.

Based on the cognitive structures illustrated in Figure 3.4, when this customer thinks about Ruby Tuesday, she connects images of it to other restaurants offering fast food and others that provide dine-in services. In this case, the individual recognizes Ruby Tuesday as a dine-in establishment. The consumer also believes that Ruby Tuesday offers excellent service, but that the service is slow. Next, when the person thinks of slow service, her thoughts turn to Mel's Diner. When she thinks of excellent service, she recalls Applebee's.

Cognitive structures contain many linkages and can exist on several levels. For instance, one level of cognition is the map with the linkages in Figure 3.5. At another level, the cognitive map is more spatial and conjures images of the actual physical location of Ruby Tuesday, as well as the surrounding businesses. A third cognitive level related to Ruby Tuesday is the person's recall of the interior of the restaurant along with other linkages that occur at that level. The consumer can even have thoughts about Ruby Tuesday that focus on employees, including a relationship she had with a server who was a friend. Therefore, cognitive processing occurs on many levels using highly complex mechanisms.

FIGURE 3.4
A Cognitive Map for Ruby Tuesday

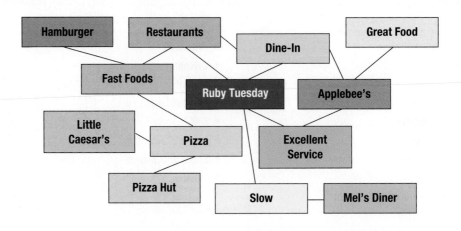

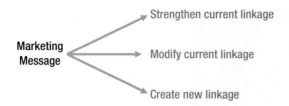

FIGURE 3.5
The Role of Marketing Messages
in Cognitive Mapping

As a marketing message reaches a consumer, the person may consider the information in several different ways. If the new information is consistent with current information, then the new information primarily tends to strengthen an existing linkage. For example, when a consumer views a Ruby Tuesday ad promoting great service, the result might be that the ad will strengthen an existing belief, because the consumer already concluded that Ruby Tuesday offers great service.

A different response can occur in other situations, including times when a message has no current linkages. For example, if a consumer sees an advertisement featuring Ruby Tuesday's seafood selection, and the consumer did not know that Ruby Tuesday offers seafood, a different reaction occurs. In order for this information to remain in the consumer's mind and to become linked to Ruby Tuesday, the customer must create a new linkage between previous Ruby Tuesday images with other images of seafood.

Hearing something once is usually not enough to cause it to be retained in a person's long-term memory. This is due to differences between short-term recall and long-term memories. The cognitive mapping process explains the knowledge structures embedded in a person's long-term memory. Ordinarily, information is retained in short-term memory for only a few seconds. As stimuli reach an individual's senses, short-term memory processes them. Short-term memory can retain only five to nine pieces of information. These new messages are either soon forgotten or added to long-term memory. When a message is repeated, an individual is more likely to remember it, because the message will be processed into long-term memory and fitted into previously developed cognitive maps.

As a result, when a company attempts to introduce consumers to a new brand, the advertisements and other marketing messages should repeat the name of the brand several times during the presentation. This repetition improves the chances of its recall at a later time. To illustrate how this works, consider what happens when a person gives a phone number to a friend. To help remember it, the individual repeats the number several times to place it into longer-term recall.

Another way a consumer can process information is to link the message to a new concept. For example, if a consumer sees an advertisement from Ruby Tuesday empha-sizing that it has great food but has never thought about the restaurant in terms of quality food, that linkage is not currently present. If the advertisement persuades the consumer, she might construct a linkage between Ruby Tuesday and good food without even traveling to the restaurant. If she does not believe the message, she will ignore or forget the information, and no new linkage evolves. A third possibility is that the consumer recalls the advertisement at a later time and decides to try Ruby Tuesday. If the food is great, then the link is established at that point. If it is not, the consumer continues thinking that Ruby Tuesday does not offer good food.

From a marketing perspective, it is easier to strengthen linkages that already exist. Adding new linkages or modifying linkages is more difficult. Regardless of how information

Consumers use cognitive mapping to assess and evaluate information.

Source: Courtesy of Sunkist Growers.

This Sunkist advertisement is designed to establish a new linkage between Sunkist lemon juice and a salt substitute.

is presented, repetition is important due to the limitations of short-term memory. Keep in mind that consumers are exposed to hundreds of messages a day. Only a few are processed into long-term memory.

Cognitive mapping and persuasion techniques designed to change attitudes or tap into strongly held values are two key ingredients in any IMC program. It is important first to understand the needs and attitudes of the target market. Then, messages should be structured to fill those needs and to capture consumers' attention by exposing them to messages that will travel effectively through a core processing channel or peripheral channels, either through solid reasoning or alluring emotional appeals.

Creatives attempt to design ads that reach the linkages consumers have already made between a product and other key ideas. For example, for a long time a linkage existed between Cadillac and quality, as witnessed by the advertising and promotional phrase "This product is the *Cadillac* . . . [of all products in the market]." Common linkages exist between products and ideas such as quality, value, low cost, expense, fun, sex, danger, practical, exotic, and many others. Carefully planned marketing campaigns look for linkages to entice the consumer to buy a given product and to believe in (or be loyal to) that product in the future. At that point, the company stays ahead of the game as consumers consider various purchasing alternatives.

EVALUATION OF ALTERNATIVES

The third step in the consumer buying decision-making process, expanded in Figure 3.6, is the evaluation of alternatives. Three models can be utilized to portray the nature of the evaluation process: (1) the evoked set approach, (2) the multiattribute approach, and (3) affect referral. Understanding how consumers make decisions allows a firm's marketing team to develop materials that lead consumers to favor the brand being promoted.

The Evoked Set Method

A person's **evoked set** consists of the brands he or she considers in a purchasing situation. An evoked set might be reviewed during both the information search and evaluation stages of the buying decision-making process. Two additional brand sets become part of the evaluation of purchase alternatives: (1) the inept set and (2) the inert set. The **inept set** consists of the brands that are part of a person's memory that are *not considered* because they elicit negative feelings. These negative sentiments are normally caused by a bad experience with a vendor or particular brand. They can also originate from negative comments made by a friend or by seeing an advertisement that the potential customer did not like.

FIGURE 3.6
Methods of Evaluating Alternatives

The **inert set** holds the brands that the consumer is aware of but the individual has neither negative nor positive feelings about the products. Using the terms from cognitive mapping, these brands have not been entered into any map, or they only have weak linkages to other ideas. The lack of knowledge about these brands usually eliminates them as alternatives. In other words, in most purchase situations the only brands considered are those that are present in the evoked set.

One of the primary goals of advertising is placing the brand name in the evoked sets of consumers. To do so normally requires promoting the brand name and the brand's primary benefit extensively and consistently. Extensively means using multiple media and avenues. The consumer should see the brand name frequently in as many locations as possible. Then, to make sure the name becomes part of an evoked set, the concepts described related to cognitive mapping can be employed. By tying the brand with its primary benefit, the intent is to embed the brand's name into the consumer's long-term memory. The message should be designed to establish or reinforce linkages between benefit and the brand name. When a consumer who is ready to evaluate alternatives uses his or her evoked set and the company's brand reaches the part of the set being considered, the advertising has been successful.

The Multiattribute Approach

Another model of the methods consumers use to evaluate purchasing alternatives is the multiattribute approach. It is especially useful for understanding high-involvement types of products. Consumers often examine sets of product attributes across an array of brands. The multiattribute model suggests that a consumer's ultimate attitude toward a brand is determined by:[9]

- The brand's performance on product or brand attributes
- The importance of each attribute to the consumer

The higher a brand rates on attributes that are important to the consumer, the more likely it becomes that the brand will be purchased. Table 3.1 notes products, along with some of the characteristics that affect their selection, each with potentially a lesser or greater value to individual consumers. Case 2 at the end of this chapter also illustrates this model.

From an integrated communication standpoint, providing consumers with information about a brand's performance on criteria that will be used should be the primary goal. This can be achieved by using a brand's Web site. Consumers making high-involvement decisions often use the Internet. Brochures and print ads can also be prepared; however, getting them into the hands of consumers just as they look for information presents the greatest challenge.

In advertising, creatives often feature a product with multiple benefits by designing a series of messages. Advertisements are developed highlighting price, style, service contract, software, memory, storage, or other product features. Only one or two of these benefits is presented in each ad. Otherwise, the ads become overloaded with information.

TABLE 3.1 The Multiattribute Model

Product	Characteristics				
Computer	Price	Style	Service contract	Software	Memory storage
Telephone	Price	Style	Speed dial	Caller ID	Cordless feature
Car	Price	Style	Safety	Room	Other features
T-bone steak	Price	Age	Fat content	Degree cooked	Seasonings
Sunglasses	Price	Style	UV protection	Durability	Prescription lenses
Sofa	Price	Style	Foldout bed	Stain resistance	Color
Credit card	Interest rate	Fees	Billing cycle	Access to ATM	Credit limit

Consider each item. Which characteristic is most important to you personally? Least important?

The multiattribute model is used in the purchase of high-involvement products, such as automobiles.

Consumers who see ads featuring one or two benefits are able to learn about the various characteristics of a particular brand. Over time, consumers then have the information they need to evaluate the product.

Affect Referral

A third model of how consumers evaluate purchase alternatives is called **affect referral**. It suggests that consumers choose brands they like the best or the ones with which they have developed emotional connections. This means the individual does not evaluate brands or think about product attributes. Instead, the consumer buys the brand he or she likes the best or the one that incites positive feelings. Toothpaste, ketchup, soft drinks, and milk are some of the products consumers normally select in this way. These purchases typically have low levels of involvement. They are also frequently purchased products.

The affect referral model also explains purchases of higher priced items as well as purchases of products that are "socially visible." It is the emotional bond that has been established between the consumer and the brand that leads to a purchase under those circumstances.

The affect referral model explains three things. First, using this approach to product evaluation saves mental energy. A quick choice seems easier than going through the process of evaluating every possible alternative. Some purchases basically don't deserve much effort. The affect referral model explains those situations.

Second, a multiattribute model type of approach might have been used previously when making a purchase. This means the person has already spent a great deal of time considering various product attributes, deciding which are most critical, and reaching a decision about the brand with the greatest number of advantages. Therefore, going through the process again would be "reinventing the wheel." For example, a teenager buying jeans may have already spent considerable time evaluating styles, prices, colors, durability levels, and "fit" of various brands. After making the purchase, this teenager continues to purchase the same brand as long as the experience remains positive. The affect referral model explains this buying behavior—the repurchase is simple and convenient.

Third, consumers often develop emotional bonds with brands. In terms of the purchase decision, an emotional bond with a product can be the strongest and most salient factor in the decision.[10] It is more important than any attribute or benefit the product can offer. Successful brands establish emotional bonds with consumers. A bond generates brand loyalty, enhances brand equity, and reduces brand parity. This means consumers do not have to evaluate alternatives because of their bond with the brand. Harley-Davidson has developed such a bond with many of the company's customers. So has Nike. For these customers, these feelings toward Harley-Davidson and Nike are so strong that they do not even think about other alternatives. Again, the affect referral model explains this type of buying behavior.

TRENDS IN THE CONSUMER BUYING ENVIRONMENT

Studying the steps consumers take while making purchasing decisions is a useful activity when creating marketing communications. At the same time, the environment in which purchases are made is always changing and evolving. Several trends in the consumer buying environment affect purchasing patterns. Some of these are listed in Figure 3.7.[11]

Age Complexity

Information has changed the way children grow up. Children are bombarded with advertisements, video games, television shows, movies, and a myriad of other sensory perceptions from an early age. Most know a great deal about sex by the age of 12. Female teenagers, and even preteens, wear cropped tops, miniskirts, and low-rider jeans. The result is that many believe children are "growing up" at a much earlier age.

At the other end of the spectrum, many adults are refusing to "grow old." They still wear the fashions that resemble those worn by college students. Some still drive fast sports cars or convertibles. Many middle-aged adults apparently do not want to grow old, so they act like younger people and buy products normally purchased by them. This trend challenges marketers to create messages that reflect these behaviors but do not offend the traditional middle-aged component of society.

Gender Complexity

A second new trend in the consumer buying environment can be called gender complexity. The traditional roles, lifestyles, and interests of men and women are becoming blurred. Women increasingly enter male-dominated occupations. Men now work in occupations that were once considered only for women. Many women attend college, delay marriage, and wait to start families. Some do not marry nor have children, choosing instead to focus on moving up the corporate ladder.

Men, meanwhile, are more likely to play an active role in parenting and help more with household chores. Today's men spend more on personal care products and plastic surgery. Traditionally, a company such as General Foods would advertise food and grocery shopping to women and an automaker such as General Motors would target car ads to men. That type of approach is no longer useful. Advertisements for food manufacturers may be targeted to the large percentage of men who do the grocery shopping. Ads for automobiles may be targeted at the large number of women who either purchase cars or have a major influence on vehicle purchases decisions.

Individualism

Individualism has become more pronounced, especially in the purchase of goods and services. Customers want companies to develop products just for them. To meet this trend, Nike now allows consumers to design their own shoes using the company's Web site. Levi Strauss allows for personalized jeans, made to fit the exact measurements given to them by the consumer, again over the Internet. Recognizing this trend, food manufacturers have increased the varieties, sizes, and flavors of foods. In the beverage industry, a total of 450

◆ Age complexity	◆ Cocooning
◆ Gender complexity	◆ Pleasure pursuits
◆ Individualism	◆ Health emphasis
◆ Active, busy lifestyles	

FIGURE 3.7
Trends Affecting Consumer Buying Behavior

Understanding the issues created by age and gender complexity, Guess created these two advertisements.

new products were introduced within a single year. Many of these new beverages were health-related items, touting that they were vitamin fortified, organic, all natural, or low calorie.[12]

Active, Busy Lifestyles

Active lifestyles have had a dramatic impact on consumer behaviors. In one survey, 47 percent of respondents stated that they would prefer additional free time over more money. In another poll, 53 percent of the respondents said they would be willing to give up one day's wages per week in exchange for a day off to spend with family and friends. Many consumers now focus less on material possessions and more on experiences such as vacations, entertainment, and events with friends and family.[13]

Time pressures account for increases in sales of convenience items, such as microwave ovens, drive-through dry-cleaning establishments, and one-stop shopping outlets, most notably Wal-Mart's Supercenters. People on the go use cell phones, Blackberries, or answering machines to make sure they stay in touch with others and do not miss any important messages during busy days. The demand for convenience continues to increase.

Cocooning

One of the side effects of a busy and hectic lifestyle is cocooning. The stress of long hours at work with additional hours spent fighting commuter traffic has led many individuals to retreat and cocoon in their homes. A major part of cocooning is making the home environment as soothing as possible. Evidence of cocooning includes major expenditures on elaborate homes, expensive sound systems, satellite systems with big-screen televisions, swimming pools, saunas, hot tubs, gourmet kitchens with large dining rooms, decks and porches, and moving to the country or to a gated community.

Many advertisements emphasize cocooning aspects of shops and services. Recently, Internet ads focused on the utility of shopping from home during the Christmas season to offer the consumer a method to avoid the hustle and bustle of the holidays.

Changes in Family Units

Divorce and remarriage have altered many family units. Remarried divorcees represent about 10 percent of the population. Divorcees tend to develop a new outlook on life. They often desire to cocoon, which changes their purchasing patterns. This group, called *second chancers,* is usually between the ages of 40 and 59 and has a higher household income. Second chancers are more content with life than are average adults. They tend to be happy with their new families but also have a different life focus. Second chancers spend less time trying to please others and more time seeking fuller, more enriching lives for themselves and their children or spouse. Although the home and cocooning is a major emphasis, entertainment and vacation services also appeal to this group.[14]

Pleasure Pursuits

Some people handle the stress caused by a hectic, busy lifestyle through occasional indulgences or pleasure binges such as expensive dinners out and smaller luxury purchases. Pleasure pursuits also include "getaway" weekends in resorts and on short cruises. These self-rewarding activities make the consumer feel that all the work and effort is "worth it." The implications for marketing experts is to note the indulgence aspects of products.

Many people respond to stress through exciting adventures. From theme parks to virtual reality playrooms, consumers enjoy the mental relaxation of experiencing things that seem almost unreal. Many gambling establishments cater to these more exotic types of vacations. IMAX theaters generate a much more exciting experience than do normal movie theaters. As the technology of fantasy continues to develop, more firms enter the marketplace to profit from consumer desires to "get away from it all."

Health Emphasis

The U.S. population continues to age. Two outcomes of this trend are a blossoming interest in health and maintaining one's youthful appearance. Many consumers are trying to develop a balanced lifestyle. This includes a regular emphasis on nutrition, exercise, and staying active without feeling too guilty about an occasional overindulgence.[15]

Developing better eating habits has had an impact on many families. Some companies were caught off guard by this change. Kraft, whose best-selling products included macaroni and cheese, Oscar Mayer hot dogs, Philadelphia cream cheese, and Kool-aid, faced a new landscape. Rising concerns about obesity caused the company to shift its approach, and Kraft began to produce healthy, diet-oriented foods. In addition, Kraft reduced the fat content in over 200 products. The marketing message was changed to promote Kraft foods as part of a proper diet.[16]

Although consumers want healthier foods, they also want convenience. Busy lifestyles mean consumers are less willing to cook from scratch. They want prepared foods that can be assembled easily and cooked quickly. Food products that combine health attributes with convenience are likely to sell well in the future.[17]

In sum, these new trends in the consumer buying environment create several challenges for marketing experts, as shown in Figure 3.8. The first is to monitor for changes so that the company is not surprised by them. The second is to create goods and services that are compatible with changing values. The third is to design marketing messages that reflect and build on the values people in various target

With the emphasis on health and remaining active, St. Francis Medical Center promotes knee replacement following an injury or arthritis.

First in Orthopedics.
Foremost in
Knee Replacement.

When injury or arthritis changes the simple act of walking or bending into chronic pain, routine work can become a difficult task. At St. Francis, restoring pain-free movement and independence is our commitment and our mission.

Our doctors and staff are experts at knee replacement and other orthopedic surgeries, performing these procedures almost daily. Even more importantly, we understand the value of compassionate care. Technology, expertise, and inspired dedication–St. Francis Medical Center... a higher standard.

ST. FRANCIS MEDICAL CENTER
Franciscan Missionaries of Our Lady Health System

309 Jackson Street • Monroe, Louisiana • (318) 327-4000 • www.stfran.com

Source: Courtesy of Necomer, Morris and Young, Inc.

FIGURE 3.8
How Marketers Should Respond to New Trends in the Consumer Buying Environment

- Monitor consumer environment for changes.
- Create goods and services that are compatible with the changes.
- Design marketing messages that reflect the changes.

markets express. The idea is to incorporate new trends into the marketing program while at the same time being careful not to alienate current customers who might not like the trends.

BUSINESS-TO-BUSINESS BUYER BEHAVIOR

The primary thing to remember about business-to-business (B-to-B) purchases is that *people* still make the decisions. At the same time, when selling to a business organization the marketing team must be aware that normally several individuals are involved in the purchase. Further, corporate policies create restrictions and decision rules that affect purchasing activities. Factors such as budgets, costs, and profit considerations also influence the final choice.

The buying decision-making process for businesses becomes more complex due to the number of people involved. The **buying center** is the group of individuals making a purchase decision on behalf of a business. The buying center consists of five different individuals playing various roles in the process, as shown in Figure 3.9. The five roles involved in the buying center are:

- **Users**   Members of the organization who actually use the good or service
- **Buyers**   Individuals given the formal responsibility of making the purchase
- **Influencers**   People who shape purchasing decisions by providing the information or criteria utilized in evaluating alternatives, such as engineers
- **Deciders**   Individuals who authorize the purchase decisions
- **Gatekeepers**   Individuals who control the flow of information to members of the buying center

These five roles often overlap. A gatekeeper might also be the user. Oftentimes, the gatekeeper is the entire purchasing department, and this group might determine what information reaches members of the buying center. The purchasing department usually controls the amount of access a salesperson has to members of the buying center.

Several individuals can occupy the same role in a buying center, especially for large or critical purchases. It is not unusual for a variety of members of the organization to serve as influencers, because these roles usually are not fixed and formal. Roles change as the purchase decision changes.

The buying behavior process is unique in each organization. It varies within an organization from one purchasing decision to the next. Salespeople calling on a business must be able to locate members of the buying center and understand their roles in the process. These roles often change from one purchase situation to another, making the marketing task more difficult than one might expect.[18]

FIGURE 3.9
The Buying Center

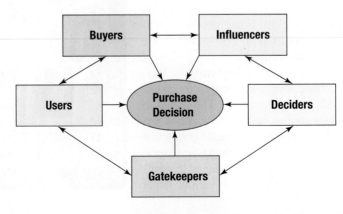

FACTORS AFFECTING MEMBERS OF BUSINESS BUYING CENTERS

The behaviors of members in the buying center are influenced by a series of organizational and individual factors.[19] These influences change the manner in which decisions are made and often affect the eventual outcome or alternative chosen.

Organizational Influences

Several organizational factors affect the ways in which individuals make purchasing decisions for a company. These organizational factors include the company's goals and its operating environment (recession, growth period, lawsuits pending, etc.). Decisions are further constrained by the organization's finances, capital assets, market position, the quality of its human resources, and the country in which the firm operates.

Studies of organizational decision making indicate that employees tend to adopt *heuristics,* which are decision rules designed to reduce the number of viable options to a smaller, manageable set. Company goals, rules, budgets, and other organizational factors create heuristics. One decision rule often employed is *satisficing,* which means that when an acceptable alternative has been identified, it is taken and the search is completed. Rather than spending a great deal of time looking for an optimal solution, decision makers tend to favor expedience.[20]

Individual Factors

At least seven factors affect each member of the business buying center: (1) personality features, (2) roles and perceived roles, (3) motivational levels, (4) levels of power, (5) attitudes toward risk, (6) levels of cognitive involvement, and (7) personal objectives (see Figure 3.10).[21] Each impacts how the individual interacts with other members of the center.

The first factor is *personality.* A decisive person makes purchase decisions in a manner different from someone who vacillates. Confidence, extroversion, shyness, and other personality traits affect both the person performing the decision-making role and others in the process. An aggressive "know-it-all" type affects the other members of a decision-making team, and such a personality feature does not always benefit the organization. An extrovert tends to become more involved in the buying process than a more introverted individual. The extrovert spends more time talking, and the introvert spends more time listening to sellers. The introvert might be too timid with salespeople, and consequently may not ask important questions.

The *roles* people play are influenced by an individual's age, heredity, ethnicity, gender, cultural memberships, and patterns of social interaction. Roles are socially

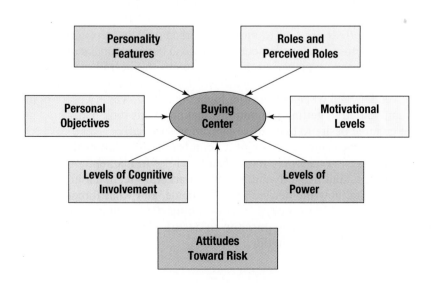

FIGURE 3.10
Individual Factors Affecting the Behaviors of Buying Center Members

constructed, which means people define how they intend to play roles as part of the negotiation process with others. A person's perception of how the role fits into the buying center process and the overall organization affects how the individual is involved in the purchase. If a buying center member perceives the role as merely giving approval to decisions made by the boss (the decider), then the individual will not actively participate. When members feel their inputs are important and are being solicited, they become more active. One person might believe that his role is to provide information. Another might perceive her role as being the person who synthesizes information provided by vendors and then relating the information to the buying center to save time. Roles and perceptions of roles are major factors determining how members of the buying center go about their business.

Motivation depends on how well the individual's goals match the organization's goals. If a factory foreman has a personal goal of becoming the vice president of operations, that foreman is more likely to become involved in all purchasing decisions that affect his performance and that of his department. If a purchasing agent has been charged by the CEO to cut expenses, that person might take a more active role to ensure that cost-cutting selections are made. Many individuals are motivated by the need for recognition. The goal of making successful purchasing decisions is to ensure that others recognize their efforts. They may think there is a link between recognition and getting promotions and pay raises.

A person's *level of power* in the buying process is derived from his or her role in the buying center, official position in the organization, and the impact of the purchase decision on a specific job. When a particular purchase decision directly affects an employee, that person tries to gain more power in the buying process. For instance, a factory foreman has greater power within the buying center in the purchase of raw materials, whereas the maintenance foreman has more power in the purchase of maintenance supplies. In these situations, each strives to influence the decision that affects his or her area.

Risk also affects members of the buying center. Many vendors are chosen because buyers believe the choice represents the lowest risk. Risk avoidance leads buyers to stay with current vendors rather than switching. In marketing to businesses, reducing risk is a major concern, especially when signing large contracts or when the purchase might affect company profits. People tend to think that taking risks (especially when a failure follows) can affect performance appraisals, promotions, and other aspects of an individual's job.

Levels of cognitive involvement influence not only consumer buyer behaviors but also business buyers. Individuals with higher levels of cognitive capacity want more information prior to making decisions. They also ask more questions when interacting with a sales rep. These individuals spend more time deliberating prior to making decisions. Clearly stated message arguments are the important ingredients in persuading people with higher cognitive levels (as noted in the discussion of consumer buyer behaviors).

Personal objectives are tied to motives, personality, perceptions of risk, and the other individual factors. Personal objectives can lead buyers to make purchases that help them politically in the organization, but that are not the best choice. For example, if someone knows his or her boss is friends with a particular vendor, the buyer might choose that vendor even when others offer higher quality, lower prices, or both. Personal objectives can be tied to getting promotions, making rivals look bad, "brown-nosing" a boss, or the genuine desire to help the organization succeed.

In sum, a buying center consists of a complex set of relationships. Members can serve different roles and may play more than one role. In marketing to businesses, it is important to understand these dynamics. The marketing team should identify who is making the decision, how the decision will be made, and what forces or factors might affect the decision-making process. By examining the organizational and individual influences that are present, it is possible to design a communications program that reaches the key people at the right time.

TYPES OF BUSINESS-TO-BUSINESS SALES

Business buyers make different types of buying decisions. The marketing team should be aware of which type of purchase decisions is being made. The three categories of buying activities are: (1) a straight rebuy, (2) a modified rebuy, and (3) a new task.[22]

A **straight rebuy** occurs when the firm has previously chosen a vendor and intends to place a reorder. This is normally a routine process involving only a few members of the buying center. Often the purchasing agent (buyer) and the users of the product are the only persons aware of a rebuy order. The user's role in this purchase situation is to ask the buyer to replenish the supply. The buyer then contacts the supplier and places an order. Little or no evaluation of alternatives or information takes place. Buyers often place orders electronically.

In making a **modified rebuy**, the company buying team will consider and evaluate alternatives. As identified in Figure 3.11, a modified rebuy purchase can be made for four different reasons. First, when a company's buyers are dissatisfied with the current vendor, they will look at new options. The greater the level of dissatisfaction, the greater the enticement to look for additional possibilities. Second, if a new company offers what is perceived by a member of the buying center to be a better buy, the purchase decision may be revisited.

A third type of modified rebuy occurs at the end of a contractual agreement. Many organizations, as dictated by corporate policy, must ask for bids each time a contract is written. This situation most often occurs when government and nonprofit organizations make purchases. The final reason for a modified rebuy is that the people in the company assigned to make the purchase might have only limited or infrequent experience with the good or service. When a company purchases delivery trucks, the typical time between decisions is 5 to 7 years. This creates a modified rebuy situation, because many factors change over that amount of time. Prices, product features, and vendors (truck dealerships) change rapidly. Also, in most cases the composition of the buying group will be different. Some may have never been part of the decision to purchase delivery vehicles.

In **new task** purchasing situations, the company buys a good or service for the first time, and the product involved is one with which organizational members have no experience. This type of purchase normally requires input from a number of people in the buying center, and a considerable amount of time is spent gathering information and evaluating vendors. In many cases, vendors are asked to assist in identifying the required specifications.

Source: Courtesy of 3M/SPD.

A 3M advertisement directed to businesses for Premium-Performance Packaging Tape.

- ◆ Dissatisfaction with current vendor.
- ◆ A different vendor makes an attractive offer.
- ◆ End of contractual arrangement with current vendor.
- ◆ Individuals involved in decision process have no or little experience with the product.

FIGURE 3.11
Reasons for a Modified Rebuy

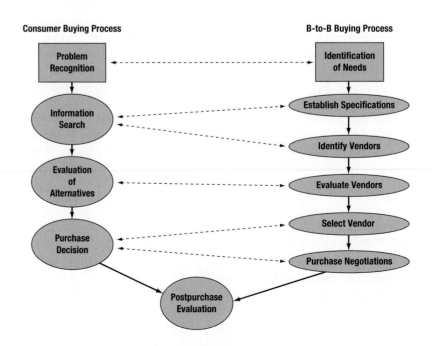

WITH SCOTT POWERLINE,

THE JOB IS IN THE BAG.

Whatever you want, Scott's got. Plus, 24/7 service anywhere on the globe!

From bucket trucks to Mantis cranes (we're the No. 1 dealer in the world), we carry the selection and inventory to get you what you need when you need it. Plus, 24/7 service to keep you running and on the job – anywhere. See all our lines online!

Rentals • Leasing • Service • Sales

SCOTT POWERLINE & UTILITY EQUIPMENT

One-Stop Scott

The demand for rental equipment offered by Scott is derived from the demand for the products and services offered by Scott's customers.

THE BUSINESS-TO-BUSINESS BUYING PROCESS

The steps involved in the business-to-business buying process are quite similar to those made by individual consumers. In new task purchasing situations, members of the buying center tend to go through each of the seven steps as part of the buying decision-making process. In modified rebuy or straight rebuy situations, one or more of the steps may be eliminated.[23] Figure 3.12 compares the consumer buying process to the business-to-business buying process. A discussion of each step follows.

Identification of Needs

Just as consumers identify needs (hunger, protection, social interaction), businesses also make purchases because of needs ranging from raw materials to professional services. The major difference, however, is the way most business needs are determined.

Many business needs are created by derived demand. **Derived demand** is based on, linked to, or generated by the production and sale of some other good or service.[24] The demand for steel is largely based on the number of cars and trucks sold each year. When the demand for vehicles goes down because the economy experiences a recession or downturn, the demand for steel also declines. Steel manufacturers find it difficult to stimulate demand because of the nature of derived demand. Derived demand results from purchases of raw materials used in the production of goods and services, such as steel, aluminum, concrete, plastic, petroleum products (e.g., jet fuel for airlines), construction materials, and so forth. Derived demand also exists for services. Most of the demand for mortgages depends on housing sales.

FIGURE 3.12
A Comparison of the Business-to-Business (B-to-B) Buying Process to the Consumer Buying Process

Consumer Buying Process: Problem Recognition → Information Search → Evaluation of Alternatives → Purchase Decision → Postpurchase Evaluation

B-to-B Buying Process: Identification of Needs → Establish Specifications → Identify Vendors → Evaluate Vendors → Select Vendor → Purchase Negotiations → Postpurchase Evaluation

Once a need has been recognized, if a straight rebuy choice is made then an order is placed with the current vendor. When the purchase is a modified rebuy or new task, members of the buying center move to the next step in the process.

Establishment of Specifications

In a new task purchase, the most complete specifications are spelled out. Many times, various vendors are involved in helping the buyer develop clear specifications. In modified rebuy situations, specifications are examined to ensure that they are current and that they meet the company's needs. Occasionally, specifications are changed, but normally these are only minor alterations.

Identification of Vendors

Once specifications have been identified, potential vendors are identified and notified to find out if they are interested in submitting bids. In most business situations, written, formal bids are required. A vendor's ability to write a clear proposal often determines whether the company will present a successful bid. Effective proposals spell out prices, quality levels, payment terms, support services, and any other condition requested by the company looking to purchase goods or services.

Vendor Evaluation

Evaluations of vendors normally occur at three levels. The first level is an *initial screening* of proposals. This process narrows the field of vendors down to three to five competitors. The number of people from the buying center involved in the initial screening depends on the dollar value of the bid and whether the product is critical to the firm's operation. As dollar values increase and the product becomes more critical, the number of individuals from the buying center involved also rises. Minor choices are often delegated to a single individual.

This city has what it takes to be an economic power.

CITY OF NEW ORLEANS
C. Ray Nagin, Mayor

It's time to care again.

595-CARE   NewNewOrleans.net

This advertisement for the American city of New Orleans is designed to encourage company leaders to consider the city for future activities.

The second level of evaluation occurs as the firm undertakes a *vendor audit*. An audit is especially important when members of the company want to develop a long-term relationship with a supplier. Vendors that are the primary sources for critical components or raw materials recognize that long-term bonds benefit both the vendor and the purchasing firm. Members of the audit team often include an engineer, someone from operations, a quality-control specialist, and members of the purchasing department. The goal of the audit is to evaluate potential suppliers and each company's ability to meet demand, provide the level of quality needed, and deliver the product on time.

The third and final level of evaluation takes place as various members of the buying center *share vendor audit information*. At that time, company leaders consider purchase procedures. A company might require the manufacturer to share its production schedule. Sharing information, such as the production schedules with suppliers, requires a degree of trust in the vendor.

Remember that vendors are people, just as members of the buying center are people. Attitudes, values, opinions, and first impressions influence evaluations made about vendors. All messages, including bids and proposals, must be carefully designed to create favorable impressions in order to achieve success.

Vendor Selection

Once company officials have carefully studied all of the vendors and the bids have been considered, it is time to make a final choice. In the decision process, members of the buying center experience all of the individual and organizational pressures discussed earlier. The final decision is normally based on a comparison of per-dollar values offered by various vendors. When selection criteria are used, the most common include quality, delivery, performance history, warranties, facilities and capacity, geographic location, and technical capability.[25] It is not likely that any one vendor will be deemed superior on all selection criteria. Therefore, the marketing team for each seller will emphasize the company's specific strengths as part of the selling process. In reality, however, politics and other forces also have a significant impact. Successful marketing requires an understanding of these forces.

Negotiation of Terms

In most purchasing situations, negotiation of terms is merely a formality, because most of the conditions have already been worked out. Occasionally, however, changes are made at this point in a contract or purchase. These tend to be minor and are normally negotiated by the purchasing agent. When the final agreement is set, goods are shipped or services provided. Assuming no further complications, the buying process is complete until the next cycle begins.

Postpurchase Evaluation

In the business-to-business arena, the post-purchase phase is a critical stage. Vendors that provide high-quality products, follow-up, and service often move into a straight rebuy situation. This means they can avoid most of the steps involved, because they are the chosen vendor until something changes. Even for products that are purchased occasionally, the firm that gives attention to the postpurchase component of the selling process is likely have an edge the next time a purchase is made.

DUAL CHANNEL MARKETING

Firms sell virtually the same goods or services to both consumers and businesses in a program known as **dual channel marketing**.[26] This approach fits several situations. Perhaps the most common scenario occurs when a product sold in business markets is then adapted to consumer markets. New products often have high start-up costs, including R&D expenditures, market research, and so forth. Businesses tend to be less price sensitive than retail consumers. Thus, it is logical to sell to them first.

As sales grow, economies of scale emerge. Larger purchases of raw materials combined with more standardized methods of production make it possible to enter consumer markets. The benefits of economies of scale entice

3M Post-it Sortable Cards are sold to both retail customers and in business-to-business markets.

3M

Growth through innovation

Post-it® Sortable Cards are redefining visual organization. They stick, stack and sort, so they're perfect for planning, organizing and brainstorming anywhere. 3M's commitment to understanding and developing markets results in a steady pipeline of innovative new products. One more reason why Post-it® and Scotch® are among the world's most powerful brands.

Post-it **Scotch**

3M, Post-it and Scotch are trademarks of 3M. © 3M 2006

manufacturers to sell products previously supplied to the business sector in the retail markets. Products such as digital cameras, calculators, computers, fax machines, and cell phones were first sold to businesses and then later to consumers. To make the move to the retail arena possible, prices must come down and products need to be user-friendly. For example, consumers can now have their photos put on a CD rather than obtaining prints. The imaging technology developed by Kodak and Intel was first sold to various businesses and now is being offered to retail customers. By forming an alliance with Intel, Kodak brought the cost down and developed the economies of scale needed for consumer markets.

Approximately 30 percent of Holiday Inn's business customers also stay with the chain on private vacations.

Another type of dual channel marketing results from *spin-off sales.* Individuals who buy a particular product at work often have positive experiences and, as a result, purchase the product for personal use. This situation often occurs with computers and computer software. Favorable feelings about more expensive items can also result in spin-off sales. A salesperson who drives a company-owned Buick LeSabre for work might like it so well that one is purchased for personal use. Holiday Inn's marketing team discovered that many of its private stays come from business-related spin-offs. Approximately 30 percent of Holiday Inn's business customers also stay with the chain on private vacations.[27]

In dual channel marketing, a primary decision that must be made is how to represent the product in each channel. The firm can either emphasize similarities between the two markets or focus on differences. Consumers and businesses looking for the same benefits and product features probably will see marketing messages quite similar in both channels. When consumers and business buyers value different product attributes or desire different benefits, the marketing strategy develops more customized messages for the separate markets.

When there are substantial differences between the two channels, the typical tactics are to:

- Use different communication messages
- Create different brands
- Use multiple channels or different channels

In many instances, the product attributes are the same, but the value or benefit of each attribute is different. Messages should focus on the benefits each segment can derive from the product. Cell phones marketed to businesses can stress the area coverage and service options. For consumers, cell phone marketing messages can center on the fashionable design of the product, its ease of use, or a lower price.

To avoid confusing individuals who might see both messages from the same producer, companies often utilize dual branding. For instance, when Black & Decker decided to launch a professional line of power tools, the DeWalt brand name was chosen. This avoided confusion with the Black & Decker name and prevented any negative image transfer from home tools to professional tools.

In most cases, business customers and consumers want the same basic benefits from products. In these situations, a single strategy for both markets is best. Tactics include:

- Integrating communications messages
- Selling the same brand in both markets
- Scanning both markets for dual marketing opportunities

In addition to creating economies of scale, integrating consumer markets has an additional advantage: the potential to create synergies. Synergies arise from increased brand identity and equity. An image developed in the consumer market can then be used to enter a business market, or vice versa. Using one brand makes it easier to develop brand awareness and brand loyalty. A business customer who uses a company-owned American Express Card is likely to have a separate card from the same company for personal use.

Scanning both types of customers for new opportunities is an important part of dual channel marketing. For example, the firm Intuit, which sells Quicken software, discovered that individuals who use Quicken at home also are willing to use a similar version for their small businesses. Capitalizing on this need or demand, Quicken added features such as payroll and inventory control to a business software package. At the same time, Quicken maintained its easy-to-use format. By finding business needs for a consumer product, Quicken adapted a current product and captured 70 percent of the small-business accounting software market.[28]

Dual channel marketing can create a major competitive advantage as products are sold in both markets. A complete IMC planning process includes the evaluation of potential business market segments as well as consumer market segments. Firms that integrate messages across these markets take a major step toward reaching every potential user of the company's goods or services.

INTERNATIONAL IMPLICATIONS

Selling to consumers and businesses requires the marketing team to understand cultural differences related to products, messages, and selling techniques. A *cultural assimilator* is an invaluable member of the marketing team in international projects. Individual buyers and members of companies from other countries will exhibit cultural differences as they consider purchasing alternatives. It is crucial to understand the nuances of the purchasing process in any transaction that takes place in a foreign country. For example, at domestic U.S. trade shows it is unlikely that an actual purchase will be finalized. Instead, information is collected and transferred between the buyer and the seller. At international trade shows, however, sales are often completed. Higher ranking members of the purchasing company attend the shows and are more inclined to buy on the spot. Knowing these kinds of differences will help a company succeed in international trade.

Remember that building a powerful brand is important in any IMC program. A strong brand means the product will become part of the consumer's initial set of brands to consider when making a purchase. A powerful brand crosses national boundaries and becomes part of an effective GMIC program. Successful global brands are built over time. It takes a combination of high-quality products and effective marketing communications to reach that point.

In business-to-business marketing, a visible global brand presence is equally crucial. The existence of multiple vendors, increasing perceptions of brand parity, and growing use of the Internet make it impossible for a company to succeed using only price differentiation. A strong brand is a necessity in the global environment.

Most markets contain numerous competitors. Each forces the other to improve the quality of the good or service being offered. Over time, fewer perceived differences exist. Perceptions of brand parity in the marketplace are the result. In those circumstances, the brand plays a vital role. A strong brand inspires recall when a purchase is about to be made. If perceptions of brand equity can be built, the company has a major advantage. The Internet allows business buyers to search for more potential providers. Without a strong brand, it becomes nearly impossible to stand out in the marketplace. As Robert Duboff writes, "It is no longer sufficient to be a great company; *you must be a great brand.*"[29]

SUMMARY

Buyer behaviors are part of the purchasing process in both consumer markets and business-to-business transactions. An effective IMC program accounts for the ways in which goods and services are purchased in both markets. The goal is to tailor marketing messages to target audiences in the appropriate media.

The consumer buying decision-making process consists of five steps. Marketing experts, and especially creatives, must be aware of each step and prepare effective communications that will lead most directly to the decision to buy. Two of the most important steps, for the purposes of creating effective marketing communications, are the information search stage and the evaluation of alternatives stage.

After a consumer recognizes a want or need, the individual searches for information both internally and externally. Marketing messages must be directed to placing the product or service in the consumer's evoked set of viable purchasing prospects. The more involved the customer is in the search, the more likely the product will have a longer-lasting impact once purchased. Those with greater needs for cognition are attracted to the process of thinking through a decision. Those with a greater degree of enthusiasm for shopping spend more time analyzing the available alternatives. Customers consider the benefits and costs of searches and make more or less rational decisions about how extensively they will seek out information.

Evoked sets, attitudes and values, and cognitive maps explain how an individual evaluates various purchasing choices. Evoked sets reveal which products "make the cut" and receive consideration. Attitudes and values predispose consumers toward some products and companies and away from others. Cognitive maps help the customer link thoughts about a company with other experiences. Marketing experts try to identify consumer attitudes and values that affect purchase decisions and make sure they do not offend prospects with messages. Stronger ties can be built with customers when the good or service is favorably attached to strongly held attitudes and values.

The new millennium presents a changing buying decision-making environment to marketers. New cultural values and attitudes, time pressures, and busy lifestyles influence what people buy, how they buy, and the manner in which they can be enticed to buy. Many families try to isolate themselves from everyday pressures by cocooning. They also try to escape through indulgences and pleasure binges, by finding excitement or fantasy, and by planning to meet social needs. An aging baby boom population is more focused on lasting values and on health issues. Marketing experts can address these needs and lead customers to purchases based on them.

By understanding business buyer behaviors, the marketing team can construct a more complete and integrated marketing communications program. Business purchases are driven by members of the buying center. These members include users, buyers, influencers, deciders, and gatekeepers. Each role is important, even when a single person plays more than one role. Members of the buying center are human beings. This means they are influenced by both organizational and individual factors that affect various marketing decisions.

Business-to-business sales take three forms. A straight rebuy occurs when the firm has previously chosen a vendor and intends to place a reorder. A modified rebuy occurs when the purchasing group is willing to consider and evaluate new alternatives. This decision is usually based on dissatisfaction with a current vendor. A new task purchase is one in which the company buys a good or service for the first time, and the product involved is one with which organizational members have no experience. The business-to-business buying process is similar to the consumer purchase decision-making process. A more formal purchasing process includes formal specifications, bids from potential vendors, and a contract finalizing the purchasing agreement.

Dual channel marketing means that the firm sells virtually the same goods or services to both consumers and businesses. Dual channel marketing creates both economies of scale and synergies for the vendor company. It also enhances the chances that a product will be sold to every available customer. The challenge to the marketing team is to create strong and consistent marketing messages to every potential buyer, accounting for how buyer behaviors are present in purchasing processes.

KEY TERMS

involvement   The extent to which a stimulus or task is relevant to a consumer's existing needs, wants, or values.

need for cognition   A personality characteristic an individual displays when he or she engages in and enjoys mental activities.

enthusiasm for shopping   Customers who like to shop will undertake a more in-depth search for details about goods and services.

attitude   A mental position taken toward a topic, person, or event that influences the holder's feelings, perceptions, learning processes, and subsequent behaviors.

values   Strongly held beliefs about various topics or concepts.

cognitive maps   Simulations of the knowledge structures embedded in an individual's brain.

evoked set   Consists of the set of brands a consumer considers during the information search and evaluation processes.

inept set   Part of a memory set that consists of the brands that are held in a person's memory but that are *not considered*, because they elicit negative feelings.

inert set   Part of a memory set of brands that hold the brands that the consumer has awareness of but has neither negative nor positive feelings about.

affect referral   A purchasing decision model in which the consumer chooses the brand for which he or she has the strongest liking or feelings.

buying center   The group of individuals who make a purchase decision on behalf of a business.

straight rebuy   Occurs when the firm has previously chosen a vendor and intends to place a reorder.

modified rebuy   The company buying team considers and evaluates new purchasing alternatives.

new task   The company buys a good or service for the first time, and the product involved is one with which organizational members have no experience.

derived demand   Demand based on, linked to, or generated by the production and sale of some other good or service.

dual channel marketing   Selling virtually the same goods or services to both consumers and businesses.

compensatory heuristics   A purchasing decision model that assumes that no one single brand will score high on every desirable attribute and that individual attributes vary in terms of their importance to the consumer.

conjunctive heuristics   A purchasing decision model that establishes a minimum or threshold rating that brands must meet in order to be considered.

phased heuristics   A purchasing decision model that is a combination of the compensatory and conjunctive heuristics models.

REVIEW QUESTIONS

1. What are the five steps of the consumer buying decision-making process? Which two steps are the most important with regard to developing quality integrated marketing communications?

2. What is the difference between an internal search and an external search in a purchasing decision?

3. Define attitude. What are the three main components of attitude, and how are they related to purchasing decisions?

4. How do values differ from attitudes? Name some personal values related to purchasing decisions.

5. Develop and explain a cognitive map of your own mind about your most recent major purchase (car, stereo, computer, etc.).

6. What is an evoked set? Why are evoked sets, inept sets, and inert sets so important to the marketing department?

7. What are the key features of the multiattribute approach to evaluating purchasing alternatives?

8. What is meant by affect referral? When is a person likely to rely on such a cognitive approach to evaluating purchasing alternatives?

9. What traditional factors and new trends in the consumer buying environment affect consumer purchasing decisions?

10. Name and describe the five roles played in a buying center.

11. What organizational and individual factors affect members of the business buying center?

12. Describe the three main forms of business-to-business sales.

13. Name the steps in the business-to-business buying process.

14. Describe dual channel marketing and explain why it is important to a company's well-being.

CRITICAL THINKING EXERCISES

Discussion Questions

1. For college students and other individuals with compulsive buying behaviors, a primary influence is the family. Often one or both parents are compulsive shoppers. Families that display other forms of dysfunctional behaviors, such as alcoholism, bulimia, extreme nervousness, or depression, tend to produce children who are more inclined to exhibit compulsive shopping behaviors. Why do dysfunctional behaviors among parents produce compulsive shopping behavior among children? Another component of compulsive buying behaviors is self-esteem. Again, self-esteem is partly inherited, but it also develops in the home environment. How would self-esteem be related to compulsive shopping behaviors? What influences other than family might contribute to compulsive shopping behaviors? If an individual has a tendency to be a compulsive shopper, what can (or should) be done?

2. Study the list of personal values presented in Figure 3.3. Identify the five most important to you. Rank them from first to last. Beside each value, identify at least two products you have purchased to satisfy those values. Then, gather into small groups of three to five students. Using the information from your list of values, discuss differences among members of the group. Identify a way to send a marketing message that will appeal to the top value from each person's list.

3. Cultural values and norms constantly change. In groups of three to five students, discuss the cultural values and norms that have changed in the last 10 years. Are these values and

norms different from those held by your parents? If so, why? What caused these changes to occur?

4. A member of the buying center for a large shoe manufacturer tries to purchase soles for shoes from an outside vendor (or vendors). Study the individual and organizational factors that affect buying center members. Discuss the effect of each factor on the roles of members in the shoe company's buying center. How does the factory foreman's role differ from that of the purchasing agent? How do these roles differ from the company president's role?

5. A purchasing agent for a clothing manufacturer is in the process of selecting a vendor (or vendors) to supply the materials to produce about 30 percent of its clothes. The clothing manufacturer employs about 300 people. As the audit nears completion, what factors are most important to the purchasing agent?

INTEGRATED LEARNING EXERCISES

1. Consumers and businesses conduct external searches when they lack sufficient internal knowledge to make a wise decision. Assume you have $50,000 to $70,000 to spend on a sailboat. Locate four Web sites that sell sailboats. Select a sailboat in your price range. Why did you select that particular brand? What features are attractive to you? Would you want any additional information before making a final purchase decision?

2. Almost everyone has an opinion about tattoos. Some attitudes are positive, whereas others are negative. Few are neutral. Go to **www.tattoos.com** and examine the material that is on the Web site. Did this information modify your attitude toward tattoos? What factors on the Web site influenced your attitude? Find at least one additional Web site of a company that offers tattoos. Discuss the components of the Web site in terms of which components of attitude it is trying to influence (i.e., cognitive, affective, or conative).

3. United Raw Material Solutions, Inc., is a business-to-business marketplace that brings together buyers and seller of textiles, petrochemicals, plastics, and electronics. Access the Web site at **www.urms.com**. Which members of the buying center would be most interested in this site? What services and benefits do you see for buyers? For suppliers?

4. Examine the following Web sites. What kind of information is provided? Which component of attitude is the site designed to affect: cognitive, affective, or conative?
   a. Kenneth Cole (**www.kennethcole.com**)
   b. Starbucks (**www.starbucks.com**)
   c. Cadillac (**www.cadillac.com**)
   d. IKEA (**www.ikea.com**)
   e. Baby Gap (**www.babygap.com**)

5. A member of the buying center has been asked to gather information about possible shipping companies for international shipments. Visit the following Web sites. What companies have the most appealing Web sites? Beyond online materials, what additional information do they need to supply to the buying center in order to win the contract?
   a. ABC India Limited (**www.abcindia.com**)
   b. SR International Logistics, Inc. (**www.srinternational.com**)
   c. Falcon Transportation & Forwarding Corp. (**www.falcontrans.com**)
   d. Global Freight Systems (**www.globalfreightsystems.com**)

STUDENT PROJECT

Creative Corner

A local travel agency has decided to advertise in the student newspaper on your campus to promote spring break packages. They have hired you to do the creative work. They are not sure which type of advertising approach to use. The agency knows that attitude consists of three parts: cognitive, affective, and conative. They also know that an advertisement can appeal to any one of the attitude components. The agency's management team is not sure which component to use. Consequently, they have asked you to design three ads, with one ad designed to appeal to the cognitive component of attitude, the second ad to the affective component, and the third ad for the conative component. After you have finished designing the ads, discuss the pros and cons of each ad and make a recommendation to the travel agency on which one to use. The ads should be for a 5-day spring break vacation on the beach in Fort Lauderdale, Florida.

CASE 1   CLEARING THE AIR

Most people want to live in a clean environment. Marketing cleaning products involves tactics ranging from rationality and logic to emotions and instincts. Some companies use the simplest possible terms, as basic as calling bacteria "germs." Advertisers use cartoons and simple diagrams to show how the product kills bad germs and makes things "sparkle." At the other extreme are the more complex and scientific explanations regarding a product's ability to clean things up.

In this context, the market for air purifiers has grown and developed in the past decade. Smaller items, such as air freshener sprays and plug-ins made by brands such as Glade, have been available for many years. Now, newer technologies, such as HEPA hydro-allergenic filtration, are available.

The Sharper Image has been a leader in the marketing of new air cleaning technologies. The company's basic product and brand, the Ionic Breeze, has been sold through retail stores and Web sites and via infomercials and inbound telemarketing for many years.

One primary feature of all the Ionic Breeze products is silent operation. The Silent Electronic Propulsion technology made the original product the number-one air-cleaner brand in America. Through this silent air circulation technology, the company promises effective removal of airborne contaminants, reduction of common household odors, no filters to replace, low energy costs, an attractive design, ease of operation, and low maintenance.

Variations on the base model now include advancements such as the Germicidal version; the QUADRA; a smaller, plug-in bathroom version; and the new MIDI, which is smaller than earlier products. Other features associated with the Ionic Breeze are its OzoneGuard with PremAir catalyst, developed by BASF Catalysts LLC, which converts the byproduct ozone to oxygen.

Not surprisingly, competition has emerged. One of the new major players is Oreck, a company that gained fame and brand strength through its line of vacuums, which are lightweight, but powerful carpet cleaners. A logical brand extension would be into air filtration.

Oreck promotes products that kill viruses, bacteria, mold, and fungi. One major difference is that the Oreck model does move the air. In advertisements and promotional materials, the air clearers are demonstrated as being superior because of this feature. Product materials strongly emphasize the health benefits of cleaner air. Oreck air cleaners are also featured in infomercials, on Web sites, and through standard television advertising.

Sharper Image carries several air purification products.

Both Oreck and Sharper Image note that the air inside a house often is much more polluted than the air outside. Consumers are warned that asthma, allergies, and respiratory illnesses or on the rise. Air cleaners are offered to help.

Now, many lower-priced air cleaners are also available through retailers such as Wal-Mart and Target. Consequently, consumers have a vast array of potential prices, product features, and promotional claims to consider when choosing an air cleaning product. The future of the air cleaning business appears to be either bright or cloudy, depending on one's perspective, and consumers will undoubtedly see the number of options for methods to clear the air continue to rise.

Sources: Case based on information available at **www.oreck.com** and **www.sharperimage.com**.

1. How would a consumer's level of involvement, need for cognition, and level of shopping enthusiasm affect the purchase of an air filtration product?

2. Explain how cognitive mapping could be used to demonstrate a consumer's reaction to either the Ionic Breeze or the Oreck Air Cleaner.

3. Which model best explains the evaluation of alternatives when it comes to air filtration products: the evoked set model, the multiattribute approach, or affect referral?

4. Should air cleaner companies focus on fear, health, or other emotions to sell products? Explain.

CASE 2   BUYING AN HDTV? IT'S NOT THAT SIMPLE

Kelli is evaluating four high-definition television brands. She knows very little about HDTVs and has spent considerable time conducting external research. The multiattribute approach to processing information helps explain Kelli's final purchasing decision and how she evaluated the information she gathered. In making this purchase, she bases her evaluations on five criteria: (1) picture quality, (2) the speakers and quality of sound, (3) the styling and appearance of the HDTV, (4) the price, and (5) the type of screen. The importance ratings in Table 3.2 indicate that Kelli is most interested in

TABLE 3.2 Example of a Multiattribute Evaluation Approach for an HDTV

Attribute[a]	Importance[b]	Pioneer	Samsung	Vizio	Westinghouse
Picture quality	5	5	4	3	4
Speakers/sound quality	4	3	4	4	5
Styling of HDTV	4	4	5	2	3
Price	3	3	3	5	4
Screen type	3	4	2	5	4
Compensatory score[c]		74	71	69	76

[a]Each attribute is ranked on a scale of 1 to 5, with 5 being high performance and 1 being low performance.

[b]Importance is ranked on a scale of 1 to 5, with 5 being very important and 1 being very unimportant.

[c]The compensatory score is the sum of the importance times the brand evaluation for each brand.

picture quality, because she gave it a rating of 5. Quality of sound with external speakers and style of the HDTV are next, with ratings of 4. The price and the type of screen are the least important to Kelli.

The next column of numbers shows her evaluation of each attribute for each brand. In terms of picture quality, the Pioneer flat-panel plasma HDTV was the best (Kelli gave it a score of 5). The Samsung and Westinghouse LCD brands were next. The score of 4 each received indicates approximately equal picture quality. The Vizio had the lowest picture quality in Kelli's evaluation, and thus she gave it a score of 3.

After evaluating all the brands across all the criteria, Kelli will make a decision. She can calculate evaluation scores in several ways. One method is to multiply each attribute's importance rating by the corresponding evaluation for each brand. Summing these results in the scores is shown in the row labeled Compensatory Score. Using this method, she would choose the Westinghouse flat panel LCD HDTV, because of its overall score. This method of evaluating alternatives is called **compensatory heuristics**.

The compensatory heuristics method assumes that no one single brand scores high on every attribute and that individual attributes vary in importance. When considering several brands, consumers make tradeoffs. Notice that in Table 3.2 Kelli rates Pioneer as having the best picture quality, her most important product attribute. At the same time, Pioneer has the lowest score for having external speakers and sound quality. She also ranked it lowest in terms of price, because it was the most costly. Although the Pioneer had the best picture quality, it was not the best brand for Kelli because of the poor ratings on other attributes.

When Kelli considers the Westinghouse, she concludes it has good picture quality, although it is not as good as the Pioneer. The Westinghouse does have the best sound, and it has external speakers. In terms of price and type of screen, it is not the best, but it is still good. The worst rating Kelli gives the Westinghouse is for its style and appearance. But even there, the Vizio brand style rating is lower. To get the best overall HDTV, Kelli has to make tradeoffs and choose the best one of the attributes evaluated. Consumers are not likely to draw a table like that in Table 3.2, but they go through a similar process mentally.

A second computational form Kelli can use to make her evaluation is called **conjunctive heuristics**. In this method, Kelli establishes a minimum, or threshold, rating. She considers only brands that meet this threshold, even when one product ranks high on individual criteria. Going back to Table 3.2, assume that Kelli has mentally established a minimum threshold of 4. She discards a brand if it scores 3 or lower on any criterion important to her. Using this method, she would eliminate all four brands because of low scores on individual attributes.

Consequently, consumers can use an *iterative approach.* Picture quality is most important to Kelli, and so she starts there. She rated the Vizio a 3, and because this is below the minimum, Kelli eliminates Vizio. Next, Kelli looks closely at the remaining three brands. All have good or excellent picture quality. Therefore, Kelli goes to her next most important criterion—quality of the sound and external speakers. She ranks both sound quality and styling of the HDTV with a 4 in terms of importance. Before Kelli can eliminate any more brands, she has to decide which of those two criteria is more important. Assuming that sound quality is next, she would eliminate Pioneer due to its rating below the threshold. Now Kelli has narrowed her choice to two models, Samsung and Westinghouse. The next attribute she considers is styling. Because the Westinghouse is below the threshold, she eliminates it. Thus, she chooses the Samsung brand because it is the only one left.

Another calculation can be made using a **phased heuristic** approach. This method is a combination of the others. Going back to Table 3.2, assume that Kelli eliminates any brand with a score lower than a 3 on any criterion. Notice Samsung's rating of 2 on type of screen and Vizio's rating of 2 on styling. Kelli immediately discards them (Samsung because it has a rear-projection screen instead of a flat-panel plasma or LCD screen, and Vizio because she does not like its styling). This leaves Pioneer and Westinghouse. To make the decision between these two brands, she can use the compensatory heuristic approach. Consumers often use a phased approach similar to this when they have many brands to evaluate. This method easily reduces the evoked set to a smaller and more manageable subset.

Buying an HDTV isn't easy. The same mental gymnastics are part of many purchases. Marketing experts spend a great deal of time trying to make sure that the characteristics consumers value appear in their products, services, and marketing messages.

1. Go through Table 3.2 and make sure you can explain how Kelli makes her purchase decision using the various heuristic models.

2. Construct a similar table for one of the following products:

   a. An automobile

   b. A night out for dinner

c. A drinking establishment

d. A new clothing outfit

3. For each product listed in Question 2, identify a recent purchase. Explain the process you used to make the purchase decision. Which heuristic model did you use?

ENDNOTES

1. Laurie Flynn, "Apple Profit Soars 73% as Sales Rise," *New York Times* (July 26, 2007) (**www.nytimes.com/2007/07/26/business/26apple.html?ei=5070&en=f4d656db68b1f20b&ex=1186977600&adxnnl=1&adxnnlx=1186880551-csf3TN4UKWf7mp+EMio+zA**); Saul Hansell, "The iTease," *New York Times* (July 24, 2007) (**http://bits.blogs.nytimes.com/2007/07/24/the-itease/**); John Markoff, "AT&T Says the iPhone Is Its Best Seller Ever," *New York Times* (July 2, 2007) (**http://bits.blogs.nytimes.com/2007/07/02/att-says-the-iphone-is-its-best-seller-ever/**); John Schwartz, "IPhone Flaw Lets Hackers Take Over, Security Firm Say," *New York Times* (July 23, 2007) (**www.nytimes.com/2007/07/23/technology/23iphone.html?ex=1186977600&en=802b4044aaa9502c&ei=5070**).

2. Jeffrey B. Schmidt and Richard A. Spreng, "A Proposed Model of External Consumer Information Search," *Journal of Academy of Marketing Science* 24, no. 3 (Summer 1996), pp. 246–56.

3. Merrie Brucks, "The Effect of Product Class Knowledge on Information Search Behavior," *Journal of Consumer Research* 12 (June 1985), pp. 1–15; Schmidt and Spreng, "A Proposed Model of External Consumer Information Search."

4. Laura M. Buchholz and Robert E. Smith, "The Role of Consumer Involvement in Determining Cognitive Responses to Broadcast Advertising," *Journal of Advertising* 20, no. 1 (1991), pp. 4–17; Schmidt and Spreng, "A Proposed Model of External Consumer Information Search"; Jeffrey J. Inman, Leigh McAllister, and Wayne D. Hoyer, "Promotion Signal: Proxy for a Price Cut," *Journal of Consumer Research* 17 (June 1990), pp. 74–81; Barry J. Babin, William R. Darden, and Mitch Griffin, "Work and/or Fun: Measuring Hedonic and Utilitarian Shopping Value," *Journal of Consumer Research* 20 (March 1994), pp. 644–56.

5. Schmidt and Spreng, "A Proposed Model of External Consumer Information Search."

6. M. Fishbein and Icek Ajzen, *Belief, Attitude, Intention, and Behavior: An Introduction to Theory and Research* (Reading, MA: Addison-Wesley, 1975).

7. Richard P. Bagozzi, Alice M. Tybout, C. Samuel Craig, and Brian Sternathal, "The Construct Validity of the Tripartite Classification of Attitudes," *Journal of Marketing* 16, no. 1 (February 1979), pp. 88–95.

8. Discussion of cognitive mapping based on Anne R. Kearny and Stephan Kaplan, "Toward a Methodology for the Measurement of Knowledge Structures of Ordinary People: The Conceptual Content Cognitive Map (3CM)," *Environment and Behavior* 29, no. 5 (September 1997), pp. 579–617; Stephan Kaplan and R. Kaplan, *Cognition and Environment, Functioning in an Uncertain World* (Ann Arbor, MI: Ulrich's, 1982, 1989).

9. Discussion of heuristics and multiattribute model based on William L. Wilkie and Edgar A. Pessemier, "Issues in Marketing's Use of Multiattribute Models," *Journal of Marketing Research* 10 (November 1983), pp. 428–41; Peter L. Wright, "Consumer Choice Strategies: Simplifying vs. Optimizing," *Journal of Marketing Research* 11 (February 1975), pp. 60–67; James B. Bettman, *An Information Processing Theory of Consumer Choice* (Reading, MA: Addison-Wesley, 1979).

10. Mark Sneider, "Create Emotional Ties with Brand for Sales," *Marketing News* 38 (May 15, 2004), pp. 44–45.

11. This section is based on "Are Latest 'Megatrends' a Road Map for New Products?" *Candy Industry* 170, no. 1 (January 2005), pp. 14–15; "The Changing Face of 2005," *International Food Ingredients* (February–March 2005), p. 20; "Global Consumer Trends," *Datamonitor* (**www.market-research-report.com/datamonitor/DMCM0683.htm**, July 21, 2004).

12. Elizabeth Fuhrman, "Consumer Trends Driving New Products," *Beverage Industry* 98, no. 4 (April 2007), pp. 4–8.

13. Mark Dolliver, "Alas, Free Time Comes at a Price," *Adweek* 45, no. 34 (September 13, 2004), p. 42; Mark Dolliver, "More Money or More Time?" *Adweek* 42, no. 11 (March 12, 2001), p. 44.

14. Discussion of second-chancers based on Richard Halverson, "The Customer Connection: Second-Chancers," *Discount Store News* 37, no. 20 (October 26, 1998), pp. 91–95.

15. "Boomers Bend the Trends," *Private Label Buyer* 21, no. 4 (April 2007), p. 14.

16. Dave Carpenter, "Diets Force Kraft to Change Marketing Approach," *Marketing News* 38 (September 15, 2004), p. 37.

17. Christine Blank, "Convenience, Health Top Consumer Trends," *Supermarket News* 55, no. 23 (June 4, 2007), p. 45.

18. Discussion based on Frederick E. Webster, Jr., and Yoram Wind, "A General Model for Understanding Organizational Buyer Behavior," *Marketing Management* 4, no. 4 (Winter–Spring 1996), pp. 52–57. Patricia M. Doney and Gary M. Armstrong, "Effects of Accountability on Symbolic Information Search and Information Analysis by Organizational Buyers," *Journal of the Academy of Marketing Science* 24, no. 1 (Winter 1996), pp. 57–66; Rob Smith, "For Best Results, Treat Business Decision Makers As Individuals," *Advertising Age's Business Marketing* 84, no. 3 (1998), p. 39.

19. Patricia M. Doney and Gary M. Armstrong, "Effects of Accountability on Symbolic Information Search and Information Analysis by Organizational Buyers," *Journal of the Academy of Marketing Science* 24, no. 1 (Winter 1996), pp. 57–66.

20. Herbert Simon, *The New Science of Management Decisions,* rev. ed. (Upper Saddle River, NJ: Prentice Hall, 1977).

21. Webster and Wind, "A General Model for Understanding Organizational Buyer Behavior"; Doney and Armstrong, "Effects of Accountability on Symbolic Information Search and Information Analysis by

Organizational Buyers"; James A. Eckert and Thomas J. Goldsby, "Using the Elaboration Likelihood Model to Guide Customer Service-Based Segmentation," *International Journal of Physical Distribution & Logistics Management* 27, no. 9–10 (1997), pp. 600–15.

22. Patrick J. Robinson, Charles W. Faris, and Yoram Wind, "Industrial Buying and Creative Marketing," *Marketing Science Institute Series* (Boston: Allyn & Bacon, 1967).

23. Adapted from Webster and Wind, "A General Model for Understanding Organizational Buyer Behavior."

24. Eugene F. Brigham and James L. Pappas, *Managerial Economics,* 2d ed. (Hinsdale, IL: Dryden Press, 1976).

25. Charles A. Weber, John R. Current, and Desai Anand, "Vendor: A Structured Approach to Vendor Selection and Negotiation," *Journal of Business Logistics* 21, no. 1 (2000), pp. 134–69.

26. Discussion of dual channel marketing is based on Wim G. Biemans, "Marketing in the Twilight Zone," *Business Horizons* 41, no. 6 (November–December 1998), pp. 69–76.

27. Ibid.

28. Ibid.

29. Robert Duboff, "True Brand Strategies Do Much More Than Name," *Marketing News* 35, no. 11 (May 21, 2001), p. 16.

4

Promotions Opportunity Analysis

Chapter Objectives

After reading this chapter, you should be able to answer the following questions:

- **What** activities are involved in completing a promotions opportunity analysis?

- **How** should a company's marketing team evaluate the relationship between a company's promotional efforts and those of the competition?

- **What** are the characteristics of the major consumer market segments?

- **How** can a company identify and reach key business-to-business market segments?

- **How** can IMC programs and promotions be expanded to the international level?

PETsMART

It's a Dog's Life (which ain't half bad)

Not so many years ago, pets kept in homes and on farms were there to serve a purpose, which typically was either to provide companionship or to serve as protective watchdogs. It wasn't unusual for a dog to sleep outdoors (no matter what the weather), to dine on the scraps that fell from the table at night, and to endure the aches and pains that accompany the aging process in silence, or with the occasional moan.

Today, the world of pet ownership consists of an entirely new form of "parent." No longer is a dog, cat, fish, potbellied pig, or snake just a diversion—the critter is considered part of the family. The pet industry has grown from simple dog and cat food, plus a few toys along the way, to a $41 billion mammoth. Companies vending goods and services to pet owners have necessarily shifted with the times.

PETsMART serves as a classic example of a company prospering in this new environment of animal indulgence. In 1986, founders Jim and Janice Dougherty secured a venture capital loan from the Phillips Van Heusen Corporation and incorporated as Pacific Coast Distributing, Inc. The primary company business, a pet owner superstore, was vending food and other basic pet supplies. As time passed, the scope of company operations grew dramatically.

By 1988, PETsMART was selling pet sweaters and emphasized cutting down on pet overpopulation. Soon after, fish and birds were added to the original line of pets for sale and the company launched a new doggie salon. The era of extravagance had begun. It wasn't long until the company's original tagline, "Where high prices have been housebroken," was outdated. The most dramatic change introduced, a new corporate vision statement, appeared in 2000. PETsMART now operates, "To provide Total Lifetime Care for every pet, every parent, every time—which means that we offer solutions, superior products, unmatched services and superb customer service."

Why the change? The market continues to evolve along with the types of pet owners in the marketplace. Pets now enjoy a new type of status, often with different types of owners, including empty-nesters, single professionals, and couples who have decided to delay starting a family consisting of actual children. Many of these new, more passionate pet lovers have a great deal of

Today's pets have become like children in the family.

income to spend on their "babies." American families spend more annually on buying, feeding, and caring for pets than they do on movies, video games, and recorded music in any form.

The range of pet-related goods and services continues to expand. The list of items available in store and online includes indoor potties, pet perfumes, trench coats for dogs, and even a patented testicular implant for dogs that have been neutered, so as to not hurt the animal's self-esteem following the surgery.

Pet psychology opens up an entirely new realm. Many find relief from the troubles and woes of a dog's life through psychotherapy and animal antidepressants. More shallow pets can rely on cosmetic procedures to keep up their self-image. Harley-Davidson branded products are available for bikers who want their pets to live on the edge.

PETsMART's competitors take animal pampering to the extreme. Doggie spas provide pedicures, professional dog walkers, and massage therapy for those aching doggie muscles. Generic dog food is no longer the norm. The market is filled with specialty foods that clearly show the vegetables and other healthy nutrients in the product. At the other end of the spectrum, entire companies have formed to take care of end-products, including service agencies named Doody Duty, Scoopy-Poo, and Pooper Trooper.

In the more traditional vein, PETsMART offers vet clinics for ailing animals and adoption centers to find homes for pets (over 200,000 are placed each year). The company also sponsors charities associated with animal well-being. Today's owner wants an animal to have an excellent quality of life from beginning to end. The net result is services oriented to ailing and dying pets along with their grieving parents.

PETsMART continues to adjust to changing conditions. The company features a strong emphasis on brand recognition and has adjusted selling techniques to meet the needs of various product lines. New signage was created in 2004. The company also opened distribution centers to make product delivery to each store more efficient.

In 2005, PETsMART began opening a series of pet hotels. Fifty pet hotels have been built, with an eventual goal of 435 hotels across the United States. Now a traveling pet owner has new options available, which means less guilt about leaving a pet behind.

In general, there has been a major shift in the marketplace. Pets are treated not in pet terms, but rather in human terms. This means that the number of marketing opportunities continues to rise and the nature of the competition continues to grow as the animal kingdom becomes more human-like each year. PETsMART vows to identify each new trend and respond accordingly, keeping pace in the dog-eat-dog world of animal comfort.[1]

OVERVIEW

Individual customers and businesses receive a myriad of promotional materials every day. From pens marked with logos to letterhead embossed with a company's mission statement to calendars containing both advertisements and tear-off discount coupons, consumers and businesses encounter marketing materials in an increasing variety of ways. These marketing contacts do not occur by accident. At some point, a marketing official decided to distribute pens or calendars or the printing department was asked to design letterhead. Beyond the world of advertising and personal selling, successful marketing efforts occur because *someone identified an opportunity to make a quality contact with a customer.* A successful IMC program identifies the places to make those contacts and presents customers with a well-defined message spoken in a clear voice.

This chapter describes the nature of a promotions opportunity analysis. The purpose is to identify customers and competitors in the marketplace and to discover new promotional opportunities. When these new opportunities are found, the firm's overall IMC message can be adapted to various target markets. An effective promotional analysis specifies the audiences and markets the company intends to serve. Locating key market segments helps the company's leaders more accurately define whom they are trying to reach with an IMC program. In this chapter, target markets and promotional opportunities are described. Each of these activities is a key component in preparing an IMC program.

PROMOTIONS OPPORTUNITY ANALYSIS

One primary task in creating an effective marketing plan is examining promotional opportunities. A **promotions opportunity analysis** is the process marketers use to identify target audiences for a company's goods and services and the communication strategies needed to reach these audiences. People are different and have unique uses for products. The same is true for businesses. These special features are especially pronounced in global markets; therefore, communication to each group requires distinct and somewhat customized approaches. An effective promotional analysis identifies the approach or appeal that is best suited to each set of customers.

A promotions opportunity analysis must accomplish two objectives: (1) determine which promotional opportunities exist for the company and (2) identify the characteristics of each target audience so that suitable advertising and marketing communications messages can reach them. The more a marketer knows about an audience, the greater the chance a message will be heard, understood, and result in the desired outcome (i.e., a purchase, increased brand loyalty, etc.).

There are five steps in developing a promotions opportunity analysis, as shown in Figure 4.1. The upcoming sections describe each part of this planning process in greater detail.

FIGURE 4.1
Promotions Opportunity Analysis Steps

Promotions Opportunity Analysis	
◆ Conduct a communication market analysis	◆ Create communications budget
◆ Establish communication objectives	◆ Prepare promotional strategies
	◆ Match tactics with strategies

COMMUNICATION MARKET ANALYSIS

The first step of a promotions opportunity analysis is a communication market analysis. A **communication market analysis** is the process of discovering the organization's strengths and weaknesses in the area of marketing communication and combining that information with an analysis of the opportunities and threats present in the firm's external environment. The analysis is from a communication perspective. A communication market analysis examines five areas:

- Competitors
- Opportunities
- Target markets
- Customers
- Product positioning

These five ingredients are studied together rather than sequentially. Each contributes key information about the marketplace.

Competitors

In examining competitors, the objective is to discover who the competition is and what they are doing in the areas of advertising and communication. The marketing tactics competitors use are identified to understand how they are contacting the marketplace. Consumers integrate information from a variety of sources. It is helpful to know what potential customers see, hear, and read about the competition.

Every domestic and foreign competitor is identified. After listing the competing firms, a competitive analysis includes gathering *secondary data* about those companies. The first items to look at are statements competitors make about themselves. These statements can be found in:

Intense competition for convention and meeting sites makes a communication market analysis important for the Morial Convention Center of New Orleans.

- Advertisements
- Promotional materials
- Annual reports
- A prospectus for a publicly held corporation
- Web sites

The idea is to obtain as much information as possible about competitors, including messages to their customers.

The next task is to study what *other people* say about the competition. Marketers often read trade journals. The library might yield additional news articles and press releases about competitor activities. The marketing team will try to discover how competing companies view them. This provides a sense of how any given company is viewed in comparison with its competition.

Another part of an analysis of the competition is *primary research*. In the retail business, it is helpful to visit competing stores to see how merchandise is displayed and to observe as the store's employees deal with customers. The marketing team should also talk to vendors and suppliers who have dealt with the competition, along with wholesalers, distributors, and agents. For businesses other than retail, marketers can contact salespeople in the field to obtain additional information about the competition.

Opportunities

A second component of a communication market analysis is the search for opportunities. This includes watching for

FIGURE 4.2
Questions for an Opportunity Analysis

- Are there customers that the competition is ignoring or not serving?
- Which markets are heavily saturated and have intense competition?
- Are the benefits of our goods and services being clearly articulated to the various customer market segments?

- Are there opportunities to build relationships with customers using a slightly different marketing approach?
- Are there opportunities that are not being pursued, or is our brand positioned with a cluster of other companies in such a manner that it cannot stand out?

This advertisement for On the Go instant coffee was developed after an opportunity analysis revealed that many travelers want convenient coffee they can carry with them.

new marketing communication opportunities by examining all of the available data and market information. Some of the questions the marketing team asks are listed in Figure 4.2.

The purpose of these questions is to explore new communication opportunities. These opportunities are present when there is an unfilled market niche, when the competition is doing a poor job of meeting the needs of some customers, when the company offers a distinct competence, or when a market niche is not being targeted with effective marketing communications.

Target Markets

A third communication market analysis activity is examining various target markets. This analysis requires the marketing department to recognize the needs of various consumer and business groups. Company marketers will identify the benefits customers are seeking and determine the various ways to reach customers.

The questions asked during this part of the analysis are similar to those posed while looking for opportunities. The focus shifts to defining target markets more precisely. Beyond target market groups, marketing experts attempt to decipher the needs and wants of individual groups. The goal is to divide the overall market into smaller market segments. The company can then develop marketing programs and advertising campaigns for each of these smaller groups.

Customers

Another ingredient in examining a target market is conducting an in-depth analysis of customers. Three types of customers should be studied:

1. Current customers
2. The competition's customers
3. Potential new customers

The point is to understand how people in each group think, why they buy, when they buy, where they buy, and how they evaluate products after purchases. Creating effective advertisements and marketing communications requires knowing what goes on in the minds of customers. The easiest group to study is a firm's current customers; however, the other two groups are equally, if not more, important. Members of these groups may think differently or make decisions differently from a firm's current customers. They might also evaluate products and advertisements differently. The objective of this part of the analysis is to find out what type of message works for each customer group.

◆ Attributes	◆ Product user
◆ Competitors	◆ Product class
◆ Use or application	◆ Cultural symbol
◆ Price–quality relationship	

FIGURE 4.3
Product Positioning Strategies

It is helpful to ascertain how customers perceive individual advertisements as well as what they think about the larger company. Service Metrics (see the advertisement in this section) examines a firm's Web site from the customer's perspective and, more importantly, compares the Web site to the competitions'. This type of analysis identifies all of a firm's communication avenues. It also tells the company how its Web site compares to the competition.

Product Positioning

The last part of a communications analysis is examining the position a firm holds relative to the competition. Product positioning is the perception in the consumer's mind regarding the nature of a company and its products relative to the competition. The seven possible positioning strategies are listed in Figure 4.3.

The quality of products, prices charged, methods of distribution, image, communication tactics, and other factors create positioning and are, in turn, affected by the brand's position. In examining the brand's positioning, the marketing firm should determine how the brand's position is viewed by consumers, businesses, and customers. It is important to make sure the position being promoted is consistent with current views by the various constituencies and with various elements of the IMC program. A problem exists when customers view the brand's position differently from the manner in which the company presents itself.

Part of a customer analysis includes an examination of a firm's Web site from the customer's perspective.

ESTABLISHING MARKETING COMMUNICATIONS OBJECTIVES

An effective communication market analysis lays the foundation for the development of communication objectives, the second step of a promotions opportunities analysis. Communication objectives guide account executives and advertising creatives in designing messages. Figure 4.4 lists some of the more common objectives found in profit-seeking organizations.

A communications plan is often oriented toward a single objective. A program can, however, accomplish more than one goal at a time. Logical combinations of communication

◆ Develop brand awareness	◆ Build customer traffic
◆ Increase category demand	◆ Enhance firm image
◆ Change customer beliefs or attitudes	◆ Increase market share
◆ Enhance purchase actions	◆ Increase sales
◆ Encourage repeat purchases	◆ Reinforce purchase decisions

FIGURE 4.4
Communication Objectives

objectives are possible. For example, the same advertisement can develop brand awareness and enhance a brand's image. Increasing sales can be accomplished through price changes, contests, or coupons. The key is to match the objective to the medium and the message.

The process of defining and establishing communication objectives is a crucial element of a promotional opportunities analysis. Communication objectives are derived from marketing objectives. They tend to be general because they relate to the entire marketing plan. They also must be measurable. Marketing objectives address:

- Sales volume
- Market share
- Profits
- Return on investment

Many marketing professionals believe that **benchmark measures** are helpful. A benchmark is a starting point that is studied in relation to the degree of change following a promotional campaign. For example, through market research a dry cleaning company's owner may discover that during its first year only 20 percent of the community's population knew about the company and that the company has a 3 percent share of the city's total market. Following a campaign featuring advertisements, coupons, and discounts for certain days of the week (Tuesday specials) and to senior citizens, the objective might be to achieve 30 percent awareness and a 5 percent share. This would indicate a level of success based on previously established benchmarks.

ESTABLISHING A COMMUNICATIONS BUDGET

The third step of a promotions opportunity analysis is preparing a communications budget. Budgets are based on communication objectives as well as marketing objectives. Communications budgets differ between consumer markets and business-to-business markets. For example, a much larger percentage of the budget for B-to-B is allocated for telephone marketing than in the consumer market.

Managers often make unrealistic assumptions about a communications budget. This occurs, for example, when a manager assumes there is a direct relationship between expenditures on advertising communications and subsequent sales revenues, which is highly unlikely. A more realistic relationship is shown in Figure 4.5. Several factors influence the relationship between expenditures on promotions and sales, including:

- The goal of the promotion
- Threshold effects
- Carryover effects
- Wear-out effects
- Decay effects
- Random events

Communication goals differ depending on the stage in the buying process that is being addressed. For instance, in Chapter 6 a model called the *hierarchy of effects* will be described. The model suggests that prior to making a purchase a consumer goes through stages of awareness, knowledge, liking, preference, and conviction. The early promotional campaign for Verizon Wireless first targeted awareness with the phrase "Can you hear me now?" prominently featured. Over time, other aspects of the company's services and comparative advantages were featured. Finally, financial incentives to buy the service were added. The entire campaign started at one place (awareness) and ended at another (the purchase). It would not be logical to expect that early promotional expenditures would create a dollar-for-dollar relationship with sales.

Instead, **threshold effects** are present. As shown in Figure 4.5, the early effects of advertising are minimal. The same is true for all communication expenditures. At first, there may be little behavioral response, especially if only advertisements are used. Over time, a

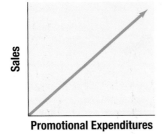

An unrealistic assumption about the relationship between promotional expenditures and sales

FIGURE 4.5
A Sales-Response Function Curve Combined with the Downward Response Curve and Marginal Analysis

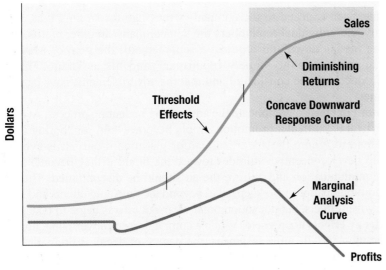

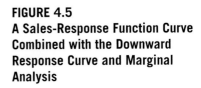

For products like boats, it is important for advertising to create carryover effects.

consumer who is exposed repeatedly to a company's marketing message recalls the company and eventually is willing to make a purchase.[2] Coupons, free samples, and other marketing tactics can help a good or service reach the threshold point sooner. Threshold effects are easy to reach in some circumstances. For instance, when the good or service is so innovative that consumers are quickly aware of its advantages and are willing to buy the item immediately. Also, when companies introduce new products under an established, strong brand name, reaching the threshold point normally occurs quicker. In others, capturing enough attention to spur sales is a lengthy process.

A point exists at which a promotional campaign has saturated the market. At that point, further expenditures have a minimal impact. The S-shaped curve displayed in Figure 4.5, which is known as the **sales-response function curve**, indicates when *diminishing returns* are present. Diminishing returns are part of the **concave downward function**. This means that incremental increases in expenditures in advertising result in smaller and smaller increases in sales. A **marginal analysis** shows that further advertising and promotional expenditures might even adversely affect profits.

Another factor that influences the relationship between promotions and sales is a **carryover effect**. Many products are only purchased when needed, such as washing machines and refrigerators. Promotions for these products must be designed to generate carryover effects. This occurs when the

Source: Courtesy of Newcomer, Morris & Young, Inc.

FIGURE 4.6
A Decay Effects Model

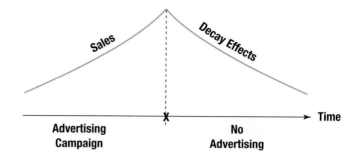

consumer has been exposed to the company's message for so long that, when the time comes to buy, the individual remembers the key company. In other words, when a washing machine breaks down and requires a replacement, the goal of Maytag is for the consumer to remember the "lonely repairman" and his assistant. This means that Maytag's products will be considered and that the advertisements have carried over until the right time.

Wear-out effects also complicate the advertising budgeting process. At a certain point, an advertisement or particular promotion simply becomes "old" or "boring." In such cases, consumers tend to ignore the advertisement or just tune it out.[3] It is even possible for consumers to develop negative attitudes toward the brand if they become annoyed at the marketing communication and believe the ad should be discontinued. The challenge for marketing communications is to keep an ad beyond the threshold effects and long enough to capture carryover effects, but not so long that wear-out effects begin to take place.

Also, **decay effects** are present. When a company stops advertising, consumers begin to forget the message. In some instances, the degree of decay is dramatic. In others, the carryover effects are strong enough that some time can lapse before the brand drops out of the consumer's consciousness. The promotional budget must be structured to avoid the problems of decay effects, which are illustrated in Figure 4.6.

Finally, random events affect promotions. A natural disaster or some other event can reduce the impact on any given campaign. Such events normally cannot be predicted.

Therefore, as the marketing team constructs the budget the assumptions that drive the process should be considered. The newness of the product, the economy, and other complicating factors must be considered during the process of tying budgeting expenditures to marketing and communication objectives.

TYPES OF BUDGETS

A communications budget can be prepared in a number of different ways. Figure 4.7 provides a list of the various methods that are used.[4]

The Percentage of Sales Method

One common approach to setting the communications budget is the **percentage of sales method**. This budget is derived from either: (1) sales from the previous year or (2) anticipated sales for the next year. A major reason for using this method is its simplicity. A percentage of sales budget is relatively easy to prepare.

The approach also has problems. First, it tends to change in the opposite direction of what is typically needed. That is, when sales go up, so does the communications budget. When sales decline, the communications budget also declines. In most cases, when sales are declining the communications budget should be increased to help reverse the trend. Further, during growth periods the communications budget may not need to be increased.

FIGURE 4.7
Methods of Determining a Marketing Communications Budget

- Percentage of sales
- Meet the competition
- "What we can afford"
- Objective and task
- Payout planning
- Quantitative models

The second major disadvantage of this method is that it does not allocate money for special needs or to combat competitive pressures. Therefore, many marketing experts believe the disadvantages of the percentage of sales method tend to outweigh its advantages.

The Meet-the-Competition Method

Some firms use the **meet-the-competition method**. The primary goal of this method is to prevent the loss of market share. It is often used in highly competitive markets where rivalries between competitors are intense.

The potential drawback to meet-the-competition budgeting is that marketing dollars might not be spent efficiently. Matching the competition's spending does not guarantee success. Market share can still be lost. It is important to remember that it is not *how much* is spent, but rather *how well* the money is allocated and how effectively the marketing campaign works at retaining customers and market share.

The "What We Can Afford" Method

A third strategy is the **"what we can afford" method**. This technique sets the marketing budget after all of the company's other budgets have been determined. Money is allocated based on what the company leaders feel they can afford. This method suggests that management may not fully recognize the benefits of marketing. Instead, company leaders may view marketing expenditures as non-revenue-generating activities. Newer and smaller companies with limited finances often use the "what we can afford" approach.

The Objective and Task Method

Another technique is the **objective and task method**. To prepare this type of communications budget, management lists all of the communication objectives to pursue during the year and then calculates the cost of accomplishing each objective. The communications budget is the cumulative sum of the estimated costs for all objectives.

Many marketing experts believe that the objective and task method is the best budgeting method because it relates dollar costs to achieving specific objectives. Unfortunately, it is difficult for a large company, such as Procter & Gamble, to use. With hundreds of products on the market, producing a budget based on objectives for each brand and product category is very time-consuming. Despite the challenge, some form of the objective and task method of setting marketing budgets is used by about 50 percent of the firms, approximately equal to the percentage of companies that use the percentage of sales technique.[5]

Payout Planning

Payout planning establishes a ratio of advertising to sales or market share. This method normally allocates greater amounts in early years to yield payouts in later years.[6] By allocating larger amounts at the beginning of a new product introduction, brand awareness and brand equity are built. Then, as the brand is accepted and sales build, a lower percentage of advertising dollars is needed to maintain a target growth. This budgeting approach is based on the threshold effects concept and the idea of diminishing returns. A company that has reached the maximum threshold point should not continue pouring money into advertising that only results in diminishing returns. Instead, a company can maintain awareness and brand equity by more effective expenditures of marketing dollars. Future promotions and advertisement will target specific market segments and consumer groups rather than simply increasing the volume of marketing dollars spent.

For a small business such as Shirlock's Inside Out, budgeting adequate dollars is essential to building brand awareness.

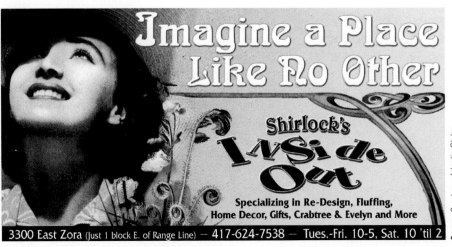

Quantitative Models

In some instances, computer simulations can be developed to model the relationship between advertising or promotional expenditures with sales and profits. These models are far from perfect. They do have the advantage of accounting for the type of industry and product as the model is created. In most cases, quantitative models are limited to larger organizations with strong computer and statistics departments.

BUDGETING EXPENDITURES

A budget is finalized when the company has specified how funds will be spent on each of the major communications tools. Media advertising normally accounts for about 41 percent of a marketing budget. Trade promotions receive about 28 percent and consumer promotions average about 28 percent (see Figure 4.8).[7] These percentages, however, vary considerably from industry to industry. Consumer product manufacturers spend more on trade promotions directed toward retailers. Service companies tend to spend more on media advertising. Budgets also vary by product types. For example, for dolls and stuffed toys the average expenditure on media advertising as a percentage of sales is 11.2 percent, whereas for men's clothing expenditures on media advertising represent only 3.3 percent of sales.[8]

The United States leads the world in annual advertising expenditures at $263.7 billion. This figure is approximately seven times more than the next closest nation.[9] See Figure 4.9 for a graph of the top 10 countries in terms of total advertising expenditures.

The ways in which advertising dollars are allocated among the various media are shown in Figure 4.10. Spot TV are ads those purchased from a local television station for that station only. Cable and network advertising are national ads and are broadcast on all systems that carry those channels. The fastest growing media outlet is the Internet.[10]

FIGURE 4.8
Breakdown of Marketing Expenditures

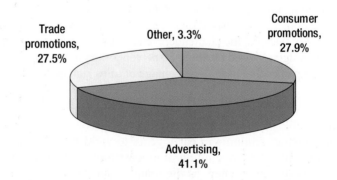

Trade promotions, 27.5%

Other, 3.3%

Consumer promotions, 27.9%

Advertising, 41.1%

FIGURE 4.9
Advertising Expenditures by Top 10 Countries

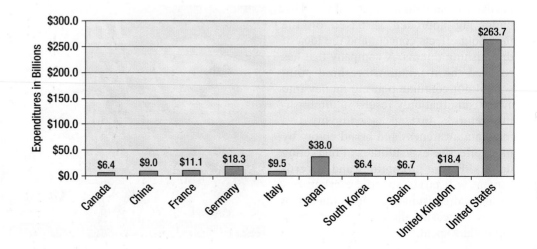

Expenditures in Billions

Canada $6.4, China $9.0, France $11.1, Germany $18.3, Italy $9.5, Japan $38.0, South Korea $6.4, Spain $6.7, United Kingdom $18.4, United States $263.7

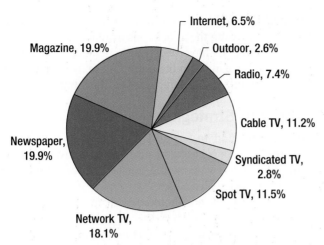

FIGURE 4.10
Advertising Expenditures
by Media

Source: Based on "100 Leading National Advertisers," *Advertising Age Datacenter 2007 Marketing Profiles Yearbook* (June 25, 2007), p. 7.

Figure 4.11 displays the total advertising expenditures for the top 10 industries.[11] As indicated by the two graphs, the ways in which advertising dollars are spent by media and within industries varies considerably. When the budgeting process is complete, company leaders should believe they have wisely allocated funds to increase the effectiveness of the marketing communications program. Although specific dollar amounts and percentages vary, the overall goal remains the same—to achieve the marketing objectives as established in the plan.

PREPARING PROMOTIONAL STRATEGIES

The fourth step of a promotions opportunity analysis program is to prepare a general communication strategy for the company and its products. **Strategies** are sweeping guidelines concerning the essence of the company's marketing efforts. Strategies provide the long-term direction for all marketing activities.

An excellent example of a general communications strategy is found in the marketing efforts of Mountain Dew. The primary market for Mountain Dew is teenagers and young adults. As a result, communications efforts are directed to that market using slogans such as "Do the Dew," "Been There Done That," and so forth. Action-oriented commercials featuring higher-risk activities are designed to attract younger people (and the young at heart), who are more willing to take "risks" in the products they sample and adopt. The overall theme of the Mountain Dew communications program guides all other activities.

It is critical that a company's communication strategies mesh with its overall message and be carefully linked to the opportunities identified by a communication market analysis.

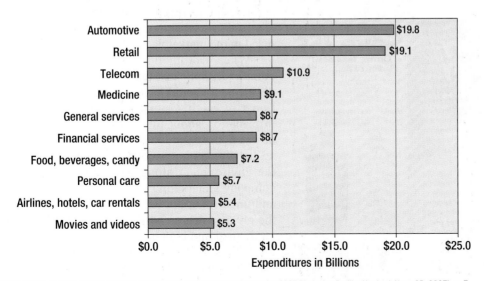

FIGURE 4.11
Advertising Expenditures
in 10 Industries

Source: Based on "100 Leading National Advertisers," *Advertising Age Datacenter 2007 Marketing Profiles Yearbook* (June 25, 2007), p. 7.

Communications strategies should be directly related to a firm's marketing objectives. Strategies must be achievable using the allocations available in the marketing and communications budgets. Once strategies have been implemented, they are not changed unless major new events occur. Only changes in the marketplace, new competitive forces, or new promotional opportunities should cause companies to alter strategies.

Matching Tactics with Strategies

Tactics are activities performed to support strategies. Tactics include promotional campaigns designed around themes based on strategic objectives. For example, Kellogg's seeks to enhance sales of cereals by designing unusual features for certain holidays, such as Halloween and Christmas Rice Krispies.

Tactics do not replace strategies, nor should they distract consumers from the consistent message or theme the company is trying to create. At the same time, they add excitement or interest to what the company is ordinarily doing. Holiday promotions, anniversary sales, and a variety of other events can be the basis for a promotional effort. Methods used in tactical campaigns include:

- Advertisements based on the major theme or a subtheme
- Personal selling enticements (bonuses and prizes for sales reps)
- Sales promotions (posters, point-of-purchase displays, end-of-aisle displays, freestanding displays)
- Special product packaging and labeling
- Price changes

Besides the methods of communicating with consumers and sales reps who offer the products, companies are able to add other enticements. The following items can be included in tactical efforts:

- Coupons
- Gift certificates
- Bonus packs (a second product attached to a first)
- Special containers (e.g., holiday decanters or soft-drink glasses)
- Contests and prizes
- Rebates
- Volume discounts (larger-size packages, "buy three, get one free" promotions, etc.)

The Gold Bond advertisement shown in this section uses a manufacturer's coupon to encourage people to purchase the product. The creative use of a snowy, winter scene highlights the product benefits of Gold Bond. The more creative the campaign, the better the chance the company can overcome clutter and become recognized in the marketplace.

When a promotions opportunity analysis is complete, company leaders and the marketing department should have a grasp of the organization's marketing situation, along with specific information about internal strengths and weaknesses in the promotions area. They should also be aware of communication opportunities present in the environment along with any threats to the company's marketing program. They must study and understand the organization's competition to the greatest degree possible. Target markets must be defined and budgets set. Then, the company's marketing leaders can establish strategies and tactics to guide efforts to reach specific marketing objectives and performance targets.

A creative message strategy is combined with the marketing tactic of a coupon to stimulate sales of Gold Bond Medicated Body Lotion.

◆ Identifying company strengths and weaknesses	◆ Focusing budget expenditures on specific consumer or business segments
◆ Locating market opportunities	
◆ Matching the company's strengths with the most lucrative sets of customers	

FIGURE 4.12
Advantages of Market Segmentation

The next sections describe two key ingredients of the promotional opportunities analysis process in greater detail. The first is the study of consumer and business-to-business market segmentation. The second is to extend promotional opportunities analysis to global or international markets.

MARKET SEGMENTATION

IMC experts use market segmentation to distinguish between specific purchasing groups. **Market segmentation** is the process of identifying specific purchasing groups based on their needs, attitudes, and interests. A **market segment** is a set of businesses or group of individual consumers with distinct characteristics. Market segmentation efforts are of great value in completing a promotions opportunity analysis. The primary advantages are listed in Figure 4.12.

Segmentation should be designed to build brand loyalty and improve the odds of success of a marketing plan. For a market segment to be considered a viable target for a specific marketing communications campaign, it should pass the following tests:

- The individuals or businesses within the market segment should be similar in nature, having the same needs, attitudes, interests, and opinions. This means persons or businesses *within* the segment are *homogenous.*
- The market segment differs from the population as a whole. Segments are distinct from other segments and the general population.
- The market segment must be large enough to be financially viable to target with a separate marketing campaign.
- The market segment must be reachable through some type of media or marketing communications method.

Market researchers spend considerable resources and amounts of time working to identify quality market segments. Market segments are grouped into two broad categories: (1) consumer markets and (2) business-to-business markets. The following section describes each of these segments in greater detail.

MARKET SEGMENTATION BY CONSUMER GROUPS

In many instances, end users are the primary target market for a firm's offerings. Effective IMC programs identify sets of consumers who are potential buyers and who have things in common, such as attitudes, interests, or needs. These consumer market segmentation approaches are listed in Figure 4.13.

◆ Demographics	◆ Geodemographics
◆ Psychographics	◆ Benefits
◆ Generations	◆ Usage
◆ Geographic	

FIGURE 4.13
Methods of Segmenting Consumer Markets

An advertisement for Bijan targeted to females.

Segments Based on Demographics

As shown in Figure 4.13, the first method of segmentation uses demographics. **Demographics** are population characteristics. Typical demographic segmentation variables include gender, age, education, income, and ethnicity. Companies create goods and services to meet the needs of individual demographic segments.

Gender

One key demographic is gender. Males and females purchase different products, buy similar products with different features (e.g., deodorants), buy the same products for dissimilar reasons (stereos, televisions), and buy the same products after being influenced by different kinds of appeals through different media.

Women have become a major market for unique getaways, and travel agencies are now marketing specific travel opportunities for women. A survey by AAA found that 24 percent of American women have gone on a getaway with one or more other women in the past 3 years and 39 percent plan on going on a girls-only getaway in the future.[12] The following are some unique female getaway packages being offered by travel agencies:

- A 3-day art safari at Carmel-by-the-Sea in California
- A gals-only week-long cruise to the Galapagos islands featuring sightseeing for giant tortoises, kayaking, scuba diving, and nature tours
- A 4-day dog-sledding adventure in the north woods of Minnesota
- A 2-day surf 'n' turf excursion at Pismo Beach in California
- A 3-day cowgirl boot camp in California's wine country that includes riding, roping, and line dancing

Marketing to women involves more than just creating and selling female-oriented products. A recent study revealed that women have an enormous impact on the spending habits of men. BMW Motorcycles recognized that women exert a considerable amount of influence on purchasing decisions for luxury touring motorcycles. A subject in one of the company's research programs explained that "If mama ain't happy, nobody's happy." Couples most often use luxury touring motorcycles for long-distance touring. This became an important factor in the development of a new motorcycle and in creating its market position. BMW's K 1200 LT has heated seats and backrests, with separate controls for both the passenger and the rider. A man tends to look at a motorcycle in terms of style, horsepower, torque, and handling. A woman has other concerns—most notably, comfort. In this case, BMW Motorcycles took what was learned from market research and made sure the motorcycle reached two target audiences: men as the primary purchasers and women as the decision-making influencers. Each was an important part of the promotional campaign.[13]

A BMW Motorcycle ad targeted toward men as the primary purchasers and women as the decision-making influencers.

Looks like two weeks vacation isn't going to cut it anymore.

BMW
Motorcycles

Age

A second demographic characteristic is age. Marketing campaigns target children, young adults, middle-age adults, and senior citizens. Some campaigns combine age-related factors with other demographics, such as gender. Creating logical

Great for growing chicks.

Want strong bones? Your bones grow until about age 35 and the calcium in milk helps. After that, it helps keep them strong. Chicks rule.

got milk?

An advertisement for milk based on
nutritional benefits directed to women.

Your bones may be in jeopardy.

One in five osteoporosis victims is male. Luckily, fat free milk has the calcium bones need to help beat it. Beating your Harvard Ph.D. opponents? Well, that's another story.

got milk?

An advertisement for milk based on
nutritional benefits directed to men.

combinations with other segments is a common segmentation approach. For example, older women may be primary targets for specific types of vitamins and other age-related products. Young working women with children are more likely to notice ads for conveniences (ready-made foods and snacks, quick lube oil change facilities, etc.). Other groups might buy vitamins, snack foods, and change their car's oil, but individual segments can be targeted with messages that reach a particular set of needs.

Children have a major impact on the purchasing decisions of their parents. Appeals to children can tie several items together, including advertisements, merchandise based on the ads, and selections from other media. Children attracted to Harry Potter can buy toys, watch the movies, buy the books, and witness advertisements using the Harry Potter theme, such as when Burger King, KFC, and Taco Bell all combined to sponsor a campaign.

Besides children, another age-based demographic group that appeals to many firms is *seniors,* defined as individuals over age 55. In the past, all seniors were treated as one market and tended to be stereotyped in ads. They were portrayed as elderly grandparents; as feeble, avid gardeners; or as enjoying a blissful retirement demonstrated by walking down the beach together holding hands. Seniors are not a homogeneous group. They do not like to be told they are getting older. Companies that have been successful with this market segment understand seniors and know how to relate to them by understanding the value seniors place on friendships, their communities, and their involvement in life. Marketing professionals recognize that the segment called "seniors" is actually a compilation of smaller groups of individuals each with different lifestyle, interests, and opinions.[14]

Income

An important demographic segmentation variable for many goods and services is an individual's or a family's income. Spending is normally directed at three large categories of goods: (1) necessities, (2) sundries, and (3) luxuries. Lower levels of income mean consumers primarily purchase necessities, such as food, clothing, cleaning supplies, and so forth. As income increases, household members can buy more items categorized as sundries, which are things that are "nice to own," but not absolutely necessary. Sundries include televisions, computers, CD players, and other durable goods. Vacations are also sundry expenditures. Luxuries are things most people cannot afford or can afford only once in a lifetime, unless the family is a high-income household. Luxuries include yachts, expensive automobiles, extravagant resort vacations, and other high-cost goods and services. Marketers work closely with creatives to tailor messages to various income groups and to select media that match those groups.

Ethnic Groups

By the year 2010, most Americans will be nonwhite. Currently, many advertisements and marketing communications are still written from a white, Anglo-Saxon perspective. This represents both an opportunity and a threat: an opportunity for companies able to adapt their messages to other cultures and heritages. It is a threat to those that do not.

Ethnic marketing includes more than spending money with ethnically owned radio stations or hiring ethnically owned advertising agencies and translating advertisements from English into Spanish. It is more than including African Americans or Asian Americans in advertisements. Successful ethnic marketing requires understanding various ethnic groups and writing marketing communications that speak to specific cultures and values.

The three major ethnic groups in the United States are African Americans, Hispanics, and Asian Americans. The buying power of these three groups is expected to reach $3 trillion by 2011.[15] In addition, a large number of immigrants are arriving from India and Pakistan. Other large groups are coming from the Middle East and Eastern European countries. Each ethnic group contains multiple subgroups. For example, the Asian community includes individuals of Korean, Japanese, Filipino, Vietnamese, and Chinese descent. The Hispanic community is made up of individuals from Latin America, Mexico, Cuba, and Puerto Rico.

Although different in many ways, several common threads exist among these ethnic groups. They all tend to be more brand loyal than their white counterparts. They value quality and are willing to pay a higher price for quality and brand identity. They value relationships with companies and are loyal to those that make the effort to establish a connection with them.

A Skechers advertisement featuring a multiethnic approach.

Source: Courtesy of Skechers USA Inc.

To market effectively to ethnic groups, marketing experts look for creative approaches that respect America's ethnic differences while also highlighting its similarities. Achieving this requires advertising and marketing agencies that understand the subtleties of multiculturalism. Becoming involved in sponsorships of minority and ethnic events helps establish ties with specific ethnic groups.

Ethnic marketing is similar in some ways to global marketing. It is important to present one overall message that is then tailored to fit the needs and values of various groups. Successfully achieving this integration of the overall message with characteristics of individual cultures should result in valuable gains in loyalty to a company and its brands and diversify the markets the company can effectively serve.

Psychographics

Demographics are relatively easy to identify. They do not, however, fully explain why people buy particular products or specific brands or the type of appeal that can be used to reach them. To assist in the marketing effort while building on demographic information, psychographic profiles have been developed. **Psychographics** emerge from patterns of responses that reveal a person's activities, interests, and opinions (AIO). AIO measures can be combined with demographic information to provide marketers with a more complete understanding of the market to be targeted.[16]

SRI Consulting Business Intelligence provides a popular classification of lifestyles using psychographic segmentation. The VALS2 typology categorizes respondents into eight different groups based on resources and on the extent to which they are action-oriented.[17] The VALS2 typology includes the following segments:

- **Innovators** Successful, sophisticated, and receptive to new technologies. Their purchases reflect cultivated tastes for upscale products.
- **Thinkers** Educated, conservative, practical consumers who value knowledge and responsibility. They look for durability, functionality, and value.
- **Achievers** Goal-oriented, conservative consumers committed to career and family. They favor established prestige products that demonstrate success to peers.
- **Experiencers** Young, enthusiastic, and impulsive consumers who seek variety and excitement and spend substantially on fashion, entertainment, and socializing.
- **Believers** Conservative, conventional consumers who focus on tradition, family, religion, and community. They prefer established brands and favor American-made products.
- **Strivers** Trendy, fun-loving consumers who are concerned about others' opinions and approval. They demonstrate to peers their ability to buy.
- **Makers** Self-sufficient consumers who have the skill and energy to carry out projects, respect authority, and are unimpressed by material possessions.
- **Survivors** Concerned with safety and security, focus on meeting needs rather than fulfilling desires. They are brand loyal and purchase discounted products.

This type of information helps marketers design more effective communications. For instance, reaching strivers requires ads that convey fun and trendy products. Ads for believers should focus more on tradition and American values.

An advertisement directed to seniors for the Geriatric Behavioral Health Program offered by McCune Brooks Hospital.

Segments Based on Generations

Many marketing efforts target generational cohorts. This approach does not require the use of psychographic information to enrich the demographics. It does possess some of the richness of the psychographics. The concept behind marketing to generational cohorts is that common experiences and events create bonds between people who are about the same age.

Segmentation based on generations notes that as people experience significant external events during their late adolescence or early adulthood, these events impact their social values, attitudes, and preferences. Based on similar experiences, these cohorts of individuals develop common preferences for music, foods, and other products. They also tend to respond to the same types of marketing appeals. Based on this idea, six cohorts or generations have been identified. Table 4.1 identifies these cohorts along with some of their basic characteristics.

Generations
"A Geriatric Behavioral Health Program"

Providing services to Seniors to promote a better quality of life

mbh
mccune-brooks hospital
Carthage, MO 64836 • 417-359-2300

TABLE 4.1 Characteristics of Generation Segments

Name of Segment	Year of Birth	Characteristics
Generation Y	1978–2002	Spend money on clothes, automobiles, college, televisions, and stereos. Ninety percent live at home or in a dorm or rent an apartment.
Generation X	1965–1977	Focus on family and children. Spend on food, housing, transportation, and personal services.
Younger boomers	1954–1964	Focus on home and family. Spend on home mortgage, pets, toys, playground equipment, and large recreational items.
Older boomers	1952–1953	Spend on upgrading homes, ensuring education and independence of their children, and luxury items, such as boats.
Seniors	Up to 1951	Most have fixed incomes. Spend heavily on health care and related medical items.

Source: Based on Dana-Nicoleta Lascu and Kennth E. Clow, *Essentials of Marketing* (Cincinnati, OH: Atomic Dog Publishing, 2007).

Segmentation by Geographic Area

Another form of segmentation is by geographic area or region. This method is especially useful for retailers seeking to limit marketing communications programs to specific areas. It also helps a company conduct a direct-mail campaign in a target area. The primary disadvantage of this approach is that everyone in a geographic area receives the marketing communication or is exposed to the advertisement, regardless of interest in the product or service. Geographic segmentation does not allow a firm to focus in on a more specific target market containing only those most likely to make purchases.

Geodemographic Segmentation

A hybrid form of geographic segmentation allows companies to enrich geographic approaches to segmentation. This powerful new form of segmentation, called *geodemographics,* identifies potential customers from demographic information, geographic information, and psychographic information.

Geodemographic segmentation is especially beneficial for national firms conducting direct-mail campaigns or using sampling promotions. It is expensive and unwise to mail a sample to every household. Through geodemographics, samples are only sent to households that match the profile of a target market. For instance, colleges and universities use geodemographics to locate ZIP codes of communities that match student profiles.

One firm, PRIZM (Potential Rating Index by Zip Marketing) specializes in geodemographics. PRIZM has identified 62 different market segments in the United States. The company has categorized every U.S. ZIP code. The concept behind PRIZM is that ZIP codes represent neighborhoods containing people with relatively uniform characteristics. Consumers tend to be attracted to neighborhoods consisting of people similar to them. Recognizing that more than one market segment might live within a ZIP code, PRIZM identifies the top market segments within each ZIP code.[18]

A PRIZM-coded map of downtown Jackson, Mississippi, identifies two primary clusters. The more predominant is the "Southside City" residents. This cluster is mainly young and elderly African Americans employed in low-paying blue-collar jobs. They tend to have lower levels of formal education, rent apartments, and read sports and fashion magazines. The second cluster within downtown Jackson is labeled as the "Towns and Gowns" neighborhoods. Towns and Gowns inhabitants also rent apartments, but members tend to be college graduates with better-paying white-collar jobs. This group likes to ski, reads beauty and fitness magazines, and frequently uses ATM cards.[19]

Geodemographic marketing has been expanded to the Internet. Adfinity is a program designed by Intelligent Interactions. It allows an advertiser to direct specific ads to Web users based on user-defined demographics. When users visit Web sites, they often provide their names and addresses along with other demographic information. While the user is surfing a site, Adfinity's software can access the user's file in order to place a targeted ad on the page. To extend its power and effectiveness, Adfinity formed a strategic alliance with PRIZM. When a user accesses a Web site, the user is matched with data from the 62 PRIZM clusters. Based on the lifestyle and interests of that cluster, messages are sent that match the user. A person from the cluster "Executive Suites" will see advertisements about jazz or business books, because people in the Executive Suites cluster prefer those items.

Benefit segmentation is often used in the wine industry.

Benefit Segmentation

Benefit segmentation focuses on the advantages consumers receive from a product rather than the characteristics of consumers themselves. Demographic and psychographic information can be combined with benefit information to identify segments. Then, the marketing team can seek to further understand each segment's consumers.

Benefit segmentation has been used in the fitness market. Regular exercisers belong in one of three benefit segments. The first group, "winners," do whatever it takes to stay physically fit. This segment tends to be younger, upwardly mobile, and career oriented. The second group, "dieters," exercise to maintain their weight and enhance physical appearance. This group tends to be females over the age of 35. They are primarily interested in reliable wellness programs offered by hospitals and weight-control nutritionists. The third group, "self-improvers," exercise to feel better and to control medical costs.[20] The understanding that individuals exercise for different reasons provides excellent material for designing marketing programs.

Usage Segmentation

The final type of consumer segmentation is based on customer usage or purchases. The goal of usage segmentation is to provide the highest level of service to a firm's best customers while promoting the company to casual or light users. Usage segmentation is also designed to maximize sales to all user groups.

Many company marketing teams identify heavy users by utilizing internal databases. With bar-code scanners, point-of-sale systems, and data from credit, debit, and transaction cards, in-house marketers can accumulate a wealth of information about customers. Many have learned that between 10 and 30 percent of a company's customers generate 70 to 90 percent of total sales. Instead of using firms such as PRIZM to create customer clusters, firms develop customer clusters from these databases. Customers are placed in clusters based on common attitudes, lifestyles, and past purchase behaviors. This technique offers a business the following advantages:[21]

1. A meaningful classification scheme to cluster customers based on a firm's actual customers.
2. The ability to reduce large volumes of customer data down to a few concise, usable clusters.

3. The ability to assign a cluster code number to each customer in the database. Each number is based on the customer's actual purchases and other characteristics (e.g., address, amount spent, credit versus cash, etc.).

4. The capacity to measure the growth and migration of customers over time and from one cluster to another, which allows for the evaluation of marketing programs.

5. The capability of using a database to develop multiple clusters based on different benefits or usages.

Not all businesses have such extensive databases. For these types of businesses, several companies sell and provide consumer databases. These consumer databases can be linked to a customer's records through a name, address, or social security number. These commercial databases contain typical information such as the household's income, the ages of household members, the length and type of residence, information about car ownership, and telephone numbers.

In summary, consumer market segments can be identified in a number of ways. The best segmentation approaches are based on the company's circumstances. In choosing market segments to approach, a marketer looks for groups that best match the company's goods and services, as well as the overall marketing message. Then the message can be structured to meet the needs of the various market segments.

BUSINESS-TO-BUSINESS SEGMENTATION

Some approaches that help identify consumer market segments can also be used to discover business-to-business market segments. Alternate methods also are available. Figure 4.14 lists the various types of business-to-business market segments. Keep in mind that, as with consumer markets, the primary goals of segmentation are to provide better customer service and to group homogeneous customers into clusters to enhance marketing efforts.

Segmentation by Industry

One method used to examine potential customers is by industry. Many marketers use the NAICS (North American Industry Classification System) coding system. NAICS allows the marketing team to examine specific industries, such as construction (23) or wholesale trade (42). They also can study segments within specific categories. For example, NAICS codes health care and social assistance services as 62. A company that manufactures health-related products can divide the market into four segments based on the subsections. These four market segments are:

621   Ambulatory Health Care Services
622   Hospitals
623   Nursing and Residential Care Facilities
624   Social Assistance

If these segments are too broad, each can be broken down into smaller subcomponents. For example, Ambulatory Health Care Services includes physicians, dentists, chiropractors, and optometrists.

The NAICS divides the economy into 20 broad sectors using a 6-digit code rather than the SIC 4-digit code. The 6-digit code allows greater stratification of industries and

FIGURE 4.14
Methods of Segmenting Business-to-Business Markets

◆ Industry (NAICS/SIC codes)	◆ Product usage
◆ Size of business	◆ Customer value
◆ Geographic location	

provides greater flexibility in creating classifications. The federal government records corporate information and data using the NAICS, making it a logical system to choose for identifying market segments.

Segmentation by Size

Market segments can be identified based on company size. Large firms have needs that are different from smaller companies, and each should be contacted in a different manner. Typically, the marketing effort is often focused on the company's purchasing department when the firm is large. For smaller firms, the owner or general manager often makes the purchase decisions and is therefore the target of marketing messages.

Segmentation by Geographic Location

As with consumer segmentation, identifying market segments by geographic location can be a successful tactic. This approach benefits businesses with customers that are concentrated in geographic pockets, such as the Silicon Valley area of California. It works for other firms as well. When the Applied Microbiology firm developed a new antimicrobial agent, the goal was to market the product to dairy farmers. The traditional agricultural marketing and distribution channel required to launch such a new product nationally was estimated at $3 million. Such a traditional marketing plan involved national advertising in agriculture magazines plus recruiting sales agents and brokers to introduce the product. Instead, Applied Microbiology used geodemographics, which combined geographic areas with demographic and psychographic data. Applied Microbiology used geodemographics to find areas with dairy herds consisting of 1,000 or more cows per ranch. These farmers were contacted for two reasons. First, large dairy farmers who adopted the product would buy greater quantities of it. Second, the company's leaders believed that the larger farmers were opinion leaders who would influence smaller farmers, thereby causing them to adopt the product as well.

Several separate direct-response pieces offering discounts for and samples of Applied Microbiology's new product were sent to larger farms. After sales started rising, farmers were asked for testimonials. The testimonials were extremely powerful, and they were then incorporated into new direct-marketing pieces. One brochure contained three testimonials and validation of the product by Cornell University. After a dairy farmer adopted the product, direct-marketing pieces were sent to farmers in the surrounding area. Not only did this method bring excellent results, but the marketing costs were one-third of the traditional approach. Using geodemographics cost only $1 million rather than the proposed $3 million.[22]

Segmentation by Product Usage

Business markets can be segmented based on the manner in which the good or service is used. Many services (financial, transportation, shipping, etc.) have a variety of uses for distinct customers. For example, in the hotel industry a major source of revenue is booking business events and conferences. A hotel or resort can identify business market segments based on various types of events. Single-day seminars require only a meeting room and refreshments. A full conference may involve renting rooms for lodging, preparing banquets, furnishing meeting rooms, and planning sightseeing excursions. By segmenting

B & J Food Service Equipment can use the NAICS code to locate firms in the food industry.

An advertisement targeted to the large business conference segment.

the market based on the use of the hotel's facilities and staff, a manager can prepare marketing materials that address the needs of each specific type of conference. The advertisement for Edgewater Beach Resort, shown in this section, is an example of this type of approach.

Segmentation by Customer Value

The final method of business segmentation is based on customer value. This approach is much easier for business-to-business firms to utilize than it is for consumer businesses, due to the availability of in-depth data about each business customer. A more precise value can be assigned to each individual business through sales records and other sources of data and information.

INTERNATIONAL IMPLICATIONS

As was first presented in Chapter 1, globally integrated marketing communications (GIMC) programs are vital for international firms. The world consists of many different languages and cultures. Brand names, marketing ideas, and advertising campaigns designed for one country do not always translate correctly to another. Consequently, understanding the international market is essential. Figure 4.15 highlights the ingredients of successful globally integrated marketing communications plans.

Recognizing the many cultural nuances throughout the world is one key. This does not mean that different marketing campaigns must always be developed for each country and each cultural group within a country. Still, marketers must understand the region and its culture in order to tailor messages to individual areas.

A borderless marketing plan suggests that the firm should use the same basic marketing approach for all of its various markets. At the same time, it allows each subsidiary the freedom to determine how to implement that marketing plan. This presents the opportunity to maintain a theme while targeting the message carefully.

Another key to a successful GIMC is developing local partnerships. Local partners can be marketing research firms or advertising firms that are familiar with the local language and culture. These partnerships sometimes are formed by hiring someone from a particular country with a full understanding of the market. Such a person is sometimes referred to as a **cultural assimilator**. It is vital that the chosen individual has a clear understanding of the English language or the language of the parent firm and the parent firm's business.

As with domestic markets, segmentation is critical. The goal is to design a communications package that effectively reaches every market segment. Target markets in other countries should be identified. In most instances, there will be both consumer and business-to-business segments.

A well-designed market communications analysis process is another key factor in the success of a GIMC program. Marketing managers must identify strengths and weaknesses of local competitors and places in which opportunities exist. They must also develop an understanding of how the firm is perceived in the international marketplace.

Finally, solid communication objectives based on an effective market communication analysis greatly improve the chances that a GIMC program will be successful. Linguistics is a major hurdle. Translating an English advertisement into another language requires expertise, because exact word translations often do not exist. For example, the slogan of Ruth's Steak House, "We sell sizzle as well as steaks," could not be translated into

FIGURE 4.15
Successful Globally Integrated Marketing Communications Tactics

- Understand the international market
- Create a borderless marketing plan
- Thinking globally but acting locally
- Local partnerships
- Communication segmentation strategies
- Market communications analysis
- Solid communication objectives

Spanish, because there is no equivalent word for "sizzle." Therefore, the translator found a Spanish idiom conveying a similar meaning in order to solve the problem.

The promotions opportunity analysis process is difficult in international settings; however, it is crucial in creating an effective GIMC. Language, culture, norms, beliefs, and laws all must be taken into consideration in the development of the GIMC program. Literal translation of a commercial's tagline might not be acceptable within a given culture. Laws concerning advertising and promotions vary by country. Further, cultures view ideas and objects differently. These differences must be considered when designing an integrated program.

Without a solid market communication analysis, international communication programs are more likely to fail. One good thing about international markets is that many of the communications objectives will be the same as those for domestic operations. In all countries, marketers must make consumers aware of the company's products. Advertisements must break through local clutter and capture the attention of the target audience. Effective communication means a product's features and advantages are clearly understood. Ads can also present the product using the emotions and imagery that speak effectively to the target audience. The ultimate goal is to persuade members of the target audience to purchase the company's products.

SUMMARY

A promotions opportunity analysis is the process by which marketers identify target audiences for the goods and services produced by the company. It consists of five steps: conduct a communication market analysis, establish communications objectives, create a communications budget, prepare promotional strategies, and match tactics with strategies. Along the way, marketing managers should review competitors, opportunities, target markets, customers, and the company's positioning.

Market segmentation is identifying sets of business or consumer groups with distinct characteristics. Segments must be clearly different, large enough to support a marketing campaign, and reachable through some type of media. Consumer groups that can be segmented include those identified by demographics, including gender, age, income, and ethnic heritage. Markets can also be identified using psychographic, generational, and geographic delineations. Geodemographic segmentation combines demographic, psychographic, and geographic information together. Other ways to categorize consumers are by the benefits they receive from goods or services and by the ways they use products.

Business-to-business segmentation can be accomplished by targeting business customers by industry, business type, the size of the company, geographic location, usage, and customer value

calculations. Marketing managers should carefully specify the company's consumer and business market segments. All other promotions opportunity analysis processes are tied to the identification of key customers.

Globally integrated marketing communications efforts must also be linked to promotions opportunities analysis programs. National differences, cultural concerns, language issues, and other challenges must be viewed in light of the target markets an individual company intends to serve.

A promotions opportunity analysis program is the first step in developing a complete IMC package. Based on an overall marketing plan, company leaders gather information and generate decisions regarding target markets and marketing opportunities. They proceed to develop a further understanding of the company's image and dig deeper into the process of revealing key consumer and business buyer behaviors. They should address the company's message to tie in with the overall IMC theme. A promotions opportunity analysis is the foundation stage for the rest of the IMC program. A solid promotions opportunity analysis program greatly increases the chances that marketing messages will reach the right audiences. This leads to increased sales, customer loyalty, and a stronger long-term standing in the marketplace.

KEY TERMS

promotions opportunity analysis The process marketers use to identify target audiences for a company's goods and services and the communication strategies needed to reach these audiences.

communication market analysis The process of discovering the organization's strengths and weaknesses in the area of marketing communication.

benchmark measures Starting points that are studied in relation to the degree of change following a promotional campaign.

threshold effects For new products, initial advertisements yield little behavioral response; however, over time, a consumer who is exposed enough times to a company's marketing message will recall the company and eventually become willing to make a purchase.

sales-response function curve   An S-shaped curve that indicates when threshold effects are present and when diminishing returns are present.

concave downward function   A model of the diminishing returns of advertising expenditures on sales.

marginal analysis   A model that shows when additional expenditures on advertising and promotions have an adverse affect on profits.

carryover effects   When products are only purchased when needed, promotions for those products must be designed to generate a situation in which the consumer has been exposed to the company's message for so long that when the time comes to buy, the consumer remembers the key company.

wear-out effects   Declines in advertising effectiveness that occur when an ad or marketing communication becomes "old" or "boring."

decay effects   Declines in advertising effectiveness that occur when advertising stops and consumers begin to forget about the company.

percentage of sales method   A form of communications budgeting in which budgeting is based on the sales from the previous year or anticipated sales for the coming year.

meet-the-competition method   A method of communications budgeting in which the primary rationale is to prevent the loss of market share, which occurs in highly competitive markets where rivalries between competitors are intense.

"what we can afford" method   A method of communications budgeting in which the marketing budget is set after all of the company's other budgets have been determined and communications monies are allocated based on what the firm feels it can afford to spend.

objective and task method   A form of communications budgeting in which management first lists all of the objectives it wants to accomplish during the year and then budgets to meet those objectives.

payout planning   A budgeting method that establishes a ratio of advertising to sales or market share.

strategies   Sweeping guidelines concerning the essence of the company's marketing efforts.

tactics   The activities companies do to support overall promotional strategies.

market segmentation   The identification of specific purchasing groups based on their needs, attitudes, and interests.

market segment   A set of businesses or group of individual consumers with distinct characteristics.

demographics   The study of population characteristics.

psychographics   The study of patterns of responses that reveal a person's activities, interests, and opinions (AIO).

cultural assimilator   A person who is familiar with the local language and culture of a given country who can help marketing efforts in that particular country.

REVIEW QUESTIONS

1. What is a promotions opportunities analysis? What makes it a critical part of a company's marketing efforts?
2. What are the five parts of a promotions opportunities analysis planning process?
3. What common marketing communications objectives do firms establish?
4. Name and describe the types of communications budgets. Which is best? Why?
5. What is a strategy? Give an example of a promotional strategy.
6. What are tactics? How are they related to strategies?
7. Define demographics. How are they used to segment consumer markets?
8. How can firms take advantage of target markets by gender?
9. What generational cohorts have marketing experts identified?
10. What problems are associated with markets segmented according to geographic areas?
11. What are geodemographics? Why have they been so successful in defining marketing segments?
12. Describe usage segmentation and benefit segmentation.
13. What are the common business-to-business market segments?
14. Describe the NAICS approach to business market segmentation.
15. Describe a usage segmentation approach in a business-to-business setting.
16. Describe a segmentation approach based on company size.
17. How does the idea of a promotions opportunities analysis fit with a GIMC program?

CRITICAL THINKING EXERCISES

Discussion Questions

1. Use a search engine to locate five companies on the Internet that sell swimwear. Perform a competitive analysis of these five companies to find the types of products sold, the types of promotional appeals that are used, and the types of special offers used to entice buyers. What type of advertising strategy would you use to sell swimwear over the Internet?

2. A promotions opportunity analysis of movie theaters revealed the primary moviegoer to be between 18 and 24 years of age. Twenty years ago, 44 percent of the individuals in this age bracket went to movies frequently. Today, less

than 34 percent are frequent moviegoers.[23] Conduct a customer analysis by interviewing five individuals between the ages of 18 and 24. Based on their responses, what suggestions would you make to movie theaters to reverse this declining trend?

3. Make a list of five consumer goods or services segmented on the basis of gender but sold to both genders. Are there any differences in the product or service attributes? Are there differences in how they are marketed? What are those differences? Do you think using a different marketing approach has worked?

4. For each of the following goods or services, identify the various benefits that consumers may derive from the good or service. Can you think of an advertisement or other marketing communication that has used the benefit as the central part of its appeal?
   a. Seafood restaurant
   b. Auto insurance
   c. Optometrist or eye-care clinic
   d. Soft drink
   e. Aspirin or other pain reliever

INTEGRATED LEARNING EXERCISES

1. Adage.com provides the latest ad agency news and account news. Go to the Web site at **www.adage.com**. Scan through the news articles about advertising, accounts, and ad agencies. Pick two that interest you and write a short summary report about the contents of each article.

2. For consumer markets, a leading geodemographic firm is Claritas. Go to the Web site at **www.claritas.com** and explore the various methods of segmentation. What information does Claritas provide? How would it help a company develop an integrated marketing communication plan?

3. Values and lifestyles (VALS) psychographic segmentation can be a valuable tool for marketers as they prepare their marketing materials. Access VALS2 through the Business Intelligence Center at **www.sric-bi.com/vals**. Once at the VALS site, examine the characteristics of each of the groups. Then take the test to determine which group you belong to. How can VALS2 help marketers develop advertising messages?

4. A current trend for many companies is the development of marketing messages for specific demographic, ethnic, or lifestyle groups. This allows for a more targeted message than is possible for the mass audience. Go to the following Web sites. What types of marketing messages are on each site? How could the information on these Web sites be used to develop integrated marketing communication plans?
   a. Women (**www.iVillage.com**)
   b. Hispanics (**www.hispaniconline.com**)
   c. African Americans (**www.targetmarketnews.com**)
   d. Gays and lesbians (**www.planetout.com**)

5. Choose one of the following companies. Examine the company's Web site to determine what segmentation strategy the firm uses. Describe the intended target market for the Web site. Using Figure 4.4 as a guide, what communication objective(s) do you think the company is trying to accomplish?
   a. Sports Spectrum Greeting Cards (**www.sportsgreeting-cards.com**)
   b. Ty Beanie Babies (**www.ty.com**)
   c. Sara Lee (**www.saralee.com**)
   d. Dr. James J. Romano (**www.jromano.com**)

STUDENT PROJECT

Creative Corner

The VALS2 typology has been used by a number of companies and advertising agencies to create marketing materials. Your task is to design two advertisements for DIRECTV. Pick one of the following pairs of VALS segments and design an advertisement promoting DIRECTV for each segment. When you are finished, write a paragraph explaining how you believe the ads you created will appeal to their respective VALS segment and how the two ads are different. Before you begin work on the ads, go to the SRI Consulting Business Intelligence Web site at **www.sric-bi.com/VALS** to obtain more information about the two segments you will be targeting with your ads.

Pair 1: Innovators and survivors
Pair 2: Thinkers and makers
Pair 3: Believers and achievers
Pair 4: Strivers and experiencers

CASE 1 BURGER WARS

The world of fast food, especially the world of hamburgers and fries, continues to evolve. The dominant force for nearly 40 years has been McDonald's. The company is practically an icon in the United States and has expanded with a nearly worldwide reach. Recently, the McDonald's empire has come under attack from a variety of sources.

Socially, films such as *Supersize Me* criticized the basic McDonald's menu, noting high levels of calories and fat in the foods offered, complaining about the suggestive selling tactics used, and arguing that advertising to children utilizing Ronald McDonald as a spokesperson has created an unhealthy, obese, malnourished new generation. McDonald's responded with products such as salads and fruit plates, while agreeing to halt the use of trans fats in French fries and other deep-fried products. Company leaders did not, however, agree that Ronald McDonald should retire. McDonald's continues to offer birthday parties, outdoor toys, and the Happy Meal to entice kids into its stores.

The number two competitor in the world of burgers is Burger King. The company is dwarfed by McDonald's in terms of locations, revenues, and dollars spent on advertising and marketing as well as in brand recognition and recall by children and teens. In 2007, Burger King began a bold new program featuring two new spokespersons. The first is the computer-animated Burger King, placed into a variety of sports events and other unusual places. The Burger King never speaks but clearly stands out. The appeal is to a slightly older generation of burger buyers than children. The second spokesperson became Homer Simpson from the television cartoon *The Simpsons*. Homer has always been a big burger-eater. He is highly recognizable to a generation of television viewers going back for 20 years. *The Simpsons Movie*, which was released as the Burger King tie-in began, created a great deal of buzz. The film was a major success in terms of tickets sold and practically ensured the Simpsons would continue on television, and possibly in movie sequels, for the next several years. The marketing genius of signing Homer Simpson is that the television show has an audience ranging from younger children to adults. Many 20-somethings grew up with The Simpsons as a weekly night-time habit.

Neither Burger King nor McDonald's can ignore other burger chains. Wendy's and Hardees have been successful in some

markets. Sonic also has a following among some customers. Each utilizes a unique marketing pitch oriented to individual target audiences.

At the same time, chains offering food items other than hamburgers also made inroads. Among the most powerful new competitors was Subway, with its "Eat Fresh" campaign, spokesperson Jared, and advertising claims regarding the lower calorie, low-fat options available. Pizza offers further competition, led by major players Pizza Hut, Papa John's, and Dominos. Taco Bell, KFC, and Long John Silver's are additional fast-food options. Under the direction of the Yum, the three are often found in the same location along the Interstate, giving a weary traveler a variety of choices under the same roof.

Both Burger King and McDonald's seek to maintain a competitive advantage through differentiation. McDonald's features include its powerful brand, accessibility across the country and around the world, and the "pull" factor, whereby children entice parents to continue to visit a unit even when other options are available. For years Burger King relied on the advertising claim that broiled burgers taste better than fried and that in taste tests people prefer the Whopper to the Big Mac.

In the next decade, the victor in the Burger wars may or may not be based on what happens on the children's front. Combinations of products, prices, delivery systems, and promotions programs might make the difference. Clearly, no company can sit still and wait to see what happens with the others.

1. Conduct a communication marketing analysis for one of the following: McDonald's, Burger King, Sonic, Wendy's, or Hardees.

2. Besides children, identify the target markets that are best suited to each of the following: McDonald's, Burger King, Wendy's, Hardees, Sonic.

3. What type of promotional budget should each major competitor use? Why?

4. Based on the information in this chapter, how would a company like Hardees or Carl's Jr (which owns Hardees) compete effectively against McDonald's? What type of communication strategy and budget would work best?

CASE 2 RED HOT MARKETING

Mary Wilson could not believe her company was suddenly facing a competitive threat. For years, her small retail shop, Red and Purple Adventures, was the only store in town catering to members of the city's numerous chapters of the Red Hat Society. Now, a rival firm had opened a competing outlet across town. Mary knew she had to work harder and smarter to keep an edge in what had always been a prosperous business.

The Red Hat Society was formed in 1998. In 1997, Sue Ellen Cooper, a resident of Fullerton, California, on vacation in Tucson, Arizona, bought a red fedora at a thrift shop. She was

acquainted with a poem, called "Warning," written by Jenny Joseph. The poem is about an older woman wearing a purple dress and a bright red hat. The poem advises older women to free themselves to be silly and have fun. Bright, daring clothes are the order of the day. Sue Ellen Cooper was so enamored with the concept that she began giving red hats and copies of the poem to friends as birthday presents. Soon after, the Red Hat Society was born when the group got together for tea.

Sue Ellen Cooper's credo for the Red Hat Society states: "We believe silliness is the comedy relief of life, and since we are all in it together, we might as well join red-gloved hands and go for the gusto together. Underneath the frivolity, we share a bond of affection, forged by common life experiences and a genuine enthusiasm for wherever life takes us next."

Besides red hats, members of the Red Hat Society wear purple outfits. Those who join the Red Hat Society before the age of 50 adorn themselves with pink hats and lavender clothes. Most activities for members of the Red Hat Society are scheduled by individual chapters, with a heavy emphasis on fun-loving events.

Mary Wilson had been selling both licensed and unlicensed red and pink hats and gloves along with purple and lavender outfits to the under- and over-50 women's crowd for several years. Her quirky store included not only clothes and hats, but also jewelry and perfume. Mary always had fresh pastries available for visiting clients. She served tea to anyone who wished to stay for a while and visit. Light "oldies" music from the 1930s, 40s and 50s played in the background. Mary always believed the key to her success was a warm, friendly atmosphere that was highly compatible with the goals of the Red Hat Society.

The new competitor in town took a different approach. The company's advertisements featured low prices and specials. Mary also believed the other store had a better location in a small but busy shopping mall where parking was easier to find. She worried new Red Hat Society members would be enticed by convenience and price. Although it made Mary uncomfortable, she knew for the first time that her business had to be more than just warm and friendly. She needed a competitive marketing strategy to fight off this new threat.

Source: Red Hat Society (**www.redhatsociety.com**, accessed April 7, 2005).

1. Conduct a promotions opportunity analysis for Red and Purple Adventures.

An example of an advertisement directed to the members of the Red Hat Society.

2. Identify the market segments that Red and Purple Adventures must continue to maintain.

3. Describe the ways to reach Mary's key market segments effectively.

4. Should Mary expand her business to the Internet and sell her merchandise nationwide via e-commerce?

ENDNOTES

1. **www.petsmart.com** (accessed November 26, 2007); Elizabeth Weise, "We Really Love—and Spend On—Our Pets," *USA Today* (December 11, 2006), p. 1-D.

2. Margaret Henderson Blair, "An Empirical Investigation of Advertising Wearin and Wearout," *Journal of Advertising Research* 40, no. 6 (November–December 2000), pp. 95–100.

3. Ibid.

4. Lionell A. Mitchell, "An Examination of Methods of Setting Advertising Budgets: Practice and Literature," *European Journal of Marketing* 27, no. 5 (1993), pp. 5–22.

5. James E. Lynch and Graham J. Hooley, "Increased Sophistication in Advertising Budget Setting," *Journal of Advertising Research* 30, no. 1 (February–March 1990), pp. 67–76.

6. James O. Peckham, "Can We Relate Advertising Dollars to Market Share Objectives?" *How Much to Spend for Advertising*, M. A. McNiver (ed). (New York: Association of National Advertisers, 1969), p. 30.

7. "Higher Gear," *Promo Industry Trends Report* (**www.promomagazine.com**, accessed January 2, 2008).

8. "2004 Advertising to Sales Ratios for 200 Largest Ad Spending Industries," *Adage* (**www.adage.com**, accessed February 26, 2005).

9. "Top Advertisers in Top 10 Countries, Excluding the U.S.," *2006 Fact Pack, Advertising Age* (February 27, 2006), p. 14.

10. "100 Leading National Advertisers," *Advertising Age Datacenter 2007 Marketing Profiles Yearbook* (June 25, 2007), p. 7.

11. Ibid.

12. Kitty Bean Yancey, "More Women Head Out, Leave the Menfolk Behind," *USA Today* (**www.usatoday.com/travel/destinations/ 2007–10–25-gal-getaways_N.htm**, October 25, 2007).

13. Interview with Kerri Martin, brand manager of BMW Motorcycles, July 18, 2000.

14. Chris Cormack, "Why Vega Got It So Wrong," *B&T Weekly* 56, no. 2574 (July 28, 2006), p. 14.

15. "Outlook 2008: Ethic Marketing," *Brand week.com* (**www.brandweek.com/bw/news/ recent_display.jsp?vnu_content_id=100369 0030**, December 31, 2007).

16. Rebecca Piirto Heath, "Psychographics," *Marketing Tools* (November–December 1995), pp. 74–81.

17. SRI Consulting Business Intelligence (**www. sric-bi.com**, accessed January 3, 2008); Dana-Nicoleta Lascu and Kenneth E. Clow, *Essentials of Marketing* (Cincinnati, OH: Atomic Dog Publishing, 2007), p. 169.

18. David Feldman, "Segmentation Building Blocks," *Marketing Research* (Summer 2006), pp. 23–29.

19. PRIZM, "My Best Segments" (**www.claritas. com/MyBestSegments/Default.jsp**, accessed January 3, 2008).

20. Ronald L. Zallocco, "Benefit Segmentation of the Fitness Market," *Journal of Health Care Marketing* 12, no. 4 (December 1992), p. 80.

21. Susan Pechman, "Custom Clusters: Finding Your True Customer Segments," *Bank Marketing* 26, no. 7 (July 1994), pp. 33–35.

22. Gene Koprowski, "Bovine Inspiration," *Marketing Tools* (October 1996), pp. 10–11.

23. Shannon Dortch, "Going to the Movies," *American Demographics* 18, no. 12 (December 1996), pp. 4–8.

PART 2

IMC Advertising Tools

5

Advertising Management

THE ANATOMY OF A PERFECT PUSHUP

Chapter Objectives

After reading this chapter, you should be able to answer the following questions:

- What activities are involved in advertising management?

- What roles do the company's overall mission, products, and services play in advertising programs?

- When is it best to use an in-house advertising approach and when is it better to employ an external advertising agency?

- What are the steps of an effective advertising campaign management program?

- How should the functions performed by the advertising account manager and the advertising creative interact in preparing an advertising campaign?

Every year around January 1, scores of people resolve to get in better shape, lose weight, and improve their body images. Diet and exercise programs flourish, creating a multimillion dollar industry. Competitors range from retailers concentrating on food products to small workout centers, such as Curves, to more elaborate exercise programs.

Some people join gyms. Others prefer to work out at home. The products that are available to the home-workout crowd include legendary products such as the ThighMaster, exercise balls, Pilates programs, and DVDs or videos. More hardcore equipment includes the highly successful Bowflex line of products, including one for an overall workout, a cardio machine, a tread climber, and dumbbells.

Entry into such a competitive market may seem daunting. Success requires innovation, a great deal of buzz, and an effective advertising program.

Alden Mills served for 7 years as a Navy Seal. As a platoon commander, he was asked to investigate the number of injuries suffered by members of his wing of the military. At that time, 73 percent of Navy Seals had been hurt to the point that they were given disability benefits. His study concluded that traditional training methods may have been part of the problem. In response, a new program was developed called Functional Training.

After leaving the military, Mills took the knowledge he had gained from these experiences and applied them to the more general fitness market. The product that emerged is called the Perfect Pushup. It is a simple set of devices, one for each hand, that allows an exerciser to maximize a push-up as it is being performed. Hands, arms, and shoulders all naturally rotate 90 degrees, as if the person is punching while pushing. The outcome is greater strength combined with better muscle definition. With this innovation, Mills founded the BODYREV company to market the product and similar items.

One clear advantage the Perfect Pushup holds is price. A Bowflex product costs hundreds of dollars. The Perfect Pushup sells for $39.95. For someone looking to work out without a large financial investment, the product became an inexpensive option.

Not long after, the Perfect Pushup was featured on numerous infomercials. Initial interest in the product created the exact type of buzz needed to move forward. Mills and his Perfect Pushup were soon featured in a variety of magazines, including *Popular Science, Men's Fitness, Men's*

The Perfect Pushup was invented by former Navy Seal Alden Mills as an alternative to regular pushups.

Journal, ESPN Magazine, and others. Appearances on *The Tonight Show with Jay Leno* and *The Big Idea with Donnie Deutsch* reached a wider audience. By the close of 2007, the Perfect Pushup had garnered unit sales in the thousands.

To establish a longer-term presence in the fitness marketplace, an advertising program was needed. The Perfect Pushup was soon featured in traditional 30-second television commercials, in numerous magazines and newspapers, on the Internet though the BODYREV Web site, as well as in cooperative advertising programs with other retailers.

The remaining challenge for BODYREV and the Perfect Pushup is longevity. The question remains whether the primary product will be viewed as a passing fad or as a continuing presence in the workout marketplace. Quality advertising combined with continued innovation is undoubtedly the key to the future.[1]

OVERVIEW

The average person encounters more than 600 advertisements per day. These messages are delivered through an expanding variety of media. Television and radio have long been the staples of advertising programs. They compete with newspaper and magazine ads, billboards, signs, direct-mail campaigns, and other traditional channels. Recently, the number of ways to contact customers has grown. Ads on the Internet, clothing lines with messages printed on them, telemarketing programs, and even messages heard while someone is on hold on the telephone create numerous new ways to attract potential customers.

Today's marketers face a tremendous challenge. A company simply cannot afford to prepare ads for every possible medium. Choices must be made. The messages must be designed to

FIGURE 5.1
Overview of Integrated Marketing Communications

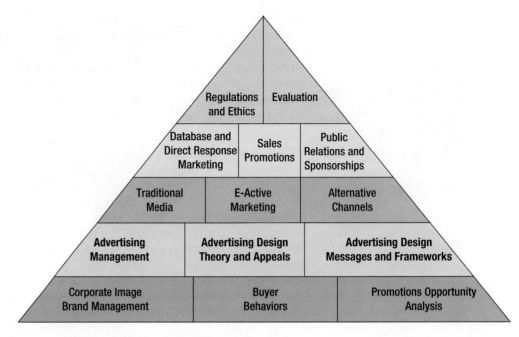

give the company an advantage in a highly cluttered world in which people are becoming increasingly proficient at simply tuning ads out.

To be effective, an ad first must be noticed. Next, it must be remembered. Then, the message of the advertisement should incite some kind of action, such as a purchase, a shift in brand loyalty, or, at the very least, find a place in the buyer's long-term memory.

Section 2 of this textbook describes the role advertising plays in an integrated marketing communications program. Figure 5.1 is a reminder of the overall IMC approach. The three chapters in this section detail the relationship, focusing on developing an advertising program that matches the company's overall IMC approach.

Three ingredients must be combined to create effective advertisements: (1) development of a logical advertising management scheme for the company, (2) thoughtful design of advertisements, and (3) careful selection of media. Media tools and media selection processes are described in the third section of this textbook. Selecting media and designing advertisements go hand in hand: One cannot be performed without the other. Although discussions of these topics (advertising design and media selection) are presented separately, they occur at the same time. The ad agency or creative department seeks to create consistent and effective advertisements and promotional campaigns.

This chapter focuses on advertising management, which lays the groundwork for the total advertising program. Advertising campaign management is the process of preparing and integrating an advertising program with the overall IMC message. One element in this process is to develop the message theme. The **message theme** is an outline of the key idea(s) that the advertising program is supposed to convey. The message theme should match the company's overall marketing and IMC strategies. The message theme component of advertising is described in greater detail later.

Chapters 6 and 7 describe the advertising design process. Several primary decisions must be made at that time. They include deciding what leverage point to use, the major appeal in the advertising campaign, and the type of executional framework to use. A **leverage point** is the key element in the advertisement that taps into, or activates, a consumer's personal value system (a value, idea, or concept). The **appeal** is how to design the advertisement that attracts attention or presents information to consumers. Typical appeals include the use of humor, fear, sexual suggestiveness, logic, and emotions. The **executional framework**, or theme, explains how the message will be delivered. Some examples of executional frameworks include the slice-of-life approach, fantasies, dramatizations, and ads constructed using animation. Figure 5.2 indicates how all of these elements fit together in the design of an advertisement.

FIGURE 5.2
Advertising Design Overview

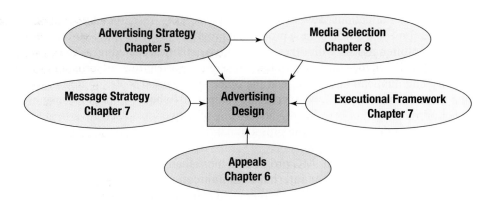

OVERVIEW OF ADVERTISING MANAGEMENT

An **advertising management program** is the process of preparing and integrating a company's advertising efforts with the overall IMC message. An effective program consists of four activities that combine to form the advertising management process. They are:

1. Review the company's activities in light of advertising management.
2. Select an in-house or external advertising agency.
3. Develop an advertising campaign management strategy.
4. Complete a creative brief.

The major principle guiding these four efforts is *consistency.* To be effective in developing successful advertisements, the company's goods or services and methods of doing business need to match the form of advertising agency chosen, the strategy of the campaign, and the work of the advertising creative. The goal is to provide a coherent message that states the theme of the entire IMC program.

ADVERTISING AND THE IMC PROCESS

Advertising is a major component of integrated marketing communications. It is also part of the "traditional" promotions mix of advertising, consumer and trade promotions, and personal selling. These functions, along with other activities such as direct marketing, public relations efforts, and alternative marketing strategies, form the basis for communicating with individual consumers and business customers. The role advertising plays varies by company, product, and the firm's marketing goals. For some products and companies, advertising is the central focus, and the other components (trade promotions, consumer promotions, and personal selling) support the advertising

Creating eye-catching ads plays a vital role in advertising management.

"Hey, there's a blue one."

Drivers wanted. VW

Source: Courtesy of Volkswagen.

campaign. In other situations, advertising plays a secondary role, such as supporting the national sales force and a firm's trade promotion program. In the business-to-business sector, advertising often assists with other promotional activities, including trade shows and personal sales calls. In the consumer sector, the reverse is often true. Advertising is usually the primary communication vehicle, and the other promotional tools (contests, coupons, sampling) are designed to back the advertising campaign. In both business-to-business and consumer promotions, the key to using advertising effectively is to see advertising as one of the "spokes" in the "wheel" of the promotional effort. The remaining "spokes" are the other components of the IMC plan.

As has been suggested, an IMC program is more than just promotions and advertising tactics. IMC includes clear internal communications among departments along with the messages sent to external customers and suppliers. IMC programs apply information technologies to develop databases that help everyone in the firm understand customer needs and characteristics. This covers the needs of both business customers and end-user consumers. Effective integrated communications programs mean that every organizational member works toward the goal of reaching customers with a clear, consistent message.

Within this framework, advertising plays a major role in sending out effective communications. This section is devoted to explaining how to prepare advertising campaigns while working with account executives, media buyers, and advertising creatives. The goal is to incorporate advertising into the IMC program in an efficient and effective manner. As advertising agencies and account managers feel growing pressures to produce tangible results, developing noticeable and measurable advertising outcomes is the major challenge for the advertising agency and for the company itself.[2]

In order to attract businesses and individuals to New Orleans, the city's leaders hired Zehnder Communications to develop a series of advertisements promoting the city.

If you want it badly enough, it will happen.

CITY OF NEW ORLEANS
C. Ray Nagin, Mayor

It's time to care again.

595-CARE   NewNewOrleans.net

CHOOSING AN ADVERTISING AGENCY

The first issue in an advertising program is deciding between an in-house advertising group and an external advertising agency. Some businesses house the integrated communications and advertising programs in internal departments. Part of the reasoning is that internal organization members have a better sense of the company's mission and message. Managers in these firms believe they can develop effective advertising programs through outsourcing some of the functions and by hiring a few key marketing and advertising experts. Activities such as writing, filming, recording, and editing advertisements in addition to planning and purchasing media time (on television and radio) and space (in magazines, in newspapers, and on billboards) can be performed by outside agencies while the remainder of the IMC program is managed internally.

Recently, Canada's property and casualty insurance industry experienced its worst 2 years in history. The management team at Co-Operators, one of Canada's largest insurance companies, grew tired of dealing with advertising agencies that did not seem to understand the company's or the industry's problems. As a result, an in-house marketing team was developed. The team was assigned the objective of

◆ Size of the account	◆ Complexity of the product
◆ Amount of money that can be spent on media buys	◆ Creativity
◆ Objectivity	

FIGURE 5.3
Variables Examined when Deciding on an External Advertising Agency or In-house Department

revitalizing the company's well-known brand and linking that awareness to specific attributes. The team developed a profile of the company's customers using in-house research and data mining. A top-notch creative director was hired to assist in the production of new advertisements. A television campaign called "Heritage" was created. The ads and accompanying marketing materials focused on an association of farmers who relied on a caring, friendly, community-minded, honest, and Canadian insurance company. The spots and the integrated campaign were highly successful.[3]

An internal approach to advertising may have some disadvantages. One problem is that the company can go "stale" and fail to identify other promotional or advertising opportunities. An internal department may also lack the expertise to carry out all of the necessary functions. The result might be the tendency to cut costs in developing ads rather than taking advantage of the knowledge and expertise that advertising agencies have to offer. In the global arena, internal members of the firm may lack the necessary understanding of language, customs, and buyer behaviors in international target markets. Therefore, a decision must be made.

Decision Variables

In deciding whether to use an external agency or in-house department, several key factors should be considered. The management team should review the variables highlighted in Figure 5.3.[4]

With regard to the *account size*, a small account usually is not as attractive to an advertising agency, because smaller accounts generate less profit. Also, with regard to *money spent on media*, smaller accounts are less economically sound for the agency, because more money must be spent on producing advertisements rather than on purchasing media time or space. A good rule of thumb is the 75–15–10 breakdown. That is, 75 percent of the money buys media time or space, 15 percent goes to the agency for the creative work, and 10 percent is spent on the actual production of the ad. For smaller accounts, the breakdown might be more like 25–40–35. This means that 75 percent of the funds go to the creative and production work, and only 25 percent is spent on media purchases. Unless 75 percent of the company's advertising budget can be spent on media purchases, it may be wise either to do the work in-house or to develop contracts with smaller specialty firms to prepare various aspects of the advertising campaign.

An agency is more likely to be *objective* than an in-house advertising department. It is difficult for an in-house creative to remain unbiased and to ignore the influences of others in the organization who might not fully understand the artistic aspects of advertising. An external creative does not face these influences and pressures.

Advertisements for highly complex products create a different set of circumstances. This is because external advertising agency members might have a difficult time understanding complicated products. To get them up to speed often requires a considerable amount of time, which costs money. Therefore, in-house departments

The creatives at the Crispin Porter & Bogusky Agency have greater objectivity in creating ads, such as this one for Volkswagen.

Source: Courtesy of Volkswagen.

can be better for more complex products. For generic or more standardized products, ad agencies usually have more to offer.

The final issue to consider in choosing an agency versus performing the work in-house is *creativity.* Most of the time advertising agencies offer greater creativity. Still, an in-house department will be able to freelance and utilize creatives just for the ad design process. The question, then, is whether to give the entire project to an agency or only use the agency's creatives and other specialists.

When the decision is made to retain an external advertising agency, the company commits substantial resources to the goal of expanding its audience through advertising and communications programs. A review of the types of agencies that can be chosen is presented next.

EXTERNAL ADVERTISING AGENCIES

Company leaders have a variety of options when choosing an advertising agency. All sizes and types of advertising agencies exist. At one end of the spectrum are the highly specialized, boutique-type agencies offering only one specialized service (e.g., making television ads) or serving only one type of client. For instance, G+G Advertising of Albuquerque, New Mexico, specializes in advertising to Native Americans, a market of an estimated 10 million people.[5]

At the other end of the spectrum are the full-service agencies that provide all types of advertising and promotional activities. These companies also offer advice and assistance in working with the other components of the IMC program, including consumer and trade promotions, direct-marketing programs, and alternative media. Figure 5.4 lists some of the services that full-service advertising agencies can provide.

In addition to advertising agencies, there are other closely associated types of firms. *Media service companies* negotiate and purchase media packages (called *media buys*) for companies. *Direct-marketing agencies* handle every aspect of a direct-marketing campaign, either through telephone orders (800 numbers), Internet programs, or by direct mail. Some companies focus on either *consumer promotions, trade promotions,* or both. These companies assist in developing promotions such as coupons, premiums, contests, and sweepstakes. They also provide assistance in making posters, end-of-aisle displays, and point-of-purchase displays. *Public relations* firms provide experts to help companies and individuals develop positive public images. Public relations firms are often called in for damage control when negative publicity arises. In-house members of the organization can render these activities, just as an in-house marketing department can perform advertising and IMC programs. In both instances, company leaders must decide how they can complete these key marketing activities efficiently and effectively.

A new trend in advertising, called the *whole egg theory,* is utilized by the Young & Rubicam Advertising Agency. The concept of the whole egg theory is to move from selling a client's products to helping the client attain total success in the marketplace. Achieving success requires integrating the marketing approach by offering a fuller array of services to both business and consumer clients. Thus, as client companies began to move toward more integrated marketing approaches, agencies such as Young & Rubicam captured more accounts.[6]

A similar company is Venture Communications of Calgary, Canada. The company's founder, Arlene Dickson, transformed Venture from a traditional advertising agency into an integrated marketing communications company by expanding to encompass every aspect of a company's marketing program. Venture is divided into six communities: advertising, technology, media buying, brand planning, public relations, and marketing and business strategies. U.S. brands, such as Lipton, Cisco, and Unisys,

FIGURE 5.4
Services Provided by Full-Service Agencies

- ◆ Advice about how to develop target markets
- ◆ Specialized services for business markets
- ◆ Suggestions on how to project a strong company image and theme
- ◆ Assistance in selecting company logos and slogans
- ◆ Preparation of advertisements
- ◆ Planning and purchasing media time and space

have bought into Venture's "synchronized" communication approach and now make up 15 percent of Venture's revenues. Agencies such as Young & Rubicam and Venture continue to succeed because they are more than just advertising agencies. Instead, these firms offer marketing experts who participate in the entire integrated marketing communications program.[7]

The process of selecting an advertising agency is difficult. A company's leaders must decide how much involvement the agency will have and how many functions the agency should perform. The next step is to develop effective selection criteria to help company leaders make wise choices in the process of hiring an advertising agency.

CHOOSING AN AGENCY

Choosing the advertising agency that best suits a company requires careful planning. Figure 5.5 lists the steps involved in this process. Additional information about these steps follows.

Goal Setting

Before making any contact with an advertising agency, company leaders identify and prioritize corporate goals. Goals provide a sense of direction for the marketing team, for the agency account executive, and for the advertising creative. Each is more likely to be "on the same page" as preparation of the advertising campaign unfolds. Without clearly understood goals, it becomes more difficult to know which agency to choose because company leaders do not have a clear idea of what they want to accomplish. Unambiguous goals help ensure a good fit between the company and the agency.

Selection Criteria

The second step in selecting an agency is stating the selection criteria to be used. Even firms with experience in selecting agencies should set selection criteria in advance. The objective is to reduce biases that may enter into the decision. Emotions and other feelings can lead to decisions that are not in the company's best interests. Although good chemistry between the agency and the firm is important, this aspect of the choice comes later in the process, after the list has been narrowed down to two or three agencies. Figure 5.6 lists some of the major issues to be considered as part of the selection process. This list is especially useful in the initial screening process, when the task is to narrow the field to the top five (or fewer) agencies.

The *size* of the agency is important, especially as it compares to the size of the company hiring the agency. If a large firm were to hire a small agency, the small agency may be overwhelmed by the account. A small firm hiring a large agency may find that the company's account could be lost or could be treated as being insignificant. A good rule of thumb to follow regarding the size of the agency is that the account should be large enough for the agency so it is important to the agency but small enough that, if lost, the agency would not be badly affected.

When Norwest Banks of Minneapolis acquired Wells Fargo of San Francisco, the company tripled in size. Norwest's agency, Carmichael Lynch, was not large enough to handle the new larger company. According to Larry Haeg, "We needed the resources and services of a larger agency."[8] In this case, it was not a matter of the firm being incompetent, but rather that the larger Norwest needed a wider variety of services and expertise.

- ◆ Set goals.
- ◆ Select process and criteria.
- ◆ Screen initial list of applicants.
- ◆ Request client references.
- ◆ Reduce list to two or three viable agencies.
- ◆ Request creative pitch.
- ◆ Select agency.

FIGURE 5.5
Steps in Selecting an Advertising Agency

FIGURE 5.6
Evaluation Criteria in Choosing an Advertising Agency

- ◆ Size of the agency
- ◆ Relevant experience of the agency
- ◆ Conflicts of interest
- ◆ Creative reputation and capabilities
- ◆ Production capabilities

- ◆ Media purchasing capabilities
- ◆ Other services available
- ◆ Client retention rates
- ◆ Personal chemistry

Relevant experience in an industry is a second evaluation criterion. When an agency has experience in a given industry, the agency's employees are better able to understand the client firm, its customers, and the structure of the marketing channel. At the same time, it is important to be certain the agency does not have any *conflicts of interest.* An advertising firm that has been hired by one manufacturer of automobile tires experiences a conflict of interest if the ad agency is hired by another tire manufacturer.

An advertising agency can have relevant experience without representing a competitor. Such experience can be gained when an agency works for a similar company that operates in a different industry. For example, if an agency has a manufacturer of automobile batteries as a client, this experience is relevant to selling automobile tires. The agency should have experience with the business-to-business side of the market, so that retailers, wholesalers, and any other channel party are considered in the marketing and advertising of the product.

All of the milk advertisements in this textbook were created by Bozell Worldwide. In addition to the milk advertisements, Bozell's clients include Datek Online, Bank of America, Unisys, Lycos, Excedrin, Jergens, and the pork industry. Notice that this list does not include competing firms within the same industry. Also note that Bozell's success in promoting milk led the pork industry to believe Bozell would have the right kind of expertise to promote pork products.

The initial screening process includes an investigation into each agency's *creative reputation and capabilities.* One method of judging an agency's creativity is to ask for a list of awards the company has received. Although awards do not always translate into effective advertisements, in most cases there is a positive relationship between winning awards and writing effective ads. Most creative awards are given by peers. As a result, they are good indicators of what others think of the agency's creative efforts. Assessing creative capabilities is very important when preparing advertising campaigns for a different country in which the firm has limited experience.

Production capabilities and *media purchasing capabilities* of the agencies should be examined if these services are needed. A firm that needs an agency to produce a television commercial and also buy media time should check on these activities as part of the initial screening process. It should also be kept in mind that many agencies either have subsidiary companies perform the media work or subcontract it to a media firm. What is important is not whether the advertising agency does the media buys itself, but that it has the capability of making sure it is done and that it fits with the ads being designed.

The type of information involved in selecting an advertising agency can be difficult to obtain. The company hiring the agency must be persistent and engage

The milk industry was just one of the accounts handled by Bozell.

In addition to the backstroke and the butterfly, I can perform a world-class chug-a-lug. With milk. It has protein for my muscles, plus essential vitamins and minerals like calcium and potassium. All of which help me get the one mineral every Olympian craves. Gold.

MILK
Where's *your* mustache?™

in thorough research. Accessing each agency's Web page, reading annual reports, and searching for news articles about individual agencies can be helpful. Most ad agencies provide prospectus sheets describing their capabilities. These reports render some information about their media buying skills.

The final three selection criteria—*other services available, client retention rates*, and *personal chemistry*—are revealed as the final steps of selection take place. These criteria help make the final determination in the selection process.

The various awards presented to the creative team of the Joplin Globe are displayed in this advertisement.

Reference Requests

Once the initial screening is complete, the company requests references from the agencies still in the running for the contract. Most agencies willingly provide lists of their best customers to serve as references. A good strategy the company can use is to obtain references of firms that have similar needs. Also, when possible, it helps to obtain names of former clients of the agency. Finding out why they switched can provide valuable information. Often changes are made for legitimate reasons. Discovering an agency's *client retention rate* helps reveal how effective the firm has been in working with various clients. Poor service is not the only reason a firm switches advertising agencies. As noted earlier in this chapter, Norwest Banks let its advertising agency go because the agency was too small to handle the increased size of Norwest.[9]

Background checks also provide useful information. Background checks start with finding firms that have dealt with each agency. Also, talking to media agents who sell media time provides insights as to how an agency buys time and deals with customers. Companies that have formed contracts with individual agencies for production facilities or other services are excellent sources of information. Background checks help the client company make sure the agency can provide quality professional services.

Creative Pitch

When the list has been narrowed to two or three finalists, the company's selection team is ready to ask for a creative pitch. Preparing a creative pitch is time-consuming and costly for the advertising agencies; therefore, agencies only want to spend time on preparing pitches with a decent chance of being accepted. It is very upsetting to spend time preparing a pitch only to find out later the company had no desire to switch agencies, but were told by upper management to solicit pitches.[10]

Although most firms narrow the list down by using the selection criteria already discussed, Lucent Technologies utilized a different method. Before choosing two or three to make a pitch for its $60 million account, the Lucent executives visited six agencies over a 2-week period. All six had met the selection criteria that had been set. The visits were made to conduct chemistry and credential checks. The idea was to see which firm would fit the best with the marketing staff at Lucent.[11]

Advertising agencies that are chosen to compete for the contract provide a formal presentation addressing a specific problem, situation, or set of questions. This is called a *shootout*. The presentations reveal how each agency would deal with specific issues that arise as a campaign is prepared. This helps a client company decide which agency best understands the issues at stake and has developed an advertising or integrated communication approach that will solve the problem or issue. When ESPA, a luxury spa treatment and beauty-product retailer in Great Britain, decided to move the company's direct marketing activities from in-house to a direct marketing agency, the management team asked the agencies involved in the pitch to produce a direct mail campaign for ESPA that would boost awareness of its range of spa-inspired products, treatments, and services.[12]

FIGURE 5.7
Pitching Do's and Don'ts

* **Do** listen. Allow the client to talk.
* **Do** your preparation. Know the client and its business.
* **Do** make a good first impression. Dress up, not down.
* **Do** a convincing job of presenting. Believe in what you are presenting.
* **Don't** assume all clients are the same. Each has a unique need.

* **Don't** try to solve the entire problem in the pitch.
* **Don't** be critical of the product or the competition.
* **Don't** overpromise. It will come back to haunt you.
* **Don't** spend a lot of time pitching credentials and references.

Source: Based on Heather Jacobs, "How to Make Sure Your Pitch Is Heard," *B&T Weekly* 57, no. 2597 (February 2, 2007), pp. 14–16.

Successful pitches do not just happen. They are the result of hard work and thorough planning. Figure 5.7 highlights some of the do's and don'ts for advertising agencies in making pitches to potential clients.

Agency Selection

During the presentation phase, the opportunity exists to meet with creatives, media buyers, account executives, and other people who will work on the account. *Chemistry* between employees of the two different firms is critical. The client companies' leaders must be convinced that they will work well together and that they will feel comfortable with each other. Chemistry can break or make the final decision.[13]

Product-specific research led to the development of this ad for Wendy's mandarin chicken salad.

When Coca-Cola put the United Kingdom business up for a pitch, the shortlist included the incumbent agency, Universal McCann, plus three other agencies. ZenithOptimedia was on the original list of possible agencies, but had to withdraw because of conflict of interests in that the company represented a competing brand. The account was to cover the Coke products of Diet Coke, Coke Zero, Sprite, Fanta, and Minute Maid. The bid went to Vizeum, because the team demonstrated during the pitch renewed thinking in key areas, particularly shopper marketing, environmental sustainability, and connecting with younger consumers in a digital age.[14]

Whenever possible, a client company's leaders should visit the advertising agency's office as part of the evaluation process. Agencies often use company executives, such as presidents or vice presidents, termed *heavy hitters* by industry insiders, to win contracts, but then turn the account over to other individuals in the agency after signing the deal. Visiting the agency's office provides an opportunity to meet personnel who might work on the account. Talking with these individuals generates quality information about how the account will be handled. The visit also can be used to hammer out specific details, such as identifying the actual person(s) who will work on the advertisements, and either agreeing to the use of freelancers (independent contractors who provide various services) to work on the project or prohibiting the agency from using such individuals.

After the selection process has been completed, the agency and the company work together to prepare the advertising campaign. Along the way, the account executive plays a key role in the process, as does the advertising creative. A brief review of the activities performed by these two individuals follows later in this chapter.

At least one thing today will exceed your expectations.

Mandarin Chicken Salad

Wendy's New Garden Sensations™   We've Raised The Bar On Salads.

ADVERTISING PLANNING AND RESEARCH

The initial meetings between the agency that has been selected and the firm's advertising management and marketing team are key moments. These meetings should be used to combine all of the advertising elements. Even then, some planning and research projects remain.

First, the agency involved should be engaged in **general preplanning input** collection. This task includes reading about the client organization in books, trade publications, research reports, and the company's Web site. Also, members of the advertising agency should, when possible, actually use the good or service involved. Also, by visiting with members of the community, employees, and other business partners, members of the advertising agency can develop a solid understanding of the client.

Next, **product-specific research** should be conducted. Two things should be identified at this point. The first is who uses this product and how is it used. It is critical to understand the typical product user, which should match with the firm's target market. In addition, how the product is used can be especially beneficial in developing a creative campaign. From this research, the agency should be able to discover the **major selling idea** that can be used in the ad campaign. The "Got milk?" theme emerged from product-specific research. Agency staff members were asked to go without milk for a week and then to report back to the creative team. The method resulted in the *deprivation approach.* The advertising agency's creative team learned that a key selling point could be to focus on how well milk fits with a person's lifestyle. Doing without it (deprivation) made people aware of the vital role milk plays in eating cereal, cookies, and other snacks and foods.

Finally, **qualitative research** is a more formal approach that can be used to assist the vendor company and its advertising agency. Focus groups are often used to bring people together to talk about a product. With a creative in attendance, it is possible to hear about the kind of person who likes a product and to discover tactics that might reach the individual. The actual collection of information can come from a variety of perspectives, including:

- Anthropology
- Sociology
- Psychology

The methods employed by *anthropologists* often involve direct observation. This helps the marketing team discover not only who is using a product, but also how it is being used. When Whirlpool employed anthropologists to study washing machines, it became clear that adult men and children also used the machines, not just the wife or mother. The researchers suggested making the controls on the units easier to use and understand for men and children, who may be less familiar with appropriate temperature and cycle settings for various kinds of fabrics.

Sociologists examine social class issues and trends. Using a sociological approach, it is clear that the market for yacht owners is primarily composed of rich, elite, and distinct people. Marketing programs are likely to focus on messages that emphasize high social class.

Psychology concentrates on motivation, cognition, and learning. When these come together, values emerge. The **values and lifestyle model (VAL)** predicts consumer behavior by concentrating on self-orientation and resources. In other words, most purchases are based on a match of lifestyle choice with funds available. A cowboy-type individual, even one who

VALS can assist Celestial Seasonings in identifying consumer groups that seek products that provide health benefits.

THIS TEA HAS MANY HEALTH BENEFITS,
NONE OF WHICH HAVE TO BE FOLLOWED BY PAGES OF POSSIBLE SIDE EFFECTS.
Since 1969, our teas have been a source of wellness, all while staying 100% natural. Celestial Seasonings Green Tea contains healthful antioxidants and antioxidants have been shown to help support a healthy heart and immune system. So, be good to yourself and enjoy a cup of our Green Tea. We guarantee you'll be able to drive a car and operate heavy machinery afterwards.

celestialseasonings.com

has moved to the city, makes purchases from western stores the person can afford, because these items reflect the individual's personal self-orientation.

Another psychological approach is called a **personal drive analysis (PDA)**. This method helps the researcher understand psychological drives toward indulgence, ambition, or individuality. These drives affect brand choices. A fine wine may be viewed as an indulgence by a consumer or as an expression of individuality. Knowing the purchasing motives of a target market can greatly enhance the effectiveness of an advertising program.

Carefully collected knowledge about the good or service and the audience for ads and advertising campaigns is crucial to success. With this information in mind, the actual campaign can be developed.

THE ROLES OF ADVERTISING ACCOUNT EXECUTIVES

The **advertising account executive** is the key go-between for both the advertising agency and the client company. This individual is actively involved in soliciting the account, finalizing details of the contract, and working with the creatives who will prepare the actual advertisements. Many times, the account executive helps the company refine and define its major message for an overall IMC program and provides other support, as needed.

Clients always want to know if they are getting a good value. Many clients believe they don't have a clue in trying to understand the relationship between an agency's cost and its actual value to the company. Ron Cox, a vice president at Wrigley Jr. Company, suggests that agencies update clients regularly on the work they are doing and the results obtained. These types of reports (called *stewardship reports*) help clients understand the process and the outcome more clearly. Updating clients on what is being done for them becomes more important as the amount being spent on advertising increases.[15]

Further, periodic reviews should be held to show that the agency is completing its work. These reviews should not be confrontational. To the client company, the updates represent the opportunity to evaluate how well the agency has done and also to become better acquainted with the personnel working on the account. As part of the process, the client firm can spend time with creatives as they work on the campaign. Client-company employees can also talk to media buyers, public relations experts, and others working on the account. In short, the account manager oversees the process in such a way that everyone involved feels comfortable and oriented toward the goal of creating an effectively integrated advertising campaign and marketing communications program.

The *traffic manager* works closely with the account executive. This person's responsibility is to schedule the various aspects of the agency's work to ensure the work is completed by the target deadline. The traffic manager serves as an important link between the account executive and the creatives.

THE ROLES OF CREATIVES

Creatives are the people who actually develop and produce advertisements. These individuals are either members of advertising agencies or freelancers. Some smaller companies provide only creative advertising services without becoming involved in other marketing programs and activities. Creatives may appear to hold the "glamour" jobs in advertising because they use many talents while producing advertisements. At the same time, creatives face long hours and work under enormous pressures to design ads that are effective and that will produce tangible results. The role of the creative is discussed in further detail in the section on creative briefs later in this chapter.

ADVERTISING CAMPAIGN MANAGEMENT

Managing an advertising campaign is the process of preparing and integrating a specific advertising program in conjunction with the overall IMC message. An effective program consists of five steps. The steps of **advertising campaign management** are:

1. Review the communication market analysis.
2. Establish advertising objectives consistent with the communication objectives developed in the promotions opportunity analysis program.
3. Review the advertising budget.
4. Select the media in conjunction with the advertising agency.
5. Prepare a creative brief.

The advertising program should be consistent with everything else in the IMC program. The idea is to make sure the firm presents a clear message to key target markets. Then, advertising efforts can be refined to gain the maximum benefit from the promotional dollars being spent. A review of the issues in each element of advertising campaign management is presented next.

COMMUNICATION MARKET ANALYSIS

In the first phase of planning, the account executive studies what the company's communication market analysis reveals (see Chapter 4). The communication analysis reveals where the firm can best focus advertising and promotional efforts by discovering company strengths along with opportunities present in the marketplace. The analysis of the various target markets and customers suggests how the firm's previous marketing communications efforts have been received by the public as well as by other businesses and potential customers. The positioning analysis explains how the firm and its products are perceived relative to the competition. The value of reviewing the communication market analysis is in focusing the account executive, the creative, and the company itself on key markets and customers, while helping them understand how the firm currently competes in the marketplace. Then the team is better able to establish and pursue specific advertising objectives.

For the purposes of advertising, two important items are outlined as part of the communication market analysis:

1. The media usage habits of people in the target market
2. The media used by the competition

When analyzing customers, knowing which media they use is vitally important. For example, teenagers surf the Web and watch television. Only a small percentage reads newspapers and news magazines. Various market segments have differences in when and how they view various media. For example, older African Americans watch television programs in patterns that are different from those of older Caucasians. Males watch more sports programs than females, and so forth.

In business-to-business markets, knowing which trade journals or business publications the various members of the buying center most likely read is essential for the development of a print advertising campaign. Engineers, who tend to be the influencers, have different media viewing habits than do vice presidents, who may be the deciders. Discovering which media reach a target market (and which do not) is a key component in a communication market analysis and an advertising program.

A component of the communication analysis is understanding the media usage habits of the product's target market.

Source: Courtesy of Summer Bradley.

FIGURE 5.8
Advertising Goals

◆ To build brand image	◆ To support other marketing efforts
◆ To inform	◆ To encourage action
◆ To persuade	

Further, studying the competition reveals how other firms attempt to reach customers. Knowing how other firms contact consumers is as important as knowing what they say. An effective communication market analysis reveals this information, so that more effective messages and advertising campaigns can be designed.

ADVERTISING GOALS

The second step of advertising planning is to establish and clarify advertising goals, which are derived from the firm's overall communication objectives. Several advertising goals are central to the IMC process. Some of these goals are listed in Figure 5.8. A discussion of each individual goal area follows.[16]

Building Brand Image

Building a strong global brand and corporate image is one of the most important advertising goals. A strong brand creates brand equity. As described in Chapter 2, brand equity is a set of characteristics that make a brand different and better to both consumers and businesses. These benefits can be enhanced when they combine effective advertising with quality products. Higher levels of brand equity are a distinct advantage as consumers make purchase decisions.

Advertising is a critical component of building brand equity. Successful brands possess two characteristics: (1) the top of mind and (2) the consumers' top choice. When consumers are asked to identify brands that quickly come to mind from a product category, one or two particular brands are nearly always mentioned. These names are the **top of mind brands**. For example, when asked to identify fast-food restaurants, McDonald's and Burger King almost always head the list. The same is true for Nike and Reebok athletic shoes. This is true not only in the United States, but also in many other countries. The term **top choice** suggests exactly what the term implies: A top choice brand is the first or second pick when a consumer reviews his or her evoked set of possible purchasing alternatives.

One of the initial parts of building brand image and brand equity is developing brand awareness. Advertising is the best method to reach that goal. Brand awareness means the consumers recognize and remember a particular brand or company name when they consider purchasing options. Brand awareness, brand image, and brand equity are vital for success.

In business-to-business marketing, brand awareness is essential to being considered by members of the buying center. It is important for business customers to recognize the brand name(s) of the various goods or services a company sells. Brand awareness is especially important in modified rebuy situations, when a firm looks to change to a new vendor or evaluates a product that has not been purchased recently. In new buy situations, members of

Campbell's Soups builds on its brand name to market a new product.

the buying center spend more time seeking prospective vendors than they do in modified rebuys. Consequently, brand equity is a major advantage for any company that has such recognition.

Providing Information

Besides building brand recognition and equity, advertising serves other goals. For example, advertising often is used to provide information to both consumers and business buyers. Typical information for consumers includes a retailer's store hours, business location, or sometimes more detailed product specifications. Information can make the purchasing process appear to be convenient and relatively simple, which can entice customers to finalize the purchasing decision and travel to the store.

For business-to-business situations, information from some ads leads various members of the buying center to consider a particular company as they examine their options. This type of information is most useful when members of the buying center are in the information search stage of the purchasing process. For high-involvement types of purchases, in which members of the buying center have strong vested interests in the success of the choice, informative advertisements are the most beneficial. Low-involvement decisions usually do not require as much detail.

In marketing to both consumers and other businesses, information can help those involved reach a decision. Information is one component of persuasion, another objective of various advertising programs.

Persuasion

Another common advertising goal is persuasion. Advertisements can convince consumers that a particular brand is superior. Ads can show consumers the negative consequences of failing to use a particular brand. Changing consumer attitudes and persuading them to consider a new purchasing choice is a challenging task. Advertisers can utilize several methods of persuasion, which will be described in a later chapter. Persuasive advertising is used more in consumer marketing than in business-to-business situations. Persuasion techniques are used more frequently in broadcast media such as television and radio rather than in print advertising.

Supporting Marketing Efforts

Advertising can be used to support other marketing functions. Manufacturers use advertising to support trade and consumer promotions, such as theme packaging or combination offers. Contests, such as the McDonald's Monopoly promotion, require extensive advertising to be effective. Retailers also use advertising to support marketing programs. Any type of special sale (white sale, buy-one-get-one-free, pre–Christmas sale) requires effective advertising to attract customers to the store. Both manufacturers and retail outlets run advertisements in conjunction with coupons or other special offers. Del Monte placed a 30-cent coupon in the advertisement shown in this section. The ad highlights a smaller-size container with a pull-top lid. These features match the ad's target market: senior citizens. The first magazine featuring this advertisement was *Modern Maturity.*

A Del Monte advertisement directed to senior customers offering a smaller size can with a pull-off lid.

Weight loss goods and services tend to be advertised using flighting advertising budget schedules.

Manufacturer coupons are regularly redeemed at grocery stores (sometimes at double their face values), and in-store coupons are part of many retail store print advertisements. When ads are combined with other marketing efforts into a larger, more integrated effort revolving around a theme, the program is called a **promotional campaign**.

Encouraging Action

Many firms set behavioral goals for advertising programs. A television commercial that encourages viewers to take action by dialing a toll-free number to make a quick purchase is an example. Everything from Veg-O-Matics to DVDs is sold using action tactics. Infomercials and home shopping network programs heavily rely on immediate consumer purchasing responses.

Action-oriented advertising is likely to be used in the business-to-business sector. When it is, often the goal is to generate sales leads. Many business advertisements provide Web addresses or telephone numbers that buyers can use to request more information or more easily make a purchase.

The five advertising goals of building image, providing information, being persuasive, supporting other marketing efforts, and encouraging action are not separate ideas. They work together in key ways. Image and information are part of persuasion. The key advertising management objective is to emphasize one goal without forgetting the others.

THE ADVERTISING BUDGET

Once the company, account manager, and creative agree on the major goals of the advertising campaign, a review of the communications budget is in order. In Chapter 4, various methods for establishing marketing communication budgets were described. After the total dollars allocated to advertising have been established, account managers and company leaders agree to uses for the funds. This includes the media to be utilized (television versus newspaper versus billboards) and the manner of distribution. Three basic tactics are:

- Pulsating schedule
- Flighting schedule
- Continuous schedule

The **pulsating schedule of advertising** involves continuous advertising with bursts of higher intensity (more ads in more media) during the course of the year, most notably during peak seasons. Companies can also select what is called a **flighting** approach or schedule, whereby ads are presented only during peak times, and not at all during off seasons.

Firms will often advertise during peak seasons such as Christmas, sending out the message when customers are most inclined to buy. When consumers are on the "hot spot," this approach makes sense for some products. For example, Weight Watchers, Diet Centers, and others advertise heavily during the first 2 weeks of January. Many New Year's resolutions include going on a diet.

Deciding to advertise during slow sales seasons is essentially oriented toward "drumming up business" when people do not regularly buy. In retail sales, slow seasons occur during January and February. Some companies advertise more during those periods to sell merchandise left over from the Christmas season and to encourage customers to shop. They also realize that many retailers are not advertising so the hope is that the ads will be noticed.

Many marketing experts believe it is best to advertise in level amounts, particularly when a product purchase is essentially a "random" event. This approach is a **continuous campaign schedule**. For example, many durable goods, such as washing machines and refrigerators, are purchased on an "as needed" basis. A family ordinarily buys a new washing machine only when the old one breaks down. Consequently, level advertising increases the odds that the buyer will remember a given name (e.g., Kenmore, Whirlpool, or General Electric). Also, there is a better chance that consumers will be exposed to ads close to the time they are ready to make purchases.

In any case, the objective should be to match the pacing of advertisements with the message, the media, and the nature of the product. Some media make it easier to advertise for longer periods of time. For instance, contracts for billboards are normally for a month or a year. They can be rotated throughout a town or city to present a continuing message about the company or its products. Budgetary constraints must also be incorporated into the strategies and tactics used in the advertising program.

MEDIA SELECTION

The next step of advertising management is to develop strategies and tactics for media selection. First, the marketing team examines the intent of the message in each specific ad. It is crucial to convey messages that are both consistent with the firm's IMC theme and that match with various media. Media buys are guided by the advertising agency or media agency, the company, and the creative. In Chapters 8 through 10, the advantages and disadvantages of various traditional and nontraditional advertising media are described. When media selection is performed correctly and messages are designed to fit with the chosen media, the chances for success greatly increase. When these issues are well coordinated, a company creates a major competitive advantage. Coordination efforts are largely outlined and described in the creative brief, which is the final element of the advertisement management program.

THE CREATIVE BRIEF

Typically, creatives work with a document called a *creative strategy* or *creative brief* as they prepare advertisements. The basic components of a creative brief are provided in Figure 5.9. The creative takes the information provided by the account executive and others in the creative brief to produce ads that convey the desired message. Details about each element of the creative brief are provided next.

The Objective

The first step in preparing the creative strategy is to identify the objective of the advertisement. Some of the most common advertising objectives include:

- Increasing brand awareness
- Building brand image

◆ The objective	◆ The support
◆ The target audience	◆ The constraints
◆ The message theme	

FIGURE 5.9
The Creative Brief

- Increasing customer traffic
- Increasing retailer or wholesaler orders
- Responding to inquiries from end users and channel members
- Providing information

The creative must understand the main objective before designing an advertisement. The objectives guide the design of the advertisement and the choice of an executional framework. An ad to increase brand awareness prominently displays the *name* of the product. An ad to build brand image can display the *actual product* more prominently.

The Target Audience

A creative must know the target audience. An advertisement designed to persuade a business to inquire about new computer software will be different from a consumer advertisement created by the same company. The business advertisement should focus on the type of industry and a specific member of the buying center. The more detail that is known about the target audience, the easier it is for a creative to design an effective advertisement.

Target market profiles that are too general are not very helpful. Rather than specifying males, ages 20 to 35, more specific information is needed (e.g., males, ages 20 to 35, college educated, professionals). Other information such as hobbies, interests, opinions, and lifestyles makes targeting an advertisement even more precise. Notice that the Playtex

An advertisement by Playtex using additional target market profile information to design a message directed to active teenagers and young adult females.

A milk industry advertisement illustrating the importance of maintaining a consistent theme over time.

advertisement in this section is designed for young females who enjoy playing sports and have active lifestyles. The additional information helped create an advertisement that appeals to this particular market segment of females.

The Message Theme

The message theme is an outline of key idea(s) that the advertising program is supposed to convey. The message theme is the benefit or promise the advertiser wants to use to reach consumers or businesses. The promise, or *unique selling point*, should describe the major benefit the good or service offers customers. For example, the message theme for an automobile could be oriented toward luxury, safety, fun, fuel efficiency, or driving excitement. The message theme for a hotel could focus on luxury, price, or unusual features, such as a hotel in Paris, France, noting the ease of access to all of the nearby tourist attractions. The message theme should match the medium selected, the target market, and the primary IMC message.[17]

Notice the advertisement for milk featuring Sarah Michelle Gellar in this section. The theme that milk provides the calcium for strong bones is consistently used in a number of "Got milk?" advertisements, as is the visual display of the white mustache. Although the model and context change, the theme is consistent.

Message themes can be oriented toward either rational or emotional processes. A "left-brain" ad is oriented toward the logical, rational side, which manages information such as numbers, letters, words, and concepts. Left-brain advertising is logical and factual, and the appeals are rational. For example, there are logical features that are part of the decision to buy a car (size, price, special features). At the same time, many cars are purchased for emotional reasons. The right side of the brain deals with the emotions. It works with abstract ideas, images, and feelings. A car may be chosen for its color, sportiness, or other less rational reasons.

Most advertising focuses on either the right-brain or left-brain. Advertising can also be effective by balancing the two sides. Rational, economic beings have difficulty defending the purchase of an expensive sports car such as a Porsche. Many product purchases are based on how a person feels about the good or service, combined with rational information.[18]

The Support

The fourth component of the creative strategy is the support. **Support** takes the form of the facts that substantiate the message theme. A pain reliever advertising claim of being effective for arthritis might support this point by noting independent medical findings or testimonials from patients with arthritis. Notice the support claims Pearle Vision makes in its advertisement in this section. The microTHINS are 30 percent thinner, 40 percent lighter, 4 times more scratch resistant, 10 times more impact resistant, antireflective, and have 99.9 percent UV protection. The creative needs these supporting facts to design effective advertisements.

The Constraints

The final step in the development of a creative strategy is identification of any **constraints**. These can be legal and mandatory restrictions placed on advertisements. Constraints include legal protections for trademarks, logos, and copy registrations.

Constraints also include disclaimers about warranties, offers, and claims. For warranties, a disclaimer specifies the conditions under which they will be honored. For example, tire warranties often state that they apply *under normal driving*

An advertisement by Pearle Vision with support information provided to substantiate the message claim.

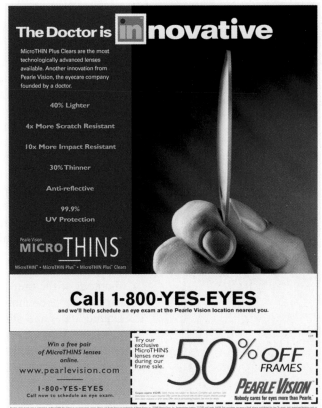

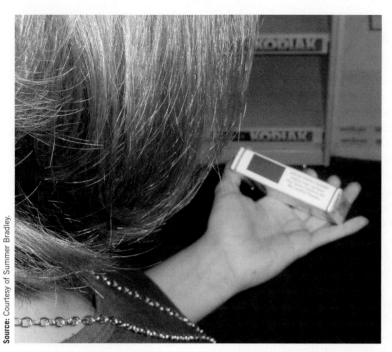

The Surgeon General's warning is an example of a constraint.

conditions with routine maintenance, so that a person cannot ignore tire balancing and rotation and expect to get free new tires when the old ones wear out quickly. Disclaimer warranties notify consumers of potential hazards associated with products. For instance, tobacco advertisements must contain a statement from the Surgeon General about the dangers of smoking and chewing tobacco. Disclaimers about offers spell out the terms of financing agreements, as well as when bonuses or discounts apply. Claims identify the exact nature of the statement made in the advertisement. This includes nutritional claims as well as statements about serving sizes and other information describing the nutrients that are actually in the product.

After these steps have been reviewed, the creative brief is complete. From this point forward, the message and the media match, and actual advertisements can be produced. Effective creative briefs take the overall IMC message and tailor it to a specific advertising campaign. This, in turn, gives companies better chances of reaching customers with messages that return measurable results and help guarantee the success of both the company and the advertising agency.

When the creative brief has been completed, the design of the campaign should move forward at a solid pace. Recent research suggests that campaigns designed in 2 months or less have the greatest likelihood of being "highly effective." Those that take longer tend not to be as effective. The goal is to move forward without rushing. Campaigns designed in 2 weeks or less are more likely to be ineffective as well.[19]

INTERNATIONAL IMPLICATIONS

Two major differences emerge when advertising management is considered from an international perspective. The first is in regard to the process itself. The second concerns preparing international advertising campaigns.

The general processes used to prepare advertising campaigns are fairly uniform. Some of the most important differences are in the areas of availability of qualified advertising agencies and how those agencies are selected. For example, in many Asian cultures the beginning of a face-to-face meeting would include an exchange of gifts. Also, business cards have differing uses and meanings across cultures. In some countries, cards are only presented to highly trusted allies. In others, they are freely passed out. The marketing team in any company would be well advised to carefully study the nuances of business meetings, including the use of formal titles, eye contact, who speaks first, and other variables, before beginning a relationship with an advertising agency in another country.

Agencies in other countries might not carefully follow typical procedures such as a shootout or the preparation of a creative brief. Forms of preplanning research may also vary. In some countries, it is not possible to conduct the same types of research as in the United States and other more Western cultures.

Advertising campaigns that are designed for an international audience require an understanding of the various languages that might be involved. In Europe, French, Spanish, Portuguese, Italian, and other languages would require translation and back-translation of advertising themes and messages to make certain the idea can be clearly presented in various countries. Media selection processes may also require adjustment; some countries have state-run television networks and others place restrictions on what can be shown in an advertisement.

A cultural assimilator is a must in the area of international advertising campaign management. This individual should provide information both about business customs and about media differences as the advertising campaign is being developed.

SUMMARY

Effective advertising requires matching a noticeable message with appropriate media. Every aspect of a company's activities, including company business cards, stationery, brochures, advertisements, and commercials, should spell out the organization's identity and image. The goal of an IMC program is to make sure that all of these elements speak with the same voice. Customers must clearly understand the nature of the company, its goods and services, and its methods of doing business.

This chapter reviews the advertising management process. Effective advertising is more likely to occur when the firm has a well-defined mission statement and targets its energies in the direction of creating goods or services to meet the needs of a target market. Then an integrated marketing communications program can build on the central theme pursued by those in the firm.

Advertising management begins with deciding whether an in-house department or group should develop advertisements or whether an external advertising agency should be retained. When choosing an external agency, the company's leaders establish clear steps to lead to the best chance that the optimal agency will be selected. The steps include: (1) spelling out and prioritizing organizational goals, (2) carefully establishing quality selection criteria, (3) screening firms based on those criteria, (4) requesting references from firms that are finalists, (5) performing background checks, (6) requesting creative pitches, (7) making an on-site visit to get to know those in the agency, and (8) offering and finalizing a contract.

Common selection criteria used in selecting agencies include: (1) the size of the agency matching the size of the company, (2) relevant experience, (3) no conflicts of interest, (4) production capabilities, (5) quality creative capabilities, (6) suitable media purchasing skills, (7) other services that can be rendered as

needed, (8) client retention rates, and (9) a good chemistry between those in the company and those in the agency. Carefully utilizing these criteria increases the odds of a match between the company and the agency, which increases the chance of success.

Within the advertising agency, the account manager performs the functions of soliciting accounts, finalizing contracts, and selecting creatives to prepare advertising campaigns. Account executives are go-betweens who mediate between the agency and the client company. Account executives also help client organizations refine their IMC messages and programs.

Creatives prepare advertisements and are guided by the creative brief. This document spells out: (1) the objective of the promotional campaign, (2) the target audience, (3) the message theme, (4) the support, and (5) the constraints. The message theme is an outline of the key idea(s) that the program is supposed to convey. The constraints include logos, warranties, disclaimers, or legal statements that are part of various advertisements.

The creative, account executive, and company should agree about which media to use in a campaign. Media are selected based on costs, types of messages, target market characteristics, and other criteria . The creatives then complete the final elements of the ad, and the campaign is prepared.

Advertising management is an important ingredient in the success of an integrated marketing communications program. A quality ad that garners the attention of people in the target audience, makes a key memorable point, and moves buyers to action is difficult to prepare. At the same time, company officials and market account executives know that designing effective ads with tangible results is a challenging but necessary activity. It is important to go through every step of the process carefully to help the company achieve its marketing goals in both the short and long term.

KEY TERMS

message theme   An outline of key idea(s) that the advertising program is supposed to convey.

leverage point   The key element in the advertisement that taps into, or activates, a consumer's personal value system (a value, idea, or concept).

appeal   How the leverage point and executional theme combine to attract attention through humor, fear, sexual suggestiveness, rational logic, or some other method.

executional framework   How the message will be delivered (musically, visually, verbally, written statements, etc.).

advertising management program   The process of preparing and integrating a company's advertising efforts with the overall IMC message.

general preplanning input   The task of studying a client organization by the advertising agency, from a rich set of sources, to gain understanding and background before preparing an advertising campaign.

product-specific research   Research that identifies information about a good or service and the major selling idea to be used in the advertising campaign.

major selling idea   The primary message concerning the good or service benefits to be transmitted to consumers in an advertising campaign.

qualitative research   Collecting subjective information and opinions about a company, its products, and services, often through the use of focus groups.

values and lifestyle model (VAL)   Research designed to predict consumer behavior by understanding self-orientation and resources.

personal drive analysis (PDA)   A model that helps the researcher understand individual psychological drives toward indulgence, ambition, or individuality, which affect brand choices.

advertising account executive   The key go-between for both the advertising agency and the client company.

creatives   The people who actually develop and produce advertisements.

advertising campaign management   The process of preparing and integrating a specific advertising program in conjunction with the overall IMC message.

top of mind brand   The brand that is nearly always mentioned when consumers are asked to identify brands that quickly come to mind from a product category.

top choice   The first or second pick when a consumer reviews his or her evoked set of possible purchasing alternatives.

promotional campaign   Combining advertisements with other marketing efforts into a larger, more integrated effort revolving around a central idea or theme.

pulsating schedule of advertising   Continuous advertising with bursts of higher intensity (more ads in more media) during the course of the year.

flighting schedule of advertising   A schedule whereby companies present ads only during specific times and not at all during other times of the year.

continuous campaign schedule of advertising   When the company advertises in level amounts throughout the year.

support   The facts that substantiate the unique selling point of a creative brief.

constraints   The company, legal, and mandatory restrictions placed on advertisements. They include legal protection for trademarks, logos, and copy registrations.

REVIEW QUESTIONS

1. What is a message theme? What role does a message theme play in an advertising campaign?
2. Define advertising management. What are the four main steps involved?
3. What is the relationship between advertising and the overall IMC process?
4. What three main company activities are involved in the advertising management process? What role does the company's mission play in this process?
5. What criteria can be used to help a company decide between an in-house advertising group and hiring an external advertising agency?
6. Besides advertising agencies, what other types of organizations play roles in the communication process?
7. What steps should be taken in selecting an advertising agency?
8. What evaluation criteria should be used in selecting an advertising agency?
9. How important is interpersonal chemistry in selecting an advertising agency?
10. Describe the roles that general planning input, product-specific research, and qualitative research play in the development of an advertising campaign.
11. What three academic disciplines can play a role in advertising research? What unique contribution does each discipline make to understanding consumers and the marketplace?
12. Describe the role of an advertising agency account executive.
13. Describe the role of the advertising creative.
14. What are the steps of an advertising campaign management process? What other process is similar in nature?
15. Describe the elements of a creative brief.

CRITICAL THINKING EXERCISES

Discussion Questions

1. Go to a magazine that you read on a regular basis. Look through the advertisements. Examine the first 10 ads in the magazine to identify the major selling point. Was the major selling idea clear or was it difficult to ascertain?
2. The deprivation approach was used by the milk industry to encourage people not to forget milk. For what other products could the deprivation approach be used? Pick one of the products you have identified and describe how you would use the deprivation approach to advertise the product.
3. Print off or open the textbook to Figure 5.8, the list of advertising goals. Create a table with three columns. In the first column you will record the brand being advertised. In the

second column you will write down which advertising goal you think the ad was designed to meet. In the third column you will assign a score based on your evaluation of each ad's effectiveness, with 10 being effective and 1 being completely ineffective. Once you have created the table, watch a 1-hour television program and record and evaluate every commercial you see. When you are finished, write a paragraph discussing which goals were used the most and which ads were the most effective at accomplishing their goal.

4. Follow the instructions given in Question 3, but instead of a television program do it for a group of 20 advertisements in a magazine. Be sure the ads are in a sequence and not ones that you randomly picked or chose.

5. Choose one of the following. Using the information in this chapter, prepare a creative brief. You can pick a brand from within the product category.
   a. Energy drink
   b. Frozen apple juice
   c. Fast food restaurant
   d. Museum
   e. Dress shoes

INTEGRATED LEARNING EXERCISES

1. Making the decision to use an external advertising agency as opposed to an in-house program for advertising or some other aspect of the advertising function is difficult. Access the American Association of Advertising Agencies (**www.aaaa.org**). From the "News and Information" section, examine articles that might help identify benefits of using an advertising agency. What type of information is available at this Web site?

2. A number of agencies assist business organizations with integrated marketing communication programs. Whereas some firms try to provide a wide array of services, others are more specialized. Access the following association Web sites. What type of information is available on each site? How would the information provided be useful in building an IMC program?
   a. Council of Public Relations Firms (**www.prfirms.org**)
   b. Promotion Marketing Association (**www.pmalink.org**)
   c. Outdoor Advertising Association of America (**www.oaaa.org**)
   d. Direct Marketing Association (**www.the-dma.org**)

3. Part of a communication marketing analysis includes understanding the media usage habits of consumers and their attitudes toward various media. An excellent source of information in Canada is the Media Awareness Network at **www.media-awareness.ca**. Review the types of information available at the Web site. Examine the news articles. What type of information is available at this Web site and how could it be used in developing an advertising campaign?

4. Many advertisers tend to direct ads toward the right side of the brain and develop advertisements based entirely on emotions, images, and pictures. Companies often advertise auto parts and tools with a scantily clad woman to attract the attention of men. The woman has nothing to do with the product, but garners attention. The rationale for using a sexy woman is that if consumers like her, they will like the product and then purchase that brand. Effective advertisements integrate elements from both the left side of the brain as well as the right. They contain elements that appeal to emotions but also have rational arguments. A laundry detergent can be advertised as offering the rational benefit of getting clothes cleaner but also contain the emotional promise that your mother-in-law will think more favorably of you. For each of the following Internet sites, discuss the balance of left-brain versus right-brain advertising appeal.
   a. Pier 1 Imports (**http://www.pier1.com**)
   b. Pig O' My Heart Potbellies (**www.potbellypigs.com**)
   c. Dark Dog (**www.darkdog.com**)
   d. Discount Cheerleading.com (**www.discountcheerleading.com**)
   e. Backcountry.com (**www.backcountry.com**)

5. You have been asked to select an advertising agency to handle an account for Red Lobster, a national restaurant chain. Your advertising budget is $30 million. Study the Web sites of the following advertising agencies. Follow the selection steps outlined in the chapter. Narrow the list down to two agencies and justify your decision. Then choose between the two agencies and justify your choice.
   a. DDB Worldwide Communications Group (**www.ddb.com**)
   b. Leo Burnett (**www.leoburnett.com**)
   c. BBDO Worldwide (**www.bbdo.com**)
   d. Lucas Design & Advertising (**www.aladv.com**)
   e. Grey Global Group (**www.grey.com**)
   f. Bozell Advertising (**www.bozell.com**)

6. A marketing manager has been placed in charge of a new brand of jeans to be introduced into the market. The company's corporate headquarters are in Atlanta, and the firm's management team has already decided to use one of the local advertising agencies. Two primary objectives in choosing an agency are: (1) the agency must have the capability to develop a strong brand name and (2) the agency must be able to help with business-to-business marketing to place the jeans into retail stores. Access Atlanta Advertising Agencies at **www.AtlantaAdAgencies.com**. Follow the steps outlined in the chapter to narrow the list to three agencies. Then design a project for the agencies to prepare as part of an oral and written presentation to the company's marketing team.

STUDENT PROJECT

Creative Corner

Use the following creative brief for this exercise.

Creative Brief for Ford Motor Company

Product:	Ford Mustang.
Objective:	To reverse lagging sales.
Target audience:	25- to 35-year-old consumers, split evenly between males and females, college educated, with annual incomes of approximately $40,000. Psychographically, the targeted market is a group known as *individualists*. They tend not to buy mainstream products. In automobile selection, they place greater emphasis on design elements, distinctiveness, and utility.
Message theme:	An automobile is like a fashion accessory. A car is selected because of the statement it makes to others.

---

1. As an account executive for an advertising agency, discuss the creative brief in terms of completeness of information provided and whether the objective is realistic. What additional information should the Ford Motor Company provide before a creative can begin working on the account?

2. The media planner for the Ford Mustang account suggests a media plan consisting of cable television, print advertising, Internet ads, and network advertising on Fox shows *The OC, House, 24, The Simpsons*, and *King of the Hill*. Evaluate this media plan in light of the creative brief's objectives. Can these shows reach the target audience?

What information does a creative and the account executive want from the media planner before starting work on actual commercials?

3. From the viewpoint of the creative assigned to this account, do the creative brief and the media plan (see Question 2) contain sufficient information to design a series of advertisements? What, if any, additional information is necessary?

4. Using the information provided in the creative brief, prepare a magazine advertisement. Which magazines might match the target audience?

CASE 1 ADVERTISING STEW

Luis Arroyo was about to begin the most exciting job assignment of his life. He had been named the brand manager for the Dinty Moore Beef Stew line of products, which is sold by Hormel Foods. His first assignment was to develop an advertising campaign for the entire line, which would be produced in the summer. The ads were scheduled to run on a pulsating schedule, with the first burst commencing in October.

The Dinty Moore brand has been in existence since 1935. Canned products in the line include Beef Stew, Chicken & Dumplings, Chicken Noodle, Chicken Stew, Meatball Stew, and Turkey Stew. A second, current set of products are microwaveable, featuring Beef Stew (7.5 ounce cup), Beef Stew (10 ounce tray), Chicken & Dumplings (7.5 ounce cup), Noodles & Chicken (7.5 ounce cup), Rice with Chicken (7.5 ounce cup), and Scalloped Potatoes & Ham (7.5 ounce cup).

The Dinty Moore page of Hormel's Web site states that its name is, "Synonymous not only with beef stew, but with a convenient and satisfying meal. Through innovations in packaging, we've made it even easier for you to enjoy by offering cups and trays for microwave cooking. And while convenience is definitely the order of the day, Dinty Moore stew meets the standards of contemporary shoppers because it has no preservatives and only 240 calories per eight-ounce serving."

Health consciousness is a major trend in the food market. Consumers are concerned about the fat, sodium, and calorie content of the foods they purchase. The Dinty Moore line clearly meets standards set by the Food and Drug Administration; however, it is possible that food producers will be required to provide more information about products in the future.

The primary competitors in the canned beef stew marketplace can be placed into four major categories:

1. Direct competitors
2. Substitute products
3. Other foods made at home
4. Restaurants

Direct competitors include Castleberry's and Armour. Both companies offer directly competing cans of stew as well as others that might compete with the Dinty Moore Line. For example, Armour offers a line of chili and chili beans. Castleberry sells barbeque pork and canned tamales through its American Originals line.

Substitute products are sold by Campbell's and other soup manufacturers. Soup can easily be substituted for stew. Also, a series of private label stews are available.

Home cooking presents an additional source of competition. Many health food trends include cooking at home with natural ingredients. Many consumers now enjoy creating meals at home as a form of social activity and relaxation.

Many restaurants vend products that compete with both homemade and canned stew. The most threatening competitors are restaurants featuring home-style, hearty foods.

Source: Courtesy of Kenneth Clow.

Dinty Moore Stew meets the standards of contemporary shoppers because it has no preservatives and only 240 calories per eight-ounce serving.

Luis decided that he needed more information before moving forward with the advertising campaign. He wanted to know more about the role price plays in purchasing decisions as well as consumers' perceptions of the quality of the Dinty Moore line as compared to Armour and Castleberry's. He also sought information about consumer promotions, especially coupons and price-off programs. He also wanted to investigate possibilities for cooperative advertising with grocery stores as well as tie-ins with other food products. He wanted to begin a new era in his company, where Dinty Moore moved to the strongest position in the marketplace as the top of mind and top choice brand.

Sources: **www.hormelfoods.com**, **www.castelberrys.com**, and **www.pinnaclefoodscorp.com** (accessed January 4, 2008).

1. Should Luis look to hire an external advertising agency or perform most of the tasks in-house? Why?

2. If an external agency is chosen, what relevant experiences would be most helpful to Luis and the Dinty Moore brand?

3. What types of advertising planning and research should be conducted to identify Dinty Moore's most loyal customers and potential new customers?

4. Design a creative brief for the upcoming Dinty Moore advertising campaign.

5. Using the list of advertising agencies provided under Question 5 of the Integrated Learning Exercises and the procedure outlined in this chapter, choose an outside advertising agency for the Dinty Moore account. Justify your selection.

HOW TO WIN (AND LOSE) AN ADVERTISING ACCOUNT

CASE 2

Being selected to manage a major advertising account is a difficult but enriching process. For instance, consider the case of Atlanta-based Charter Behavioral Systems. Charter is the largest provider of alcoholism and depression treatment services in the United States. The goal was to select an agency to handle a $20 million television advertising account. Charter identified some basic goals and developed a selection process that included the criteria to use in the screening process. The six agencies identified for initial screening were McCann Erickson, BBDO, Rubin Postaer, Carat ICG, Tauche Martin, and Bates USA. The initial screening process was based on the following items:

- Size
- Capabilities
- Credentials and references
- Documented experience and past successes

Tauche Martin was dropped from the list because it was too small. Although the management team at Charter believed the staff at Tauche Martin consisted of some very bright people, the size of the account would have overwhelmed the firm. Bates USA was rejected, because Bates' major client was Korean. A recent lag in the Asian economy caused the leaders of Charter to fear that Bates might be forced to close its Atlanta office if it lost its Korean client. Charter eliminated another agency based on reference checks. From television station reps to media buyers, the consistent word was "run!" At the end of the initial screening process, two agencies remained: Rubin Postaer and Carat ICG.

Rubin Postaer is a $550 million full-service agency based in Los Angeles. The firm is known primarily for work with Honda, Charles Schwab, and *Discover* magazine. Carat ICG is a $600 million agency with clients such as Ameritech, Midas, Primestar, and DHL Worldwide.

To decide between Rubin Postaer and Carat ICG, Charter asked each to make a creative pitch addressing a series of 10 questions. They were further instructed to think of it as a "mock buy" in the Atlanta market. The companies were asked to provide their projected list of media buys and the rationale for the buys. The most challenging aspect of the creative pitch requirement was a roundtable discussion with at least five of the agency's media buyers. Although each agency's management team could be present, the managers were told not to answer questions posed to the buyers.

Carat ICG included employees in the final presentation who were not going to be part of the account team. Although Charter's management team felt that it was flattering to have Carat ICG's chairman present for the 3-hour presentation, Charter believed ICG's approach was more of a sales presentation than a mock media buy.

ICG demonstrated a solid command of the strategies the agency believed Charter should use in the Atlanta market. Unfortunately, ICG skimped on some logistical details. Charter's leaders also thought that when ICG presented the mock buy, its representatives were quick, superficial, and had not spent a great deal of time laying out a total approach. On the positive side, ICG's senior vice president Jim Surmanek led the agency's presentation. Surmanek, the author of a media textbook, knew the media issues extremely well. In the final evaluation, Charter concluded ICG clearly was superior at developing an advertising strategy. The agency's recommendations highlighted the company's deep understanding of Charter's business.

In contrast, Rubin Postaer made a presentation using employees who would be servicing the account. Chairman Jerry Rubin did not attend the meeting, although he did meet with Charter's management briefly to assure them of his commitment. Charter felt Rubin Postaer made a serious mistake during the presentation. The presentation team did not bring in a buyer for the direct-response media. ICG did. At the same time, Rubin's vice president of spot buying, Cathleen Campe, grasped quickly what was most important. Campe flew in buyers from Chicago, New York, and Los Angeles to assist in the presentation. These buyers spoke often, expressing their views. Charter concluded that Rubin was more powerful in "branding" its media style with a label called "active negotiation." Rubin's basic philosophy was that the toughest negotiations begin after buying the media time. Rubin made the claim that the agency was willing to spend more time monitoring media purchases than making the actual purchases. This advantage was substantiated by all of the references.

1. Which agency should Charter Behavioral Systems hire? Justify your answer.
2. Should Carat ICG do anything differently the next time company representatives make a presentation? Why or why not?
3. Should Rubin Postaer do anything differently the next time the firm makes a presentation? Why or why not?
4. Should "fuzzy" variables such as trust and confidence be the deciding factor in choosing an advertising agency? Why or why not?

Source: Michael Alvear, "On the Spot," *Mediaweek* 8, no. 13 (March 30, 1998), pp. 26–28.

ENDNOTES

1. Perfect Pushup (**www.perfectpushup.com**, accessed January 3, 2008); *The Big Idea with Donnie Deutsch*, September 4, 2007.
2. Based on Charles F. Frazier, "Creative Strategies: A Management Perspective," *Journal of Advertising* 12, no. 4 (1983), pp. 36–41.
3. Paul Mlodzik, "An Inside Job," *Communication World* 21, no. 5 (September–October 2004), pp. 22–27.
4. Al Ries, "Should Your Ads Be an Inside Job?" *Sales and Marketing Management* 147, no. 2 (February 1995), pp. 26–27.
5. G+G Advertising (**www.gng.net**, accessed January 4, 2008); "Ad Firm's Focus: Native Americans," *Editor & Publisher* 132, no. 28 (July 10, 1999), p. 28.
6. Beth Snyder and Laurel Wentz, "Whole Egg Theory Finally Fits the Bill for Y&R Clients,"
   Advertising Age 70, no. 4 (July 25, 1999), pp. 12–13.
7. Norma Ramage, "Calgary's Excellent Ad-Venture," *Marketing Magazine* 109, no. 26 (November 22, 2004), p. 26.
8. James Zoltak and Aaron Baar, "Norwest–Wells Fargo to DDB," *Adweek Western Edition* 49, no. 19 (May 10, 1999), p. 50.
9. Ibid.

10. Heather Jacobs, "How to Make Sure Your Pitch Is Heard," *B&T Weekly* 57, no. 2597 (February 8, 2007), pp. 14–16.

11. Andrew McMains, "Six to Pitch for $60 Mil. Account," *Adweek Midwest Edition* 41, no. 15 (April 10, 2000), p. 125.

12. "Spa Company ESPA in DM Agency Hunt," *Campaign (UK)*, November 2, 2007, p. 3.

13. Jacobs, "How to Make Sure Your Pitch Is Heard."

14. Jemima Bokaie, "Coca-Cola Appoints Vizeum," *Marketing*, November 7, 2007, p. 6.

15. Laura Petrecca, "Agencies Urged to Show the Worth of Their Work," *Advertising Age* 68, no. 15 (April 14, 1997), pp. 3–4.

16. Robert J. Lavidge and Gary A. Steiner, "A Model for Predictive Measurements of Advertising Effectiveness," *Journal of Marketing* 24 (October 1961), pp. 59–62.

17. Henry A. Laskey and Richard J. Fox, "The Relationship Between Advertising Message Strategy and Television Commercial Effectiveness," *Journal of Advertising Research* 35, no. 2 (March–April 1995), pp. 31–39.

18. Herbert E. Krugman, "Memory Without Recall, Exposure Without Perception," *Journal of Advertising Research* 40, no. 6 (November–December 2000), pp. 49–55; David Kay, "Left Brain Versus Right Brain," *Marketing Magazine* 108, no. 36 (October 27, 2003), p. 37.

19. "Picking up the Pace," *Marketing News* 36, no. 7 (April 1, 2002), p. 3.

6

Advertising Design
Theoretical Frameworks and Types of Appeals

Chapter Objectives

After reading this chapter, you should be able to answer the following questions:

- How do advertising theories help the creative move a consumer from awareness of a product to the eventual purchase decision?

- What roles do attitudes and values play in developing advertising messages?

- When should visual and verbal elements be integrated into advertisements?

- What factors might influence the effectiveness of an advertising appeal?

- Are there differences in creating advertisements for business-to-business and in international markets?

ECKO ENTERPRISES

Dressing the Hip Hop World and Beyond

It is a safe bet to guess that the majority of people over 40 years old have not heard of Marc Ecko or Ecko Enterprises. The world of hip hop belongs to a new generation, one with its own unique form of clothing, known to many as "urban apparel."

Ecko Enterprises was formed in 1993 when three friends began creating T-shirt fashions using cans of spray paint. By 2004, the same company reported sales of nearly $1 billion. Items from Ecko Enterprises and the Ecko Unlimited brand are sold in more than 5,000 department and specialty stores domestically and in over 45 countries internationally. There are now 30 Ecko Unlimited full-price company annex stores, 16 of which are located outside of the United States. The Ecko Unlimited clothing line often features the stark silhouette of a rhinoceros on T-shirts, baggy jeans, and other products.

Ecko's company competes with firms that rely on the cred (credibility) that comes from being a performer, such as the Sean John line featuring P. Diddy, Rocawear from Jay-Z and Damon Dash, and Phat Fashions offered by Russell Simmons. Marc Ecko, in contrast, is simply a fan of the music who grew up living in cul-de-sac type neighborhoods. Although he is sometimes described as a "former graffiti artist," the reality is that his company was formed while he was studying at Rutgers University to become a pharmacist.

A variety of products are featured through Ecko Unlimited, Marc Ecko Formalwear, and Eckored Kids, including outerwear, footwear, watches, eyewear, underwear, belts, bags, hats, small leather goods, and formalwear. The Marc Ecko Cut & Sew brand is a contemporary menswear line consisting of casual and dress separates designed to blend street-inspired edginess with more sophisticated designs and fabrics. Cut & Sew offers semi-tailored separates, sweaters, urban spa-inspired active wear, woven shirts, and premium denim.

A newer brand, the G-Unit Clothing Company, is an independent venture operated by Ecko and multiplatinum-selling artist 50 Cent. The G-Unit line includes items for men, women, boys, and girls. It features denim, T-shirts, fleece, outerwear, hats, and sportswear. Also, Marc Ecko Enterprises formed an exclusive U.S. and Canadian licensing agreement with Avirex Ltd. to introduce a sportswear collection. The line carries a full collection of apparel, including fashion

denim, tees, knits, and outerwear. Other licensing agreements have been formed with Geoffrey Allen, Skechers, Paul D'Avril, Inc., Kid Headquarters, and Viva International.

The company also offers skateboards and skater-influenced clothing and accessories through the Zoo York label. The brand was launched in 1993 and is now part of the MEE line, which is the East Coast's largest action sports company. Ecko also publishes *Complex Magazine*, a bimonthly urban lifestyle publication with a circulation of 325,000. Another new venture is Contents Under Pressure, a game developed in partnership with Atari, Inc. The game has stories and characters in a futuristic universe in which graffiti plays a key role.

Marc Ecko was born as Marc Milecofsky. He grew up south of New York City in Lakewood, New Jersey. His parents were real-estate agents. Ecko has two sisters, one of whom is his twin, Marci. The name Ecko is the result of a family story. When Ecko's mother was pregnant with Marci, the doctor informed her of an "echo" on an ultrasound, which turned out to be Marc.

Urban apparel can be viewed as a form of "lifestyle merchandising." Ecko was able to translate his own enthusiasm for hip hop into something new and different in the fashion world. By placing ads in hip-hop magazines such as *The Source* and *Vibe,* the Ecko rhino grew based on relationships with a wide range of maverick recording artists, including Talib Kweli and the Beatnuts. Although many retailers feared the urban look, Federated Department Stores, the owner of Macy's and Bloomingdale's, became an enthusiastic seller of Ecko Unlimited.

Russell Simmons, founder of Phat Fashions and the godfather of hip-hop culture, was quoted as saying, "Marc is a very, very creative designer. He's got more edge than most." Simmons describes Ecko's line as having an "alternative" quality or a "more suburban edge." In other words, the Ecko brands were able to gain market share of the hip-hop audience.

The net result is that Marc Ecko is able to live a fantasy life in his castle-like home in New Jersey. He is the sole benefactor of the Tikya Children's Home, which is a Ukrainian orphanage.

He is noted for his Star Wars memorabilia collection. In 2007, he purchased the baseball Barry Bonds hit to record his 757th home run. Then, Ecko created a Web site on which fans were allowed to vote on whether the ball should be given to the Baseball Hall of Fame, branded with an asterisk, or shot into space (the asterisk won). As his success continues, the marketing lesson is clear: Finding the right target market and effectively communicating in that market can lead to amazing things.[1]

OVERVIEW

Which advertising message made the biggest impression on you in the past 5 years? Was it a funny ad? Was it something shown during the Super Bowl? Was the ad sexy, like some of the more recent GoDaddy ads? Or did a local commercial get your attention? Did you end up buying a product or using a service because you saw the ad, or was it just entertaining? Do you think business-to-business buyers respond to ads differently from those oriented toward consumers?

These questions show how the process of designing an advertising campaign can be one of the most challenging elements of an integrated marketing communications program. For an advertisement to be successful, people need to do more than just enjoy what they see. The ad should change their behaviors and attitudes. At the least, viewers should remember the good or service being advertised, so that the next time they make a purchase the company or brand will come to mind.

Chapter 5 described the overall advertising management program. The advertising agency is led by the account executive, who assists in making a pitch for the account, conducts media selections, and works with creatives, media planners, and media buyers. In this chapter, the focus is on the actual message design. This work is completed by the agency's creative staff.

The message design process is not performed in isolation. It is based on the creative brief, which is prepared by the client in conjunction with the account executive, and also takes into consideration the media that will be utilized. By combining all of these elements, the creative can design effective advertisements.

Two major topics are covered in this chapter. The first is to describe three theoretical approaches to advertising design. They are:

- Hierarchy of effects model
- Means–end theory
- Visual and verbal imaging

The second topic is to review, in detail, the major appeals advertisers use. Many of these approaches may seem familiar. The goal of the advertising agency is to select the appeal that has the best chance of achieving a desired outcome. From there, the actual message content is developed. Before beginning the process of creating the ad, it is important to remember the steps taken up to this point. These activities can be summarized by reviewing the items in a creative brief.

THE CREATIVE BRIEF

Figure 6.1 summarizes the elements of the creative brief that were introduced in Chapter 5. The document provides the background for the creative work. Designing an effective advertising message begins with understanding the *objective* of the ad and the *target audience*. Then, the advertising group agrees on the *message theme*, which is the outline of the key ideas the commercial will convey. The account executive or client must provide the *support* and documentation for the advertising theme or claim. Finally, the creative must be aware of any *constraints* to be included. With these key components in mind, the creative can move forward and prepare the ad. The following section describes three theoretical approaches that may assist the creative in the design process.

◆ The objective	◆ The support	**FIGURE 6.1** **Creative Brief**
◆ The target audience	◆ The constraints	
◆ The message theme		

ADVERTISING THEORY

In developing an advertisement for an advertising campaign, several theoretical frameworks are useful. The first is the hierarchy of effects model. The second is a means–end chain. Both the hierarchy of effects model and a means–end chain can be used to develop leverage points. A leverage point moves the consumer from understanding a product's benefits to linking those benefits with personal values. Finally, the third theoretical perspective involves the visual and verbal images present in an advertisement.

Hierarchy of Effects

The **hierarchy of effects model** aids in clarifying the objectives of an advertising campaign and the development of individual ads. The model suggests that there are six steps a consumer or a business buyer moves through when making a purchase. The steps are:

1. Awareness
2. Knowledge
3. Liking
4. Preference
5. Conviction
6. The actual purchase

These steps are sequential. A consumer will spend a period of time at each step before moving to the next. Thus, before a person can develop a liking for a product, he or she must first have sufficient knowledge of the product. Once the individual has the knowledge and develops liking for the product, the advertiser can try to influence the consumer to favor a particular brand or company.

The hierarchy of effects approach can help a creative understand how a consumer reaches purchase decisions; however, some of the theory's assumptions have been questioned. For one, it is possible that these six steps are not always the route taken by consumers. For instance, a person makes a purchase (such as an impulse buy) and then later develops knowledge, liking, preference, and conviction. Also, shoppers may purchase products when little or no preference is involved, because coupons, discounts, or other purchase incentives cause them to choose one brand instead of another. At other times, someone may not even remember the name of the brand purchased. This is often the case with commodity products such as sugar and flour or even clothing purchases such as socks and shirts.

Still, the major benefit of the hierarchy of effects model is that it is one method used to identify the typical steps consumers and businesses take when making purchases. To encourage brand loyalty, all six steps must be included. A consumer or business is unlikely to be loyal to a particular brand without sufficient knowledge of the brand. Purchasers must like the brand and build a strong preference for it. Next, they must cultivate strong convictions that the particular brand is superior to the other brands on the market. None of this occurs without first becoming aware of the product. Thus, the components of the hierarchy of effects approach highlight the various responses that advertising or other marketing communications must stimulate. This is true in both consumer and business-to-business markets.

The hierarchy of effects model has many similarities with theories about attitudes and attitudinal change, including the concepts of cognitive, affective, and conative elements. The *cognitive* component is the person's mental images, understanding, and interpretations of the person, object, or issue. The *affective* component contains the feelings or emotions a person has about the object, topic, or idea. The *conative* component is the individual's intentions, actions, or behavior. The most common sequence that takes place when an attitude forms is:

Cognitive → Affective → Conative

Any combination of these components is possible. This suggests that the structured six-step process of the hierarchy of effects model may be more rigid than is actually the case. Sometimes an advertisement breaks out of the mold. An ad can be very different and highly successful because of how it captures an individual's attention. As a general guideline, however, cognitive-oriented ads work best for the advertising objectives of brand awareness and brand knowledge. Affective-oriented ads are superior in developing liking, preference, and conviction for a product. Conative-oriented ads are normally the best for facilitating actual product purchases or other types of buyer actions.

Means–End Theory

A second theoretical approach a creative can use to design an advertisement is a **means–end chain**. This approach suggests that an advertisement should contain a message, or *means,* that leads the consumer to a desired end state. These *end* states include the personal values that are listed in Figure 6.2. The purpose of the means–end chain is to start a process in which viewing the ad leads the consumer to believe that using the product will help him or her reach one of these personal values.

Means–end theory is the basis of a model called the **Means–End Conceptualization of Components for Advertising Strategy (MECCAS)**.[2] The MECCAS model suggests using five elements in creating ads:

- The product's attributes
- Consumer benefits
- Leverage points
- Personal values
- The executional framework

The MECCAS approach moves consumers through the five elements. The attributes of the product are linked to the specific benefits consumers can derive. These benefits, in turn, lead to the attainment of a personal value.

To illustrate the MECCAS method, consider Figure 6.3 and the milk advertisement shown. The product attribute calcium is linked to the benefits of being strong and healthy. The personal value the consumer obtains from healthy bones is feeling wise for using the product. The leverage point in the advertisement is the link between the benefit of health and the personal value of feeling wise. The white mustache and the text in the advertisement are designed to help the viewer remember that drinking milk is healthy. In this case, the specific issue is preventing osteoporosis in women.

FIGURE 6.2
Personal Values

◆ Comfortable life	◆ Inner peace	◆ Self-fulfillment
◆ Equality	◆ Mature love	◆ Self-respect
◆ Excitement	◆ Personal accomplishment	◆ Sense of belonging
◆ Freedom	◆ Pleasure	◆ Social acceptance
◆ Fun, exciting life	◆ Salvation	◆ Wisdom
◆ Happiness	◆ Security	

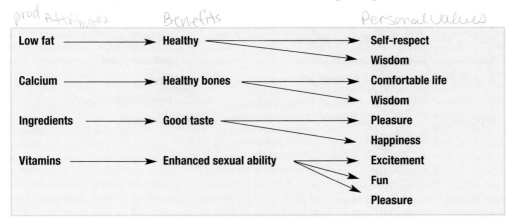

prod Attributes   Benefits   Personal Values

Low fat ⟶ Healthy ⟶ Self-respect, Wisdom

Calcium ⟶ Healthy bones ⟶ Comfortable life, Wisdom

Ingredients ⟶ Good taste ⟶ Pleasure, Happiness

Vitamins ⟶ Enhanced sexual ability ⟶ Excitement, Fun, Pleasure

FIGURE 6.3
Means–End Chain for Milk

The MECCAS approach can also be applied to business-to-business advertisements. Members of the buying center can be influenced by personal values, organizational values, and corporate goals. Consider the advertisement for Greenfield Online in this section and the means–end chain in Figure 6.4. Each attribute is presented in terms of the benefits business customers can obtain. Although not explicitly stated, the personal values of members of the buying center choosing Greenfield Online might include job security for making good decisions, self-fulfillment, wisdom, and social acceptance by other members of the buying group.

Leverage Points

Both the hierarchy of effects model and the means–end chain approach lead to leverage points. A leverage point is designed to move the consumer from understanding a product's benefits to linking those benefits with personal values. To construct a quality leverage point, the creative builds the pathway that connects a product benefit with the potential buyer's value system.

In terms of the hierarchy of effects model, the initial level of awareness begins the process of exposing consumers to product benefits. As the viewer moves through the six stages, he or she eventually develops the conviction to buy the product. At that point, the benefit has indeed been linked with a personal value. In the milk advertisement used to illustrate the means–end chain, the leverage point is the phrase "There's one person I won't be," which is tied with the copy message "a woman with osteoporosis." The copy goes on to explain that because of calcium (a product attribute), women can have healthy bones (product benefit). Making a conscious decision to use milk to prevent osteoporosis demonstrates the personal values of wisdom and seeking a healthy lifestyle.

In the Greenfield Online business-to-business advertisement, the leverage point is the picture of an old-fashioned woman using an old telephone sandwiched between the headline "Are you still buying marketing research done the old-fashioned way?" and the first sentence of the copy explaining that companies can "Do it better on the Internet." The

A Got Milk? advertisement illustrating the use of a means-end chain.

There's one person I won't be.

A woman with osteoporosis. So it's bloody marvelous that fat free milk has the calcium to help prevent it. Thank goodness there's enough to go around.

got milk?

TRACEY ULLMAN ©1999 NATIONAL FLUID MILK PROCESSOR PROMOTION BOARD

FIGURE 6.4
B-to-B Means–End Chain for Greenfield Online

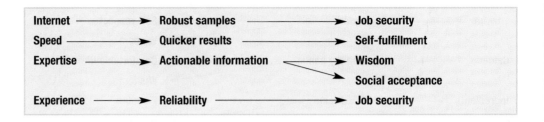

picture creates an excellent mental image of marketing research done the old-fashioned way and the opportunities Greenfield Online can provide.

The means–end chain and MECCAS approaches are based on the product's attributes and its benefits to the consumer. The leverage point is the message that links these attributes and benefits with consumer values. In the ad itself, the executional framework is the plot or scenario used to convey the message designed to complete the linkage. Chapter 7 presents executional frameworks in detail, in which dramatizations and other methods of telling the ad story help build successful leverage points.

An effective leverage point can also be associated with an attitudinal change, especially when the sequence is cognitive → affective → conative. As the attitude is formed, the individual first understands, then is moved emotionally, and then takes action. A leverage point can help the viewer of an ad move through these three stages, thereby tying cognitive knowledge of the product to more emotional and personal values.

Creatives spend considerable amounts of time designing ads with powerful leverage points. Executional frameworks and various types of appeals, as described in the upcoming pages, are the tools creatives use to help consumers make the transition from being aware of a product's benefits to incorporating them with personal value systems.

A Greenfield Online business advertisement illustrating the use of a means–end chain in a business ad.

Verbal and Visual Images

A third theoretical approach to advertising design includes the decision the creative makes about the degree of emphasis given to the visual part of the ad versus the verbal element. Most major forms of advertising have both visual and verbal or written elements. A visual ad places the greatest emphasis on the picture or visual element of the ad. A verbal or written ad places the most emphasis on the copy.

Visual images often lead to more favorable attitudes toward both the advertisement and the brand. Visuals also tend to be more easily remembered than verbal copy. They are stored in the brain as both pictures and words. This dual-coding process makes it easier for people to recall the message. Further, images are usually stored in both the left and right sides of the brain; verbal messages tend be stored in the left side of the brain only.

Visual images can range from concrete and realistic to highly abstract. A concrete visual is one in which the subject is easily recognizable as a person, place, or thing. In an abstract image, the subject is more difficult to recognize. Concrete pictures have a higher level of recall than do abstract images because of the dual-coding process whereby the image is stored in the brain as both a visual and a verbal representation. For example, viewers process an ad with a picture of spaghetti used in promoting a restaurant as both a picture and a verbal representation. Ads with concrete images lead to more favorable attitudes than those with no pictures or abstract pictures. Research offers many reasons for creatives to include visual images in advertisements.[3]

Radio advertisers often seek to create visual images for the audience. Pepsi produced an ad in which listeners hear a can being opened, the soft drink being poured, and the sizzle of the carbonation—an excellent example of creating a visual image. If consumers can see the image in their minds, the effect is greater than an actual visual portrayal. An actual visual event requires less brain activity than using one's imagination to develop the image. The secret is getting the person to think beyond the ad and picture the scene being simulated.

Visual imagery is especially important in international marketing. Global advertising agencies try to create what is called **visual Esperanto**, a universal language that makes global advertising possible for any good or service. Visual Esperanto advertising recognizes that visual images are more powerful than verbal descriptions. Visual images are more likely to transcend cultural differences.[4] To illustrate the power of a visual image compared to a verbal account, think of the word *exotic*. To some, *exotic* means a white beach in Hawaii with young people in sexy swimsuits. To others, it may be a small cabin in the snow-capped mountains of Switzerland. To others still, exotic may be a close-up of a tribal village in Africa. The word *exotic* can vary in meaning. At the same time, a picture of a couple holding hands in front of Niagara Falls has practically the same meaning across all cultures. A young child smiling after eating a piece of candy also conveys an almost universal message.

Finding the appropriate image is the most important task in creating visual Esperanto. The creative looks for an image that conveys the intended meaning or message. The goal is to create a brand identity through visuals rather than words. Then the creative uses words to support the visual image. For example, the creative may decide that a boy and his father at a sports event illustrate the priceless treasure of a shared family moment. In Mexico, the setting could be a soccer match instead of a baseball game in the United States. The specific copy (the words) can then be adapted to the country involved. The difficult part of obtaining visual Esperanto is choosing an image that transcends cultures. Once a universal image is found, creatives in each of the countries represented can take the visual image and modify it to appeal to the local target audience.

In the past, creatives designing business-to-business advertisements relied heavily on the verbal element rather than on visuals. The basis of this approach was the idea that business decisions are made in a rational, cognitive manner. In recent years, more business ads have incorporated strong visual elements to heighten the emotional aspects of making a purchase.

In summary, all of the theoretical models presented in this section provide useful ideas for the advertising creative. Each one suggests that some kind of sequence must be followed as the ad is prepared. The endpoint of the ad should be a situation in which the viewer is enticed to remember the product, to think favorably about it, and to look for that product when making a purchase decision. Various kinds of advertising messages, or appeals, can be utilized to reach such key advertising objectives.

This ASICS ad blends visual imagery with verbal copy.

TYPES OF ADVERTISING APPEALS

Throughout the years, advertisers have employed a wide variety of advertising approaches. Seven major types of **advertising appeals** have been the most successful. Advertisers usually select from one of these types of appeals as they develop the advertisement (see Figure 6.5).

The decision about which type of appeal to use should be based on a review of the creative brief, the objective of the advertisement, and the means–end chain to be conveyed. The final choice depends on a number of factors, including the product being

FIGURE 6.5
Advertising Appeals

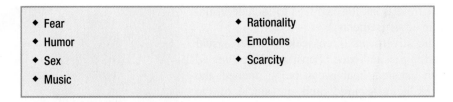

- Fear
- Humor
- Sex
- Music

- Rationality
- Emotions
- Scarcity

sold, the personal preferences of the advertising creative and the account executive, as well as the wishes of the client. In determining the best appeal to use, it is often a question of which type of appeal is most *inappropriate*. Advertising experts know that certain appeals are less successful at various times. For example, research indicates that sex appeals are not very effective for goods and services that are not related to sex.

This section provides descriptions of the types of advertising appeals that are available. Each has been successfully used in some ads but failed in others. The key responsibility of the marketer is to make sure, to whatever degree is possible, that the appeal is the best choice for the brand and the target audience.

Fear

Advertisers use fear to sell numerous products. Life insurance companies focus on the consequences of not having life insurance when a person dies. Shampoo and mouthwash ads invoke fears of dandruff and bad breath. These problems can make a person a social outcast. Fear is used more often than most casual observers realize.

Simply stated, advertisers use fear appeals because they work. Fear increases both the viewer's interest in an advertisement and the ad's persuasiveness. Many individuals remember advertisements with fear appeals better than they do warm, upbeat messages.[5] Consumers who pay more attention to an advertisement are more likely to process the information it presents. This information processing makes it possible to accomplish the ad's main objective.

A theoretical explanation regarding the way fear works is the *behavioral response model* (see Figure 6.6).[6] As shown, various incidents can lead to negative or positive consequences, which then affect future behaviors.

In developing fear advertisements, the idea is to include as many aspects of the behavioral response model as possible. A business-to-business advertiser offering Internet services tries to focus on the **severity** of downtime if a company's Internet server goes down. Another ad describes the firm's **vulnerability** by showing the high probability that a company's server is going to crash. The Service Metrics advertisement in this section features a picture of a blindfolded man ready to step into a manhole to illustrate the danger of e-business pitfalls. The goal of the advertisement is to make business leaders realize

FIGURE 6.6
Behavioral Response Model

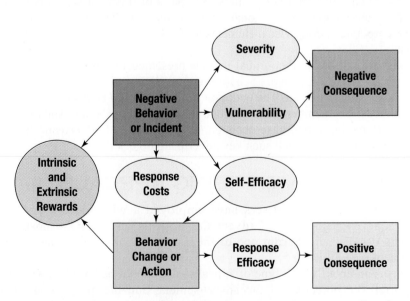

their companies are more vulnerable than they think. Service Metrics can help them identify these potential problems before they turn into disasters.

When using fear, one issue is the strength of the appeal. Most advertisers believe a moderate level of fear is the most effective. A low level of fear may not be noticed, and the fear level may not be convincing in terms of severity or vulnerability. Further, an advertisement with too high of a fear level can backfire, because the message is so strong that it causes feelings of anxiety. This leads the viewer to avoid watching the ad, by changing the channel or muting the sound.[7] Therefore, the goal for a fear ad should be to make it powerful enough to capture a viewer's attention and to influence his or her thinking, but not so scary that the person avoids seeing the advertisement.

Fear ads match well with certain types of goods and services, especially products that eliminate problems or threats to a consumer's sense of personal security. Account executives, creatives, and company leaders must decide if fear is a good choice or if some other type of appeal offers greater promise.

Humor

Clutter is a significant problem in every advertising medium. Capturing a viewer's attention is difficult. Even after an advertiser has garnered the audiences' attention, keeping that attention is even more challenging. Humor has proven to be one of the best techniques for cutting through clutter. Humor can be effective at both getting attention and keeping it. Consumers, as a whole, enjoy advertisements that make them laugh. Something that is funny has intrusive value and grabs attention.[8]

A business-to-business advertisement using a fear appeal.

Humor is used in about 24 percent of prime time television advertisements and 35 percent of radio ads. Humorous ads often win awards and tend to be favorites among judges at the International Advertising Film Festival at Cannes as well as for other types of advertising awards. At a recent Clio Awards ceremony for radio ads, 62 percent of the winners used some type of humor.[9] In *USA Today*'s consumer survey of the most likeable advertising campaigns for the year, simplicity and humor were the key ingredients.[10]

The success of humor as an advertising appeal is based on three things. Humor causes consumers to: (1) watch, (2) laugh, and, most importantly, (3) remember. In recall tests, consumers most often remember humorous ads. To be successful, the humor should be connected directly to the product's benefits. It should tie together the product features, the advantage to customers, and the personal values of the means–end chain.

Humorous ads pique viewer interest. This makes it is easier to gain more careful consumer consideration of the advertisement's message. A funny ad captures the viewer's attention, which leads to improved comprehension and recall of the advertising message and tagline. Advertising research indicates that humor elevates people's moods. Happy consumers associate a good mood with the advertiser's products. Humor helps fix the company in the consumer's cognitive structure with links to positive feelings.

Although humor captures the viewer's attention, cuts through ad clutter, and enhances recall, unfortunately, humorous ads can also go wrong. Advertisers must be

Brand manager eliminates pilot costs, becomes hero

Testing new package designs online with rotating 3-D images not only saved the client expensive tooling costs but also saved time. Now manufacturers can design today and test tomorrow. Eliminating pilot costs and shortening "time to market" are just some of the many ways that Greenfield Online quantitative research beats the old-fashioned kind.

Put our expert consultants and advanced technology to work for you.

www.greenfield.com

888.291.9997

Greenfield Online
Leading the Research Revolution®

• Quantitative Studies
• Qualitative Studies
• Media Research
• Self-Directed Research
• Syndicated Studies
• Website Evaluations

HERO

A Greenfield Online ad using a humor appeal.

careful to avoid letting the humor overpower the advertisement. When humor fails, it is usually because the joke in the ad is remembered but the product or brand is not. In other words, the ad is so funny that the audience forgets or does not catch the sponsor's name. Although humorous ads often win awards, they can fail in terms of accomplishing advertising objectives. To avoid this problem, the humor used in the ad should focus on a component of the means–end chain. The humor should relate either to a product's attributes, a customer benefit, or the personal value obtained from the product. The most effective ads are those in which the humor incorporates all three elements.

Humor is often used to rise above the clutter of ads, but occasionally the humor goes bad. Such was the case with the Snickers ad during the 2007 Super Bowl. The ad featured two mechanics eating from opposite ends of the same candy bar until they accidentally ended up kissing. The two men responded in disgust by ripping out their own chest hairs. The outcry against the ad was so loud and strong that it was immediately pulled from television.[11]

Some evidence suggests that humor is universal; however, there are particular executions of humor that may not be. Humor is often culturally based. It may be difficult to transfer wit from one culture to another. Not all audiences will see a humorous ad in the same way. It is important for advertisers to pretest an advertisement before it is launched in another country to ensure it will be liked and, more important, that it will be considered funny and not offensive.

Humor is being used more frequently in various countries. A humorous ad developed for McDonald's in Singapore had the highest recall rate (90 percent) of all other ads shown in the month it was released. In Germany, Ford deviated from traditional ads that concentrated on promoting product quality and value to a humorous ad approach. The humorous ad shows a pigeon sitting on tree branch with a Ford Ka parked nearby. The bird swoops down to bomb the car, but at the last minute the car hood springs up and knocks the bird out. The advertisement was first shown on Ford's U.K. Web site. Word about the ad quickly spread until more than 1 million people had visited the Web site to see the ad. German dealers requested the ad so they could show it on television. The feedback and popularity of the ad in the United Kingdom caused Ford's marketing bosses to agree to run the ad in Germany. The ad resonated with young, affluent buyers, which Ford had been trying to reach. The new ad was seen as witty, gutsy, and edgy, which worked well with Ford's theme of projecting the Ka as a stylish car.[12]

Humorous ads are difficult to design. One cynic once noted that there are only 12 funny people in the United States. Humor that doesn't work often creates a negative image for the company. But, humor that works can bring great success to a company and provide great dividends in terms of brand equity. Figure 6.7 summarizes the major reasons for using humor.

FIGURE 6.7
Reasons for Using Humor in Ads

• Captures attention.
• Holds attention.
• Often wins creative awards.
• High recall scores.
• Consumers enjoy ads that make them laugh.
• Evaluated by consumers as likeable ads.

FIGURE 6.8
Sexuality Approaches Used in Advertisements

◆ Subliminal techniques
◆ Sensuality
◆ Sexual suggestiveness
◆ Nudity or partial nudity
◆ Overt sexuality

Sex

Sexual appeals are often used to break through clutter. Advertisements in the United States and other countries throughout the world contain more visual sexual themes than they have in the past. Nudity and other sexual approaches are common. Sexual themes in ads, however, no longer sell the way they used to. Sex no longer has shock value. Today's teens are growing up in societies immersed in sex. Seeing another sexually oriented ad gets very little attention. Currently, many advertisers are shifting to more subtle sexual cues, suggestions, and innuendos.[13] Sexuality has been employed in advertising in the five ways listed in Figure 6.8.

Subliminal approaches place sexual cues or icons in advertisements in the attempt to affect a viewer's subconscious mind. In an odd paradox, truly subliminal cues are not noticed nor do they create any effects. Consumers pay little attention to ads already. A subliminal message that registers only in the subconscious mind is not going to be effective. If it did, there would not be the need for stronger sexual content in advertising.

Sexual appeals can also be based on *sensuality*. Many women respond more favorably to a sensual suggestion than an overtly sexual approach. An alluring glance across a crowded room can be sensual and draw attention to a product. Many view sensuality as a more sophisticated approach, because it relies on the imagination. Images of romance and love can be more enticing than raw sexuality.

Many ads feature a *sexually suggestive* approach. The Bijan ad shown on the next page features Bo Derek. The ad states, "Bo Derek is wearing Bijan Eau de Parfum and nothing else," which is a sexually suggestive message. In a similar

An advertisement for Old Orchard featuring a sensuality appeal.

Forever on the lips, never on the hips.

A Bijan perfume advertisement using the "sexual suggestiveness" approach.

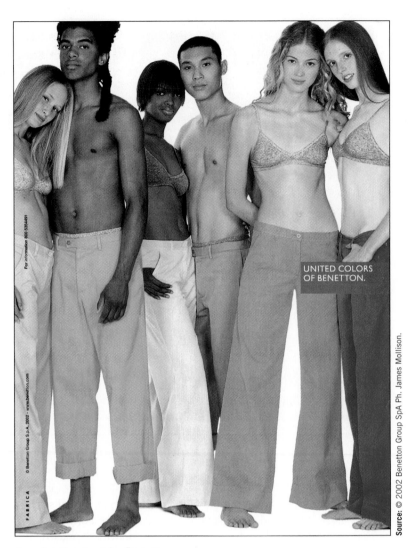

An advertisement by Benetton using partial nudity.

manner, the Clairol Herbal Essence Shampoo ads borrowed the "yes, Yes, YES!" scene from the movie *When Harry Met Sally* to make the product seem more sensuous by suggesting sexual activity.

A recent trend in sexual suggestiveness is to use gay and lesbian themes. Swedish retailer IKEA was the first in the United States to use a gay theme. A television commercial showing two gay men shopping for a dining room table together first appeared in 1994. Many other ads hint at gay themes.[14]

Nudity or *partial nudity* is still used to sell products that have sexual connotations, such as clothing, perfume, and cologne. Some ads are designed to solicit a sexual response. Others are not. For example, starting in 1987 underwear companies could use live models in television ads. The first commercials were modest and informational, emphasizing the design or materials used in the undergarment. The first Playtex bra commercials using live models drew strong criticism from organizations such as the American Family Association. Now, advertisements for undergarments go much further and involve superstars, such as actress Jennifer Love Hewitt who appeared in television and print ads for Hanes for their All-Over Comfort bra and their Perfect Panty. The campaign even included an online element with footage from the photo shoots, a "bad bra toss" game, and a blog about bad bra moments.[15]

♦ The presence of female (or male) decorative models improves ad recognition, but not brand recognition.

♦ The presence of a decorative model influences emotional and objective evaluations of the product among both male and female audiences.

♦ Attractive models produce a higher level of attention to ads than do less attractive models.

♦ The presence of an attractive model produces higher purchase intentions when the product is sexually relevant than if it is not sexually relevant.

FIGURE 6.9
Factors to Consider Before Using Decorative Models

A common sexual approach in advertising is to use decorative models. **Decorative models** are individuals in an advertisement whose primary purpose is to adorn the product as a sexual or attractive stimulus. The model serves no functional purpose in the ad except to attract attention. In the past, commercials for automobiles, tools, and beer often used female models dressed in bikinis to stand by their products. A number of studies have been conducted to determine how effective decorative models are. The basic conclusions are listed in Figure 6.9.[16]

Using *overt sexuality* in ads for products that are sexually oriented is normally accepted, but it often becomes controversial when used for other types of products. When Procter & Gamble launched a television advertising campaign for Dentyne, eyebrows were raised. The ad shows two teens in a living room. The girl pops a piece of Dentyne Fire bubble gum into her mouth and then rips off her blouse and jumps on her boyfriend. At first the parents stare in shock. Then, the mom tries a piece of Dentyne Fire and promptly jumps on the dad. The controversy centered on whether the ad promoted teenage sexuality by suggesting that parents should openly display sexual feelings and desires.[17]

Are Sex Appeals Effective?

In addition to research on the use of decorative models, numerous studies have examined the effectiveness of sexual appeals and nudity in advertising. Almost all of them have concluded that sex and nudity do increase attention, regardless of the gender of the individual in the advertisement or the gender of the audience. Normally, the attention is greater for opposite-sex situations than same-sex situations. That is, a male viewing a female in a sexually provocative advertisement pays more attention than a male viewing another male in a sexually provocative ad. The same is true for females. To encourage both males and females to pay attention to its ads, Guess often uses both a male and female in a sexually provocative manner in a single advertisement.

Although sexually oriented ads attract attention, brand recall for ads using a sex appeal is lower than ads using some other type of appeal. Thus, it appears that although people watch the advertisement, the sexual theme distracts them from paying attention to the brand name.[18]

A Guess advertisement featuring both a male and a female model using a sexual appeal.

Sexually oriented advertisements are often rated as being more interesting. Those ads deemed to be highly controversial in terms of their sexual content were rated as more interesting by both males and females. The paradox, however, is that although the controversial ads are more interesting, they fail to increase the transmission of information. Respondents are less likely to remember any more about the message.[19]

Advertisements using overt sexual stimuli or containing nudity produce higher levels of physiological arousal responses. These arousal responses have been linked to the formation of both affective and cognitive responses. If the viewer is male and the sexual stimulus is female, such as a naked female in an ad for cologne, then the viewer tends to develop a strong feeling toward the ad based on the arousal response his body experiences. Female viewers of male nudity in an ad often experience the same type of response, although the arousal response tends not to be as strong.

The cognitive impression made on viewers of a sexually oriented ad depends on whether the viewer feels the advertisement is pleasant or offensive. If a viewer likes the ad, then a positive impression of the brand will result. If, however, the viewer thinks the ad is in poor taste, then negative feelings and beliefs about the brand may result. When sex works, the ad increases sales. When it does not, the ad may create strong negative feelings toward the company.[20]

In determining the level of sex appeal to use in an advertisement, it is important to consider society's view and level of acceptance.[21] Just as economies go through cycles, attitudes toward sex in advertising experience acceptance swings. The use and acceptance of sexual themes in advertising had swung to a high level of tolerance in the early part of the 2000s, until the Super Bowl of 2004. The public reaction to Janet Jackson's breast-baring halftime show sent ripples all the way to Madison Avenue. Shortly afterward, Victoria's Secret dropped its TV lingerie fashion show. Abercrombie & Fitch killed the company's quarterly catalog, which had been strongly criticized for featuring models in sexually suggestive poses. Anheuser-Busch dropped some of its risqué ads.[22] The pendulum was still swinging in the opposite direction a year later when ads for Super Bowl 2005 were unveiled. Fewer ads used sexual appeals. Those that featured sex were much tamer. The only controversial ad was by GoDaddy.com. Only one of the two ads for GoDaddy.com was shown; the other was rejected by the network because of its highly sexual content. The network feared upsetting the Super Bowl audience.

Many researchers, both in academia and in industry, believe society is becoming more conservative and that youth are returning to more traditional values. Recent research suggests that many teens are offended by the widespread use of sexually provocative advertising and are often embarrassed by sexual innuendos. As one study concluded, "Sexually explicit advertising has lost its potency. Young people of today are more interested in traditional family values and wholesome ad messages than the flash of a breast to sell shampoo or the promise of limitless sex if your engine is big enough."[23]

This sensual ad for Stetson cologne was placed in a woman's magazine.

Source: Courtesy of J.B. Stetson Company.

In contrast, a study of clothing ads geared to teens revealed that teens had a stronger, more favorable opinion of brands featuring sexually oriented messages. A 17-year-old male, upon seeing a non–sexually oriented clothing ad, complained that the ad was " . . . too boring. If I saw it somewhere, it wouldn't stick in my mind. A good ad is either funny, sexy, or provocative. This is neither. The models aren't even sexy—what is this, a Wal-Mart ad?"[24]

It is clear that the use of sex in advertising will continue. Advertisers must carefully determine the level and the type of sexuality to use and the target audience. What will work at one particular point in time may not work at another.

Sex Appeals in International Advertising

What is deemed appropriate in terms of sexual appeal varies across countries. Something that is acceptable in one country may not be in another. In Chile, a campaign featuring nude celebrities touting the benefits of drinking milk was recently launched. The ads' producers stated, "Chile is a country of stuffed shirts, so this campaign is going to shake them up, and at a relatively low cost, thanks to nudity." The Chilean dairy federation believed the idea of rebellion rather than nudity is an easy sell to Chilean youth. As more Chilean kids travel and see a world filled with teens wearing green and blue hair and body piercings, public nudity will become associated with freedom. Despite opposition by conservatives, the new "naked" milk campaign aroused the attention of Chilean young people and milk sales grew.[25]

Religions, cultures, and value systems determine the levels of nudity, sexual references, and gender-specific issues that are permitted in a country. Moslem nations tend to reject any kind of nudity and any reference to sexuality and other gender-related issues. They also do not permit any type of advertising for personal goods, such as female hygiene products, contraceptives, and undergarments. Any hint of sexuality or display of the female body is strictly forbidden.

In many Middle Eastern countries, sex and gender issues are taboo subjects. Sexual appeals are not used in advertising, and even sexually related products are difficult to advertise. In Egypt, Procter & Gamble hosted a call-in TV show directed toward young girls. The show's panel contained health experts, and topics ranged from marriage to menopause. The call-in show was followed up with a TV talk show (called *Frankly Speaking*) about feminine hygiene. The goal of the show was to tackle some of the more sensitive issues facing young Egyptian girls. Although the show discussed what happens during puberty, it was P&G's policy not to discuss sexuality. P&G sponsored the show and the primary product advertised was P&G's feminine sanitary pads, Always.[26]

In other countries, standards on sexually oriented advertising are quite liberal but sometimes confusing. In France, sex is everywhere. Advertisers can feature seminude or completely nude models in advertisements if they can be justified; a relationship must exist between the product and the nude model. It does not take much of a justification in France, where sex is viewed as healthy, innocent, and natural. One difference in France, however, is that sex and humor are not mixed. The French do not see sex as silly or funny.[27]

Disadvantages of Sex Appeals

Everyone has heard that "sex sells." Although this may be true, it is a less powerful force today. Seeing another naked person in an advertisement is much less likely to cause a viewer to pay more attention.

One major criticism of sexually based advertising is that it perpetuates dissatisfaction with one's body. Females in print advertisements and models in television advertising are often thin. The key to success seems to be the thinner the better. As advertising models have gotten thinner, body dissatisfaction and eating disorders among women have risen. Research indicates that women feel unhappy about their own

An effective example of a sexual appeal to promote milk.

bodies and believe they are too fat after viewing advertisements showing thin models. What is interesting is that these same ads have an impact on men, but the reverse. Men feel they are not muscular enough and are too thin or too fat. It does not make any difference whether the male is viewing a male model or a female model in advertisements.[28]

In response, some firms have begun using "regular person" models in ads. Wal-Mart and Kmart have employees pose in clothing to be sold and with other products. This approach has met with many positive results, which means other companies may need to rethink their positions on body image advertising.

The problem with the stereotyping of females in ads takes a different twist in other countries. For example, in Saudi Arabia and Malaysia women must be shown in family settings. They cannot be depicted as being carefree or desirable to the opposite sex. In Canada, France, and Sweden, sexism should be avoided in any advertising directed toward children. Advertisers refrain from associating toys with a particular gender, such as dolls for girls or soldier figures for boys.[29]

In general, the use of sex to make products more appealing is a legitimate tactic for many companies, products, and advertising firms. The goal should be to use sex in a manner that is interesting, germane to the product, and within the ethical standards of the region. From there, taste and other more personalized standards serve as guides. The U.S. milk industry advertisement shown in this section has been very effective. Although the model is dressed in a swimsuit, it is germane to the product. It is a very effective way to persuade women that milk not only is good for healthy bones, but that it also enhances one's appearance. By telling women that bones continue to develop until the age of 35, the ad reinforces one of the reasons to consume milk.

Musical Appeals

Music is an extremely important advertising ingredient. Music helps capture the listener's attention. It is easily linked to emotions, memories, and other experiences. Music can be intrusive, which means it will gain the attention of someone who previously was not listening to or watching a program. Music can be the stimulus that ties a particular musical arrangement, jingle, or song to a certain product or company. As soon as the tune begins, consumers know what product is being advertised because they have been conditioned to tie the product to the music. For example, the song "Like a Rock" is often quickly linked to Chevrolet's trucks for many people, and the Intel "tune" is readily noticed by computer buffs.

Music gains attention and increases the retention of information as it becomes strongly intertwined with the product. Even when consumers do not recall the ad message argument, music can lead to a better recall of an ad's visual and emotional aspects. Music can also increase the persuasiveness of an argument. Subjects asked to compare ads with music to identical ads without music almost always rated those with music higher in terms of persuasiveness.[30]

Musical memories are often stored in long-term recall areas of the brain. Most people can remember tunes even from their childhood days. Figure 6.10 lists some popular songs now being used in commercials. Several decisions are made when selecting music for ads. They include answering questions such as the following:

- What role will music play in the ad?
- Will a familiar song be used, or will something original be created?
- What emotional pitch should the music reach?
- How does the music fit with the message of the ad?

Music plays a number of roles in advertisements. Sometimes the music is incidental. In others, it is the ad's primary theme. Occasionally, the use of music misdirects the audience so a surprise ending can be used. The creative must select the correct type of music, from whimsical to dramatic to romantic. Just as using the wrong plot or wrong actors in an advertisement can mean disaster, so can selecting the wrong music. Conversely, a quality match between the music and the ad theme can lead to a strongly favorable reaction by the viewer or listener.

Another important decision involves the selection of a familiar tune versus creating original music for the ad. The most common method is to write a jingle or music specifically for the advertisement. Background or mood-inducing music is usually instrumental, and advertisers often pay musicians to write music that matches the scenes in the ad. Also, some companies use the same instrumental tune for each commercial, such as United Airlines, which for years featured "Rhapsody in Blue" in television and radio ads.

Using a well-known song in an ad has certain advantages. The primary benefit is that consumers already have developed an affinity for the song. Brand awareness, brand equity, and brand loyalty are easier to develop when consumers are familiar with the music. This happens when consumers transfer an emotional affinity for the song to the product. One variation on this approach is to purchase an existing song and adapt the ad to the music.[31] Using popular songs is often costly. The price for rights to a very popular song is into six or seven figures.[32] The Internet company Excite paid $7 million for the rights to Jimi Hendrix's song "Are You Experienced," and Microsoft paid about $12 million for "Start Me Up."[33]

Not all writers and musicians are willing to sell their songs for advertising. Ben McDonald rejected a $150,000 offer from Bausch & Lomb and $450,000 from Clairol for the Top 40 hit "The Future's So Bright I Gotta Wear Shades." Bruce Springsteen rejected offers in the millions for his hit song "Born in the USA." These and other songwriters feel strongly about preventing their music from becoming part of an ad. To them, it would be selling out.[34]

An alternative method of developing music is now emerging, primarily because of the Internet. There is now more cooperation among musicians and marketers. Musicians now view advertisements as a way to get their songs heard. Marketers see an opportunity to tie a new, emerging song to a product. Many consumers are also interested in finding out who performs the music in various ads. The Internet provides the

---

- "Revolution" by Beatles (Nike)
- "Real Love" by John Lennon (JCPenney)
- "We're All in This Together" by Ben Lee (Kohl's)
- "Hush" by Deep Purple (Jaguar)
- "Just Fine" by Mary J. Blige (Chevrolet)
- "I'm in the Mood for Love" by Brenda Lee (Victoria's Secret)
- "Thriller" by Michael Jackson (Sobe)
- "Da Ya Think I'm Sexy?" by Rod Stewart (Chips Ahoy)
- "Eyes on Me" by Celine Dion (Celine Dion Sensational)

FIGURE 6.10
Popular Songs Used in Ads

opportunity not only to find out, but to post it for others to enjoy. When an ad only contains part of the song, many companies place the entire tune on their Web sites so individuals can download it. The song "Sir Duke" sung by Stevie Wonder was part of a Lee Jeans commercial and is now available on the company's Web site.[35]

Occasionally, a song that is written for a commercial will crack Billboard's Top 100 list. Jason Wade, a singer in the band Lifehouse, had never written a song for a commercial before. After viewing a copy of the 60-second commercial for Allstate Insurance produced by Leo Burnett Agency, Wade wrote a song entitled "From Where You Are." The commercial promoted Allstate's safe driving program for teenagers. After the commercial aired, the song was made available on iTunes. Within 2 weeks, sales were high enough for the song to reach No. 40 on Billboard's charts.[36]

Rational Appeals

A rational appeal follows the hierarchy of effects stages of awareness, knowledge, liking, preference, conviction, and purchase. Creatives design ads for one of the six steps. An ad oriented to the knowledge stage will transmit basic product information. In the preference stage, the ad shifts to presenting logical reasons why one particular brand is superior, such as the superior gas mileage of an automobile or a better safety record. A rational ad leads to a stronger conviction about a product's benefits, so that the purchase is eventually made.

Rational appeals rely on consumers actively processing the information presented in the advertisement. The consumer must pay attention to the commercial, comprehend the message, and compare the message to knowledge embedded in a cognitive map. Messages consistent with the current concepts in the cognitive map strengthen key linkages. New messages help the person form cognitive beliefs about the brand and establish a new linkage from his or her current map to the new product. A business customer who sees a Kinko's advertisement about videoconferencing services already may have the company in his cognitive structure. The customer may have used Kinko's in the past but was not aware that the company offers videoconferencing. When Kinko's is already established in this person's cognitive map, it is only a matter of creating a new linkage to entice the customer to try its videoconferencing services.

Print media offer the best outlets for rational appeals. Print ads allow readers greater opportunities to process copy information. They can pause and take time to read the verbal content. Television and radio commercials are so short that it is difficult for viewers to process message arguments. Also, if television viewers miss the ad they must wait until the ad is broadcast again to view it.

Business-to-business advertisers use print media extensively. These advertisers take advantage of print's ability to feature rational appeals. Many advertising account executives believe trade publications are the best way to reach members of the buying center. Those in the industry read trade publications carefully. Placing an ad in a trade publication means the firm has an excellent chance of hitting its primary target market. Further, trade publications allow advertisers the opportunity to convey more details to potential buyers.

Buying center members who scan trade journals while in the information search stage of the buying process are quite likely to notice the ad, read it, and process the information. Buying center members who are not

Notice that rational ads often contain more copy.

Source: Courtesy of Newcomer, Morris & Young, Inc.

Devoted to healing those who depend on us the most.

It begins with imagination and grows from compassion. It inspires devotion...
Caring for little ones is our special calling.

You want what's best for your child...happiness at play and the finest in pediatric care.

St. Francis North Hospital is devoted to providing the highest level of pediatric care, including this region's **only Pediatric Intensive Care Unit (PICU)**. After all, our **pediatric subspecialists, pediatric hospitalists,** nurses, and staff are not only experts in their field, but many of them have children of their own. They understand your concerns when your child needs hospitalization. They realize that caring for sick little ones takes compassion and an appreciation for imagination.

So when your little nurse needs some extra care, we're here to get her back to caring for those she loves.

ST. FRANCIS NORTH HOSPITAL
An Affiliate of St. Francis Medical Center
3421 Medical Park Drive • Monroe
(318) 388-1946   www.stfran.com

First in Pediatrics.
Foremost in Caring for Kids.

looking for information about the particular product probably will ignore the same ad. Magazines do not have intrusion value and readers can easily skip or ignore an advertisement. A rational appeal usually focuses on a primary appeal, and no strong peripheral cues grab the reader's attention.

Conventional advertising wisdom states that rational appeals are well suited for high-involvement and complex products. High-involvement decisions require considerable cognitive activity, and consumers spend more time evaluating the attributes of the individual brands. Thus, a rational appeal is the best approach to reach them. For some consumers, however, emotions and feelings even influence high-involvement decisions. For instance, life insurance involves both rational and emotional elements. Various insurance companies can use both in seeking to influence consumers.

In general, rational appeals are effective when consumers have high levels of involvement and are willing to pay attention to the advertisement. Message arguments and product information can be placed in the copy. Consumers can then more fully absorb information.

A rational appeal is superior to other appeals in developing or changing attitudes and establishing brand beliefs. This is mainly true when a consumer has a particular interest in the product or brand advertised. Otherwise, the consumer will often ignore an ad using a rational appeal.

Emotional Appeals

Emotional appeals are based on three ideas (see Figure 6.11). First, consumers ignore most advertisements. Second, rational appeals go unnoticed unless the consumer is in the market for a particular product at the time it is advertised. Third, and most important, emotional advertising can capture a viewer's attention and cause an attachment to develop between the consumer and the brand.

Most creatives view emotional advertising as the key to brand loyalty. Creatives want customers to feel a bond with the brand. Emotional appeals reach the more creative side of the brain. Visual cues in ads are important in emotional appeals. Notice how the visual elements in the New Balance ad in this section contribute to a feeling or mood of serenity. Also, peripheral cues, such as the music and the actor, are crucial. Although individuals develop perceptions of brands based largely on visual and peripheral stimuli, it does not happen instantly. With repetition, perceptions and attitudinal changes emerge. Figure 6.12 displays some of the more common emotions presented in advertisements.

Western Union used emotional appeals in advertisements targeted to U.S. Spanish-language television channels and Latin American countries. The television ads featured testimonials from people reminiscing about their relatives in Latin America whom they had left behind when they came to the United States. Using scenes in kitchens, gardens, and local streets, relatives point out that they all receive money from relatives in the United States via Western Union. In one commercial, a mother and daughter make pastries in their kitchen in El Salvador. The mother talks about her son in the United States sending her money each month. Western Union's previous ads focused on product attributes. Customer focus groups in the United States revealed that many had not seen their children, parents, or cousins in Latin America for 10 years. Western

◆ Consumers ignore most ads.
◆ Rational appeals generally go unnoticed.
◆ Emotional appeals can capture attention and foster an attachment.

FIGURE 6.11
Reasons for Using Emotional Appeals

FIGURE 6.12
Emotions Used in Advertisements

- ◆ Trust
- ◆ Reliability
- ◆ Friendship
- ◆ Happiness
- ◆ Security
- ◆ Glamour–luxury
- ◆ Serenity
- ◆ Anger

- ◆ Protecting loved ones
- ◆ Romance
- ◆ Passion
- ◆ Family bonds
  - ◆ with parents
  - ◆ with siblings
  - ◆ with children
  - ◆ with extended family members

Union used this emotional appeal to convey the concepts of trust and reliability, and sales grew dramatically as a result.[37]

The Effie Awards are sponsored by the New York Chapter of the American Marketing Association. In a recent awards ceremony, of the 34 Effie Gold Awards presented 21 used emotional appeals. The most common approach winners used was to combine humor with emotions. The second most common approach among the emotional-appeal ads was a focus on the consumer's life and feelings.[38] The MasterCard "Priceless" campaign uses this approach.

The Priceless campaign was created by Joyce King Thomas of the McCann-Erickson Ad Agency. The basic tagline is "There are some things money can't buy. For everything else, there's MasterCard." One of the most popular ads featured a father and son at a baseball game. The ad successfully created warm feelings in viewers. It also increased both awareness and use of the MasterCard. Mothers responded as favorably as men to the spot. The same theme is used in international markets. Commercials are adjusted to local customs. In Australia, instead of a baseball game, the father and son attend a cricket match.[39]

Business-to-business advertisers are now beginning to use emotional appeals. In the past, only 5 to 10 percent of all business-to-business ads had emotional appeals. Today, the figure is around 25 percent. A magazine advertisement created by NKH&W Advertising Agency for a product to treat racehorses switched from a rational appeal to an emotional appeal. The target market for the ad was veterinarians. In the past, the ad would have opened with such ad copy as "For swelling in joints use . . ." The emotional ad has the horse thinking, "I will prove them wrong. I will run again. I will mend my spirits."[40]

The underlying principle for changing to more emotional business-to-business ads is that emotions can be part of every type of purchase decision. Members of the buying center consider product information in making decisions but, at the same time, they are likely to be affected by emotions. Although a member of the buying center may try to minimize the emotional side of a purchase, the person is still likely to be affected. The affective component of attitudes is just as important as the cognitive component. In the past, business-to-business advertisers tended to ignore the affective element.

An advertisement by State Farm using an emotional appeal.

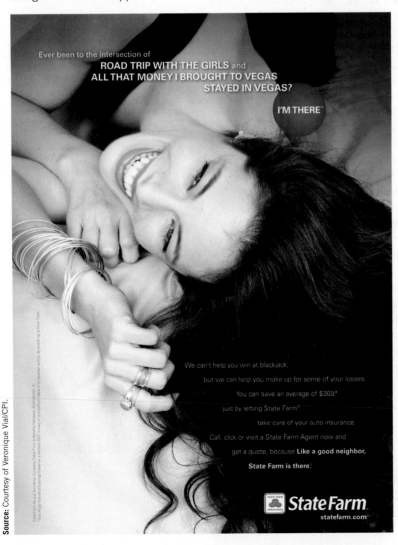

Television is one of the best media for emotional appeals. Television offers advertisers intrusion value and can utilize both sound and sight. Models in the ads can be "real people." Facial expressions can convey emotions and attitudes. Consumers learn about a particular product and develop attitudes based on these vicarious experiences. Television ads also are more vivid, more lifelike, and they can create dynamic situations that pull the viewer into the ad. Music can be incorporated to make the ad more dramatic. Peripheral cues are important components of emotional appeals. These peripheral cues (such as music and background visuals) also capture the viewer's attention.

Emotions are tied with humor, fear, music, and other appeals to make a compelling case for a product. The same ad can influence a consumer both emotionally and rationally. The goal of the creative is to select the most appropriate emotional appeal for the product and company.

Scarcity Appeals

Scarcity appeals urge consumers to buy a particular product because of a limitation. It can be a limited number of the products available or, more often, that the product is available for only a limited time. When there is a limited supply of a product, the value of that product increases.

Source: Courtesy of New Balance Athletic Shoes Inc. Photographed by Paul Wakefield.

New Balance uses visual elements in this advertisement to create an emotional appeal of serenity and peace.

For the Olympics, General Mills introduced USA Olympic Crunch cereal and Betty Crocker Team USA desserts for a limited time. Then, at the turn of the century, General Mills introduced a Cheerios line called *Millenios* as a limited-time product. Tiny "2s" were added to the familiar O-shaped Cheerios.[41] McDonald's, Wendy's, and Burger King offer sandwiches (McRib, Hot N' Spicy Chicken, Dollar Whoppers) for limited-time periods throughout the year. The scarcity concept is also used for musical compilations, encouraging consumers to buy the product because of its limited availability. By making sure it is not available in retail stores, marketers increase its scarcity value.

A scarcity appeal is often tied to other promotional tools. For example, a manufacturer may advertise a limited price discount offer to retailers who stock up early for Christmas or some other holiday season. Contests and sweepstakes also run for limited times. The primary benefit of scarcity appeals is that they encourage consumers to take action. Creatives normally receive information about scarcity issues in the creative brief or from the account executive who has consulted with the company.

THE STRUCTURE OF AN ADVERTISEMENT

The majority of ads prepared for publication or broadcast tend to contain five elements. These ingredients create the structure of an advertisement. They are:

- The promise of a benefit (the headline)
- The spelling out of the promise (a subheadline)
- Amplification
- Proof of the claim
- Action to take

In print advertising, the *headline* is crucial. A typical reader is going to look at the artwork, figure, or illustration first. Next, the reader scans the headline. To keep the potential customer interested means finding some method (rational, emotional, humor, etc.) that moves the reader to the rest of the copy. Typical features of a headline are that the words are short, simple, and limited (less than 12); inviting or interest-provoking; action oriented; and supply enough information to let the buyer know about the product while appealing most directly to the target audience.

A headline should not be mistaken for a tagline. The **tagline** is a key phrase that is usually placed near the end of an advertisement's copy. Examples of headlines and subheadlines are shown in Figure 6.13. The *subheadline*, or spelling out of the promise, accompanies the headline. In some instances, the headline is powerful enough by itself, so this step is skipped. A subheadline is similar to a second headline in a newspaper story. It delivers additional information and leads the reader to the copy.

The *amplification* is the text or body copy of the advertisement. The wording should be concise. The *unique selling proposition* or the *major selling idea* is portrayed in the copy. The company can be factual, imaginative, or emotional in its approach. Factual copy often is part of comparison advertising, where one product or company is directly contrasted with another. Amplification copy is especially important in business-to-business advertisements, in which more complex features of a product must be explained or summarized.

Proof of the claim can be generated from many sources. These include seals of approval (e.g., Good Housekeeping), guarantees (money back if not fully satisfied), trial offers and samples, warranties, demonstrations, and testimonials. A company with strong brand equity is in a better position to make a claim because of the brand's power.

Finally, the consumer must be made aware of the *action to take.* "Buy now," "stop by for a free sample," and "tell your friends" are statements declaring the action the consumer should take. Less direct actions might be to "give us a try" or "stop by for a test

FIGURE 6.13
Advertising Headlines and Subheadlines

STAND-ALONE HEADLINES
Now you can shave your legs half as often. *(the promise of a benefit by Jergens)*
Just when you thought laundry couldn't get any more fun. *(benefit promised by Tide)*
It's so delicious you'll wish bagels didn't have holes. *(enticement, Brummel & Brown spread)*
Can Opener *(provocative, Maxwell House—the opener is one finger)*
Why macaroni was invented. *(presents an existing benefit, Kraft Macaroni and Cheese Dinner Deluxe)*

HEADLINES WITH SUBHEADINGS	
Headline:	Whipped up. Fluffy. Now with better-tasting chocolate. *(presents a new benefit, 3 Musketeers)*
Subheadline:	It could be better if Mr. Right fed it to you. *(targets women in Redbook, a magazine oriented to women)*
Headline:	Chemo was stealing the energy I needed for my grandson. *(emotional, Procrit)*
Subheadline:	Until I talked to my doctor about getting it back.
Headline:	Free face-lifts. *(creates intrigue, FTD florists)*
Subheadline:	With every bouquet from your FTD florist.

drive." The action should mirror the stage in the hierarchy of effects model: awareness, knowledge, liking, preference, conviction, or purchase.

These five parts of the structure of an advertisement must also be contained in the use of message strategies and executional frameworks, which are presented in the following chapter. The account executive, creative, and company presenting the ad know that every advertisement cannot contain every component. Instead, these factors and features should appear as an advertising campaign progresses over time.

INTERNATIONAL IMPLICATIONS

Many of the international implications of both advertising theory and the various types of appeals have already been described. In summary, leverage points lead to customer values. These values may be influenced by the culture or country in which the consumer lives. Therefore, advertisements must be constructed in ways that will express those values appropriate for the market.

The advertising appeals must also be adjusted for cultural differences. As a small example, fear of body odor is often used in selling products in the United States. In other cultures, body odor does not carry the same meaning. Sexual appeals, as noted, must be adjusted to fit the laws and customs of a region. Musical tastes vary, as do perceptions of rationality and scarcity. Emotions may be stronger in some cultures, whereas in others, people are much more reserved.

An international company or a firm seeking to expand into additional countries must adapt and adjust both the theoretical approach and type of appeal in order to create effective advertisements. Finding universal themes, such as visual Esperanto, may be a great help to the international advertising creative.

SUMMARY

Developing effective advertisements is the culmination of a series of integrated marketing communications efforts. They include knowing the objective of the ad, the target audience, the message theme used, the type of support needed, and any constraints that apply. Then, a creative must work within the context of key advertising theories in selecting the correct media and designing the leverage point and message appeal that work effectively within each medium.

Three important theoretical approaches drive the development of many advertisements. The hierarchy of effects model suggests consumers move through a series of stages as they are persuaded to make a purchase. The steps are: (1) awareness, (2) knowledge, (3) liking, (4) preference, (5) conviction, and (6) the actual purchase. Although the process probably is not a lock-step model that every buyer follows, the hierarchy of effects approach does provide important information about which mental issues to account for in various advertising campaigns. The hierarchy of effects model can be combined with the three main elements present in attitudes: (1) cognitive, (2) affective, and (3) conative components. Ads are designed to influence affective feelings, cognitive knowledge, or conative intentions to act or behave based on an attitude. A means–end chain displays the linkages between a means to achieve a desired state and the end or personal value at issue. Advertisers can select personal values that mesh with the key characteristics of the target market and then construct ads designed to provide them the means to achieve these ends by purchasing the good or service. These ideas help the creative develop a leverage point to move the buyer from understanding the product's benefits to incorporating those benefits with his or her personal values.

Visual and verbal issues should also be considered in the formation of an ad. Concrete visual images are easily recognized and recalled. Abstract images may be linked with values or emotions the product creates or the feeling the buyer should experience that may be associated with the product or company. Visual elements are key components in almost every form of advertising. Verbal elements must reach the more rational, central route of the audience's mental processing procedures.

Beyond these components, advertising creatives must form messages using one (or more) of the seven major appeals: (1) fear, (2) humor, (3) sex, (4) music, (5) rationality, (6) emotions, or (7) scarcity. Just as there are logical combinations of media, there are logical combinations of these appeals for various messages. Often, music is the backdrop for messages invoking fear, humor, sex, and emotions. Humor can be linked with sex, music, rationality (by showing how being illogical is silly or funny), and scarcity. Rationality combines with fear in many commercials. The goal of the creative is to design a message argument that takes advantage of the various characteristics of these appeals, breaks through clutter, and convinces the audience to buy the item involved. Mismatches of message tactics are to be avoided, such as combining sex with humor in France, as mentioned in this chapter.

Business-to-business ads often appear in print and many times include rational approaches in the copy because the purchase decision variables are more complex. At the same time, many advertisers have recently discovered that emotional ads can be effective, which expands business-to-business advertising into other venues, such as television, radio, and the Internet.

The process of designing ads for international markets is quite similar to that for domestic ads. The major difference is careful consideration of local attitudes and customers, with due care given to the language, slang, and symbols of the area. For example, Sega recently discovered that its product's name is slang for "masturbation" in Italian, after a major advertising campaign had started. These types of mistakes should be carefully avoided.

Every marketer knows that some ad campaigns, no matter how carefully conceived, still fail. The goal is to try to reach a point where the failure of one specific ad or campaign does not have long-lasting effects on the company. To do so, a thoughtfully designed IMC program can build a firm's image in such a manner that brand and product loyalty, along with customer recognition, can reduce the ill effects of one "lead balloon" advertising campaign. In the end, advertising is only one component of an IMC program. Although it is clearly a major and important ingredient, it should be considered in the context of a long-term plan to strengthen the company, its products, and its overall image in the customers' mind.

KEY TERMS

hierarchy of effects model   A marketing approach suggesting that a consumer moves through a series of six steps when becoming convinced to make a purchase: (1) awareness, (2) knowledge, (3) liking, (4) preference, (5) conviction, and (6) the actual purchase.

means–end chain   An advertisement approach in which the message contains a means (a reasoning or mental process) to lead the consumer to a desired end state, such as a key personal value.

Means–End Conceptualization of Components for Advertising Strategy (MECCAS)   An advertising approach that suggests using five elements in creating ads: (1) the product's attributes, (2) consumer benefits, (3) leverage points, (4) personal values, and (5) the executional framework.

visual Esperanto   A universal language that makes global advertising possible for any good or service by recognizing that visual images are more powerful than verbal descriptions.

advertising appeals   Approaches to reaching consumers with ads. The seven major appeals are: (1) fear, (2) humor, (3) sex, (4) music, (5) rationality, (6) emotions, and (7) scarcity.

severity   Part of the fear behavioral response model that leads the individual to consider how strong certain negative consequences of an action will be.

vulnerability   Part of the fear behavioral response model that leads the individual to consider the odds of being affected by the negative consequences of an action.

decorative models   Models in an advertisement whose primary purpose is to adorn the product as a sexual or attractive stimulus without serving a functional purpose.

tagline   The final key phrase in an ad, used to make the key point and reinforce the company's image to the consumer.

REVIEW QUESTIONS

1. What are the five main elements of a creative brief? How do they affect the choice of advertising appeals?

2. What are the six stages of the hierarchy of effects model? Do they always occur in that order? Why or why not?

3. How are the three components of attitudes related to the hierarchy of effects model?

4. In a means–end chain, what are the means? The ends? How do they affect advertising design?

5. What is a leverage point? How are leverage points related to the hierarchy of effects model, attitudinal changes, and means–end chains?

6. Why are visual elements in advertisement important? What is the relationship between visual and verbal elements? Can there be one without the other?

7. What are the advantages and disadvantages of fear appeals in advertising?

8. When does humor work in an ad? What pitfalls should companies avoid in using humorous appeals?

9. What types of sexual appeals can advertisers use?

10. When are sexual appeals most likely to succeed? To fail?

11. What should international advertisers consider when thinking about using sexual appeals?

12. Name the different ways music can play a role in an advertisement. Explain how each role should match individual appeals, media, and the other elements in the design of the ad.

13. What are the advantages and disadvantages of rational appeals? Which media do they best match?

14. How can emotions accentuate advertisements? Why are they being used more often in business-to-business advertisements?

15. What is scarcity? How do scarcity ads lead to buyer action?

16. Name four combinations of appeals that are logical combinations for advertisers.

17. What five components make up the structure of an advertisement? Explain each one.

CRITICAL THINKING EXERCISES

Discussion Questions

1. Develop a means–end chain similar to the one in Figure 6.3 for each of the following branded products:

   a. Clorox bleach

   b. Zippo lighters

   c. Kool-Aid

   d. Sony stereos

Share your results with the class. How were your means–end chains similar or dissimilar to others in class?

2. Evaluate the balance of visual and verbal elements of five advertisements shown in this chapter. Which is predominant? Which images are considered appropriate for international advertising because they have the characteristic of visual Esperanto?

3. Try to recall five outstanding television commercials. Identify the appeal used in each one. Why were these five ads effective? Compare your list with those of other classmates. What was their reaction to your list? How did you feel about theirs?

4. Locate a print ad or television ad that uses a fear appeal. Using the behavioral response model in Figure 6.6, identify various elements in the ad that correspond with the components in the model. Some of the elements will require thinking beyond what is visually or verbally present in the ad itself.

5. Hardee's and Carl's Jr. recently used a television commercial featuring a schoolteacher dancing on top of her desk while a room full of guys performed a rap song entitled "I Like Flat Buns." The song seemed appropriate since the ad was for the Patty Melt on a flat bun. Instead, the ad received considerable flack because the sexy blonde school teacher was wearing a short, tight skirt. Teacher's associations complained that it was inappropriate because it was a "sexually exploitive assault" on teachers, students, and schools.[42] Do you agree or disagree? Why?

6. Record five television commercials. Identify which appeal each advertisement uses. Discuss the quality of the advertisement and its best and worst aspects. For each ad, present another possible appeal and how it could be used. What personal values and customer benefits does each advertisement present?

7. Record five television commercials or find five print advertisements that use sex appeal. Identify which of the five ways sexuality was used. Evaluate each ad in terms of the appropriateness and effectiveness of the sex appeal.

INTEGRATED LEARNING EXERCISES

1. Greenfield Online is one of the leading online research firms. Access the Web site at **www.greenfieldcentral.com**. What types of products does the company offer? How would this information help a creative in developing an advertisement? How would this information assist an advertising agency in understanding the target audience for an advertisement?

2. Examine Figure 6.3, and then access the following Web sites for the milk industry. What differences do you see in the Web sites? What do you believe is the intended audience for each Web site?

   a. www.got-milk.com

   b. www.gotmilk.com

   c. www.whymilk.com

3. Visit the following Web sites. Identify which type of appeal each site uses. Evaluate the quality of that appeal. What other appeals can be used to make the site more appealing? Discuss the balance of visual and verbal elements on the Web site and ad.

   a. Service Metrics (**www.servicemetrics.com**)

   b. Trashy Lingerie (**www.trashy.com**)

   c. Skechers (**www.skechers.com**)

   d. Bijan Fragrances (**www.bijan.com**)

   e. Guess (**www.guess.com**)

   f. Aetna Inc. (**www.aetna.com**)

   g. Liz Claiborne (**www.lizclaiborne.com**)

4. Access an online database search engine through your library. Pick one of the appeals listed in the chapter. Find at least three different articles that discuss the appeal. Write a report of your findings.

STUDENT PROJECT

Creative Corner

It is time to try your creativity with a television advertisement. Borrow a camcorder and develop a 30- or 45-second television spot for one of the following products, using the suggested appeal. Be sure to develop a means–end chain prior to creating the advertisement.

a. Denim skirt, sex appeal

b. Tennis racket, humor appeal

c. Ice cream, emotional appeal

d. Vitamins, fear appeal

e. Golf club, rational appeal

f. Spring break trip package, scarcity appeal

g. Restaurant, music appeal

CASE 1 LIGHTING UP KINDLE

The world of book publishing and book reading is currently undergoing radical changes that are largely being driven by new technologies. Authors who previously found themselves shut out of traditional publishing can now use the Internet to distribute their books on topics ranging from self-help to political ideology.

After the initial wave of e-book releases, including one by well-known author Stephen King, changes in consumer book-purchasing patterns slowed. Noted New York literary agent Peter Rubie believed that the secret was mobility. He stated that "as soon as someone can carry an e-book to the beach without needing a lap top, the industry is going to change."

That day may have arrived. In late 2007, Jeff Bezos, the founder and CEO of Amazon.com, announced the release of a revolutionary new product—the Kindle. The Kindle is a wireless, portable reading device that offers instant access to more than 90,000 books, blogs, magazines, and newspapers. The technology behind the Kindle is the same as contained in cell phones, which means that users do not need to find a Wi-Fi hotspot to use it. The Kindle weighs 10.3 ounces and can carry 200 books at any time. Readers can download books, magazines, blogs, and newspapers from any location.

The device offered a variety of new features. For example, if a person does not know the meaning of a word in a text, the word can be highlighted and then found in an instant dictionary. Links to other sources, such as Wikipedia, are also available.

The great benefit of Kindle to authors is that their books remain available in perpetuity. No longer will a book go "out of print." Each book download costs the reader about $10.00, and the author receives a royalty, just as in the past. For some authors, an additional benefit is the ability to revise a book over time, because the entire content is digital rather than print.

The Kindle debuted with some buzz, despite its hefty price tag ($400). Bezos appeared on *Charlie Rose*, and several newspaper and magazine articles about the product created some publicity. The company will need to build on that early momentum, because it clearly did not generate the same kind of interest as the MP3 player or the iPhone. Further, competition soon became available in the form of the Sony Portable Reading System.

Author Kevin Maney summarized the Kindle this way: "It's too early to tell whether this is the book's future. The Kindle isn't even set up to do all that just yet. But it is the first e-book reader built to be wirelessly connected to the Internet at all times. It's the first system that shows that living, connected books—some combination of traditional books and Wikipedia—are possible. And, in fact, that's the first reason to think that e-books could evolve into something other than paper books." Consumers will undoubtedly decide the rest.

Sources: **www.amazon.com**, accessed January 5, 2008; Kevin Maney, "A Book That Never Ends?" *USA Today,* December 6, 2007, p. 19A.1.

1. As an advertising executive who is working with a creative, which advertising theory do you think best fits the release and subsequent advertising for Kindle?

2. What should be the leverage point in a commercial for Kindle?

3. What type of advertising appeal, or sets of appeals, should be used in promoting Kindle?

4. What should be the headline of a Kindle ad? Why?

5. Design a print ad promoting Kindle. Identify which appeal you used and explain why you chose it.

CASE 2 THE AUTO ADVANTAGE

Barry Farber has pretty much "seen it all" in his 30 years of selling used cars. His business, The Auto Advantage, had experienced a series of high and low points related to buyer whims and the nature of the industry. Barry is quick to point out that his strongest ally has always been a local advertising company in Sacramento that has helped him negotiate the troubled waters.

From the beginning, Barry has seen opportunities rise up and drift away. When he opened his modest lot in 1973, the first gas crisis was just emerging. People were dumping gas-hog cars and diligently looking for high-mileage cars and those fueled by diesel. In fact, Barry distinctly remembers offering a practically brand-new Ford LTD II, one of the most popular models of the time, at $3,000 below its "blue book" value and not being able to find a buyer for weeks due to consumer fears about oil shortages and rising gas prices.

At that time, Barry's new advertising agency manager, Wendy Mozden, pointed out an old technique that had worked wonders for years. She called it "turning a disadvantage into an

Both advertising and effective salesmanship are important in selling cars.

advantage." She learned the tactic by watching old Volkswagen commercials. The original "bug" was promoted as being ugly, but economical. Many restaurants during that era bought ads pointing out that the reason they were so "slow" was due to their higher-quality food, making it "worth the wait."

Consequently, The Auto Advantage placed ads in newspapers and on the radio focusing on the "value" an individual could obtain by trading down or across. Sales reps were instructed to convey to individual buyers that a person would have to buy an awfully large amount of gas at 55 cents per gallon before a large car would actually be costly, especially when mpg (miles per gallon) differences between midsize and smaller cars were so small. The Auto Advantage managed to buy cars that other companies did not want to carry at drastically reduced prices and sell them to the customers they could educate concerning the shift from disadvantage to advantage. Within a few years, those high-priced (and hard to maintain) diesel cars disappeared, and people once again fell in love with larger gas hogs. By then Barry's company was well established in the marketplace.

Barry weathered the invasion of foreign cars into the United States by once again seeing an advantage in the disadvantage. Using patriotic themes, his company subtly pointed out that people buying foreign-made cars hurt the local economy, especially because one of the major manufacturers in the Sacramento area made replacement parts for GM cars. Sales presentations always included the question "Are you in a union?" Those who responded "yes" were easy targets for the company's "Buy American" theme during the early 1980s.

From there, Barry spent a great deal of energy making sure he understood the needs of his aging client base. Those who started families in the 1980s needed minivans in the 1990s. Those who were older and facing retirement often wanted low-maintenance cars. By carefully constructing his original

message, that a person would gain an advantage by shopping at his lot, the business continued to succeed.

The next major challenge for The Auto Advantage may become the same one in which the company began. Oil prices are rising, and the U.S. government has created tighter pollution standards for almost every make and model of car. Some consumers are again looking for more fuel-efficient autos, even hybrid gas–electric models ones. Barry knows he needs to continue to adapt as the marketplace evolves. He continues to look for turnaround situations to find the edge to keep his clients happy with what they bought from The Auto Advantage.

1. Describe an advertisement that you have seen in which the firm attempted to turn a disadvantage into an advantage.

2. If gas prices doubled in a 1-year time period, how should The Auto Advantage respond? Design an ad using the various strategies described in this chapter that promote fuel economy.

3. Should The Auto Advantage continue to advertise to baby boomer and older clients? How would they attract Generation X or Generation Y customers to the lot? In other words, how would the advertisements be different? Design an advertisement for the Generation X or Generation Y customers.

4. Pick one of the following appeals. Design a print advertisement for The Auto Advantage using that appeal.

   a. Fear

   b. Humor

   c. Sex

   d. Emotional

ENDNOTES

1. Rob Walker, "Cul-de-sac Cred," *New York Times Magazine*, July 10, 2005.

2. **www.marceckoenterprises.com**, accessed October 1, 2007.

3. Jerry Olson and Thomas J. Reynolds, "Understanding Consumers' Cognitive Structures: Implications for Advertising Strategy," *Advertising Consumer Psychology*, L. Percy and A. Woodside, eds. (Lexington, MA: Lexington Books, 1983), pp. 77–90; Thomas J. Reynolds and Alyce Craddock, "The Application of the MECCAS Model to Development and Assessment of Advertising Strategy," *Journal of Advertising Research* 28, no. 2 (1988), pp. 43–54.

4. Laurie A. Babin and Alvin C. Burns, "Effects of Print Ad Pictures and Copy Containing Instructions to Imagine on Mental Imagery That Mediates Attitudes," *Journal of Advertising* 26, no. 3 (Fall 1997), pp. 33–44.

5. Marc Bourgery and George Guimaraes, "Global Ads: Say It with Pictures," *Journal of European Business* 4, no. 5 (May–June 1993), pp. 22–26.

6. Olson and Reynolds, "Understanding Consumers' Cognitive Structures"; Reynolds

and Craddock, "The Application of the MEC-CAS Model to Development and Assessment of Advertising Strategy."

7. Based on Rosemary M. Murtaugh, "Designing Effective Health Promotion Messages Using Components of Protection Motivation Theory," *Proceedings of the Atlantic Marketing Association* (1999), pp. 553–57; R. W. Rogers and S. Prentice-Dunn, "Protection Motivation Theory," *Handbook of Health Behavior Research I: Personal and Social Determinants*, D. Gochman, ed. (New York: Plenum Press, 1997), pp. 130–32.

8. Michael S. Latour and Robin L. Snipes, "Don't Be Afraid to Use Fear Appeals: An Experimental Study," *Journal of Advertising Research* 36, no. 2 (March–April 1996), pp. 59–68.

9. Martin Eisend, "A Meta-Analysis of Humor Effects in Advertising," *Advances in Consumer Research–North American Conference Proceedings* 34 (2007), pp. 320–23.

10. Karen Flaherty, Marc G. Weinberger, and Charles S. Gulas, "The Impact of Perceived Humor, Product Type, and Humor Style in Radio Advertising," *Journal of Current Issues*

and Research in Advertising 26, no. 1 (Spring 2004), pp. 25–37.

11. Theresa Howard, "Windex Birds Make Clean Sweep as Most-Liked Ads," *USA Today* (December 18, 2006), p. 7B (Money).

12. Matthew Creamer, "Marketing's Era of Outrage," *Advertising Age* 78, no. 7 (February 12, 2007), pp. 1, 26.

13. Jimmy Yap, "McDonald's Finds Humor a Hit with Singapore Viewers," *Media Asia* (February 7, 2004), p. 22; Bill Britt, "Ford Tries Witty, Edgy Advertising to Promote the Kia," *Automotive News Europe* 9, no. 2 (January 26, 2004), p. 4.

14. "Sex Doesn't Sell," *The Economist* 373, no. 8399 (October 30, 2004), pp. 62–63.

15. Laurel Wentz, "Global Village," *Advertising Age* 68, no. 10 (March 10, 1997), p. 3; Michael Wilke, "A Kiss Before Buying," *Advocate* (April 27, 1999), pp. 34–35.

16. Sandra O'Loughlin, "Hanes Shows Some 'Love' in Battle for Intimates," *Brandweek* 48, no. 9 (February 26, 2007), p. 11.

17. Based on G. Smith and R. Engel, "Influence of a Female Model on Perceived Characteristics

of an Automobile," *Proceedings of the 76th Annual Convention of the American Psychological Association* 15, no. 3 (1968), pp. 46–54; Leonard Reid and Lawrence C. Soley, "Decorative Models and the Readership of Magazine Ads," *Journal of Advertising Research* 23, (April–May 1983), pp. 27–32; R. Chestnut, C. LaChance, and A. Lubitz, "The Decorative Female Model: Sexual Stimuli and the Recognition of Advertisements," *Journal of Advertising* 6 (Fall 1977), pp. 11–14.

18. Bob Garfield, "Dentyne Spot Makes It Seem That Naysayers Have a Point," *Advertising Age* 76, no. 5 (January 31, 2005), p. 41.

19. Jessica Severn, George E. Belch, and Michael A. Belch, "The Effects of Sexual and Non-Sexual Advertising Appeals and Information Level on Cognitive Processing and Communication Effectiveness," *Journal of Advertising* 19, no. 1 (1990), pp. 14–22.

20. Tom Reichart, "Sex in Advertising Research: A Review of Content, Effects, and Functions of Sexual Information in Consumer Advertising," *Annual Review of Sex Research* 13 (2002), pp. 242–74; D. C. Bello, R. E. Pitts, and M. J. Etzel, "The Communication Effects of Controversial Sexual Content in Television Programs and Commercials," *Journal of Advertising* 3, no. 12 (1983), pp. 32–42.

21. "Note to Chrysler: Gutter Humor Has No Place in Ads," *Automotive News* 78, no. 6064 (October 27, 2003), p. 12.

22. Tom Reichart, "Sex in Advertising Research: A Review of Content, Effects, and Functions of Sexual Information in Consumer Advertising," *Annual Review of Sex Research* 13 (2002), pp. 242–74; Andrew A. Mitchell, "The Effect of Verbal and Visual Components of Advertisements on Brand Attitude and Attitude Toward the Advertisement," *Journal of Consumer Research* 13 (June 1986), pp. 12–24.

23. Bruce Horovitz, "Risqué May Be Too Risky for Ads," *USA Today* (April 16, 2004), p. 1B.

24. Bruce Horovitz, "Risqué May Be Too Risky for Ads," *USA Today* (April 16, 2004), p. 1B; Claire Beale, "What Now for Ad Industry As Sex No Longer Sells?" *Campaign (UK)*, no. 36 (September 3, 2004), p. 23.

25. Kelly Lynne Ashton, "Wise to the Game," *Marketing Magazine* 108, no. 28 (August 11, 2003), pp. 22–23; "Teens Deconstruct Two Clothing Ads," *Marketing Magazine* 108, no. 28 (August 11, 2003), p. 22.

26. Daniel A. Joelson, "Rebel Sell," *Latin Trade* 12, no. 8 (August 2004), p. 16.

27. Elizabeth Bryant, "P&G Pushes the Envelope in Egypt with TV Show on Feminine Hygiene," *Advertising Age International* (December 14, 1998), p. 2.

28. Gerard Stamp and Mark Stockdale, "Sex in Advertising," *Advertising Age's Creativity* 7, no. 6 (July–August 1999), pp. 35–36; Bob Garfield, "Pushing the Envelope: The Performing Penis," *Advertising Age International*, (July 12, 1999), p. 4. Jean J. Boddewyn, "Sex and Decency Issues in Advertising: General and International Dimensions," *Business Horizons* 34, no. 5 (September–October 1991), pp. 13–20.

29. Howard Levine, Donna Sweeney, and Stephen H. Wagner, "Depicting Women as Sex Objects in Television Advertising," *Personality and Social Psychology Bulletin* 25, no. 8 (August 1999), pp. 1049–58.

30. Boddewyn, "Sex and Decency Issues in Advertising: General and International Dimensions."

31. Steve Oakes, "Evaluating Empirical Research into Music in Advertising: A Congruity Perspective," *Journal of Advertising Research* 47, no. 1 (March 2007), pp. 38–50.

32. Felicity Shea, "Reaching Youth with Music," *B&T Weekly* 54, no. 2491 (October 1, 2004), pp. 16–17.

33. Brian Steinberg, "The Times Are a-Changin' for Musicians and Marketers," *Advertising Age* 78, no. 43 (October 29, 2005) p. 43.

34. Michael Miller, "Even out of Context, the Beat Goes On (and On)," *Pittsburgh Business Times* 18, no. 18 (November 27, 1998), p. 12.

35. Simon Morrissey, "Jingles in the Jungle," *Campaign (UK)*, no. 38 (September 17, 2004), p. 37; John Marks, "Shake, Rattle, and Please Buy My Product," *U.S. News & World Report* 124, no. 20 (May 25, 1998), p. 51.

36. Nicole Rivard, "Maximizing Music," *SHOOT* 48, no. 4 (February 23, 2007), pp. 17–21.

37. Douglas Quenqua, "What's That Catchy Tune? A Song for Car Insurance Makes the Charts," *The New York Times,* December 31, 2007 (**www.nytimes.com/2007/12/31/business/media/31 allstate.html**).

38. Joy Dietrich, "Western Union Retraces Roots: The Emotions of Money Transfers," *Advertising Age International* (October 1999), pp. 24–25.

39. Scott Rockwood, "For Better Ad Success, Try Getting Emotional," *Marketing News* 30, no. 22 (October 21, 1996), p. 4.

40. Mae Anderson, "A Priceless Promotion," *Adweek* 45, no. 44 (November 22, 2004), pp. 24–25.

41. Joanne Lynch and Leslie de Chernatony, "The Power of Emotion: Brand Communication in Business-to-Business Markets," *Journal of Brand Management* 11, no. 5 (May 2004), pp. 403–420; Karalynn Ott, "B-to-B Marketers Display Their Creative Side," *Advertising Age's Business Marketing* 84, no. 1 (January 1999), pp. 3–4.

42. Stephanie Thompson, "Big Deal," *Mediaweek* 7, no. 44 (November 24, 1997), p. 36; Judann Pollack, "Big G Has Special Cheerios for Big '00,'" *Advertising Age* (June 14, 1999), pp. 1–2. Gregg Cebrzynski, "Teachers Hot about Hot Teacher Dancing in 'Sexually Exploitive' Hardee's TV Spot," *Nation's Restaurant News* 41, no. 37 (September 17, 2007), p. 12.

7

Advertising Design
Message Strategies and Executional Frameworks

Chapter Objectives

After reading this chapter, you should be able to answer the following questions:

- **How** do cognitive, affective, and conative message strategies differ?

- **How** do message strategies affect the development of leverage points and executional frameworks?

- **What** is an executional framework?

- **How** many executional frameworks are there, and what are their names?

- **Which** characteristics are most important when selecting a source or spokesperson?

- **What** are the principles of effective advertising design?

DOVE'S SOCIAL AND FASHION ADVERTISING

In late 2007, *Time* magazine listed its choices for the top 10 advertisements of the year. Fourth on that list was a 60-second spot entitled "Onslaught." The commercial opens with the words "a Dove film" and displays a close-up of a smiling, innocent, red-headed girl for nearly 20 seconds.

Then the onslaught begins. With music featuring a modern sound and the words "Here it comes" frequently repeated in the background, cuts from various pseudo advertisements display slinky, fashionable, beautiful models. The attributes needed to reach such a status are mentioned, "younger, smaller, lighter, thinner, tighter, softer" among them. "It works" is highlighted again and again by the advertising pitchwomen. The inevitable pathway to yo-yo dieting, eating disorders, and various forms of cosmetic surgery follow.

Finally, as a group of young girls around the age of 10 cross a street, the commercial closes with the words, "Talk to your daughter before the beauty industry does." The compelling message does not mention Dove soap or any of its product features. Instead, it offers a strong indictment of the social pressures young girls and young women face.

Advertising and marketing to women and girls may be at a crossroad. Clearly pressures to grow up more quickly, to look older at a younger age, and to fit in socially drive a great deal of product design and what is now being called *age-compression marketing.* Some responsible parents and those who offer social commentary are pushing back with the essential message, "Let girls be girls."

Complaints about body image issues are not new. In the 1960s, a young supermodel named Twiggy captured international attention by looking girlish and paper thin. Movies and movie remakes of the tale of *Lolita* stirred additional controversy and debate. In 2007, the Disney Channel's *Hannah Montana* highlighted the mega power associated with marketing to young girls. The stage show that traveled across the United States resulted in price gouging and ticket-scalping prices into the hundreds of dollars. One side of Hannah, of course, is the glamorous world of a rock star.

CHAPTER SEVEN

Source: Courtesy of Summer Bradley.

Dove's "Onslaught" advertisement is designed to tap into the competing message. The Dove Web site includes pages called "Campaign for Real Beauty" for young girls and "Dove Pro-age" for older women. Visitors can make charitable contributions to the Dove Self-Esteem fund through the Web site. Clearly, this division of the company is tapping into an emotion held by many women, especially mothers.

Time cynically notes that Dove is owned by Unilever, which "advertises its Axe Body Spray to men using a lingerie-and-stiletto-clad rock band called Bom Chicka Wah Wahs," and then asks, "What do we tell our daughters about that?"[1]

OVERVIEW

The essence of an integrated marketing communications program is designing messages that effectively reach the target audience. Many of these messages are, in a very real sense, quite personal. They are designed to change or shape attitudes. They must be remembered. They should lead to some kind of short- or long-term action.

Marketing messages travel in two ways. First, a personal message can be delivered through a personal medium. A sales rep closing the deal, shaking the hand of the buyer, giving a reassuring tap on the shoulder, and smiling while talking is delivering a message in an intimate, warm, human fashion. Clearly, personal media (sales reps, repair department personnel, customer services representatives, etc.) must be included in the overall IMC program and approach.

The second way marketing messages travel is through the various forms of advertising media. Many of these media are completely *impersonal*. Television sets are indifferent as to what appears on the screen. Radios deliver any sound that can be transmitted. Computer screens are nothing more than special-purpose television screens. The challenge to the marketing

Source: © Big Cheese Photo LLC/Alamy.

account executive, the company, and especially the creative is to design a personal message, even while it is being delivered through an impersonal medium.

Account executives are acutely aware of the importance of effectively reaching a target audience. It is not simply a matter of reach, frequency, and continuity. The message must engage the targeted buyer and influence the individual to the point that he or she will recall and purchase the product.

Beyond the goal of making a message personal, many marketers are interested in tangible, measurable results that can be reported to clients and to prospective new customers. Therefore, the relationship between the executive and the creative reaches a critical point at the stage in which an advertisement is developed.

This chapter focuses on several major topics. First, three types of message strategies are described. Each may be used to help convince the consumer to make a purchase, either through reason, emotion, or an action-inducing advertisement. Second, the major types of executional frameworks are noted. These forms of advertising presentations help the creative prepare original, convincing, and memorable ads. Third, the four types of sources or spokespersons that appear in various advertisements are described, and the criteria used to select them are reviewed. Fourth, and finally, the principles of effective advertising campaigns are presented. When advertisements are combined with other elements of the promotions mix in an integrated fashion, the net result is a stronger company image and a clear IMC theme.

MESSAGE STRATEGIES

The **message theme** is the outline of the key ideas in an advertisement. It is a central part of the creative brief. The message theme can be created using a number of message strategies. A **message strategy** is the primary tactic or approach used to deliver the message theme. The three broad categories of message strategies are:[2]

1. Cognitive strategies
2. Affective strategies
3. Conative strategies

The categories represent the components of attitudes, as described earlier. All three of the message strategies are described in this section. Figure 7.1 lists various forms or approaches from each category.

Cognitive Strategies

A **cognitive message strategy** is the presentation of rational arguments or pieces of information to consumers. These ideas require cognitive processing. When a cognitive message strategy is used, the advertisement's key message is about the product's attributes or benefits. Customers can obtain these benefits by using the product.[3]

The goal of the cognitive message strategy approach is to design an ad that will have an impact on a person's beliefs and/or knowledge structure. This can be accomplished by suggesting any one of a wide variety of potential product benefits. Foods may be described as healthful, pleasant tasting, or low calorie. A tool can be shown as durable,

FIGURE 7.1
Message Strategies

◆ Generic	◆ Resonance ⎫ Affective
◆ Preemptive	◆ Emotional ⎭
◆ Unique selling proposition	◆ Action-inducing ⎫ Conative
◆ Hyberbole	◆ Promotional support ⎭
◆ Comparative	

convenient, or handy to use. A drill press machine used in a manufacturing operation may be portrayed as being more reliable or faster than comparable machines on the market. Cognitive message strategies make these benefits clear to potential customers. The five major forms of cognitive strategies are:

1. Generic messages
2. Preemptive messages
3. Unique selling proposition
4. Hyperbole
5. Comparative advertisements

Generic messages are direct promotions of product attributes or benefits without any claim of superiority. This type of strategy works best for a firm that is clearly the brand leader and is the dominant company in the industry. The goal of the generic message is to make the brand synonymous with the product category. Thus, Campbell's Soups can declare "Soup is good food" without making any claim to superiority. This is because the company so strongly dominates the industry. When most consumers think of soup, they think of Campbell's. Of the 10 billion bowls of soup consumed each year, 69 percent are a variety of Campbell's.[4] Nintendo uses a similar strategy because the company dominates the handheld game category with more than 98 percent of the market share.[5]

Generic message strategies are seldom found in business-to-business advertisements, because few firms dominate an industry to the extent of Campbell's or Nintendo. One major exception is Intel, which currently controls 80.2 percent of the microchip market.[6] The generic message "Intel inside" has been used for years to convey to both businesses and end users that the processor inside is made by Intel.

This advertisement uses a generic message strategy by stating *Grace* is a magazine for today's woman.

Generic message strategies can also be used to create brand awareness. The goal of the advertiser may be to develop a cognitive linkage between a specific brand name and a product category, such as Skechers and sporty footwear. The ad may contain very little information about the product's attributes. The intent of the ad is simply to put the brand name in a person's cognitive memory and cognitive map.

Preemptive messages claim superiority based on a product's specific attribute or benefit. The idea is to prevent the competition from making the same or a similar statement. For example, Crest toothpaste is well known as "the cavity fighter." The brand preempts other companies from making similar-sounding claims, even though all toothpastes fight cavities. The key to effectively using a preemptive strategy is to be the first company to state the advantage. This keeps competitors from saying the same thing. Those that do are viewed as "me-too" brands or copycats.

A **unique selling proposition (USP)** is an explicit, testable claim of uniqueness or superiority that can be supported or substantiated in some manner. In the Bonne Bell advertisement shown on the next page, the company proposes a unique selling proposition aimed at teenagers. The message that Bonne Bell Lipshade is "your 1 and only, 1 handed, sleek sweep flipstick!" stresses a unique product feature.

The **hyperbole** approach makes an untestable claim based upon some attribute or benefit. When NBC states that its programming contains America's favorite comedies, the claim is a hyperbole. These claims do not have to be substantiated, which makes this cognitive strategy quite popular.

The final cognitive message strategy is a **comparative advertisement**. When an advertiser directly or indirectly compares a good or service to the competition, it is the comparative method. The advertisement may or may not mention the competitor by name.

An advertisement for Bonne Bell featuring a unique selling proposition.

Sometimes, an advertiser simply presents a "make-believe" competitor, giving it a name like brand *X*. This approach, however, is not as effective as comparative advertising that states the actual competitor's name. To provide protection from lawsuits, company leaders must be sure any claim concerning the competition can be clearly substantiated.

AT&T and MCI compare rates. VISA notes that many merchants will not accept American Express. Burger King explains the advantages of flame broiling as opposed to frying, which McDonald's and Wendy's use. In the business-to-business sector, shipping companies compare delivery times and accuracy rates.

The major advantage of comparative ads is that they often capture the consumer's attention. When comparisons are made, both brand awareness and message awareness increase. Consumers tend to remember more of what the ad says about a brand than when the same information is presented in a noncomparative ad format.

The negative side of using comparative ads is in the areas of believability and consumer attitudes. Many consumers think comparative ads are less believable. They view the information about the sponsor brand as exaggerated and conclude that the information about the comparison brand probably is misstated to make the sponsor brand appear superior.

Another danger of comparative ads is the negative attitudes consumers may develop toward the ad. If viewers acquire negative attitudes toward the advertisement, these negative attitudes can transfer to the sponsor's product. This is especially true when the sponsor runs a *negative comparative ad*. This form of advertisement portrays the competition's product in a negative light. Research has shown that negative comparative ads typically result in lower believability of the ad claims and create less favorable attitudes toward the brand.[7]

In psychology, the concept of *spontaneous trait transference* suggests that when someone calls another person dishonest, other people tend to remember the speaker as also being less than honest. When a comparative ad criticizes the competition's brand based on some particular attribute, viewers of the ad may attribute that deficiency to the sponsor brand as well. This is most likely to occur when the consumer uses the comparative brand, not the sponsored brand.[8] Company leaders must be careful in choosing an appropriate comparison firm and must be even more careful about using a negative comparative ad format.

The comparative message strategy can be beneficial if used with caution. The comparison brand must be picked carefully to ensure consumers see it as a viable competing brand. Actual product attributes and customer benefits must be used, without stretching the information or providing misleading information. If there are actual differences to compare, then comparative advertising works well. If the comparisons are all hype and opinion, with no substantial differences, comparative advertising does not work as well. If the comparison is misleading, the Federal Trade Commission (FTC) may step in and investigate. The largest number of complaints that the FTC hears are about potentially misleading comparison advertisements.

In general, comparing a low-market share brand to the market leader works well, because viewers concentrate more carefully on the content and message of the ad. On the other hand, comparing a high-market share brand with another high-market share brand is often not effective. In these cases, a better strategy may be to simply make the comparison without naming the competitor.

Several years ago, comparative advertising worked well for Avis. When Avis was 10th in market share in the rental car industry, a series of ads was developed for Avis, comparing its service to the market leader, Hertz, mentioning the Hertz name specifically. Consumers began to believe that Avis provided the same level of quality as Hertz.

After gaining market share and becoming one of the top three brands, Avis changed its approach and now usually does not mention Hertz in advertisements. Still, when comparisons are made, consumers still know which competitor is involved.[9]

All five of these cognitive message strategies are based on some type of rational logic. The message is designed to make sure consumers pay attention to the ad and take the time to cognitively process the information. In terms of attitudes, the sequence of *cognitive* → *affective* → *conative* is the plan of attack when developing a rational approach. The intention of a cognitive message strategy is first to present consumers with rational information about a good, service, or company, and then to help them develop positive feelings about the same product or company.

Affective Strategies

Affective message strategies invoke feelings or emotions and match those feelings with the good, service, or company. Such ads are prepared to enhance the likeability of the product, recall of the appeal, or comprehension of the advertisement. Affective strategies elicit emotions that, in turn, lead the consumer to act, preferably to buy the product, and subsequently affect the consumer's reasoning process.

An emotion such as love can be featured in order to convince consumers that a product such as Cheerios is a superior breakfast cereal for loved ones. The consumer group is then led to believe Cheerios is a rational choice because the company's advertisements mention the cereal's positive effects on cholesterol levels. This approach is demonstrated by the advertisement for Cheerios in this section. The ad features a photo of three generations of a family combined with the words "Your heart has better things to do than deal with heart disease." Family memories and emotions combine with the product feature of being a heart-smart cereal. Affective strategies fall into two categories: (1) resonance and (2) emotional.

Resonance advertising connects a product with a consumer's experiences to develop stronger ties between the product and the consumer. The use of music from the 1980s takes echo boomers back to that time. Any strongly held memory or emotional attachment is a candidate for resonance advertising.

Emotional advertising attempts to elicit powerful emotions that eventually lead to product recall and choice. Many emotions can be connected to products, including trust, reliability, friendship, happiness, security, glamour, luxury, serenity, pleasure, romance, and passion.

Emotional appeals are used in both consumer-oriented and business-to-business ads. Members of the buying center in a business are also human. They do not make decisions based solely on rational thought processes. Emotions and feelings also affect decisions. If the product's benefits can be presented within an emotional framework, the advertisement is normally more effective, even in business-to-business ads.[10]

Affective strategies are a common approach to developing a strong brand name. When an advertisement gets you to like a brand and have positive feelings for a brand, then the hope is that you will also purchase that brand. Cognitive beliefs about the brand then follow. This approach relies on the attitude development sequence of *affective* → *conative* → *cognitive*. For some products, affective ads are an effective approach

Source: Courtesy of Gerald Lopez © Dorling Kindersley.

The AVIS "We Try Harder" campaign was an effective comparative advertising approach.

A Cheerios advertisement utilizing a resonance affective message strategy.

Your Heart Has Better Things To Do Than Deal With Heart Disease

Eating heart-healthy whole grain oat foods like Cheerios as part of a low-fat diet, may be a good way to lower your cholesterol and reduce your risk of heart disease. So make health a habit for your heart, body and soul. And let your heart do something it's better at...holding your family together.

Cheerios

"The One and Only Cheerios"

Source: Courtesy of General Mills.

An advertisement for Skechers Sport Footwear using an emotional message strategy.

because there are no real tangible differences among the brands. Skechers Sport Footwear is using an affective strategy in the advertisement in this section. The ad depicts social acceptance and the idea that Skechers shoes will make you a part of the in-crowd. The ad is supposed to create positive feelings for the Skechers Sport brand.

Conative Strategies

Conative message strategies are designed to lead more directly to some type of consumer response. They can be used to support other promotional efforts, such as coupon redemption programs, Internet "hits" and orders, and in-store offers such as buy-one-get-one-free. The goal of a conative advertisement is to elicit behavior. A conative strategy is present in any television advertisement for music CDs that seeks to persuade viewers to call a toll-free number to purchase the music. These ads typically encourage quick action by stating that the CD cannot be purchased at stores and is available for only a limited time.

Action-inducing conative advertisements create situations in which cognitive knowledge of the product or affective liking of the product may come later (after the actual purchase) or during product usage. For instance, a point-of-purchase display is designed (sometimes through advertising tie-ins) to cause people to make *impulse buys.* The goal is to make the sale, with cognitive knowledge and affective feelings forming as the product is used. In terms of an attitude sequence, conative message strategies typically utilize the *conative → cognitive → affective* approach.

Promotional support conative advertisements are used to support other promotional efforts. Besides coupons and phone-in promotions, a company may advertise a sweepstakes that a consumer enters by filling out the form on the advertisement or by going to a particular retail store.

Cognitive, affective, and conative strategies can be matched with the hierarchy of effects approach described in the previous chapter. The hierarchy of effects model suggests that consumers pass through a series of stages, from awareness to knowledge, liking, preference, conviction, and, finally, to the purchase. As shown in Figure 7.2, each message strategy can highlight a different stage of the hierarchy of effects model.

FIGURE 7.2
The Hierarchy of Effects Model, Message Strategies, and Advertising Components

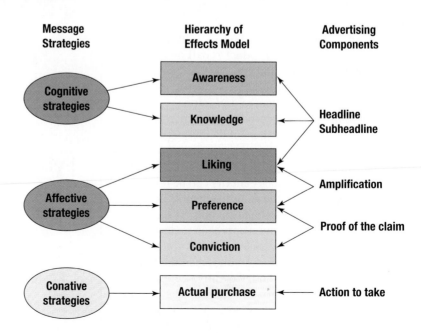

Choosing the right message strategy is a key ingredient in creating a successful advertising program. To be effective, the message strategy must be carefully matched with the leverage point and executional framework that have been selected as well as with the media that will be utilized. The creative and the account executive must remain in constant contact throughout the process to be certain all of these advertising ingredients are consistent. In the following section, the next element, the executional framework, is described.

EXECUTIONAL FRAMEWORKS

An **executional framework** is the manner in which an ad appeal is presented. The executional framework is chosen in conjunction with an advertising appeal. The types of appeals that are most commonly used were described in Chapter 6, and they include fear, humor, sex, music, rationality, emotions, and scarcity. Each appeal can be matched with the appropriate executional framework. Figure 7.3 displays the various frameworks that are described in this section.

Animation

Animation is a popular type of executional framework. In recent years, the use of animation in advertising has increased dramatically. This is due, in part, to the growing sophistication of computer graphics programs. The animation technologies available to advertising creatives are far superior to the cartoon-type that was previously used.

One new animation technique is *rotoscoping*. Rotoscoping is the process of digitally painting or sketching figures into live sequences.[11] This makes it possible to present both live actors and animated characters in the same frame. The creative can also merge or modify various live scenes within the same frame. Another animation method, *clay animation*, was made popular by commercials featuring the Pillsbury Doughboy.

Animation characters can be human, animal, or product personifications. Animation was originally a last-resort technique for advertisers who did not have money to prepare a live commercial. Most agencies did not hold it in high regard. Animation has become one of the most popular advertising techniques. Successful films such as *The Incredibles* and *Bee Movie* continue to create a great deal of interest in animation advertising.

Animation is used mostly in television spots. It is also used in movie trailers and Internet ads. Single shots of animated characters, such as Tony the Tiger, are also placed into print ads. For years, animation was rarely used in business-to-business advertising. Many advertising agencies had negative views of it. Agency leaders tended to believe animation appealed to children but not to businesspeople. These views have changed. Business ads shown on television can now take advantage of

A Green Giant advertisement using animation.

◆ Animation	◆ Authoritative
◆ Slice-of-life	◆ Demonstration
◆ Dramatization	◆ Fantasy
◆ Testimonial	◆ Informative

FIGURE 7.3
Executional Frameworks

HIKING BOOTS, A BOTANY TEXTBOOK, AND AN OLD PICK-UP.
THIS WAS VENTURE CAPITAL FOR A TEA COMPANY IN 1969.
We may have had an unorthodox business plan when we started making tea in 1969, but we worked hard to create the most delicious blends of herbs the Rocky Mountains had to offer. Today our operation is a little more sophisticated, but we still create our tea the old-fashioned way, hand-blended from the finest ingredients in the world.

celestialseasonings.com

A Celestial sleepytime tea advertisement featuring an animated bear on the package label.

high-quality graphics technologies to illustrate a product's uses with animated figures and graphics.

A recent example of animation in business-to-business advertising comes from United Airlines. A commercial shows a father gently adjusting the blankets where his son is sleeping, just as he is getting ready to leave on a business trip. The son is dreaming that the father is flying away on the wings of a swan. The point is to make an emotional connection with the viewer through animation.[12]

Slice-of-Life

In slice-of-life commercials, advertisers attempt to provide solutions to the everyday problems consumers or businesses face. This format was made famous by Procter & Gamble during the early days of television advertising in the 1950s. The advertisements normally show the common experiences, and especially the problems, people encounter. Then, the good or service is made available to solve the problem. The most common slice-of-life format has the four components identified in Figure 7.4. In some of the ads, the actors portray the dilemma or problem and solve the problems themselves. In others, a voice-over explains the benefits or solution to the problem that the good, service, or company provides.

A typical slice-of-life commercial could start with a child playing soccer and her parents cheering (the encounter). Her dirty uniform is then shown with comments by the child that it will never come clean for the championship game or a voice-over can be used to state the same message (the problem). Another parent or the announcer then introduces the benefits of the new laundry detergent (the interaction). The commercial ends with the proud parents taking their daughter to a championship game in a clean uniform (the solution). Note that this commercial could be shot in various ways. The actors can talk to each other in the scenario, making the audience the third party who essentially is "eavesdropping" on the conversation. Or, the commercial can be shot using a voice-over to highlight the problem and solution portions of the commercial, with the announcer speaking directly to the audience.

In print advertisements, slice-of-life frameworks are difficult, but not impossible, to prepare. In the business-to-business advertisement for Messagemedia shown in this section, the encounter is the potential female customer. The problem is that the "average single female breaks up with 4.3 men, avoids 237 phone calls, and ignores approximately 79 red lights per year." The interaction occurs through the copy "What are the chances she'll read your e-mail message?" The solution to this problem is Messagemedia's "E-messaging campaign."

Business-to-business advertisements also heavily use the slice-of-life method. The execution is popular because it allows the advertiser to highlight the ways a product can

FIGURE 7.4
Components of a Slice-of-Life Ad

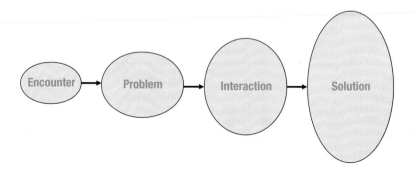

meet business needs. For example, a typical business-to-business ad begins with a routine business experience, such as a sales manager making a presentation to the board of directors. Then, the projector being used by the salesperson does not have a clear picture. The ad offers the solution: a projector from Sony. The presentation is made with great clarity, and the board of directors accepts the customer's bid for the account. As with all slice-of-life commercials, a disaster is avoided. By using the advertised brand, a happy ending is the result.

Slice-of-life executions are possible in most media, including magazines or billboards, because a single picture can depict a normal, everyday situation or problem. The challenge is creating one image that can tell the entire story, with the product being the solution.

Dramatization

A dramatization is similar to the slice-of-life executional framework. It uses the same format in which a problem is first presented and then a solution is offered. The difference lies in the intensity and story format. Dramatization uses a higher level of excitement and suspense to tell the story. A dramatization story normally builds to a crisis point leading to a suspenseful climax.

An effective and dramatic advertisement is difficult to create, because the drama must be completed in either 30 or 60 seconds. Building a story to a climatic moment is challenging, given such a short time period. The early "What's in Your Wallet" advertisements for Capital One credit cards did manage to create the level of excitement needed. They were, however, later replaced with humorous executions. Not all dramatic execution styles can, however, accomplish the high level of suspense required to make them successful. It is often easier to simply produce the ad using the slice-of-life framework.

A business-to-business advertisement for Messagemedia.com containing a slice-of-life execution.

Testimonials

The testimonial type of executional framework has been successful for many years, especially in the business-to-business and service sectors. When a customer is presented in an advertisement telling about a positive experience with a product, it is a testimonial. In the business-to-business sector, testimonials from current customers add credibility to the claims being made. In many business buying situations, prospective vendors are asked for references. Testimonials provide references in advance. Further, most buyers believe what others say about a company more than they believe what a company says about itself. Thus, testimonials by someone else offer greater credibility than self-proclamations.

Testimonials also are an effective method for promoting services. Services are intangible; they cannot be seen or touched. Consumers cannot examine services before making decisions. A testimony from a current customer is an effective method of describing the benefits or attributes of the service. This matches the method most consumers use in selecting a service. When choosing a dentist, an attorney, or an automobile repair shop, consumers often ask friends, relatives, or co-workers. A testimonial ad for a service simulates this type of word-of-mouth recommendation.

One major reason companies choose testimonials is that they enhance company credibility. Endorsers and famous individuals do not always have high levels of credibility, because consumers know they are being paid for their endorsements. In testimonials, everyday people, often actual customers, are the main characters. At other times, they are paid actors who look like everyday consumers.

An authoritative execution combined with a humor appeal.

Authoritative

When using the authoritative executional framework, the advertiser is seeking to convince viewers that a given product is superior to other brands. One form is **expert authority**. These ads employ a physician, dentist, engineer, or chemist to state the particular brand's advantages compared to other brands. Firms also can feature less recognized experts such as automobile mechanics, professional house painters, nurses, and aerobics instructors. Advertising presents each of these as an expert or authority in a particular field. These experts normally talk about the brand attributes that make the product superior.

Many authoritative advertisements include some type of scientific or survey evidence. Independent organizations such as the American Medical Association undertake a variety of product studies. Quoting the results gives an ad greater credibility. Survey results are less credible. Stating that four out of five dentists recommend a particular toothbrush or toothpaste is less effective, because consumers do not have details about how the survey was conducted or even how many dentists were surveyed (5 or 50). In contrast, when the American Medical Association states that an aspirin a day reduces the risk of a second heart attack, it is highly credible. A company such as Bayer can take advantage of the finding by including the information in the company's ads. The same is true when a magazine such as *Consumer Reports* ranks a particular brand as the best.

Any scientific, independent, unpaid source makes an advertising claim more powerful. For example, Wachovia Bank recently created advertisements featuring its ranking as the number one community development lender in the United States. The ranking was given by the Federal Financial Institutions Examining Council.[13] The ad was more credible because the rating was made by a federal agency, which was an independent source.

Authoritative advertisements have been widely incorporated into business-to-business sector ads, especially when scientific findings are available to support a company's product claims. Independent test results are likely to have a more profound influence on members of the buying center, especially if they are actively looking for rational information to help them make decisions.

The authoritative approach assumes consumers and business decision makers rely on cognitive processes when making purchase decisions. This means that they will pay attention to an ad and carefully think about the information conveyed in the advertisement. The authoritative approach works in print ads, because the buyers are willing to take the time to read the claim or findings provided in the advertisement.

Authoritative ads perform especially well in specialty magazines and on specific Web sites. For example, in a hunting magazine, having an expert hunter discuss the superiority of a particular gun is effective, because readers have an interest in hunting. Brides observe the endorsements of wedding experts in special bridal magazines and bridal Web sites. Readers notice these specialized advertisements, and the claims made have greater credibility. The same is true in business-to-business magazines. Trade journals in the business world are similar to specialty magazines in the consumer world.

Demonstration

A demonstration execution shows how a product works. A demonstration is an effective way to communicate the attributes of a product to viewers. Other product benefits can be described as the product is exhibited. For example, one recent advertisement featured a new form of dust cloth that could be attached to a handle or used separately.

The demonstration highlighted the product's multiple uses by cleaning a television screen, a wooden floor, a saxophone, and light fixtures on the ceiling. Thus, consumers were being shown how to use the product while at the same time hearing about its advantages.

Business-to-business ads often present demonstrations. They allow a business to illustrate how a product can meet the specific needs of another business. For example, GoldTouch, Inc. can demonstrate the InstaGold Flash System, which deposits a bright and uniform gold surface finish on products, such as jewelry, through a nonelectrical current process of immersion plating. Such demonstrations can be offered via television ads or Flash media ads on the Internet.

Demonstration ads are especially well suited to television and Internet video ads. To a limited extent, the print media can feature demonstrations, especially when a series of photos outlines the sequence of product usage.

A Jantzen ad utilizing a fantasy executional framework.

Fantasy

Some products lend themselves to a fantasy-type executional framework. Fantasy executions are designed to lift the audience beyond the real world to a make-believe experience. Some fantasies are meant to be realistic. Others are completely irrational. Often, the more irrational and illogical ads are, the more clearly consumers recall them. Fantasies can deal with anything from a dream vacation spot or cruise ships to a juicy hamburger or an enticing DiGiorno pizza. The Jantzen ad in this section encourages consumer fantasies. People are even encouraged to share their fantasies by contacting Jantzen at **www.jantzen.com**.

The most common fantasy themes, however, still involve sex, love, and romance. According to some marketing experts, raw sex and nudity in advertisements are losing their impact. Instead, advertisers can feature a softer, more subtle presentation of sex. Fantasy fits nicely with target audiences that have a preference for a tamer presentation of sexuality. Instead of raw sex and nudity that may be offensive, fantasy takes them into a world of romantic make-believe.

One product category that frequently uses fantasy executions is the perfume and cologne industry. In the past, the most common theme was that splashing on a certain cologne causes women to flock to a man. For women, the reverse was suggested. Although used extensively, these ads were not particularly effective because people didn't believe them. Currently, perfume advertisers tend to portray the product as enhancing the love life of a couple or even making a man or woman feel more sensuous, rather than turning a man into a "babe magnet" or a woman into a "diva."

Television fantasy ads for cruise lines show couples enjoying romantic, sensuous vacations together; swimming; jet skiing; and scuba diving. The goal is to make the cruise into more than just a vacation—it should become a romantic fantasy trip. Fantasy ads also can show people experiencing the thrill of winning a major sports event or sharing a common product (e.g., beer, pizza) with a beautiful model. Effective fantasies can inspire both recall and action.

The business-to-business advertising field has not used fantasy a great deal, primarily because of fear that members of a buying center will not take it seriously. At the same time, creatives are sometimes able to feature a fantasy in a business-to-business ad by showing a product helping the buyer achieve some type of unrealistic result or outcome. For example, being promoted from janitor to president because of the correct choice of a cleaning product would be a fantasy aimed at people using or purchasing janitorial supplies.

This advertisement for Security Finance combines animation with an informative execution.

Informative

A common advertising executional framework is an informative advertisement. Informative ads present information to the audience in a straight-forward manner. Agencies prepare informative messages extensively for radio advertisements, where only verbal communication is possible. Informative ads are less common in television and print, because consumers tend to ignore them. With so many ads bombarding the consumer, it takes more than just the presentation of information to capture someone's attention.

Consumers who are highly involved in a particular product category pay more attention to an informational ad. Such is often the case when business buyers are in the process of gathering information for either a new buy or a modified rebuy. If the business is not in the market for a particular product, buying center members do not pay much attention to informative ads. Thus, informative ads tend to work well only in high-involvement situations. Many advertisers believe that business buyers need detailed information to make intelligent buying decisions. As a result, the informative framework continues to be a popular approach for business-to-business advertisers.

One of the keys to informative advertising is the placement of the ad. An informative advertisement about a restaurant placed on a radio station just before noon is listened to more carefully than if it runs at 3:00 P.M. An informative ad about a diet product in an issue of *Glamour* that has a special article on weight control or exercising will be noticed more than if it is placed in the fashion section of the magazine. An informative business ad featuring a new piece of industrial equipment works well next to an article about the capital costs of equipment. Consequently, informative ads have limited uses but can be effective when placed properly.

Beyond these types of executional frameworks, the creative selects all of the other ingredients, including music, copy, color, motion, light, and the size of a print ad. Remember that almost any of these executional frameworks can be used within the format of one of the various appeals. A slice-of-life can depict fear, as can a dramatization. Informative ads can be humorous, but so can animations. Testimonials or demonstrations are rational or emotional, and so forth. As the advertisement comes together, one element remains: the choice of a source or spokesperson.

SOURCES AND SPOKESPERSONS

One final major issue remains for the creative, the company, and the account executive. Selecting the right **source and spokesperson** to use in an advertisement is a critical decision. Figure 7.5 identifies four types of sources available to advertisers. Of the four

FIGURE 7.5
Types of Sources and Spokepersons

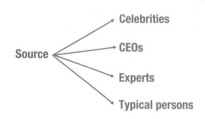

FIGURE 7.6
Top Hollywood Celebrity Endorsers

- ◆ **Catherine Zeta-Jones,** T-Mobile, $20 million
- ◆ **Angelina Jolie,** St. John clothing, $12 million
- ◆ **Nicole Kidman,** Channel 5 perfume, $12 million
- ◆ **Jessica Simpson,** Guthy-Renker direct response tv, cosmetics, $7.5 million
- ◆ **Gwyneth Paltrow,** Estee Lauder fragrances, $6 million
- ◆ **Charlize Theron,** Dior fragrance, $6 million
- ◆ **Julia Roberts,** Gianfranco Ferre fashion, $5 million
- ◆ **Brad Pitt,** Heineken beer, $4 million

Source: Based on Gail Schiller, "Top 10 Ad Deals," *Adweek* 47, no. 17 (April 24, 2006), pp. 20–22.

types listed, *celebrity spokespersons* are the most common. Their appearance in ads has been declining. According to the research firm Millward Brown, 17 percent of all television ads in 2001 used some type of celebrity endorser. Today, that percentage is around 6 percent.[14]

Companies still use celebrity endorsers because his or her stamp of approval can enhance the product's brand equity. Celebrities also help create emotional bonds with the products. The idea is to transfer the bond that exists between the celebrity and the audience to the product being endorsed. This bond transfer often is more profound for younger consumers. Older consumers are not as likely to be influenced by celebrity endorsements. Still, many advertisers believe they are effective. Figure 7.6 lists the top eight Hollywood celebrities and their recent endorsements.

Agencies also use celebrities to help establish a "personality" for a brand. The trick is to tie the brand's characteristics to those of the spokesperson, such as Elizabeth Taylor's love of the finer things in life being attached to her line of scents and perfumes, as well as other products. In developing a brand personality, the brand must already be established. The celebrity merely helps to define the brand more clearly. Using celebrities for new products does not always work as well as for already established brands.

There are three variations of celebrity endorsements: (1) unpaid spokespersons, (2) celebrity voice-overs, and (3) what may be called *dead-person endorsements.* Unpaid spokespersons are those celebrities who support a charity or cause by appearing in an ad. These types of endorsements are highly credible and can entice significant contributions to a cause. Politicians, actors, and musicians all appear in these ads. VH1's "Save the Music" ads are a recent campaign of this type.

Many celebrities also provide voice-overs for television and radio ads without being shown or identified. Listeners often respond to the ads and try to figure out who is reading the copy. This adds interest to the ad but may also serve as a distraction, when the individual does not hear the message while trying to identify the speaker.

A dead-person endorsement occurs when a sponsor uses an image or past video or film featuring an actor or personality who has died. Dead-person endorsements are somewhat controversial but are becoming more common. Bob Marley, Marilyn Monroe, John Wayne, John Lennon, Elvis Presley, and many others have appeared in ads and have even become spokespersons for products after dying. Colonel Sanders has become a spokesperson in animation for KFC. Figure 7.7 identifies the top-earning dead celebrities and the amount each of their estates earned in just one year.

An advertisement for a new album featuring the artist as a celebrity spokesperson.

Source: Courtesy of Elberson Partners.

FIGURE 7.7
Top Earning Dead Celebrities

◆ Curt Cobain	$50 million	◆ Andy Warhol	$19 million
◆ Elvis Presley	$42 million	◆ Theodor Geisel (Dr. Seuss)	$10 million
◆ Charles M. Schultz	$35 million	◆ Ray Charles	$10 million
◆ John Lennon	$24 million	◆ Marilyn Monroe	$ 8 million
◆ Albert Einstein	$20 million	◆ Johnny Cash	$ 8 million

Source: Based on "Top Earning Dead Celebrities" (October 20, 2006) (**www.forbes.com/2006/10/20/tech-media_06deadcelebs**).

Instead of celebrities, advertisers can use a CEO as the spokesperson or source. Dave Thomas of Wendy's was possibly the most famous CEO in commercials in the 1990s. Michael Dell has appeared as the spokesperson for Dell. A highly visible and personable CEO can become a major asset for the firm and its products. Many local companies succeed, in part, because their owners are out front in small-market television commercials. They then begin to take on the status of local celebrities.

Expert sources include physicians, lawyers, accountants, and financial planners. These experts tend not to be famous celebrities or CEOs. Experts provide backing for testimonials, serve as authoritative figures, demonstrate products, and enhance the credibility of informative advertisements.

The final category of spokesperson is *typical-person sources*. Typical persons are one of two types. The first category consists of paid actors or models who portray or resemble everyday people. The second is actual, typical, everyday people used in advertisements. Wal-Mart, as already mentioned, features its own store employees in freestanding insert advertisements. Agencies also create "man-on-the-street" types of advertisements. For example, PERT shampoo recently prepared ads showing an individual asking people if they would like to have their hair washed. Dr. Scholl's interviews people about foot problems that might be resolved with cushioned shoe inserts.

Real-people sources are becoming more common. One reason for this is the overuse of celebrities. Many experts believe that consumers have become saturated with celebrity endorsers and that the positive impact today is not as strong as it was in the past. One study conducted in Great Britain indicated that 55 percent of the consumers surveyed reported that a famous face was not enough to hold their attention. Celebrities held a greater appeal for the 15- to 24-year-old age bracket. Sixty-two percent of that group stated that a famous person in an ad would get their attention.[15]

Source Characteristics

In evaluating sources, most account executives and companies consider several characteristics. The effectiveness of an advertisement that utilizes a spokesperson depends on the degree to which the person has one or more of the characteristics. As illustrated in Figure 7.8, the source-selection characteristic of a spokesperson's *credibility* is derived from the composite of attractiveness, similarity, likability, trustworthiness, and expertise.[16] Credibility affects a receiver's acceptance of the spokesperson and message. A credible source is believable. Most sources do not score highly on all four attributes, yet they need to

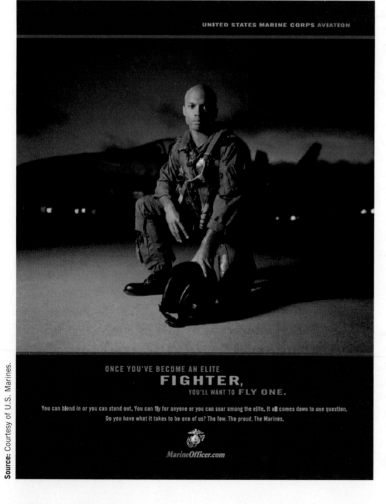

An advertisement for the U.S. Marines with a typical person spokesperson.

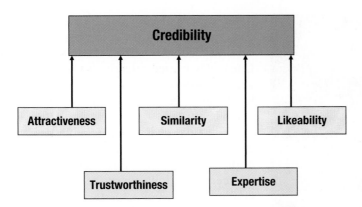

FIGURE 7.8
Characteristics of Effective Spokepersons

score highly on multiple characteristics to be viewed as credible. One reason for using celebrities is that they are more likely to possess at least an element of all characteristics. A CEO, expert, or typical person probably lacks one or more of them.

Attractiveness has two forms: (1) physical characteristics and (2) personality characteristics. Physical attractiveness is usually an important asset for an endorser. Bijan used Michael Jordan's and Bo Derek's physical attractiveness to promote its line of menswear, perfume, and jewelry. Advertisements with physically attractive spokespersons fare better than advertisements with less attractive people. This is true for both male and female audiences. At the same time, the attractiveness of the spokesperson's personality is also important to many consumers. This personality component helps viewers form emotional bonds with the spokesperson. If the spokesperson is seen as having a sour personality, even if physically beautiful, consumers are less likely to develop an emotional bond with the individual and the product.

Closely related to attractiveness is the concept of **similarity**. Consumers are more inclined to be influenced by a message delivered by a person who is somehow similar. For example, a "stay at home" mom is more likely to be influenced by an advertisement that starts out with a woman saying, "Since I made the decision to stop working and care for my family full-time . . ." Similarity allows the viewer to *identify* with the spokesperson in some manner. At times this may involve the fantasy of identifying with a rich person buying a BMW. At others, **identification** is based on believing the source has similar beliefs, attitudes, preferences, or behaviors or is in the same or a similar situation as the customer.

Closely related to the personality components of attractiveness and similarity is *likeability*. Consumers respond more positively to spokespersons they like. This liking arises from various sources, including situations in which viewers like either the actor or the character played by the actor in a movie. An athlete gains likeability if he or she plays on the consumer's favorite team. Other individuals are likeable because they support the favorite charities of consumers. If consumers do not like a particular spokesperson, they are likely to transfer that dislike to the product the celebrity endorses. This is not an automatic transfer, because consumers recognize that endorsers are paid spokespersons. Still, there is almost always a negative impact on attitudes toward the brand.

A celebrity may be likable or attractive, but he or she may not be viewed as *trustworthy*. Trustworthiness

Attractiveness is often used as a source characteristic.

Source: Courtesy of Bijan Fragrances, Inc.

Michael Jordan is a rare celebrity who can endorse multiple products and maintain a high level of credibility.

is the degree of confidence or the level of acceptance consumers place in the spokesperson's message. A trustworthy spokesperson helps consumers believe the message. One highly trusted celebrity is Oprah Winfrey. Likeability and trustworthiness are highly related. People who are liked tend to be trusted and people who are disliked tend not to be trusted.

The final characteristic advertisers look for when examining sources is *expertise.* Spokespersons with higher levels of expertise are more believable than sources with low expertise. Richard Petty and Jeff Gordon are seen as experts when automobile products and lubricants are advertised. Often when expertise is desired in an ad, the ad agency opts for the CEO or a trained or educated expert in the field. American Express features Maria Barraza, a small-business owner and designer, to promote its Small Business Services.

A potential negative side to using a CEO as the spokesperson may be present. Although he or she has a high degree of expertise, the individual may lack some of the other key characteristics (attractiveness, likeability, or trustworthiness). Expertise can be valuable in persuasive advertisements designed to change opinions or attitudes. Spokespersons with high levels of expertise are more capable of persuading an audience than someone with zero or low expertise.[17]

Matching Source Types and Characteristics

The account executive, ad agency, and corporate sponsor, individually or jointly, may choose the type of spokesperson. They can choose a celebrity, CEO, expert, or typical person, and the specific individual must have the key characteristics. This section matches source types with various characteristics.

Celebrities tend to score well in terms of trustworthiness, believability, persuasiveness, and likeability. These virtues increase if the match between the product and celebrity is a logical and proper fit. For example, Phil Mickelson endorsing golf merchandise is a good fit. An athlete endorsing any type of athletic product fits well. Companies can be creative but also use common sense in making quality matches. For instance, the match of boxer George Foreman to his Lean Mean Grilling Machine is a great success.[18]

Several dangers exist in using celebrities. The first is negative publicity about the celebrity caused by inappropriate conduct. For example, Michael Vick's arrest and conviction for dog fighting created considerable negative press. Britney Spears' battles with depression and the courts have created a superstar that brands do not want to touch. Then there was Lindsey Lohan's drunken-driving arrests and subsequent jail stint. Although advertisers like celebrity endorsers because of the potential they have for developing an attraction to their brands, they have to weigh the positive benefits against the potential risks.[19]

The potential for negative publicity has led some advertisers to use deceased celebrities. Companies have concluded that there is no need to risk bringing embarrassment or injury to themselves or the brand. It is also a reason that more ads use cartoon characters. Practically everyone likes cartoons.

The second danger of using celebrities is that their endorsement of too many products can tarnish their credibility. Consumers know celebrities are paid, which detracts from their believability. If the celebrity endorses a number of products, consumer evaluations of that person's credibility decline further. Some advertising research indicates that when a celebrity endorses multiple products, it tends to reduce his or her credibility and likeability as well as consumers' attitudes toward the ad.[20]

As a result, careful consideration must be given to the choice of a celebrity. The individual cannot simply be famous. The person should possess as many of the characteristics as possible, match the good or service being advertised, not be "spread too thin" or overexposed, and promote a positive image that can be transferred to the good, service, or company.

A *CEO* or other prominent corporate official may or may not possess the characteristics of attractiveness and likeability. CEOs should, however, appear to be trustworthy, have expertise, and maintain a degree of credibility. A CEO is not a professional actor or model. It might be difficult for the CEO to come across well in a commercial.

Companies must be aware of the trustworthiness issue. For example, many times the owner of a local auto dealership represents it as the spokesperson. The primary problem is that many consumers view used-car salespeople as untrustworthy. Other local business owners may be highly trustworthy, such as restaurant owners, physicians, eye care professionals, and so forth.

Advertising creatives and account executives should be careful about asking a CEO or business owner to serve as a source. They first must be convinced that the individual has enough key characteristics to promote the product and gain the consumer's interest and trust.

Experts, first and foremost, should be credible. The ad agency should seek out an expert who is attractive, likable, and trustworthy. Experts are helpful in promoting health-care products and other high-involvement types of products. Recent research has indicated that experts are more believable than celebrities when it comes to high-technology products, and as a result, the use of an expert will reduce consumers' level of perceived risk in purchasing the product.[21] These types of endorsers can be effective when consumers or businesses perceive there are higher levels of risk involved in making purchases. Therefore, when selecting an expert spokesperson, agencies should be certain that the person has valid credentials and will be able to clearly explain a product's benefits. Doing so will reduce the level of perceived risk.

Typical-person ads are sometimes difficult to prepare, especially when they use real persons. First, typical-person sources do not have the name recognition of celebrities. Consequently, advertisers often use multiple sources within one advertisement to build credibility. Increasing the number of sources in the ad makes the ad more effective. Hearing three people talk about a good dentist is more believable than hearing it from only one person. By using multiple sources, viewers are motivated to pay attention to the ad and to process its arguments.[22]

Real-person ads are a kind of double-edged sword. On the one hand, trustworthiness, similarity, and credibility rise when the source is bald, overweight, or has some other physical imperfections. This can be especially valuable when the bald person promotes a hair replacement program or the overweight source talks about a diet program. On the other hand, attractiveness and likeability may be lower.

Using customers in ads can be difficult, because they will flub lines and look less natural on the screen. These difficulties with actual customers and employees lead

Source: Courtesy of Jockey International.

This Jockey advertisement features an older typical person model.

many ad agencies to turn to professional models and actors to portray ordinary people. Professional actors make filming and photographing much easier. Also, the agency is in the position to choose a likable, but plain, person. The desired effects (trustworthiness, similarity and credibility) are often easier to create using professional actors and models.

In general, the ad agency should seek to be certain that the source or spokesperson has the major characteristics the ad needs. When the appeal is humor, likeability is very important. In a rational or informational ad, expertise and credibility are crucial, especially in business-to-business ads. In each case, the goal is to try to include as many of the characteristics as possible when retaining a spokesperson.

CREATING AN ADVERTISEMENT

Figure 7.9 illustrates the process a creative uses in preparing an advertisement. The work begins with the creative brief, which outlines the message theme of the advertisement, as well as other pertinent information. Using the creative brief blueprint, the creative develops a means–end chain, starting with an attribute of the product that generates a specific customer benefit and eventually produces a desirable end state. This means–end chain is the foundation on which all other decisions will be made.

Following the development of the means–end chain, the creative selects a message strategy, the appeal, and the executional framework. The creative also chooses a source or spokesperson at this point, because the choice usually affects other creative decisions. Development of the leverage point is usually undertaken after the creative begins work on the advertisement. The leverage point moves the consumer from the product attribute or customer benefit to the desired end state. The type of leverage point used depends on the message strategy, appeal, and executional framework.

Although certain combinations tend to work well together, the creative has an almost infinite number of options when preparing an advertisement or campaign. For example, if the creative wants to use a cognitive message strategy, the most logical appeal is rationality. The creative, however, could use fear, humor, sex, music, or even scarcity. The one appeal that would not work as well is emotions. The emotional part of the advertisement tends to overpower the cognitive message the creative is trying to send to the viewer. If the creative decides to use a humor approach with a cognitive strategy, other logical and illogical combinations emerge. In terms of an executional framework, the dramatization and authoritative approaches tend not to work as well

FIGURE 7.9
Creating an Advertisement

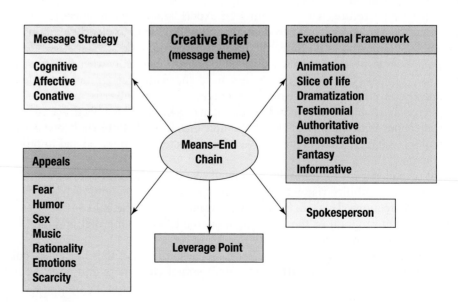

with humor. Any of the other executional frameworks are suitable. This flexibility allows a variety of advertisements to emerge from a single means–end chain. The combination to use depends on the creative's expertise and experience as well as his or her opinion about the best way to accomplish the client's advertising objectives.

ADVERTISING EFFECTIVENESS

Producing effective ads requires the joint efforts of the account executive, creative, media planner, and media buyer. Working independently can produce some award-winning ads, but often they will not be effective ads that meet a client's objectives. One major problem ad agencies face is producing a commercial that will stand out among the thousands of existing ads. If an advertisement can break through the clutter, half the battle is won. All that remains is finding a way to lead consumers or businesses to react to the ad in the desired manner.

An effective advertisement accomplishes the objectives desired by the client. The task of making sure the ad accomplishes the IMC objectives is a major challenge. The seven basic principles of advertising effectiveness, shown in Figure 7.10, should be followed. Each of these principles is described in greater detail next.

Notice the visual consistency present in these two advertisements for tourism in North Carolina.

The first principle is to maintain **visual consistency**. Repeatedly seeing a specific image or visual display helps to embed it in long-term memory. Visual consistency is important because consumers, whether individual consumers or members of a business buying center, spend very little time viewing or listening to an advertisement. In most cases, it is just a casual glance at a print advertisement or a cursory glimpse at a television ad. Visual consistency causes the viewer to move the advertising message from short-term to long-term memory. Consistently used logos and other long-standing images help fix the brand or company in the consumer's mind. For example, people remember Frosted Flakes because of the visually consistent use of Tony the Tiger. They know Green Giant products by the cartoon spokesperson. Logos such as the Nike swoosh and the Prudential Rock emblem are well established in the minds of many consumers.

The second principle of effective advertising is concerned with *campaign duration*. Consumers often do not pay attention to advertisements. This makes the length or duration of a campaign important. Using the same advertisement for an appropriate period of time helps embed the message in the consumer's long-term memory. Account executives give careful thought to how long to run an advertisement. The ad

- ◆ Visual consistency
- ◆ Campaign duration
- ◆ Repeated taglines
- ◆ Consistent positioning—avoid ambiguity
- ◆ Simplicity
- ◆ Identifiable selling point
- ◆ Create an effective flow

FIGURE 7.10
Principles of Effective Advertising

should be changed before it becomes stale and viewers become bored with it; however, changing ads too frequently impedes retention. Reach and frequency affect the duration of a campaign. Higher frequency usually leads to a shorter duration. Low reach may be associated with a longer duration. In any case, typical campaigns last about 6 months, but there are exceptions.

The third method used to build effective advertising campaigns is *repeated taglines*. Visual consistency combined with consistent taglines can be a powerful approach. The advertisement may change, but either the visual imagery or the tagline remains the same. The U.S. Army has promoted the tagline "Be all that you can be" for many years, and the Marines are known as "The few. The proud. The Marines." Taglines help consumers tie the advertisement into current knowledge structure nodes that already exist in their minds. Figure 7.11 contains some of the more common taglines. See how many you can identify.

A fourth advertising principle is *consistent positioning*. Maintaining consistent positioning throughout a product's life makes it easier for consumers to place the product in a cognitive map. When the firm emphasizes quality in every ad, it becomes easier to tie the product into the consumer's cognitive map than if the firm stresses quality in some ads, price in others, and convenience in a third campaign. This inconsistency in positioning makes the brand and company more difficult to remember. Consistent positioning avoids ambiguity, and the message stays clear and understandable.

Simplicity is the fifth principle of effective advertising. Simple advertisements are easier to comprehend than are complex ads. A print ad with a simple tagline and limited copy is much easier to read than an overloaded or complex one. Consequently, advertisers must resist the temptation to relate all of a product's attributes in a single advertisement. This practice is more prevalent in business-to-business print advertisements, but it should be avoided there as well. Further, consumer ads on radio or television spots often are so verbally overloaded that the announcer is forced to talk faster. This is usually ineffective, because the listener has too much information to grasp in such a short time period.

The principle of simplicity should be carefully applied to Internet advertising. The primary reason for simplicity with the Internet is load time. Individuals surfing the Internet will not wait more than a few seconds for something to load; if it doesn't load quickly, they move on to another site.

The next principle of effective advertising is the concept of an *identifiable selling point*. The emphasis should be placed on all three of the words: (1) identifiable, (2) selling, and (3) point. The advertisement should have a selling point (price, quality, convenience, luxury, etc.) that is easily identifiable to the viewer of the ad. It is important to remember that an advertisement should sell a product's *benefits* as much as the product itself. Also, the concept is a selling point, not selling *points*. The best advertisements are those that emphasize one major point and do not confuse the viewer by trying to present too many ideas. An advertisement's primary goal is to fix the product into the viewer's cognitive map through establishing new linkages or strengthening current linkages. An identifiable selling point helps reach that goal.

FIGURE 7.11
Which Taglines Can You Identify?

1. A diamond is forever.	6. Look Mom, no cavities.
2. Be all you can be.	7. The ultimate driving machine.
3. Can you hear me now?	8. What can Brown do for you?
4. Don't leave home without it.	9. We try harder.
5. Just do it.	10. You deserve a break today.

Answers: (1) DeBeers, (2) U.S. Army, (3) Verizon, (4) American Express, (5) Nike, (6) Crest, (7) BMW, (8) UPS, (9) Avis, (10) McDonald's

The final principle is to *create an effective flow.* In a print ad, the reader's eye should move easily to all of the key points in the ad. In a television ad, the points to be made should flow in a manner that leads the consumer to the appropriate action or conclusion. Ads without flow confuse the consumer or are simply tuned out.

Beating Ad Clutter

Overcoming clutter is a major challenge when creating an effective advertising campaign. The presence of a competitor's ad within the same medium or time slot makes the ad clutter problem worse. A recent survey of television advertising revealed that during prime-time programming, 42 percent of the ads shown had one or more of their competitors also advertising during the same hour. Research suggests that an advertisement's effectiveness is significantly reduced when a competitor's advertisement runs during the same time slot.[23]

One method advertisers use to overcome this brand interference is repetition. Repeating an ad can increase brand and ad recall. In advertising studies, repetition is effective in increasing recall if no competitor ads are present. When competitor ads are

These two advertisements for St. Patrick's use variability theory concepts to beat ad clutter.

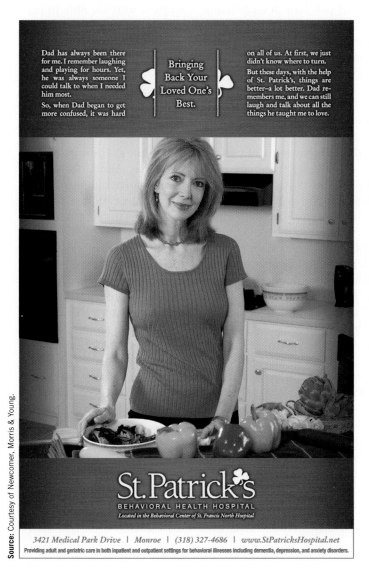

present, repetition does not help the competitive ad interference problem and does not stimulate greater recall.

Mere repetition of an ad does not always work. Therefore, advertisers have begun to emphasize the principles present in **variability theory**.[24] The theory suggests that variable encoding occurs when a consumer sees the same advertisement in different environments. These varied environments increase an ad's recall and effectiveness by encoding it into the brain through various methods. Creatives can generate the effect by varying the situational context of a particular ad. For example, the MasterCard campaign noted previously uses various settings to convey the same basic message, "There are some things money can't buy. For everything else, there's MasterCard." Varying the context of the ad increases recall and is an effective method for overcoming competitive ad interference.[25]

Another method designed to decrease the impact of competing ads is to use a second medium. Using two media to convey a message generally is more effective than repeating an advertisement within the same medium. An ad placed in more than one medium also reduces competing ad interference. In other words, an ad that appears on television and in magazines works better than one that appears only on television. Consumers seeing an advertisement in a different medium are more likely to recall the ad than if it is always seen in only one medium.

Clutter remains a difficult problem in advertising. Creatives who are able to capture the attention of the audience and transmit messages successfully are in great demand. Companies constantly experiment with various approaches to reach audiences. When a program works, the advertising firm and its client have a great deal to celebrate.

INTERNATIONAL IMPLICATIONS

Many common themes and messages translate well across cultures. The major challenge is to make sure that the message strategy and form of executional framework match the tendencies and preferences in a region. For example, some cultures tend to be more rational in decision-making processes, whereas others favor more emotional approaches. This may, in turn, affect the selection of a message strategy in a given nation.

Comparison ads are less common in other countries. This is due to both social and cultural differences as well as legal restrictions. It is critical to be aware of these issues. For example, in many European countries comparative advertising is illegal. In Japan, it is not illegal, but it runs against the society's cultural preferences. In Brazil, the advertising industry is so powerful that any attempt to create a comparative advertisement has been challenged and stopped. Often, international consumers not only dislike the advertisements, but often transfer that dislike to the company sponsoring the ad.[26]

Choices of message strategies will affect selections of executional frameworks. Once again, someone familiar with the tendencies of a given country should be consulted before the creative begins work. A cultural assimilator who is familiar with advertising practices becomes invaluable.

The slice-of-life executional framework has become popular in Japan in recent years. The slice-of-life style is suited to Japan's soft-sell approach to marketing. A more hard-sell attitude is often found in the United States. Japanese advertising tends to be more indirect, and the slice-of-life approach allows advertisers to present a product in a typical everyday situation. Benefits can be presented in a positive light without making brazen or harsh claims and without directly disparaging the competition.[27]

Other patterns and changes in preferred forms of executions can be discovered by watching local media and reading about trends in magazines and trade journals in the country involved. While maintaining an overall message and idea, the advertiser must adjust to social customs present in a region.

SUMMARY

Advertising is the process of transmitting a personal message through one or more impersonal media. The message should reflect the image that occurs throughout an IMC program. Three types of message strategies are present in advertisements. Cognitive strategies emphasize rational and logical arguments to compel consumers to make purchases. Affective strategies are oriented toward buyer emotions and feelings. Conative strategies are linked to more direct responses, behaviors, and actions. These strategies should be integrated with various types of appeals through the media selected for the campaign.

Executional frameworks tell the story in the ad. Animation has become more sophisticated and provides many new creative approaches in the design of ads. The slice-of-life approach and dramatizations are problem-solving types of ads, leading the consumer to something better by using the product. Testimonials are rendered by individuals who have realized the benefits of a product. An authoritative expert can build consumer confidence in a product or company. Demonstrations show how products can be used. A fantasy takes people away from the real world to a make-believe place. This makes the product more exotic and desirable. Informative ads render basic information about the product. Each execution can be used effectively to persuade consumers and business-to-business buyers to consider a company's offerings.

Celebrities, CEOs, experts, and typical persons can be chosen to be "out front" in the advertisement. Each has advantages and disadvantages. The marketing team selects sources or spokespersons based on the individual's attractiveness, similarity, likeability, trustworthiness, expertise, or credibility. The more of these characteristics that are present, the better off the advertiser will be.

Effective ad campaigns are based on the seven principles of visual consistency, sufficient campaign duration, repeated taglines, consistent positioning, simplicity, presentation of an identifiable selling point, and creation of an effective flow. Creatives and account executives must incorporate these principles into the advertising campaign to enhance the odds of success. Also, clutter must be overcome by repeating ads and showing them in various media or in some other way.

Many consider ad design to be the most glamorous part of the advertising industry, and in many ways it is. Remember, however, that the other side of the glamour coin is hard work and the constant pressure to perform. Many people think being a creative is a burnout-type of job. At the same time, those who have proven track records of success are well rewarded for their efforts. Utilizing the principles presented in this chapter can be key to success in the highly competitive and exciting business of advertising design.

KEY TERMS

message theme   The outline of the key idea(s) that the advertising program is supposed to convey.

message strategy   The primary tactic used to deliver the message theme.

cognitive message strategy   The presentation of rational arguments or pieces of information to consumers.

generic messages   Direct promotions of product attributes or benefits without any claim of superiority.

preemptive messages   Claims of superiority based on a specific attribute or benefit of a product that preempts the competition from making the same claim.

unique selling proposition   An explicit, testable claim of uniqueness or superiority that can be supported or substantiated in some manner.

hyperbole   Making an untestable claim based upon some attribute or benefit.

comparative advertisement   The direct or indirect comparison of a good or service to the competition.

affective message strategies   Ads designed to invoke feelings and emotions and match them with the good, service, or company.

resonance advertising   Attempting to connect a product with a consumer's experiences to develop stronger ties between the product and the consumer.

emotional advertising   Attempting to elicit powerful emotions that eventually lead to brand recall and choice.

action-inducing conative advertisements   Advertisements that create situations in which cognitive knowledge of the product or affective liking of the product follow the actual purchase or arise during usage of the product.

promotional support conative advertisements   Ads designed to support other promotional efforts.

executional framework   The manner in which an ad appeal is presented.

expert authority   When an advertiser seeks to convince viewers that a given product is superior to other brands in some authoritative manner.

sources and spokespersons   Persons in the advertisement who make the actual presentation.

similarity (source)   Consumers are more inclined to be influenced by a message delivered by a person who is somehow similar.

identification (source)   Occurs when the receiver is able, in some manner, to identify with the source, either through a fantasy or by similar beliefs, attitudes, preferences, behaviors, or by being in the same or a similar situation.

visual consistency   Occurs when consumers see a specific image or visual display repeatedly.

variability theory   A theory stating that when a consumer sees the same advertisement in different environments, the ad will be more effective.

REVIEW QUESTIONS

1. Name the three types of message strategies creatives can use. How are message strategies related to the message theme?

2. What types of products or services best match cognitive message strategies? List the five types of cognitive approaches.

3. When will an affective message strategy be most effective? What two types of affective messages can creatives design? Give an example of each.

4. What is the primary goal of a conative message strategy?

5. How is an executional framework different from an ad appeal? How are they related?

6. List as many uses of animation-based advertisements as possible. What forms of animation are possible with the available technology?

7. How are slice-of-life and dramatization executional frameworks similar? How are they different?

8. How are authoritative and informational executional frameworks similar? How are they different?

9. What types of testimonials can advertisers use? Give an example of each.

10. Which media are best for demonstration-type ads?

11. What kinds of products or services are best suited to fantasy-based executional frameworks? What products or services are poor candidates for fantasies?

12. Identify the four main types of sources or spokespersons. What are the advantages and disadvantages of each?

13. List the five key criteria used when selecting a spokesperson. Which four build to the fifth?

14. Identify the tactics available to overcome clutter. How does variability theory assist in this process?

CRITICAL THINKING EXERCISES

Discussion Questions

1. Select five advertisements in a magazine. Identify the message strategy, appeal, and executional framework in each. Did the creative select the right combination for the advertisement? What other message strategies or executional frameworks could have been used?

2. Record five television advertisements. Identify the message strategy, appeal, and executional framework each uses. Did the creative select the right combination for the advertisement? What other message strategies or executional frameworks could have been used?

3. Studies involving comparative advertisements as compared to noncomparative ads produced the following findings.[28] Discuss why you think each statement is true. Try to think of comparative ads you have seen that substantiate these claims.
   a. Message awareness was higher for comparative ads than for noncomparative ads if the brands were already established brands.
   b. Brand recall was higher for comparative ads than for noncomparative ads.
   c. Comparative ads were viewed as less believable than noncomparative ads.
   d. Attitudes toward comparative ads were more negative than those toward noncomparative ads.

4. Suppose the marketing team for Charles Schwab wants to develop an advertisement with the message theme that Charles Schwab understands the needs of individual consumers and can design an investment strategy to meet each person's particular needs. Which type of message strategy should Schwab choose? Why? Based on the message strategy chosen, which executional framework should the company use? Why? What type of source or spokesperson should Schwab use? Why? Would the type of media being used for the advertisement affect the message strategy choice? Explain your answer.

5. A resort in Florida wants to develop an advertisement highlighting scuba diving classes. The target market will be college students. Discuss the merits of each of the following approaches. In your opinion, which one would be the best? Why? Describe a television ad that could be created using the strategy you chose.
   a. Hyperbole cognitive message strategy, humor appeal, and demonstration execution
   b. Emotional message strategy, emotional appeal, and slice-of-life execution
   c. Conative message strategy, scarcity appeal, and informative execution
   d. Emotional or resonance message strategy, sex appeal, and fantasy execution
   e. Comparative message strategy, fear appeal, and a testimonial execution

6. Name three influential commercial spokespersons. For each one, discuss the five characteristics used to evaluate spokespersons and their overall level of credibility. Next, make a list of three individuals who are poor spokespersons. Discuss each of the five evaluation characteristics for each of these individuals. What differences exist between an effective and a poor spokesperson?

7. Find a copy of a business journal, such as *Business Week* or *Fortune,* or a trade journal. Also locate a copy of a consumer periodical such as *Glamour, Time, Sports Illustrated,* or a specialty magazine. Look through an entire issue.

What differences between the advertisements in the business journal and consumer journals are readily noticeable? For each of the concepts that follow, discuss specific differences you noted between the two types of magazines. Explain why the differences exist.

a. Message strategies

b. Executional frameworks

c. Sources and spokespersons

8. Identify an advertisement that uses each of the following executional frameworks. Evaluate the advertisement in terms of how well it is executed. Also, did the appeal and message strategy fit well with the execution? Was the ad memorable? What made it memorable?

a. Animation

b. Slice-of-life

c. Dramatization

d. Testimonial

e. Authoritative

f. Demonstration

g. Fantasy

h. Informative

INTEGRATED LEARNING EXERCISES

1. Web sites often include animation to make them more appealing. Two sources of free animation that can be used for your personal Web site or for a commercial Web site are **www.camelotdesign.com** and **www.animationlibrary.com**. Access each site. What types of animation are available? How could animation be used to enhance a commercial Web site?

2. Current as well as past Super Bowl ads are available at **www.superbowl-ads.com**. Access the site and compare Super Bowl ads for the last several years. What types of message strategies were used? What types of executions were used? Who and what types of endorsers were used? Compare and contrast these three elements of ads.

3. Most advertising agencies provide examples of advertisements on company Web pages. The goal is to display the agency's creative abilities to potential clients. Using a search engine, locate three different advertising agencies. Locate samples of their work. Compare the ads produced by these three agencies in terms of message appeals, executions, and spokespersons. What similarities do you see? What differences do you see? Which agency, in your opinion, is the most creative? Why?

4. Access the following Web sites. For each, identify the primary message strategy used. Does the site use any sources or spokespersons? From Chapter 6, what type of appeal is being used? For each Web site, suggest how the site could be improved. Be specific. Explain how the change would improve the site.

a. Georgia–Pacific (**www.gp.com**)

b. Playland International (**www.playland-inc.com**)

c. MGM Grand (**www.mgmgrand.com**)

d. The Exotic Body (**www.exoticbody.com**)

e. CoverGirl (**www.covergirl.com**)

f. American Supercamp (**www.americansupercamp.com**)

g. Windmill Hill Tennis & Golf Academy (**www.windmillhill.co.uk**)

5. Access the following Web sites. For each, identify and evaluate the primary executional framework used. Is it the best execution, or would another execution work better? Does the site use any sources or spokespersons? From Chapter 6, what type of appeal is being used? For each Web site, suggest how the site could be improved. Be specific. Explain how the change would improve the site.

a. Kellogg's Frosted Flakes (**www.frostedflakes.com**)

b. Bonne Bell (**www.bonnebell.com**)

c. MessageMedia (**www.message-media.com.au**)

d. Jantzen (**www.jantzen.com**)

e. Jockey International (**www.jockey.com**)

STUDENT PROJECT

Creative Corner

For a number of years, LendingTree.com used the tagline "When banks compete, you win." In the mid-2000s, when the housing market tumbled, mortgage companies faced financial problems, and consumers defaulted on home mortgages, LendingTree.com changed its approach. The company developed new ads and modified the Web site to educate consumers about "smart borrowing." Other financial and mortgage companies followed suit. JPMorgan Chase asserted "Whether you are saving money, looking for a loan, or managing a business, you can always depend on Chase." Astoria Federal Savings promoted its longevity, telling consumers it had been in business "more than 118 years" and using phrases such as "We're part of your community" and "We're here when you need us."[29]

The marketing department for First National Bank wants to promote its home mortgage business. They are unsure about what type of approach to use. They are not sure about which creative message strategy to use, which execution would work best, and which appeal to use. They would also like to use some type of spokesperson, but are not sure which of the four types would be the most effective.

Based on the information provided, design a print advertisement for the local newspaper for First National Bank. Describe a television campaign for the bank. Before launching into these two creative assignments, identify and justify your choice of creative message strategy, executional framework, appeal, and spokesperson.

CASE 1   PEERLESS MARKETING

In the United States, the majority of homes have indoor plumbing. Sinks, faucets, toilets, and other pieces of hardware are largely taken for granted. Only in two circumstances are they prominently in the minds of customers. The first is when a plumbing product is being purchased for the first time, such as when a home is being built or an area is being refurbished. The second is when an item is defective and must be replaced.

The challenge to manufacturers is to make certain that a company's brand is remembered by consumers and preferred by builders and plumbers. The products must be placed in stores such as Home Depot or Lowes in a way that makes them easy to find and always accessible.

One of the major players in the plumbing fixture marketplace is Delta Faucet Company. A strange path brought the company to prominence. In the 1920s, an immigrant named Alex Manoogian founded Masco Company, which provided auto parts. Twenty-five years later, Manoogian was contacted by an inventor who had created the first washerless faucet. Although it was not related to his current business, Manoogian saw the potential and refined the item, which was first sold out of the trunks of salesmen's cars, as the first Delta Faucet. The name was chosen because a key part of the product resembled the shape of the Greek letter delta.

The Delta Faucet Company became a separate part of the original Masco Company and relocated. Over the next two decades, it expanded quickly to an entire line of products. Currently, Delta Faucet Company is a multinational firm with four primary locations: Indianapolis, Indiana; Jackson, Tennessee; London Ontario, Canada; and Panyu, China. It sells over 1 million faucets per month. The overall Masco Company now sells door hardware and locks, cabinets, and glass products in addition to faucets.

The Delta line includes two other names: Brizo and Peerless. Brizo is the high-end line of faucets, Delta is the flagship and primary brand, and Peerless is the lower-end line of items.

The primary advertising challenges appear to exist in four main areas. First, company leaders must make sure that one brand does not cannibalize the others. The brands must remain as distinct products offered to separate sets of consumers. Second, the brands must be viewed as the primary choices and must be remembered by consumers when the time comes to buy a plumbing fixture. Third, there cannot be brand confusion. Builders and plumbers must believe that the fixtures are distinct along several lines, including quality and durability, ease of installation, and strong warranties, but they must also be perceived as being fashionable. Fourth, innovation has become a new part of the plumbing fixture industry. A wide variety of options exist. Delta's products must compete with all the new faucet variations and retain its position as the one of the premier manufacturers.

Complications occur due to differences in markets and customers. Many contractors and builders are simply looking for a low-cost option, especially when lower-end rental properties and similar units are being developed. Plumbers may be willing to install a wide variety of products. They will consider the costs of a product but also want something that will be easy to install and that will be durable. Individual consumers

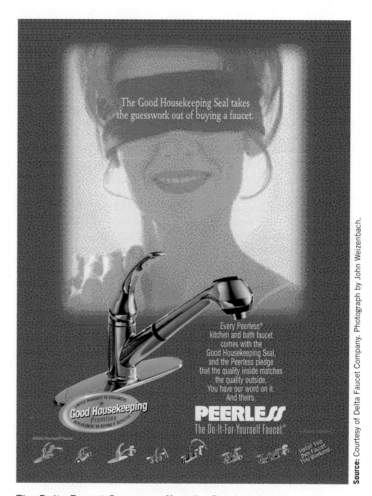

The Delta Faucet Company offers the Peerless brand.

are the most likely to be interested in other product qualities, such as novel features and the look of the product.

Source: www.deltafaucet.com, accessed January 8, 2008.

1. What type of message strategy should Delta Faucet Company utilize? Should it be the same for all of the brands and in all of the markets (builders, plumbers, consumers)?

2. What leverage point makes the most sense for Delta Faucet Company advertising?

3. What type of executional framework should be used in traditional advertisements aimed at consumers?

4. What type of executional framework should be used for print advertisements aimed at contractors, builders, and plumbers? Why might it be different (or the same) from ads aimed at consumers?

5. Should the company use a spokesperson? If so, which one of the four types should be used? Justify your answers.

HANK'S FURNITURE MART

Hank Freeman was excited. His new store, Hank's Furniture Mart, was about to open. Hank had been in the furniture business for more than 10 years, first as a delivery and setup man and then as an in-store salesperson. This was his big chance to launch out on his own. Using some money that he inherited, various loans, and the investment of a silent partner, the mid-price-range retail furniture store was ready for business.

Hank's Furniture Mart was located outside the city limits of a large metropolitan area. Being outside the city limits meant customers would not have to pay city sales tax. The store was part of a large corner cluster. Hank's agreement with the other tenants was to stay out of the mattress and bedding business, because another retailer sold those items exclusively. For the same reason, he also agreed that he would not sell television sets or stereos. A "country-kitchen" chain restaurant was located across the parking lot from the retail stores. The entire shopping complex could be reached easily, because of its convenient location next to the interstate.

Hank knew any furniture store faced a variety of competitors. On the high end, stores such Ethan Allen attracted the affluent customers. On the lower end were large warehouse-style operations offering low prices and prompt delivery of lower-quality pieces. In the middle, several retail chains sold various furnishings. Specialty stores that focused solely on recliners were also close by.

Two advantages gave Hank hope that his store would be a grand success. The first was his extensive knowledge of the retail furniture business. He knew how various stores competed, whether through price, quality, "deals," or any other tactic. His knowledge extended to the various manufacturers. Hank knew which ones gave the best deals, which ones delivered merchandise on time (or late), and the quality levels of the pieces each sold.

The second advantage was Hank's extensive potential customer base. Hank had been working in the retail furniture marketplace for more than a decade. He believed he had a series of loyal buyers and that word-of-mouth would be a big help.

At the same time, Hank knew he would have to advertise. He had set aside enough money to fund television spots and radio, newspaper, Internet, and specialty ads, including direct mail. Hank had chosen a local agency to develop a consistent theme across all the store's ads. He suggested the tagline "Hank's Furniture Mart: Our prices are right and our deals are real."

1. What type of message strategy should Hank's Furniture Mart feature?

2. What type of executional framework should Hank's ads utilize? Which type of appeal will the framework feature?

3. Who should be the spokesperson for the store, Hank or a paid professional actor?

4. Design a print ad for Hank's Furniture Mart.

ENDNOTES

1. Rebecca Winters Keegan, "Top 10 TV ads" (**www.time.com/specials/2007/top 10/article**, accessed January 9, 2008).

2. Henry A. Laskey, Ellen Day, and Melvin R. Crask, "Typology of Main Message Strategies for Television Commercials," *Journal of Advertising* 18, no. 1 (1989), pp. 36–41.

3. David Aaker and Donald Norris, "Characteristics of TV Commercials Perceived As Informative," *Journal of Advertising Research* 22, no. 2 (1982), pp. 61–70;

4. **www.campbellsoupcompany.com/atw_usa.asp**, accessed January 12, 2008.

5. Kenneth Hein, "Nintendo Takes Charge with DS," *Brandweek* 46, no. 6 (February 7, 2005), p. 15.

6. Tony Smith, "Intel Extends Market Share Gains," *Register Hardware* (**www.reghardware.co.uk/2007/04/20/intel_vs_amd_q1_07/print.html**), April 20, 2007.

7. Shailendra Pratap Jain and Steven S. Posavac, "Valenced Comparisons," *Journal of Marketing Research* 41, no. 1 (February 2004), pp. 46–56.

8. Dhruv Grewal and Sukumar Kavanoor, "Comparative Versus Noncomparative Advertising: A Meta-Analysis," *Journal of Marketing* 61, no. 4 (October 1997), pp. 1–15;

Shailendra Pratap Jain and Steven S. Posavac, "Valenced Comparisons," *Journal of Marketing Research* 41, no. 1 (February 2004), pp. 46–56.

9. Joseph R. Priester, John Godek, D. J. Nayakankuppam, and Kiwan Park, "Brand Congruity and Comparative Advertising: When and Why Comparative Advertisements Lead to Greater Elaboration," *Journal of Consumer Psychology* 14, no. 1/2 (2004), pp. 115–24; Grewal and Kavanoor, "Comparative Versus Noncomparative Advertising: A Meta-Analysis."

10. Joanne Lynch and Leslie de Chernatony, "The Power of Emotion: Brand Communication in Business-to-Business Markets," *Journal of Brand Management* 11, no. 5 (May 2004), pp. 403–420.

11. Jim Hanas, "Rotscope Redux," *Creativity* 10, no. 1 (February 2002), pp. 40–41.

12. "Drawing Attention to Animation," *BtoB* 91, no. 7 (June 12, 2006), p. 46.

13. Amilda Dymi, "Wachovia Claims First Place in Community Development," *Financial News* 28, no. 14 (December 29, 2003), p. 6.

14. Matthew Warren, "Do Celebrity Endorsements Still Work?" *Campaign (UK)* 44 (November 2, 2007) p. 13.

15. Claire Murphy, "Stars Brought Down to Earth in TV Ads Research," *Marketing* (January 22, 1998), p. 1.

16. Kamile Junokaite, Sonata Alijosiene, and Rasa Gudonaviciene, "The Solutions of Celebrity Endorsers Selection for Advertising Products," *Economics & Management* 12, no. 3 (2007), pp. 384–90.

17. Roobina Ohanian, "Construction and Validation of a Scale to Measure Celebrity Endorsers' Perceived Expertise," *Journal of Advertising* 19, no. 3 (1990), pp. 39–52.

18 Cathy Yingling, "Beware the Lure of Celebrity Endorsers," *Advertising Age* (**www.adage.com/print?article_ide=120560**), September 24, 2007.

19. Carolyn Tripp, Thomas D. Jensen, and Les Carlson, "The Effects of Multiple Product Endorsements by Celebrities on Consumers' Attitudes and Intentions," *Journal of Consumer Research* 20 (March 1994), pp. 535–47.

20. Dipayan Biswas, Abhijit Biswas, and Neel Das, "The Differential Effects of Celebrity and Expert Endorsements on Consumer Risk Perceptions," *Journal of Advertising* 35, no. 2 (Summer 2006), pp. 17–31.

21. David J. Moore and John C. Mowen, "Multiple Sources in Advertising Appeals: When Product

Endorsers Are Paid by the Advertising Sponsor," *Journal of Academy of Marketing Science* 22, no. 3 (Summer 1994), pp. 234–43.

22. Raymond R. Burke and Thomas K. Srull, "Competitive Interference and Consumer Memory for Advertising," *Journal of Consumer Research* 15 (June 1988), pp. 55–68.

23. A. W. Melton, "The Situation with Respect to the Spacing of Repetitions and Memory," *Journal of Verbal Learning and Verbal Behavior* 9 (1970), pp. 596–606.

24. H. Rao Unnava and Deepak Sirdeshmukh, "Reducing Competitive Ad Interference," *Journal of Marketing Research* 31, no. 3 (August 1994), pp. 403–411.

25. Naveen Donthu, "A Cross-Country Investigation of Recall of and Attitudes Toward Comparative Advertising," *Journal of Advertising* 27, no. 2 (Summer 1998), pp. 111–21.

26. Grewal and Kavanoor, "Comparative Versus Noncomparative Advertising: A Meta-Analysis."

27. Michael L. Maynard, "Slice-of-Life: A nPersuasive Mini Drama in Japanese Television Advertising," *Journal of Popular Culture* 31, no. 2 (Fall 1997), pp. 131–42.

28. Grewal and Kavanoor, "Comparative Versus Noncomparative Advertising: A Meta-Analysis."

29. Stuart Elliott, "With Economy Volatile, Financial Firms Start to Stress Stability," *The New York Times* (**www.nytimes.com/ 2007/09/19/business/media/19adco.html**), September 19, 2007.

PART 3

IMC Media Tools

8

Traditional Media Channels

M&M'S

The Sweet Task of Media Selection

Can you remember the first time you ate M&M's? Most probably cannot, because it happened so early in life. The M&M's brand is one of the most famous and popular candies offered by Mars, Incorporated. Today, the brand enjoys an international presence that continues to grow.

M&M's began with a global flavor. According to corporate legend, Forrest Mars Sr. was in Spain visiting soldiers fighting the Spanish Civil War. He noted that they were eating pieces of chocolate that were encased in a hard, sugary coating. Using this as inspiration, Mars returned to the United States and refined the recipe for M&M's. The first packages were sold in 1941 in the United States. They were a favorite of many GIs serving in World War II. The original candies were sold in a cardboard tube. The famous brown-and-white package didn't emerge until the late 1940s.

The legend of M&M's grew when colors were added to the original brown. In the 1960s, red, green, and yellow were introduced. Eventually, these and other colors developed into advertising "spokescandies," including the egomaniac, Red; the lovely female, Green; and the amazing crispy Orange, cool Blue, and nutty Yellow.

Red disappeared for a time from the M&M's mix after research suggested problems with red food dye, even though the problem was not associated with M&M's. In 1987, Red triumphantly returned, much to the joy of candy lovers around the world.

The advertising program for M&M's has been long lasting, noteworthy, and award winning. Practically any baby boomer remembers the original M&M's tagline: "Melts in your mouth, not in your hand." Television advertisements have long been the staple of M&M's marketing. Using a natural tie-in with candy consumption at Christmas, an intense burst of M&M's advertising takes place each December. Most of these ads include a guest visit from Santa.

The effectiveness of the M&M's characters has allowed many additional forms of support advertising. Print ads featuring Red, Blue, Green, Yellow, and Orange are placed in magazines for both children and adults. The M&M's Web site celebrates the characters, even offering a bio for each individual color. The characters are featured in a "Virtual Hollywood" site that includes M&M's Studios. By 1996, the characters were more popular than Mickey Mouse and Bart Simpson. M&M's merchandise, such as stuffed "candy" pillows, is available online and in other retail locations.

Chapter Objectives

After reading this chapter, you should be able to answer the following questions:

- **What** activities are involved in creating a media strategy?

- **How** do the roles played by media planners and media buyers differ from others in the marketing department?

- **What** are reach, frequency, continuity, impressions, and CPM?

- **What** are the advantages and disadvantages of the various forms of traditional media used in advertising?

- **Why** is the mix of media a key part of an advertising campaign?

CHAPTER EIGHT

Several exciting advertising and promotional programs have been used to advertise the M&M's brand. In 1998, M&M's became the "Official Spokescandies of the New Millennium," due, in part, to the good fortune of two "M"s (MM) being the equivalent of the Roman numeral for "2000." Also in 2000, the official candy name switched from M&M's *Plain* Chocolate Candies to M&M's *Milk* Chocolate Candies, a major victory for Red, who supported the more accurate brand name.

During the tragedy of September 11, 2001, M&M's were provided in a special package containing only red, white, and blue colors. The candies were distributed to rescue workers and others working near Ground Zero. Approximately $3 million of the proceeds from the sale of the limited edition were given to victims and survivors of the attacks.

At the close of 2004, all of the M&M's lost their color on *Dick Clark's Rockin' New Year's Eve* television show. The question was posed, "Will the colors come back?" Only black and white M&M's were on the market for about 2 months. Then, the colors returned with a grand celebration, noting, "Chocolate is better in color!"

Beyond advertising in print, electronic, and television media, M&M's is involved with several charitable efforts. One is the Special Olympics; a "Keep Wrappers to Keep Dreams Alive" promotion raised more than $1 million dollars for the charity. In 2003, M&M's "Groovy Summer" program was used to support the Susan G. Komen Breast Cancer foundation. Special pink and white candies were created as part of the effort.

The future of M&M's continues to be bright. Everything from a vote to choose a new color (purple won) to news that the candy flies on the Space Shuttle keeps M&M's a popular, memorable, fun brand in the eyes of candy lovers around the world.[1]

"

OVERVIEW

If a tree falls in the forest and no one is present, does it make a sound? This philosophical question has been asked for many years. In the world of advertising, far too many "trees" fall as unheard and unseen advertisements. Successful marketing account executives help a firm identify target markets and then find media that reach the members of those markets, in both retail situations and business-to-business marketing efforts. Once they identify the right media, creatives design clever, memorable, exciting, and persuasive advertisements to help convince customers to purchase products.

The third section of this textbook is devoted to the IMC media tools. This includes both traditional media channels and newer approaches. The concepts of e-active marketing and alternative channels are explained in the upcoming chapters (see Figure 8.1).

Traditional media continue to play an important role in developing a fully integrated marketing program. This chapter explains the various traditional media channels, including the following topics:

- The media strategy
- Media planning processes and the roles of the media planner and buyer
- Advertising objectives
- Media choices based on the advantages and disadvantages of each medium
- Media selection in business-to-business and international settings

Developing an advertising campaign within the framework of an integrated marketing communications program is a vital function that high-quality advertising agencies provide. Client companies depend on effective ads to attract customers and entice them into purchasing various goods and services. The goals are to build a firm's image and to create a larger consumer base. Advertising media selection is an important element in this process. A review of the elements of the selection process follows.

MEDIA STRATEGY

One of the most important ingredients in matching an advertising campaign with the overall integrated marketing communications program is to prepare an effective media strategy. A **media strategy** is the process of analyzing and choosing media for an advertising and promotions campaign.

FIGURE 8.1
Overview of Integrated Marketing Communications

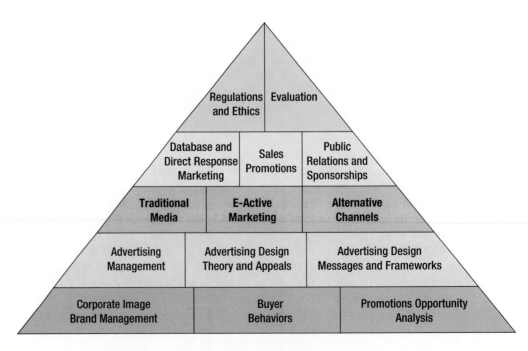

The average consumer reads or looks over only 9 of the more than 200 consumer magazines on the market. A radio listener usually tunes in to only three of the stations available in a given area. Television viewers watch fewer than 8 of the 30-plus stations available via cable or satellite and average network prime-time ratings have declined by more than 30 percent over the last decade. Simply finding the right places to speak to potential customers is challenging.

To make the account executive and media buyer's jobs more difficult, prices for advertising time or space have risen. Client budgets for advertising have not kept up with inflation. And, there are stronger demands for results and accountability. This means that the marketing team faces difficulties in locating media outlets. Once the media strategy is in place, other aspects of media selection can proceed.

MEDIA PLANNING

Media planning begins with a careful analysis of the target market. It involves understanding the process consumers and businesses use in making a purchase and what influences the final decision. One method of addressing media planning is to study the media choices that members of a specific, defined target market might make at different times during the course of a day. Some of the more common choices are listed in Figure 8.2.

Specific details of this type are extremely valuable when developing a media strategy. Simply knowing demographic information such as age, sex, income, and education is not enough to determine the media habits of a person in a target market. Information about the listening and viewing patterns of customers helps the marketing team design messages that appeal to the right people. The message can also be made available at the best times and in the best places.

No two media plans are alike. Each plan should integrate the overall IMC strategy with specific marketing tactics. The typical components of a media plan include the following elements, which are also identified in Figure 8.3.

A *marketing analysis* is a comprehensive review of the fundamental marketing program. It includes a statement of current sales, current market share, and prime prospects to be solicited (by demographics, lifestyle, geographic location, or product usage). These elements should reflect a compatible pricing strategy based on the product, its benefits and distinguishing characteristics, and an analysis of the competitive environment.

An *advertising analysis* states the fundamental advertising strategy and budget to be used in meeting advertising objectives. The *media strategy* spells out the media to be used and the creative considerations. The *media schedule* notes when ads will appear in individual vehicles. The *justification and summary* states the measures of goal achievement. It also states the rationale for each media choice. Each of the media plan's elements is described in greater detail in the upcoming sections.[2]

Several individuals are involved in media planning. In addition to account executives and creatives, most agencies utilize media planners and media buyers. In smaller agencies, the media planner and media buyer can be the same person. In larger companies, they are usually different individuals.

- ◆ A favorite wake-up radio station or one listened to during the commute to work
- ◆ A favorite morning news show or newspaper
- ◆ Trade or business journals examined while at work
- ◆ A radio station played during office hours at work
- ◆ Favorite computer sites accessed during work
- ◆ Favorite magazines read during the evening hours
- ◆ Favorite television shows watched during the evening hours
- ◆ Internet sites accessed during leisure time
- ◆ Shopping, dining, and entertainment venues frequented

FIGURE 8.2
Examples of Times Workers Are Exposed to Advertisements

FIGURE 8.3
Components of a Media Plan

- ◆ Marketing analysis
- ◆ Advertising analysis
- ◆ Media strategy

- ◆ Media schedule
- ◆ Justification and summary

Media Planners

The **media planner** formulates a media program stating where and when to place advertisements. Media planners work closely with creatives, account executives, agencies, and media buyers. The creative must know which media will be used due to the impact on advertising design. Television ads are constructed in a different way than radio or newspaper ads.

Media planners provide extremely valuable functions and are in high demand. The issue of accountability for advertising results combined with the need to create a "return on investment" on marketing dollars has led to a shift in greater power being held by the media buying side. Less is held by the creatives.

Media planning drives much of the strategic planning. Marketing experts at companies such as Procter & Gamble and Unilever consider media planning to be the heart of a communications strategy. In the Unilever division of P&G, the first step is to set brand priorities and objectives. Next, a media channel communications plan is agreed upon before the actual communications plan and creative brief are prepared.[3] The challenge for media buyers in this environment, according to Carl Fremont of the worldwide media services company Digitas, is "to integrate marketing messages across a range of media, and sometimes this involves working with several agencies to accomplish the client's goals."[4]

In most instances, the media planner conducts research to help match the product with the market and media. If a product's target market is 18- to 25-year-old males with college degrees who love the outdoors, then the media should match those characteristics. The media planner then identifies the most ideal locations for the advertisements. The New Balance running shoe ad in this section was placed in *Runner's World* near an article about running. The media plan should be designed to find the best ways to reach the client's customers.

Part of the media planner's research is gathering information about various media. This includes newspaper and magazine circulation rates and the characteristics of those who use the medium. The audience for a television show may be quite different from those of a radio station or a magazine. Careful research improves the chances of selecting appropriate media.[5]

Almost everyone has heard of S.O.S. soap pads. A few years ago, however, S.O.S. sales began to decline. The product was no longer the top-of-mind brand. The task of rebuilding awareness for the S.O.S. soap pads in Canada was assigned to the Palmer Jarvis DDB agency. The agency's media planners began by examining the media habits of the primary target market for S.O.S. soap pads. The group consisted of women, ages 35 to 54 that work, have kids, and are in a busy, active household. Women in this target group are heavy magazine readers. They have interests in home décor, entertaining, gardening, and cooking. As a result, media buys were made in

An advertisement featuring New Balance shoes that was placed in *Runner's World* magazine.

Canadian Living, Cooking at Home, Canadian House & Home, and *Homemaker's*. These magazines were the best match of product, market, and media habits of the main consumer group.[6]

Media Buyers

After the media are chosen, someone must buy the space and negotiate rates, times, and schedules for the ads. This is the work of the **media buyer.** Media buyers stay in constant contact with media sales representatives. They have a great deal of knowledge about rates and schedules. Media buyers also watch for special deals and tie-ins between different media outlets (e.g., radio with television, magazines with the same owner, etc.).

The media planner works with the media buyer, the creative, and the account executive in the design of an advertising campaign. Each plays a critical role in the development of an integrated marketing communications program. The challenge of coordinating the efforts of these individuals intensifies when they are from different companies, which is typically the case for large clients and national brands.

The size of the advertising agency or media buying firm alone does not ensure effective media purchases. Research indicates that there is little connection between the size of an advertising firm and the prices it can negotiate. One study indicated that differences in media costs are based on the time of the actual purchase (closer to the day the ad is to run) rather than the size of the agency.[7] Other major factors in cost differences are knowledge of the marketplace and the ability to negotiate package deals. Spot television media plans vary by as much as 45 percent in the price of the spot. A **spot ad** is a one-time placement of an ad on a local television station. Rates are negotiated individually by the number of times ads appear with individual stations. For example, a media plan costing one firm $10 million can cost another firm $12 million. Radio time slots vary by as much as 42 percent and national print ads by as much as 24 percent.[8] More importantly, differences in effectiveness of advertising are often related to:

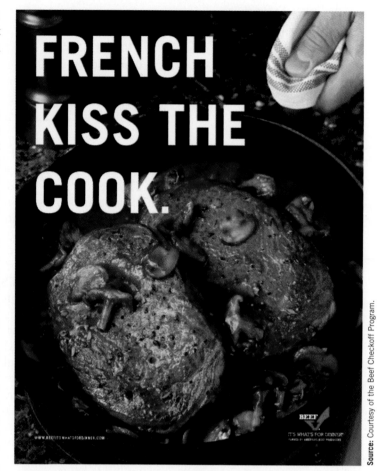

Source: Courtesy of the Beef Checkoff Program.

The media buyer will purchase space in various print media for ads such as this.

- The quality of media choices (the right ones) made by each agency
- Creativity
- Financial stewardship ("bang" for your advertising buck)
- Agency culture and track record
- Computer systems to analyze data
- Relationships between the agency and the medium's sales representative

The negotiated price is only one element in the success of an advertising program. Effectiveness in advertising is also determined by quality of the selections made by the marketing team and the content of the ad itself. Media should be selected and purchased with specific advertising objectives in mind.

ADVERTISING OBJECTIVES

In selecting media, a review of the communications objectives established during the development of the IMC program occurs. These objectives guide media selection decisions as well as the message design. The technical terms used to describe outcomes are listed in Figure 8.4.

Reach is the number of people, households, or businesses in a target audience exposed to a media vehicle or message schedule at least once during a given time period.

FIGURE 8.4
Advertising Objective Terminology

- ◆ Reach
- ◆ Frequency
- ◆ Opportunities to see (OTS)
- ◆ Gross rating points (GRP)
- ◆ Cost per thousand (CPM)

- ◆ Cost per rating point (CPRP)
- ◆ Ratings
- ◆ Continuity
- ◆ Gross impressions

A time period is normally 4 weeks. In other words, how many targeted buyers did the ad reach at least once during a 4-week period?

Frequency is the average number of times an individual, household, or business within a particular target market is exposed to a particular advertisement within a specified time period, again, usually 4 weeks. Or, how many times did the person see the ad during the campaign? A regular viewer sees the same ad shown each day on *Wheel of Fortune* more frequently than an ad shown once on *Grey's Anatomy*, even though the program has a far greater reach. In media planning, instead of frequency, **opportunities to see (OTS)** is commonly used. Opportunities to see refers to the cumulative exposures achieved in a given time period. For example, if a company places two ads on a television show that is televised weekly, then during a 4-week period there are 8 OTS (4 shows × 2 ads per show).

Gross rating points (GRP) are a measure of the impact or intensity of a media plan. Gross rating points are calculated by multiplying a vehicle's rating by the OTS, or number of insertions of an advertisement. GRP gives the advertiser an idea about the odds of the target audience actually viewing the ad. By increasing the frequency, or OTS, of an advertisement, the chances of a magazine reader seeing the advertisement increase. An advertisement featured in each issue of *Time* during a 4-week period is more likely to be seen than one that appears only once in a monthly periodical.

Cost is a measure of overall expenditures associated with an advertising program or campaign. But, to be able to compare how cost effective one medium or ad placement is to another, a measure called **cost per thousand (CPM)** is calculated. CPM is the dollar cost of reaching 1,000 members of the media vehicle's audience. CPM is calculated by using the following formula:

$$\text{CPM} = (\text{Cost of media buy}/\text{Total audience}) \times 1{,}000$$

Table 8.1 shows some basic cost and readership information. The first three columns of the table provide the name of the magazine, the cost of a four-color full-page advertisement, and the magazine's total readership. The fourth column contains a

TABLE 8.1 Hypothetical Media Plan Information for Select Magazines

Magazine	Cost for 4-Color Full-Page Ad	Total Readership (000s)	CPM Total	Target Market (20M) Rating (Reach)	Target Market (20M) Cost per Rating Point (CPRP)
National Geographic	$ 346,080	21,051	$16.44	16.1	$21,496
Newsweek	780,180	15,594	50.03	12.2	63,949
People	605,880	21,824	27.76	9.4	64,455
Southern Living	11,370	5,733	1.98	2.4	4,738
Sports Illustrated	965,940	13,583	71.11	10.5	91,994
Time	1,324,282	21,468	61.69	15.9	83,288
Travel & Leisure	183,216	2,205	83.09	2.3	79,659
U.S. News & World Report	100,740	8,929	11.28	8.3	12,137

measure of the CPM of each magazine. Notice that the CPM for *National Geographic* is $16.44. This means that it takes $16.44 to reach 1,000 *National Geographic* readers. Notice the CPM for *Sports Illustrated* is $71.11 and for *Travel & Leisure*, $83.09. The readership of *Travel & Leisure* is the lowest, and yet its CPM is the highest of all eight magazines. In terms of cost per thousand readers, the best buy is *Southern Living*, at only $1.98 per thousand.

Another cost calculation can be made besides CPM. One critical concern is the cost of reaching a firm's target audience. Therefore, a measure called the **cost per rating point (CPRP)** was developed. The cost per rating point is a relative measure of the efficiency of a media vehicle relative to a firm's target market. **Ratings** measure the percentage of a firm's target market that is exposed to a show on television or an article in a print medium. The following formula is used to calculate the cost per rating point:

$$CPRP = \text{Cost of media buy/Vehicle's rating}$$

The ratings in Table 8.1 were generated for potential buyers of a 35 mm digital camera. The table shows the rating for *National Geographic* is 16.1, which means that 16.1 percent of the defined target market for 35 mm digital cameras read *National Geographic*. The CPRP for *National Geographic* is $21,496. This is the average cost for each rating point, or of each 1 percent of the firm's target audience (35 mm digital camera buyers). Not all readers of a magazine are part of the firm's target market. The CPRP more accurately measures an advertising campaign's efficiency than does CPM. Notice that the CPRP is the lowest for *National Geographic, Southern Living,* and *U.S. News & World Report.*

CPRP provides a relative measure of reach exposure in terms of cost. For example, it costs $21,496 to reach 1 percent, or 200,000, of the 20 million in this firm's target market using *National Geographic*. It costs $91,994 to reach 1 percent, or 200,000, using *Sports Illustrated*. To reach 1 percent, or 200,000, using *Southern Living* costs only $4,738. Because *Southern Living* is so efficient, why wouldn't a media planner just do all of the advertising in that magazine? The answer lies in the rating for *Southern Living*. Advertising in only that magazine reaches just 2.4 percent (or 480,000) of the target audience, meaning 97.6 percent of the target market does not read *Southern Living*, and would not be exposed to the ad. Thus, another magazine or media outlet is necessary to reach them. This example explains why diversity in media is essential to reach a large portion of a firm's target market.

To further analyze whether an ad has reached the target market effectively, a **weighted (or demographic) CPM** value can be calculated, as follows:

$$\text{Weighted CPM} = \frac{\text{Advertisement cost} \times 1,000}{\text{Actual audience reached}}$$

For example, if the cost of an advertisement in *Sports Illustrated* is $115,000 and the magazine reaches 4,200,000 readers, the standard CPM would be $27.38. If the ad targets parents of Little League baseball players and research indicates that 600,000 of *Sports Illustrated*'s readers are Little League parents, the result would be:

$$\text{Weighted CPM} = \frac{\$115,000 \times 1,000}{600,000} = \$191.66$$

This figure could be compared to figures for *Sporting News, ESPN Magazine,* and other sports magazines.

Continuity is the exposure pattern or schedule used in the ad campaign. As explained in Chapter 5, the three types of patterns are continuous, pulsating, and discontinuous. A continuous campaign uses media time in a steady stream. The Skechers ad shown in this section could be presented on a continuous schedule. To do so, the media buys would be for ad space in specific magazines for a period of 1 to 2 years. By using different ads and rotating them, readers will not get bored, because they will see more than one ad for the same product. A retailer such as JCPenney might

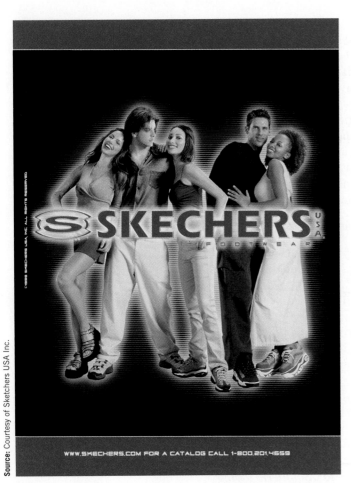

An advertisement promoting the Skechers brand.

use a pulsating schedule by placing ads in various media throughout the entire year, but then increasing the number of advertisements in small, short bursts around holidays, including Christmas, Thanksgiving, Memorial Day, Labor Day, Mother's Day, Father's Day, and Easter. The goal of pulsating advertising is to reach consumers when they are most likely to make purchases or buy special merchandise, such as during the holiday shopping season. Thus, a Barnes and Noble advertisement just prior to Christmas can encourage consumers to purchase Barnes and Noble gift cards. A flighting (or discontinuous) campaign schedule is likely to be used by a ski resort that runs ads during the fall and winter seasons but none during the spring and summer.

The final objective advertisers consider is the concept of *impressions*. The number of **gross impressions** is the total exposures of the audience to an advertisement. It does not take into consideration what percentage of the total audience will see the advertisement. Table 8.1 indicates that the total readership of *National Geographic* is 21,051,000. If six insertions were placed in *National Geographic,* multiplying the insertions by the readership would yield a total of 126 million impressions.

ACHIEVING ADVERTISING OBJECTIVES

One continuing issue facing advertisers is deciding how many times a person must be exposed to an ad before it has an impact. Most agree that a single exposure is not enough. Discovering the actual number has inspired a great deal of debate. Some argue it takes three exposures. Others say as many as 10. The basic rule, developed by Herbert Krugman, states that it takes a minimum of three exposures for an advertisement to be effective. This is the *three-exposure hypothesis*. Most media planners have assumed it for many years.[9]

Now, many advertisers think three exposures are not enough to create an impression in the consumer's mind, primarily because of the amount of clutter that exists. Clutter also affects the types of objectives firms try to accomplish. For instance, increasing brand awareness is usually easier than building brand image. Attention-getting is easier than holding someone's interest long enough to make a point about the firm's image. Also, a well-known brand that is the first choice of the majority of consumers can accomplish its objective with fewer ad exposures than a less well-known brand.

Seeking to discover the minimum number of exposures needed to be effective is based on two concepts: effective frequency and effective reach. **Effective reach** is the *percentage of an audience* that must be exposed to a particular message to achieve a specific objective. **Effective frequency** refers to the *number of times* a target audience must be exposed to a message to achieve a particular objective. The concept of effective frequency implies that some minimum number of exposures exists.

Effective frequency and effective reach are crucial. Too few exposures means the advertiser will fail to attain its intended objectives. On the other hand, too many exposures waste resources. The goal is to discover the optimal reach and frequency mix to accomplish the intended objectives without experiencing diminishing returns from extra ads. Remember that the optimal mix for an objective dealing with brand recognition is different than if the objective involved is brand recall.

When the objective is to increase brand recognition, the emphasis will be on the visual presentation of the product and/or logo. The goal is to create or strengthen a linkage in the person's knowledge structure between the brand and other nodes of knowledge that already exist. Rather than have the individual recall the brand name from memory, the advertiser wants the person to recognize the brand name and logo at the retail store or in an advertisement. In this situation, advertisers want to increase reach, exposing a maximum percentage of the target audience to the brand's name, logo, and selling point. Media that are good at maximizing reach include television, billboards, magazines, the Internet, and direct mail.[10]

When the objective is to increase brand recall, frequency is more important than reach. Repetition is required to embed a brand in the consumer's cognitive memory. Repetition increases the odds that a particular brand will come to mind. When the name of a restaurant is mentioned seven times in a 30-second commercial, it is more likely the name will be remembered than if it is stated only once or twice. In terms of media selection, television, radio, newspapers, and the Internet offer the potential for high frequency.[11] Figure 8.5 compares brand recall with brand recognition.

Other elements can also enhance effective frequency and effective reach. They include the size, placement, and the length of an ad. A small magazine advertisement does not create the same impact as a larger ad. In television advertising, a spot in the middle of an ad sequence usually has less of an impact than the ads shown at the beginning and end of the series. If a firm uses 15-second television ads, effective frequency may require six exposures. In comparison, a longer 45-second spot may require only four exposures to be remembered.

Another important factor that affects these objectives is the number of different media used in an advertising campaign. In general, a campaign featuring ads in two types of media, such as television and magazines, has greater effective reach than a campaign in only one medium, such as magazines only.

In recent years, numerous media companies have designed computer models to optimize reach and frequency, including *Nielsen SAVE*, which examines cable TV alternatives and calculates the value of each using criteria such as Nielsen TV audience data (ratings), product purchasing information, customer preference cluster data, and specific systems data. Another version, *ADPlus* software, combines reach and frequency information with media mix information, budgeting data, and customized information for the individual advertiser. *Adware* provides Arbitron and Nielsen rating information, calculates media costs, and is designed to project GRP.

The programs that evaluate effective reach and frequency are based on probability theory and are designed to help the marketing team effectively allocate advertising dollars. An interaction of an attention-getting television ad with a magazine ad with copy explaining a product's features may have a synergistic effect in which the combined ads are more potent than the impact of either ad alone.

Recency Theory

A new theory challenges the traditional three-exposure hypothesis. It is called *recency theory*. The theory suggests that a consumer's attention is selective and focused on his

Effective reach and effective frequency are important measures to evaluate ads, such as this one for Keepsake.

Objective	Brand Recognition	Brand Recall
Goal	Create or strengthen mental linkages	Place brand in evoked set
Method	Increase reach	Increase frequency (repetition)
Best media	Television	Television
	Billboards	Radio
	Magazines	Newspapers
	Internet	Internet
	Direct mail	

FIGURE 8.5
Brand Recognition Versus Brand Recall

Based on recency theory, a female looking for ski boots is likely to notice this ad.

or her individual needs and wants. It is also based on the idea that because of clutter advertising has only a short-term effect and responses to advertising dissipate rapidly, with few carryover effects.[12]

The traditional three-exposure hypothesis is based on the intrusion value of advertisements and the idea that advertisements can make an impact on an audience regardless of individual needs or wants. **Intrusion value** is the ability of media or an advertisement to intrude upon a viewer without his or her voluntary attention.

Recency theory's premise is that consumers have selective attention processes as they consider advertisements. They give the most attention to messages that might meet their needs or wants. The closer or more recent an ad is to a purchase, the more powerful the ad will be. Also, when a consumer contemplates a future purchase of the product being advertised, it becomes more likely that the consumer will pay attention to and react favorably toward an ad. This means that a member of a buying center from a business in the market for a new copier will more readily notice copier advertisements. An individual who is not in the market for a copier ignores the same ad. The same is true in consumer markets: An individual needing a new pair of jeans notices clothing ads, especially ones that feature jeans.

Recency theory also suggests that the impact of advertising dissipates over time, even if the ad is noticed by individuals. The clutter and information overload that consumers experience means that the carryover effects of advertising tend to be low. Therefore, companies must advertise on an almost continuous basis to ensure an advertisement is in front of the buyer when he or she is thinking of making a purchase.

One primary difference in recency theory is the idea that one ad exposure is enough to affect an audience when that person or business needs the product being promoted. Additional exposures actually may not be necessary. The advertising strategy that matches recency theory spreads the message around using a variety of media, each one providing limited exposure per week or time period. In the case of selling supplemental health insurance to the elderly, magazines such as *Senior Living*, televisions spots on local news and weather programs, and newspaper ads can quickly reach the target audience in a cost-effective manner. Such an approach, which maximizes reach, accomplishes more than increasing frequency.

In the business-to-business arena, applying recency theory means that ads should appear in a number of outlets and over a longer period of time rather than running a series of ads in one trade journal. Many times, a number of individuals are members of the buying center, each with different responsibilities. To make sure each one sees the ad, placing ads in all of the journals that might be read by buying center members is the key. To facilitate the purchasing process for a company seeking to buy an audio-conferencing system, the media buyer purchases space in trade journals, human resource journals, sales journals, and business journals. This increases the odds that the message will effectively reach the buying center members. One exposure might be enough for each person, because the member is looking for information and is ready to make a purchase decision. To reach business personnel while traveling, Polycom recently placed an advertisement in the Delta Airline's *Sky* magazine, because of the higher odds that more than one buying center member might see the ad while flying.

Once the media buyer, media planner, account executive, and company leaders agree about basic objectives of the advertising campaign, they can select the actual media. The goal is to identify logical media combinations. The next section examines the traditional media that are available.

MEDIA SELECTION

A variety of advertising media are available. Effectively mixing these media is an important part of designing quality advertising. To do so, the advantages and disadvantages of each individual medium must be understood.

Television

For many years, television had the reputation of being the most glamorous advertising medium. A company featuring a television advertising campaign enjoyed more prestige. To some, television advertising is still the best option. Today, television advertisement may or may not be the best option.

Table 8.2 lists the advantages and disadvantages of television advertising. As shown, television offers advertisers the most extensive coverage and highest reach of any of the media. A single ad can reach millions of viewers simultaneously. Even though the total cost of running the ad is high, the cost per contact is relatively low. This *low cost per contact* justifies, for example, spending $2 million for a 30-second spot on the Super Bowl.

Further, television has the advantage of *intrusion value*, which is the ability of a medium or advertisement to intrude upon a viewer without his or her voluntary attention. Television ads with a catchy musical tune, sexy content, or humor can quickly grab a viewer's attention. Television provides many opportunities for creativity in advertising design. Visual images and sounds can be incorporated to capture the viewer's attention and present persuasive messages. Products and services can be demonstrated on television in a manner not possible in print or using radio advertisements.

Clutter is the primary problem with television advertising. Five years ago, prime-time averaged 16 minutes and 26 ads per hour of programming. That has slowly crept upward to about 19 minutes and 31 ads per hour. One particular television show had a total of 24 ads within the 30-minute show, which meant 11 minutes out of the 30 was devoted to advertising. Four- and 5-minute commercial breaks are no longer unusual.[13] As a result, many viewers switch channels during commercial breaks. Thus, messages at the beginning or near the end of the break have the best recall. Those in the middle often have virtually no impact. Therefore, clutter makes it difficult for a single message to have much influence.

Another method some viewers use to cope with clutter is a DVR, recording favorite programs and watching them later. Currently, 20 percent of television viewers use a DVR. The fear advertisers have is that consumers will skip over the commercials. Some research indicates, however, that fewer than half fast-forward through commercials. Also, the majority watches the television show the same day it is recorded, and 75 percent have watched it by the end of the next day. This means that time-sensitive ads are being seen close to when they first were shown.[14]

Television commercials have *short life spans.* Sixty-nine percent of the national ads produced during the past year were 30-second ads. Occasionally an advertiser purchases a 15-, 45-, or 60-second ad, but those are rare. Another

---

TABLE 8.2 Television Advertising

Advantages	Disadvantages
1. High reach	1. Greater clutter
2. High frequency potential	2. Low recall due to clutter
3. Low cost per contact	3. Channel surfing during commercials
4. High intrusion value (motion, sound)	4. Short amount of copy
5. Quality creative opportunities	5. High cost per ad
6. Segmentation possibilities through cable outlets	

"A Brand New Day"
2008 InCourage

Silent house. Ceiling fan is turning while restless lady tosses and turns.

Flashback to home that has been completely destroyed by the hurricane.

Restless lady glances at an alarm clock to see it is early in the morning and she still cannot fall asleep.

She sits up in bed and decides it is time to get help.

InCourage
1-800-437-0303

Display logo with phone number for those who were affected by the hurricane to get help.

Woman grins with the thought that she can have a brand new day with the help of InCourage, as the morning light shines upon her face.

A storyboard produced by Zhender Communications for a television commercial.

disadvantage of television is the high cost per ad not only for the media time, but also in terms of production costs. Outstanding commercials often are expensive to produce. The average cost to produce a 30-second national ad is $358,000. Production fees account for the largest portion of the cost, an average of $236,000. Other costs include director fees ($23,000), editing and finishing the ad ($45,000), and creative/labor fees and music ($34,000).[15]

When television advertising spots are shown too frequently they quickly lose the ability to attract the viewer's interest. Companies are forced to replace the ads with something new before consumers get tired of them and tune them out even though the marketing team wants to run an ad long enough to recover production costs.

Choosing the best television advertising outlets for an ad is challenging. The goal is to match a firm's target audience with specific shows. Many cable television programs provide well-defined audiences.

To gain a sense of how well an advertisement fared in terms of reaching an audience, a given program's *rating* can be calculated. The typical ratings formula is:

$$\text{Rating} = \frac{\text{Number of households turned to a program}}{\text{Total number of households in a market}}$$

In the United States, approximately 109.7 million households have television sets. To calculate the rating of an episode of *American Idol*, if the number of households tuned to the season finale was 17.8 million the rating would be:

$$\text{Rating} = \frac{17,800,000}{109,700,000} = 16.2$$

Next, if the advertiser were interested in the percentage of households that actually were watching television at that hour, the program's share could be calculated. If 71 million of the 109.7 million households had a television turned on during the hour in which *American Idol* aired the share would be:

$$\text{Share} = \frac{\text{Number of households tuned to \textit{American Idol}}}{\text{Number of households with a television turned on}} = \frac{17,800,000}{71,000,000} = 25$$

A 16.2 rating would mean that 16.2 percent of all televisions in the United States were tuned to *American Idol*. A 25 share means 25 percent of the households with a television actually turned on were watching the program.

There is no guarantee that the viewers saw the commercial. Ratings and shares are only indicators of how well the program fared. Ratings are used to establish rates for advertisements. The higher a show's rating over time, the more that is charged. For example, *American Idol* had ratings between 15 and 20 for most weeks, and a 30-second spot cost around $600,000. *Grey's Anatomy* had a rating around 16.1, with a 30-second ad costing $419,000. In contrast, the cost of a 30-second spot on *Two and a Half Men*, which has a rating of 10.3, was around $231,000.[16] Figure 8.6 provides some popular television shows and the cost of a 30-second ad.

ACNielsen is the primary organization that calculates and reports ratings and shares. The company also provides local channel information regarding shares of stations in local markets known as *designated marketing areas* (DMAs). Data gathering techniques used by ACNielsen include diaries written by viewers who report what they watched, audience meters that record what is being watched automatically, and people meters that allow the viewing habits of individual members of families to be tracked.

TV Show	Cost
American Idol	$600,000
Grey's Anatomy	419,000
Desperate Housewives	394,000
The Simpsons	315,000
Heroes	296,000
CSI	248,000
Two and a Half Men	231,000

FIGURE 8.6
Cost of a 30-Second Ad

Source: Based on Brian Steinberg, "Ads on ABC Most Expensive at Season Bow," *TV Week* (September 30, 2007). (**www.tvweek.com/news/2007/09/exclusive-sunday_night_costs_t.php**).

These numbers can be further refined to help advertisers understand whether an advertisement reached a target market. Within rating and share categories, viewers can be subdivided by certain demographics, such as:

- Age
- Income
- Gender
- Educational level
- Race or ethnic heritage

Organizations that prepare this kind of information include Nielsen Media Research; Starch INRA; Hooper, Inc.; Mediamark Research, Inc.; Burke Marketing Research; and Simmons Market Research Bureau. An advertising team may find it extremely helpful to know that viewers of *CSI: Miami* tend to be college educated, older than the age of 40, and have annual incomes of more than $50,000. If psychographic information can be added in (such as that the show is mostly watched by people who voted for Democrats in the previous election), then the advertiser has a good sense of whether this is the best audience for a given advertisement or campaign.

For local and regional advertisers, spot TV is the best option for television advertising. In many cases, national brands supplement national commercials with spot TV purchases in select markets. Media planners do this primarily because of the high cost of national ad time and because 75 to 80 percent of prime-time slots are sold out during the spring, shortly after they go on the market. By selecting local early news, late news, and local prime access, a media planner can generate higher GRP at a lower cost than if only national ad time is purchased.

Two measures, the brand and category development indices, can be used to help pick spot TV times. The *brand development index* (BDI) is the market's percentage of sales of a particular brand divided by the percent that local market represents of total U.S. households. The *category development index* (CDI) is the particular market's percentage of a category sales divided by the percent of the market's share of the U.S. households.[17] To illustrate, the city of Miami has 1.4 percent of the total U.S. population. To calculate the BDI and CDI for a product such as Ivory bar soap, several figures are needed. First, 4.6 percent of Ivory's total U.S. sales occur in Miami. This yields a BDI of 329 (4.6/1.4). The category sales of bar soap in Miami are 3.3 percent of total U.S. sales of bar soap. This makes the CDI 236 (3.3/1.4). The BDI and CDI indices indicate that Ivory has a higher percentage of the total bar soap of the Miami market than it does in other U.S. markets. This information can then be compared to sales figures in other markets in order to gain a sense of where Ivory is doing well and where sales are less strong.

Another factor that may be considered before making a decision to purchase spot TV time in Miami is *trend information*. If the BDI has been declining during the last few months or years, additional spot TV time may be purchased to reverse the declining trend. On the other hand, if the trend analysis shows a steady market share or increasing market share, Ivory's marketing team may reduce spot TV time in Miami and shift those advertising dollars to other local markets where sales are less robust.

Snack foods are often advertised on television.

In general, television still has a wide audience that appeals to companies selling goods and services with general target markets. These markets include most durable goods (washers, dryers, cars, etc.), staple items (detergent, soap, deodorant), general appeal products (snack foods, beers, soft drinks, and Internet sites), and various luxuries marketed to larger groups (cruise ships, theme parks, and credit cards).

Business-to-business advertisers use television for several reasons. First, members of the business buying center watch television. Second, increasing ad clutter in trade journals and traditional business outlets makes television spots more desirable. Third, business advertisements now use more emotional appeals and television portrays emotions effectively. Fourth, a strong brand identity is a growing factor in the business-to-business sector and television ads can increase it. Finally, television reaches members of the buying center when they are not preoccupied with other business concerns. Consequently, they may be more open to advertising messages.

Radio

Radio is not as glamorous as television. It is more difficult to attract talented creatives to prepare radio ads. At the same time, a well-placed, clever ad is a one-on-one message (announcer to driver in a car stuck in traffic). Many smaller local companies rely heavily on radio advertising. Most radio ads are produced locally and with small budgets. Table 8.3 summarizes the advantages and disadvantages of radio advertising.

Radio offers several advantages. Skillful radio advertisers help the listener remember the message by creating a powerful image to visualize or by using repetition. It is important to help the consumer move the ad from short-term to long-term memory. Various sound effects and lively tunes assist in this process. Through repetition a person hears an advertisement often enough to assist in recall—just like repeating a phone number or e-mail address helps you remember numbers or letters.

A radio station has definable target markets based on its format. Certain formats (talk radio, lite mix, oldies, etc.) attract similar audiences. This means a firm can advertise on a specific type of station across the country. Campbell's found radio spots were an effective way to promote its Chunky Soup using a tie-in with the National Football League. The company advertised on sports stations with primarily male audiences and featured professional football players praising Chunky Soup.[18]

TABLE 8.3 Radio Advertising	
Advantages	**Disadvantages**
1. Recall promoted	1. Short exposure time
2. Narrower target markets	2. Low attention
3. Ad music can match station's programming	3. Few chances to reach national audience
4. High segmentation potential	4. Target duplication when several stations use the same format
5. Flexibility in making new ads	5. Information overload
6. Able to modify ads to fit local conditions	
7. Intimacy (with DJs and radio personalities)	
8. Mobile—people carry radios everywhere	
9. Creative opportunities with music and other sounds	

Radio has become a viable alternative for reaching Hispanic Americans, who tend to listen to radio more than the general population. Currently, there are more than 600 Spanish-speaking radio stations reaching more than 95.5 percent of all Hispanics age 12 and older. National advertising on Hispanic stations has increased by double digits. The Miller Brewing Company recently signed a $100 million deal with Univision. The package included radio, TV, and online advertisements aimed at the Hispanic market. Miller Brewing integrated the TV, radio, and online ads to reflect messages that were specially designed for Hispanics.[19]

Radio advertisers can also examine the rating and share of a program as well as the estimated number of people listening to a program. The primary organization that calculates these numbers for local stations is Arbitron. Radio's All-Dimension Audience Research (RADAR) reports ratings for national radio networks.

Radio stations offer considerable *flexibility* and a short lead time. Commercials can be recorded and placed on the air within a few days, and sometimes within hours. Ads can be changed quickly. This is especially helpful in volatile markets or in the retail sector for companies that want to change the items featured on sale. A national company can modify advertisements to fit local conditions. A manufacturer can develop one national advertisement and change it for each dealer or retailer that carries the manufacturer's merchandise. General Motors offered its 3,800 U.S. dealers nationally produced radio spots to advertise the GM certified brand of used vehicles. The national ad was higher quality than can usually be produced locally and provided consistency across the United States for GM. Local dealers can customize the spots with local information, such as the dealer's address, phone number, or Web site.[20]

Another major advantage of radio is *intimacy*. Listeners often feel personally close to some DJs and radio personalities. This closeness grows over time. Listening to the same individual becomes more personal and intimate, especially if the listener has a conversation with the DJ during a contest or when requesting a song. The bond or intimacy level gives the radio personality a higher level of credibility and an edge to goods and services the radio celebrity endorses. No other medium offers this advantage.

Elizabeth Arden used radio to launch the Skinsimple line of skin-care products. Sales increased by an average of 18 percent in the 3 weeks following the run of advertisements in 30 markets. According to Greg Griffin, vice president of marketing for Elizabeth Arden, "The radio listener is more open to your message . . . especially when the DJs are given leeway to have fun with the promotions and chat about the brand, consumers don't feel like it's an ad."[21]

Radio is also *mobile*. People carry radios to the beach, the ballpark, work, and picnics. They listen at home, at work, and on the road in between. No other medium stays with the audience quite like radio.

Radio also has disadvantages. One is the *short exposure time* of an ad. Like television, most radio advertisements last only 15 or 30 seconds. Listeners involved in other activities, such as driving or working on a computer, may not pay attention to the radio. Further, people often use radio as a background to drown out other distractions, especially at work.

Radio also suffers from advertising *clutter*. A U.S. study indicated that after six ads in a block only 20 percent of the listening audience is still there. Yet, radio advertisers continue to build larger and larger blocks of ads. In Australia, ad blocks

Source: Courtesy of KMXL–Mix 95.1.

This advertisement for Mix 95.1 highlights the market niche served by the station.

Radio enjoys the advantage of intimacy.

Source: Courtesy of Pearson Education/PH College.

have reached a high of 13 straight ads. With the advance of MP3 players and digital technology, ad clutter in radio is going to become an even more serious problem, because listeners will have new alternatives for listening to music.[22]

For national advertisers, covering a large area with radio advertisements is challenging. To place a national advertisement requires contacting a large number of companies. Few large radio conglomerates means contacts must be made with multiple stations. Negotiating rates with individual stations based on volume is difficult. Local businesses can often negotiate better rates than national advertisers because of the local company's relationships with the radio stations.

The four main national radio networks in the United States are Westwood One, ABC, CBS, and Unistar. These are joined by a few other strong networks, such as ESPN radio and CNN. Nationally syndicated programs such as those on the Fox radio network and Don Imus offer some opportunities to national advertisers.

In large metropolitan areas, another problem is target duplication. Several radio stations may try to reach the same target market. For instance, Chicago has several rock stations. Advertising on every station is not financially feasible, yet reaching everyone in that target market is not possible unless all rock stations are used. The rock music audience is divided among those stations, with each having its own subset of loyal listeners.

Another new challenge to traditional radio is satellite radio. These stations charge a fee for listening, but then do not run advertisements. The growth in satellite radio may hurt both national and local radio stations and networks.

Finally, many locally produced commercials often have too much information crammed into the spot. It overloads the consumer and very little is retained.

Radio advertising is a low-cost option for a local firm. Ads can be placed at ideal times and adapted to local conditions. The key to radio is careful selection of stations, times, and quality construction of the ad. Tests can be created to see if ads effectively reach customers. Immediate response techniques, contest entries, and other devices provide evidence about whether customers heard and responded to ads. Radio *remotes* occur when the station broadcasts from a business location. Remotes are a popular method of attracting attention to a new business (restaurants, taverns, small retail shops, etc.) or to a company trying to make a major push for immediate customers. Effective radio promotions can be combined with other media (local television, newspapers, etc.) to send out a more integrated message.

For business-to-business advertisers, radio provides the opportunity to reach businesses during working hours, because many employees listen to the radio during office hours. More important, radio can reach businesspeople while in transit to or from work. Both radio and television usage has increased for business-to-business marketing.

Outdoor advertising in Times Square.

Outdoor Advertising

Billboards along major roads are the most common form of outdoor advertising. They have been used since the late 1800s. Billboards, however, are only one form of outdoor advertising. Signs on cabs, buses, park benches, and fences of sports arenas are other types of outdoor advertising. Some would argue that even a blimp flying above a major sporting event is a form of outdoor advertising.

Outdoor advertising has changed dramatically with advances in technology. Annual expenditures on outdoor advertisements now total more than $5.5 billion. Global positioning systems, wireless communications, and digital display technology have transformed outdoor advertising. The most popular outdoor technology, LED, is used by companies such as Procter & Gamble and McDonald's. LED technology is used to create video screens for

TABLE 8.4 Outdoor Advertising	
Advantages	**Disadvantages**
1. Able to select key geographic areas	1. Short exposure time
2. Accessible for local ads	2. Brief messages
3. Low cost per impression	3. Little segmentation possible
4. Broad reach	4. Cluttered travel routes
5. High frequency on major commuter routes	
6. Large, spectacular ads possible	

animated videos in locations such as Times Square in New York and the Strip in Las Vegas. It can create both static messages and visuals that change electronically.[23] In Times Square in New York, Toshiba recently signed a 10-year lease for the anchor spot on top of the building at the southern end of the district. The cost is in the neighborhood of $300,000 per month.[24]

The cosmetics industry spends heavily on outdoor advertising. On average, 6.7 percent of a cosmetics company's budget is reserved for outdoors, compared to an industry average of 2.6 percent. In the past few years, billboards have been used to feature Dove and Neutrogena. Taxi-top ads helped launch the Visibly Even line of products for Neutrogena.[25] Other fast-growing outdoor ad programs are found in the fashion industry. The Gap, Calvin Klein, Ralph Lauren, and DKNY regularly buy outdoor space. Table 8.4 lists the advantages and disadvantages of outdoor ads.

One primary advantage of billboard advertising is *long life*. For local companies, billboards are an excellent advertising medium because the message is seen primarily by local audiences. Services such as restaurants, hotels, resorts, service stations, and amusement parks are heavy users of billboards. Billboards provide an effective way to communicate a firm's location to travelers. Individuals who want to eat at a particular restaurant (Wendy's, Shoney's, Burger King) while on the road can normally spot a billboard for that restaurant.

In terms of cost per impression, outdoor advertising is a low-cost media outlet. Outdoor advertising also offers a broad reach and a high level of frequency if multiple billboards are purchased. Every person who travels past a billboard or sees an advertisement on a taxi has the potential for being exposed to the message. Many billboard companies provide rotation packages in which an ad moves to different locations throughout an area during the course of the year, thereby increasing the ad's reach.

Billboard ads can be *large* and *spectacular*, making them major attention-getting devices. A billboard's large size creates the impression that the product and message are important. Movement and lighting through LED technology add to the attention-capturing qualities of billboards. At the other extreme, outdoor advertising can be small, yet stir attention.

A major drawback of outdoor advertising is the *short exposure time*. Drivers must pay attention to the traffic as they travel by an outdoor ad. When the ad is on a vehicle, pedestrians often get only a quick look. Most either ignore outdoor ads or give them just a casual glance. Ironically, in large cities along major arteries the cost of billboard spots is increasing. The reason: traffic jams. People stuck in slow-moving traffic spend more time looking at billboards. If this space is not available, a firm can seek billboard locations where traffic stops for signals or at stop signs.

To counter the short exposure time and take advantage of traffic jams, another outdoor technique that is now being used is a mobile billboard, which is a truck covered with a two-sided billboard. For $500 to $800 a day, customers can tailor a mobile billboard to exact routes they want driven, to specific ZIP codes, or to even park outside a specific event. Although some cities ban mobile billboards and some citizens are raising concerns about added pollution and drivers being distracted by reading billboards on moving vehicles, the popularity of mobile billboards is rising.

A billboard for Wendy's breakfast meal.

Source: Courtesy of Newcomer, Morris & Young.

YOU CAN JUDGE AN ORANGE BY ITS STICKER

Produce of USA

A billboard advertisement for Sunkist.

Mobile billboards provide the opportunity to beat ad clutter and the short exposure times of static billboards. They reach consumers where they are—stuck in traffic.[26]

Outdoor ads provide limited *opportunities for creativity.* A short exposure time means the message must be extremely brief. People usually ignore a complicated or detailed message. Further, outdoor ads offer limited segmentation opportunities. A wide variety of people may view the billboard's message. To help overcome this problem, some companies use geodemographic software technologies to identify the profile of individuals who will pass by a particular outdoor location. Such an approach works well on local streets of cities and towns but is not very effective along major interstates, because of long-distance traffic.

In the past, outdoor advertising was seldom considered in the planning of an integrated marketing communications program or the development of the media plan. Today, outdoor advertising is seen as a critical component of an IMC program and, in some cases, the primary medium. Saturn launched what was called a "total landscape domination campaign" in Los Angeles, California, for the Saturn Vue and Aura hybrid cars. The campaign involved increasing the number of billboards by seven. In addition, ads were placed on 400 buses and in 329 gas stations. The company also printed 500,000 insulating coffee-cup sleeves, which had a picture of the two hybrid Saturn vehicles and the message "135 more safety features than this 205 degree cup of coffee."[27]

Figure 8.7 highlights the major industries and how much each spent on outdoor advertising during one quarter. As the chart indicates, local services and amusements spend considerably more than any other industry.

Magazines

For many advertisers, magazines have always been a second choice. Recent research indicates that in some cases magazines are actually a quality option. One study concluded that every dollar a company spends on magazine advertising yields an average of $8.23 in sales. The average return on investment for all other media is $3.52 per dollar spent on advertising. The reason given for this difference is magazine advertising's ability to target consumers more efficiently by demographics and lifestyles.[28] Naturally, the validity of these results has been staunchly debated by executives from other media. Table 8.5 displays the pros and cons of magazine advertising.

FIGURE 8.7
Expenditures on Outdoor Advertising During the First Quarter of 2004

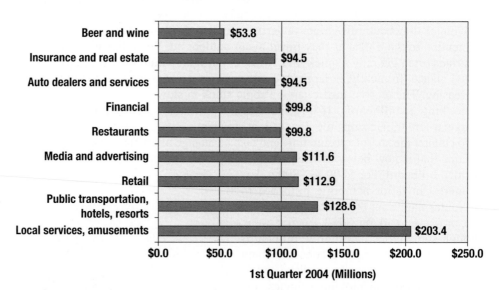

Industry	1st Quarter 2004 (Millions)
Beer and wine	$53.8
Insurance and real estate	$94.5
Auto dealers and services	$94.5
Financial	$99.8
Restaurants	$99.8
Media and advertising	$111.6
Retail	$112.9
Public transportation, hotels, resorts	$128.6
Local services, amusements	$203.4

Source: Deborah L. Vence, "Outdoor Ads Leverage New Technology," *Marketing News* 38, no. 15 (September 15, 2004), pp. 11–13.

TABLE 8.5 Magazine Advertising

Advantages	Disadvantages
1. High market segmentation	1. Declining readership (some magazines)
2. Targeted audience interest by magazine	2. High level of clutter
3. Direct-response techniques (e.g., coupons, Web addresses, toll-free numbers)	3. Long lead time
4. High color quality	4. Little flexibility
5. Availability of special features (e.g., scratch and sniff)	5. High cost
6. Long life	
7. Read during leisure time (longer attention to ad)	

One major advantage of magazines is the high level of *market segmentation.* Magazines are highly segmented by topic area. Specialized magazines are much more common than general magazines with broad readerships. Even within certain market segments, such as automobiles, a number of magazines exist. High audience interest becomes another advantage. An individual who subscribes to *Modern Bride* has an attraction to weddings. People reading magazines also tend to view and pay attention to advertisements related to their needs and wants. Often, readers linger over an ad for a longer period of time because they read magazines in waiting situations (e.g., doctor's office) or during leisure time. This high level of interest, segmentation, and differentiation are ideal for products with precisely defined target markets.

Trade and business journals are a major medium for business-to-business marketing. Businesses can target advertisements to buying center members. The ad copy can then provide a greater level of detail about products. Readers, if interested, take time to read the information in the ad. Ads can provide toll-free telephone numbers and Web addresses so that interested parties can obtain further information.

Magazines offer *high-quality color* and more sophisticated production processes, providing the creative with the opportunity to produce intriguing and enticing advertisements. Motion, color, and unusual images can be used to attract attention. Magazines such as *Glamour, Elle,* and *Cosmopolitan* may include scratch-and-sniff ads to entice women to notice the fragrance of a perfume or cologne. Even car manufacturers have ventured into this type of advertising by producing the smell of leather in ads.

Magazines have a *long life* that reaches beyond the immediate issue. Subscribers read and reread them. It is not unusual for an avid magazine reader to examine a particular issue several times and spend a considerable amount of time with each issue. This appeal is attractive because advertisers know the reader will be exposed to the ad more than once and is more likely to pay attention. Other individuals may also look at the magazine. In the business-to-business sector, trade journals are often passed around to several individuals or members of the buying center. As long as the magazine lasts, the advertisement is still there to be viewed.

This Treetop advertisement targets new mothers.

Nurtured from the start.

Source: Courtesy of Tree Top, Inc.

Grace magazine targets women of all ages.

One major disadvantage facing magazine advertisers is a *decline in younger readers.* The Leo Burnett Company's *Starcom Report* stated that magazines lost 61 million readers from the 18- to 49-year-old age bracket in just a year.[29] But overall, magazine readership for the top 300 magazines is down only 0.5 percent from 1997.[30]

Although circulation has remained relatively stable, the number of ad pages has declined in recent years. Ad pages for the top 300 magazines are down 21 percent from 1997 and 26 percent from 2000. Despite the decline in ad pages, total ad revenue has not declined nearly as much due to the increased cost of magazine ads. For national magazines, color ad rates now run approximately $10,000 per ad page for every 100,000 circulation. A magazine such as *Sports Illustrated*, therefore, charges $243,000 for a full-page color ad; *Parade* (newspaper supplement) charges $830,000. The full-page rate for *Better Homes and Gardens* is $339,000. *LIFE* magazine charges $310,000, and for *ESPN, the Magazine*, it costs $148,000.[31]

Clutter is another big problem for magazine advertisers. A recent 318-page issue of *Glamour* contained 195 pages of advertising and only 123 pages of content. Ads can be easily lost in those situations. To be noticed, the advertisement must be unique or stand out in some way.

Long lead times are a major disadvantage of magazines, because advertisements must be submitted as much as 6 months in advance of the issue. Consequently, making changes in ads after submission is very difficult. Also, because of the long life of magazines, images or messages created through magazine advertising have long lives. This is good for stable goods or services, but not for volatile markets or highly competitive markets wherein the appeal, price, or some other aspect of the marketing mix changes more frequently.

Magazines continue to proliferate even with the problems of *declining readership.* The wide variety of special interests makes it possible to develop and sell them. Many advertisers still can target audiences and take advantage of various magazine features, such as direct-response Internet addresses and coupon offers. This is especially true in the business market. Although business-to-business marketers increasingly use other media, trade journals and business magazines remain an effective method of reaching their target markets. As a result, the nature of advertising in magazines may change, but individual companies still will find effective uses for the outlets.

Newspapers

When *USA Today* was launched, few believed a national daily newspaper could succeed. Obviously it has. The nature of news reporting has changed. Many small local papers no longer exist, and conglomerates, such as Gannett, own most major city newspapers. Still, daily readership continues.

For many smaller local firms, newspaper ads, billboards, and local radio programs are the most viable advertising options, especially if television ads are cost prohibitive. Newspapers can be distributed daily, weekly, or in partial form as the advertising supplements found in the front sections of many grocery stores and retail outlets. Table 8.6 displays the basic advantages and disadvantages of newspaper advertising.

Many retailers rely heavily on newspaper ads because they offer *geographic selectivity* (local market access). Promoting sales, retail hours, and store locations is easy to accomplish in a newspaper ad. Short lead time allows retailers to change ads and promotions quickly. This *flexibility* is a major advantage. It allows advertisers the ability to keep ads current. Ads can be modified to meet competitive offers or to focus on recent events.

TABLE 8.6 Newspaper Advertising

Advantages	Disadvantages
1. Geographic selectivity	1. Poor buying procedures
2. High flexibility	2. Short life span
3. High credibility	3. Major clutter (especially holidays)
4. Strong audience interest	4. Poor quality reproduction (especially color)
5. Longer copy	5. Internet competition with classified ads
6. Cumulative volume discounts	
7. Coupons and special-response features	

Newspapers have *high levels of credibility.* Readers rely on newspapers for factual information in stories. Newspaper readers hold high interest levels in the articles they read. They tend to pay more attention to advertisements as well as news stories. This increased audience interest allows advertisers to provide more copy detail in their ads. Newspaper readers take more time to read copy, unless simply too much information is jammed into a small space.

Realizing the good match between newspaper readers and its customer base, Starbucks launched a unique newspaper campaign designed by the agency Wieden + Kennedy of Portland, Oregon. Starbucks invited coffee drinkers to stop at their local Starbucks for a free cup of coffee on March 15. Four-page full-color ads were placed in daily newspapers of 11 major markets, including New York, Los Angeles, Chicago, Boston, and Dallas. The ads were placed in the newspapers one week before the giveaway and again the day before. Then, on the day of the giveaway, Starbucks hired street vendors to pass out free copies of the newspapers that contained the Starbucks ad. The newspapers were banded with the distinctive Starbuck's coffee cup sleeve. The campaign cost $545,000, but resulted in a half-million customers going into a Starbucks store. In some locations lines wrapped around the block. Starbucks estimated the newspaper campaign resulted in 12 million impressions.[32]

Newspaper advertisers receive volume discounts for buying larger *column inches* of advertising space. Many newspapers grant these volume discounts, called *cumulative discounts,* for 1-month, 3-month, or even yearlong time periods. This potentially makes the cost per exposure even lower, because larger and repeated ads are more likely to garner the reader's attention.

There are limitations and disadvantages to newspaper advertising. First, newspapers cannot be targeted as easily to specific market segments (although sports pages carry sports ads, entertainment pages contain movie and restaurant ads, and so forth). Newspapers also have a *short life.* Once read, a newspaper normally is cast to the side, recycled, or destroyed. If a reader does not see an advertisement during the first pass through a newspaper, it probably will go unnoticed. Readers rarely pick up papers a second time. When they do, it is to continue reading, not to re-read or re-scan a section that has already been viewed.

Newspaper ads often suffer from *lower production quality.* Many companies do not buy color ads because

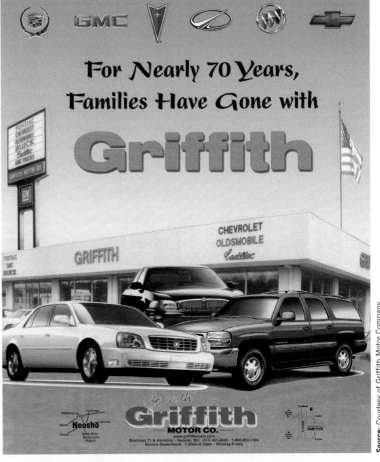

This award winning newspaper advertisement promotes Griffith Motor Co.

GREAT TASTE COMES WITH CHOICES

Newspaper advertising is used by many food producers.

they are much more expensive. Photos and copy tend to be harder to read and see clearly compared to other print media, especially magazines. Newspaper ads tend not to be wild or highly creative. Newspaper editors normally avoid and turn down anything that may be controversial. Many newspaper editors try to avoid offending readers.

Newspapers suffer *poor national buying procedures.* For a national advertiser, this means contacting numerous companies and using rate cards that vary by market. Also, newspapers tend to favor local companies instead of national firms. Local businesses generally receive better advertising rates than do national advertisers, because local companies advertise on a more regular basis and receive volume discounts. Also, newspapers want to have a strong local appeal. By favoring local companies in ad rates, they can meet this goal and seem more desirable to local patrons. To counter this difficulty, the Newspaper National Network (NNN) and Newspapers First have been formed to make national buys. NNN helps national advertisers reach virtually every daily U.S. newspaper with one buy and one bill. Newspapers First is a cooperative that places ads in more than 40 large, daily newspapers.[33] As a result, national advertising, which makes up only 17 percent of all newspaper ad spending, is growing faster than any other category of newspaper advertising.[34]

MEDIA MIX

Selecting the proper blend of media outlets for advertisements is crucial. As campaigns are prepared, decisions are made regarding the appropriate mix of media. Media planners and media buyers are both excellent sources of information about the most effective type of mix for a particular advertising campaign. It is the creative's challenge to design ads for each medium that speak to the audience and that also tie in with the overall theme of the integrated marketing communications program. Table 8.7 displays considerable differences in media mixes used by various industries. Restaurant owners spend considerably more on television advertising than on any other medium. Apparel manufacturers, however, spend the largest percentage of budgets on magazines. Choosing the appropriate advertising channels and then effectively combining outlets requires the expertise of a media planner who can study each outlet and match it with the product and overall message.

Recent studies by Millward Brown and ACNielsen highlight the benefits of combining different media.[35] In a telephone survey, Millward Brown reported that ad awareness was

TABLE 8.7 Advertising Expenditures for Select Categories

Category	Total	Magazines	Newspapers	Outdoor	Television	Radio	Internet
Automotive	$19.799	11.0%	25.4%	1.7%	50.4%	7.8%	3.7%
Retail	$19.114	11.0%	35.4%	2.0%	33.8%	11.2%	6.6%
Telecommunications	$10.950	8.2%	19.8%	2.5%	48.7%	7.1%	13.6%
Financial services	$ 8.689	13.7%	21.8%	2.8%	36.3%	8.3%	17.0%
Food, beverages, candy	$ 7.225	27.6%	0.7%	1.1%	64.2%	4.5%	1.8%
Restaurants	$ 5.291	2.5%	3.5%	4.5%	78.4%	10.1%	0.9%
Apparel	$ 2.911	75.1%	2.0%	1.0%	19.8%	0.7%	1.3%

Source: Based on "100 Leading National Advertisers," *Advertising Age* (June 25, 2007), p. 9.

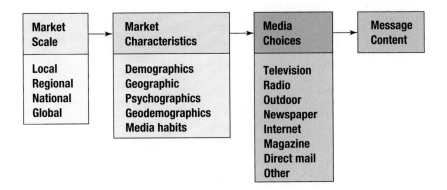

FIGURE 8.8
Developing Logical Combinations of Media

strongest when consumers were exposed to an advertisement on television and in a magazine. Ad awareness was much lower for only those who read the magazine ad and even less for those who only saw the television ad. The increased impact of using two or more media is called a **media multiplier effect**, which means that the combined impact of using two or more media is stronger than using either medium alone. Business-to-business firms apply this concept by buying ad space in places other than traditional trade journals. The key is finding effective combinations of media when designing a media mix.

Figure 8.8 shows the process for choosing the best media for a particular advertising message. Consider the many possible options and combinations. Media experts work continually to decide which go together for individual target markets, goods and services, and advertising messages.

MEDIA SELECTION IN BUSINESS-TO-BUSINESS MARKETS

Identifying differences between consumer ads and business-to-business ads is becoming more difficult, especially in television, outdoor, and Internet ads. In the past, it was easy to spot business-to-business ads. The content was clearly aimed toward another company, and television, outdoor, and the Internet were seldom used. Currently, over half of all business advertising dollars are spent in nonbusiness environments.[36]

Several items explain this shift to more nonbusiness media. First, business decision makers are also consumers of goods and services. The same psychological techniques used to influence and gain consumer attention can also be used for business decision makers.

Second, and probably the most important, business decision makers are very difficult to reach at work. Gatekeepers (secretaries, voice mail systems, etc.) often prevent information flow to users, influencers, and decision makers. This is especially true for straight rebuy situations whereby orders are given to the current vendor. If a company is not the chosen vendor, it is extremely difficult to get anyone's attention. To avoid various gatekeepers, business-to-business firms try to reach the members of the buying center at their homes, in their cars, or in some other non-business venue.

A third reason for this shift to non-business media is that the clutter among the traditional business media has made it more difficult to get a company noticed. Business advertisers recognize that a strong brand name is a major factor in making a sale. Taking lessons from brand giants such as Nike, Campbell's Soups, Wal-Mart, and Procter & Gamble, business marketers see the value of strong brands, because the name helps a company gain the attention of members of the buying center.

Office Depot recently launched an advertising campaign directed toward the business buyers that make up approximately 80 percent of the company's customer base. The campaign, titled "Takin' Care of Business," highlighted the company's commitment to business customers. The campaign included TV spots, along with radio, print, online, and search marketing ads. Office Depot also signed a sponsorship deal to be the official office products partner of NASCAR.[37]

FIGURE 8.9
Business-to-Business Advertising
Expenditures

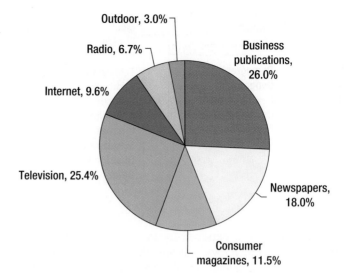

Source: Based on Kate Maddox, "Top 100 B-to-B Advertisers Increased Spending 3% in '06," *B to B* 92, no. 11 (September 10, 2007), pp. 25–30.

In the past, business ads were fairly dull. They now are more likely to resemble ads aimed at consumers. Creative appeals and the use of music, humor, sex, and fear are used. The boldest business ads sometimes include nudity or other more risqué material.

Figure 8.9 identifies how business-to-business advertising expenditures are divided among the various media. In the past, business publications would account for most of the expenditures, often assuming half of the dollars. Business publications now account for only 26 percent of the $14.39 billion that was spent last year on business-to-business advertising. As more dollars are shifted to nonbusiness types of media, the amount being spent on television, newspapers, and consumer magazines has steadily increased.[38]

The media multiplier effect is equally important in business-to-business advertising. In a survey conducted by American Business Media, 89 percent of the business respondents indicated that an integrated marketing approach raised their awareness of a company or brand. Seeing advertisements in more than one medium caused the company or brand name to become top-of-mind. It also resulted in more individuals making purchases.[39]

The top six business-to-business advertisers are dominated by firms in the telecommunications and computer industries. Figure 8.10 highlights the amount each of these companies devoted to business advertising.

FIGURE 8.10
Top Six Business-to-Business
Advertisers

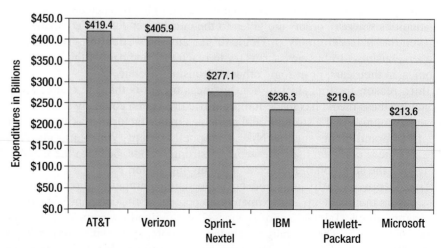

Source: Based on Kate Maddox, "Top 100 B-to-B Advertisers Increased Spending 3% in '06," *B to B* 92, no. 11 (September 10, 2007), pp. 25–30.

Although the use of business publications has decreased, trade journals still provide an excellent opportunity to contact members of the buying center whom salespeople cannot reach. Gatekeepers typically do not prevent trade journals from being sent to members of the buying center. Unfortunately, if the firm is in a straight rebuy situation, it is doubtful the ad will be noticed. If the firm is in a modified rebuy and the buying center is in the information search stage, then the ad has a better chance of success.

In addition to trade journals, business-to-business advertisers also use business magazines such as *Business Week* and consumer magazines. The primary reasons for these high levels of expenditures in print media are because they have highly selective audiences and the ads have longer life spans in print. Business decision makers and members of the buying center spend more working time examining print media than any other medium. Business buying center members are more likely to notice the WingspanBank.com ad shown on this page when it is located in a trade journal than they would if the same ad ran in a more general-audience type magazine such as *Time*. A trade journal's readers are more likely to notice and read the advertisement, because they are more likely to have been working with or thinking about banking or financial services within their companies.

Many goals in business-to-business advertisements are the same as those devoted to consumers. It remains important to identify key target markets, to select the proper media, and to prepare creative, enticing ads resulting in some kind of action, such as a change in attitude toward the company or movement toward a purchase decision. Many of the variables shown in Figure 8.8 apply equally well to business advertising.

An advertisement for Internet banking.

INTERNATIONAL IMPLICATIONS

Understanding media viewing habits in international markets is important for successful advertising programs. In Japan, television is a major advertising tool; in other countries, it is not as prevalent. In Europe, the best way to reach consumers is through print media; magazines and newspapers account for 51.5 percent of total ad spending. Figure 8.11 illustrates differences in media usage in the United States, Europe, and Japan.

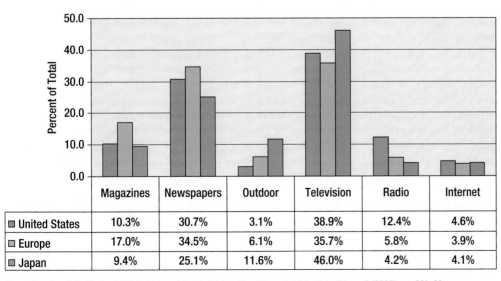

FIGURE 8.11
Media Usage in the United States, Europe, and Japan

	Magazines	Newspapers	Outdoor	Television	Radio	Internet
■ United States	10.3%	30.7%	3.1%	38.9%	12.4%	4.6%
■ Europe	17.0%	34.5%	6.1%	35.7%	5.8%	3.9%
■ Japan	9.4%	25.1%	11.6%	46.0%	4.2%	4.1%

Source: Based on Colin MacLeod, "Global Adspend Trends," *International Journal of Advertising* 24, no. 2 (2005), pp. 261–62.

Although there are a large number of media buying agencies throughout the world, nearly three-quarters of all media buying is conducted by only six large global agencies or their holding agencies. The largest global media company is the WPP Group, which holds 22 percent of the market share.[40] To combat these large media networks, a global media consortium has been formed. The consortium is made up of a number of smaller independent agencies and offers services in Europe, North America, the Russian Federation, and Asia. Central offices are located in New York and London to serve business clients' and to pitch for regional and national accounts.[41]

The large global media agencies have faced some criticism in recent years by marketing managers. They complain about the inability to provide effective media buys throughout all the countries where the clients operate. Although a few agencies do cover the world, it is difficult to be strong in every country where an agency may have a presence. The global agency just cannot be the best option in every country. For this reason, local media agencies and the consortium of independent agencies believe they have a chance to increase their market share.

China offers an excellent example of the difficulties the global media agencies face. A recent study revealed that the average multinational agency has a relationship with Chinese clients for 2.4 to 2.8 years, which is two to three times shorter than the typical agency–client relationship in the United States and Europe. The challenge the multinational agencies face is to provide a seamless delivery to far-flung cities and provinces throughout China and to provide it cheaper, faster, and better than the local Chinese agencies. It is a monumental task. For instance, one client required media buys in 120 Chinese cities. With 55,000 local Chinese agencies vying for business in China, the global companies face a stiff challenge.[42]

In general, the tactics used to develop advertising campaigns and choose appropriate media in the United States apply to other countries throughout the world. What differs is the nature of the target markets, consumer media preferences, and the processes used to buy media. Also, company representatives must carefully attend to cultural mores to make sure the buying process does not offend the cultural and religious attitudes prevalent in any given region. It is important to fully understand the target market as a company purchases advertising time or space and prepares ad campaigns.

SUMMARY

The traditional view of advertising has been to design a message that will accomplish the intended IMC objective and then find the best media channel. This view is slowly being replaced as the roles of media planners and media buyers grow in importance. According to Bob Brennan, chief operating officer of Chicago-based Leo Burnett Starcom USA, in the past "Ninety-five percent of your success was great creative and 5 percent was great media. Now it's much closer to 50–50."[43]

This chapter reviews the media selection process. A media strategy is the process of analyzing and choosing media for an advertising and promotions campaign. Media planners and buyers complete much of this work. The media planner's primary job is to formulate a program stating where and when to place advertisements. Media planners work closely with creatives and account executives. Media buyers purchase the space, and they negotiate rates, times, and schedules for the ads.

The goals of reach, frequency, opportunity to see, gross rating points, effective rating points, cost, continuity, and gross impressions drive the media selection process. Reach is the number of people, households, or businesses in a target audience exposed to a media vehicle or message schedule at least once during a given time period. Frequency is the average

number of times an individual, household, or business within a particular target market is exposed to a particular advertisement within a specified time period. Gross rating points (GRP) measure the impact or intensity of a media plan. Cost per thousand (CPM) is one method of finding the cost of the campaign by assessing the dollar cost of reaching 1,000 members of the media vehicle's audience. Cost per rating point (CPRP) is a second cost measure, which assesses the efficiency of a media vehicle relative to a firm's target market. Ratings measure the percentage of a firm's target market that is exposed to a show on television or an article in a print medium. Continuity is the schedule or pattern of advertisement placements within an advertising campaign period. Gross impressions are the number of total exposures of the audience to an advertisement.

In addition to these basic concepts, advertising experts often utilize the concepts of effective frequency and effective reach. Effective frequency is the number of times a target audience must be exposed to a message to achieve a particular objective. Effective reach is the percentage of an audience that must be exposed to a particular message to achieve a specific objective.

In seeking advertising goals, marketing experts, account executives, and others must assess the relative advantages and disadvantages of each individual advertising medium. Thus, television, radio, outdoor, magazines, and newspapers should all be considered as potential ingredients in a campaign. Other new media can be used to complement and supplement the more traditional media outlets. Logical combinations of media must be chosen to make sure the intended audience is exposed to the message. The three-exposure hypothesis suggests that a consumer must be exposed to an ad at least three times before it has the desired impact; other experts believe even more exposures are necessary. In contrast, recency theory suggests that ads truly reach only those wanting or needing a product and that the carryover effect of advertising diminishes rapidly. It is necessary, therefore, to advertise on a continuous basis to ensure that the message is retained by consumers when a purchase decision is made.

In business-to-business settings, companies can combine consumer media outlets with trade journals and other business venues (trade shows, conventions, etc.) to attempt to reach members of the buying center. In many cases, enticing ads using consumer appeals such as sex, fear, and humor have replaced dry, dull, boring ads with an abundance of copy.

When designing business advertising, remember that advertising is just one component of the integrated marketing communications plan. It must be integrated with the sales force, sales promotions, trade promotions, and public relations. Business-to-business advertising using traditional consumer media cannot accomplish all of the communications objectives a business needs to accomplish. They help develop brand awareness and build brand equity, but are usually not the best for providing information the buying center needs.

International advertising media selection is different in some ways from that which takes place in the United States, because media buying processes differ as do media preferences of locals in various countries. At the same time, the process of media selection is quite similar: Marketing experts choose media they believe will reach the target audience in an effective manner.

Media selection takes place in conjunction with the message design and within the framework of the overall IMC approach. Effective media selection means the company spends enough money to find the target audience and does not waste funds by overwhelming them with the same message. Account executives, creatives, media planners, media buyers, and the company's representative must all work together to make certain the process moves as effectively and efficiently as possible.

KEY TERMS

media strategy The process of analyzing and choosing media for an advertising and promotions campaign.

media planner The individual who formulates the program stating where and when to place advertisements.

media buyer The person who buys the space and negotiates rates, times, and schedules for the ads.

spot ad A one-time ad placed on a local television station.

reach The number of people, households, or businesses in a target audience exposed to a media vehicle or message schedule at least once during a given time period.

frequency The average number of times an individual, household, or business within a particular target market is exposed to a particular advertisement within a specified time period.

opportunities to see (OTS) The cumulative exposures to an advertisement that are achieved in a given time period.

gross rating points (GRP) A measure of the impact or intensity of a media plan.

cost per thousand (CPM) The dollar cost of reaching 1,000 members of the media vehicle's audience.

cost per rating point (CPRP) A measure of the efficiency of a media vehicle relative to a firm's target market.

ratings A measure of the percentage of a firm's target market that is exposed to a show on television or an article in a print medium.

weighted (or demographic) CPM A measure used to calculate whether an advertisement reached the target market effectively.

continuity The schedule or pattern of advertisement placements within an advertising campaign period.

gross impressions The number of total exposures of the audience to an advertisement.

effective reach The percentage of an audience that must be exposed to a particular message to achieve a specific objective.

effective frequency The number of times a target audience must be exposed to a message to achieve a particular objective.

intrusion value The ability of media or an advertisement to intrude upon a viewer without his or her voluntary attention.

media multiplier effect The combined impact of using two or more media is stronger than using either medium alone.

REVIEW QUESTIONS

1. What is a media strategy? How does it relate to the creative brief and the overall IMC program?

2. What does a media planner do?

3. Describe the role of media buyer in an advertising program.

4. What is reach? Give examples of reach in various advertising media.

5. What is frequency? How can an advertiser increase frequency in a campaign?

6. What are gross rating points? What do they measure?

7. What is the difference between CPM and CPRP? What costs do they measure?

8. What is continuity?

9. Describe the three-exposure hypothesis.

10. How does recency theory differ from the three-exposure hypothesis?

11. What is effective frequency? Effective reach?

12. What are the major advantages and disadvantages of television advertising?

13. What are the major advantages and disadvantages of radio advertising?

14. What are the major advantages and disadvantages of magazine advertising?

15. What are the major advantages and disadvantages of newspaper advertising?

16. Is the strong intrusion value of television an advantage? Why or why not?

17. Name a product and three media that would mix well to advertise that product. Defend your media mix choices.

18. What special challenges does media selection present for businesses? What roles do gatekeepers play in creating those challenges?

19. What special challenges does media selection present for international advertising campaigns? What differences and similarities exist with U.S. media selection processes?

CRITICAL THINKING EXERCISES

Discussion Questions

1. To be effective, multiple media should be chosen and integrated carefully. Individuals who are exposed to advertisements in combinations of media selected from television, radio, the Internet, and outdoor are more inclined to process the information than when only a solitary medium is used. Fill in the chart below. Put your probability of being exposed to an advertisement from each medium into the appropriate column. The percentages across each row should add up to 100 percent.

2. Billboard advertising in Times Square is so popular that space has already been sold for 10 years. Coca-Cola, General Motors, Toshiba, Prudential, NBC, Budweiser, and *The New York Times* are paying rates in excess of $100,000 per month to hold these spaces. Inter City built a 50-story hotel at Broadway and 47th Street. The building will accommodate 75,000 square feet of advertising. Even before the completion of the hotel or tower, companies, including FedEx, Apple, AT&T, HBO, Levi Strauss, Morgan Stanley, and the U.S. Postal Service, purchased space. Why would companies pay so much for outdoor advertising? What are the advantages and disadvantages of purchasing billboards at Times Square?

3. Repetition and a short, catchy name are the keys for an effective radio spot. Sports equipment retailer Fogdog.com has been very successful with its radio spots. The URL is easy to remember and is reinforced with the sound of a howling dog. People don't have to fumble with finding a pencil to write it down. After a few repetitions, they remember it.[44] *USA Today* has developed a fantasy sports game site called Sandbox Fantasy Games. It is looking to develop a radio and billboard campaign for its online fantasy baseball game. Describe a radio and a billboard advertisement that will catch people's attention and that will be easy to remember. What are the advantages of combining a radio campaign with billboards?

4. Xerox offers a color printer that sells for $1,200. The goal is to market it to business buyers. What media mix would you suggest for a $20 million advertising campaign? Justify your answer.

Product	Television	Radio	Newspaper	Magazine	Outdoor	Internet	Other
Movie							
Restaurant							
Clothing							
Jewelry							
Nightclub							

INTEGRATED LEARNING EXERCISES

1. From the following tables, choose either the cosmetics companies or the clothing companies. Access each firm's Web site. Indicate how many advertisements you have seen in each of the media listed within the last month. Then discuss each company's media plan. Does the company project an integrated message? What target market does the Web site attract? Does the Web site convey the same message broadcast in the other media?

Cosmetics Companies

Company (Web Address)	TV	Radio	Newspaper	Magazine	Outdoor	Internet
Estee Lauder (www.esteelauder.com)						
Maybelline (www.maybelline.com)						
Sephora (www.sephora.com)						
Clinique (www.clinique.com)						
Revlon (www.revlon.com)						

Clothing Companies

Company (Web Address)	TV	Radio	Newspaper	Magazine	Outdoor	Internet
Polo (www.polojeans.com)						
Pepe (www.pepejeans.com)						
Squeeze (www.sqz.com)						
Guess (www.guess.com)						
Lee (www.leejeans.com)						
Wrangler (www.wrangler.com)						

2. The following table provides the population of the top 10 demographic marketing areas (DMAs). The target market for a particular company is yuppie boomers, or those 35 to 54 years old who are professionals or managers. Based on the percentage of adults in each DMA that fits the target market profile, calculate the size of the target market in each DMA. Washington, D.C. has been completed for you. If you had funds to advertise in only 5 of the 10 DMAs, which five would you choose? Why?

DMA	Population	DMA Percent	Number in Target Market
Washington, D.C.	3,965,200	18.4%	729,600
San Francisco–Oakland	4,824,600	14.2	
Boston	4,495,600	13.6	
Dallas–Ft. Worth	3,669,900	13.3	
Houston	3,251,100	13.1	
New York	14,432,500	12.0	
Chicago	6,483,800	11.7	
Philadelphia	5,655,800	11.6	
Los Angeles	11,391,200	11.3	
Detroit	3,549,600	11.1	

3. A major supplier of media research information is Nielsen Media Research. Access its Web site at **www.nielsen-media.com**. Go to the "Inside TV Ratings" and summarize the meaning of TV ratings. Access the "Products and Services" section. Elaborate on the products and services Nielsen Media Research offers. What other information is available at the Web site?

4. In Canada, a valuable source of information is BBM (Bureau of Broadcast Measurement). Access this Web site at **www.bbm.ca**. What type of information is available on the site? How can it be used to develop a media plan for Canada?

5. Achieving advertising media objectives normally requires a blending of the various media within the advertising plan. Access Benchmark Communications at **www.bmcommuni-cations.com** and examine the information that is provided in the site, especially about the traditional media of newspapers, radio, and television. What types of services does Benchmark Communications provide? How can Benchmark Communications assist in the development of a media plan?

6. Two Web sites that are important for radio advertising are the Radio Advertising Bureau at **www.rab.com** and the top 100 radio sites at **www.100topradiosites.com**. Access both sites. What information is available in each site? Discuss how the information can be used to develop an advertising plan using radio.

7. A major company for outdoor advertising is Lamar Advertising Company. Access its Web site at **www.lamar.com**. Access the outdoor component of the company and locate the rates for your area. What type of outdoor advertising is available? Access the transit component of the company. What services does Lamar offer? What other services does Lamar offer?

8. One of the best sources of information for business-to-business advertisers is *BtoB* at **www.btobonline.com**. What type of information is available at this Web site? How can it be used? What benefits would a business-to-business advertiser derive from the Web site?

STUDENT PROJECT

Creative Corner

Advertising and marketing of colleges and universities is a recent phenomenon. Promoting a College of Business or a marketing department within a university is even rarer. One of your recent marketing alumni donated $10,000 for media buys to advertise the marketing program. She is especially interested in the nontraditional student who is married, has a family, and is working full time. What message would you want to convey about the marketing program to this specific target market? Design a media package that would utilize the media discussed in this chapter. Contact your local television stations, radio stations, and newspaper for their rates. Develop a media plan that would maximize the use of the $10,000. Identify when, where, and how many ads you would place in each medium.

CASE 1 MAINSTREAMING HEAD SHAVING

Todd Green's hair history features a common story. At a relatively young age, he began to experience male-pattern baldness, a development that affects nearly 20 million men in the United States. Todd considered the options such as hair plugs, medicines, and creams, and of course, a rug. Eventually he decided to go with the flow and became a head shaver.

Inspiration then met the situation. Todd's frustrations were twofold. First, traditional razors are hard to manage because the handle moves awkwardly when cropping the day's growth. Other products, such as clippers, electric shavers, and depilatories just didn't suit his needs. Second, being a night shaver meant he was often faced with a five o'clock shadow the next afternoon. While pondering the dilemma, Todd did the natural thing and rubbed his head. Inspiration arrived. He concluded that it would be much easier to shave his head if he could just put the blade above his finger.

Not long after, the HeadBlade was born. Todd first tried selling the innovation to companies such as Gillette and Schick. When they showed no interest, he formed his own company with money he borrowed from his father and his friends. He quit his job and worked for 2 years to develop the first version (go to **www.headblade.com** to see an actual photo).

The HeadBlade was first sold through an e-commerce program. A great deal of free publicity followed with features in a wide variety of magazine articles and mentions on television programs. The HeadBlade received several awards for innovation, including prizes from Summit Creative, *Time* magazine, *I.D. Magazine*, and eventually from the Museum of Modern Art.

The HeadBlade Company now offers the basic product for about $13.00, plus HeadShed Lotion and HeadShade Sun Screen, plus fashion merchandise, most notably T-shirts. The company sells travel kits and other methods to carry the product.

Green does not believe his product will be just a fad. His company's sales have reached $10 million annually. He has developed ties with the International Fight League, with comedian Howie Mandel, and with former NBA player John Amaechi. As he put it, "We're going after both the X Games demographic and the average guy who shaves his head. We want to be the Home Depot of head care." From a marketing perspective, The HeadBlade faces two challenges. The first is the likelihood of being copied by similar products, possibly from larger, mainstream companies. The second is finding ways to advertise the

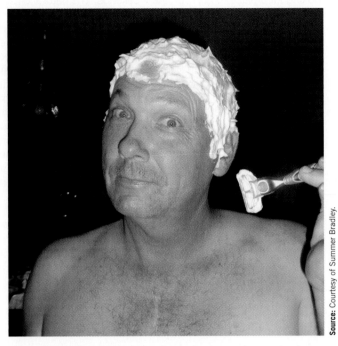

Source: Courtesy of Summer Bradley.

The HeadBlade provides an excellent alternative to shaving with a traditional straight edge razor.

company's product on a national and international scale. This will undoubtedly include greater use of traditional media.

Sources: www.headblade.com, accessed January 10, 2008; "First Person: A Cut Above: Todd Green Makes a Business out of Baldness," *BusinessWeek,* December 2007 (**www.businessweekonline.com**, accessed January 10, 2008).

1. Discuss the concepts of reach and frequency as they would apply to advertising The HeadBlade.
2. Would the three-exposure hypothesis or recency theory best explain the purchase of The HeadBlade?
3. Which traditional media are best suited to advertising The HeadBlade? Which do not fit?
4. Design a national and an international advertising program for The HeadBlade, identifying the target markets and methods to reach them.

CASE 2 OPRYLAND AMERICA

Mark Jones was about to begin an interesting aspect of his advertising career. His agency had been chosen to represent a new client—Opryland America. The country and western, gospel, and bluegrass music show was located near the Lake of the Ozarks in central Missouri.

For many years, Opryland America was not only the best choice for live country and western music, but it was also the only choice. Visitors came from nearby towns such as

Jefferson City and Columbia, Missouri, and from the Kansas City and St. Louis metropolitan areas. From 1960 to 1980, Opryland thrived using a small television advertising program for local markets and the metropolitan areas. Word-of-mouth brought in a great deal of business. Campers and lake-lovers who visited the Lake of the Ozarks would drive by the music theater as they reached the Bagnell Dam area, creating another set of potential audience members.

The 1990s brought new challenges to the show. First, the Lake of the Ozarks area had evolved from a "family" area to a major hangout for college students (especially from the University of Missouri, which was about 60 miles away) and 20-somethings looking for a place to party on the weekends. The natural draw of families had declined.

The bigger problem was new, regional competitors. Among the most dangerous was a new music mecca called Branson. The Branson region featured several cleaner, less crowded lakes along with other family enticements, especially the Silver Dollar City theme park. Silver Dollar City's advertising stretched across the Midwest and attracted many visitors who would then attend one of the many music shows nearby. Market research indicated that people attend Branson music shows for three reasons: nostalgic fun, religion, and patriotism. Many political candidates (especially Republicans) scheduled campaign stops in Branson. For several years Branson had also been a satellite site for the Jerry Lewis Muscular Dystrophy Telethon during the Labor Day weekend.

Other competitors were also beginning to advertise on a wider scale, especially Pigeon Forge, Tennessee, which was close to the Dollywood theme park. Nashville also became more of a threat as roads to the city were widened. Access to quality country music had become much easier for people in Missouri, Tennessee, Arkansas, and other nearby states.

Mark's challenge was to find a way to bring people back to Opryland. Essentially, he had a much smaller budget than the competition. He needed to find a way to attract local music lovers and reach the tourists who still came to the Lake of the Ozarks.

Opryland had two major advantages. First, those who had seen the show over the years were loyal fans. These people would bring their children and grandchildren to see the program. Second, Mark knew that the actual music and show were every bit as good as those offered by competitors, who charged higher prices. Tickets to prime shows with good seats in Branson, Pigeon Forge, and Nashville ran in excess of $40. Opryland still only charged $25 for the best seats in the house.

Against this backdrop, Mark began to think about his media choice options. He knew the future of Opryland America might very well depend on the quality of the advertising program he developed.

1. Which media should Mark use in advertising Opryland America? Defend your choices.

2. What should be the primary message sent out in Opryland's advertising?

3. Besides advertising, what else should Opryland do to bring back business and find new customers?

ENDNOTES

1. Mars Incorporated, M&M's homepage (**www.mms.com**, accessed May 4, 2005).

2. Mickey Marks, "Millennial Satiation," *Advertising Age* 14 (February 2000), p. S16; J. Thomas Russell and W. Ronald Lane, *Kleppner's Advertising Procedure*, 15th ed. (Upper Saddle River, NJ: Prentice Hall), 2002, pp. 174–75.

3. Larry Percy, John R. Rossiter, and Richard Elliott, "Media Strategy," *Strategic Advertising Management* (2001), pp. 151–63.

4. Kate Maddox, "Media Planners in High Demand," *BtoB* 89, no. 13 (November 8, 2004), p. 24.

5. Jack Neff, "Media Buying & Planning," *Advertising Age* 70, no. 32 (August 2, 1999), pp. 1–2.

6. Melanie Johnston, "That Little Blue Pad," *Marketing Magazine* 107, no. 4 (April 8, 2002), p. 10.

7. Arthur A. Andersen, "Clout Only a Part of Media Buyer's Value," *Advertising Age* 70, no. 15 (April 5, 1999), p. 26.

8. Ibid.

9. Herbert E. Krugman, "Why Three Exposures May Be Enough," *Journal of Advertising Research* 12, no. 6 (1972), pp. 11–14.

10. Larry Percy, John R. Rossiter, and Richard Elliott, "Media Strategy," *Strategic Advertising Management* (2001), pp. 151–63.

11. Ibid.

12. Erwin Ephron and Colin McDonald, "Media Scheduling and Carry-over Effects: Is Adstock a Useful Planning Tool," *Journal of Advertising Research* 42, no. 4 (July–August 2002), pp. 66–70; Laurie Freeman, "Added Theories Drive Need for Client Solutions," *Advertising Age* 68, no. 31, p. 18.

13. Diane Holloway, "What's On? Ads, Ads, and Maybe a TV Show," *Austin American States man* (**www.austin360.com/tv/content/movies/television/2005/10/11tvcolumn.html**, accessed January 17, 2008).

14. Gregory Solman, "Forward Thought: Ads A-Ok on DVRs," *Hollywood Reporter* (**http://hollywoodreporter.com**), December 27, 2007.

15. "AAAA Survey Finds Eight Percent Hike in Cost to Produce 30-Second TV Commercials," *Film & Video Production & Postproduction Magazine (ICOM)* (**www.icommag.com/november-2002/november-page-1b.html**, accessed January 14, 2005).

16. Brian Steinberg, "Ads on ABC Most Expensive at Season Bow," *Television Week* (September 30, 2007) (**www.tvweek.com/news/2007/09/exclusive-sunday_night_costs_t.php**); "Nielsen Ratings for Jan. 7–13," *USA Today* (**www./usatodaycom.life/television/news/nielsens-charts.htm**, accessed January 17, 2008).

17. Roger Baron, "Spot TV Strategy No Simple Matter," *Television Week* 23, no. 39 (September 27, 2004), p. 57.

18. Stephanie Thompson, "Food Marketers Stir Up the Media," *Advertising Age* 70, no. 42 (September 11, 1999), p. 18.

19. Kate Fitzgerald, "Beer, Auto, Retail Energizing Radio Airwaves," *Advertising Age* 76, no. 5 (January 31, 2005), p. S–6; Gary Fries, "Radio Is the Tool to Tune Into Ethnic Consumers," *DSN Retailing Today* 43, no. 22 (November 22, 2004), pp. 10–11.

20. Arlena Sawyers, "GM Certified Offers Dealer Ads," *Automotive News* 79, no. 6138 (March 14, 2005), p. 58.

21. Stephanie Thompson, "Arden Scores with Radio Promotions," *Advertising Age* 75, no. 47 (November 22, 2004), p. 8.

22. Camille Alarcon, "War of Words over Radio Ads," *B&T Weekly* 54, no. 2508 (February 25, 2005), p. 9.

23. Deborah L. Vence, "Outdoor Ads Leverage New Technology," *Marketing News* 38, no. 5 (September 15, 2004), pp. 11–13.

24. Stuart Elliott, "Back in Times Square, Toshiba Stands Tall," *The New York Times* (**www.nytimes.com/2007/12/03/business/world-business/03toshiba.html**), December 3, 2007.

25. Dana Wood, "The Great Outdoors," *WWD: Women's Wear Daily* 188, no. 121 (December 10, 2004), p. 6.

26. "Mobile Billboards Get Exposed in Traffic," *Marketing News* 38, no. 14 (September 1, 2004), p. 12.

27. Alana Semeuls, "Saturn Ad Blitz Set for L.A.'s Outdoors," *Los Angeles Times* (**www. latimes.com/business/la-fi-saturn3dec03. html**), December 3, 2007.

28. Jamie LaReau, "Magazines Are Pricey—But a Bargain, Publishers Say," *Automotive News* 79, no. 6139 (March 21, 2005), p. 46.

29. Ann Marie Kerwin, "Magazines Blast Study Showing Reader Falloff," *Advertising Age* 70, no. 10 (March 8, 1999), pp. 3–4.

30. "Reports of Mag-Industry Demise Greatly Exaggerated," *Advertising Age* 78, no. 14 (April 2, 2007), p. 14.

31. Lisa Granatstein, "Ups and Downs," *Brandweek* 45, no. 34 (September 27, 2004), p. SR11; Jamie LaReau, "Magazines Are Pricey—But a Bargain, Publishers Say," *Automotive News* 79, no. 6139 (March 21, 2005), p. 46.

32. Bill Gloede, "Best Use of Newspapers," *Adweek* 48, no. 25 (June 18, 2007), pp. SR22–23.

33. Pete Wetmore, "National Ads Kick It Up a Notch," *Advertising Age* 75, no. 16 (April 19, 2004), p. N–4.

34. Todd Shields, "Slow Growing," *Brandweek* 45, no. 34 (September 27, 2004), p. SR–12.

35. Lindsay Morris, "Studies Give 'Thumbs Up' to Mags for Ad Awareness," *Advertising Age* 70, no. 32 (August 2, 1999), pp. 16–17; Rachel X. Weissman, "Broadcasters Mine the Gold," *American Demographics* 21, no. 6 (June 1999), pp. 35–37.

36. Kate Maddox, "Top 100 B-to-B Advertisers Increased Spending 3% in '06," *BtoB* 92, no. 11 (September 10, 2007), pp. 25–30.

37. Carol Krol, "Office Depot Puts Focus on 'Business' in New Year," *BtoB* 90, no. 1 (January 17, 2005), p. 3.

38. Kate Maddox, "Top 100 B-to-B Advertisers Increased Spending 3% in '06," *BtoB* 92, no. 11 (September 10, 2007), pp. 25–30.

39. "ABM Releases Harris Study Data: B2B Advertising Highly Effective," *Min's B2B* 9, no. 26 (June 26, 2006), p. 8.

40. Joe Mandese, "Power Shift," *Broadcasting & Cable* 135, no. 53 (December 12, 2005), p. 12.

41. Martin Croft, "Media Indies Take on Networks with Consortium," *Marketing Week* 29, no. 28 (July 13, 2006), p. 13.

42. Greg Paull, "Act Local, Think Local as China Gets Even Tougher," *Media: Asia's Media & Marketing Newspaper* (April 21, 2006), p. 19.

43. Neff, "Media Buying & Planning."

44. Noah Liberman, "Web Marketers Use Radio to Net Audience Members," *Atlanta Business Chronicle* 22, no. 16 (September 24, 1999), p. 73A.

9

E-active Marketing

Chapter Objectives

After reading this chapter, you should be able to answer the following questions:

- **What** is e-active marketing?

- **How** can an e-commerce program be utilized to complement and supplement other selling and promotional activities?

- **Why** is it important to incorporate incentives into e-commerce programs?

- **What** is meant by the term interactive marketing?

- **How** can a marketing department adjust to the presence of social networks, blogs, and other new forms of Internet marketing?

HOW GOOGLE HAS CHANGED OUR LANGUAGE

Every once in awhile, a product or a company's name becomes so famous it gets added to our vocabulary. A generation ago, people started making "xerox" copies. Before that, people started taking "aspirins" instead of "pain medicine" and covering wounds with "band aids" rather than "adhesive strips."

Today, it is common to hear someone say they "googled" something. The name Google was taken from the word *googol*. A googol is a 1 followed by 100 zeros. And now, a new term has emerged: *Narcissurfing,* the habit of surfing the Web looking for your own appearances. Narcissurfers are those who Google themselves on a daily or weekly basis.[1]

Google has achieved success and changed our language in a world first filled with failures—Internet companies. Google works because it uses a different business model. The company's primary edge is its ability to organize a vast amount of information into a system that can be easily accessed using the Web, and Google provides information to users for free. The company sells advertising that is linked to the free information.

The search engine provides access to a vast variety of Web sites that help connect customers with information about products, ideas, social trends, and an endless variety of additional services. Need something translated from Russian to English? Go to Google, and numerous free translation services are quickly at your disposal. Of course, those translation services are more than willing to sell you courses to help you learn various foreign languages at the same time.

"A search" according to Steve Cohen, a vice president in charge of products at Basis Technology, "is made up of two stages: indexing and retrieval." One primary advantage held by Google is that the company has been able to expand indexing and retrieval searches into nearly 100 languages. It was not an easy task. For example, many Asian languages, in their print forms, do not have spaces between words. This created a major challenge for word box search engines. Using tools from Basis Technology, Google is able to offer searches in Asian languages as well as other challenging languages. The net result is a global company with a worldwide reach.

The year 2004 was especially significant at Google. The company sold stock for the first time, raising $1.67 billion in capital. The stock price then soared. Many major firms have learned that

advertising on a search engine like Google provides a targeted audience with profitable results. Naturally, advertising dollars are quick to follow, and in this case they moved to Google, the market leader in search engine use. One industry leader commented that Google has created almost a "new world order" in advertising.

To maintain its strong pattern of growth, executives at Google have expanded into new territories. First, the firm began advertising to build brand strength. Previously, Google relied solely on word-of-mouth. Now the company advertises using radio and print in numerous markets. Next, Google is entering the "local search market." Local classified advertising is a major source of revenue for many companies. Google's technology makes it possible to see all of the dry cleaners in just one city. The primary challenge in this expansion effort has been brand awareness. Google's marketing team has moved to solve the problem by using local advertising. A final launch in 2005 was in the area of business computing.

Google's management team is acutely aware of competitors. Microsoft and Yahoo! are two main search engine providers that could affect Google's share. New competitors emerge every day. Firefox, Opera, and Apple's Safari are some of the latest entrants. Still, Google's power in the marketplace makes company leaders optimistic about the future. Google is an excellent example of how to succeed using creativity, energy, and an effective marketing program to turn a brand into a cultural icon.[2]

OVERVIEW

The Internet has changed many aspects of U.S. culture. Web sites such as YouTube, Facebook, JibJab, MiGente, AsianAve, and MySpace have affected interpersonal relationships, politics, views toward personal privacy, and numerous other aspects of everyday life. The Internet is especially attractive to younger people, who access it on personal computers, through telephone services, and an ever-growing set of new technologies.

In marketing, a new era has emerged. A company in practically any location can compete globally, and the size of an organization's operation makes little difference. The Internet is an open environment, just a click away. A buyer can locate numerous sellers offering practically the same merchandise at a comparable price and with similar offers at any time. As more people and businesses become comfortable with the Internet, the marketing landscape continues to evolve. The various applications of Web technology are now essential elements in any fully integrated marketing communications program. These activities are typically directed by the **Webmaster**, the individual assigned to manage a firm's Web site.

What is **e-active marketing**? The term is used to suggest two major components of Internet marketing: (1) e-commerce and (2) interactive marketing. Both activities are vital to an organization's online presence. Many of today's consumers rely heavily on the Internet to research products, to shop, to make comparisons, and to read both favorable and unfavorable comments by other consumers. An effective IMC program incorporates these new elements into an advertising and promotions plan.

The first part of this chapter examines e-commerce programs, including the incentives used to attract customers as well as consumer concerns with Internet shopping. Next, business-to-business e-commerce programs are described. Finally, the various interactive marketing methodologies being used by companies, including online advertising, brand spiraling, blogs, online social networks, e-mail campaigns, and viral marketing, are presented. With each, the goal is to increase the company's brand presence and to influence purchase decisions. Web site design issues and international challenges are also described.

E-COMMERCE

Selling goods and services on the Internet is the focus of **e-commerce** programs, of which there are many types. A retail store can, for example, offer items by Internet when there is no outlet nearby or simply as a convenience. E-commerce can also take the form of a retail operation selling entirely on the Web without any physical store or even inventory. Services are offered, deals are mediated, and products are shipped through a wide range of e-commerce operations. Figure 9.1 identifies the top 10 cyber shopping categories.

Many established retail operations add e-commerce programs in order to offer customers an alternative mode for making purchases. Not everyone makes purchases on the Internet, but more than half of U.S. households regularly shop there. Online purchases now make up 7 percent of total retail sales in the United States. Consumers are increasingly comfortable with online shopping.[3]

Further, many consumers make purchases at retail stores after first using the Internet to collect information. Thus, a shopper may research stereos on the Internet and then visit a store with a list of finalists. Another person may go online to find a fishing rod with a special set of features. Using a store locator on the manufacturer's Web site, the individual identifies the closest store offering the product and goes there to make the actual purchase. In that case, even though the customer did not make the purchase via e-commerce, he or

FIGURE 9.1
Top 10 Cyber Shopping Categories

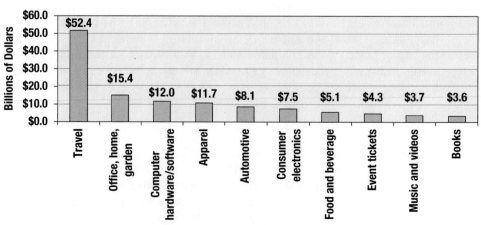

Billions of Dollars

Travel	$52.4
Office, home, garden	$15.4
Computer hardware/software	$12.0
Apparel	$11.7
Automotive	$8.1
Consumer electronics	$7.5
Food and beverage	$5.1
Event tickets	$4.3
Music and videos	$3.7
Books	$3.6

Source: Based on "Cyber Shopping," *License* 7, no. 10 (November 2004), p. 12.

◆ Catalog	◆ Customer service information
◆ Shopping cart	◆ Public relations information
◆ Payment system	◆ Optional components

FIGURE 9.2
Components of an E-Commerce Web Site

she has used the Internet as part of the buying decision-making process. Consequently, the leaders of most established businesses know they must develop high-quality e-commerce sites in order to remain competitive.

E-Commerce Components

As shown in Figure 9.2, e-commerce programs feature several components. The first is a *catalog*. A catalog may display only a few items or be a complex presentation of thousands of products. The nature of the firm's operation determines the type of catalog required. In every case, customers should be able to easily locate products of interest. Photos, streaming videos, and product information can be used to create an appealing online catalog. If the company has a printed catalog, it is important to tie the printed catalog to the Web catalog. Victoria's Secret has a "catalog quick order" system that allows customers to enter the product number from the print catalog and then go straight to checkout. The shopping program saves considerable time in trying to find and buy a product on the Web.[4]

Second, each site contains a *shopping cart* to assist consumers as they select products. Again, the shopping cart can range from checking a circle for an item when only a few products are offered to more complicated shopping carts that are designed to keep records of multiple purchases.

Third, each site contains a *method of payment* for items purchased. For consumers, this may be a credit card system or a payment service such as PayPal or Google Checkout. E-retailers offering multiple methods of payment have experienced greater increases in sales than those providing fewer options. Currently, the average number of different payment options offered by online retailers is 2.6, up from 2.1 in 2005.[5]

For business-to-business operations, payments are normally made using a voucher system. In other situations, a bill is generated or a computerized billing system is used to direct the invoice to the buyer. In more trusting relationships, the invoice is added to the customer's records without a physical bill ever being mailed.

Most sites carry a *customer service* component. The objective is to support the consumer after the sale. This part of the Web site is used to document purchases and provide operating information about the product. Shoppers who have questions can use the e-mail function of a Web site to obtain information or scroll through the **FAQs (frequently asked questions)** page. Portions of these sites may be password protected in order to ensure that only customers who have purchased products can access certain information.

Another component found on many sites is a *public relations* link that is tied to a cause or charity supported by the organization. Individuals can view what altruistic activities a company supports. They may also be able to volunteer for or donate money to the cause. The charity may be presented within the company's site or in a separate place. Many Web sites provide a hyperlink to the homepage of the charitable organization.

Many marketing efforts include ways to provide value-added services to customers as part of an e-commerce program. The idea is to develop greater customer loyalty. Barnes & Noble, Charles Schwab, and others have launched a value-added service that is proving to be extremely popular—free education. Barnes & Noble offers free online courses on subjects such

Barnes & Noble offers more than 50 courses per year through its online university.

Source: Courtesy of Chen Chao © Dorling Kindersley.

as playing the guitar and enjoying Shakespeare. The site is called Barnes & Noble University. More than 50 courses per year are offered, each tied to a book in its inventory that must be purchased by students. Classes are often taught by the authors and consist of assigned reading materials, communication with classmates, and quizzes. Since June 2000, over 500,000 students have taken classes, with the average student enrolling in two classes.

Charles Schwab offers more than 50 online courses through the Charles Schwab Learning Center. Some courses are self-paced learning exercises; others are live, virtual classrooms that utilize conferencing software such as WebEx Communications. More than 200,000 people have enrolled, with recent enrollments averaging 1,000 per week.[6] These types of programs encourage repeat visitors who are more likely to make purchases and become regular customers.

E-COMMERCE INCENTIVES

Any lure or attraction that brings people to a Web site is called **cyberbait**. The various forms of cyberbait include incentives designed to encourage consumers (or businesses) to visit a Web site and to make online purchases. Cyberbait incentives can be classified into three categories:

- Financial incentives
- Convenience incentives
- Value-based incentives

These features do not appear separately; they are normally combined into an overall approach.

E-commerce retailer Bluefly.com often provides financial incentives to encourage online purchases.

tuesday, 11:15 p.m. buying a new dress.

bluefly

Women's, men's and kid's designer fashions. Save up to 75%.   90-day money back guarantee.

www.bluefly.com℠
the outlet store in your home℠

Financial Incentives

Financial incentives are especially helpful in persuading an individual or business to make a first-time purchase via e-commerce. The incentive can take the form of a reduced price, free shipping, or an e-coupon. Financial incentives may not hurt a firm's profit margin because of the reduced costs of doing business online. Once the individual or company takes advantage of the financial incentive and makes the switch, continuing the incentive may not be necessary. At that point, the convenience and added-value features of the e-commerce program help keep the customer.

When consumers or businesses make purchases via the Internet, the vendor often saves time and money. These savings can be passed along as financial incentives. This is because the firm that fills orders via the Internet is cutting costs in several ways, including:

- Reduced shipping costs, because the costs are passed along to the buyer
- Decreased labor costs, because shelves do not have to be restocked
- Lower personnel costs (sales force), because in-store salespeople are not needed

The Bluefly ad in this section states that the company is "the outlet store in your home." Bluefly (**www.bluefly.com**) is a successful New York–based upscale apparel and home furnishings discounter. The company's philosophy is that more site traffic equals more business.

Bluefly regularly uses various types of cyberbait to drive traffic to the company's Web site in order to collect names for a database as well as to boost sales.

Bluefly took advantage of the value of a hard-to-get fashion accessory that even celebrities and socialites had been waiting months to purchase. A sweepstakes, named "30 Bags in 30 Days," was created for the company's Web site. Customers could enter as many times as they wanted, but were restricted to only one entry per day. The sweepstakes increased traffic to the site by 100 percent as compared to the same month from the previous year. Fifty percent of the visitors asked Bluefly to send them a daily reminder to play the sweepstakes. Forty percent referred their friends to the site and the sweepstakes. The end result was a 62 percent increase in sales due to the new customers that the sweepstakes brought in and existing customers who continued to make purchases even after the sweepstakes was over.[7]

Typically, the most effective financial incentives offer something free or at a discount. According to a survey by BizRateResearch, the most popular online promotion is free shipping, which was preferred by 80 percent of the respondents.[8] Whatever financial incentive is used, two things should be kept in mind. First, the incentive must be meaningful to individuals visiting the site. Second, the incentive should be changed periodically to encourage new visitors to buy and to encourage repeat purchases by current visitors.

Convenience Incentives

Another incentive that encourages customers to visit a Web site is making shopping easier. Instead of making a trip to a retail store, a consumer can place the order in the office or at home. More important, the order can be placed at any time; 24-hour availability is also a major reason why ATMs are popular. The convenience and speed of purchasing merchandise online drives many consumers to e-retailers.

Convenience becomes an advantage when the consumer seeks specific product information. The Internet is undoubtedly quicker and easier than using *Consumer Reports* or talking to a salesperson. The majority of consumers research major purchases online before going to a store. Most shoppers have looked at least once at an online peer review before finalizing a purchase, and roughly 40 percent have compared product features and prices across outlets online before buying.[9]

Where do individuals go when they look for product information? The most frequently employed site is Google. It is accessed in about one-third of all information searches. No other Internet source is used more than 7 percent of the time. Whether it is Google or another method, the most frequently given reason for the method chosen is that it was easier. Figure 9.3 provides a list of the various reasons for choosing a particular method of information research. Notice that easier, convenient, and quicker are three of the top four reasons. Today's consumers are driven by the convenience that e-commerce provides.

Web sites are continually updated and changed to encourage return visits.[10] Prices and product information are kept up-to-date. In addition, the appearance of the site will be routinely changed so that consumers will return to see what is new. The front page of a Web site can be revised just as a display at a retail store is regularly altered. The difference, however, is that in changing the Web site, the marketing team must be careful not to change links or the location of merchandise. Consumers become accustomed to finding things on the site. It is best not to make it hard for them to locate familiar items. Just as a grocery store seldom moves merchandise around just to create a different look, designers also must

This advertisement by iParty.com highlights the convenience of finding all of a person's party needs at one location.

i want everything at my party to be yellow. i want yellow balloons, yellow cups, and yellow icing on my cake because yellow is the prettiest color ever. except for pink. i want everything at my party to be pink.

www.iparty.com > birthdays > basics > **pink** > cups/plates/napkins/favors > order

i want. i click. iparty.com

aol keyword: iparty

FIGURE 9.3
Reasons for Choosing a Particular Method of Researching a Product

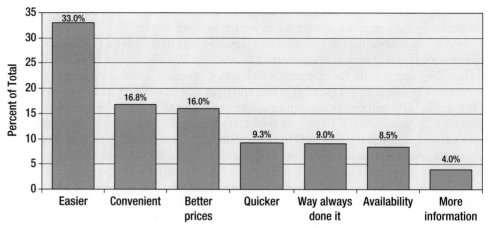

Percent of Total

| Easier | Convenient | Better prices | Quicker | Way always done it | Availability | More information |
| 33.0% | 16.8% | 16.0% | 9.3% | 9.0% | 8.5% | 4.0% |

Source: Based on Andrew Burgess, "At Your Convenience," *Marketing Week* 29, no. 38 (September 21, 2006), pp. 34–35.

be aware that shoppers will become annoyed if they cannot find their favorite products. Consequently, convenience remains an important feature as a Web site is being redesigned. The Web site should also consistently emphasize the IMC theme and the company's image.

As company leaders become more Internet savvy, new types of e-commerce programs have emerged. For example, many retail stores now offer online wedding gift registries. Out-of-town friends can conveniently choose, wrap, and ship presents to the couple. Victoria's Secret has a gift guide that lists various items either by price or popularity. Apparel cataloger J. Crew has easy-to-use "how to measure" charts to assure consumers that what they are buying will fit.[11] Such conveniences stimulate sales and encourage visitors to return to a company's Web site.

This advertisement offers the convenience of making travel arrangements online and paying for them with a credit card.

Value-Added Incentives

Value-added incentives are used to lead consumers to change purchasing habits over the long term. The added value may be personalized shopping, whereby the software system recognizes patterns in customers' purchasing behaviors. The same specialized software may inform customers about special deals. These offers are matched to past purchasing behaviors or a customer's search patterns. For example, a consumer going through the mystery section of an online bookstore may see a banner pop up advertising a special deal on a new mystery novel. In addition to instant banners, consumers and businesses also may receive e-mails offering new information and other special deals that are available.

One common value-added approach many e-retailers use is offering merchandise on the Web site that is not available in a print catalog. Design Within Reach, a modern furniture retailer, advertises, "Our Web site offers numerous products not always included in the catalog, as well as weekly features of new items." An antique hardware retailer places sale items and new products on the Web site before including them in the print catalog.[12]

It is frequently the combination of incentives that makes the difference. The cyberbait may include a discount or special price on a pair of jeans (a financial-based incentive), and at the same time creates the freedom to place an order at 3:00 A.M. (a convenience-based incentive). The same site may feature a game or offer a weekly or daily tip on some topic (value-added incentive). To entice consumers and businesses to return to the site on a regular basis, all three incentives are needed. E-shoppers find it easy to surf the Internet and search competing sites. When they do so, brand names and particular Web sites are not as important. Consumers need a reason to return to the site on a regular basis.

CONSUMER CONCERNS WITH E-COMMERCE

Some consumers are still wary of purchasing products via the Internet. The primary reasons are highlighted in Figure 9.4.[13] Although these concerns are not as widespread as they were 10 years ago, they exist for certain individuals.

Seller Opportunism

One of the major economic benefits of the Internet also results in one of consumers' worst fears. The Internet allows a company from anywhere to conduct business with an individual or another business anywhere in the world. This freedom of access also creates buyer apprehension. Is the business legitimate or is the Web site merely an attempt to make illegal gains, through fraud, identity theft, or some other activity? The key issue is trust. Can the Internet be trusted to facilitate sales of goods or services safely?

Security Issues

Consumer concerns about security are based on past incidents in which credit card numbers have been stolen as well as from cases of identity theft. A review of the past may be helpful in understanding this concern. When telephone orders were first encouraged by mail-order firms, people were hesitant because of fears about giving out a phone or credit card number to a stranger they couldn't see. Now, nearly everyone is willing to provide the information while placing orders on the phone. Also, it was not that long ago when shoppers expressed anxiety about store employees stealing their credit card numbers. Originally, customers were instructed to "take the carbon" from a credit card purchase to make sure it was torn up in order to prevent an employee from using the credit card number later.

The same pattern is likely to follow with Internet shopping. As more consumers become accustomed to using the Web, fears about giving out credit card information will probably become no greater than they now are for telephone orders or in-store credit card sales. Credit card companies have created a series of independent television commercials designed to calm and reassure people about the quality of their Internet security programs. Online retailers have also provided additional payment methods. This flexibility provides assurance to worried consumers, because it allows shoppers to choose the method of payment.

These efforts have paid off. Consumer confidence in e-commerce Web site security is on the rise. A recent survey revealed that three-fourths of all online shoppers have faith in Web security.[14]

I remember her in blue jeans and a T-shirt in high school. I remember her in a thrift store leather jacket in college. I remember her in a rain jacket in Oregon. I remember her in a swimsuit on the beach in Florida. I remember her without a swimsuit on the beach in Greece. I remember her in a sleeping bag in a tent in Yellowstone, refusing to come out. But I can't say that I remember ever seeing her in a dress like that.

Date set: _May 20th_

Plan your wedding | Buy a gift | Find your dress | Book your honeymoon | More

Thousands of gowns. And everything else you need to plan the perfect wedding.

WeddingChannel.com™

A magazine ad for WeddingChannel.com encouraging individuals to visit their Web site.

* Seller opportunism
* Security concerns
* Information privacy issues
* Brick-and-mortar purchasing habits

FIGURE 9.4
Reasons Consumers Are Wary of Purchasing Products on the Internet

Privacy Issues

Many people are also apprehensive about privacy issues. Beyond apprehension about regarding identity theft and fraud is the concern that unscrupulous firms will sell sensitive personal information to others. Once this information is readily available to others, the individual has lost control over who sees it and how it used. A person might not wish to have his shopping patterns known, especially when the individual buys personal care products such as those for baldness, sexual dysfunction, weight loss, or other private matters.

Further, many consumers are frustrated by being bombarded with advertising and marketing information. Internet tracking technology and software programs allow a firm's marketing team to learn a great deal of information about an individual. Programs can track where they visit and what they do on the Internet. Products can be suggested based on this information. Specific information and advertisements can be generated based on this knowledge. Although this may offer the consumer a number of benefits, it is still is an invasion of privacy.

Many people do not want these marketing materials, especially when they are based on personal information. Some consumers believe that such marketing tactics are an invasion of their privacy rights as an individual and as a member of society. Many consumers strongly express the desire to maintain control over their personal information. They believe they should be able to decide who should use it and how it should be used.

Therefore, company leaders should be extremely careful about what types of data and information are collected from Web site visitors. More important, they should insist that the IT department guard that information. Customers now are demanding that firms inform them if any information is sold or passed on to other Web sites, companies, or individuals, which goes back to the issue of trust. Successful online retailers must gain the confidence of browsers who visit a Web site.

This advertisement for Duofold encourages consumers to obtain further information online.

Purchasing Habits

The final issue has strong ramifications for the ultimate success of e-commerce. Currently, many consumers are most comfortable when they buy merchandise at retail stores. Some are also comfortable buying through catalogs. It takes time to change these habits, especially the preference for retail shopping.

At the retail store, consumers can view and touch the merchandise. They can inspect it for defects and compare brands. Clothes can be tried on to make sure they fit. In addition, the customer can see how the clothing item looks while being worn. Changing these habits requires the right kinds of incentives. Consumers must have valid reasons for switching to the Internet to make a purchase.

To reach consumers who are reluctant to switch purchasing habits, retailers rely on several tactics. Some retailers, such as Circuit City, allow consumers to purchase a product online but then pick the item up at the retail store. The customer does not need to wait for Fed Ex or UPS to deliver it. The same is true for an item of clothing from a retailer. A customer can order an item and then go to the store to try it on before taking the item home. To complete these types of sales, retailers send text messages and e-mails informing customers that the product has arrived at the store.[15]

Purchase habits are already changing. Many consumers are far more comfortable with e-commerce purchases, especially during busy times of the year, such as the Christmas shopping season. It is clear e-commerce will not replace brick and mortar stores. At the same time, it has become a vital supplement for many retail chains and stores.

BUSINESS-TO-BUSINESS E-COMMERCE

For business-to-business organizations, e-commerce is critical. In many buying situations, purchasing agents go to the Internet and compare prices and product information. Once a business account is established, a business customer finds it easy to place orders, and the prices may be lower than those offered by more traditional outlets. Consequently, to compete in e-commerce, a business-to-business firm must have an effective e-commerce site and work to establish a strong, distinct brand name.[16]

The number of hits on a business-to-business Web site is directly related to the amount spent on advertising and sales promotions. Recently, one large business-to-business company went from 20,000 visits per month to 80,000 visits per month during a 6-month period by doubling the company's annual advertising budget for print, direct mail, and trade shows. A small company went from 2,000 to 6,000 hits per month by increasing the company's budget for print ads from $25,000 to $65,000 per year.[17]

Financial, convenience, and value-added incentives are also offered to business buyers. In the iGo.com Internet advertisement shown in this section, a 10-percent discount is offered as a financial incentive for orders placed via the Internet at **www.igo.com** or by telephone.

Why clothes have pockets.

What good is a pocket if it's empty? iGo offers over 7,900 mobile technology products from hard-to-find batteries, chargers and adapters to the coolest cell phones and digital cameras. To receive a 10% discount, visit us at www.igo.com/esvp or call 1-888-205-0065 and mention code IGOESVP.

iGo
Mobile Technology Outfitter™

10% discount on any product or service purchased through employeesavings.com

| Batteries and Power Gear | Laptop Gear | Cellular Gear | PDA and Handheld | Hot Products | Travel Gear |

An Internet advertisement for iGo.com featuring a financial incentive to encourage business-to-business purchases.

For businesses, ordering merchandise, supplies, and materials using the Internet can save purchasing agents considerable time. Businesses can also check the status of an order, shipment information, and billing data online. In most cases, getting information about a purchase online is considerably quicker than making a telephone call. In the fast-paced world of business, convenience is a highly attractive incentive for many companies. E-commerce programs offer many other benefits for business-to-business companies, including those described next.

A growing form of e-commerce in the business-to-business sector is online exchanges and auctions. These exchanges allow business buyers to purchase a variety of commodities and goods at bargain prices. The Internet enables vendors to speed up time to market, to sell directly to other businesses, and to cut transaction and inventory costs. Buyers can find both non-production goods, such as office supplies, as well as production-related supplies, raw materials, and equipment. Sites offering oil, natural gas, electricity, coal, chemicals, steel, and other raw materials also are available. Many online markets are operated by intermediary companies that match buyers and sellers.[18]

Interactive marketing reaches a worldwide community of shoppers.

INTERACTIVE MARKETING

There is a new term in marketing—*interactive marketing*. **Interactive marketing** is the development of marketing programs that create interplay between consumers and businesses rather than simply sending messages to potential customers. The programs feature two-way communication and customer involvement.

The Internet is the ideal medium for interactive marketing because of the ability to accurately track

FIGURE 9.5
Online Interactive Tactics

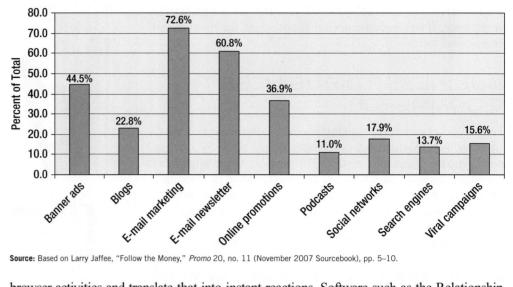

Source: Based on Larry Jaffee, "Follow the Money," *Promo* 20, no. 11 (November 2007 Sourcebook), pp. 5–10.

browser activities and translate that into instant reactions. Software such as the Relationship Optimizer and Prime Response by NCR uses powerful data analysis techniques to personalize marketing messages. The NCR software analyzes customer interactions such as click-stream data traffic—any type of customer interaction with the firm—and combines it with demographic information from external or internal databases. As the data are being processed, the software can launch complex interactive and personalized marketing materials.

Levi Strauss employs Blue Martini E-Merchandising software to customize both the Levis.com and the Dockers.com Web sites. The Home Shopping Network uses Edify's Smart Options software to track user preferences and suggest products based on the customer's past activities and current purchases. These technologies blur the line between selling and marketing, because the messages and products a customer sees are based on past purchasing and browsing activities. These programs are designed to increase the odds that the customer will discover something he or she wants rather than being forced to wade through scores of products he or she has no interest in purchasing at a more standardized Web site.[19]

Interactive marketing emphasizes two primary activities. First, it allows marketers to target individuals with personalized information, specifically the customers that are most likely to be interested in a company and its products. Second, it engages the consumer with the company and product in some way. As a result, the consumer becomes an active participant in the marketing exchange and not just a passive recipient. Figure 9.5 provides a list of various online interactive tactics used by companies today and what percentage of companies utilizes each method.

Interactive marketing can help accomplish a number of additional objectives. Figure 9.6 identifies various marketing objectives and the percentage of companies that

FIGURE 9.6
Interactive Marketing Objectives

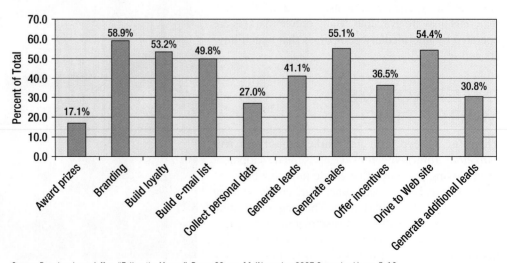

Source: Based on Larry Jaffee, "Follow the Money," *Promo* 20, no. 11 (November 2007 Sourcebook), pp. 5–10.

use interactive marketing campaigns to accomplish them. As shown, interactive marketing can achieve a wide variety of objectives and serve many purposes. The next few sections examine the primary interactive methods used by companies.

ONLINE ADVERTISING

Since the early 1990s, budgets for online advertising have steadily increased. Funds devoted to online advertising have become a larger portion of overall advertising and marketing budgets. Many marketing experts believe it is a highly effective method for reaching today's consumers, especially the younger, more Internet-savvy market.

Forms of Online Advertising

Four distinct categories of online advertising have emerged, as shown in Figure 9.7. The first to be used was a display or banner ad. It was usually in graphic form. Banner ads are now often embedded with videos. Today, these types of ads account for 32 percent of online advertising. The second form is classified ads, which comprise 17 percent of online ad budgets. The third and largest category of online expenditures is for spots on search engines. These are the text ads that appear next to search results when a specific word is keyed in. Funds devoted to search engines make up about 41 percent of online advertising expenditures. The final category of online advertising is media/video ads. Although it comprises only about 10 percent of online spending, it is the fastest growing category. This growth will escalate as mobile phones and other handheld devices develop increased capabilities to display videos.[20]

Reach Students created a series of Internet ads to promote an offer from one of the major parcel delivery services. The ads ran in May and June, just as students were deciding what to do with their personal items over the summer. Should they keep them or ship them home? The timing seemed perfect for such a campaign. Unfortunately, only 0.04 percent—only 4 out of every 10,000—students who saw the Web ad responded. Luke Mitchell, who ran the campaign, had anticipated at least a 1 percent response rate.[21]

The Impact of Online Advertising

As more dollars are shifted to online advertising, there is concern about the impact of those ads. Web users, just like television viewers, are becoming immune to advertisements. The percentage of people who respond to banner ads is steadily shrinking. The click-through rate on major Web destinations such as Microsoft, AOL, and Yahoo! has declined to less than 1 percent. A recent measurement showed a response rate of 0.27 percent.[22] Despite their declining effectiveness, many companies use banner ads to promote brands (see Figure 9.7).

BRAND SPIRALING

What does it take to create an effective online branding campaign? According to Abbey Klaassen at Advertising Age, "Think pictures, not words. Keep it simple. And tie it in with your off-line efforts."[23] Effective online advertising must be tied in with offline advertising to maintain a uniform brand presence and advertising message. It involves integrating online and offline branding tactics that reinforce each other to speak with one

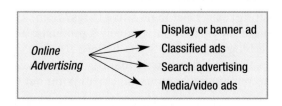

FIGURE 9.7
Types of Online Advertising

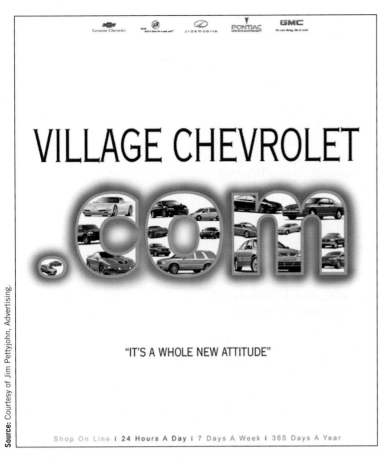

VILLAGE CHEVROLET
.com

"IT'S A WHOLE NEW ATTITUDE"

Shop On Line ι **24 Hours A Day** ι 7 Days A Week ι 365 Days A Year

A print advertisement encouraging consumers to visit the company's Web site.

voice. This process is called **brand spiraling**, which is the practice of using traditional media to promote and attract consumers to a Web site. Television, radio, newspapers, magazines, billboards, and carry-home shopping bags are all designed to encourage consumers to visit the firm's Web site. A fully integrated advertising campaign is essential, along with the creation of online ads that are highly visual and simple.

While many companies continue to utilize online advertising, there is also a movement into more interactive technologies. Blogs, e-mail marketing programs, podcasts, social networks, and search engines are emerging as effective new advertising channels.

BLOGS

It started with chat rooms, which allowed consumers to discuss and share information about items to purchase and the brands that perform the best, or the worst. People were turning to other people for information—confirmation and disconfirmation—about products. Chat rooms became a new form of word-of-mouth communication, and peer-to-peer influence continued to grow. To marketers, it first appeared to just be people talking, as if on some corner in some town, except it was online. Then it grew. As more people went online, thousands began to share the ideas, thoughts, and opinions about an endless array of topics. Today, millions of people might read about another person's experiences or thoughts.

From chat rooms came **blogs**, a term derived from *Web logs*. Blogs are basically online musings. Blogs have been created on a wide range of topics. Some blogs permit visitors to post comments; others are just the ramblings of an individual. What makes blogs powerful is that one consumer dissatisfied with a particular brand can now tell thousands, and in some cases millions, of others. Previously, a bad shopping experience meant that 12 to 15 people would be told about it. Now, however, an individual's complaint can be sent to more than just friends and family. A discontented consumer can speak to anyone who is willing to listen (read) via the Internet.

The power of online buzz has grown at an exponential rate. The result is the development of a number of unique methods of communication between individuals that attract advertisers looking for ways to tap into these venues. A recent survey by the American Marketing Association illustrates the tremendous growth in these intrapersonal online communication channels. An online survey of 1,174 people revealed that:[24]

- 47 percent go to a social network site to download coupons or to search for information about a product.
- 45 percent go to a social network site to find out about upcoming sales in retail stores and discounts on particular brands of products.
- 22 percent read or write a product review on a blog.

Reactions to Negative Comments

How should the marketing team react to negative blogs? Some companies hire people to search the Internet for blogs about a company's products. The next issue is what to do when a negative blog is located. Some believe the best approach is to join in the discussion. When they do, some will identify themselves as working for the company. Others try to remain anonymous and try to point out the good things about the brand.

Company-Sponsored Blogging

Some marketing managers have tried to turn the situation around by looking for ways to use blogs to promote products. They try to find methods of blogging that spread positive word-of-mouth communications about the company's brand, including setting up company-sponsored blogs. The goal is to realize the potential marketing power of blogs and how they emulate word-of-mouth communication.

The online retailer Bluefly regularly updates customers with fashion news through its Flypaper blog (**http://flypaper.bluefly.com**). The blog encourages customers to visit the site often for postings on new styles, upcoming designers, and fashion faux pas. In the past Bluefly customers would have relied on magazines such as *Vogue* for fashion information. Now they can get information quicker, and more importantly, it is interactive. This allows the marketing team to develop a two-way channel of communication with customers.

Do company-sponsored blogs work? Research conducted by ComScore Networks revealed that shoppers who visit blogs spend more than the average shopper. For Bluefly, the individuals who access the Flypaper blog are the company's very best customers. In addition to spending more money, the ComScore study indicated that the average visitor to a blog spends nearly 23 hours per week online, compared to 13 hours per week for the average Internet user.[25]

A company-sponsored blog can provide a number of benefits. It may ease shopper fears about purchasing from a particular company, especially an unknown e-retailer or less well-known brand. The postings and responses from customers give individuals reading the blog a glimpse of how the company deals with customers and the relative level of customer satisfaction of those who have purchased products. A blog can provide the company with an avenue to release information about its products. It also can provide an avenue for customers to voice their opinions. The biggest advantage is that all of this remains under the control of the company.

The company's marketing team must be extremely careful to be honest with the blog and not censor everything that is negative. If it does, consumers will quickly see it as a sham. When a negative comment appears, the marketing department then has the opportunity to respond. This provides an avenue for other customers to join in on the discussion, pro and con. Such a dialogue can be very rewarding for a company if it is conducted in an honest and open way. It also provides valuable insights into how customers view the company, its brands, and its products.

Source: Courtesy of Skyjacker Suspensions.

Suspension systems sold by Skyjacker are discussed in both company-sponsored and consumer blogs.

ONLINE SOCIAL NETWORKS

Online social networks have become extremely popular with people and with companies seeking to communicate with consumers. The most well-known social networking sites are Facebook and MySpace. Facebook has 59 million active profiles; MySpace has 110 million active profiles. Both sites allow companies to place ads and to target them to the interests, habits, and friends of members based on their profiles.

Seventy percent of social network advertising dollars goes to MySpace and Facebook. As ad clutter started to become a bigger problem, some marketers began using smaller

Source: Courtesy of Summer Bradley.

Coca-Cola offers a social network page for Sprite called "Sprite Sips."

social networking sites with a narrower focus and those that are more in tune with specific target audiences. There is a social network for just about every possible theme that can be imagined. Yub.com is for shopaholics; Fuzzstar is for pet lovers; YogaMates is for people who like Yoga; ONLoq.com is for hip-hop fans; and PassportStamp.com is for avid travelers. Membership can vary widely, from a few hundred to millions.[26] These smaller sites provide companies the opportunity to zero in on an audience that provides an optimal match with what is being offered.

Brands such as Calvin Klein, Nike, Adidas, Victoria's Secret, and Ralph Lauren are increasingly featured on sites such as YouTube and MySpace. These types of sites allow companies to post videos, advertisements, and other marketing materials. For fashion designers, the sites provide venues for posting behind-the-scenes footage and fashion shows. People can choose which videos they want to watch and share them with friends. And, these videos are being watched. In 2008, YouTube had 160 million unique visitors in just 1 month. This figure does not include individuals who go back numerous times to watch or post videos.[27]

Developing a Social Network Presence

The initial steps most marketers take in developing a social network presence for a company is starting a profile page and then accepting "friend requests" from people logging onto the network. Other companies have specific product pages. Coca-Cola, for example, has a page for Sprite, called "Sprite Sips," where people can play with an animated character. Facebook and other social networks treat these brand pages just like other pages; the company can add photos, videos, reviews, and comments, just like individual users.[28]

Nike regularly posts new commercials on YouTube and other sites through either the company's own brand page or a profile page. In addition to commercials, Nike posts videos that typically are generated behind the scenes. These postings provide Nike with additional exposure and allows Nike's marketing department to monitor feedback and get a feel for what the public thinks. The feedback is immediate. The marketing department quickly knows what connects with consumers and what does not. If viewers like the video, it will often generate word-of-mouth buzz. Visitors to the site tell their friends about the video or send them the link. Nike is at the forefront in featuring this type of interactive marketing, and the company's commercials and videos normally generate a huge demand.

CONSUMER-GENERATED ADVERTISING

Most of the commercials, videos, and marketing information placed on social network sites have been generated by the company or a professional advertising agency. Now a new method is being used to develop advertisements. For the 2007 Super Bowl, Doritos featured a commercial that was the result of an ad-making contest for consumers. Converse, Firefox, and Diet Coke have also used materials generated by consumers. Encouraging consumers to create advertisements is a creative version of interactive marketing. The idea is that the viewers of the ad tend to accept a consumer-generated advertisement as being more genuine than a company-produced commercial. Some marketing and advertising experts believe that the future of advertising is in user-generated content rather than agency-produced ads.

To illustrate the power of consumer-generated advertising, consider Nick Haley, an 18-year-old student. Haley is an Apple computer loyalist who received his first Macintosh at the age of 3. A few years ago, he was inspired to make a commercial about the Apple iPod Touch upon hearing the song "Music Is My Hot, Hot Sex" and a lyric in the song that said, "My music is where I'd like to touch." Using the song as a background, Haley created a fast-paced tour of the abilities of the iPod Touch. He uploaded the video to YouTube. He received 4 stars out of a possible 5 and comments such as "That's awesome" and "Makes me want to buy one." Among the viewers of the commercial was an employee at Apple, who asked the staff to contact the company's advertising agency TBWA/Chiat/Day. The agency liked the commercial, contacted Haley, and invited him to their office to make a high-definition version of his commercial.[29]

Nick Haley's story is beginning to be repeated as companies and advertising agencies realize the power of consumer-generated advertising. In the words of Haley, "That's the whole point of advertising; it needs to get to the user. If you get the user to make ads, who better?" According to Lee Clow, chairman and chief creative at TBWA Worldwide, consumer-generated ads is part of the new world in which we live: "It's an exciting new format for brands to communicate with their audiences. People's relationship with a brand is becoming a dialog, not a monolog."[30]

CONSUMER-GENERATED REVIEWS

The nature of word-of-mouth endorsements has changed. In the past, it was simply a satisfied or dissatisfied consumer telling close friends and relatives about a purchasing experience. Now, many companies that vend multiple goods or services solicit consumer-generated reviews of those products.

Amazon.com is at the forefront of consumer-generated reviews. Each book offered online holds a space where individual customers can write reviews, both with words and a one- to five-star rating. The site informs the shopper of the number of reviews, the average star rating, and notes if the reviews are written by anonymous critics or those who provide their real names. A person wishing to place his or her name on a review must authenticate it by presenting Amazon with a credit card number. The benefit to customers is that they can read the reviews before making purchases. Obviously the system is not perfect, because an author may use a pseudonym to write a highly favorable review and encourage friends and family members to do the same. At the same time, the author cannot control any outside review that is posted.

Circuit City is another retailer that has incorporated consumer feedback into online retailing. Circuit City offers a blog section for consumers to read about and discuss various topics. For each product category, such as cameras, Circuit City provides a discussion forum on a variety of topics that relate to that product. In the digital camera discussion forum, consumers can post photos they have taken with various cameras. Circuit City provides customer reviews of each product. Some are positive, some are negative. These reviews have considerable influence on which brands consumers consider and eventually purchase. By providing blogs, discussion forums, and consumer reviews, Circuit City's goal is to offer consumers a variety of ways to search for and evaluate products and to make final purchase decisions without ever leaving the company's Web site.[31]

Consumer-generated reviews and discussions can be important vehicles for reaching early adopters of products. They provide a forum that allows for the dissemination of information among consumers.[32]

Circuit City's Web site provides consumer reviews of numerous products, such as video cameras.

Source: Courtesy of Summer Bradley.

There are several key implications of customer-generated reviews. First, too many negative reviews and low-star ratings will be harmful to the company. The marketing team should carefully monitor them to see what is being said about the company. Second, reviews stress the importance of consistent, high-quality customer products and services. Third, reviews provide important information on how a company's product is being evaluated by customers and how the brand compares to competing brands. This information is critical in developing marketing plans, product modifications, and service strategies.

Clearly, the use of consumer-generated reviews is on the rise. The challenge for marketing departments is to manage this aspect of consumer word-of-mouth endorsements in a way that will enhance brand equity and increase sales.

E-MAIL

Another aspect of a company's interactive marketing strategy is to effectively use e-mail (see Figure 9.8). To be successful, an e-mail marketing program must be: (1) integrated with other marketing channels, (2) based on Web analytics, and (3) combined with future Web monitoring systems. It is also helpful if the e-mail campaign is integrated with the Web site's content management and customer relationship management systems.[33]

Integration with Other Channels

E-mail marketing should be integrated with other marketing channels. It cannot simply be a program where a list of e-mail addresses is purchased and mass e-mails are sent to individuals on the list. This is because response rates are low.

Response rates increase when e-mail messages resemble the information on the company's Web site and in its advertisements and direct mail messages. Consumers are more likely to respond if the e-mail looks familiar. The message should be designed to move consumers along in the purchase decision-making process and help them evaluate alternatives or even think about making the actual purchase. E-mail campaigns are not suited to building brand awareness or liking for a product. Instead, an e-mail program should focus on the latter stages of the purchase process. That is where Web analytics comes into the picture.

Web Analytics

Web analytics is the process of analyzing where consumers went at a brand's Web site, what they did within the Web site, and what other sites were visited. If an individual spent 10 minutes examining merchandise within a particular section of the Web site, then that person is an excellent target for an e-mail about the products he or she examined. If an individual visited several Web sites to look at similar merchandise, then that person is likely in the latter stages of the purchase process and is close to making the purchase decision or actual purchase. Web analytics allows a company to develop e-mail campaigns that offer the greatest chance of response.

E-mail campaigns can be directed at consumers who abandon shopping carts without making a purchase while visiting a Web site. Recent research indicates that about 40 percent of online shoppers abandon the shopping cart just prior to the checkout. Only about 30 percent of these shoppers ever return to complete the transaction. The IT department can identify

FIGURE 9.8
Building a Successful E-Mail Campaign

It is *essential* to:	It is *beneficial* to:
◆ Integrate with other marketing channels	◆ Integrate with Web site's content management
◆ Be based on Web analytics	◆ Integrate with a customer relationship program
◆ Combine with future Web analytics	

those individuals who have abandoned a shopping basket. An e-mail sent to these individuals offering free shipping, a discount if they complete the order, or a simple reminder that they have items in their shopping basket can lead to greater sales.

Converting these individuals to customers is much easier and more lucrative than sending mass e-mails. Targeted e-mails have a conversion rate 5 to 10 times higher than mass e-mails sent to the firm's customers. In addition, revenues from these follow-up e-mails are 3 to 9 times higher.[34]

Source: Courtesy of Chen Chao © Dorling Kindersley.

Monitoring Future Actions

The third essential component of an e-mail interactive marketing program is monitoring of future actions. Web analytics are used to determine the percentage of individuals from an e-mail campaign that accessed the Web site, what they did at the site, where they went within the site, and the purchases made. This information is valuable in determining what works and what doesn't work along with information about how to design future e-mail campaigns.

Hotel chains, such as Hyatt, can use Web analytics to monitor the effectiveness of e-mail campaigns.

Another tactic that can be used to strengthen an e-mail marketing campaign is making sure that e-mail information is integrated with Web content. An e-mail that matches the content of the Web site is likely to increase the response rate. Sometimes, instead of modifying the primary site, the marketing team creates a micro-site to match the e-mail. Thus, if an e-mail offers a 15 percent discount on a new stereo system, then the URL that is placed in the e-mail can take the person directly to a micro-site that was developed specifically for the discount offer. The site will be linked to the company's primary Web site in case the person wants to browse further. This strategy is especially beneficial if the e-mail encourages the individual to play some type of game or enter a contest or sweepstakes. It prevents clutter on the main site and allows the e-mail to effectively transport the recipient to the targeted message.

The final component of an e-mail program is a customer relationship management (CRM). CRM is discussed in depth in Chapter 11 as part of direct response marketing.

E-Mail Newsletters

An e-mail newsletter can help to create brand awareness and to drive traffic to a Web site. Newsletters are especially beneficial when consumers sign up to receive them. The newsletter must be constructed in a way that it offers value to recipients. It must go beyond product information. The more valuable the content is to the recipients, the more likely the newsletter will yield results.

The brand's Web site is the best place to build an e-mail subscription list. The newsletter should be offered free and tie in with the company's products. Subscription lists can be used to gather demographic, behavioral, and psychographic information about consumers. The information can be used for targeting future e-mails and in designing the actual newsletter. All of the newsletters are not the same. Each is customized to match customer profiles from the company's e-mail database.

Advertising on Other Newsletters

Another option is to advertise on another company's newsletter. Doing so can be an excellent way to build brand awareness and to drive traffic to the company's Web site. For business-to-business marketers, advertising in this way can generate leads for future e-mails, telephone calls, or sales call visits. The key is to pick the newsletters that are relevant to the firm's target audience. In addition to advertising in the newsletter, it may help to place a banner ad on the newsletter's Web site or other marketing materials sent by the creator of the newsletter. For instance, a business-to-business company that sells restaurant supplies may want to place ads in the e-newsletter sent out by *Nation's Restaurant News*. The same company may feature ads in the *Nation's Restaurant News* trade journal and Web site.

SEARCH ENGINE OPTIMIZATION

When individuals look for specific information or products on the Internet, they often begin by accessing a search engine. In fact, nearly 80 percent of all Web traffic begins at a search engine.[35] Therefore, one key marketing goal is to make sure that a company's name or brand is one of the first ones listed when a person performs a search. **SEO**, or **search engine optimization**, is the process of increasing the probability of a particular company's Web site emerging from a search.

SEO can be reached in one of three ways. The first is through a paid search insertion that comes up when certain products or information are sought. Companies can speed this process by registering with various search engines in order to have the site indexed. Even paying for insertions takes time. It can take months for a site to be listed prominently.

The second approach is to increase identification through the natural, or organic, emergence of the site. The idea is to develop efficient and effective organic results that will arise from the natural search process. Each search engine uses a slightly different set of algorithms to generate results. At the same time, these programs identify key phrases that match what the person types into the search box. To be listed first in an organic search requires time and effort. When a Web site is first built, it is unlikely that the site will emerge at the top of the search results. It takes time for the search engines to locate the site.

Some studies suggest that the impact of organic listings can be impressive. For sites that come up on the first page of a search or within the top 10, Web traffic increases ninefold. For second- and third-page listings, Web traffic increases sixfold. In terms of sales, being a top 10 listing has resulted in a 42 percent increase in sales the first month and a 100 percent increase the second month.[36]

The third approach is to use paid search ads. Paid search advertising can be small text boxes that pop up when a particular word is typed in or it can be paid link boxes at the top or side of a search result. Search advertising now accounts for 40 percent of online advertising dollars. More money has been shifted to search advertising, because it is more effective than regular online advertising. The typical click-through rate for online advertising is around 0.2 percent; for search advertising it is around 5 percent.[37]

Many dollars are being spent on search engine optimization. Although the early results are impressive, it is important to remember that SEO should be considered a long-term investment. The effects do not occur quickly. Getting into the top 10 listings of a search can take months or years. It requires optimizing content, programming, and code that will be picked up by search engines.

Finally, there is a danger. As more dollars are spent on search advertising, it will be become more cluttered and expensive. The potential exists that Web browsers will begin to ignore them just as they do other forms of advertising.

VIRAL MARKETING

Technology has created another new form of interactive marketing—*viral marketing*. **Viral marketing** is preparing a marketing message that in some way is passed from one consumer to another. A viral campaign can take the form of an e-mail or it can be a video that is posted to a personal blog and passed through to other blogs or site visitors. It is a form of advocacy or word-of-mouth endorsement marketing. Viral marketing takes place as one customer passes along a message to other potential buyers. The term *viral* is derived from the image of a person being infected with the marketing message and then spreading it to friends, like a virus. The major difference, however, is that the customer voluntarily sends the message to others.

Viral marketing messages may include advertisements, hyperlinked promotions, online newsletters, streaming videos, and various games. For instance, Blue Marble created a viral marketing program for Scope mouthwash. Consumers were able to send a customized, animated e-mail "kiss" to their friends. The attached marketing message reinforced the brand message that Scope brings people "kissably close." People who received the e-mail kiss could then forward the message to someone else. Scope's tracking technology indicated that most people who received an e-mail kiss forwarded the message. Mazda created a viral marketing campaign that included a video clip attachment about parking cars—a Mazda, of course—and the differences between males and females. The clip and link were passed on to thousands and sparked an international debate on blogs and in other forums about male and female parking capabilities. Globally, the viral marketing campaign generated over a million views in less than a month.[38]

Figure 9.9 provides some suggestions on how to create successful viral campaigns. The viral message must *focus on the product or business* so it is not lost. Mazda's campaign focused on parking cars; Scope's campaign focused on the importance of good breath for a kiss. The marketing team must determine *why an individual would want to pass the message along* or tell friends about it. OfficeMax created a viral campaign close to the Christmas holiday season that centered around a quartet of dancing elves with cutout photos pasted on their bodies. Visitors to the special micro-site were encouraged to paste their pictures on the elves and pass it along to friends. The viral campaign drew more than 110 million visitors, because it was unique and it provided something that people wanted to pass along to others. Even the *Today Show* and *Good Morning America* created their own dancing holiday greetings for viewers.

Individuals must have an *incentive* to pass the message along. One incentive is to create a message with entertainment value. Or, the incentive can be financial, such as free merchandise or a discount if the message is passed along to friends who make a purchase, log onto a Web site, or register for an e-newsletter. The incentive could also just be the campaign's uniqueness. A message that can be *personalized* has a great chance of being sent on.

With the many forms of interactive marketing available to companies, some believe viral marketing campaigns have lost some of their luster. Consumers may also have lost their enthusiasm and are less willing to pass along messages. It is important, therefore, to track the results of a viral campaign and to analyze the resulting data to determine what works and what does not.[39]

Your mom just bought a portable CD player. It's time to move on.

Introducing the RCA LYRA Personal Digital Player
Make your own CD-quality mixes by downloading music files and CD tracks from your PC. It's digital Skip Free™ memory music to go. So you're not just keeping up with the times, you're keeping one step ahead of Mom.

RCA Changing Entertainment. Again. www.lyrazone.com

Source: Courtesy of RCA.

Teenagers are a prime target for a viral campaign.

◆ Focus on the product or business.	◆ Offer an incentive.
◆ Determine why individuals would want to pass the message along.	◆ Make it personal.
	◆ Track the results and analyze the data.

FIGURE 9.9
Keys to Successful Viral Marketing Campaigns

WEB SITE DESIGN ISSUES

The primary Web site design issues are to make sure that the site functions properly and that it can serve as a springboard for interactive marketing programs. E-commerce companies spend an average of $100 to acquire each new customer, and some companies spend up to $500.[40] It may appear that developing an effective Web site is cheap; however, it is not. As a result, it is essential that company leaders specify the key function to be served by the Web site before it is created. The site should be designed to effectively support the function that is to be provided. If the primary function is e-commerce, then the site should be easy for customers to navigate. It must also be simple for customers to select products and place orders.

A Web site should match the constituency it serves. Too often, a site is designed by a computer whiz who likes fancy graphics and images, but the users of the site hate it because they cannot find what they are looking for or the pages take too long to load. Figure 9.10 offers some tips on how to create winning Web sites.

The high usage of search engines to locate products, brands, and companies has led to changes in the ways Web sites are designed. A search engine often will direct an individual straight to the page with the product on it. The front page will be skipped entirely. Therefore, it is important to design each page of the Web site as if it is the front page and the consumer is coming through on that page. Menus should be available to allow the site visitor to easily access other parts of the site. Brand awareness and marketing messages must be reinforced at every level.

INTERNATIONAL IMPLICATIONS

One of the major advantages e-commerce has over brick and-mortar retail stores is the ability to reach consumers everywhere, even in other countries. Unfortunately, some online companies are forced to turn away international orders because they do not have processes in place to fill the orders. Therefore, although the Internet makes it possible to sell items in an international marketplace, many companies are not prepared to go global. Many obstacles to selling across national boundaries exist, including communications barriers, cultural differences, global shipping problems due to a lack of sufficient infrastructure, and varying degrees of Internet capabilities in other countries.[41]

Shipping Issues

One key to the effective launch of a global e-commerce site is preparing to make international shipments. Air transport is affordable for smaller products; DHL Worldwide Express, FedEx, and UPS offer excellent shipping options. Larger merchandise normally is shipped by some type of freight forwarder, who finds the best mode of delivery, from ships to trucks to rail. Both air transport companies and freight forwarders offer specialized logistics

FIGURE 9.10
Tips to Creating Winning Web Sites

- The Web site should follow a strategic purpose such as to acquire new customers, serve existing customers, or to cross-sell goods and services.
- Make the Web site easy to access and quick to load.
- Written content should be precise with short words, short sentences, and short paragraphs.
- Remember that content is the key to success, not fancy graphics and design.
- Be certain graphics support content, and do not detract from it.

- Make some type of marketing offer to encourage a response.
- Ask for site evaluation.
- Provide easy-to-use navigation links on every page.
- Use gimmicks such as moving icons or flashing banners to gain attention at the beginning but do not use them deeper in the Web site.
- Change the Web site on a regular basis to keep individuals coming back.
- Measure results continually, especially designs and offers.

Source: Based on Ray Jutkins, "13 Ideas That Could Lead to Successful Web Marketing," *Advertising Age's Business Marketing* 84, no. 6 (June 1999), p. 27.

software and provide the proper documentation and forms to meet the importing and exporting regulations in every country they serve. Internet companies must follow local exporting and importing laws.

Payment Methods

Shipping arrangements are not the only concern. Payment mechanisms must also be addressed. Each country has a different currency, and methods of payment also vary. For example, in Europe debit cards are preferred to credit cards. Europe also has a high rate of credit card theft, which increases the risks associated with accepting them.

Communication Issues

Another task in the international arena is developing a Web site that appeals to the audience in each country. This includes adding information that someone in another country would need, such as the country code for telephone numbers. It also requires removing or changing any colors, words, or images that might be offensive to a particular group of people in another country.

New globalization software has been developed for companies expanding into other countries. One software package translates an English-language Web site into a large number of foreign languages. Another valuable feature that the software offers is "cultural adaptation," which adjusts a Web site's terminology, look, and feel to suit local norms. The software also has a feature in which the content that is developed in one location can easily be deployed to all sites around the world. This provides a more consistent look to the Web sites, without someone spending time modifying every foreign site. Such software makes it easier to create a Web site prepared in the proper native language that also conforms to local customs.[42]

Technology Issues

The technical side of international e-commerce remains a difficult challenge. Software compatibility is an unresolved technical issue. Eventually, the hope is that these various technologies will be merged into one system. Currently, the bandwidth for handling Internet traffic varies considerably. Information technology (IT) people must be involved in every step of an internationalization process in order to overcome all of the potential technical glitches.

Another major key to successful global e-commerce is a coherent IMC strategy utilizing local input from the various countries involved. The brand on an Internet site must be consistent from one country to the next. Each site should also consistently present the company's primary marketing message. For IBM, this meant using local companies in each country to design individual Web sites and provide the information used on each site. To ensure consistency, IBM designs the main marketing messages at its central office, but then local companies translate the messages and add reseller contact and pricing information.

In the future, the growth of international e-commerce will continue to rise. Firms that get in on the ground floor are likely to enjoy a major marketing advantage.

SUMMARY

Increased usage of the Internet by both consumers and businesses has led many marketing teams to develop a Web site or Internet presence. The key is to identify the functions that the Web site should perform. This chapter explained how a Web site can be integrated into the overall integrated marketing communications plan.

The primary marketing functions performed by various Web sites include advertising, sales support, customer service, public relations, and e-commerce. An e-commerce Web site includes a catalog, a shopping cart, and a payment collection method. In e-commerce and other Internet ventures, customers must feel the process is secure and be enticed to change their buying habits. Three incentives that help people alter buying patterns are financial incentives, greater convenience, and added value.

The Internet changes the traditional ways that buyers and sellers deal with each other. In business-to-business markets, field salespeople have traditionally called on customers and prospects. Information is shared, prices are negotiated, and orders are taken. On the Internet, buyers can purchase directly from suppliers. Middlemen can be eliminated. Buyers can obtain quotes from a number of vendors and obtain product information from each, all on the Internet. Although it saves the selling company money in terms of sales calls, it also risks losing customers. Loyalty and strong relationships are endangered as buyers search the Web to meet corporate needs.

The Internet blurs many internal functional boundaries. An effective Web site can do more than advertise and send sales messages; it can also provide public relations announcements, offer press releases to the media, talk about the company, provide answers to frequently asked questions, provide information to investors, dispense product catalogs complete with product descriptions and prices, take orders from customers, process payments, receive e-mail messages, handle customer service queries, and entertain Web viewers.

The primary goal of any online program is to expand and enhance the message portrayed by the company's IMC plan. Careful attention must be paid to issues of brand image and loyalty. Web sites must be designed to support selling efforts and customer service programs as well as deliver consumer promotions of value to potential buyers. Brand spiraling may be used to combine the Internet program with advertising in traditional media. The quality of a Web site is a primary factor in the success of the entire Internet program. Many company leaders are beginning to grasp the potential of these marketing efforts as interest and activity on the Web continue to grow.

International markets may also be served by e-commerce enterprises, especially when cultural differences, shipping problems, and Internet capability problems can be solved. Information technology departments will play a key role in solving the Internet problems. Shipping issues and language differences also require attention in this lucrative and growing marketplace.

KEY TERMS

Webmaster   The person who manages a firm's Web site.

e-active marketing   The two major components of Internet marketing: e-commerce and interactive marketing.

e-commerce   Selling goods and services on the Internet.

FAQs (frequently asked questions)   Questions people have about various items or services.

cyberbait   Some type of lure or attraction that brings people to a Web site.

interactive marketing   Individualizing and personalizing Web content and e-mail messages for various consumers.

brand spiraling   The practice of using traditional media to promote and attract consumers to a Web site.

blogs   Online musings by an individual or group; the term is derived from *Web logs.*

search engine optimization (SEO)   The process of increasing the probability of a particular company's Web site emerging from a search.

viral marketing   An advertisement that is tied to an e-mail or other form of online communication in which one person passes on the advertisement or e-mail to other consumers.

REVIEW QUESTIONS

1. Define e-commerce. What are the common components of e-commerce programs?

2. What is cyberbait? What are the three main forms of cyberbait?

3. What concerns do some consumers still have about e-commerce?

4. What benefits do e-commerce programs offer to business-to-business operations?

5. What is interactive marketing?

6. What four forms of online advertising are used by marketing teams?

7. What is brand spiraling?

8. What is a blog? How can blogs be used in marketing communication programs?

9. How can online social networks be used to supplement advertising and communication tactics?

10. Describe consumer-generated advertising.

11. Identify and describe three elements of an effective e-mail campaign in marketing.

12. What is meant by the term search engine optimization (SEO)? How can it be accomplished?

13. What is viral marketing? What is the goal of a viral marketing program?

14. What tactics should companies avoid in designing Web sites? What should they do to make effective Web pages?

15. What challenges must be overcome to establish an international e-commerce operation?

CRITICAL THINKING EXERCISES

Discussion Questions

1. What types of goods or services have you purchased online during the past year? Have your parents purchased anything online? If so, compare your purchases and attitudes toward buying via the Internet with theirs. If neither you nor your parents have used the Internet to make purchases, why not?

2. Access four different Web sites for one of the following products. Locate the FAQ section. Was the FAQ section difficult to find? How is the FAQ section organized? Does it provide effective answers for questions? Do the four sites have similar questions listed?

   a. Antivirus software

   b. Cosmetic surgery

   c. Automobile parts

   d. Cameras

   e. Financial services

3. Many people are concerned about credit card security. Interview five people of various ages and genders. Does age or gender make any difference in the person's feelings, especially about the fear of using a credit card to make purchases over the Internet? Are there specific products or Web sites that people do not trust? More important, how do you judge whether a Web site provides the necessary credit security?

4. First Energy Corporation, the nation's 12th largest utility, purchases about 30 percent of its coal via the Internet. The purchasing process, which used to take 60 days to complete, has been compressed to just 2 weeks. Bidding takes place on a single day, and suppliers know within 2 to 3 days whether they have won the order.[43] What risks does First Energy take in purchasing coal over the Internet? How can those risks be minimized? Why would a supplier want to sell coal over the Internet instead of developing a strong personal relationship with First Energy Corporation?

5. Interview 10 individuals of different ages about blogs. What percent have read, launched, or participated in blogging on the Internet? What was each person's motivation?

6. Online social networks exist for almost any purpose. What motivates individuals to be a part of a social network? What are the pros and cons of joining a social network?

7. Have you ever participated in a viral marketing campaign? If so, discuss why you participated and your evaluation of the viral campaign from the company or brand's perspective. If you have not participated in a viral campaign, what type of incentive would it take for you to participate? How effective do you think viral campaigns are with consumers in your market segment?

INTEGRATED LEARNING EXERCISES

1. Best Buy was a late e-commerce entrant, but it has developed a strong e-commerce component. The key to Best Buy's success, according to Barry Judge, vice president of marketing, is, "We do a lot of one-to-one marketing. We're not overly focused on where the consumers buy." The Web site carries every product that Best Buy stocks. It uses personalized services, along with convenient pickup and fair return policies to entice consumers to shop. Consumers can purchase items on the Internet and either have them shipped directly to them or pick them up at the closest store. Shoppers can use the Internet to see if Best Buy stocks a particular item, to determine what the item costs, and to gather product information. What is the advantage of this strategy? Access the Web site at **www.bestbuy.com**. Evaluate it in terms of ease of use and product information, and then locate the Best Buy closest to you. Next, access Circuit City's Web site at **www.circuitcity.com**. Compare it to Best Buy's site. Select a product, such as a camcorder, to compare the two Web sites.

2. Pick one of the following product categories and access the Web sites of two companies that sell the product. What types of financial incentives are offered on each company's Web site to encourage you to purchase? What about the other two types of incentives, greater convenience and added value?

What evidence do you see for them? Compare and contrast the two companies in terms of incentives offered.

   a. Contacts or eyeglasses

   b. Water skis

   c. Jeans

   d. Computers

   e. Camping supplies

3. The three main companies businesses use to ship small packages either overnight or 2-day delivery are FedEx, UPS, and the U.S. Postal Service. Access the Web sites of each shipping solution provider: **www.fedex.com**, **www. ups.com**, and **www.usps.gov**. What delivery guarantees does each offer? Which site is the most user-friendly? Which site appears to offer the best customer service? In looking at the different functions of a Web site discussed in this chapter, indicate the function for which each Web site was designed.

4. Web sites serve a number of different functions. Access the following sites. What is the primary function of each? For each site, list other functions it offers.

   a. Travelocity (**www.travelocity.com**)

   b. Trebnick Systems (**www.trebnick.com**)

   c. Wells Fargo Bank (**www.wellsfargo.com**)

d. WeddingChannel.com (**www.weddingchannel.com**)

e. Bluefly (**www.bluefly.com**)

5. Customer interactive software is an important part of many Web sites. Access the following two companies that sell interactive software. What capabilities does each software package offer? What other services are available?

a. Escalate RetailEs (**www.escalate.com**)

b. Intervoice (**www.intervoice.com**)

6. Blogs provide opportunities for both individuals and businesses to share information, thoughts, and opinions. Go to Google Blog Search at **http://blogsearch.google.com**. Type in a topic that you are interested in exploring that is related to advertising and marketing communications, such as "advertising to children." Locate three blogs on the topic you chose. Discuss who initiated the blog and the value of the information on the blog.

7. Go to the front page of MySpace at **www.myspace.com**. What information is on the main page? Access one of the menu pages and discuss what information is provided. If you have accessed MySpace in the past, discuss how often you go to the site and what types of activities you participate in while there. If you have not accessed MySpace in the past, discuss why you have not and after looking at the site identify areas that may be of interest to you. Notice that MySpace features advertising. How effective is it? How do you feel about the advertising that is on the site?

8. Access each of the following search engines. For each one, discuss how it handles paid search advertising when you type in a search, such as "running shoes." What ads do you see as display ads and what ads are part of the search results? Discuss the differences among the four search engines. Which one do you like the best? Why?

a. Google (**www.google.com**)

b. Yahoo (**www.yahoo.com**)

c. Altavista (**www.altavista.com**)

d. AOL Search (**http://search.aol.com**)

STUDENT PROJECT

Creative Corner

Suppose Bluefly wants to enhance the company's brand name and Internet presence. Further, assume that the company's marketing department has asked you to be an Internet advertising consulting. Access the Web site at **www.bluefly.com**. Once you feel comfortable with the company, prepare the following creative material and information for Bluefly.

1. Bluefly wants to use brand spiraling to increase brand awareness and enhance the brand name. Outline a media plan that you believe will accomplish this objective.

2. The company is interested in placing an advertisement on a social network, such as YouTube or MySpace. Advise them as to which social network would be the best. Then design the display ad that should be placed on the site.

3. The company believes a viral marketing campaign would be effective in drawing new visitors to the site. Design a viral marketing campaign.

4. Search engine optimization seems to be an effective tool for driving individuals to the company's site. Which search engine should be used? Identify five key words that you believe Bluefly should advertise. Design the display or listing ad that should be used.

CASE 1 SOMETHING SALTY FOR THE HOT TUB MARKET

Bernie Johnson was about to begin a new business venture. After working for years in the pool and spa industry as a salesperson in a local store, he decided to launch his own line of products, a series of hot tubs with the brand name Salt Spa.

Bernie was convinced that the future of the hot tub marketplace was in selling saltwater systems, actually saline-based, rather than traditional tubs using chemicals and chlorine. Saltwater systems work by creating their own chlorine. An electric current passes through saltwater in a chlorinator cell, which splits the salt into sodium and chloride. It then releases a chlorine gas that dissolves in the water. This process not only sterilizes the water, it prevents the growth of algae.

Saline-based systems offer a number of benefits. First, the water is not as harsh, so it does not hurt a person's eyes. It is also less irritating to the skin. It feels softer and does not create drying effects on the skin after the person leaves the tub. People who have reactions to chlorinated tubs are generally reacting not to the chlorine, but to other chemicals and by-products. They generally do not encounter the same problem lounging in a saline hot tub. Also, swimming suits worn in salt-based hot tubs last much longer than do those exposed to chlorine.

A saline-based system means the consumer does not have to buy expensive and dangerous chemicals. Instead, the maintenance process is adding common salt to the system, and it is not added often, because the system recycles the salt. Sometimes it requires adding acid to balance the pH levels. In essence, saline hot tubs are more environmentally friendly. In general, a saltwater tub is safer, less expensive to maintain over time, healthier, and better for the environment.

The major disadvantage of a saline-based tub is the cost. The price of installing a saline system to an existing chlorine hot tub is high. Doing so also voids any factory warranty. When running salt through a hot tub filter, the consumer must be very conscientious about cleaning the filter. Also, the consumer must also watch out for any corrosion, which is the primary problem when trying to maintain a saltwater hot tub. It is similar to what happens to a car after several winters. The salt from the road is like acid on the hull of a new car.

Bernie intended to sell both salt-based hot tubs and conversion kits. His primary markets were going to be: (1) online buyers through his Web site, (2) any retail outlets that would carry his line, and (3) spas and other places offering hot tubs to clients.

The challenges to his new business would be to build a recognizable brand, make inroads with retailers, and find ways to reach business-to-business clients. Hot tubs are sold as primarily luxury items, which means that the people who buy

Swimming pools and hot tubs are sold primarily to higher-income consumers.

them have higher incomes and live in nicer homes. Finding ways to reach them was one key.

Bernie had to make sure that retail sales people did not say that a saltwater hot tub system is chemical free—a myth perpetuated on many Web sites. Salt is a chemical compound. It is not on the periodic table. When the electrodes separate the salt, it becomes two chemicals, which means the tub is not chemical free.

Attracting spas and other businesses to buy saline-based systems would require both an Internet presence and a small sales force to make calls, possibly one or two salespeople at first. Still, he was excited, because Bernie believed he was getting in on the ground floor of a major change in the marketplace.

Sources: www.home-repair.com/Saltwater_hot-tubs.html, accessed January 15, 2008; Anne Clark, "Saline Versus Chlorine: Which Is Better for Your Pool or Hot Tub?" (**www.ezinearticles.com**, accessed January 15, 2008).

1. Can Salt Spas be sold through a traditional e-commerce program?

2. What should be the major features of the Salt Spa Web site?

3. Describe how a blog, social network, or e-mail program could be used to drive traffic to the Salt Spa Web site.

4. What types of relationships must Bernie build to make sure his products are sold in any new home being built with a spa room? How can his Internet program help him in this area?

SHELLY'S CONNECTION

K. Michele Kacmar (who goes by Shelly) loved love. She enjoyed introducing people to see if any kind of spark would fire. She had "set up" several friends who wound up dating and even marrying each other. Shelly's other major talent was Web design. These two skills led Shelly to believe her calling was to set up an Internet dating service. She created one for the Los Angeles area, where she lived, called "Shelly's Connection."

Shelly's Connection had two twists. First, the site was designed only for local people, those living in Los Angeles and the surrounding counties. She was not trying to set up a national service. Second, besides simply making high-tech introductions, Shelly's Connection offered social events. These included evening "meet ups," where people sipping coffee or soft drinks circulated through the room and visited with 5 to 10 potential dating partners in a 90-minute time span. Also, Shelly's Connection had singles parties and mixers where people who had expressed interest in three or four potential dating partners could pay a cover charge and then attend the event; light snacks were served, dance music was played at a volume low enough for people to talk, and a cash bar was available. Shelly's marketing idea was to create a "fully integrated" dating program.

Internet dating services are not new. Two of the more popular ones are eHarmony and Chemistry.com. They are plagued by several problems. First, unless properly screened, married people sign up to start dating "on the side." Second,

some people confuse dating services with online escort services and prostitution rings. Third, most dating services offer nationwide prospects rather than just local arrangements. Sifting through all of the clients to find one close to home can be a problem. Fourth, some people shy away from the services because they feel like joining makes them seem "desperate."

To combat these problems, Shelly believed a high-quality advertising campaign would be needed. The ad should clearly spell out what type of service she offered, warn away married people, and emphasize that dating and meeting people are time-consuming. Shelly's Connection was set up to offer convenience, help people who want to use their spare time wisely, and have fun. Armed with some venture capital from local investors, Shelly's Connection began operations. Time would tell if love would bloom and Shelly would enjoy a successful Internet business operation.

1. Are there any other potential problems that Shelly has not considered in creating her company?

2. How would the use of a social network be helpful to Shelly?

3. Create the ad copy for Shelly's Connection that features the Web site address. Write an effective tagline for the ads.

4. How could e-mail be used to enhance Shelly's business?

ENDNOTES

1. **www.narcissurfing.com**, accessed January 12, 2008.

2. Heidi Gautschi, "Search in Any Language," *EContent* 28, no. 5 (May 2005), p. 29; "Google Is Standing on the Brink of Global Dominance," *Marketing Week* (April 28, 2005), p. 31; Thomas Claburn and Tony Kontzer, "Google Wants a Piece of the Business Market," *InformationWeek*, no. 1040 (May 23, 2005), p. 29; Mathew Creamer and Kris Oser, "Google Breaks Down and Decides to Advertise," *Advertising Age* 76, no. 18 (May 2, 2005), p. 3.

3. Kimberly Palmer, "Shop Online for Everything," *U.S. News & World Report* 143, no. 21 (December 17, 2007), p. 61.

4. David Sparrow, "Get 'em to Bite," *Catalog Age* 20, no. 4 (April 2003), pp. 35–36.

5. Christine Dugas, "E-Retailers Increase Alternative Pay Options," *USA Today* (November 13, 2007).

6. Elisabeth Goodridge, "E-Businesses Hope to Learn That Edu-Commerce Pays," *InformationWeek*, no. 877 (February 25, 2002), pp. 76–77.

7. Maya Dollarhide, "Bluefly Buzz Bags Shoppers," *Incentive* 180, no. 1 (June 2006), p. 10.

8. Lisa Cervini, "Free Shipping Offers Fueling Online Sales," *This Week in Consumer Electronics* 20, no. 24 (November 21, 2005), p. 16.

9. Nanette Byrnes, "More Clicks at the Bricks," *BusinessWeek*, no. 4063 (December 17, 2007), pp. 50–52.

10. Jeffrey Gangemi, "Secrets of Online Business Success," *BusinessWeek Online*, (September 6, 2006), p. 18.

11. David Sparrow, "Get 'em to Bite," *Catalog Age* 20, no. 4 (April 2003), pp. 35–36.

12. Mark Del Franco, "Mailers Say, Webward Ho!" *Catalog Age* 19, no. 4 (March 15, 2002), pp. 1–3.

13. Paul A. Pavlou, Huigang Liang, and Yajiong Xue, "Understanding and Mitigating Uncertainty in Online Exchange Relationships: A Principal-Agent Perspective," *MIS Quarterly* 31, mo. 1 (March 2007), pp. 105–36.

14. Suzanne Beame, "Consumer Confidence in Online Shopping Sites is on the Rise," *New Media Age* (November 15, 2007), p. 15.

15. Nanette Byrnes, "More Clicks at the Bricks," *BusinessWeek*, no. 4063 (December 17, 2007), pp. 50–52.

16. Bob Donath, "Web Could Boost Branding in B-to-B Marketing," *Marketing News* 32, no. 10 (May 11, 1998), p. 6.

17. Carol Patton, "Marketers Promote Online Traffic Through Traditional Media," *Advertising Age's Business Marketing* 84, no. 8 (August 1999), p. 40.

18. Doug Harper, "Net Gains, Net Pains," *Industrial Distribution* 89, no. 9 (September 2000), pp. E4–6.

19. Jeff Sweat and Rick Whiting, "Instant Marketing," *InformationWeek*, no. 746 (August 2, 1999), pp. 18–20.

20. Rory J. Thompson, "Can't Skip This: Consumers Acclimating to Internet Ads," *Brandweek* 48, no. 7 (December 31, 2007), p. 5; "Word of Mouse," *Economist* 385, no. 8554 (November 10, 2007), pp. 77–78.

21. Catherine Holahan and Robert D. Hof, "So Many Ads, So Few Clicks," *BusinessWeek*, no. 4058 (November 12, 2007), p. 38.

22. Ibid.

23. Abbey Klaaseen, "When Web Branding Works," *Advertising Age* 78, no. 28 (July 16, 2007), pp. 1, 33.

24. Rory J. Thompson, "Study: Chat Rooms Influence Holiday Purchases," *Marketing Power* (**www.marketingpower.com/content/ OPTEDRELEASE12–06.pdf**), December 13, 2007.

25. Lorrie Grant, "Retailers Hope Shoppers Buy Blogs as the Place to Go," *USA Today,* August 25, 2005, Money Section, p. 5b.

26. Kim Hart, "Online Networking Goes Small, and Sponsors Follow," *Washington Post,* December 29, 2007, p. D01.

27. Lisa Lockwood, "Talking to a Generation: Brands Turn to YouTube to Spread the Message," *Women's Daily Wear* 193, no. 114 (May 29, 2007), pp. 1, 9–10.

28. "Word of Mouse," *Economist* 385, no. 8554 (November 10, 2007), pp. 77–78.

29. Stuart Elliott, "Student's Ad Gets a Remake, and Makes the Big Time," *New York Times,* (**www.nytimes.com/2007/10/26/business/ media/26appleweb.html**), October 26, 2007.

30. Ibid.

31. Brian Quinton, "Beyond Page Reviews," *Direct* 19, no. 6 (June 1, 2007), pp. 28–30; **www.circuitcity.com**, accessed February 21, 2008.

32. "Questex Media Launches AllThings HiDef.com," *Response* 15, no. 3, p. 10.

33. Mary E. Morrison, "Integration a Powerful Tool," *BtoB* 92, no. 12 (September 24, 2007), p. 28.

34. "Re-Marketing Helps Boost Online Shoppers' Baskets," *Data Strategy* 3, no. 7 (May 2007), p. 9.

35. "Problem Solved," *BtoB* 92, no. 15 (November 12, 2007), p. 21.

36. Ibid.

37. Josh Quittner, Jessi Hempel, and Lindsay Blakely, "The Battle for Your Social Circle," *Fortune* 156, no. 10 (November 26, 2007), pp. 11–13.

38. Justin Kirty, "Getting the Bug," *Brand Strategy,* no. 184 (July–August 2004), p. 33.

39. Brian Morrissey, "The Rules of Viral Web Success, At Least for Now," *Adweek* 49, no. 1 (January 7, 2008), p. 13.

40. Donna L. Hoffman and Thomas P. Novak, "How to Acquire Customers on the Web," *Harvard Business Review* 78, no. 3 (May–June 2000), pp. 179–85.

41. Lynda Radosevich, "Going Global Overnight," *InfoWorld* 21, no. 16 (April 19, 1999), pp. 1–3.

42. "The Worldly Web," *CFO* 19, no. 7 (June 2003), p. 30.

43. Tobi Elkin, "Best Buy Takes Cue from Retail Shops," *Advertising Age* 71, no. 10 (March 6, 2000), p. 8.

10

Alternative Marketing

RED BULL'S BUZZ

In today's active world, people need help. At least, that would be the position presented by any of the companies that sell energy drinks. No longer will simple soft drinks serve the purpose of waking people up and getting them moving. Instead, Red Bull and other products are designed to jolt a consumer into action.

Red Bull's ingredient list begins with taurine. Taurine occurs naturally in the human body. Red Bull helps to replace the taurine that is lost during conditions of high stress or physical exertion, which, in turn helps the person recover more quickly. Carbohydrate glucuronolactone, which also is found naturally in the human body, is added to help with detoxification processes as well as support the body in eliminating waste substances. The amount of caffeine in a serving of Red Bull is nearly double the amount present in Mountain Dew, which is perceived by many as the highest-energy soft drink. Red Bull also contains acesulfame K, sucrose, glucose, B-vitamins, and aspartame, which is well-known as the key ingredient in NutraSweet. The company's marketing materials emphasize that the formula took 3 years to develop. The 8.3-ounce canned drink was first launched in Australia in 1984. Red Bull tastes sweet and lemony, and as one fan put it, "like a melted lollypop." The price of a single can is typically much higher than a 16-ounce bottle of soda.[1]

The new product clearly struck a chord in some markets. Those pulling all-nighters for school, work, or partying, as well as those engaged in extreme sports quickly gravitated to Red Bull. By 2001, the drink held a 70 percent share of the U.S. market for similar drinks and annual sales topped $140 million.

Red Bull's entry into the United States is viewed by many marketing experts as one of the first and classic uses of alternative and buzz marketing. Red Bull's brand management team began by identifying a target audience—those who would most likely want the buzz created by an energy drink. One key constituent group would be college students. Consequently, the company gave free samples of the drink to college and university students, who were encouraged to throw big parties where cases of Red Bull would be provided.

Red Bull's marketing team created a group of "consumer educators" who traveled to various locations giving out free samples. The brand managers also organized and sponsored extreme sporting events, such as skateboarding and cliff diving, for consumer educators to attend. The concept was that the participants and fans of these types of sports had buzz-seeking desires and an interest in products that were positioned as "sleek, sweet, and full-throttle."[2] From the

Chapter Objectives

After reading this chapter, you should be able to answer the following questions:

- **How** do buzz marketing, guerrilla marketing, product placements and branded entertainment, and lifestyle marketing fit into an IMC program?

- **What** is the difference between a product placement and branded entertainment?

- **What** conditions must be present in order to develop a successful guerrilla marketing program?

- **How** can alternative marketing methods be integrated with in-store programs?

- **Why** is it important to attempt to strengthen customer brand communities?

parties and the extreme sports, word-of-mouth communications about the brand spread. The buzz-seeking target audience became Red Bull's first customer base.

The traditional soft drink companies were slow to react. Eventually, Pepsi created a competing product called Adrenaline Rush; Coca-Cola entered the market with KMX; and Anheuser Busch developed 180, which is supposed to turn a person's energy level around by 180 degrees. Pepsi may be less concerned with Red Bull due to its ownership of Gatorade. Still, both Coke and Pepsi have concentrated efforts on garnering shelf space in convenience stores and superstores.

More recently, Red Bull's marketing efforts have been expanded to include more traditional forms of advertising. At the same time, endorsers tend to be edgier figures, such as famed kayaker Tao Berman, and the commercials themselves remain offbeat. Red Bull creator Dietrich Mateschitz summarized it best, "If we don't create a market, it doesn't exist." And $1.6 billion later, it is clear that he has a point.

"

OVERVIEW

Traditional mass media advertising faces many challenges. Although many, if not most, company leaders are not ready to abandon radio, television, magazines, newspapers, and outdoor programs, they also know that consumers are increasingly adept at tuning out these venues. Even the Internet is beginning to suffer from increasing clutter.

As a result, alternative media programs are on the rise. Increasing numbers of dollars are spent finding ways to reach potential customers in new and innovative formats. And, as suggested by the Red Bull experience, it is possible to begin an advertising and promotional program relying heavily on these new approaches.

Ugg is the brand name for an Australian company that sells big, bulky sheepskin boots. The company's marketing team wondered if it would be possible to get fashion-conscious consumers to even consider the boots. Instead of advertising to the fashion-conscious consumer, Ugg's marketing team targeted high-profile fashion influencers. They successfully contacted and convinced Kate Hudson and Sarah Jessica Parker to wear the items. Then Oprah Winfrey praised Uggs on one of her shows. At that point, the boots became fashionable and retailers couldn't keep them in stock. Sales reached $30 million in just a few months, without a single commercial being run.[3]

In this chapter, four main topics are presented. First, the four main types of alternative media programs are identified: buzz marketing, guerrilla marketing, product placements and branded entertainment, and lifestyle marketing. Next, a series of tactics associated with alternative media plans are described. Third, the nature of in-store marketing is described. Finally, brand communities are discussed. The international implications of these new forms of alternative media are also presented.

ALTERNATIVE MEDIA PROGRAMS

Developing alternative media programs requires creativity and imagination. The goal is to identify new places where a consumer's path intersects with a brand's presence. Then a marketing message can be developed for those points. The idea is to supplement mass media advertising with more targeted media options. In essence, the goal remains the same. Marketing professionals must find ways to get noticed that reach a target audience. Alternative media programs and alternative marketing venues are widely accepted options. What exactly are the alternative media choices? Figure 10.1 lists some of the more common.

Alternative media relies on buzz, word-of-mouth, lifestyles, and times when consumers are relaxing and enjoying hobbies and events. These programs and venues are described in this chapter. Many times the programs and tactics overlap. The goal is to integrate them into one coherent program with a clear voice and message.

BUZZ MARKETING

Buzz marketing is one of the fastest growing areas in alternative media marketing. Estimated expenditures for buzz marketing are now at $1 billion annually. **Buzz marketing**, which is also known as word-of-mouth marketing, emphasizes consumers passing along information about a product. A recommendation by another person carries higher levels of credibility than does an advertisement. It is also more powerful than the words of a paid spokesperson or endorser. Buzz, or word-of-mouth, can be generated in one of the following ways:

- Consumers who truly like a brand and tell others
- Consumers who like a brand and are sponsored by a company to tell others
- Company or agency employees posing as customers of the company, telling others about the brand

FIGURE 10.1
Forms of Alternative Marketing

Alternative Media Programs
- Buzz marketing
- Product placement and branded entertainment
- Guerrilla marketing
- Lifestyle marketing

Alternative Media Venues
- Video game advertising
- In-tunnel subway advertising
- Escalator advertising
- Leaflets and brochures
- Carry-home bag advertising
- Mall signs
- Ads by fax
- Cinema advertising
- Parking lot advertising
- Airline in-flight advertising
- Carry-home menus
- Advertising on clothes
- Kiosk ads

Consumers Who Like a Brand

The ideal situation occurs when a consumer truly likes a particular brand and tells others. This can take place in person or it can occur via the Internet in chat rooms, blogs, or by e-mails. Many musical groups have gained fame and fortune through the word-of-mouth support of those who have seen the bands in bars or as part of a small concert or tour.

Sponsored Consumers

Many companies sponsor individuals as agents or advocates to introduce new products. When Procter & Gamble launched a new cleaning product called Dawn Direct Foam, a set of consumers that were called *connectors* was identified. The group, which was named Vocalpoint, consisted of 450,000 mothers who were assigned the task of starting discussions about P&G products. When Dawn Direct Foam launched, the pitch to these moms was that it would make dishwashing fun for children. Members of Vocalpoint received coupons and "fun for children" talking points. The moms quickly spread the word, increasing the sales of the new detergent by 50 percent.[4]

Sony used buzz marketing and brand advocates to launch its GPS camera. The product featured an emerging technology, and Sony's marketing department believed it was important to get people to physically try the product. The company selected 25 "ambassadors" from a pool of 2,000 applicants. The individuals chosen displayed high levels of interest in cameras, in taking pictures, and had plans to either travel or participate in sporting events. Each ambassador was given a free camera and lessons on how to use it. The Sony ambassadors were encouraged to hand out discount coupons, show the cameras to anyone who asked, and blog weekly about their adventures on the Sony micro-site. One of the ambassadors, Cheryl Gillet, described and photographed her trip to Australia, adding a map of her journey. Juxtaposed with destinations on the map were photos of beach scenes and her tanned friends in swimsuits. Even those applicants who were not selected were pleased because each was sent a 20-percent discount coupon for the GPS camera.[5]

Brand ambassadors or customer evangelists are typically individuals who already like the products that they are asked to sponsor. The company offers them incentives and rewards in exchange for advocacy. Companies select these ambassadors based on devotion to the brand and the size of their social circles. Once recruited, they are expected to deliver messages to their social circles, families, friends, reference groups, and work associates. Some are expected to develop grassroots, no- or low-cost marketing events and to promote the brand on the Internet through blogs or on social networks such as MySpace. Brand advocates are asked to be upfront and honest about their connections with the brand.

When the marketing team at Lee jeans decided to find ways to strengthen the brand's connection with younger, contemporary consumers, the company identified 1,000 brand ambassadors. Each received a free pair of One True Fit jeans, a promotional kit, a suggested list of people to contact, and a DVD. Six months later 88 percent of the agents still wore the jeans and 50 percent bought at least one more pair.[6]

Company Employees

The final group of advocates, employees posing as customers, has been used by some companies. Doing so is risky. According to the Word of Mouth Marketing Association (WOMMA), the practice is dishonest and unethical, unless the person is upfront and clearly identifies him or herself as being with the company. In the past, Wal-Mart used the tactic on a blog about two ordinary people, Laura and Jim, trekking across the Unites States in an RV staying in Wal-Mart parking lots. The blog received considerable attention, especially after *BusinessWeek* exposed Jim as a professional

Source: Courtesy of Kenneth Clow.

The House of Blues in New Orleans often generates buzz marketing activity over the Internet as well as person-to-person.

Dawn Direct Foam launched a buzz marketing campaign involving "fun for children" talking points for mom ambassadors.

Source: Courtesy of © Dorling Kindersley.

photojournalist employed by Edelman, Wal-Mart's public relations firm. Both Wal-Mart and Edelman received considerable criticism regarding the program.[7]

WOMMA provides guidelines for companies that want to generate word-of-mouth communications through its employees, agency employees, or even sponsors or agents. It encourages:

- Honesty of relationship—be honest about the relationship between consumers, advocates, and marketers.
- Honesty of opinion—be honest in presenting opinions about the brand, both good and bad.
- Honesty of identity—identify honestly who you are.[8]

Buzz Marketing Stages

Buzz marketing can be compared to a virus, consisting of three stages: inoculation, incubation, and infection.[9] The inoculation stage corresponds to the product being introduced. During incubation, the product is being used by a few innovators or trendsetters. In the infection stage, there is widespread use of the product.

Only a few companies have been successful with buzz marketing during the inoculation stage, or product introduction, such as Procter & Gamble with Dawn Direct Foam. In most cases, buzz marketing is not successful at this stage, unless it is with brand agents or brand ambassadors. It is virtually impossible to generate word-of-mouth communication from actual customers. Previous research suggests that the true customer-generated buzz occurs only after awareness of the product has developed and that awareness requires advertising through the traditional channels.[10]

Buzz Marketing Preconditions

Neither advertising nor buzz communication programs from actual customers can, by themselves, create a successful buzz program. Other conditions must exist. First, the *product* must be unique, new, or perform better than current brands. The *brand* must stand out and have distinct advantages over current products on the market. Although not essential, *memorable advertising* helps to generate buzz. The advertising must be *intriguing*, *different*, and *unique* and capture attention and generate talk among people. *Getting consumers involved* can enhance the creation of word-of-mouth communications.

Stride Sugarless Gum developed a Web site to complement the company's traditional advertising. The campaign used the tagline "Stride gum lasts a ridiculously long time." Consumers were invited to share what they would like to do for a ridiculously long time and to post photographs of these activities on the Stride micro-site developed for the Sugarless Gum.[11]

Buzz marketing works for two primary reasons. First, people trust someone else's opinion more than paid advertising. Second, people like to give their opinions. They like to share their thoughts because as human beings there is an innate desire for social interaction and a concern about the welfare of others. Also, one's ego and self-worth are elevated through sharing an opinion with others, especially, if that opinion generates happiness through satisfaction with a particular branded product.

National and international buzz will generate higher movie ticket sales.

GUERRILLA MARKETING

Historically, one of the most successful alternative media marketing programs is guerrilla marketing, as first developed by marketing guru Jay Conrad Levinson. **Guerrilla marketing** programs are designed to obtain instant results while using limited resources. The tactics rely on creativity, quality relationships, and the willingness to try unusual approaches. These programs were originally aimed at small businesses; however, now guerrilla

FIGURE 10.2
Traditional vs. Guerrilla
Marketing

Traditional Marketing	Guerrilla Marketing
◆ Requires money	◆ Requires energy and imagination
◆ Geared to large businesses with big budgets	◆ Geared to small businesses and big dreams
◆ Results measured by sales	◆ Results measured by profits
◆ Based on experience and guesswork	◆ Based on psychology and human behavior
◆ Increases production and diversity	◆ Grows through existing customers and referrals
◆ Grows by adding customers	◆ Cooperates with other businesses
◆ Obliterates the competition	◆ Aims messages at individuals and small groups
◆ Aims messages at large groups	◆ Uses marketing to gain customer consent
◆ Uses marketing to generate sales	◆ "You Marketing" that looks at how can we help "You"
◆ "Me Marketing" that looks at "My" company	

marketing tactics are found in wide array of firms. Guerrilla marketing emphasizes a combination of media, advertising, public relations, and surprise tactics to reach consumers.

Figure 10.2 compares guerrilla marketing to traditional marketing. Guerrilla marketing tends to focus on specific regions or areas. It is not a national or international campaign, and instead features personal communication. The idea is to create excitement that will spread to others by word-of-mouth. Guerrilla marketing often involves interacting with consumers, not just sending out a message. The idea is to build relationships with customers. By getting consumers to react or to do something, the program enhances the chance that the message will hit home. Advertisements are made accessible to consumers, where they live, play, and work in a way that it is noticed. The eventual relationships that evolve help create brand loyalty and positive recommendations to other consumers.

A notable example of guerrilla marketing was used by the Harley-Davidson franchise in Gloversville, New York. The company advertised a "cat shoot," to be held at the store. Local police, the Humane Society, the mayor, and the Society for Prevention of Cruelty to Animals all inquired, and the event generated front-page stories for 3 straight days in local papers. The event was actually a three-for-a-dollar paintball shoot at a 6-foot-high cartoon cat, with proceeds benefiting the local Humane Society. It was tremendously successful in helping customers find their way to the store. Although bizarre, the approach used by Van's Harley-Davidson illustrates the concept of guerrilla marketing.[12]

Guerrilla marketing should be an aggressive, grassroots approach to marketing. It promotes a one-to-one relationship with consumers through innovative, alternative means of branding. Touchmedia CEO Mickey Fung used guerrilla marketing tactics by placing more than 3,000 interactive PDA-type screens on the back of taxi cabs headrests in Shanghai, China. The touch screens play ads and videos, but passengers in the taxi can also choose the content they want to view through multiple icons on the screen. Follow-up research on the program indicated that 89 percent of the passengers accessed the screen in some way.

The location of the touch screens is ideal for companies attempting to reach wealthy Chinese consumers. Only the top 10 percent of Chinese citizens in Shanghai can afford to ride in a taxi. The passengers are mostly 21 to 49 years of age, white collar workers, and 45 percent have managerial-level jobs. Brands such as Heineken, Chivas, Virgin, Nokia and companies like Estee Lauder, Procter & Gamble, KFC, and Volkswagen have advertised on the taxi screens. More than 4 million people watched an ad while in the taxi promoting a Christina Aguilera concert in Shanghai. Of those who purchased tickets, 49 percent were reserved by individuals who used the hot line listed on the taxi touch screens.[13] The touch screens are not only an alternative media, but they are also touching consumers with an innovative approach that allows the consumer to interact and choose what they want to watch.

Guerrilla marketing not only utilizes alternative media tactics and venues; the program focuses on finding creative ways of doing things. The objective is to change the thinking process in the marketing department itself. The first step is to discover "touch points" with customers. In other words, where do the customers eat, drink, shop, hang out, and sleep? This makes it possible to reach customers at the points the product interconnects with their lives in creative and imaginative ways. Figure 10.3 identifies six reasons to use guerrilla marketing.

FIGURE 10.3
Reasons for Using Guerrilla Marketing

- To find a new way to communicate with consumers
- To interact with consumers
- To make advertising accessible to consumers
- To impact a spot market
- To create buzz
- To build relationships with consumers

Source: Based on Lin Zuo and Shari Veil, "Guerrilla Marketing and the Aqua Teen Hunger Force Fiasco," *Public Relations Quarterly* 51, no. 4 (Winter 2006–2007), pp. 8–11.

PRODUCT PLACEMENTS AND BRANDED ENTERTAINMENT

It is common knowledge in marketing that getting a product noticed has become increasingly difficult. In response, many firms have increased expenditures on product placements and branded entertainment. **Product placement** is defined as the planned insertion of a brand or product into a movie, television show, and some other media program with the purpose of influencing viewers. **Branded entertainment** is the integration of entertainment and advertising by embedding brands into the storyline of a movie, television show, or other entertainment medium.[14]

Product Placements

Product placements have been a part of motion pictures since the beginning in the 1890s. Lever Brothers placed the company's soap brand in some of the early films. In the 1930s, Buick had 10-picture deal with Warner Brothers for placements. Several tobacco companies paid actors to endorse and use the brands. Early television programs were sponsored by brands, such as the *Colgate Comedy Hour.* The biggest surge in product placement may have occurred in 1982, when Reese's Pieces were used to lure E.T. out of hiding as part of the plot of the movie E.T. The placement of the Reese's Pieces spurred a 65 percent rise in sales following the movie's release.[15]

Advertisers believe that product placements lead to increased awareness and more positive attitudes toward the brand. In a few isolated cases, sales of a brand have increased. In most instances, however, there is not an immediate impact on sales. Research by Nielsen reveals the following about product placements:[16]

- Brands placed within "emotionally engaging" television programs were recognized by 43 percent more viewers.
- Brand recognition increased 29 percent for brands place in highly enjoyed programs compared to 21 percent for commercial spots.
- Positive brand feelings increased by 85 percent for brands placed in programs compared to 75 percent for commercial spots.

One key advantage of brand placement is the low cost-per-viewer. This is especially true for movies. After a movie has finished at the cinema, it is usually converted to a DVD for movie rental. From there, it is not unusual for the movie to be converted to television for viewing on syndication outlets or one of the premium movie channels. It may also be available on TV through video-on-demand. The end result is that the movie expands beyond the cinema screen to various venues and may be seen multiple times by individuals.

The top-rated brand placement in 2007 was by Tyson Foods, which purchased a brand placement on ABC's *Extreme Makeover: Home Edition.* Tyson provided a year's supply of meat to the family featured on the show and donated 20,000 pounds of meat to the community in which the family lived. The company received highly favorable ratings for the effort. Another successful brand placement was for Sue Bee Honey. Contestants on the *Apprentice* harvested, bottled, and sold Sue Bee Honey in a supermarket. Figure 10.4 identifies the top 10 product placements on television during 2007.

Branded Entertainment

In branded entertainment, the brand is woven into the storyline of the movie or television show. For instance, in an episode of the CTC drama *The Eleventh Hour*, Nicorette was

Rank	Brand	Program	Index
1.	Tyson	*Extreme Makeover*	394
2.	Sue Bee Honey	*The Apprentice*	368
3.	Soft Scrub	*The Apprentice*	332
4.	Kraft	*Top Chef*	324
5.	Propel Fitness Water	*Work Out*	319
6.	SmartMouth	*The Apprentice*	316
7.	Nexxus	*Shear Genius*	311
8.	Second Life	*The Office*	308
9.	VISA	*What Not to Wear*	308
10.	Kenmore	*Top Chef*	306

FIGURE 10.4
Most Effective TV Brand Placements in 2007

Source: Based on Gail Schiller, "Tyson's 'Makeover' Integration Top Placement," *The Hollywood Reporter* (December 26, 2007) (**http://hollywood reporter.com/tyson**).

integrated into a story about a character trying to quit smoking. By integrating the brand into the story, it is much more noticeable to the viewing audience. The use of branded entertainment increased sharply with the rise of reality television shows where there is a lack of scripts and the focus is on creating "real world" situations. The success of branded entertainment in reality shows has led to its use in scripted television shows. Branded entertainment is now also found in novels, plays, songs, and movies.

Achieving Success with Individual Consumers

Figure 10.5 identifies the major factors that influence the success of brand placements and branded entertainment. Notice that the media used has an impact on their effectiveness. Some television programs are losing clout because of placement clutter. For instance, there were 4,349 product placements during Fox's *American Idol* shows that ran from January to May in the 2006–07 season.[17] Unless a brand was prominent, like the red plastic cups of Coca-Cola in front of the judges, most were lost in the clutter of other brands appearing on the show.

Product placements and branded entertainment work because there is no call to action. The primary goal is to increase brand awareness and liking. When a consumer's favorite actor uses a particular brand or her favorite show contains a particular brand, it becomes more likely that the individual will transfer those positive feelings to the brand.

Some consumers are more receptive to brand placements than others. People between the ages of 15 and 34 are more likely to notice brands placed in a movie or show. Also, individuals in North America and the Asia-Pacific area are more receptive than people in Europe.

When a consumer sees a brand placement of a product that he or she has purchased, it may reinforce that idea that a wise decision was made, which further validates the original purchase decision.[18]

Company Tactics

The actual manner in which a brand is placed into a movie or show is important. Brand insertions work best when they seem logical. In other words, the most effective placements are those woven into the program in such a way that it appears to be a natural part

- ◆ Media
- ◆ Supporting promotional activities
- ◆ Consumer attitudes toward placements
- ◆ Placement characteristics
- ◆ Regulations

FIGURE 10.5
Key Factors Influencing Effectiveness of Product Placement and Branded Entertainment

Source: Based on Simon Hudson and David Hudson, "Branded Entertainment: A New Advertising Technique or Product Placement in Disguise?" *Journal of Marketing Management* 22, no. 5/6 (July 2006), pp. 489–504.

of the story. Brands shown in the background that seem to be artificially inserted are not nearly as effective.

It is also important to examine the scene where the brand placement will occur. Will the viewer see the brand in a positive manner, or will it be a negative situation? For instance, in the movie *The Hoax* staring Richard Gere, McGraw-Hill is not seen in a positive light, because the star in the show deceived the publisher by proposing a fake biography of Howard Hughes.[19]

For some companies, an advantage to product placement in movies is that it bypasses most of the legislation and guidance that is intended to control advertising for children and young adults. A study of the top 25 box office movies found 32 percent were rated for viewing by adolescents and contained prominent brand placements for tobacco products. If these companies would have tried to advertise directly to teens, they would have been met with numerous regulations and severe penalties.[20]

Many companies buy advertising spots on television programs that feature product placements of the brand. Additional promotional incentives may also be offered. The goal is to move beyond recognition and liking to the actual purchase.

Budgets for product placements and branded entertainment have been increasing for several reasons. First, a brand's appeal is stronger when it is shown in a nonadvertising context. Second, the perception of what others think of a brand is important to consumers. For many it is more important than how the consumer views the brand. Seeing the brand being used in a television show, a movie, or a book makes the brand look acceptable and even desirable. Third, seeing the brand used by others provides postpurchase reassurance for individuals who have already purchased the item. Fourth, for individuals who place little value in brand names and branded products, having a brand placed in a program can provide evidence of the brand's advantages and this evidence may be strong enough for them to consider purchasing the brand. In these cases, the brand does not have to persuade the consumer of its merits directly. It does so through the acceptance and use of the brand by the actor or program.

The Media's Perspective

For moviemakers and television producers, the primary motivation behind product placements and branded entertainment is money. In the past, brand mentions were incidental or used by movie producers to create realism in a film. They now generate additional income. Martha Stewart charges $10,000 for a 30-second placement on her show. For a one-time mention in the show with a product close-up, the price goes up to $100,000. For a 2-minute branded entertainment segment with two or three talking points, the price is $250,000 plus.[21]

In summary, brand placements offer an excellent method to increase share of mind and build brand awareness. Although some are concerned that some programs are becoming saturated with product placements, they continue to be utilized. If clutter does become too severe usage is likely to decline. The key will be consumer responses and attitudes.[22]

LIFESTYLE MARKETING

A final program that can be used to make contacts with consumers in more offbeat and relaxed settings is **lifestyle marketing**, which involves identifying marketing methods associated with the hobbies and entertainment venues of the target audience. Lifestyle marketing includes contacting consumers at places such as farmer's markets, bluegrass festivals, city-wide garage sales, flea markets, craft shows, stock car races, and other places where there are large concentrations of potential customers.

Farmer's markets can be used in lifestyle marketing.

There are many consumer lifestyles, from relatively standard habits to more edgy and extreme behaviors. In a manner similar to Red Bull, the producers of the energy snack PowerBar offered free samples to persons attending sports events, including football and baseball games. The simple concept was that people who watch sports might be most inclined to give the product a try. Firms vending fertilizers and pesticides are most likely to set up operations at 4-H events and state fairs. In all cases, lifestyle marketing's key goal is to identify a venue where the target market goes for relaxation, excitement, socialization, or enjoyment.

Lifestyle marketing has a great deal in common with event marketing. An opera or symphonic performance creates a venue for music lovers. Those attending the performance can be reached with marketing materials unique to their interests and passions.

ALTERNATIVE MEDIA VENUES

The four alternative media programs discussed in this chapter incorporate numerous promotional activities into an overall approach. Thus, a lifestyle event such as a company's presence at a stock car race could feature coupons, samples, or an attempt to garner free publicity through a tie-in with a charity or cause, along with other creative tactics. There are other ways to reach consumers other than by relying on a traditional advertising program. In this section, the alternative media venues that were shown in Figure 10.1 are described.

Video Game Advertising

One specialized form of product placement is in video games. Products can be part of a stand-alone game purchased at a retail store and played on the computer or they can be placed in an Internet video game. In-game brand placement has all of the advantages of brand placements and branded entertainment. In addition, it has the added feature of interactivity. Approximately $1 billion per year is now being spent on in-game advertising. It has become a very attractive market for the following reasons:[23]

- 75 percent of all U.S. Internet users spend at least 1 hour a month playing online games.
- 27 percent average 30 hours a month playing games.
- The primary game-playing market segment is 16- to 34-year-old males.
- The fastest growing market segment is females, now about 20 percent of the total gaming market.

Video game advertising allows marketers to reach young males, who have become difficult to get to through traditional media. With an increasing number of women playing video games, the audience has become even more attractive. Men tend to play shooting games; women tend to play puzzle and cerebral games.

Video game advertising takes several forms (see Figure 10.6). The original and most widespread form of video game advertising is to have a brand placement in the game. It can be in the form of a billboard in a racing game, a Coke vending machine, or McDonald's restaurant that is permanently integrated into the game's design. With the cost of producing a game now in the $20 to $30 million range, game producers welcome product placement advertising as a source of revenue generation.

The Po-Boy Preservation Festival is an excellent venue for lifestyle marketing.

◆ In-game advertisements	◆ Game-related Web sites
◆ Rotating in-game advertising	◆ Advergames
◆ Interactive ads	◆ Sponsored downloads

FIGURE 10.6
Video Game Advertising

The number of game-related Web sites has exploded in recent years. Rather than placing ads in the game itself, advertisers can place ads on these gaming Web sites. Although the exact number of gaming Web sites is not known, estimates are that there are in excess of 6,000. Some have as many as 7 million visits per year.[24]

A number of companies are creating video games to be played on branded Web sites. These branded video games are called **advergames**. Axe, which is a brand of men's deodorant, offers an online game for men. The game allows the individual to test their "pickup" skills with 100 different "hot" women. Players collect and use pickup moves to try to woo the various women featured in the game. Other companies that have created advergames include Maxwell House, Holiday Inn, Baskin-Robbins, and Suave. Instead of creating a special micros-site for the game, the advergames can be placed on free gaming portals, such as Kewlbox (**www.kewlbox.com**), where 90 percent of the games are advergames. These advergames are played 500,000 to 700,000 times per day. According to Kewlbox founder Dan Ferguson, "People want free games."[25]

Another option for companies is sponsored downloads for games. This form is especially popular for automotive manufacturers. The games include video downloads for racing games that insert automaker's brand as the cars driven by each player.

Benefits of Video Game Advertising

Online video games offer advertisers the luxury of using Web metrics that are not available with other forms of product placement. Advertisers can track the length of ad exposure in an online game. In most cases, the company can tie in demographic information to find out who is viewing the in-game ad, how long they play, and how often. These metrics then make it possible to target ads specifically to the consumer. For instance, an advertiser can now place in games ads targeted toward females aged 18 to 30 living in Dallas, Texas. Ads can be targeted to specific demographic groups, location profiles, or a specific type of game player.[26]

Disadvantages of Video Game Advertising

The primary disadvantage of the product placement within a game is that the ad soon becomes static and often is no longer noticed by the player. To combat this problem, a new technology is available that rotates in-game ads. Massive is a company that has pioneered the technology to change ads in online video games in real time. As a result, advertisers are able to insert new ads and products into the game each time the person plays it. The player will not see the same billboard or same product placement ad. By being able to change the ads, the marketing team can deliver time-sensitive promotions into the game. Advertising can be current. It does not have to be ads that were prepared a year in advance. Massive is also able to make the ad in the game interactive, allowing the player to click on the ad for additional information.[27]

Cinema Advertising

Moviegoers now watch more than just promotional trailers and offers for concession stand products. Many theaters run several commercials mixed in with coming feature segments, ads for popcorn, and requests for audience members to be respectful to others. The products being offered may have direct relationships with movie-watching, such as gum or a soft drink, or they may be unrelated. Although clutter exists in the sense that the commercials may run consecutively, they are being shown to what is essentially a "captive" audience waiting for the main feature to start.

In-Tunnel Subway Advertising

Cities with well-developed subway systems offer numerous promotional opportunities. Ads may be placed on the walls of entryways into the subway system, at terminal locations, and on benches for travelers. Direct response materials, such as order placement cards, may also be attached to the wall. Additional advertisements are placed within the subway trains themselves. The newest version of subway technology allows a "moving" advertisement to be displayed on the walls of the subway as the train travels to the next destination. The ads may be a welcome distraction for an otherwise bored commuter waiting for a train to arrive or while on the journey.

Parking Lot Advertising

Park bench advertising has been in existence for over half a century. One new trend is to place park bench advertising near parking lots along with standard bus stop locations. Advertisements may also be placed strategically within parking garages on walls, in stairwells leading to and from the parking lot, or even on the parking place itself. Doing so has the advantage of creating *novelty*, where a new stimulus is viewed in a familiar location, which has an attention-getting quality.

Escalator Advertising

Escalators are found within stores, malls, airports, and in other settings. Consumers riding on them essentially have a few free moments to review ads placed on the hand rails or the walls that they travel past. The newest trend is placement of advertisements on the steps themselves. A customer typically looks down to make sure she lands squarely on the step. What better place for a quick reminder about a product or service?

Advertising is common on the walls of the Paris metro.

Airline In-Flight Advertising

As airline travel becomes a more popular venue for both businesspeople and persons on vacation, advertising to those potential customers continues to increase. Numerous ads are placed on the walls of airport terminals. Ads are placed on the in-flight television services offered to entertain travelers. Behind each seat on the plane, two advertising materials are typically found. The first is the airline's own magazine, featuring stories about cities where the line flies along with advertisements from restaurants, resorts, and real estate companies. The second is the *Sky Mall* magazine, which sells items from numerous top-end producers. Upon entering and leaving the aircraft, each passenger is thanked via intercom and in person by attendants for patronizing a particular carrier. In essence, a passenger can expect to be bombarded with messages every step of the way, from entering the airport to sitting on a bench waiting for a cab or bus, to the bus ride itself, and on any vehicle which helps the individual find her car or a car rental agency.

Leaflets and Brochures

Leaflets are hardly new. For many years, however, leafleting consisted of someone standing on a street corner handing out papers to those who may or may not be interested. Today, leaflets and brochures are targeted to specific events and audiences. Thus, a group of senior citizens may be invited to attend a wine and cheese party combined with a seminar on estate planning and the brochures are offered at the event. The goal is to be sure the paperwork is likely to be taken home and read.

Advertisements are often placed alongside of escalators.

Carry-Home Menus

Many restaurant owners provide carry-home menus to customers. The goal is to entice the individual to place the menu in a prominent place, such as on the refrigerator or by the phone. To make the menu more user-friendly, some are magnetized. Carry-home menus are also offered to business owners, especially those near a given site. Building a loyal lunch crowd bodes well for any food establishment.

Carry-Home Bag Advertising

A wide variety of retailers advertise on carry-home bags. Grocers print ads featuring food items made in the store, such as sausage or taco meat, as well as ads for name-brand items and private-label products. The objectives can be to increase consumer recognition that a given item exists or to build brand loyalty. Other retailers, such as Sak's Fifth Avenue and Macy's, send customers out the door with more expensive carry-home bags featuring the company's name. A new trend is to sell cloth bags that can be reused as carry-home bags that also provide an advertising space.

Advertising on Clothing

When someone wears a T-shirt or hat featuring a product, the individual becomes a walking billboard. Many manufacturers and retailers have created clothing items featuring advertising on them. Some are given away as purchasing enticements; others are sold. Many sports figures wear caps that are then offered to individual consumers for purchase, such as the Nike Swoosh worn by Tiger Woods as a golf cap. When an advertisement is placed on an item to be sold to the consumer, the technique is referred to as *merchandising the advertising.*

Other clothing designers place logos in a prominent place on the shirt, pair of pants, or even on pajamas. This notifies others that the consumer has purchased a high-end item, such as Tommy Bahama or Polo clothing item. The Echo Rhino is also prominently displayed on a number of fashions, often in conjunction with specific product brands.

Mall Signs

A new trend in malls is to sell advertising space on walls. Also, freestanding signs are placed in various strategic places within the mall. The cost to the advertiser is low and shoppers see the ad each time they visit a given location.

Kiosks

Kiosks are set up within many shopping malls as well as at various street locations. They can be similar to bulletin boards, in which a wide variety of company business cards, advertisements, and other materials are pinned. They can also be themed kiosks, such as one devoted solely to real estate. Advertisers can display individual houses or other pieces of property, as well as business cards and other messages. Consumers who stop to read advertising pieces on kiosks are either interested in a specific theme or are waiting for something or someone. In either case, the shopper is likely to linger and pay more attention to the messages.

In summary, the popularity of using methods to deliver advertising messages in nontraditional formats continues to increase. Each time an innovative marketing professional identifies a new venue, a certain segment of the advertising community jumps on board. The goal is to find ways to send out messages that either cut through or go around clutter to reach people in moments when they may be more receptive to the content of the ad.

A street kiosk in Spain.

IN-STORE MARKETING

Despite all the money spent on advertising in traditional and nontraditional media, approximately 70 percent of all purchase decisions are still made in the retail store. Except for point-of-purchase (POP) displays, in-store marketing has not received much attention. Funds devoted to it represent a very small percentage of advertising and marketing budgets. This may represent the failure to take advantage of a real opportunity.

To understand the potential of in-store advertising, consider what influences consumer decisions in purchasing clothing. In a survey of 599 consumers, 52.6 percent said that in-store signage, displays, or point-of-purchase displays influenced their decision. This far outdistances print advertising, and even word-of-mouth communications.[28] A complete list of these influences is provided in Figure 10.7. In this section, new in-store marketing tactics, as well as the more traditional point-of-purchase (POP) approach, are described.

New In-Store Marketing Tactics

The use of color, light, and sound has long been a part of in-store marketing. Retailers brighten and soften products using displays and photos often featuring the current and most popular colors. Music, from the elevator-type to popular new forms for trendy stores, has long been a part of retail shopping. What is new in this area is to add *motion.*

The newest and most expensive in-store marketing tactic is carefully placing and using video screens and television monitors. Many static signs are being replaced with high-technology mediums. Even shopping carts with static signs that are broken or unreadable are being replaced with video screens. Spending on digital signage is estimated to double to $2.8 billion annually by 2011. Digital media within the store offers retailers the opportunity to customize messages to fit the particular retail store and even the aisle where the display is located.[29]

Airplay America is the producer of The Salon Channel, which is a new retail television channel and digital signage network for beauty salons. Programming consists of human interest and lifestyle stories. Salon patrons spend an average of 30 to 45 minutes per salon visit. The Salon Channel provides them with entertainment, including features about nationally recognized hairstyles and the latest styles, as well as advertisements for products and services, many of which are related to beauty and fashion.[30]

Wal-Mart follows the same path. In the past, Wal-Mart's ads appeared on all in-store televisions at the same time. Using new technologies, the marketing department is able to distribute ads geared to each department within a store and even for specific aisles. The approach is now used in 1,200 Wal-Mart stores on over 100,000 television monitors. Television monitors are no longer hung from the ceiling. The new monitors are flat screen panels and are placed at eye level in the aisles, because it leads to greater recall of ads. Digital monitors are also being installed at end-caps and at point-of-purchase displays. These television monitors contain advertising pertinent to the end-cap or POP display.[31]

Unilever has tested the Wal-Mart in-store network system. The company's advertising team created a commercial specifically to be shown in Wal-Mart stores. The ad was part of Unilever's "real beauty" campaign. Instead of using young and slinky female models posing in the underwear, an elderly Wal-Mart employee talks about how pretty she feels, even with her wrinkles.[32]

To fully appreciate the potential impact of this new form of in-store advertising, consider this: Each week 68 million viewers watch the national television newscasts of Katie Couric, Brian Williams and Charles Gibson. The number of shoppers at Wal-Mart each week is 127 million. The potential audience for an ad placed on the Wal-Mart television system is

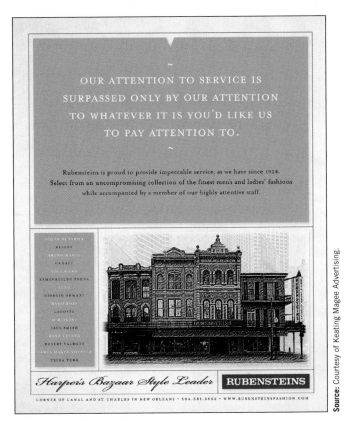

Rubensteins of New Orleans recognizes that advertising great service must be followed up with appropriate in-store signage and attention by employees.

- In-store advertising (52.6%)
- Print ads (23.9%)
- Word-of-mouth communications (15.8%)
- Television ads (14.1%)
- Internet ads (10.4%)
- Direct mail (7.4%)
- Radio ads (1.8%)

Source: Based on Amy Johannes, "Snap Decisions," *Promo* 18, no. 11 (October 2005), p. 16.

FIGURE 10.7
Types of Advertising that Most Influenced Clothing Purchases

almost twice as large as an ad on the national newscasts.[33] In addition, the Wal-Mart ad reaches consumers as they are shopping and when they are making purchase decisions.

A final new in-store tactic relies on yet other senses, *taste* and *smell*. The use of scents to enhance a shopping experience is not new. What is new is that some stores release pheromones into the air to make customers feel aroused and sexy. Others rely on less controversial approaches by baking and selling pastries and offering specialty coffees and teas. High-end retailers often present buyers with hot tea as part of the shopping experience. The goal is to both personalize the shopping experience and to make it more enticing, which may cause the customer to return.

POINT-OF-PURCHASE TACTICS

Traditionally, one of the most important components of in-store marketing has been the creation of quality **point-of-purchase displays (POP)**. POP is any form of special display that advertises merchandise. POP displays are often located near cash registers in retail stores, at the end of an aisle, in a store's entryway, or any other place where they will be noticed. POP advertising includes displays, signs, structures, and devices used to identify, advertise, or merchandise an outlet, service, or product. POP displays serve as an important aid to retail selling.

POP displays remain highly effective tools for increasing sales. About 70 percent of all purchasing decisions are made in the retail store. Nearly 50 percent of the money spent at mass-merchandisers and supermarkets is unplanned. These purchases are called *impulse buys*. When consumers make purchases, they often do not decide on the particular brand until the last minute. For food purchases, 88 percent of the decisions about brands are made in the store at the time of the purchase. In many instances, point-of-purchase materials and other in-store advertising materials influenced the decision.[34]

Coca-Cola reports that only 50 percent of soft drink sales are made from the regular store shelf. The other 50 percent results from product displays in other parts of the store. American Express discovered that 30 percent of purchases charged on the American Express card came from impulse decisions by customers seeing the "American Express Cards Welcome" sign. Other research indicates that an average increase in sales around 9 percent occurs when one POP display is used. Only about half of POP displays create an impact on sales. For the half that does make an impact, however, the average increase in purchases is about 20 percent. Consequently, POP advertising is quite attractive to manufacturers.[35]

Currently, manufacturers spend more than $17 billion each year on point-of-purchase advertising materials. The largest users of POP advertising are restaurants, food services, apparel stores, and footwear retailers. The fastest-growing categories are fresh, frozen, or refrigerated foods, and professional services.[36]

Manufacturers view POP displays as an attractive method of getting a brand more prominently displayed before customers. Many retailers have a different perspective. Retailers believe POP materials should either boost sales for the store or draw customers into the store. Retailers are not interested in the sales of one particular brand, but instead want to improve overall sales and store profits. Retailers prefer displays that educate consumers and provide information. As a result, retailers are most inclined to set up POP displays to match the retailer's marketing objectives.

Designing Effective POP

To be effective, POP displays must clearly communicate the product's attributes. Pricing and other promotional information is also helpful. The display should encourage the customer to stop

POP displays are very helpful when selling products such as cosmetics, perfume, or cologne.

Source: Courtesy of Bijan Fragrances, Inc.

FIGURE 10.8
Effective POP Displays

- Integrate the brand's image into the display.
- Integrate the display with current advertising and promotions.
- Make the display dramatic to get attention.
- Keep the color of the display down so the product and signage stand out.
- Make the display versatile so it can be easily adapted by retailers.
- Make the display reusable and easy to assemble.
- Make the display easy to stock.
- Customize the display to fit the retailer's store.

and look, pick up the product, and examine it. A customer who stops to examine a product on display is more likely to buy that product.

The POP display should make a clear, succinct offer that customers immediately understand. Many times the POP display only has three-tenths of a second to capture the customer's attention. If it fails, the customer simply moves on to other merchandise. Colors, designs, merchandise arrangements, and tie-ins with other marketing messages are critical elements of effective POP displays.

The best POP displays are those integrated with other marketing messages. Logos and message themes used in advertisements should appear on the POP. The POP display should reflect any form of special sales promotion. Customers more quickly recognize tie-ins with current advertising and promotional themes as they view displays. Figure 10.8 lists some additional pointers for point-of-purchase advertising.

Remember that the size of a display is important to retailers. Store space is limited. Customers do not respond well when freestanding displays at the ends of aisles block traffic through the store. Consequently, individual retailers normally will use only POP displays that fit the space that is allocated. Retailers prefer easy to assemble, easy to stock, and adaptable displays. A manufacturer's marketing team should remember that if a retailer does not like a display, it won't be used, no matter how great it looks.

Retailers want displays to be durable. Corrugated cardboard (which is often used) tends to wear out and tear. Poorly built displays are often thrown away. Retailers do not have time to repair displays. They also take down worn, shabby-looking exhibits. Retailers give preference to manufacturers offering customized displays for individual stores.

The most common reason retailers do not use displays furnished by manufacturers is that they are inappropriate for the channel. In other words, a display that works well in a discount store may not be appropriate for a supermarket or a specialty store. Various retailers and channel members have different needs in terms of what they want in a POP display design. Manufacturers should consult with each type of channel member to ensure the display meets these needs.

Measuring POP Effectiveness

Both retailers and manufacturers look for methods to measure the effectiveness of POP displays. Retailers have limited space and can set up only a fraction of the displays sent to them. They want to use the most effective displays. Manufacturers invest money into building, shipping, and promoting POP displays. The manufacturer wants its display to be utilized and not set in a storeroom or simply thrown away. Thus, it is in the best interests of both parties to develop methods for measuring effectiveness.

One method to measure results is tying the POP display into a point-of-sale (POS) cash register. Items on the display are coded so that the POS system picks them up. Then individual stores measure sales before and during a POP display program by using cash register data. The data also help the retailer decide that it is time to withdraw or change a POP display because sales have begun to decline. This technology allows retailers to identify the POP displays with the largest impact on sales. A retailer even could use this method to test-market different types of POP displays in various stores. The most effective displays can then be used nationally.

From the manufacturer's viewpoint, using POS data can help improve POP displays. The data can also be used to strengthen partnerships with retailers. These bonds help the manufacturer weather poor POP showings. Retailers are more willing to stay with a manufacturer that tries to develop displays that benefit both parties.

Combination Approaches

Some of the tactics presented in this chapter are being integrated into point-of-purchase displays. Static point-of-purchase displays are on their way out. Retailers want digital interactive displays that consumers will notice and displays with the capability of changing the message. Messages are now being changed daily, weekly, or, in some cases, several times per day.

One method manufacturers use to make changes is by featuring LED electronic signs, which can be altered via computer. This allows the manufacturer or retailer to frequently present new messages to keep the POP fresh to consumers. To the retailer, the major advantage is that messages can be localized and designed to meet changing local needs. To the manufacturer, it offers an opportunity to partner with retailers looking for ways to maximize sales. Consequently, some of the new combination approaches include:

- Utilization of interactive digital POP displays
- Integration of the POP with the brand's advertising and marketing campaigns
- Interface of digital technology with in-store networks
- Interface with retail computers to permit measurement of results

There has also been a greater effort to integrate POP displays with a brand's advertising and marketing materials. Consumers are more likely to notice a POP display if they recognize a logo, character, or other communication they have seen elsewhere. A study by the Saatchi & Saatchi advertising agency revealed that consumers' purchase decisions are made in just 4 seconds and they will only look at a display or signage from 3 to 7 seconds.[37] Tying a POP display into current advertising and marketing will increase the chances of it being noticed.

Many big box retailers have moved to in-store television networks featuring POP displays that are integrated with television advertising. Wal-Mart even sells advertising time on its in-store network to manufacturers. These ads can be displayed at the POP display, in aisles adjacent to the display, or throughout the entire store. Tying a display to in-store signage, video screens, or in-store TV networks increases the effectiveness of the display.

In the future, POP may evolve even further. The use of 3-D technologies and holograms is just now being explored. It will not be long until these new tactics are part of a shopper's retail experience.

Point-of-purchase displays are often located near cash registers.

BRAND COMMUNITIES

Brand communities are the ultimate demonstration of brand loyalty and brand devotion. In most cases there is a symbolic meaning behind the brand that links individuals to the brand community and to other owners of the brand. The identity and belonging are formed through interactions between customers and with the product. The result is a set of shared values and experiences that integrate with feelings about the brand.

Brand communities do not form around every brand. They cannot be created by the brand itself; however, a marketing department can facilitate and enhance the community experience. A company with a strong brand community maintains a positive image, has a rich and long tradition, occupies a unique position in the marketplace, and enjoys a group of loyal, dedicated followers.[38] Figure 10.9 highlights some of the reasons that brand communities exist. Most brand communities require some type of face-to-face interactions, although the Internet does provide a venue for members to contact each other and to blog about the product.

FIGURE 10.9
Reason Brand Communities Form

◆ Affirmation of the buying decision

◆ Social identity and bond

◆ Swap stories

◆ Swap advice and provide help to others

◆ Feedback and new ideas

Jeep, Harley-Davidson, and Apple are firms with loyal brand communities. In each case, the brand owners are diverse. This can be seen in the Jeep Jamborees and Camp Jeep events, which are events sponsored by Jeep. Both allow Jeep owners the opportunity to share driving experiences, tell stories, and share ideas. Most of the interactions among customers occur during the company-sponsored barbecue. They also take place during roundtable discussions hosted by a Jeep engineer or other Jeep employee.

It is not unusual for many, if not most, of the attendees at a Camp Jeep event to have no experience driving their Jeep off-road. Then among those who had driven their Jeep off-road, some have a "tread lightly" ethos, whereas others have mud-covered vehicles from heavy off-road use. First timers at the camp are often timid and afraid they won't fit in, but soon find they do as repeaters fully welcome anyone and everyone to the Jeep community. The vehicle provides the common bond that brings individuals together regardless of demographic and psychographic differences.

Perhaps the best example of brand community is Harley-Davidson. The company's leadership team has done an excellent job of creating a unique brand community spirit. An organization called HOG has formed around the Harley brand. In return, Harley-Davidson offers benefits, such as information about community gatherings along with special marketing offers for accessories, to HOG members. The benefits are only available to the HOG group. This encourages new Harley-Davidson owners to join the HOG brand community.

Although it is virtually impossible for companies to create a brand community, they can facilitate and enhance the community in which owners can interact. Figure 10.10 provides information on ways a marketing team can assist in creating a brand community.

Building a brand community begins with sponsoring events that bring product owners together. Jeep sponsors both the jamborees and a camp. Harley sponsors rides, rallies, and even local events. These events are critical for the creation of a brand community spirit and allow for bonding between owners. Eventually this produces a sense of social identity.

It is important to involve company representatives in club events. Jeep engineers always attend Jeep events and mingle with customers. They provide advice and encouragement to any new owner who is taking his or her vehicle off-road for the first time. Harley managers, including the CEO, ride Harleys to rallies to talk with owners.

Skyjacker has developed a brand community with off-road enthusiasts.

Source: Courtesy of Skyjacker Suspensions.

◆ Create member benefits to encourage new customers to join a group.

◆ Provide materials to the group that are not available anywhere else.

◆ Involve firm representatives in the groups.

◆ Sponsor special events and regular meetings.

◆ Promote communications among members of the group.

◆ Build a strong brand reputation.

FIGURE 10.10
Ways to Enhance a Brand
Community Spirit

Source: Based on "Brand Communities," *Bulletpoint*, no. 133 (July 2006), pp. 12–16.

In addition to company-sponsored events, other venues for interaction should be encouraged. The Internet offers another place for owners to interact. They can visit through blogs, chat rooms, or social network micro-sites. It is important that the company be involved in these exchange venues and to openly identify themselves. Brand communities want company involvement and want an honest exchange of comments.

Finally, while providing venues and means for developing a brand community spirit, the company must continue other advertising and marketing programs. A brand community is normally the outgrowth of a brand with a strong image. That image must be maintained. The pride of owning the brand must be prominent in the advertising. Its uniqueness and position in the marketplace should be clear.

INTERNATIONAL IMPLICATIONS

The use of alternative media is growing in marketing to minority groups within the United States. An example of buzz marketing occurred when a company called Clamato sought to increase brand awareness among U.S. Latinos. The company gave 2,000 agents a 32-ounce bottle of Clamato and 10 coupons. The agents reached 34,000 potential customers, and positive opinions of the drink rose from 32 percent to 78 percent.

Alternative media are being used in other countries. Starbucks and Pepsi combined efforts to produce a movie series called "A Sunny Day." It is about a girl from the Chinese countryside who moves to the big city and discovers love, blogging, and Starbucks. The series was tailored for Shanghai's subway and the 2.2 million who ride the subway every day. The story was made into a soap opera-style script featuring short daily segments. A Web site featured the story snippets each day for those missed seeing it on the subway and wanted to know what happened. The Shanghai subway has a network of 4,000 flat-screen monitors that provide train information, clips of soccer highlights, entertainment news, and advertising. Marketers pay to run ads, just like they would on television. The "A Sunny Day" was the first venture into a short mini-series, with episodes each day for 40 weeks. The purpose of the movie was to promote Pepsi and Starbucks and introduce Starbucks' new bottled Frappuccino drinks.[39]

Brand communities are also developing in other nations. Jeep is using the brand community concept to build a brand presence in China. The first Jeep was introduced in 1983 by American Motors through a joint venture in Beijing; however, recent sales of Jeep have slowed. In response, the first 3-day Camp Jeep was created. It attracted 700 Jeep owners and 3,000 participants. The event included off-road courses, bungee jumping, a hiking course, wall climbing, a soccer field, and off-road ATV course. There was also musical entertainment and time slots for Karaoke enthusiasts.[40] The purpose of the event was to renew Jeep's strong brand name and to create a strong sense of community among current Jeep owners in China. Through these individuals, Jeep hopes to generate word-of-mouth, or buzz, for the Jeep brand, driving new customers to the Jeep brand.

It is apparent that the clutter problems which plague U.S. advertisers are present around the world. Not surprising, then, the tactics used domestically will grow in two ways. First, firms from other nations will adapt alternative media tactics. Second, international conglomerates will also respond with new and creative alternative marketing programs.

SUMMARY

Alternative media has many success stories. Well-known brands, such as Ben & Jerry's and Starbucks, have emerged using very little traditional advertising. Each found new methods to establish a brand presence, including alternative media and alternative marketing methods. Starbucks built an entire community of coffee lovers through local involvements and word-of-mouth.

There are four forms of alternative marketing programs. Buzz marketing, or word-of-mouth marketing, places the emphasis on consumers passing along information about a brand. The consumers can be those who like a brand, sponsored consumers, or company insiders. Some consider using company insiders to be unethical.

Guerrilla marketing programs are those designed to obtain instant results while using limited resources, instead utilizing creativity, quality relationships, and the willingness to try unusual approaches. Product placements are planned insertions of a brand or product into a movie, television program, or some other media program. Branded entertainment is the integration of entertainment and advertising by embedding brands into the storyline of a movie, television show, or other entertainment medium. Lifestyle marketing is using marketing methods associated with the hobbies and entertainment venues of the target audience.

Numerous alternative media venues are available. They include video game advertising and advergames, cinema advertising, in-tunnel subway advertising, parking lot advertising, escalator advertising, airline in-flight advertising, leaflets, brochures, carry-home menus, carry-home bag advertising, advertising on clothing, mall signs, and kiosks. Use of these media has been on the increase as the impact of traditional media and the Internet continue to decline.

In-store marketing programs take two forms. New tactics include the use of high-tech video screens and television monitors in new and more visible places. This also includes tailoring messages to individual parts of the store. Traditional point-of-purchase advertising (POP) continues to be widely utilized. Recently, POP has been combined with newer technologies to increase the impact of these in-store marketing devices.

Brand communities evolve when consumers feel a great deal of brand loyalty and devotion. They form around events, programs, and exchanges of information. A company with a strong brand and a devoted marketing team can assist in the formation and continuance of brand communities.

Alterative media choices are being utilized to reach minority groups in the United States in unique new ways. They are also expanding into international markets. As traditional clutter increases, the use of these media is likely to grow, and they will become cluttered as well.

KEY TERMS

buzz marketing   Emphasizes consumers passing along information about a product to others, and is also known as *word-of-mouth marketing.*

guerrilla marketing   Programs designed to obtain instant results using limited resources by relying on creativity, quality relationships, and the willingness to try new approaches.

product placement   The planned insertion of a brand or product into a movie, television show, or some other media program.

branded entertainment   The integration of entertainment and advertising by embedding brands into the storyline of a movie, television show, or other entertainment medium.

lifestyle marketing   Marketing methods associated with the hobbies and entertainment venues of the target audience.

advergames   Branded video games.

point-of-purchase displays (POP)   Any form of special display that advertises merchandise.

brand communities   A link that forms due to an association between the brand, a consumer, and others who own or purchase the brand.

REVIEW QUESTIONS

1. What are the four main alternative media programs described in this chapter?

2. What is buzz marketing?

3. What three types of consumers can pass along buzz marketing messages?

4. Why is buzz marketing effective? What preconditions should be met to ensure its effectiveness?

5. What is guerrilla marketing? How does it differ from traditional marketing?

6. What are product placements and branded entertainment? What do they have in common?

7. What is lifestyle marketing? How is it similar to event marketing?

8. Describe the forms of video game advertising, including advergames.

9. Identify the alternative media venues described in this chapter.

10. What is in-store marketing? Why is it important?

11. What new in-store marketing tactics are being utilized?

12. What is POP? Why is it important?

13. How have new technologies changed some forms of POP?

14. What is a brand community?

15. What should a company's marketing team do to assist in the development and growth of brand communities?

16. Is the use of alternative media growing or declining in international markets? Explain why.

CRITICAL THINKING EXERCISES

Discussion Questions

1. Consider a set of products to which you have a high level of loyalty. Would you consider being a brand advocate, ambassador, or evangelist for a brand? Pick the brand where your loyalty is the highest. What type of offer would it take from the company for you to become a brand ambassador? What would you do to be an effective advocate for that brand?

2. Consider a recent purchase you made at the recommendation of someone else. Why did you trust that person's

recommendation? How important is the recommendation of others in your purchase decisions?

3. In making a purchase decision, have you accessed the Internet to read blogs or customer reviews before the purchase decision? If so, discuss the outcome. If not, why not?

4. Suppose you were approached by a local small business owner of a small clothing boutique. She has heard about guerrilla marketing and wants to try it. First, why she should use guerrilla marketing? What are the pros and cons? Second, what guerrilla marketing techniques would you suggest?

5. Find a movie that you have already watched and enjoyed. Watch it again, but this time make a list of all of the product placements you see. Identify if it was a prominent placement, if the actor used the brand, or if it was just in the background. When you finish, discuss the product placements that were the most effective and the placements that were the least effective. What made the placement effective? What made it ineffective?

6. Do you play video games? If so, approximately how many hours a month do you play games (including online games)? What advertising have you noticed in the game? How effective was the advertising?

7. Review Figure 10.7, which presents the types of advertising that most influence clothing purchases. Rank the list based on your own personal situation. What ranked first in terms of influence? What ranked second? If your list is different from Figure 10.7, explain why it is different for you.

8. Go to a nearby retail store. Examine the point-of-purchase displays in the store. Which ones were the most impressive? Why? Which ones did not succeed at getting your attention? Why not? Go back to the store a week later. How many of the displays had changed? What is your overall evaluation of the POP displays used by the retailer?

9. Go to a nearby retail store and talk to the manager or one of the employees. Ask them about the store signage, including POP displays. Ask the employee to discuss what signage is effective and why. As a customer, did you agree with the manager's or employee's viewpoint? Why or why not?

INTEGRATED LEARNING EXERCISES

1. Access the Red Bull Web site at **www.redbull.com**. What is your opinion of the Web site? Find examples or illustrations of buzz marketing or guerrilla marketing. What other types of nontraditional advertising techniques does the company appear to use? Reread the opening vignette about Red Bull; then comment on the way the product was launched in the United States.

2. Access the Web site of Ugg at **www.uggaustralia.com**. Evaluate the Web site in terms of its effectiveness, freshness, and the use of alternative marketing methods. What traditional marketing methods did you see? Do you think Ugg has effectively merged traditional and nontraditional advertising methods? Why or why not?

3. Access the Word of Mouth Marketing Association Web site at **www.womma.org**. List the alternative names used for word-of-mouth marketing. Do you think these are good synonyms for word-of-mouth communications? Why or why not? What features did you find on the site? What benefits does the site provide? What value would the site be to a business? Is there any value for a consumer?

4. Type "buzz marketing" into an online search engine. Pick two different sites that are of advertising agencies or marketing agencies that offer buzz marketing expertise to its clients. Which company do you think offers the best buzz marketing program? Why?

5. Online gaming has become very popular, especially with the 16- to 34-year-old demographic. Access the Kewlbox Web site at **www.kewlbox.com**. Discuss the various games that are available. Locate some advergames. Who were the sponsoring brands? What is your evaluation of the game site?

6. Point-of-purchase displays should be an important component of a firm's IMC program. Research indicates that effective POP displays have a positive impact on sales. Access the following firms that produce POP displays. Which firm's site is the most attractive? Which firm would be the best from the standpoint of developing displays for a manufacturer? Why?
   a. Acrylic Designs, Inc. (**www.acrylicdesigns.com**)
   b. Vulcan Industries (**www.vulcanind.com**)
   c. Display Design & Sales (**www.displays4pop.com**)

STUDENT PROJECT

Creative Corner

Ugg has become successful because of unique alternative marketing methods. Access Ugg's Web site at **www.uggaustralia.com** to learn about the company's products and the company itself. Suppose Ugg wanted to initiate a buzz marketing campaign at your university and that they contacted you for marketing advice. First, they would like to recruit some brand ambassadors as advocates for their brand. Your first task, therefore, is to design a flyer to post around campus announcing Ugg wants to hire brand ambassadors. But, before you can design the flyer, you must decide on the relationship the ambassador will have with Ugg and the type of reward or payment they will receive. After you design the flyer, your second task is to develop a buzz marketing program that you believe Ugg and the new brand ambassador should use on your campus.

CASE 1 THE NATURE OF BUZZ

One of the more challenging aspects of buzz marketing is found within its very nature. Encouraging word-of-mouth communication makes it possible to reach a vast number of consumers in a hurry. Also, those receiving the messages may be found in concentrations of potential customers. At the same time, many times conversations change. What was hot soon is not.

The manuscript for this book was prepared in late 2007 and early 2008. At that point, three media phenomena were taking place, the movie *Snakes on a Plane*, the *Hannah Montana* craze (including the tour), and the release of the final Harry Potter book and movie (see Chapter 13).

By the time this text reaches your hands, it is entirely possible that none of these will be subjects of interest, even to the most devoted fans of the time. Consider *Snakes on a Plane*. The film, starring Samuel L. Jackson, contained many firsts. For openers, the title attracted a great deal of attention by itself and was the primary reason Jackson agreed to appear in the film. Also potential moviegoers were teased with partial releases and premises about the film for nearly a year before it was released. Potential audience members were invited to help write and revise the script and to create alternative endings. There was even an album released entitled *Soundtrack for the Motion Picture Snakes on a Plane*.

When the film was actually released, a substantial amount of buzz had already occurred, in Internet chat clubs, public relations releases, press stories, television blurbs, and more traditional forms of marketing. It seemed nearly impossible for the movie to be anywhere as good as the hype. Box office numbers were disappointing, but the film did result in ticket sales totaling nearly $60 million worldwide. There was a subsequent comic book, and no one in the film industry is likely to forget Samuel L. Jackson's famous line about being ". . . tired of these **** on this **** plane!"

One year later, *Hannah Montana* took the country by storm. The popular Disney television show about a regular girl by day and a rock star by night had evolved into a major phenomenon. The title character was played by Miley Ray Cyrus, who appeared as a feature interview on the *Barbara Walter's Special* on the night of the 2008 Academy Awards, and Cyrus was a presenter for one of the trophies.

The 2007–2008 "Best of Both Worlds" tour generated tremendous publicity. Many families struggled to obtain high-price tickets, some of which were sold by scalpers for amounts as high as $1,000. Presidential candidate Barack Obama noted that his status as a national figure did allow him the opportunity to obtain seats, thereby enhancing his status with his daughters.

Hannah Montana merchandise includes music CDs, T-shirts, games, movies, chat rooms, e-mail contact points, and numerous other items. Young girls and their parents flocked to the G-rated form of entertainment.

By 2010, Cyrus will be 18 years old and fully grown. Will the buzz continue? After all, the original fans will also be older.

In the past, marketing experts noted the difference between a *fad*, which is quick to develop and quick to end, and a *fashion*, which has a longer-lasting impact and life span. Teen idols come and go. Creating buzz around entertainers and certain types of products may be highly profitable, but also short-lived.

1. What are the differences between the type of buzz that was created for *Snakes on a Plane* and *Hannah Montana*, as compared to the Red Bull success story at the opening of this chapter?

2. What types of products are most likely to benefit from buzz marketing that can be sustained through more traditional forms of marketing, promotions, and advertising?

3. What types of products are least likely to be sustainable, thus becoming more like fads and less like fashions?

4. Does the potential exist for *Snakes on a Plane 2*? Could *Hannah Montana* end up having a younger sister or cousin that could sustain the story? If so, how?

5. What brand, product, movie, or individual has received considerable buzz activity lately? What caused the buzz to occur? In your opinion, how long will it last?

CASE 2 TANNING AND VOLLEYBALL: REVITALIZING A LIFESTYLE

Jessica Jones faced a difficult challenge as she took control of the Sun Products, Inc., account. As a relatively new account executive, Jessica knew it was important to establish measurable results when conducting various marketing communication campaigns. Sun Products sells items primarily oriented toward beach-related activities, the most successful of which is the company's line of sunscreen products.

The tanning industry faces a unique set of challenges as a new generation of consumers emerges. First, more than ever consumers are aware of the dangerous long-term effects of tanning. These include more wrinkles along with vastly increased chances of developing skin cancer in later life. In Australia, where the ozone layer is the most depleted, exposure to the sun is even more hazardous. More important, however, is a potential shift in cultural values regarding appearance.

As the new millennium commences, it is possible that a certain set of consumers will begin to believe that tanning is equal to foolishness—or, at least, that a suntan is no longer as "sexy" as it has been for many years. Beach bums and bunnies continue to run counter to this trend. The question remains, however, whether being brown is a good idea.

One way to counter this problem is by developing new products designed to screen out the sun rather than enhance the sun's tanning properties. Lotions with higher SPF (sun protection factor) values generally sell at higher prices. Higher-quality sunscreens do not wash off in a pool or while swimming. Further, items containing herbal ingredients and new aromas are designed to entice new interest. Sun Products with aloe vera and vitamin E may help reduce the pain and heal sunburns more quickly. Products that "tan" without exposure to the sun are being developed for those who want the beach look without doing time in the sand.

At the same time, to promote more "traditional" products to college students on spring break and others who still enjoy a deep, dark tan requires careful promotion. Advertisements often stress the "fun" aspects of being outdoors.

Hawaiian Tropics, one of the chief competitors in the tanning industry, has taken a unique approach to the promotion of its products. The company holds an annual contest in which the Tropics team of beach girls is chosen to represent the firm. Contestants are female, beautiful, and have good tans. Those who win the contest tour the country promoting Hawaiian Tropics products and appear on television programs. At individual events held at beaches across the United States and in other locations, free samples of Hawaiian Tropics are given out, along with coupons and other purchase incentives. Giveaways of beach towels and other beach equipment are used to heighten interest in the product at various stores.

Beach Volleyball Magazine notes that it features not a sport, but a lifestyle. The activity has the benefit of being included as part of the Summer Olympics. Some women, such as Misty May-Treanor and Kerri Walsh, have recognizable names on the national stage and enjoy immense popularity within the women's volleyball fan base. In addition, there are professional beach volleyball tournaments across the United States each year.

Promotion of women's beach volleyball tends to focus on tans, bikinis, and what has to be viewed as a sexy sport. Many of the marketing materials available online, on posters, and in other places feature photos of participants in the skimpiest of bathing suits. Fans also tend to attend events wearing outfits designed to show off a fit body and a great tan.

Jessica suspects there is a natural tie-in available with beach volleyball, especially on the women's side. Instead of tanning for its own sake, getting a tan while doing something healthy seems like a great appeal. The primary issue is whether the appeal can move beyond volleyball fans to the larger public. The secret would be to find a theme for the tie-in that appeals to a larger audience.

An entire range of promotional items is possible. Items include coupons, premiums and giveaways, contests, samples, bonus packs (with various ranges of SPF values in the same pack), and refunds for higher-priced lotions.

Jessica knows the key is to maintain a consistent message and theme for her company. It must stand out in the crowd of Coppertone, Bain de Soleil, and Hawaiian Tropics. She realizes that to succeed she needs Sun Products' POP displays placed prominently in as many places as possible, from drugstores to swimming specialty stores.

1. Is a buzz marketing program possible for Sun Products? Why or why not?

2. Design a complete lifestyle marketing program for Sun Products based on a tie-in with women's beach volleyball.

Source: Courtesy of Greg Huglin; Stock Connection.

A combination of beach volleyball and sun tanning creates unique marketing opportunities.

Include both traditional and nontraditional advertising venues.

3. Name any opportunities you can identify for product placements or brand entertainment for Sun Products.

4. Is there a potential overlap between the brand community that loves beach volleyball and a brand community for Sun Products? Describe the ways that Sun Products' marketing department could build and enhance a connection between the two.

ENDNOTES

1. "Red Bull's Good Buzz," *Newsweek* (May 14, 2001), p. 83.

2. Jeff Weiss, "Building Brands Without Ads," *Marketing Magazine* 109, no. 32 (October 4–11, 2004), p. 22.

3. Ibid.

4. Sinclair Stewart, "More Marketers Using Word of Mouth to Whip up Sales," *The Seattle Post-Intelligencer* (**http://seattlepi.nwsource.com/business/344656_wordofmouth24.html**), December 23, 2007.

5. Joan Voight, "The New Brand Ambassadors," *Adweek.com* (**http://adweek.com/pt/cpt/The + New + Brand+Ambassadors**), December 31, 2007.

6. Sinclair Stewart, "More Marketers Using Word of Mouth to Whip up Sales."

7. Angelo Fernando, "Transparency Under Attack," *Communication World* 24, no. 2 (March– April 2007), pp. 9–11.

8. Ibid.

9. Jim Matorin, "Infectious 'Buzz Marketing' Is a Smart Way to Build Customer Loyalty at Your Operation," *Nation's Restaurant News* 41, no. 18 (April 30, 2007), pp. 18–20.

10. Kate Niederhoffer, Rob Mooth, David Wiesenfeld, and Jonathon Gordon, "The Origin and Impact of CPG New-Product Buzz: Emerging Trends and Implications," *Journal of Advertising Research* 47, no. 4 (December 2007), pp. 420–26.

11. Ibid.

12. Shari Caudron, "Guerrilla Tactics," *Industry Week* 250, no. 10 (July 16, 2001), p. 52.

13. Normandy Madden, "Upstart's Taxi Play Helps Brands Flag Down Rich Chinese," *Advertising Age* 78, no. 43 (2006), p. 46.

14. Simon Hudson and David Hudson, "Branded Entertainment: A New Advertising Technique or Product Placement in Disguise?" *Journal of Marketing Management* 22, no. 5/6 (July 2006), pp. 489–504.

15. Ibid.

16. Linda Moss, "Nielsen: Product Placements Succeed in "'Emotionally Engaging' Shows," *Multichannel News* (**www.multichannel.com/index.asp**), December 10, 2007.

17. Cecily Hall, "Subliminal Messages," *Women's Wear Daily* 195, no. 2 (January 3, 2008), p.12.

18. Simon Hudson and David Hudson, "Branded Entertainment: A New Advertising Technique or Product Placement in Disguise?"

19. Jean-Marc Lehu, "Seamless Brand Integration," *Brand Strategy,* no. 211 (April 2007), pp. 34–35.

20. Raj Persaud, "The Art of Product Placement," *Brand Strategy,* no. 216 (October 2007), pp. 30–31.

21. Burt Helm, "Marketing: Queen of the Product Pitch," *BusinessWeek* (April 30, 2007), pp. 40–41.

22. Rebecca Harris, "Brand Watchers," *Marketing Magazine* 111, no. 18 (May 15, 2006), p. 6.

23. Theresa Howard, "As More People Play, Advertisers Devise Game Plans," *USA Today* (July 11, 2006), p. Money, 3b.

24. Ibid.

25. Ibid.

26. Susan Catto, "Are You Game?" *Marketing Magazine* (November 26, 2007, Supplement), pp. 18–19.

27. Ibid.

28. Amy Johannes, "Snap Decisions," *Promo* 18, no. 11 (October 2005), p. 16.

29. Tim Dreyer, "In-Store Technology Trends," *Display & Design Ideas* 19, no. 9 (September 2007), p. 92.

30. Ibid.

31. Steve McClellan, "Wal-Mart Takes Its Ads to a New Level: The Aisle," *Adweek* 47, no. 38 (October 16, 2006), p. 9.

32. Laura Blum and Steve McClellan, "Selling Where People Buy: The Rise of In-Store TV," *Adweek* 47, no. 28 (July 17, 2006), p. 11.

33. Michael Bellas, "Shopper Marketing's Instant Impact," *Beverage World* 126, no. 11 (November 15, 2007), p. 18.

34. Ibid.

35. "POP Sharpness in Focus," *Brandweek* 44, no. 24 (June 6, 2003), pp. 31–36; David Tossman, "The Final Push—POP Boom," *New Zealand Marketing Magazine* 18, no. 8 (September 1999), pp. 45–51.

36. Betsy Spethmann, "Retail Details," *Promo SourceBook 2005* 17 (2005), pp. 27–28.

37. RoxAnna Sway, "Four Critical Seconds," *Display & Design Ideas* 17, no. 11 (November 2005), p. 3.

38. Catja Prykop and Mark Heitmann, "Designing Mobile Brand Communities: Concept and Empirical Illustration," *Journal of Organizational Computing & Electronic Commerce* 16, No. 3/4 (2006), pp. 301–23.

39. James T. Areddy, "Starbucks, PepsiCo Bring 'Subopera' to Shanghai," *The Wall Street Journal Online* (**http://online.wsj.com/public/article_print/SB119387410336878365.html**), November 1, 2007, p. B1.

40. Thomas Clouse, "Camp Jeep Comes to China," *Automotive News* 82, no. 6281 (November 12, 2007), p. 48.

PART 4

IMC Promotional Tools

11

Database and Direct Response Marketing

Chapter Objectives

After reading this chapter, you should be able to answer the following questions:

- **How** can a marketing team match a database program with an IMC program?

- **What** is meant by "database-driven marketing communications"?

- **Name** the ways a company's database can be used to create permission marketing, frequency programs, and customer relationship management programs.

- **Which** direct response marketing programs are most effective and least effective?

LEVI STRAUSS & CO.

Using Quality Information to Build Relationships

Levi Strauss & Co. has been in business since 1853, when a Bavarian immigrant by the name of Levi Strauss opened his clothing operation. Since that time, the firm has continued to operate, guided by four principles: empathy, originality, integrity, and courage. The goal of integrity has led to a strong emphasis on social responsibility. Empathy and originality fit with designing innovative clothing and knowledgeable customers. Courage is the desire to take bold steps that company leaders believe are right, such as the move toward providing health insurance to same-sex domestic partners.

The company's three primary brands are Levi's, Dockers, and Levi Strauss Signature. The Dockers brand is targeted at older customers. The brand helped maintain sales to consumers who need a little more room in a pair of pants. The Dockers line features pants that are comfortable, fashionable, and acceptable in many workplaces, at least on casual days. Dockers are sold at Sears, JCPenney, and slightly more upscale clothing stores that don't necessarily target just teenage buyers. The Levi Strauss Signature brand is emphasized in Europe and other parts of the world.

For many years, the original Levi's brand was a dominant force in the U.S. teenage and young adult marketplace. In the past two decades, however, some brand erosion has taken place. Many younger buyers began to express the sentiment that Levi's were the jeans worn by their parents. Firms such as Old Navy, Calvin Klein, and other brands were gaining sales at Levi's expense, because younger customers didn't view Levi's as a hip brand.

The company responded to these challenges by developing a strong database marketing program. Levi's marketing team recognized that to be effective, a company's database must be much more than a collection of names and addresses. Levi's reacted by emphasizing relationship marketing, with a goal of understanding what consumers wanted and giving them a voice that would be heard by company leaders. To meet these objectives, the firm used a survey to identify five consumer groups. These groups became part of a pilot program.

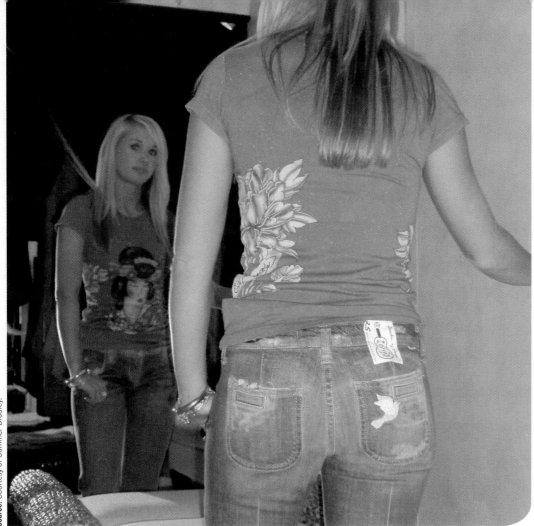

CHAPTER ELEVEN

Source: Courtesy of Summer Bradley.

Using the existing database, the company's marketing team contacted various shoppers and enticed them to fill out questionnaires. In total, nearly 100,000 consumers completed questionnaires, which were distributed at stores, colleges, the Lilith Fair, and via customer service lines. Levi's carefully recorded the "doorway" each respondent used and tied it to other information, which eventually yielded the five major groups of shoppers. Each of the five groups expressed differing needs when it came to jeans.

Next, Levi's targeted the groups individually. Promotions were structured to match the nature of the customer profile that emerged. For example, one group, known as Valuable Shoppers, represented individuals who were willing to spend $60 or more on a pair of pants. These patrons received thank-you gifts following purchases of custom-fit jeans. The gift was a planter with flower bulbs and a card signed by the clerk who took the fitting. Responses from this group were impressive. A Valuable Shopper who was sent a gift purchased, on average, 2.3 more pairs of jeans within the next few weeks.

Online shoppers, who largely came from a group identified as Generation Y, consumers ages 15 to 25, were not given this type of premium. Instead, the marketing team delivered fashion messages to them. Thus, the promotional approach matched the buyer group's characteristics.

By contacting consumers through questionnaires, gifts, promotions, and service lines, Levi's marketing team believed it was able to establish a more intimate form of communication with the company's clientele. This, in turn, helped the company combat declining interest in Levi's products.

Levi's success started with having a fairly well-established database to begin the program, enhancing the database, and listening to what consumers had to say. Any organization that is willing to utilize the talents and programs made available from an effective database management team may be in the position to reap similar rewards.[1]

OVERVIEW

Loyal customers are valuable to every company. They purchase more often and spend more money. Maintaining repeat business is far less expensive than constantly replacing those who turn to other companies. The secrets to developing loyalty include recognition, relationships, and rewards. *Recognition* means knowing who your customers are. *Relationships* means keeping in contact with them over time. *Rewards* make relationships more valuable in consumers' minds.

This fourth section reviews a variety of promotional tools, as displayed in Figure 11.1. Database programs, direct response marketing, and sales promotions are examined next. Also, public relations and sponsorship programs are used to support the overall IMC program.

Database marketing provides the link by which vital communication channels are opened with customers. This, in turn, helps to produce higher levels of customer retention and customer loyalty. Database marketing has become increasingly crucial in the twenty-first century. Fortunately, new technologies associated with the Internet and computer software have made it easier to build and develop strong database programs for communications and marketing.

The first part of this chapter examines database marketing, including methods for building data warehouses, data coding, data mining, as well as data-driven communications and marketing programs. Three data-driven marketing programs are described: permission marketing, frequency programs, and customer relationship management systems. Finally, direct response marketing techniques are presented, including direct mail, television programs, other traditional media, alternative media, and telemarketing.

Today's customers clearly value personalized marketing efforts. Creating programs that both individualize messages and marketing offers but that also do not bombard them or make them feel overloaded represents the essence of successful database and direct response efforts.

DATABASE MARKETING

Database marketing involves collecting and utilizing customer data for the purposes of enhancing interactions with customers and developing customer loyalty. Successful database marketing emphasizes two things: identifying customers and building relationships

FIGURE 11.1
Overview of Integrated Marketing Communications

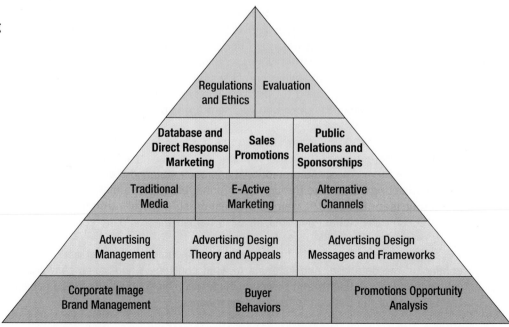

with them. This includes understanding the lifetime values of various customers and the development of customer retention efforts, especially for the firm's best customers. The primary benefit of database marketing is the enhancement of customer loyalty. While database marketing can be used for selling products, retention and relationships should remain the primary focus.

Mitchell's of Westport is a high-end clothing store. When shoppers visit the store, the sales staff has access to data regarding their preferences, sizes, previous purchases, and other information. Purchases are followed-up with thank-you notes. Customers receive notices when new shipments of clothes arrive, and they are given invitations to special events. Loyalty to the store remains high. Even customers who have moved to new cities return to buy clothing.[2] One vital ingredient in this success story stands out: Data are used to make customers feel special and for developing relationships them. While selling occurred, it did not drive the database program.

The tasks associated with database marketing are displayed in Figure 11.2. Of these, building the data warehouse and data coding are key activities. These two tasks are described next.

BUILDING A DATA WAREHOUSE

Successful database marketing requires a quality data warehouse. The **data warehouse** holds all of the customer data. In building one, the IT department and marketing team first distinguish between an operational database and the marketing database. The operational database contains the transactions individuals have with the firm and follows accounting principles. The marketing department manages the marketing database, which contains information about current customers, former customers, and prospects. Examples of data and analyses found in a standard marketing data warehouse include:

- Customer names and addresses
- E-mail addresses and the cookies that record Web visits to the company's Web site
- History of every purchase transaction
- History of customer interactions, such as inquiries, complaints, and returns
- Results of any customer surveys
- Preferences and profiles supplied by the customer
- Marketing promotions and response history from marketing campaigns

Building relationships with business customers is a valuable role of database marketing.

• Building a data warehouse	• Data-driven marketing communications
• Database coding and analysis	• Data-driven marketing programs
• Data mining	

FIGURE 11.2
Tasks in Database Marketing

- Appended demographic and psychographic data from sources such as Knowledge Base Marketing or Claritas
- Database coding through customer analyses, such as lifetime value, customer segment cluster, and RFM (recency, frequency, monetary) analysis

Collecting customer names and addresses is the easiest part of developing the database. The challenge is collecting all of the other information that turns the data warehouse into a powerful marketing and communication tool.

The marketing team typically has a system for updating addresses, because approximately 20 percent of Americans move each year. When individuals fill out a change of address form with the U.S. Postal Service, the information is sent to all of the service bureaus authorized to sell the information to businesses. A company that sends database names to one of these service bureaus receives address updates for only a few cents per hit, or per individual that moves. Updating mailing addresses should occur at least once each year, depending on how the database is used and the frequencies of contacts.

E-Mail and Internet Data

E-mail addresses are essential elements of a quality database. The Internet and e-mail provide excellent, cost-effective channels of communication to be used in building relationships with customers. Most database programs take advantage of cookies to register and store Web site visits and browsing patterns. This information makes it possible to personalize the firm's Web site for each customer. When someone logs onto the site, a greeting such as "Welcome back Stacy" can appear on the screen. The cookie technology makes it possible for the system to recognize that Stacy, or at least someone using her computer, is accessing the Web site. If Stacy has purchased products or browsed the catalog, then the content of the pages can be personalized to contain the products she has an interest in purchasing.

Purchase and Communication Histories

Effective database programs maintain detailed purchase histories of customers. The database records every interaction the company has with a customer. If the customer sends an e-mail to tech support, this information should be placed in the database. If the person returned a product or called customer service with a complaint, the information is documented. Purchases and interaction histories determine future communications with customers and assist the marketing department in evaluating each customer's lifetime value, as well as the other customer value metrics.

Personal Preference Profiles

Purchase and visit histories are not sufficient. Quality database marketing programs include customer profiles with specific information regarding each customer's personal preferences. The manner in which these profiles and personal preference files are constructed varies from company to company. Some may

Purchase and communication history provides important database information for a company such as Scott.

THINK OF SCOTT AS **THE MOTHER LODE.**

scottpowerline.com • Monroe, LA - 877-388-9269 • McDonough, GA - 877-396-1500

Whatever you want, Scott's got. Plus, 24/7 service – anywhere!
From bucket trucks to Mantis cranes (we're the No. 1 dealer in the world), we carry the selection and inventory to get you what you need when you need it. Plus, 24/7 service to keep you running and on the job – anywhere. See all our lines online!

Rentals • Leasing • Service • Sales

SCOTT
POWERLINE & UTILITY EQUIPMENT
One-Stop Scott

be obtained from customer surveys. Others gather information on the Web site or in retail stores.

Every time the company initiates contact with customers, the information is placed in the database, along with the customer's response. This information provides a rich history of what works and what does not. It further allows for customization of communication methods for each customer, which leads to the highest probability of success.

Customer Information Companies

Many times demographic and psychographic information is not available through internal company records. In these cases, the information can be obtained by working with a marketing research firm that specializes in collecting customer data. Knowledge Base Marketing, Donnelly, Dialog, and Claritas are four of the many companies that market this type of information.

Geocoding

One way to append demographic information is **geocoding**, which is the process of adding geographic codes to each customer record so that customer addresses can be plotted on a map. Geocoding helps decision makers finalize placements of retail outlets and can be used to direct marketing materials to specific geographic areas. Geocoding allows for combining demographic information with lifestyle data. This assists the marketing team in selecting media where ads are most likely to be noticed.

One version of geocoding software is named *CACI Coder/Plus*. The software identifies a cluster in which an address belongs. A group such as Enterprising Young Singles in the CACI system contains certain characteristics, such as enjoying dining, spending money on DVDs and personal computers, and reading certain magazines. A retailer could then target this group with mailings and special offers.[3]

Dialog is an online database service that can supply a company with customer information.

Knowing the lifetime value of customers is important in developing a useful database for retailers like Chic Shaque.

DATABASE CODING AND ANALYSIS

The next component in building a database is database coding and analysis. These codes provide critical information for the development of personalized communication. They also assist in creating marketing promotional campaigns. Two common forms of database coding are lifetime value analysis and an RFM analysis.

Lifetime Value Analysis

The first procedure that may be used is the calculation of the lifetime value of a customer or market segment. **Lifetime value** is a figure that represents the profit revenue of a customer throughout the lifetime of a relationship. Some companies calculate the value for individual customers. Others calculate it for customer segments. Many marketing experts believe the latter value is more accurate, because it sums costs across a market segment. Individual lifetime value calculations normally only contain costs for single customers.

The key figures in calculating the lifetime value of a consumer or set of consumers are revenues, costs, retention rates, and visits or purchases per time period, normally

1 year. Revenue and costs are normally easy to obtain, because many companies record these numbers for accounting purposes. Retention rate and purchases per year require an accurate marketing database system.

The cost of acquiring a new customer is important. It is calculated by dividing the total marketing and advertising expenditures in dollars by the number of new customers obtained. As an example, if $1,000 dollars are spent and the company acquires 10 new customers as a result, then the acquisition cost is $100 per customer.

Another key figure is the cost of maintaining a database. This figure represents the number of dollars spent to keep records and enter new information. Typically its does not include any costs associated with customer retention or dollars spent on marketing efforts targeted at customers in the database.

One method for calculating lifetime value is shown in Figure 11.3. The table presents a lifetime value calculation for the database customers of Lilly Fashions. This small retailer has 3,200 customers in its database. Approximately 50 percent of the customers who provide information and join Lilly's database through a membership card stay with the club during the first year. In the second year following the sign up, 60 percent continue with the club. By the third year, approximately 70 percent stay with the club. As indicated by the data from Lilly's Fashions, loyal customers make more purchases and also increase the amounts they spend on each visit. Retaining customers is clearly more efficient and effective than constantly seeking to acquire new customers.

Lilly Fashions chose to calculate a customer's lifetime value for 3 years. There is nothing magic about that figure. A firm can use any number of years, but the longer the period the more difficult it is to estimate future behavior. The calculations for Year 2 and Year 3 are for the Year 1 cohort only. Each year Lilly Fashions adds new members. The lifetime value for each year is kept separately.

Notice that the lifetime value of this set of customers over a 3-year period is $220.60. This is the average amount of profit each of the loyal customers generates for Lilly Fashions. It gives Lilly Fashions an idea of what it can spend on maintaining the loyalty of these customers.

RFM Analysis

A second common metric used in database marketing is **RFM analysis**. RFM refers to the use of the terms *recency, frequency,* and *monetary,* which are used to predict customer behaviors. *Recency* notes the date of the last purchase. *Frequency* is the number of purchases within a specific time period, normally 1 year. *Monetary* refers to the

FIGURE 11.3
Lifetime Value for Lilly Fashions

	Year 1	Year 2	Year 3
Customers	3,200	1,600	960
Retention rate	50%	60%	70%
Visits per year	4	5	6
Sales per visit	$78.00	$94.00	$110.00
Total revenue	$998,400	$752,000	$633,600
Variable costs %	60%	60%	60%
Variable costs $	$599,040	$451,200	$380,160
Acquisition costs ($72)	$230,400		
Database costs ($3)	$9,600	$4,800	$2,880
Total costs	$839,040	$456,000	$383,040
Gross profit	$159,360	$296,000	$250,560
Cumulative gross profit	$159,360	$455,360	$705,920
Lifetime value per customer	**$49.80**	**$142.30**	**$220.60**

monetary expenditures with a firm and is usually expressed as expenditures per year, or other suitable time period.

To code the database in terms of recency, the database will be sorted from the most recent purchase date to the most historic date. The data are then typically split into five equal groups, with each group being assigned a value of 5, 4, 3, 2, or 1. A code of "5" is given for the most recent purchasers, "4" for the second most recent group, and so forth, with the group making the *least* frequent purchases coded "1." The same procedure is used for the frequency, where "5" is assigned to the most frequent purchasers and "1" is assigned to the least frequent purchasers. Finally, the data are coded based on the total amount of money spent using the same procedure.

The end result of the RFM analysis is that each customer is assigned a three-digit code corresponding to recency, frequency, and monetary. Codes for an individual person would range from 555 to 111. A person with a score of 235, for instance, has not recently made a purchase, makes an average number of purchases in terms of frequency, but has spent a large amount of money in total.

The codes provide excellent information as a whole and for each separate number. Clearly a customer with a value of 555 holds the highest value to the company. Further, marketers know that recency has the most significant impact on future purchases. Individuals who have purchased recently (those with a score of "5" as the first number in the code)

An RFM analysis can be used by retailers such as Flair Jewelers.

are more inclined to purchase again. The longer the time since the last purchase, the less likely they will make a purchase or respond to a marketing initiative. The same is true for frequency, although frequency is not as precise in predicting future behavior as is recency. The more frequently an individual makes a purchase (with a score of "5" as the second number in the code), the more likely the person is to make another purchase.

The least predictive figure in the RFM analysis is monetary, the third number in the code. Past purchase size does not necessarily predict that the person will make a future purchase. Consequently, it gives a less clear indication of how valuable that customer may be.

DATA MINING

Another aspect of database marketing, data mining, normally involves two activities: (1) building profiles of customer segments, and/or (2) preparing models that predict future purchase behaviors based on past purchases. **Data mining** is the program used to develop a profile of the company's best customers. The profile, in turn, helps identify prospective new customers. The profile can be used to examine "good" customers to see if they are candidates for sales calls that would move them from "good" to a higher value. Companies offering different types of goods and services will develop multiple profiles. These profiles are used to target sales calls and to look for situations in which cross-selling is possible.

The marketing team at First Horizon National Bank used data mining to expand the company's wealth management business by studying consumer groups. Data about existing customers from the mortgage side of the firm's business made it possible to locate the best prospects for the firm's investment services. The data mining program combined

Haggar placed this ad in women's magazines after data mining revealed many women purchase clothes for their men.

with cross-selling resulted in an increase in company revenues from $26.3 million to $33.8 million in just 1 year.[4]

Retailer American Eagle used data mining to study how consumers responded to price markdowns. The information helped the marketing team determine when to cut prices and by how much in order to optimize sales. Markdown programs were geared to individual stores, because consumers responded differently in each outlet.

Goody's data mining program analyzed baskets of merchandise purchased by individual shoppers. The goal was to determine the types of items customers purchase together.[5] The information helped the marketing team develop advertising and consumer promotions programs, point-of-purchase displays, and store layouts.

The second data mining method involves developing models that predict future sales based on past purchasing activities. Staples, Inc., used a modeling program to examine the buying habits of the company's catalog customers. The program identified the names of frequent buyers. Customized mailings were sent to those customers.

The method used to mine the data is determined by specific informational needs. Once the data have been mined for information, individual marketing programs can be designed. Profiles and models assist in designing the database best suited for each purpose or program. A direct-mail program to current customers is different from one designed to attract new customers. The data provide clues about the best approach for each customer segment.

Data coding and data mining serve two purposes. First, they can be used to develop marketing communications. The marketing team utilizes the information to choose types of promotions, advertising media, and the type of message to be presented to each group of customers. Second, they will be helpful in developing marketing programs. Both of these purposes are discussed in the following sections.

DATABASE-DRIVEN MARKETING COMMUNICATIONS

The primary reason for building a database, coding the information, and data mining is to use the output to establish one-on-one communication with each customer. Personalized communication builds relationships and leads to both repeat business and customer loyalty. The goal is to move the company and its products from brand parity to brand equity. A database marketing program provides the tools to personalize messages and keep records of the types of communications that work and those that do not.

The key technology for database-driven communications is the Internet. Figure 11.4 highlights reasons why the Internet is important in customer interactions. The Internet provides instant communications, easy and viable analyses, and messages can be adapted to specific customers.

FIGURE 11.4
Why the Internet Is Important in Customer Communications

- It is the cheapest form of communication.
- It is available 24/7.
- Metric analysis reveals that the customer read the message, the time it was read, and how much time was spent reading it.
- Customers are able to access additional information whenever they want.
- It can build a bond with customers.

Identification Codes

A database-driven marketing program starts with assigning individual customers IDs and passwords that allow them to access components of the Web site that are not available to those who simply log on to the site. The IDs and passwords are tied to cookies in order to customize pages and individual offers. When the system works properly, the customer does not have to log in each time. Instead, the cookie automatically does it for the user. For example, each time a user accesses Barnes and Noble, he receives a personalized greeting, such as "Welcome, Ken." Next, when an order is placed, the user does not have to type in address or credit card information. It is in the database and comes up automatically. This saves the customer time and effort and increases the probability he or she will make a purchase.

Specialized communications should be sent after the sale. Each time a purchase is made a series of communications follows. First, an e-mail confirming the order and thanking the buyer for the making the purchase is sent. An estimate of shipping date should be included. When the order is pulled and shipped, another e-mail containing the tracking number follows. Some companies include an e-mail at the in-between time, stating that the order is at the warehouse and is being pulled and made ready for shipment.

Customer Profile Information

An effective database-driven communication program relies on customer profiles and any other information about customer preferences to help individualize messages. Lilly Fashions and Bluesky send e-mails about new fashions that have arrived to those in the data file. But, these e-mails do not go to every person in the database. E-mails are sent only to those individuals who have indicated a desire to receive such information or who have indicated they have an interest in fashion news. The goal is to make these customers feel they are receiving special "inside" information.

Customer profiles can also be used to send birthday greetings to loyal customers. Recently, a steak and seafood restaurant sent a card and offered a $10 birthday discount to 215,600 customers who had provided their birthdates. The cost of mailing the birthday card and discount was $90,000. Approximately 40 percent of the cards were redeemed. Each birthday customer brought about 2 other people with them, and those individuals paid full price for their meals. The result was $2.9 million in revenues derived from the program.[6]

The profiles, cookies, and ID numbers are also critical when the customer initiates contact with the company. When a customer contacts the company on the Web or through e-mail, the company already knows something about the individual. Responses can then be created that are tailored to that particular customer.

In-Bound Telemarketing

Contacts made by telephone work in the same way as Internet contacts. The service-call operator knows immediately who is calling. Customer data appears on the screen in front of the in-bound

Through customer profile information, Columbia can identify individuals with high levels of interest in hiking.

TAKE THE ROAD LESS PLOWED.

Columbia
Sportswear Company.

TESTED TOUGH

Every road is a thruway when you're sporting the **Bugabootoo™ Boot**. Seam sealed waterproof leather upper • Omni-Grip® rubber outsole for traction in the snow and on the ice • Thinsulate™ Insulation and a cushioning midsole provide comfort along the way. Visit columbia.com for more information.

Junk in the trunk.

This Volkswagen is carrying an extra burden.

Several hundred actually.

We're not talking weight, or the various awards Jetta has won—most recently Autosite.com's Best Car for the Environment—or even the responsibility of being North America's best-selling Volkswagen.

Those aren't exactly tough burdens to bear.

We're talking about the hundreds of German-engineered advancements we've wedged inside it over the years.

Features like uni-body construction, 8-speaker sound system, 6 standard airbags, traction control and ABS brakes.

Not to mention an extra large trunk. Each one adds a level of performance to the Jetta. But each one can also add weight to its price—if we're not careful.

Lucky for us, we are.

Introducing the jam-packed Jetta at a new low price. Because an award-winning car that's gotten expensive isn't much of an achievement in our book.

 The world has come to expect more from a Volkswagen. The 2008 Jetta. Priced for the people at $16,990.

A company such as Volkswagen can use trawling to correspond with buyers on each yearly anniversary of their purchase.

telemarketer. This allows the operator to treat the caller in a more personal way. When the company calculates either an RFM or a lifetime value code, the operator also knows the value and status of this customer. The operator can ask about a recent purchase or communicate about information provided on the preference or profile lists. The means the operator can greet and treat each customer as an individual, not as just some random person making a call.

Trawling

Database marketing includes a procedure called **trawling**, which is the process of searching the database for a specific piece of information for marketing purposes. Home Depot uses trawling to locate individuals who have recently moved. Home Depot's marketing team believes that with any move there are often expenditures that have to be made for the new home. Most of the time, these items include merchandise sold at Home Depot.

Other marketers trawl a database to find anniversary dates. For instance, a letter with a free gift or special offer may be sent to individuals on the 5th or 10th anniversary with the company. Some car dealerships send a correspondence on each year's anniversary of a car purchase to see if the customer is satisfied or is interested in trading for a new vehicle. Trawling can be used in a wide variety of ways to communicate with specific individuals that meet a particular criterion.

Lifetime Value Segments

A lifetime value segment refers to a group of individuals with a specific value to the firm. Consider the lifetime segments illustrated in Figure 11.5. The Gold segment is a company's very best customers. They shop frequently and spend a lot of money. The Silver segment is slightly less valuable customers; they have a lower lifetime value. Thus, the goal is to continually move customers upward into the next value segment. The company will want to move Silver customers into the Gold customer category. Similarly, the goal should be to move Bronze customers to Silver customers.

Segmenting customers based on lifetime value allows a company to customize marketing programs for each segment. For example, the focus for the Gold segment should be customer reward programs. They are already the best customers, so it makes no sense to spend money trying to get them to purchase more. Instead, the focus is on

FIGURE 11.5
Segmenting Customers by Lifetime Value

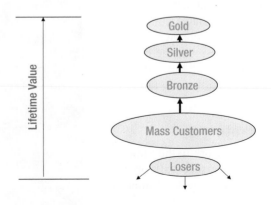

how to retain them. For the Silver group, the focus is on providing rewards, but also on increasing purchase levels to move them into the Gold group. The same strategy is used for the Bronze customers, with incentive marketing programs that will entice them to increase purchases. The incentives are different from those for Silver customers. For the largest group of customers, the mass customers, the goal is to provide incentives that will encourage them to become part of the company's database. Then, the company's marketing team can begin to create personal communications and develop relationships with them.

DATABASE-DRIVEN MARKETING PROGRAMS

Database-driven marketing programs take many forms. They may be used in conjunction with other marketing activities. Some of the more common programs include permission marketing, frequency programs, and customer relationship management efforts. These methods are described next.

Permission Marketing

There has been a strong backlash by consumers regarding spam and junk mail. Consequently, many marketing departments have turned to **permission marketing**, a program in which promotional information is only sent to consumers who give the company permission to do so. Permission marketing programs can be offered on the Internet, by telephone, or through direct mail. Response rates are often higher in permissions programs, because consumers are receiving only the marketing materials they have asked for. Results are further enhanced if permission marketing programs utilize database technology and segment customers. Not everyone who signs up for a permission marketing program is a good customer.

Figure 11.6 lists the steps of a permission marketing program. Permission is normally obtained by providing an incentive for volunteering. Information, entertainment, a gift, cash, or entries in a sweepstakes are common incentives. The information provided is primarily educational and is focused on the company's product or service features. Reinforcing the incentive involves an additional new incentive beyond the original gift. Permission levels are increased by obtaining more in-depth information about a consumer, such as hobbies, interests, attitudes, and opinions. This information can be used to entice additional purchases by offering the individual participant a special deal, which creates a win–win situation for both parties.

Quris, Inc., of Denver, Colorado, solicited travelers and frequent fliers for an e-mail permissions marketing program. The permission marketing e-mails were opened and read regularly by 54 percent of the enrollees in the program. In one year, 64 percent made online purchases that were a direct result of the e-mail permission marketing program. Frequent fliers who participated in the e-mail permission program spent an average of an extra $1,210 per year.[7]

Keys to Success in Permission Marketing

For a permission marketing program to succeed, the marketing team must make sure that the recipients have agreed to participate. Unfortunately, some consumers have been tricked into joining permission marketing programs. A common tactic is used when a

---

1. Obtain permission from the customer.
2. Offer the consumer an ongoing curriculum that is meaningful.
3. Reinforce the incentive to continue the relationship.
4. Increase the level of permission.
5. Leverage the permission to benefit both parties.

FIGURE 11.6
Steps in Building a Permissions Marketing Program

customer completes an online survey or when the person makes an online purchase. To opt out of the permission marketing part of the program, the person must uncheck a box on the site. Although this increases the number of individuals enrolled in the program, the technique often creates negative feelings.

An e-mail marketing piece must be relevant to the consumer receiving it in order for the program to work. Far too many people have joined a permission marketing program that turns into a situation where the consumer has no input and is bombarded with extraneous marketing messages. This does not create loyalty and runs counter to the purpose of a permission program.

One recent survey revealed that 80 percent of consumers stopped reading permission e-mails from companies because they were shoddy or irrelevant. Another 68 percent said the e-mails came too frequently, and 51 percent said they lost interest in the goods, services, or topics of the e-mails. On the whole, consumers delete an average of 43 percent of permission e-mails without ever reading them.[8]

To overcome these challenges, the marketing team should monitor responses and customize the permission program to meet the needs of individual customers. Database technology allows for such customization by tracking responses. For example, if a customer regularly accesses a Web site through a link in an e-mail sent by the company to read the latest fashion news, then this behavior can trigger e-mail offers and incentives on fashions related to the news stories. An individual who does not access the Web site and does not appear to be interested in fashion news receives a different type of e-mail offer. By capitalizing on the power of database technology, a company can enhance the permissions marketing program and make it beneficial to the company and the customer.

Permission Marketing Enticements

What attracts a person to an e-mail permission marketing program? Figure 11.7 lists the top reasons for opting into e-mail programs. At the top of the list is a chance to win something in a sweepstakes. Also, when the individual is already a customer of the company, the person feels favorably predisposed to the company's products.[9] It is normally much easier to entice a current customer into the permissions marketing program than it is to attract a new customer.

When asked what motivates them to remain loyal to a permission marketing relationship, consumers shift their answers. The most frequent reason is the content of the e-mail is particularly interesting, followed by account status updates. Contests and sweepstakes remain an important factor at 34 percent. Figure 11.8 provides the complete list.[10]

Permission marketing programs have the potential to build strong, ongoing relationships with customers when the program offers something of value to the customer. To optimize permission marketing, firms must feature empowerment and reciprocity.[11] **Empowerment** means consumers believe they have power throughout the relationship

FIGURE 11.7
Reasons Consumers Opt into an E-Mail Frequency Program

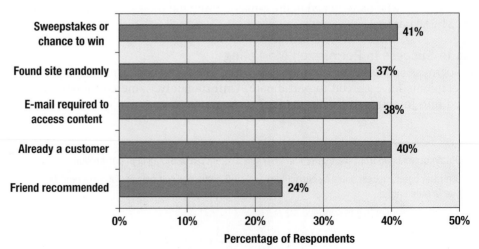

Source: Joseph Gatti, "Most Consumers Have Reached Permission E-Mail Threshold," *Direct Marketing* (December 2003), pp. 1–2.

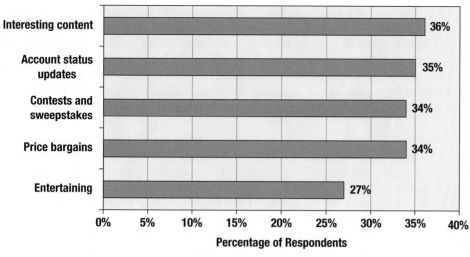

FIGURE 11.8
Reasons Consumers Remain Loyal to a Permission Relationship

Source: Joseph Gatti, "Most Consumers Have Reached Permission E-Mail Threshold," *Direct Marketing* (December 2003), pp. 1–2.

and not just at the beginning when they agreed to join the program. They can make decisions and have choices about what is received.

To maintain positive attitudes, consumers should be given instant rewards along the way, not just at the beginning. This creates feelings of **reciprocity**, which is a sense of obligation toward the company. One mistake that is often made is rewarding consumers only for joining a permission marketing program. Empowerment and reciprocity lead the customer to believe the company values the relationship. This enhances the quality of the program and increases the chances that the consumer will remain an active participant in the program.

Frequency Programs

When a company offers free merchandise or services for a series of purchases, the technique is known as a **frequency program** or **loyalty program**. These efforts encourage customers to make repeat purchases. Frequent flyer programs in the airline industry offer free flights after a certain number of miles have been accumulated by a traveler. Many photo development shops give consumers punch cards that track the number of times the individual brings in film or electronic versions of pictures. Following a certain number (usually 10), the next set will be developed for free.

Airlines use frequent flyer programs due to the presence of brand parity, or the perception that the service is basically the same regardless of which company is being given patronage. Figure 11.9 lists various reasons for developing frequency programs. Frequency programs were first developed to differentiate one brand from its competition; however, now they tend to be common across all competitors in an industry (credit cards, airlines, hotels, etc.).

Goals

Frequency programs target three goals. The first is developing customer loyalty. Matching or preempting the competition is a second objective. Third, higher income individuals tend to join loyalty or frequency programs more than lower income households, which make

---

- ◆ Maintain sales, margins, or profits.
- ◆ Increase loyalty of existing customers.
- ◆ Preempt or match a competitor's frequency program.
- ◆ Induce cross-selling to existing customers.
- ◆ Differentiate a parity brand.
- ◆ Preempt the entry of a new brand.

FIGURE 11.9
Frequency Program Objectives

Source: Grahame R. Dowling and Mark Uncles, "Do Customer Loyalty Programs Really Work?" *Sloan Management Review* 38, no. 4 (Summer 1997), pp. 71–82.

them an inviting market segments to reach. As evidence, marketers point out that 92 percent of households with incomes of $125,000 or higher are actively enrolled in a frequent flyer program compared to only 51 percent for households with incomes below $125,000. Further, participating in a frequency program influences future purchase decisions. About 90 percent of the high-income households said a membership in a frequency program had a moderate to strong impact on purchase decisions.[12] Keeping customers creates repeat purchases. It also makes it possible to cross-sell other goods and services.

Principles

Three principles guide the development of a loyalty program. The first principle, *design the program to enhance the value of the product*, means the program should add value to what the product offers or provide a unique new feature. For example, Miller Brewing offers a loyalty program for beer. The Miller High Life Extras loyalty program allows consumers to earn points by purchasing specially marked 12-packs and 30-packs of Miller High Life. The points can be redeemed for merchandise ranging from High Life screen savers to branded fire pits. Much of the merchandise reinforces the Miller brand. The company's name is featured prominently on branded apparel, including Miller High Life deliveryman shirts, boxer shorts, hooded sweatshirts, and baseball caps.[13]

The more effort a customer expends to participate in a frequency program, the greater the value of the reward should be. Many consumers are willing to put forth greater effort to obtain luxury rewards as opposed to necessity rewards. Shoppers at a grocery store are more likely to be willing to give a higher level of effort in order to receive a free overnight stay at nearby local resort or a free meal at nice restaurant than they would for a $50 gift certificate for food.[14]

The second principle in building a loyalty program is to *calculate the full cost of the program*. This means the marketing team considers record-keeping as part of the cost. Many times the cost of maintaining a frequency account is greater than any additional profits.

The third principle is to *design a program that maximizes the customer's motivation to make the next purchase*. Moderate users of a product are most likely to be enticed by a frequency program. The added incentive encourages loyalty to a particular company or brand.

Harrah's Entertainment, one of the world's largest casino operators, generates $4 billion annually through 45,000 slot machines in 28 casinos. Seventy-five percent of Harrah's 250,000 daily customers are members of the company's rewards program and use the company's "loyalty card." With every push of a button and every swipe of the loyalty card, data are sent to Harrah's computing center. Over 100 million pieces of data are collected daily. The card can be used to track the machines or games a customer plays, how much that customer spends, how long the person stays at a particular machine, and how often the customer goes to a Harrah's casino. The marketing team tracks the gambling behavior of 30 million people. By combining the information with slot records, the marketing team determines the games that are the most popular with various groups, such as men, women, tourists, and locals. The Harrah's staff also knows which slot machines are hot and which are not. The information is used to place slot machines in the best locations at each casino. Other data helps the managers decide which types of machines should be purchased and which ones should be phased out. Finally, the information suggests which customers should receive frequency rewards, such as room upgrades, show tickets, or free-dinner vouchers.[15]

The marketing team should monitor members within a frequency program. RFM analysis is a useful tool. For example, a locally owned restaurant did a recency analysis of its Frequent

Many restaurants, such as The Pasta House, have frequency or loyalty programs for diners.

Diner Club and located 4,000 club members who had not earned any points during the previous 3 months. The restaurant sent a letter to each of the 4,000 offering a $5 discount on dinner. The offer was good for 35 days and the mailing cost $1,800. The results were as follows:

- The average number of member visits per day increased from 25 to 42 during the promotion and to 29 per day after the promotion ended.
- Average visits by individual members holding cards increased both during and after the promotion.
- Incremental sales increased by $17,100 during the promotion and by $4,700 after the 35-day promotion.

By spending $1,800, this promotion led to reactivations by 599 people who had not dined at the restaurant in 3 months. Of the 599 who came back during the promotion, 147 dined at the restaurant after the promotion was over.[16]

Customer Relationship Management

A third database-driven marketing program is customer relationship management (CRM), which generated a great deal of interest in the 1990s. Many companies invested millions of dollars in CRM software, employee training, and implementation. The basic idea behind **customer relationship management** was that companies could use databases to customize products and communications to customers that would result in higher sales and profits. Unfortunately, however, most CRM endeavors were not successful. Many reasons have been given for the poor results; the central key to its failure seems to be that many CRM programs focused on sales rather than on enhancing relationships with customers.

The basic tenets of CRM are sound. The objectives of CRM and its implementation are the ingredients that are usually flawed. Successful CRM programs are designed to build long-term loyalty and bonds with customers through the use of a personal touch, facilitated by technology. CRM programs were designed to go beyond the development of a database and traditional selling tactics to the mass customization of both communications and products.

Two primary metrics of CRM are the lifetime value of the customer and share of customer. The lifetime value concept has already been discussed. The second underlying metric, share of customer, is based on the concept that some customers are more valuable than others and that over time the amount of money a customer spends with a firm can increase. **Share of customer** refers to the percentage of expenditures a customer makes with one particular firm compared to total expenditures in that product's category. Share of customer is a measure of a customer's potential value. The question becomes, "If more is invested by the company in developing a relationship, what will the yield be over time?" When a customer makes only one-fourth of his or her purchases of a particular product with a specific vendor, increasing the share of the customer would mean increasing that percentage from 25 percent to a higher level, thus generating additional sales revenues. The ultimate goal would be leading the customer to make 100 percent of his or her purchases with one vendor.[17]

Glaxo Pharmaceutical's CRM program includes a product information hotline.

If the tenets of CRM were correct, why did so many programs fail? The Gartner Group, a research and advisory firm, found four factors that contributed to these failures. First, the program was often implemented before a solid customer strategy was created. Market segments must be identified so that customization programs can proceed. Failing to understand market segments creates a "ready, fire, aim" approach.[18]

Second, rolling out a CRM program before changing the organization to match it creates problems. A CRM program affects views of how to treat customers as well as how to deliver goods and services to them. This means a new management philosophy is essential. Failing to educate the entire staff about this new perspective and approach quickly leads to problems.

Third, some CRM programs fail because they are technology-driven rather than customer-driven. Technology can only assist in record keeping and some aspects of order fulfillment. The rest is the responsibility of the employees, who must understand the customer and develop customized approaches.

Fourth, CRM programs fail when customers feel like they are being "stalked" rather than "wooed." Trying to build a relationship with a disinterested customer will be more annoying than helpful. For example, the *Dallas Morning News* discovered that its telemarketing program to gain subscribers was annoying people rather than winning them over.

Thus, although the principles of CRM are sound, the execution has not been. Many marketing departments have abandoned its use and are searching for new ways to build relationships with customers.

In general, database-driven marketing programs should be designed to enhance customer loyalty. When a hotel's check-in person knows in advance that a business traveler prefers a nonsmoking room, a queen-size bed, and reads *USA Today*, these items could be made available as the guest arrives. Training hotel clerks and other employees to use the database helps them to provide better service, thereby building loyalty from regular customers. Any organization's marketing department can adapt these techniques to fit the needs of its customers and clients.

Remember that in addition to permission marketing, frequency programs, and CRM systems, other marketing programs can result from database analysis. Internet programs, trade promotions, consumer promotions, and other marketing tactics can be facilitated by carefully using the database.

DIRECT RESPONSE MARKETING

A program that is closely tied to database marketing is direct response marketing. **Direct response marketing** (or **direct marketing**) is vending products to customers without the use of other channel members. Figure 11.10 identifies the most typical forms of direct marketing and percentages of companies using them. Notice that direct marketing is targeted toward customers as well as prospects. According to the Direct Marketing Association, about 60 percent of a typical direct-marketing budget is used for prospecting for new customers; the other 40 percent is spent retaining current customers.[19]

Many companies use multiple forms of direct marketing to increase response rates and sales. In every type of program, a toll-free number and the company's Web site address are frequently displayed so that consumers know how to contact the company for additional information and also to place orders.[20]

Dell created a strong brand and reputation through direct response marketing. Dell's primary direct-marketing tool is its catalog. Several versions of the catalog are mailed each month to current customers and small and medium-size businesses. The catalog program is supplemented by television advertising focused either on the Dell brand or on direct-response offers. Dell's marketing team recently discovered that the company's television spots had a much greater impact on sales than was anticipated. Television generated the largest number of responses, as measured by inbound calls and hits on the company's Web site after seeing an advertisement. Dell also places ads in freestanding inserts (FSIs) in newspapers and on the radio. Both have also proven to be more successful than anticipated in driving traffic to Dell's Web site.[21]

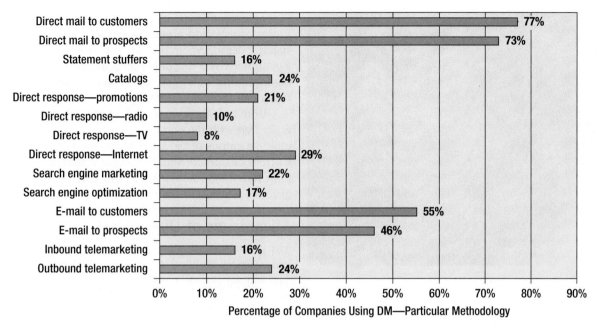

FIGURE 11.10
Methods of Direct Marketing
Source: Richard H. Levey, "Prospects Look Good," *Direct* 16 (December 1, 2004), pp. 1–5.

Direct response advertising, especially television and magazine advertising, is used extensively by pharmaceutical companies. A recent study revealed that this direct response approach works. Ads for prescription medications by pharmaceuticals prompted almost one-third of Americans to ask their doctors about a particular brand of medicine and 82 percent of those who asked their doctors received some type of prescription. The prescription was for the advertised brand 44 percent of the time; for another drug, 56 percent of the time. Sometimes doctors prescribed both the advertised brand as well as another brand.[22]

DIRECT MAIL

As shown in Figure 11.10, mail remains the most common form of direct marketing. Direct mail can be targeted to both consumers and business-to-business customers. The success of a direct mail program is often determined by the quality of the mailing list. Companies have two sources when compiling a mailing list: the firm's internal database or a commercial list.

When the company's internal list is used, the marketing department should carefully parse the list and separate active members from inactive members. The direct mail piece used to prospect for new customers is different from the direct mail piece used to gain repeat purchases. Mailing direct offers to individuals (or businesses) who have not purchased recently but who have purchased in the past will often yield a higher response rate than a cold-call mailing list from a broker.

Types of Lists

The most common approach to direct mail is to purchase a list, either a response list or a compiled list. A **response list** consists of customers who have made purchases or responded to direct mail offers in the past. Brokers selling these lists provide information on the composition of the list and how much was spent by buyers on it. In addition, a "hot list" can be requested that contains the names of individuals who have responded within the past 30 days. Based on the discussion of recency in the previous section, individuals from the hot list are more likely to make purchases. This type of list will cost more, perhaps up to $250 per thousand while the regular response list may sell for $100 per thousand.

A key to a successful direct mail campaign is having a quality target list.

The direct mail piece sent by Diamond Security & Communications.

The second type of list, a **compiled list**, provides information about consumers who meet a specific demographic profile. The disadvantage of a compiled list is that although someone might fit a demographic category, only about one-half of Americans purchase items by mail.

Both response lists and compiled lists are compared with the company's in-house list so that multiple entries of the same name can be removed. Current customers should receive different direct mail flyers than noncustomers or customers who have not purchase recently.

Advantages of Direct Mail

The primary advantage of direct mail is that mail can be easily targeted to various consumer groups. The impact is easily measurable. The marketing team compares the number of mailings to the number of responses. The team can test every component of a direct-mail campaign, including the type of offer, the copy in the ad, graphics used, color, and the size of the mail packet.

Direct mail is an important driver of online sales. A recent study by Pitney Bowes revealed that direct mail is the primary tool for promoting company Web sites. Direct mail was used to advertise a firm's Web site by 70 percent of firms with annual sales of at least $1 million. In addition, 43 percent of Internet sales were driven by some type of direct mail.[23]

Disadvantages of Direct Mail

Clutter is a primary disadvantage of direct mail. Most consumers receive numerous direct-mail offers on a daily basis. Therefore, one key aspect of direct marketing is to make certain only viable prospects receive mailings. A second disadvantage can be cost, especially if the program does not carefully and correctly identify prospective customers.

The technology of direct marketing has greatly improved. Mailings can be customized to the individual recipient through **digital direct-to-press**, a software program that instructs the computer to send a tailor-made message. Digital direct-to-press is popular in the business-to-business sector, where there are fewer total customers to contact than consumer markets. Sending a customize message to each business customer may help the message be viewed. The expense of the software limits the number of companies that can afford it.[24]

CATALOGS

Many consumers enjoy catalogs, and they view them at their leisure. Catalogs have a longer-term impact because they are kept and shared. Catalogs are a low-pressure direct response marketing tactic that allows consumers time to consider goods and prices. Many marketers believe that online shopping has replaced catalog mail-order shopping; however, research by the U.S. Postal Service reveals that although the number of consumers purchasing online has increased, consumers continue to prefer to receive catalogs by mail. In many cases, receiving a catalog is the first step in the buying cycle.[25]

Successful cataloging requires an enhanced database. Many catalog companies such as L.L.Bean, Spiegel, and JCPenney create specialty catalogs geared to specific market segments. The items have a lower cost and a higher yield, because they target individual market segments.

Catalogs are essential selling tools for many business-to-business marketing programs. They provide more complete information to members of the buying center as well as prices for the purchasing agent. When combined with the Internet, a catalog program can provide a strong connection with individual customers.

DIRECT RESPONSE MEDIA

Television, radio, magazines, and newspapers are common tools for direct response advertising. Direct response commercials can be presented on many channels and stations. Often, these commercials are slightly longer (60 seconds), which allows a potential buyer time to find a pen to write down a toll free number, address, or Web site. Catchy, easy-to-remember contact information is often used, such as "1–800-Go-Green" or "www.gogreen.com." The response format is repeated frequently to help the customer remember how to respond. Often a "call-now" prompt concludes the ad.

Television also features infomercials. Cable and satellite systems have led to the creation of numerous direct response channels, with the *Home Shopping Network* as one of the most successful examples. The channel is, in essence, a 24-hour infomercial station. Other channels feature jewelry, foods, and other items.

The second form of direct response infomercial is taped and run on more traditional stations. Many times these programs are featured late at night. Others are placed in spots where rates for running a 30-minute program are low.

Direct response techniques also are used on radio stations and in magazines and newspapers. Radio does not have the reach of television, but it can be targeted by the type of station format. Radio ads must repeat the response number frequently so consumers can make contact.

Print media can be sent to various market segments. Newspaper advertisements may feature Web site information and other quick-response formats. The same is true for magazines. Both provide Web site information and toll-free numbers.[26]

INTERNET

The Internet has become a valuable form of direct marketing. Not only can consumers respond directly to ads placed on a Web site, direct response advertisements can be placed on search engines and used in e-mails.

Notice in Figure 11.10 that e-mail is the third most frequently used form of direct response marketing. E-mail provides a cost-effective method of reaching prospects. It also provides a means of building relationships with current customers through personalization of communication and providing marketing offers tailored to the needs, wants, and desires of each consumer.

Placing ads on search engines and using search engine optimization procedures enable firms to make direct response offers directly to individuals and businesses that are in the market for a particular product. A direct response ad for fruit trees that appears when a person types in "apple trees" is significantly more effective. The same is true for a purchasing agent who types in "computer furniture."

ALTERNATIVE MEDIA

Direct-marketing programs using alternative media represent new ways to reach consumers. **Package insert programs (PIPs)** are materials placed in order-fulfillment packages, such as when a record club includes direct response order forms for jewelry, customized checks, or CD players in a package of CDs or tapes. **Ride-alongs** are materials that are placed with another company's catalog or direct-mail piece, such as the

They love flying
(saved 10% on airline tickets)

ice cream
(saved 75 cents on their favorite sundae)

amusement parks
(saved $20 on family admission)

and the blue envelope.

Valpak

There's something in it for you.

Discover great savings like these inside the envelope and online at www.valpak.com.
To advertise, call 800-368-6476, today.

Valpak offers businesses a unique method to reach customers, who are, in turn, more likely to make purchases.

additional marketing materials packaged with a record club's catalog. **Statement stuffers** are direct mail offers placed inside of a statement, or bill. Credit card bills, utility bills, and many other types of statements will contain one or more direct mail offerings. A **card pack** is a deck of 20 to 50 business reply cards, normally 3 1/2 by 5 inches, placed in a plastic pack. These can be sent to consumers or as part of a business-to-business program.[27] Another successful alternative media program is offered by Valpak, which creates what are called "cooperative direct mail" products. Advertisers place ads into an envelope called "The Blue Envelope of Savings." Postage is shared among the advertisers. Consumer responses have been favorable and strong.

TELEMARKETING

Telemarketing takes place in two ways: inbound or outbound. Inbound telemarketing occurs when an individual initiates a call to a company. When a customer places an order, cross-selling can occur by offering other products or services. Many times inbound calls take place because the customer has a complaint or problem. Direct response marketing can be used to offer the customer a method to solve the problem. For example, when a customer calls a mortgage company because of a late fee, the person can be encouraged to sign up for a direct pay program, which means the customer does not have to worry about possible delays because of the U.S. mail system.

The least popular method for direct marketing is outbound telemarketing. Cold-calling of consumers yields few buyers and alienates many people. No-call list legislation, whereby a person or organization can designate a telephone number that may not be contacted by business organizations using telemarketing programs, has been passed to reduce the number of calls individuals receive. Many people even object to calls from companies with which they do business.

Outbound direct response telemarketing is most successful when it is tied into a database and either customers or prospects are being contacted. An outbound telemarketing program that contacts customers who have not purchased in a year can be successful at bringing those customers back and learning why they have not purchased recently. A company that purchases a copy machine can be called to see if they are interested in a contract that would supply it with paper and toner.

INTERNATIONAL IMPLICATIONS

Database marketing faces the same challenges as other aspects of an IMC program when a firm moves into the international arena. These include differences in technology, which make data collection and analysis more difficult due to issues such as language and Internet availability. Further, local laws may limit the methods by which information can be collected as well as the types of information a company seeks and/or shares with other companies.

In many parts of the world, customers may only live a few miles apart yet at the same time are in a different country. For example, the European Union consists of many nations in close proximity. Therefore, decisions must be made as to whether data will be country specific.

Programs such as permission marketing, frequency, and CRM are subject to legal restrictions as well as cultural differences. In some instances, they may be highly accepted. This is the case for permission marketing in Japan. In many Asian cultures, the giving of gifts takes on added meaning. This may include stronger bonds between customers and companies.

Direct marketing programs also must be adapted to local conditions. Mail delivery systems may be easier to access in some countries than others. The same is true for telephone systems, Internet access, and other technologies. Infomercials may not be possible in countries with state-run television systems. A company's marketing team should consider all local legal, social, cultural, technological, and competitive conditions before embarking on an international database market or direct marketing program.

SUMMARY

Database marketing has become a vital element of creating a complete IMC program. The two key activities involved at the most general level, identifying customers and building relationships with them, have an impact on numerous other IMC tasks. It is clearly more cost-effective to retain customers than to continually seek out new ones. Further, the actual message will change when communicating with long-time, loyal customers.

Building a data warehouse begins with collecting data to be used by the marketing department. Beyond basic information, such as a customer's name, address, and e-mail address, other key data include the customer's purchase history and preferences. Geocoding is the process of adding geographic codes to customer records, which assists in selecting media and creating messages targeted to specific groups.

Database coding and analysis leads to either a lifetime value analysis of customers and customer groups, or RFM analysis of customer spending patterns, or both. Data mining programs involve building profiles of customer segments and/or preparing models that predict future purchase behaviors based on past purchases. The information gathered from data coding and data mining leads to the development of data-driven marketing communications and marketing programs.

Database-driven marketing communication programs are facilitated by effective identification codes that allow for personalization of messages and interactions. An effective database-driven communication program relies on customer profiles combined with other information available regarding specific customers. In-bound telemarketing programs, trawling, advertising, and lifetime value segment programs can be fine-tuned for individual customers.

Database-driven marketing programs include permission marketing, frequency programs, and CRM systems. Permission marketing is a selling approach in which the customer agrees to receive promotional materials in exchange for various incentives. Frequency programs are incentives customers receive for repeat business. Both are designed to create customer loyalty over time. CRM is designed to build long-term loyalty and bonds with customers through the use of a personal touch facilitated by technology.

Closely related to database marketing is direct response (or direct) marketing. These efforts may be made by mail, catalog, phone, mass media, the Internet, or e-mail. Direct mail programs remain most popular as out-bound telemarketing programs continue to diminish.

In the new age of marketing communications, a case can be made that individual consumers desire greater intimacy with the companies that serve them. They are drawn to firms that take the time to build relationships through quality, customized communications and marketing programs. It seems likely that this trend will continue and that successful marketing teams must continue to emphasize methods for identifying customers and personalizing relationships with them.

KEY TERMS

data warehouse The place where customer data are held.

geocoding Adding geographic codes to customer records to make it possible to plot customer addresses on a map.

lifetime value Sales revenues generated by a customer throughout the lifetime of his or her relationship with a company.

RFM analysis The use of recency, frequency, and monetary figures to predict consumer behaviors.

data mining The process of searching a database to develop a profile of the company's best customers.

trawling The process of searching the database for a specific piece of information for marketing purposes.

permission marketing A form of database marketing in which the company sends promotional materials to customers who give the company permission to do so.

empowerment Consumers believe they have power throughout the seller–consumer relationship, not just at the beginning when they agreed to join a frequency program.

reciprocity A sense of obligation toward a company that results from receiving special deals or incentives such as gifts.

frequency (or loyalty) program A marketing program designed to promote loyalty or frequent purchases of the same brand (or company).

customer relationship management (CRM)   Programs designed to build long-term loyalty and bonds with customers through the use of a personal touch facilitated by technology.

share of customer   The percentage of expenditures a customer makes with one particular firm compared to total expenditures in that product's category.

direct response (or direct) marketing   Vending products to customers without the use of other channel members.

response list   A list of customers who have made purchases or who have responded to direct mail offers in the past.

compiled list   A list consisting of information about consumers who meet a specific demographic profile.

digital direct-to-press   Software that instructs the computer to create a tailor-made direct mail message to a customer.

package insert programs (PIPs)   Marketing materials placed in order fulfillment packages.

ride-alongs   Marketing materials that are placed with another company's catalog or direct-mail piece.

statement stuffers   Direct mail offers placed inside of a statement or bill.

card pack   A deck of 20 to 50 business reply cards, normally 3 1/2 by 5 inches, placed in a plastic mail pack.

REVIEW QUESTIONS

1. What two activities are part of a successful database marketing program?
2. What is a data warehouse? What is the difference between an operational database and a marketing database?
3. Name the steps involved in building a data warehouse.
4. What is geocoding?
5. Define lifetime value. How is it determined?
6. What does RFM stand for? Explain what an RFM code describes.
7. What are the two primary functions of data mining?
8. Explain the importance of identification codes in database-driven marketing communications.
9. Explain the roles consumer profile information plays in in-bound telemarketing, trawling, and advertising.
10. Describe a permission marketing program. What are the key benefits of this approach?
11. What are the keys to an effective permission marketing program?
12. Describe a frequency program. Which type of user pays off the best in a frequency program—light, medium, or heavy users?
13. What is customer relationship management? Explain why most CRM programs have not been successful.
14. What is meant by the term share of customer?
15. What is direct response marketing?
16. Explain how response lists and compiled lists are used in direct mail programs.
17. Why is digital direct-to-press popular in business-to-business direct marketing?
18. Explain the two ways infomercials are presented as parts of a direct response program.
19. Describe the use of package insert programs, ride-alongs, statement stuffers, and card packs in direct response marketing.
20. What is a no-call list? How is it related to outbound telemarketing?

CRITICAL THINKING EXERCISES

Discussion Questions

1. Assume that you are the account executive at a database marketing agency. A music retailer has asked you to develop a database for the company. How would you go about building a data warehouse? What information should be in the databases? Where and how would you obtain the data?
2. Review the section entitled "Lifetime Value" and study Figure 11.3, which presents data on the lifetime value of customers in Lilly Fashions' database. The manager of Lilly Fashions knows that each customer in the database generates an average of $220.60 in profit over 3 years. In order to encourage loyalty, retention, and increased spending, the manager has decided to devote $30 per year per customer to this effort. Based on material presented in this chapter, what types of marketing and retention efforts would you encourage for Lilly Fashions? Justify your recommendations.
3. Lilly Fashions has a database of customers. This means the marketing team can use data mining to improve its marketing efforts. Suggest ways data mining can be used to develop marketing programs for the company's current customers. How can it be used to attract new customers?
4. ForeverWed sells wedding supplies via the Internet to individuals as well as wedding coordinators and planners. Access the company's Web site at **www.foreverwed.com**. ForeverWed realizes that personalized communications with individuals who visit its Web site are important in building relationships and sales. Review the concepts presented in the section "Database-Driven Marketing Communications." What steps should the company take to develop data-driven communications with visitors to the Web site, as well as individuals who make a purchase?
5. Using the information provided in the previous question, discuss how ForeverWed could develop a permission

marketing program. How can the marketing team encourage individuals to give permission to receive e-mail marketing materials? Once the company has the customer's permission, how can the relationship be continued to make it beneficial to both the consumer and to ForeverWed?

6. A primary reason for developing a frequency program is to encourage customers to be loyal to a business or brand. For each of the following products, discuss the merits of a frequency program. What types of incentives would individuals need to join the frequency club and then participate in the program?

   a. Local restaurant

   b. Auto repair service

   c. Printing service

   d. Clothing retailer

7. Examine the forms of direct response marketing shown in the graph in Figure 11.10. Which ones have you responded to in the past? Which ones are most likely to influence a purchase decision? Which ones are the least likely? Discuss the type of direct response offer and ad that influences your purchase decision.

8. Suppose ForeverWed wants to use direct response advertising to accomplish two goals: (1) to sell specific merchandise and (2) to encourage individuals to visit the Web site. Which types of direct response advertising would be the most effective? Why? What type of direct response offer should ForeverWed make?

9. Examine the direct marketing methods highlighted in Figure 11.10. Evaluate each method for the following types of businesses. Which ones would be the best? Which ones would not work as well? Justify your answers.

   a. Shoe store

   b. Sporting goods retailer

   c. Internet hosiery retailer (sells only via the Internet)

   d. Manufacturer of tin cans for food-processing companies

10. Form a group of four to five students. Ask each person in the group to list the catalogs that have come into his or her home during the past 2 weeks. Have each person discuss why he or she receives certain catalogs. Next, discuss how often each of you orders something out of a catalog and how the order was placed. Is anyone in the group accessing the Internet for information given in a catalog or ordering from a catalog after accessing a Web site? Discuss how important the catalog market is to you and what you see as the future of catalog marketing.

INTEGRATED LEARNING EXERCISES

1. Pick one company that sells blue jeans. Go to the company's Web site. What evidence do you see of database marketing and of personalization of the Web site? Describe a database marketing program that the company could use.

2. Go to Web site for Scotts Miracle Gro at **www.scott.com**. What evidence do you see of database marketing and of personalization? Review the concepts presented in the section "Database-Driven Marketing Communications." What steps should Scotts take to develop data-driven communications with visitors to the Web site as well as individuals who make purchases?

3. A number of companies specialize in database marketing. You are the manager of a small chain of 25 restaurants. Review the Web site of each of the following companies. Outline what each company offers. Which one would be the best for your company? Why?

   a. Database Marketing Solutions (**www.database marketing.com**)

   b. Advanced Marketing Consultants (**www.marketing principles.com**)

   c. Dovetail (**www.dovetaildatabase.com**)

4. *DM News* is a trade journal for database marketing and customer relationship management programs. Access the Web site at **www.dmnews.com**. What types of information are available on the site? How could this help companies with database marketing and CRM programs? Access and read one of the articles from the journal. Write a paragraph about what you learned.

5. CentricData is a database marketing firm that specializes in mid-to-large size retailers. Access the Web site at **www.centricdata.com**. What type of services does CentricData offer? How could this company help a retail store develop a database marketing program?

6. The Direct Marketing Association (DMA) is a global trade association of business and nonprofit organizations that use direct marketing tools and techniques. Access the trade organization's Web site at **www.the-dma.org**. What services does the DMA provide its members? What value would this be to a business in developing a direct marketing response program?

7. A primary key in successful direct marketing is the quality of the list that is used. One company that specializes in compiling lists is US Data Corporation. Access the company's Web site at **www.usdatacorporation.com**. What types of lists does the company offer? Access one of the lists and describe how that list can be compiled. Discuss how a company could use US Data Corporation for a direct response marketing campaign.

8. Almost all hotels have some type of frequency or loyalty program. Examine the loyalty programs of the following hotels. Critique each one. Which ones are best? Why?

   a. Best Western (**www.bestwestern.com**)

   b. Days Inn (**www.daysinn.com**)

   c. Doubletree Inn (**doubletree.hilton.com**)

   d. Marriott (**www.marriott.com**)

   e. Radisson (**www.radisson.com**)

   f. Wyndham Hotels & Resorts (**www.wyndham.com**)

CREATIVE CORNER

Student Project

Lilly Fashions sells fashionable clothes in the mid-to-upper price range to females ages 15 to 30. Lilly's wants to capitalize on the concepts of database marketing and direct response marketing. Design a newspaper advertisement that encourages females in the company's target market to visit the retail store and join Lilly's database program. In addition, design a direct mail piece that would go out to individuals who are currently in their database but have not made a purchase within the last 3 months. Design an e-mail that can be sent out to members in the database on the person's birthday offering them a free meal at a local restaurant. All they have to do is come to the store to pick up the meal voucher. This promotion is a joint promotion with the restaurant, which shares in the cost of the promotion. Thus, the restaurant must also be part of the e-mail letter.

CASE 1 FOLLOW THE BEST

George Coffman's entrepreneurial adventure began in a pattern that was similar to many other start-ups. He had grown increasingly tired of answering to a supervisor that he did not respect and believed simply lacked the knowledge to manage his department. At the same time, an idea continued to preoccupy his mind: What if he started a company that was essentially a male version of Lillian Vernon? After all, Lillian Vernon had been named to the Direct Marketing Hall of Fame in 1994 and continued a successful run to the present day.

Rather than using a person's name, George chose to brand his company Maximus. He believed the name conjured up images of maleness and virility. The range of products offered by Lillian Vernon includes personalized gifts, holiday items, home and office products, garden and outdoor items, bags, jewelry and accessories, and toys. Maximus would offer many of the same products, with an emphasis on masculine products for home and office and sportswear fashions.

The evolution of Lillian Vernon was of particular interest to George. Ms. Vernon had begun her company by personalizing items for women out of her garage. Initially she solicited business with magazine advertisements. Eventually her company grew to the point where a full catalog was developed. A large number of the sales came from call-in orders. As new technologies emerged, Lillian Vernon expanded into Web sites, some retail stores, and Internet communications.

Maximus would follow a similar route. The first items to be offered would be personalized sportswear, focused on hunting, fishing, and other outdoor activities. George believed many hunters and fishermen would enjoy seeing their initials embossed on boots, coats, super-warm socks, and other items. He would begin by advertising in *Field and Stream* and similar magazines. He would also try look for ways to reach the women who might wish to buy these items as gifts for Father's Day, Christmas, and birthday celebrations.

The idea was to expand into other lines as the brand gained recognition. The first target market, male sportsmen, would eventually expand into men who preferred other activities, such as gardening. Also, those with home offices who wanted to personalize some space would be targeted.

George had pitched his idea to several investment capital companies. He had struck a chord with some investors. They had bought in, which provided Maximus with start-up funds and monies for his original advertising and promotions. The investors insisted that George consider building a database marketing program as part of his start-up.

1. How can George gather names, addresses, and e-mail addresses of potential customers?

2. What types of database-driven marketing communications will be most successful for Maximus?

3. Can Maximus utilize a permission marketing program or a frequency program? If so, how?

4. Using the Lillian Vernon Web site as a guide (**www.lillianvernon.com**), construct the opening screen of a Web site for Maximus.

CASE 2 LINCOLN MEDICAL SUPPLY

Sara Holmes has just taken on a unique dual role in her job at Lincoln Medical Supply. She was to be in charge of the marketing database for the company and also would serve as liaison with the advertising firm and marketing group that provided promotions for the organization. Sara was told her input would be heavily counted on to help with key decisions to build the size and scope of the company in the next several years.

Lincoln Medical Supply was located in Lincoln, Nebraska. The company served both retail and business-to-business markets by selling and servicing various types of medical equipment, from items as basic as ankle braces to those as sophisticated as fetal monitors. The company had achieved a great deal of success simply through the sheer demand for various products, but the management team was concerned that no coherent marketing plan had ever been developed.

Sara was told that the company had three basic customer groups:

- Retail walk-in buyers
- Physicians' offices
- Hospitals

Retail customers purchased the lower-cost, less intricate items, such as braces, bandages, and cold packs. Physicians bought more elaborate equipment and also provided referrals for patients. Hospitals ordered the big-ticket items. Each customer type generated a solid source of revenue for the organization.

Sara's first challenge was to develop a database for each type of customer. Her potential sources for retail customers were insurance forms (many filed for insurance to pay for the items involved) and sales ticket information requested from each person. Doctors' offices could be sources of a great deal of information, but the company often had to "push" the staff to provide statistics on numbers of patients, types of expenditures, and other key facts. Hospitals could be assessed through internal company reports and as well as by accessing data from external sources.

Following the simple generation of data, Sara would need to decide if all this information should be compiled into one overall data warehouse, or if it should be separated by customer type. Clearly the needs of each group were different, and therefore it seemed plausible that the marketing tactics used for each customer type would also vary. At the same time, Sara wanted a consistent message sent out that Lincoln Medical Supply stood for consistent, high-quality, and excellent service advantages. She knew the name "Lincoln" didn't help, because so many companies in the city also used the name (e.g., Lincoln Electric Supply, Lincoln Party Favors, and so forth).

Source: Courtesy of Ron May; Pearson Education/PH College.

Sophisticated medical equipment as well as simple medical supplies, such as leg braces, are sold by Lincoln Medical Supply.

Sara held a meeting with the marketing team. The group told her the primary goal was to build greater brand equity in the name, because a new medical supply house had just opened near one of Lincoln's biggest hospitals. Next, the company's leaders wanted to know how to get walk-in buyers to purchase more items and how to expand purchases from the other two segments of the business at the same time. The leaders discussed the use of catalogs and an Internet site to widen the scope of product offerings. They also considered the possibility of opening satellite locations in Omaha (50 miles away), Grand Island (90 miles west), and North Platte (400 miles away). They wanted to develop an understanding of the type of individual who would venture into a medical supply store, what the person might buy, and what the person would not buy. They also needed to know if they were meeting the needs of physicians and hospitals. With all of these challenges in mind, Sara took a deep breath and started working.

1. Identify the sources of internal and external data for all three types of customers.

2. What types of data should Sara collect from each type of customer?

3. How can Sara meet the goals imposed on her by the marketing group?

4. What kinds of marketing programs could be developed from the data Sara generates? Should the data be separated by customer type or combined into one major database? Why or why not?

5. Is Lincoln Medical Supply a candidate for a CRM program? Why or why not?

ENDNOTES

1. Betsy Spethmann, "Can We Talk?" *American Demographics* 21, no. 3 (1999), pp. 42–45; Levi Strauss (**www.levistrauss.com**, accessed June 6, 2005).

2. Brian Sullivan, "Winners Focus on Customers," *Computerworld* 35, no. 24 (June 11, 2001), pp. 50–51.

3. Leo Rabinovitch, "America's 'First' Department Stores Mines Customer Data," *Direct Marketing* 62, no. 8 (December 1999), pp. 42–45.

4. Howard J. Stock, "Connecting the Dots," *Bank Investment Consultant* 13, no. 3 (March 2005), pp. 28–31.

5. Jordan K. Speer, "Digging Deep: Extreme Data Mining," *Apparel Magazine* 45, no. 12 (August 2004), p. 1; Eric Cohen, "Database Marketing," *Target Marketing* 22, no. 4 (April 1999), p. 50.

6. Arthur M. Hughes, "The Importance of Customer Communications," *Database Marketing Institute* (**www.dbmarketing.com/articles/ART233.htm**, August 23, 2007).

7. "High-Fliers Are Attractive Buyers," *Marketing News* 38, no. 1 (September 15, 2004), p. 2.

8. Joseph Gatti, "Poor E-Mail Practices Provoking Considerable Customer Defection," *Direct Marketing* (December 2003), pp. 1–2.

9. Joseph Gatti, "Most Consumers Have Reached Permission E-Mail Threshold," *Direct Marketing* (December 2003), pp. 1–2.

10. Ibid.

11. J. Walker Smith, "Permission Is Not Enough," *Marketing Management* 13, no. 3 (May–June 2004), p. 52.

12. Arthur M. Hughes, *Strategic Database Marketing* (New York: McGraw Hill, 2006).

13. Mike Beime, "Miller Launches Year-Long Loyalty Program," *Brandweek.com* (**www.brandweek.com/bw/news/recent_display.jsp?vnu_content_id=1003719329**, March 4, 2008).

14. Ran Kivetz and Itamar Simonson, "Earning the Right to Indulge: Effort As a Determinant of Customer Preferences Toward Frequency Program Rewards," *Journal of Marketing Research* 39, no. 2 (May 2002), pp. 155–70.

15. Daniel Lyons, "Too Much Information," *Forbes* 174, no. 12 (December 13, 2004), pp. 110–14.

16. Arthur M. Hughes, "The Importance of Customer Communications," *Database Marketing Institute* (**www.dbmarketing.com/articles/ART233.htm**, August 23, 2007).

17. "CRM Metrics," *Harvard Management Update* 5, no. 3 (March 2000), pp. 3–4.

18. Darrell K. Rigby, Frederick F. Reichheld, and Phil Schefter, "Avoid the Four Perils of CRM," *Harvard Business Review* 80, no. 2 (February 2002), pp. 101–108.

19. Richard H. Levey, "Prospects Look Good," *Direct* 16, no. 6 (December 1, 2004), pp. 1–5.

20. "Publishers Witness Mailing Boost," *Precision Marketing* 16, no. 16 (February 13, 2004), p. 9.

21. Carol Krol, "Dell Sees Continued Success with DM," *BtoB* 89, no. 12 (October 25, 2004), p. 8.

22. Julie Appleby, "As Drug Ads Surge, More Rx's Filled," *USA Today* (**www.usatoday.com/news/health/2008–02–29-drugs-main_N.htm**, February 29, 2008).

23. Cara Beardi, "E-Commerce Still Favors Traditional Techniques," *Advertising Age* 71, no. 43 (October 16, 2000), pp. 2–3.

24. Patrick Totty, "Direct Mail Gets a New Lease on Life," *Credit Union Magazine* 66 no. 4 (April 2000), pp. 36–37.

25. Carol Krol, "USPS Magazine Touts Direct Mail," *BtoB* 90, no. 3 (March 14, 2005), p. 20.

26. Based on Jay Kiltsch, "Making Your Message Hit Home: Some Basics to Consider When . . . ," *Direct Marketing* 61, no. 2 (June 1998), pp. 32–34.

27. John Ahern and Rachel McLaughlin, "What You May Not Have Known, But Were Afraid to Ask," *Target Marketing* 21, no. 9 (September 1998), pp. 14–15.

12

Sales Promotions

Chapter Objectives

After reading this chapter, you should be able to answer the following questions:

- **What** are the two main categories of sales promotions and how do they differ?

- **What** are the advantages and disadvantages of the various types of consumer promotions?

- **What** are the major categories of trade promotions and how are they used?

- **How** can a marketing team tie consumer promotions to trade promotions and other elements of the promotions mix?

- **What** are the potential limitations when sales promotions programs are being developed for international customers?

SALES PROMOTIONS AND MORE HOOK FANS

"What is your favorite word?" This question was posed by baseball executive Jay Miller at a recent management and marketing conference. "If you think about it, it might be that one of your favorite words is your own name," he said with a smile. Miller continued, "When you come to our ballpark, we are going to know your name." In truth, Jay Miller is talking about two ballparks with which he is associated, one in Corpus Christi, Texas, and the other in Round Rock, Texas. The ballparks are home to minor league professional baseball teams.

The Corpus Christi team, the Hooks, is a stellar success. The organization, an affiliate of the Houston Astros, averages more than 7,000 fans per game over 72 home dates each summer. This ranks among the top franchises at the Double-A level of professional baseball. Beyond the statistics, however, is the sense of civic pride that permeates the team, the fans, and the entire organization. In a city with a large Hispanic community, the term *la familia* clearly applies. The Hooks are a family that hosts a large number of guests at each game.

Professional baseball thrives on consumer promotions. For fans, numerous discounts and giveaways are part of the scene. In 2008, the Hooks staged over 30 promotional nights. The free gifts included bobbleheads, baseball card sets, duffle bags, blankets, photos, autographed souvenirs, and more. In addition, the team offers "One Dollar Hot Dog and Soda Night," "Half-Price Group Night," "Thirsty Thursdays," and "Friday Fireworks."

Sponsorships and trade promotion tie-ins are widely utilized. The ballpark is known as "Whataburger" field, due to the sponsorship of the popular hamburger chain. Whataburger hosts its own fan day. Other sponsors place advertising on the scoreboard, field, walls, and other places. Special corporate box seats are available for entertaining clients and rewarding employees. Various business organizations are featured on the videoboard and on items given to fans. In addition, the Hooks have created ties with several local charities and civic organizations, including the "Get Hooked on Reading" program for young fans.

All of these sales promotions serve to enhance the rest of the organization's marketing efforts. Jay Miller and CEO Reid Ryan strongly emphasize the importance of "awesome customer service." At a Hooks game, everyone from parking attendants to the ticket takers to the ushers

CHAPTER TWELVE

Source: Courtesy of Ryan Sanders Baseball.

and concessions personnel focuses on friendly, first-name care. Miller and Ryan routinely circulate through the stands to mingle with fans, solve any problems, and provide an occassional extra thrill. One of their favorites is to find a family sitting in the cheapest (most distant) seats in the stadium and move them to the owner's box next to the field.

The team also hosts a "postgame catch" in which many lucky kids are brought down to the field to play catch with the players. On Sundays, or "Kids Day," fans are allowed on the field prior to the game. Many times disadvantaged children, Little Leaguers, and others are paired with a player to go out on the field as the game is about to begin to stand during the national anthem. Other attendees participate in the "Dizzy Bat Race" or in races with the Hooks mascot. Even those who stay in the stands may find themselves featured in "Kiss Cam" or "Fan Cam" on the 16-by-22-foot video screen between innings.

Reid Ryan's father is Hall of Fame pitcher Nolan Ryan, who is one of the principle owners of the team. Reid believes the success of the organization, known as Ryan Sanders Baseball, is based on promoting a summer-long experience rather than a single event. Instead of focusing on wins and losses or even on players, the enjoyment of attending a series of games in a low-cost, family friendly environment remains

Source: Courtesy of Ryan Sanders Baseball.

Reid Ryan

Jay Miller

the key to long-term fan loyalty. Players come and go, teams win and lose, but a fun summer evening with family and friends creates a long-lasting impression. The Hooks' advertising tagline, "Catch a Memory-Hooks Baseball," expresses this feeling.

Jay Miller has been associated with professional baseball for over 24 years. He has been named "Executive of the Year" on more than one occasion. He is proud to report that sales of memorabilia for the Hooks is higher than the majority of minor league teams, an indication of the strong loyalty in the community. A walk down the streets of Corpus Christi or a visit to the ballpark confirms the devotion fans show by proudly wearing caps, T-shirts, and jerseys with the Hooks insignia and logo.

Both Miller and Ryan stress the importance of brand and image building. In a marketplace where a wide variety of summertime activities are possible, they emphasize the goal of being top-of-mind, or the family's first choice. A stadium full of happy customers for every home game provides all the evidence they need that their approach is working.[1]

OVERVIEW

Some marketers may be tempted to think that once a high-quality advertising program has been put in place, the task of promotion is almost complete. Of course, this is not the case. A fully integrated marketing communications program includes additional activities. This chapter describes sales promotions programs. **Sales promotions** consist of all of the incentives offered to customers and channel members to encourage product purchases.

Sales promotions take two forms: consumer promotions and trade promotions. **Consumer promotions** are the incentives that are directly offered to a firm's customers or potential customers. Consumer promotions are aimed at those who actually use the product, or end-users. They may be individuals or households. Another end-user may be a business that consumes the product, and the item is not resold to another business. In other words, consumer promotions are offered in both consumer markets and business-to-business markets.

Trade promotions are used only in the distribution channel. **Trade promotions** consist of the expenditures or incentives used by manufacturers and other members of the marketing channel to purchase goods for eventual resale. Trade promotions provided to other firms help push products through to retailers.

In the past, some marketing experts believed that any type of sales promotion, whether consumer or trade, eroded brand equity. They suggested that the incentives simply encouraged customers, businesses, and the distribution channel to focus on price. Recently, however, that view has changed. Many company leaders recognize that promotions can differentiate a brand from the competition. This increased differentiation builds brand awareness and improves a brand's image.[2]

The marketing team carefully designs promotional programs that help the company reach its IMC objectives and that support a brand's position in the marketplace. In the early stages of a product's life cycle, promotions are typically designed to match advertising and other efforts focused on brand awareness, creating opportunities for trial purchases and stimulating additional purchases. Later, the goal may shift to strengthening a brand, increasing consumption, fending off competition, or finding new markets.

This chapter examines consumer promotions first, followed by trade promotions. Although the presentations are separate, keep in mind that the marketing team designs both at the same time. The adjustments that are made to sales promotions programs in international markets are also described.

CONSUMER PROMOTIONS

Enticing a consumer to take the final step and make the purchase is one of the primary goals of a consumer promotions program. Advertising creates the interest and excitement that brings the consumer into the store. Marketers then use other tactics. In addition to

- ◆ Coupons
- ◆ Premiums
- ◆ Contests and sweepstakes
- ◆ Refunds and rebates
- ◆ Sampling
- ◆ Bonus packs
- ◆ Price-offs

FIGURE 12.1
Types of Consumer Promotions

leading to the final decision to buy an item, consumer promotions programs can be highly effective in generating traffic to a store and enhancing brand loyalty.

In 2007, Taco Bell created a unique promotion program. The restaurant chain offered every person in the U.S. a free taco if one of the players in the World Series stole a base during the game. In the fourth inning of the second game, Boston Red Sox rookie Jacoby Ellsbury stole second base. The free tacos were given out between 2:00 to 6:00 P.M. the next day. The estimated cost of the giveaway was $1 million; however, when customers purchased a drink or other food with the free taco, the actual cost to the company was lower.[3] Marketing professionals estimated the value of the buzz and publicity to be $5.6 million. The figure was based on the idea that the giveaway created news that was featured on ESPN and other sports channels. It also resulted in chatter on blogs and social networks. The ensuing publicity was far better than any advertising the company could have purchased.

As the Taco Bell example suggests, consumer promotions can be highly effective. The two most general categories of consumer promotions are franchise-building promotions and sales-building promotions. *Franchise-building promotions* are designed to increase awareness of and loyalty to a brand. Building a favorable image by pointing out unique features and selling points is the goal. This also reduces reliance on discounts to increase sales.

Sales-building promotions focus on immediate sales, rather than brand equity or loyalty, through discounts, prizes, or other enticements. From the list of consumer promotions in Figure 12.1, franchise-building promotions would be premiums, contests, sweepstakes, sampling, and bonus packs. Sales-building promotions would include coupons, refunds, rebates, and price-offs. Each of these forms of promotions is described next.

COUPONS

A coupon is a price reduction offer to a consumer. It may be a percentage off the retail price, such as 25 or 40 percent, or an absolute amount, such as 50 cents or $1. In the United States, 323 billion coupons were distributed and 3 billion were redeemed within just a year. The 0.93 percent redemption rate represents approximately $3.47 billion in savings for consumers, or about 89 cents per coupon.[4] Approximately 78 percent of all U.S. households use coupons, and 64 percent are willing to switch brands with coupons.[5] Figure 12.2 provides a more detailed breakdown of coupon usage.

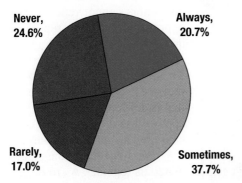

FIGURE 12.2
Percentage of Consumers Coupon Usage

Source: Karen Holt, "Coupon Crimes," *PROMO* 17, no. 5 (April 2004), pp. 23–29.

FIGURE 12.3
Methods of Distributing Coupons

- ◆ Print media
- ◆ Direct mail
- ◆ On- or in-package
- ◆ In-store
- ◆ Sampling
- ◆ Scanner delivered
- ◆ Cross-ruffing
- ◆ Response offer
- ◆ Internet
- ◆ Fax
- ◆ Sales staff

Coupon Distribution

Approximately 80 percent of all coupons are issued by manufacturers. Figure 12.3 lists the various forms of coupon distribution. Nearly 90 percent of all coupons are sent out through print media. Approximately 88 percent are distributed through **freestanding inserts (FSIs)**. FSIs are sheets of coupons distributed in newspapers, primarily on Sunday. The average person receives 850 freestanding inserts per year. Other methods of distribution include in-store, on-shelf, and electronically dispensed coupons, along with coupons attached to free samples of a product. The remaining coupons are distributed in or on product packages, by direct mail, and in magazines and newspapers.[6]

FSIs and print media are used to distribute coupons for several reasons. First, a consumer must make a conscious effort to clip or save the coupon. Second, coupons create brand awareness. The consumer sees the brand name on the coupon even when the coupon is not redeemed. Third, FSIs encourage consumers to purchase brands on the next trip to the store. Consumers are more likely to purchase a couponed brand and remember the brand name when they redeem a coupon, which helps move the brand to a consumer's long-term memory. The consumer is more likely to recall the brand and buy it the next time the need arises, even without a coupon.

A manufacturer's coupon for 50 cents off the new Snax Stix.

Source: Courtesy of Keebler Company.

Types of Coupons

Coupons are often distributed in retail stores and placed on or near packages. The consumer can immediately redeem the coupon while making the purchase. This type of coupon is called an *instant redemption coupon.* These coupons often lead to trial purchases and purchases of additional packages of a product. Many grocery stores allow a company to cook a new food product and offer free samples along with coupon giveaways. Coupons are also placed in dispensers near various products, which provide convenient access for customers. All of these are forms of instant redemption coupons, because customers can use them immediately.

Coupons can also be placed inside packages so that customers cannot redeem them quite as quickly. This approach encourages repeat purchases. These coupons are called *bounce-back coupons.*

Some companies issue coupons at the cash register. These are called *scanner-delivered coupons,* because they are triggered by an item being scanned. The coupon that is delivered is often for a competitor's product. This approach is designed to encourage brand switching the next time a consumer makes a purchase.

Cross-ruffing is the placement of two promotional materials together. A cross-ruff coupon is placed on one product for another product. A coupon for a French onion dip placed on a package of potato chips is a cross-ruff coupon. Cross-ruff coupons should be on products that fit together logically and that are often purchased and consumed simultaneously. Occasionally, a manufacturer uses cross-ruffing to encourage consumers to purchase another one of its products. For example, Kellogg may place a coupon on a Rice Krispies box for another cereal, such as Frosted Flakes or an oatmeal product. This type of couponing tactic encourages consumers to purchase within the same brand or family of products.

Response offer coupons are issued following requests by consumers. Coupons then are mailed, faxed, or sent by Internet to the consumer. A fax is the most common method of response offer coupon in the business-to-business sector. Office supply companies and other vendors use them to entice business customers to make purchases or place orders. Some firms distribute coupons through sales representatives. This creates instant redemptions, because the salesperson also takes the order.

Problems with Coupons

The use of coupons as a promotional tactic does have some drawbacks, including:

- Reduced revenues
- Mass-cutting
- Counterfeiting
- Misredemptions

A cross-ruffing coupon for Tyson and Betty Crocker.

Source: Courtesy of Betty Crocker and Tyson.

Customers who already have a preference for a brand redeem approximately 80 percent of all coupons.[7] Some argue that offering a price discount to customers who are willing to pay full price does not make sense. Manufacturers, however, point out that these consumers may be willing to stock up on the item, which means they won't use the competition's coupons or products. Consequently, manufacturers recognize that these brand-preference customer redemptions are a "necessary evil" if mass distribution is used. Some firms use direct mail to distribute the coupon primarily to customers who are not brand loyal. The goal is to target nonusers and the competitor's customers. The primary disadvantage of this method is the high cost of direct mail, especially in light of the low response rate associated with direct-mail coupons.

Of the $3.6 billion paid annually for coupon redemptions, $500 million is in the form of illegal reimbursements, according to Coupon Information Council estimates.[8] A common form of coupon fraud is *mass-cutting*. Coupons are "redeemed" through a fraudulent, nonexistent retail outlet, which is a mailbox set up by an illegal coupon-redemption ring. At $.50 to $3 per coupon, mass-cutting of coupons can be lucrative. Many times these rings take advantage of charitable organizations and religious groups that think they are helping a worthy cause by sending in coupons to the mailbox to receive a percentage of the proceeds. Instead, they actually are aiding an illegal activity.

Counterfeiting occurs when coupons are copied and then sent back to the manufacturer for reimbursement. The manufacturer pays for phony coupons. Newspaper-generated black-and-white coupons are the easiest to counterfeit. Color copiers, however, have made other forms of counterfeiting easier. The major source of counterfeiting is the Internet. High-quality printer technology makes it possible for people to create bogus coupons and then sell or distribute them via the Internet. In most cases, the counterfeit coupons are sold in bulk and they often are for inflated discounts or even free merchandise.

Retailers usually are not involved in mass-cutting or counterfeiting of coupons. They can, however, engage in the *misredemption* of coupons. For instance, a coupon for soup often states the size of can for which the discount applies. If the discount is used for another size, such as a 12-ounce can instead of the 24-ounce can, then a misredemption occurs. This may be due to an error on the part of the clerk who did not check the coupon carefully. Or, the clerk might have known it was the wrong-size can but did not want to bother finding the correct size or risk making the customer mad by denying the coupon. Other times, clerks honor coupons for merchandise that was not purchased when they take the coupon and subtract it from the customer's total without matching it to any actual product.

PREMIUMS

A second form of consumer promotion is the offer of a premium. Premiums are prizes, gifts, or other special offers consumers receive when purchasing products. When a company presents a premium, the consumer pays full price for the good or service, in contrast to coupons, which grant price reductions.

Some marketing experts believe overusing coupons damages a brand's image. Conversely, premiums can actually enhance an image. The key is to pick the right type of premium. Premiums can be used in the attempt to boost sales; however, they usually are not as successful as coupon sales. Nevertheless, premiums remain a valuable consumer promotional tool. In the United States, over $4.5 billion is spent on premiums each year.[9]

A free-in-the-mail premium by Fisher Boy for "cool" prizes and a coupon for 55 cents off.

Source: Courtesy of Fisher Boy.

Types of Premiums

The four major types of premiums are shown in Figure 12.4. *Free-in-the-mail premiums* are gifts individuals receive for purchasing products. To receive the gift, the customer mails in a proof of purchase to the manufacturer, who then mails the gift to the customer. Sometimes more than one purchase is required to receive the gift. Notice the premiums being offered in the Fisher Boy advertisement shown in this section. Consumers collect points from the front of Fisher Boy packages to be redeemed for "cool" prizes. To further encourage sales, the advertisement has a coupon attached.

Credit card companies use premiums to entice individuals to sign up for credit cards. Instead of providing a proof of purchase, the consumer needs only to activate the card to receive the incentives, which can range from cash back on purchases to merchandise and frequent-flier miles.

In- or *on-package premiums* are usually small gifts, such as toys in cereal boxes. The gift may be disguised or packaged so the consumer must buy the product to find out which premium it contains. The most famous of these may be Cracker Jack's prizes. At other times the gift is attached to the package, such as a package of blades with the purchase of a razor.

Store or manufacturer premiums are gifts given by either the retail store or the manufacturer when the customer purchases a product. Fast-food restaurants offer children a toy with the purchase of a child's meal. To entice individuals to purchase high-end homes and real estate in Prime Nature Villa in Thailand, the contractors offered a number of unique premiums. One premium was

FIGURE 12.4
Types of Premiums

◆ Free-in-the-mail	◆ Store or manufacturer
◆ In- or on-package	◆ Self-liquidating

FIGURE 12.5
Keys to Successful Premiums

- ◆ Match the premium to the target market
- ◆ Carefully select the premiums (avoid fads, try for exclusivity)
- ◆ Pick a premium that reinforces the firm's product and image
- ◆ Integrate the premium with other IMC tools (especially advertising and POP displays)
- ◆ Don't expect premiums to increase short-term profits

Source: Based on Don Jagoda, "The Seven Habits of Highly Successful Premiums," *Incentive* 173, no. 8 (August 1999), pp. 104–105.

a 525i BMW automobile that was given to individuals who purchased land plots larger than 1,600 square meters in the company's luxury-home project area. Individuals who purchased smaller plots of between 800 and 1,600 square meters received gift certificates for diamond jewelry.[10]

The fourth major type is called a *self-liquidating premium*. These require the consumer to pay an amount of money for a gift or item. For example, the premium may be offered for only $4.99 plus shipping and handling and two proofs of purchase from boxes of Cheerios. The premium is called self-liquidating because the $4.99 covers the cost of the premium. The manufacturer also receives money for shipping and handling. This means that consumers pay most or all of the actual cost of the item.

Keys to Successful Premium Programs

Successful premium programs have several common elements (Figure 12.5). First, the premium should match the target market. A target market such as older, high-income individuals can be reached with a premium such as china or fine crystal. If the market is children, a cartoon figure or a character from Disney or Sesame Street is more attractive.

The best premiums reinforce the firm's image. They should not be low-cost trinkets. Offering cheap merchandise insults customers and can damage the firm's image Premium programs succeed when they tie-in with the firm's products in order to enhance the image of the product and the firm.[11]

Premiums should be integrated with the other components of the IMC program. Premiums provide an excellent means of adding value to a product instead of slashing prices or using coupons. Premiums can serve as a "thank you" to current customers or to attract new customers. *Sports Illustrated* has a rich history of premium programs, from DVDs to watches to phones, which are presented for either renewing a subscription to the magazine or ordering one for the first time.

Although premiums are an excellent method of adding value or enhancing a brand, they are not as effective at increasing profits. Therefore, a clear relationship between the premium's intention and IMC goals should be established. Logically, the goal is more about image than profit.

CONTESTS AND SWEEPSTAKES

Contests and sweepstakes are popular consumer sales promotions. Approximately $1.8 billion is spent on various games, contests, and sweepstakes each year, which appear in consumer markets as well as business markets.[12] The prize list is the primary factor that determines the success or failure of these appeals. Members of the target market for the contest or sweepstakes find the prizes to be desirable in order to entice them to participate. A prize with a low or zero value does not work.

The words *contest* and *sweepstakes* tend to be used interchangeably, yet there are some differences, primarily legal. *Contests* normally require the participant to perform some type of activity. The winner is selected based on who performs best or provides the most correct answers. Often, contests require a participant to make a purchase to enter. In some states, however, it is illegal to force a consumer to make a purchase to enter a contest. In developing contests, the marketing team should investigate the state and federal laws that apply.

Contests

Contests range from the controversial bikini or suntan contests at local nightclubs to popular television shows such as *Jeopardy* or *American Idol* in which contestants must answer questions or win competitions to earn prizes. Although some contests are mostly chance (e.g., *Wheel of Fortune*), others require skill. For example, ACH Food Company sponsored a Karo Syrup Recipe Contest for students. To enter, students had to create original recipes using Karo syrup. In a similar type of contest sponsored by Florida's Tomato Association, participants created original recipes utilizing tomatoes. The grand prize winner for the latter contest was Steve Barnhart's "Fresh Florida Tomato Orange Soup."[13]

Sweepstakes

No purchase is required to enter a sweepstakes. Consumers can enter as many times as they wish, although it is permissible for firms to restrict customers to one entry per visit to the store or some other location. The chances of winning a sweepstakes are based on a probability factor. The probability of winning must clearly be stated on all point-of-purchase (POP) displays and advertising materials. In a sweepstakes, the probability of winning each prize is published in advance. This means the firm must know how many winning entries, as compared to total entries, have been prepared.

People enter contests and sweepstakes that they perceive as being worth their time and attention. Consumers do not enter every contest or sweepstakes they encounter. Instead, they selectively choose. The decision is often based on the perceived value of the contest or sweepstakes prize combined with the odds of winning. The greater the perceived odds of winning, the more likely a person will participate in the contest or enter the sweepstakes.

This advertisement for fantasy fishing by Bassmaster is designed to appeal to outdoorsmen.

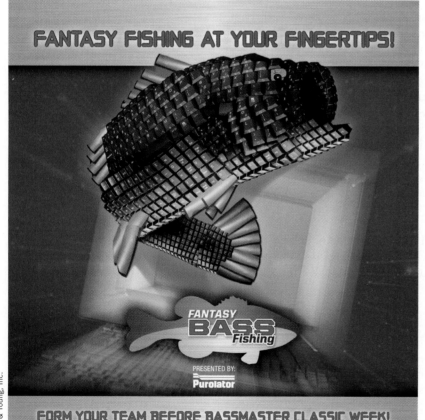

Components of Prizes

The perceived value of a prize has two components: extrinsic value and intrinsic value. The *extrinsic value* is the actual attractiveness of the item (a car versus a free sandwich). The greater the perceived value, the more likely the person will participate. *Intrinsic values* are those associated with participating. A contest requiring the use of a skill, such as the one with recipes or an essay contest, entices entry by individuals who enjoy demonstrating a skill. In that case, extrinsic rewards become secondary. Instead, participants enjoy competing and demonstrating their abilities, which in part explains the popularity of fantasy football and baseball leagues and "pick the winner" sports contests.

A factor in the success level of a contest or sweepstakes is finding the right prizes. Marketers can be creative when choosing prizes. For example, in Ohio a sweepstakes was created for a small, local company, the Velvet Ice Cream Company. Ohio was a gateway to the West in the early 1800s. A number of inns were built along stagecoach routes traveling through the state. Many of these inns still exist. Six inns were solicited and agreed to participate in the sweepstakes. The inns provided prizes, which consisted of one free night stay for two, dinner, and a dessert containing a Velvet Ice Cream product. Each winner also received a booklet with pictures of the inn, a brief history of the inn, and various recipes for Velvet Ice Cream products. The sweepstakes ran from Memorial Day to Labor Day and was considered a rousing success by Velvet, as well as by the six inns that participated. Traffic and revenues for all participants increased during the sweepstakes.[14]

The Internet has become a popular location for contests and sweepstakes. The Internet can provide opportunities for individuals to participate for a prize's intrinsic value. It also can be used to create interactive games that can challenge a contestant's ability. The Internet provides promoters with data-capturing capabilities. Internet contests are less costly to set up and run than other types of promotions.

To encourage consumers to continue participating in a contest, the extrinsic values of prizes can be increased by allowing small, incremental rewards. A consumer who wins a soft drink or a sandwich in a sweepstakes at Subway is more likely to continue participating. Scratch-and-win cards tend to be effective because the reward is instant.

A mobile phone promotion developed by Hip Cricket, a mobile marketing and event company, provided instant notification of winning via text messaging. Hip Cricket developed a sweepstakes for Miller Brewing Company's Icehouse brand. The sweepstakes was the first to be conducted live, during a rock concert. Music fans, 21 years old or older, could enter the sweepstakes by text messaging the words "Pick Me" during the concert. At 10:00 P.M., one concertgoer, Melissa Hasty, received word via text message that she had won the grand prize, a 5-day, 4-night Caribbean cruise on the "Rock Boat." Other concert fans won secondary prizes throughout the night, again, receiving notification via their cell phone's instant messaging system. Winning is always fun. For Melissa and others at the concert, winning instantly was even more exciting.[15]

Goals of Contests and Sweepstakes

To fully ensure the success of the contest or sweepstakes, the marketing team coordinates the promotion with advertising, POP displays, and other marketing tools. All of these elements are directed at the same target audience and convey a united message. These features add to the cost of the contest; however, such integration is a crucial ingredient in achieving the desired goals.

Primary goals of contests and sweepstakes include encouraging customer traffic and boosting sales. Contests and sweepstakes routinely increase customer traffic. The question is whether they actually boost sales. Some do, others do not. Marketers are beginning to realize that intrinsic rewards tend to draw consumers back. This means many online games are exciting prospects, because they can be structured to create intrinsic rewards.

Marketing research has demonstrated that brand awareness increases with multiple exposures to an advertisement or contest. Therefore, although contests and sweepstakes may not boost sales in the short run, they can be a driving force behind brand awareness and brand image development for longer periods of time, such as the McDonald's Monopoly game promotion that has run for several years. As a result, these games are often key weapons in the marketing arsenals of many organizations.

A new media trend for contests and sweepstakes is offering them over the Internet.

REFUNDS AND REBATES

Refunds and rebates are cash returns offered to consumers or businesses following the purchase of a product. Consumers pay full price for the product but can mail in some type of proof of purchase. The manufacturer then refunds a portion of the purchase price. A *refund* is a cash return on what are called "soft goods," such as food or clothing. *Rebates* are cash returns on "hard goods," which are major ticket items such as automobiles and appliances.

This ad for Skyjacker offers a $35.00 rebate on 4 Skyjacker Hydro or Nitro Shocks.

Normally, refunds are smaller and rebates are larger. For example, the typical refund offered on a food item may be $1; the typical rebate on a car may be $500, $1,000, or more, depending on the price and size of the car.

Only about 30 percent of all rebates are ever claimed. For rebates valued at $50 or more, however, the percentage of claims rises to about 65 percent. The major reason for the low response rate is the inconvenience associated with getting the rebate. Too many steps or long waiting times because of "snail mail" are common complaints about rebates. It is not unusual for consumers to wait up to 6 months to receive a rebate check.[16]

Many rebate programs suffer from diminished effectiveness, because consumers have come to expect them. For example, car dealers often find that customers won't buy until rebates are offered. As a result, there is no new purchase activity associated with the rebate, but rather a delay in the purchase process as consumers "wait out" auto manufacturers. According to J.D. Power and Associates, slightly more than 60 percent of all vehicle purchases in the United States involve some type of cash rebate.[17] Further, increasing the amount of a rebate no longer seems to spur additional sales activity, yet discontinuing or reducing rebate levels tends to have an immediate negative impact on sales.

Refunds and rebates achieve the greatest successes when they are perceived as being new or original. When they become an entrenched part of doing business, they are expected discounts. Rebates and refunds must have the impact of changing the buyer's behavior, either by leading to more immediate purchases or by causing the customer to change brands.

SAMPLING

A popular method for enticing consumers to try new products is sampling. Sampling is the actual delivery of a product to consumers for their use or consumption. Most samples are provided free of charge. A coupon or price-off incentive is often given with the sample to persuade the consumer to purchase a larger version of the product, such as a full-size package.

In business-to-business markets, samples of products may be provided to potential clients. Sampling also can be featured in the service sector. For example, a tanning salon may offer an initial visit free to encourage new customers to try its facilities. Dentists and lawyers use sampling when they offer an initial consultation free of charge.

Figure 12.6 lists various ways samples are distributed. The most common consumer method is *in-store distribution,* such as when food product companies have personnel cooking the food and passing it out to individuals in the store. *Direct sampling* is a program in which samples are mailed or delivered door to door to consumers.

- ◆ In-store distribution
- ◆ Direct sampling
- ◆ Response sampling
- ◆ Cross-ruff sampling

- ◆ Media sampling
- ◆ Professional sampling
- ◆ Selective sampling

FIGURE 12.6
Types of Sampling

Types of Samples

Various demographic target markets can be identified for free samples. In the business-to-business sector, salespeople often deliver direct samples. *Response samples* are made available to individuals or businesses responding to a media offer on television, on the Internet, from a magazine, or by some other source. *Cross-ruff* sampling plans provide samples of one product on another. A laundry detergent with a free dryer sheet attached to the package is a cross-ruff sample. *Media sampling* means the sample is included in the media outlet. For example, a small sample of perfume can be included in a magazine advertisement or with a newspaper. *Professional samples* are delivered to professionals, such as doctors, who may then provide patients with the free drug samples. *Selective samples* are distributed at a site such as a state fair, parade, hospital, restaurant, or sporting event. For instance, many times Power Bars are given to people attending football or basketball games. There is a tie-in between the product (nutrition) and the event (athletics).

In recent years, marketers have increased usage of FSIs for the distribution of samples. A variety of products have been distributed in newspapers, such as breakfast bars, coffee, shampoo, snacks, tea, and automotive cleansers. Companies using newspapers utilize the FSI insert method because it breaks through the clutter and gets the attention of consumers. The newspaper is an "invited medium." Therefore, consumers are more receptive when samples are distributed with the paper.[18]

Benefits of Sampling

Product sampling is an effective way to introduce a new product, generate interest in that product, and collect information about consumers. Internet-based response sampling programs have also become popular with both consumers and manufacturers. Bristol-Myers/Squibb was one of the first companies to utilize the Internet for product sampling. The company offered a free sample of Excedrin to individuals who requested the sample and were willing to provide their names, addresses, and e-mail information. In addition to the 12-pack sample of Excedrin, consumers received coupons for additional Excedrin purchases, along with the quarterly *Excedrin Headache Relief Update Newsletter*. The advantage of this form of response sampling is that only consumers who requested the product received it. Also, companies normally can gather additional information to be added to a database. Seventy percent of consumers who requested a sample online were willing to complete a survey to receive the sample.[19]

Problems with Sampling

The primary disadvantage of sampling is cost. Often, a special sample-size package must be developed. The package must be very similar to the regular-size pack, so consumers will be able to identify the product after using the sample. Many times samples are mailed, adding to the expense of the program. A sample given out in a store requires an individual to distribute it and some kind of permission from the store.

This B-to-B Polycom ad offers a free 30-day, risk-free trial.

Source: Courtesy of Polycom, Inc.

Successful Sampling Programs

As with the other consumer promotions, sampling must be a central part of the IMC plan. The primary purpose of sampling is to encourage a trial use by a consumer or a business. Sampling is most effective when it introduces a new product or a new version of a product to a market. Samples also help promote a current product to a new target market or to new prospects.

Successful sampling means targeting the right audience. Mass sampling is not nearly as cost-effective as targeted sampling. Recently, Green & Black launched a sampling campaign for organic chocolates at 21 outdoor concerts in England. Each audience member was given a bar of Green & Black's organic chocolate at the entrance. More than 80 percent of the audience, a total of 105,000 people, received sample bars. A tasting marquee was also set up in the concert area so that concert attendees could try other flavors. The goal was to build a brand experience between concert attendees and the Green & Black brand name and to boost sales, which it did. Sales of the organic chocolate bar increased 79 percent in the months immediately following the concerts.[20]

A bonus pack offer for two packages of Lean Slices by Carl Buddig.

Source: Courtesy of Carl Buddig & Company.

BONUS PACKS

When an additional or extra number of items are placed in a special product package, it is called a bonus pack. When a consumer buys four bars of soap for the price of three, it is a bonus pack promotion. Recently, Rayovac offered three free AA batteries in a bonus pack containing nine batteries. Typical bonuses range from 20 percent to 100 percent of the normal number of units in a package. A 30 percent bonus is the most common.

Types of Bonus Packs

Figure 12.7 identifies the major objectives of bonus packs. Increasing the size or quantity of the package can lead to greater product use. For example, if a cereal box is increased in size by 25 percent, the consumer is likely to eat more cereal, because it is readily available. This is not true for products that have a constant rate of consumption. For instance, if Colgate increases the size of a toothpaste container by 25 percent, consumers will not use more toothpaste. In effect, this delays the customer's next purchase. Still, manufacturers offer these types of bonus packs, because they may preempt the competition. A consumer with a large quantity of the merchandise on hand is less likely to switch to another brand, even when offered some type of deal.

Benefits of Bonus Packs

A firm's current customers often take advantage of a bonus pack offer. When customers stockpile a quantity of a

---

FIGURE 12.7
Reasons for Using Bonus Packs

◆ Increase usage of the product	◆ Develop customer loyalty
◆ Match or preempt competitive actions	◆ Attract new users
◆ Stockpile the product	◆ Encourage brand switching

particular brand, they are less likely to purchase from a competitor. Bonus packs reward customer loyalty by offering, in effect, free merchandise.

Bonus packs can lead to brand switching if the consumer has used the brand previously. Facing purchase decisions, consumers may opt for brands that offer a bonus pack at the regular price. These products have an advantage that competitive brands are not offering.

Bonus packs tend to be popular with manufacturers, retailers, and customers. A retailer can build a good relationship with a manufacturer that uses a bonus pack to increase brand switching and stockpiling. Retailers gain an advantage because the bonus pack is a "bargain" or "value" offered through the retail outlet. Customers like bonus packs because they get additional product at the same price. For ongoing products with high competition, the bonus pack approach is one way to maintain brand loyalty and reduce brand switching at a minimal cost.

Problems with Bonus Packs

Bonus packs rarely attract new customers because the consumer is less likely to have previously purchased the brand. Obtaining an extra quantity does not reduce the purchase risk. In fact, it adds to the risk, especially when the customer does not like to waste a product by throwing it away if he or she is dissatisfied with the product.

Some marketing research indicates that consumers are skeptical of bonus pack offers. When the bonus is small (20 to 40 percent), consumers often believe the price has not truly changed. Unfortunately, when the bonus is large, such as a two-for-the-price-of-one sale, consumers tend to believe that the price was first increased to compensate for the additional quantity. Even though increasing the size of a bonus catches the consumer's attention, it may not convey the desired message.[21]

A price-off and coupon offer for Papa John's pizza.

PRICE-OFFS

A price-off is a temporary reduction in the price of a product to the consumer. A price-off can be physically marked on the product, such as when a bottle of aspirin shows the regular retail price marked out and replaced by a special retail price (e.g., $4.99 marked out and replaced by $3.99). Producing a label with the price reduction premarked forces the retailer to sell the item at the reduced price. This ensures the price-off incentive will be passed on to the consumer. At other times, the price-off is not on the actual item, but on a POP display, sign, or shelf.

Benefits of Price-Offs

Price-offs are excellent at stimulating sales of an existing product. They can entice customers to try new products because the lower price reduces the financial risk of making the purchase. They can encourage customers to switch brands in brand parity situations or when no strong brand loyalty exists. In cases where consumers do have a brand preference, a price-off on a favorite brand encourages stockpiling of the product and possibly increased consumption of the item.[22] A consumer who purchases additional breakfast bars because of a price-off tends to consume more breakfast bars. Again, this will not be true for products such as deodorant or toothpaste. Stockpiling for those types of products just delays the next purchase. It does not increase consumption. Similar effects are seen in the business-to-business arena when price-offs are used.

Price-offs have proven to be successful consumer promotions for two reasons. First, the price-off has the

appeal of a monetary savings to consumers. Second, the reward is immediate. Unlike rebates, refunds, contests, sweepstakes, and other promotional incentives, consumers do not have to wait for the reward.

Problems with Price-Offs

While price-offs are easy to implement and can have a sudden impact on sales, they can also cause problems. Although sales may increase, it can have a negative impact on a company's profit margin. It normally takes at least a 20-percent increase in sales to offset each 5-percent price reduction.

Another danger of price-off programs is that they encourage consumers to become more price-sensitive. In the same way that customers respond to rebates, they can either wait for a price-off promotion or choose another brand that happens to be on sale. In addition, when used too often, price-offs can have a negative impact on a brand's image. As always, price-off programs should be incorporated into the firm's overall IMC program.

OVERLAYS AND TIE-INS

At times companies combine two or more consumer promotions activities into a single campaign, called an *overlay*. To attract Chinese consumers in Canada, Tropicana combined sampling with coupons. Free samples (50,000 cups of orange juice) were given out along with 30,000 coupons at a Chinese New Year's celebration in Vancouver. Asians who live in the United States and Canada are not typically large users of coupons; however, Tropicana Canada's research showed that the Chinese consider oranges to be harbingers of good luck. A few weeks after the promotion, 40 percent of the coupons were redeemed, and sales of Tropicana orange juice among the Chinese community in Canada increased considerably.[23]

Another common strategy is to develop a consumer promotion with another product or company. This is called a *tie-in*. *Intracompany tie-ins* are the promotion of two different products within one company using one consumer promotion. An alternative method is partnering with another company which is an *intercompany tie-in*. Fast-food restaurants often use tie-ins with movies and toys to creative attractive children's promotions. Whether a promotion is a stand-alone, overlay, or tie-in program, careful attention must be given to planning the event to maximize its effect.

PLANNING FOR CONSUMER PROMOTIONS

In planning the consumer promotions component of the IMC, the promotions should support the brand image and the brand positioning strategy. To ensure this occurs, bear in mind the target audience. Research should be conducted to identify the core values present in the target audience, as well as opinions regarding the firm's products, especially as they relate to the competition. After gathering this information, the marketing team can finalize the consumer promotions plan. In terms of promotions, consumers can be divided into three general categories: promotion prone, brand loyal, and price sensitive (see Figure 12.8).

Promotion-prone consumers regularly respond to coupons, price-off plans, and premiums, which means they are not brand loyal and primarily purchase on-deal items. A **brand-loyal consumer** purchases only one particular brand and does not substitute, regardless of any deal being offered. Few consumers are completely promotion prone or brand loyal. Instead, buying resembles a continuum anchored at its ends by promotional proneness and brand loyalty. People lean toward one approach but sometimes lapse into the other. The tendency toward being promotion prone or brand loyal may depend on the product being purchased. A beer drinker may be extremely promotion prone; a wine drinker may be quite brand loyal. The same beer drinker may be extremely loyal to a

FIGURE 12.8
Types of Consumers in Relation to Consumer Promotions

- ◆ Promotion prone
- ◆ Brand loyal
- ◆ Price sensitive

Source: Courtesy of Alan Keohane © Dorling Kindersley.

pizza brand, and the same wine drinker may be quite promotion prone when it comes to buying potato chips.

For the **price-sensitive consumer**, price remains the primary, if not only, criterion used in making a purchase decision. Brand names are not important, and these individuals will not pay more for a brand name. They take advantage of any type of promotion that reduces the price. It is important to identify the set of promotion prone or price-sensitive consumers who will be targeted by a consumer promotions program.

For brand-loyal consumers, sales promotions can be crafted to boost sales and reinforce the firm's image. For example, a small local restaurant has a monthly drawing for a free meal for two. To enter, patrons place a business card in a jar upon leaving. Each month the restaurant draws a name. The more often a person dines at the restaurant, the greater the chance of winning. A simple promotion such as this can boost sales for the restaurant by tying chances of winning with additional meals. The additional cost to the restaurant to run this promotion is minimal and can result in excellent goodwill from customers.

In planning promotions, it is important for manufacturers to understand retailers' incentives in using promotions. It does little good to create a promotion that is popular with consumers if retailers are not willing to work with the manufacturer to enhance the promotional offer. Retailers prefer promotions that will benefit them in some way. The primary reasons retailers give for supporting a manufacturer's consumer promotions program are to:[24]

- Increase store traffic
- Increase store sales
- Attract new customers
- Increase the basket size

It is important to tie the promotions program with the theme of the IMC program while keeping in mind where the promotions will be seen by the consumer. Specific goals associated with the product, the target market, and the retail outlets should be formulated.

For instance, building brand image is more of a long-term goal; generating sales is more short range. Price-based offers normally are designed to attract new customers or to build sales. Other consumer promotions such as high-value premiums can be used to enhance a firm's image.

TRADE PROMOTIONS

Trade promotions are incentives members of the trade channel use to entice another member to *purchase goods for eventual resale.* Trade promotions are aimed at retailers, distributors, wholesalers, brokers, or agents. A manufacturer can offer trade promotions to convince another member of the trade channel to carry its goods. Wholesalers, distributors, brokers, and agents use trade promotions to entice retailers to purchase products for eventual resale.

Trade promotions account for a significant percentage of a supplier's or retailer's gross revenues. Twenty years ago they accounted for about 25 percent of a manufacturer's marketing budget; today it is nearly 70 percent of the budget. Trade promotions are often the second-largest expense for a manufacturer after the cost-of-goods-sold. Trade promotions account for 17.4 percent of gross sales of manufacturers.[25]

Trade promotions are an integral part of an IMC program. Unfortunately, in many companies, the individual handling trade promotions is not involved in the IMC planning process. Leaders in these firms often view trade promotions as being merely a means for getting products onto retail shelves or satisfying some channel member's request. As a result, little consideration may be given to matching the IMC program when trade promotions programs are developed.

A variety of trade promotions tools exist. Individual companies select trade promotions techniques based on several factors. These factors include the nature of the business (manufacturer versus distributor), the type of customer to be influenced (e.g., selling to a retailer versus selling to a wholesaler), company preferences, and the objectives of the IMC plan. The primary types of trade promotions are listed in Figure 12.9.

Trade Allowances

The first major type of trade promotion manufacturers and others use in the channel is a trade allowance. **Trade allowances** provide financial incentives to other channel members to motivate them to make purchases. Trade allowances can be packaged into a variety of forms, including the ones described in Figure 12.10. Each makes it possible for the channel member to offer discounts or other deals to customers.

Off-Invoice Allowances and Slotting Fees

Off-invoice allowances are financial discounts given for each item, case, or pallet ordered. They encourage channel members to place orders. Approximately 35 percent of all trade dollars are spent on off-invoice allowances, making them the largest expenditure among trade promotions tools.[26] Companies often feature off-invoice allowances during holiday seasons. This encourages retailers to purchase larger quantities. Orders must be placed by a specific date to receive a holiday off-invoice allowance. Manufacturers also can place a minimum order size as a further condition.

FIGURE 12.9
Types of Trade Promotions

- ◆ **Off-invoice allowance:** A per-case rebate paid to retailers for an order.
- ◆ **Slotting fees:** Money paid to retailers to stock a new product.
- ◆ **Exit fees:** Money paid to retailers to remove an item from their SKU inventory.

FIGURE 12.10
Types of Trade Allowances

The most controversial form of trade allowance is a slotting fee. **Slotting fees** are funds charged by retailers to stock new products. Most retailers charge slotting fees and justify them in several ways.[27] First, retailers spend money to add new products to inventories and to stock merchandise. A product that is not successful means the retailer's investment in inventory represents a loss, especially when the retailer has stocked the product in a large number of stores.

Second, adding a new product in the retail store means giving it shelf space. Most shelves are already filled with products. Adding a new product means either deleting brands or products or reducing the amount of shelf space allocated to them. In both cases, the retailer spends both time and money on creating space for a new product.

Third, slotting fees make it easier for retailers to finalize decisions about new products. A typical supermarket carries 35,000 SKUs (stockkeeping units). The supermarket's managers must evaluate at least 10,000 to 15,000 new products per year. Most will fail. Consequently, retailers believe charging slotting fees forces manufacturers to weed out poor product introductions. The average total cost in slotting fees for a nationally introduced product ranges from $1.5 million to $2 million.[28] Consequently, retailers contend that slotting fees force manufacturers to conduct careful test marketing on products before introducing them. Such testing reduces the number of new products offered each year. This, in turn, drastically reduces the number of new product failures.

Fourth, and finally, slotting fees add to the bottom line. Many products have low margins or markups. Slotting fees provide additional monies to support retail operations. It has been estimated that between 14 and 27 percent of trade promotion monies given to retailers go directly to the retailer's bottom line.[29]

The other side of the argument comes from manufacturers, who claim slotting fees are practically a form of extortion. Many manufacturers believe slotting fees are too costly and are unfair in the first place. These fees compel manufacturers to pay millions of dollars to retailers that could be used for advertising, sales promotions, or other marketing efforts.

Slotting fees can prevent small manufacturers from getting products into stores simply because they cannot afford them. Some large retail operations have small vendor policies; however, placing merchandise remains extremely challenging.

In addition to keeping small manufacturers out of the market, slotting fees favor incumbent suppliers. New entrants into the market face tremendous investment of up-front money already, and then must add on slotting fees. Unless company leaders are absolutely certain the new brand can compete, the firm may not enter a market simply because of slotting fees.

Instead of paying a slotting allowance, some retailers ask for **exit fees**, which are monies paid to remove an item from a retailer's inventory. This approach is often used when a manufacturer introduces a new size of a product or a new version, such as a 3-liter bottle of Pepsi or Pepsi Diet Vanilla. PepsiCo already has products on the retailer's shelves. Adding a new-sized container or new variety of the product involves lower risk and is not the same as adding a new product. Rather than charging an up-front fee such as a slotting allowance, retailers request exit fees if the new version of the product fails or if one of the current

New products, such as a new salad dressing offered by Ott's, are often charged slotting fees.

Source: Courtesy of Ott Food Products LLC.

versions must be removed from the inventory. Only 4 percent of retailers use exit fees, compared to the 82 percent that use slotting fees.[30]

Trade Allowance Complications

In offering trade allowances to retailers, manufacturers assume that a portion of the price reduction will be passed on to consumers. This occurs only about half of the time. When a portion of the price allowance is passed on to consumers, retailers often schedule competing brands, so they can have at least one special offer going at all times. It is not an accident that one week Pepsi offers a reduced price and the next Coke offers a discount. The two products are rarely promoted *on-deal* (passing along trade allowance discounts) at the same time. By offering only one on-deal at a time, the retailer always has a reduced price competitor for the price-sensitive consumer. The retailer also can charge the brand-loyal consumer full price 50 percent of the time. While accomplishing these goals, the retailer receives special trade allowances from both Pepsi and Coke.

In an effort to increase their profit margins, retailers often engage in two activities: forward buying and diversion. *Forward buying* occurs when a retailer purchases extra amounts of a product while it is on-deal. The retailer then sells the on-deal merchandise after the deal period ends, saving the cost of purchasing the product at the manufacturer's full price. *Diversion* occurs when a retailer purchases a product on-deal in one location and ships it to another location where it is off-deal. For example, a manufacturer may offer an off-invoice allowance of $5 per case for the product in Texas. Diversion tactics mean the retailer purchases an excess quantity in Texas and has it shipped to stores in other states. To do so, retailers first examine the potential profits to be earned, less the cost of shipping the product to other locations. Shipping costs tend to be relatively high compared to trade allowances offered. Consequently, retailers do not use diversion nearly as much as forward buying.

Trade Contests

To achieve sales targets and other objectives, manufacturers sometimes use trade contests. Rewards are given as contest prizes to brokers, retail salespeople, retail stores, wholesalers, or agents. These funds are also known as **spiff money**. The prizes offered in a trade contest can be items such as luggage, a stereo, a television, or a trip to an exotic place such as Hawaii.

A contest can be held at various levels within the channel. It can be between brokers or agents who handle the manufacturer's goods. It can be for wholesalers, or it can be a sales volume contest among individual retail stores. Although contests can be designed between retail organizations (e.g., Target versus Wal-Mart), they are seldom used because of conflict of interest policies in many large organizations. Buyers in large organizations are often prohibited from participating in vendor contests because they create conflicts of interest and unfairly influence their buying decisions. Although this is exactly what a contest is designed to accomplish, many large retail organizations do not want buyers participating, because these buyers make purchase decisions for as many as 500 to 2,500 stores. This places undue pressure on the buyer.

Demand for cruise ship vacations has steadily increased in the past few years. There is intense competition among the cruise lines. Cruise ship companies use a combination of advertising, consumer promotions, and trade promotions to attract patrons. For example, Royal Caribbean International offered travel agents cooperative advertising programs featuring TV commercials, newspaper ads, as well as an e-mail template to contact potential travelers. Norwegian Cruise Lines enrolled 5,500 agents in a "Sale of All Sails" promotional contest. Prizes were based on bookings. Each agent that set up a Holland America cruise was enrolled in the trade contest. The prizes offered included a free cruise with five veranda staterooms.

The Princess Cruise line offered booking agents the chance to win a West Coast sailing cruise with a minisuite. One cruise was awarded each day during a 90-day period. This combination of advertising, consumer promotions, and trade promotions led to a year in which advanced bookings for summer cruises reached an all-time high. It is not surprising that offering travel agents the chance to win prizes and cruises for themselves causes them to be highly motivated to book cruises for the lines holding the contests.[31]

When conducting a contest at the individual store level, most channel members agree that these contests work best when restricted to a specific region. Many times, they are also limited to exclusive dealerships, such as auto, truck, or boat dealers that sell a particular brand. For example B.F. Goodrich may run a contest among its retail operations within a specific region for highest sales within a given time period.

Trade Incentives

Trade incentives are similar to trade allowances. The difference is that **trade incentives** involve the retailer performing a function in order to receive the funds. The purpose, however, is the same as it was for trade allowances: to encourage retailers either to push the manufacturer's brand or to increase retailer purchases of that brand. The three major types of trade incentives are identified in Figure 12.11.

Cooperative Merchandising Agreements

The most comprehensive trade incentive is a *cooperative merchandising agreement (CMA),* which is a formal agreement between the retailer and manufacturer to undertake a two-way marketing effort. The CMA can be for a wide variety of marketing tasks. For instance, a CMA can feature the manufacturer's brand as a price leader in an advertisement. A cooperative agreement can be made to emphasize the manufacturer's brand as part of an in-house offer made by the retail store or a by using a special shelf display featuring a price incentive. The advantage of creating a CMA agreement that features a price break is that the manufacturer is assured that the retailer will pass along the price allowance to the customer.

CMAs are popular with manufacturers because the retailer performs a function in order to receive the allowance or incentive. The manufacturer retains control of the functions performed. Also, if price allowances are made as part of the CMA, the manufacturer knows that the retailer passes a certain percentage of the price discount on to the consumer. CMAs allow manufacturers to create annual contracts with retailers. These longer-term commitments reduce the need for last-minute trade incentives or trade allowances.

CMAs also benefit retailers. The primary benefit of a CMA from the retailer's perspective is that it allows them to develop calendar promotions. *Calendar promotions* are promotional campaigns the retailer plans for customers through manufacturer trade incentives. By signing a CMA, a retailer can schedule the weeks a particular brand will be on sale and offset the other weeks with other brands. By using calendar promotions, the retailer will always have one brand on sale while the others are off-deal. Calendar promotions allow the retailer to rotate the brands on sale. This arrangement is attractive for price-sensitive customers, because one brand is always on sale. For the brand-loyal

Trade contests were used to increase cruise ship bookings.

Trade Incentive → Cooperative merchandising agreement
→ Premium or bonus pack
→ Co-op advertising programs

FIGURE 12.11
Types of Trade Incentives

consumer, the retailer carries the preferred brand at the regular price sometimes and on sale at others. By arranging sales through trade incentives, the margins for the retailer are approximately the same for all brands, both on-deal and off-deal, because they rotate. Retailers can effectively move price reductions given to the customer to the manufacturer rather than absorbing them themselves. A store may feature Budweiser on-deal one week and Heineken the next. Loyal beer drinkers stay with their preferred brand, while price-sensitive consumers can choose the on-deal brand, and the store retains a reasonable markup on all beers sold.

Premiums and Bonus Packs

The second major type of trade incentive is a *premium or bonus pack*. Instead of offering the retailer a discount on the price, the manufacturer offers free merchandise. For example, a manufacturer can offer a bonus pack of one carton for each 20 purchased within the next 60 days. The bonus packs are free to the retailer and are awarded either for placing the order by a certain date or for agreeing to a minimum-size order. Often, to receive the free merchandise the retailer must meet both conditions: a specified date and a minimum order size.

Cooperative Advertising

The final trade incentive is co-op advertising. In a *cooperative advertising program,* the manufacturer agrees to reimburse the retailer a certain percentage of the advertising costs associated with advertising the manufacturer's products in the retailer's ad. To receive the reimbursement, the retailer follows specific guidelines concerning the placement of the ad and its content. In almost all cases, no competing products can be advertised. Normally, the manufacturer's product must be displayed prominently. There may be other restrictions on how the product is advertised as well as specific photos or copy that must be used.

In most cooperative advertising programs, retailers accrue co-op monies based on purchases. This is normally a certain percentage of sales. For example, B.F. Goodrich, a manufacturer of automobile tires, offers a 4.5 percent co-op advertising fund on all purchases. This money can be accrued for a year, and then it starts over again. B.F. Goodrich pays 70 percent of the cost of an approved advertisement. Any of the media can be used for the advertisement, including radio, newspaper, magazines, television, and outdoor advertising. This unlimited media choice does not hold true for all manufacturers. For example, Dayton, another tire manufacturer, does not allow co-op dollars to be used for magazine advertising. B.F. Goodrich allows group ads for co-op monies; Dayton does not. Further, Dayton requires preapproval for some of the media buys and advertisements; B. F. Goodrich does not require any preapprovals. Thus, each manufacturer has a unique set of restrictions that must be followed by retailers seeking to qualify for co-op monies.[32]

Co-op advertising programs allow retailers to use the manufacturer's dollars to expand advertising programs. In a co-op ad, the retailer gains additional advertising coverage at minimal cost. Retailers also benefit from the image of a national brand, which can attract new or additional customers to the store. From

Cooperative advertising programs are used heavily by automobile manufacturers such as Volkswagen.

the retailer's perspective, there is little to lose in co-op programs. The only negative side is that the retailer is reimbursed following the placement of the ad, which could lead to a cash flow problem for a smaller company.

Manufacturers also benefit from co-op ads. By sharing advertising costs with retailers, the manufacturer gains additional exposure at a reduced cost. More important, almost all co-op advertising programs are tied to sales. The retailer accrues co-op advertising dollars based on a certain percentage of sales. Thus, to get the co-op money, the retailer must not only promote the brand prominently, but must also purchase the product for resale. As a result, it is not surprising to see the wide variety of cooperative advertisements appearing regularly in every medium, for both consumer and business-to-business products.

Over $12 billion is spent on trade shows each year.

Source: Courtesy of Jeff Scheid; Getty Images, Inc.

Trade Shows

Trade shows are used extensively in business-to-business marketing programs. They benefit both manufacturers and retailers. From a manufacturer's standpoint, a trade show offers the opportunity to discover potential customers and sell new products. Also, relationships with current customers can be strengthened at a show. A trade show often provides the chance to find out what the competition is doing. Many times, trade shows present a situation in which the manufacturer's sales team can meet directly with decision makers and buyers from business-to-business clients. A trade show can be used to strengthen the brand name of a product as well as the company's image.

From the retailer's perspective, a trade show allows buyers to compare merchandise and to make contacts with several prospective vendors in a short period of time. In some cases, the retailer can negotiate special deals. Trade shows represent an ideal place for buyers and sellers to meet in an informal, low-pressure setting to discuss how to work together effectively.

Some national and international trade shows are attended by thousands of buyers. To be sure the trade show will be successful, manufacturers seek out key buyers and try to avoid spending too much time with nonbuyers. Narrowing down the large number of contacts to those most promising is called *prospecting*. Figure 12.12 identifies five categories of buyers who attend trade shows. Many marketers try to weed out the education seekers who are not interested in buying. Manufacturer's agents concentrate efforts on three groups: solution seekers, buying teams, and power buyers. Asking the right questions identifies solution seekers and buying teams. The power buyers are more difficult to find because they do not want to be identified. They often do not wear badges at trade shows, which means vendors are never sure who they are.

- ◆ **Education seekers:** Buyers who want to browse, look, and learn but are not in the buying mode

- ◆ **Reinforcement seekers:** Buyers who want reassurance they made the right decision in past purchases

- ◆ **Solution seekers:** Buyers seeking solutions to specific problems and are in the buying mode

- ◆ **Buying teams:** A team of buyers seeking vendors for their business; usually are in the buying mode

- ◆ **Power buyers:** Members of upper management or key purchasing agents with the authority to buy

FIGURE 12.12
Five Categories of Buyers Attending Trade Shows

In the United States, few deals are finalized during trade shows. Buyers and sellers meet, discuss, and maybe even negotiate, but seldom are buys completed. Instead, manufacturers collect business cards as leads to be followed up later. This procedure varies for international customers. International attendees tend to be senior executives with the authority to make purchases. They fit into the power buyer category listed in Figure 12.12. American manufacturers know that the international attendee often wishes to conduct business during the trade show, not afterward. The international attendees also spend more time at each manufacturer's booth. They stay longer in order to gather and study information in greater detail. The international guest, who pays more for travel expenses, wants more in-depth information than an American counterpart usually needs.

The number of international trade show visitors has increased as competition continues to expand globally. The increase in international participants has caused trade show centers to set up more meeting spaces, conference centers, and even places to eat where buyers and sellers can meet and transact business.

Trade shows have changed in other ways. Large national and international shows are being replaced by niche and regional shows. For example, in the 1990s many megasports trade shows were attended by everybody in the sporting goods business. The National Sporting Goods Association World Sports Expo in Chicago attracted in excess of 90,000 attendees during the mid-1900s. The number has dwindled to fewer than 40,000 today. Now manufacturers and retailers attend specialty trade shows that focus on only one sport or regional shows that focus on one section of the country. Smaller shows are cheaper to set up. Many company leaders believe they provide higher-quality prospects, better opportunities to bond with customers, and provide more quality one-to-one time with customers and potential customers. In contrast, it is relatively easy to get lost in the crowd at a bigger show.[33]

Many pesticides are featured in agricultural trade shows.

A trade show is an excellent place to locate prospective buyers.

CONCERNS WITH TRADE PROMOTIONS

Every member of a company should find ways to incorporate trade promotions into an overall IMC effort. This occurs only when top management buys into the integrated marketing communications concept and insists on including the trade promotions manager on the marketing team. The manager must also make sure all the team members work together with a common marketing agenda.

In most organizations, employee pay structures encourage the use of trade promotions, irrespective of the IMC plan. Sales managers face quotas, and if sales fall behind the easiest way to boost them is to offer retailers a trade deal. Further, brand managers are often evaluated based on the sales growth of a brand. The easiest way to ensure continuing growth is to offer trade deals. The pattern of using trade deals to reach short-term quotas rather than long-term image and theme-building will not change until top management adopts a new approach. The IMC model only succeeds when a long-term horizon is considered and compensation structures change with them.

To illustrate why a new management philosophy is necessary, consider the following situation: A sales manager or brand manager has about a month left in the fiscal year and is 12 percent behind on a sales quota. To ensure that the quota is reached, the sales manager requests a trade deal to encourage retailers to buy excess merchandise. In the short term, the goal has been achieved. In the long run, however, the brand's image may have eroded. It takes a long-term perspective for management to say that increasing trade promotions to meet the quota is not part of the IMC plan and should not be used, because it is not in the company's best long-term interest.

A strong brand image causes retailers to stock the product even when fewer trade deals are offered. This is because a strong brand by itself can help pull customers into retail stores. For example, if a customer believes Sony is a strong brand name in the stereo marketplace, an electronics retailer stocking Sony has an advantage, even when no current trade promotions are on the table.

Meanwhile, as company leaders consider ways to include trade promotions into the IMC plan, they should be aware of other potential problems associated with trade promotions programs. These include costs and the tendency to rely too much on trade promotions to move merchandise.

The first concern is the cost of trade promotions. Manufacturers spend billions of dollars each year on them. These costs are often passed on to consumers in the form of higher prices. It is estimated that 11 cents out of every dollar spent for a consumer product goes directly for the cost of trade promotions.[34] The goal should be to keep the cost at a reasonable level. Money should be spent wisely, rather than simply getting into "bidding wars" with competitors. Trade promotions dollars are best used when they build relationships and help achieve other key IMC goals.

The use of trade promotions has led to a situation in which merchandise does not move until a trade promotion incentive is offered. In the grocery industry, an estimated 70 to 90 percent of all purchases made by retailers are on-deal with some type of trade incentive in place. The constant use of deals has trimmed manufacturer margins on products and created competitive pressures to conform. If a manufacturer tries to quit or cut back on trade promotions, retailers replace the manufacturer's products with other brands or trim shelf space to allow more room for manufacturers offering better deals. Recently, Procter & Gamble cut back on trade promotions in an effort to sell more products off-deal in order to boost profit margins. In a retaliatory action, Safeway cut some of the less popular P&G sizes and brands from its stores. Curbing trade promotional expenditures is extremely difficult because trade promotions are a critical part of moving goods from manufacturers to retailers.[35]

The best way to correct these problems is to spend more on advertising focused on building or rebuilding a brand's image. Also, it is important to be certain promotions fit the brand's image. "If it doesn't fit," writes Brian Sullivan in *Marketing News,* "don't use it."[36] Unfortunately, to spend more on advertising means cutting trade promotions incentives. The risk becomes that other competitors will move in by offering trade promotions to retailers, and shelf space is lost as a result. Then, the vicious cycle begins again.

The management of trade promotions programs is a challenging part of the marketing planning process because such a large percentage of the marketing budget is spent on trade promotions. Effective IMC programs achieve a balance between all elements of the promotions mix and identify clear goals and targets for trade promotions programs. Only then is the company able to compete on all levels and not just through a cycle of trade promotions bidding wars.

INTERNATIONAL IMPLICATIONS

Consumer promotions should be adapted to any country in which they are offered. There are two complications: legal and cultural. Any coupon, premium, contest, sweepstakes, or price change must fit with local legal regulations. The marketing team should investigate any potential legal problems before launching an international consumer promotions program.

Culturally, citizens in some countries may take a dim view of some promotions, most notably coupons. Those who redeem them may be viewed as being of lower socioeconomic status, which may dissuade some from using them. Participation in contests or sweepstakes may violate religious norms in some nations. When considering a consumer promotions program, a cultural assimilator should be consulted to make sure the promotion is both legally and culturally viable.

The same holds true for trade promotions. Laws will vary regarding discounts, spiff money, slotting fees, and exit fees. These issues may also be reflected in cultural values. And, as previously noted, the ways in which managers in companies around the world participate in trade shows varies.

Finally, the emphasis placed on sales promotions will be different, depending on the company involved and the country in which that company operates. Both small companies seeking to do business in foreign countries and large international conglomerates will need to adjust to local conditions when employing these marketing tactics. At the same time, the goal remains to be certain that the efforts match the company's image and overall approach to marketing communications.

SUMMARY

An IMC program should incorporate all four elements of the promotions mix. Advertising may be considered to be the main "voice" of the IMC message. At the same time, the sales promotion part of the mix, including trade and consumer promotions, plays a crucial role in the success or failure of the overall marketing program.

This chapter reviewed the techniques available to attract customers by using consumer promotions. These tactics include coupons, premiums, contests and sweepstakes, refunds, rebates, samples, bonus packs, and price-off deals. These items should be combined with specific promotional goals to have the right impact on customers.

Consumer promotions are often used to boost sales. They can be an excellent short-term method to increase sales or a firm's market share. They can also be an excellent means of introducing new products. Often, a consumer promotion prompts consumers to at least try the product where selling it at the regular price will not. Coupons and contests have been successful tactics for attracting new customers. Consumer promotions can boost sales of a particular brand, and

evidence suggests that they increase sales of the overall product category rather than just take sales away from competitors.

Trade promotions complement consumer promotions. The use of trade allowances, trade contests, trade incentives, and participation in trade shows helps the manufacturer or member of the marketing channel maintain positive contact with other organizations and moves products toward the retailer. Trade promotions work best when they are integrated into other IMC efforts rather than being viewed as a necessary evil or simply as a short term tool to increase sales.

Internationally, sales promotions can be used when they are chosen based on the characteristics, attitudes, laws, regulations, and cultural nuances of a given geographic region. The primary objective of any promotions program must always be to enhance the message sent forth in other aspects of the IMC program in a manner that helps the company reach its long-term marketing objectives in a cost-effective and positive fashion.

KEY TERMS

sales promotions   All of the incentives offered to customers and channel members to encourage product purchases.

consumer promotions   Incentives directly offered to a firm's customers or potential customers.

trade promotions   Expenditures or incentives used by manufacturers and other members of the marketing channel to purchase goods for eventual sale.

freestanding inserts (FSIs)   Sheets of coupons distributed in newspapers, primarily on Sunday.

cross-ruffing   The placement of two promotional materials together.

promotion-prone consumers   Consumers who are not brand loyal and regularly respond to promotions, such as coupons price-off plans, or premiums, only purchasing items that are on-deal.

brand-loyal consumers   Consumers who purchase only one particular brand and do not substitute, regardless of any deal being offered.

price-sensitive consumers   Consumers for whom price is the primary, if not the only, criterion used in making a purchase decision.

trade allowances   Financial incentives to other channel members to motivate them to make purchases.

slotting fees   A form of trade allowance in which are funds charged by retailers to stock new products.

exit fees   Monies paid to remove an item from a retailer's inventory.

spiff money   Rewards given as contest prizes to brokers, retail salespeople, stores, wholesalers, and agents.

trade incentives   Funds given that require the retailer to perform a function in order to receive the dollars.

REVIEW QUESTIONS

1. Define sales promotion. What are the two main categories of sales promotions?
2. Name and describe five types of coupons. Which is the most popular with manufacturers? Which has the highest redemption rate?
3. What problems are associated with coupon programs?
4. What is a premium? What four types of premium programs can companies use?
5. What are the keys to successful premium programs?
6. What is the difference between a contest and a sweepstakes?
7. What are the two main components of prizes rendered in contests and sweepstakes?
8. What tactics can be used to improve the success rates of contests and sweepstakes? What role might the Internet play in this process?
9. How is a refund different from a rebate?
10. What are the primary types of samples?
11. What benefits and problems are associated with sampling?
12. What are the benefits of offering bonus packs?
13. What benefits and problems are associated with price-off tactics?
14. What is an overlay?
15. What are the major types of trade allowances?
16. What is a slotting fee? An exit fee?
17. What is meant by the term on-deal?
18. What complications are associated with trade allowances?
19. How does the term spiff money relate to trade contests?
20. What are the main types of trade incentives?
21. Describe a cooperative merchandising agreement.
22. How are premiums or bonus packs used as trade incentives?
23. How can a cooperative advertising program benefit both a manufacturer and a retailer?
24. How have trade shows changed in recent years?
25. Describe how to effectively utilize trade promotions.
26. What problems must be overcome when developing international sales promotions programs?

CRITICAL THINKING EXERCISES

Discussion Questions

1. According to Kim James, sales promotion manager for Eckerd Drug, "The teen and preteen segments are important because they (teens) are developing buying habits and loyalties during these ages and are our future loyal consumers." In addition to established brands such as Cover Girl and Maybelline, Eckerd Drug now stocks brands such as Bonne Bell, Jane, and Naturistics.[37] Which

consumer promotions would be the best to attract teens and preteens to the cosmetics department of Eckerd Drug? What tie-ins or overlays would you recommend?

2. Many manufacturers believe the best method for differentiating company brands from competitors is advertising. It is true that consumer and trade promotions cannot replace advertising in brand development. At the same time, well-chosen promotional tactics can support brand differentiation. Discuss which consumer promotions a manufacturer should and should not use to develop a brand. Justify your answer.

3. Design a magazine advertisement with a detachable coupon or premium for one of the following products. Compare your offer with those of other students in your class. Discuss the differences between the offers.

   a. SunBright Tanning Salon

   b. Dixie Printing

   c. Hamburger Haven

   d. Blue Bell Ice Cream

4. The Rawlings Sports Equipment Company plans to increase sales of baseball gloves this season. The company intends to use a coupon program. Discuss the pros and cons of each method of distributing coupons for Rawlings listed in Figure 12.3. Which methods should be used? Why?

5. To maintain its strong brand image, Revlon's marketing team decides to use a premium for each of its lipstick products. What type of premium would you suggest for Revlon for each of the target markets listed here? Which premium would you use? Justify your answers.

   a. Caucasian females, ages 50+

   b. African American females, ages 14 to 19

   c. Hispanic females, ages 25 to 40

   d. Professional females, ages 30 to 50

6. Meet in groups of four to six students. Ask each group member to identify the last contest and the last sweepstakes he or she entered. What was the enticement to enter? What was the extrinsic reward? What was the intrinsic reward?

7. Video games generate huge revenues for many companies. One manufacturer decided to use sampling as a method to reach the primary target market—males between the ages of 15 and 30. The sampling could have been distributed in one of two ways. First, the actual game could be loaded on a computer for targeted individuals. Second, potential customers could be sent an abbreviated version of the game. Which sampling method would be the best? Using Figure 12.6, discuss the pros and cons of each sampling method in terms of this new video game. Which type and method of sampling would you recommend? Why?

8. Consumers can be divided into three broad categories in terms of how they respond to consumer promotions: (1) promotion prone, (2) brand loyal, and (3) price sensitive. Identify two services or goods that would fit into each category for you personally. For example, you may be promotion prone when you buy soft drinks (your favorite brand is "What's on Sale"), but be very brand loyal when you buy shoes (Nike, Reebok). Compare your completed list with those of other students. Discuss the differences you observe.

9. Interview three people who have lived in another country about the use of consumer promotions in those countries. Make a list of those promotions heavily used and those not used. Present your findings to the class.

10. As with the other consumer promotions, international expansion requires understanding the laws and customs of each country and culture. In Saudi Arabia and other Muslim countries, Clinique had to modify its sampling techniques. In the United States and Western cultures, Clinique provides cosmetics samples in retail outlets for customers to try. In the United States, females normally sell retail cosmetics; in Saudi Arabia, males do. At the same time, Muslim custom prohibits a male from touching a female. Female customers must either apply the cosmetics themselves or bring their husbands to the store with them.

   Asking a female customer "What color are your eyes?" constitutes a grave offense in Saudi Arabia, because the eyes are believed to be the gateway to the soul. Asking her about skin tone does not make sense, because females keep their faces covered after they reach the age of 14. Sampling is very important for Clinique in Saudi Arabia.[38] How would you organize a sampling program in light of these cultural factors? What other consumer promotions could be used? If you have someone in your class from a Muslim country, ask your classmate to discuss the use of consumer promotions in his or her home country.

INTEGRATED LEARNING EXERCISES

1. Coupons are one of the most popular forms of consumer promotions. Access three of the following Web sites. What are the advantages and disadvantages of each to a consumer? How do the Web sites impact manufacturers? How do they impact retailers?

   a. Eversave (**www.eversave.com**)

   b. CoolSavings (**www.coolsavings.com**)

   c. SmartSource (**www.smartsource.com**)

   d. Valpak (**www.valpak.com**)

   e. Coupons (**www.coupons.com**)

   f. Coupon Country (**www.couponcountry.com**)

2. Sweepstakes and contests are excellent methods for building customer traffic to a retail outlet and for building interest in a brand. Certain firms can assist in the development of sweepstakes and contests. This is important due to a variety of legal restrictions imposed by different states. Access the following Web sites. What types of services does each offer? How can the companies assist in developing a contest or

sweepstakes? Which firm would you choose if you were responsible for developing a contest or a sweepstakes program?

a. Promotions Activators Inc. (**www.promotionactivators. com**)

b. Centra Marketing (**www.centramarketing.com**)

c. Ventura Associates (**www.sweepspros.com**)

3. Many companies offer special consumer promotions on company Web sites. Examine the following company Web sites. What types of promotions are available? What are the objectives of the various consumer promotions? Do the promotions on the Web sites mesh with the company's advertising and consumer promotions at retail outlets?

a. Taco Bell (**www.tacobell.com**)

b. Hershey's (**www.hersheys.com**)

c. Quaker Oats (**www.quakeroats.com**)

d. Papa John's (**www.papajohns.com**)

4. One widely read journal featuring promotional marketing is called *PROMO*. Access the Web site at **www. promomagazine.com**. Examine the table of contents and access the various areas. After exploring the site, write a short report on what is available at the Web site and how it can be used to assist companies wanting to develop various promotions.

CREATIVE CORNER

Student Project

Reread the opening vignette that featured the Corpus Christi Hooks. Design an advertising program for the following events:

Opening Day
Cinco de Mayo
Mother's Day
Father's Day

Fourth of July
Labor Day
Play-off Games
Championship Celebration

Make sure that each advertisement features a consumer promotion that is either mentioned in the vignette or that you come up with on your own.

BEN'S COMPLETE LAWN CARE SERVICE

Ben Folds had turned a part-time college job into a full-time business. As a student, he maintained a solid client list of people using his lawn-mowing service. Following graduation, he knew the type of business that best matched his skills and personality: a complete lawn care service.

Lawn care is typically divided into three main types of companies: (1) those that mow lawns and provide trimming; (2) firms that provide fertilizers, insect control, and weed control; and (3) sod and seeding companies. Ben's idea was to provide every single aspect of lawn care, from the first spring feeding to mowing, trimming, weeding, leaf removal, and even a winter fertilization program. He would also offer sod and seed services for lawns with bare spots or brand new lots.

Ben's vision was to service two main types of customers: (1) residential homeowners who do not want to do lawn work, either because they don't enjoy it or because they do not have the time, and (2) businesses requiring lawn care, including any construction contractors and house builders that want to subcontract the grass-growing part of finishing a home.

Companies that provide lawn-mowing services tend to compete with price and quality. Most offer free bids for a residential mowing job. The more successful firms are those that make a lawn look as good as possible, including trimming around hard-to-reach spots.

Fertilization, weed control, and insecticide providers normally offer a full price and then discount in a variety of ways. Prepayment discounts are given for those who pay in advance. Quantity discounts are given for customers who use the services more frequently, such as a price-per-treatment for eight summer-time treatments that is substantially lower than the price-per-treatment for a customer who only schedules four. Referral discounts are given when a customer finds a new client for the company. Specials are run for extra services when needed. The major national companies will also offer larger price discounts to those customers who decide to terminate services. A follow-up call is made or a coupon is sent to the customer, proposing substantial price discounts to get the reluctant customer to re-establish a relationship with the company.

Sod and seeding companies charge what the market will bear. A customer with only a few options pays more for sod and

A well-manicured lawn is a source of pride.

seed than one who lives where there are more competitors. Many sod companies primarily service wealthy homeowners and contractors.

Ben knew his company faced several challenges. First was brand-name awareness. He had to reach a wide audience of potential buyers. Second would be convincing homeowners to use his services rather than those of national chains. His biggest advantage was being a full-service lawn care company, offering more than just one or two types of services. Ben's Complete Lawn Care Service began operations in Minneapolis in the winter. The company had four employees. Ben knew that he had to build a strong client list quickly and keep those clients happy so that word-of-mouth referrals would help his firm grow in the future.

1. What kinds of promotions are used by Ben's competitors?

2. Design a consumer promotions campaign for Ben's Complete Lawn Care Service.

3. What types of advertisements should be used in conjunction with the company's consumer promotions campaign?

HOT ROD MARKETING

Terry Walsh knew the time was right to move from being a small, "garage-based" company to a much larger enterprise. After spending years as a research chemist, Terry had launched out on his own. His goal was to develop a top-of-the-line fuel injector cleaner for both domestic and foreign automobiles. For 2 years, he worked with various formulas until the right one emerged. The product was named Hot Fire Fuel Injector Cleaner, and the company's name was Hot Fire. Terry was positive Hot Fire would perform well against any competitive product.

The market for fuel-injector cleaners is diverse. Numerous backyard mechanics sell limited amounts of their concoctions to local merchants and over the Internet. Several formulas are even available on eBay. There is no guarantee of quality for these products, some of which may actually harm engine performance. At the other extreme, major companies such as

STP, Gumout, and Dupont offer various grades of cleaners, from low-end products selling for around $3 per unit up to high-end versions priced as high as $30. The primary price determinant is the degree to which the product reduces congestion in a fuel injector. The higher-priced entries are more powerful and remove more "gunk."

Terry's Hot Fire Fuel Injector Cleaner was at the high end. The price would be $17 wholesale, per can. He hoped that dealers would charge no more than $25 as a retail price. Hot Fire sold in single containers as well as in multipacks of 6 and 12 cans. Each can held two treatments or applications.

Several potential markets are available for fuel-injector cleaners. The first is auto repair shops, including simple "lube and oil" change stores and more traditional repair shops. Many times, the proprietors of these stores welcome the idea of a small display of an auto repair or maintenance product, as long as the owner believes the product actually works.

The second type of outlet consists of all of the retailers that sell replacement parts and auto supplies, such as Napa Auto Parts, Dallas Auto Parts, and O'Reilly Auto Parts. Most of these retailers only sell nationally based products from major manufacturers. Getting them to stock Hot Fire would be a major victory.

A third potential customer base is convenience stores. Again, the primary challenge would be convincing a chain, such as 7-Eleven or Circle K, to carry Hot Fire along with other, cheaper products such as STP's and Gumout's low-end products.

Terry knew that buyers in all of these outlets are extremely price sensitive. At the same time, the buyers want to be sure the product works and will not harm other engine parts. Once these objectives have been reached, the goal is to convince them to order larger quantities and continually stock the product. To encourage sales, seasonal discounts, such as for the summer driving season, may move more product to the shelves.

Hot Fire currently employs 20 workers in the production department and has a sales force of 5 people to cover the entire country. The company's Web site is designed to attract people who are willing to buy auto products online and to provide information to business customers.

Terry had a large enough budget to do some advertising. He mostly bought ads in magazines that featured high-performance cars and trade journals for auto body shop managers. One major advantage that had emerged was that Hot Fire sold well locally and was emerging as a product known by local and regional race-car drivers. Hot Fire decals were placed on cars at races across the region.

With some additional funding, it was now time to try to move Hot Fire to national prominence. Winning over each type of retailer was the key to success.

1. What should be the main trade promotions objectives for Hot Fire Fuel Injector Cleaner? What challenges or obstacles might keep the company from reaching those objectives?

2. Design a trade promotions program for Hot Fire Fuel Injector Cleaner.

3. Create a trade magazine advertisement and tagline for Hot Fire that ties in with the trade promotions program.

ENDNOTES

1. Personal interview of Reid Ryan and Jay Miller by Donald Baack, March 12, 2008. **www.cchooks.com**, accessed June 20, 2008.

2. Mariola Palazon-Vidal and Elena Delgado-Ballester, "Sales Promotions Effect on Consumer-Based Brand Equity," *International Journal of Market Research* 47, no. 2 (2005), pp. 179–205.

3. Emily Bryson York, "Why Taco Bell's World Series Play Was a Steal," *Advertising Age* (**http://adage.com/article_id=121563**, October 29, 2007).

4. "Clippings Slow," *Promo* (**www.promomagazine.com/mag/marketing_clipping_slows/index.html**, accessed January 2, 2008).

5. "Do Coupons Make Sense," *Incentive* 177, no. 5 (May 2003), p. 19.

6. Noreen O'Leary, "Dealing with Coupons," *Adweek* 46, no. 8 (February 21, 2005), p. 29.

7. Elizabeth Gardener and Minakshi Trivedi, "A Communication Framework to Evaluate Sales Promotion Strategies," *Journal of Advertising Research* 38, no. 3 (May–June 1998), pp. 67–71.

8. Karen Holt, "Coupon Crimes," *PROMO* 17, no. 5 (April 2004), pp. 23–29.

9. "Upward Bound," *PROMO* 17, no. 5 (April 2004), pp. AR3–5.

10. Srimalee Somluck, "Prime Nature Villa: Cars, Jewelry on Offer," *The Nation (Thailand)* (**www.nationmultimedia.com**, accessed September 29, 2004).

11. Don Jagoda, "The Seven Habits of Highly Successful Promotions," *Incentive* 173, no. 8 (August 1999), pp. 104–105.

12. "Industry Trends Report 2007," *Promo* (**www.promomagazine.com/september2007**), pp. AR1–27.

13. "Contest News," *Restaurant Hospitality* 89, no. 2 (February 2005), p. 110.

14. Lee Esposito, "Sweepstakes Can Run As Smoothly As Velvet," *Frozen Food Age* 53, no. 7 (February 2005), p. 46.

15. Kathleen Joyce, "Not Just a Novelty," *PROMO* 17, no. 12 (November 2004), pp. 52–56

16. Sandra Block, "Rattled About Rebate Hassles? Regulators Starting to Step In," *USA Today* (March 22, 2005), p. 3b.

17. Lindsay Chappell, "Rebates Eventually Become Ho-Hum, Researcher Says," *Automotive News* 79, no. 6133 (February 7, 2005), p. 36.

18. Pete Wetmore, "Inserts Branch Out Beyond Print Fliers," *Advertising Age* 75, no. 16 (April 19, 2004), p. N-6.

19. Betsy Spethman, "Introductory Offer," *PROMO* 16 (2004), p. 27; Jennifer Kulpa, "Bristol-Myers Squibb Breaks Ground with Direct Response Product Sampling Website," *Drug Store News* 19, no. 7 (April 7, 1997), p. 19.

20. Jennifer Hiscock, "The Two Faces of Sampling," *Event* (April 2004), pp. 25–26.

21. Beng Soo Ong and Foo Nin Ho, "Consumer Perceptions of Bonus Packs: An Exploratory Analysis," *Journal of Consumer Marketing* 14, no. 2–3 (1997), pp. 102–12.

22. David R. Bell, Ganesh Iyer, and V. Padmanaghan, "Price Competition Under Stockpiling and Flexible Consumption," *Journal of Marketing Research* 39, no. 3 (August 2002), pp. 292–304.

23. Showwei Chu, "Welcome to Canada, Please Buy Something," *Canadian Business* 71, no. 9 (May 29, 1998), pp. 72–73.

24. Walter Heller, "Promotion Pullback," *Progressive Grocer* 81, no. 4 (March 1, 2002), p. 19.

25. Miguel Gomez, Vithala Rao, and Edward McLaughlin, "Empirical Analysis of Budget and Allocation of Trade Promotions in the U.S. Supermarket Industry," *Journal of Marketing Research* 44, no. 3 (August 2007), pp. 410–24.

26. Ibid.

27. K. Sudhir and Vithala Rao, "Do Slotting Allowances Enhance Efficiency or Hinder Competition?" *Journal of Marketing Research* 43, no. 2 (May 2006), pp. 137–55.

28. Paula Bone, Karen France, and Richard Riley, "A Multifirm Analysis of Slotting Fees," *Journal of Public Policy & Marketing* 25, no. 2 (Fall 2006), pp. 224–37.

29. "Study: Trade Dollars Up," *Frozen Food Age* 50, no. 2 (September 2001), p. 14.

30. Walter Heller, "Promotion Pullback," *Progressive Grocer* 81, no. 4 (March 1, 2002), p. 19.

31. "Cruise Selling Season Kicks Off with Agent Promotions and Optimism," *Travel Agent* 319 (January 3, 2005), p. 9.

32. Roger A. Slavens, "Getting a Grip on Co-Op," *Modern Tire Dealer* 75, no. 3 (March 1994), pp. 34–37.

33. Jennifer Gilber, "The Show Must Go On," *Sales & Marketing Management* 155, no. 5 (May 2003), p. 14.

34. Walter Heller, "Promotion Pullback," *Progressive Grocer* 81, no. 4 (March 1, 2002), p. 19.

35. Jack K. Kasulis, "Managing Trade Promotions in the Context of Market Power," *Journal of the Academy of Marketing Science* 27, no. 3 (Summer 1999), pp. 320–32.

36. Brian Sullivan, "Make Sure Promotional Items Fit Brand Perfectly," *Marketing News* 35, no. 19 (September 10, 2001), p. 15.

37. Liz Parks, "Chains See Today's Wealthy Teens as Tomorrow's Loyal Customers," *Drug Store News* 21, no. 15 (September 27, 1999), p. 84.

38. Donald Baack, "International Business," New York: Glencoe-McGraw Hill (2008), pp. 28–49.

13

Public Relations and Sponsorship Programs

Chapter Objectives

After reading this chapter, you should be able to answer the following questions:

- **What** types of relationships are possible between a public relations department and a marketing department?

- **Why** is it important to understand the natures of various organizational stakeholders?

- **When** should a marketing team consider cause-related marketing and green marketing programs?

- **How** can a sponsorship program hurt or enhance a firm's image?

- **When** are event marketing programs most and least likely to succeed?

EVERYONE'S WILD ABOUT HARRY

On July 21, 2007, thousands of anxious fans crowded into bookstores around the world, hoping to be among the first to buy *Harry Potter and the Deathly Hallows*, the final installment of the fabled series. The scheduled release at midnight in each time zone around the world led to long lines, fans and employees dressed in Potter costumes, and coverage in every venue, from local papers to national news stories.

Prior to the book's release, speculation about the fate of Harry created an amazing level of buzz. Some enjoyed trying to guess his fate. Others hoped to spoil it for everyone by reporting they had stolen advance copies and publishing the outcome before the release of the book. One person claimed that he was able to hack into the computers at Bloomsburg Publishing in order to reveal the outcome. Another bragged about shooting photos of the page proofs. Either way, these attempts only added to the suspense and the amount of publicity the book received.

The *Deathly Hallows* came out the same week that the fifth novel (*Harry Potter and the Order of the Phoenix*) was released as a motion picture. The interplay between the two added to both the excitement and the long lines in bookstores and movie theaters.

In the first 10 days, over 11.5 million copies of the *Deathly Hallows* were sold. Some avid readers quickly turned to the final page to read how the story turned out. Others carefully sequestered themselves in hideaways, where they were guaranteed the chance to take in the entire story without having someone accidentally (or on purpose) reveal the ending. Within the next few weeks, sales soared to over 14 million copies.

Reviews of the final edition were largely positive. Most readers seemed relieved that Harry lived on, while most critics noted the literary quality of the story and the writing. For the most part, the majority of readers appeared to be satisfied with the ending. When it became common knowledge that Harry had survived, speculation quickly emerged that the door was being left open for a new saga.

The *Harry Potter* series generated sales of over 350 million books. Movies were made for each edition, leading to millions more in ticket revenues. Costumes, posters, magnets, wands and

CHAPTER THIRTEEN

Source: Courtesy of Summer Bradley.

other toys, plus even Christmas tree ornaments added to the revenues generated by the characters created by author JK Rowling.

The books and merchandise were a bonanza for not only the publishing company and manufacturers—the reach extended to local bookstores, national chains such as Barnes and Noble, and even to larger retailers such as Wal-Mart. Many social analysts noted that the *Harry Potter* series caused many children to take up reading at an early age. The ripple affected numerous companies associated with book publishing. After the *Deathly Hallows* had been on the market for 1 month, the publishing industry reported that over 100 million copies of the various *Harry Potter* books were still in print and available.

From a marketing perspective, it is clear that *Harry Potter* is more than just a successful book series. The final chapters of the saga were accompanied by word-of-mouth, free publicity through news stories, Internet chatter, release events, and a degree of buzz with an impact that cannot be overestimated. Mugwarts enjoyed a special status in popular culture. *Harry Potter* is a powerful brand that will continue to be a force for many years to come.[1]

OVERVIEW

The traditional promotions mix consists of advertising, sales promotions, personal selling, and public relations efforts. At this point in the textbook, the first three elements in the mix have been presented. This chapter is devoted to the fourth element—public relations. Sponsorship and event programs are also examined.

Public relations efforts, sponsorships, and event programs are part of the overall IMC approach. The same unified message appears in every marketing endeavor, from the appearance of the company's letterhead and stationery to advertisements, promotional items, information in press releases, and in any sponsorship program. The goal of an IMC plan is to make sure that each component of a firm's communication plan speaks with one voice. Extending this goal to public relations and sponsorships is an important task for the marketing team.

This chapter begins with a discussion of the nature of a public relations function within an integrated marketing plan. Second, sponsorship programs and event marketing tactics are outlined to show how the company can make quality contacts with existing customers, new prospects, vendors, and others. The goal of these activities is to reach the general public with the same clear voice that has been developed in other marketing activities. When the company succeeds at building positive public relations and sponsorship programs, the firm's image is enhanced and its brands are better known and perceived more favorably in the marketplace.

PUBLIC RELATIONS

In Hollywood, one well-worn phrase is "There's no such thing as bad publicity." This may be true for a bad-boy actor trying to get his name out to the public; however, in the world of marketing and communications bad publicity is *worse* than no publicity. Many business organizations spend countless hours fending off negative news while trying to develop positive and noticeable messages and themes.

The **public relations (PR) department** is a unit in the firm that manages publicity and other communications with every group that is in contact with the company. Some of the functions performed by the public relations department are similar to those provided by the marketing department. Others are quite different. Often, the public relations department is separate from the marketing department. The two may cooperate with and consult each other, yet each has a separate role to perform.

Some marketing experts argue that public relations should be part of the marketing department, just as advertising, trade promotions, and consumer promotions are under the jurisdiction of the marketing manager. Others suggest that public relations activities are different and cannot operate effectively within a marketing department. Instead, a member of the public relations department should serve as a consultant to the marketing department. Still others contend that a new division, called the "department of communications," should be created to oversee both marketing and public relations activities.

Internal Versus External Public Relations

In any case, the first major decision company leaders must make concerning public relations is who will handle the various activities involved. They can be managed by an internal public relations officer or department. Other companies hire public relations firms to handle either special projects or all of the public relations functions. When a public relations agency is retained, normally someone is placed in charge of internal public relations, because most public relations firms deal only with external publics.

The decision criteria used in selecting advertising agencies can be applied to selecting a public relations firm. It is important to develop a trusting relationship with the public relations agency and to carefully spell out what the firm expects from the agency.

Public Relations Tools

A number of tools are available to the public relations department. These include company newsletters, internal messages, public relations releases, correspondence with stockholders, annual reports, and various special events. Even the bulletin board in the company's break room can be used to convey messages to internal stakeholders.

One common goal of a public relations firm is to get hits. A **hit** is the mention of a company's name in a news story. Hits can be positive, negative, or even neutral in terms of their impact on a firm. The concept behind getting hits in the news is that the more a consumer sees the name of a company in a news-related context, the higher the brand or company awareness will become. This may be true, but it is important to consider the

◆ Identify internal and external stakeholders	◆ Create positive image-building activities	
◆ Assess the corporate reputation	◆ Prevent or reduce image damage	
◆ Audit corporate social responsibility		

FIGURE 13.1
Public Relations Functions

type of image that is being developed. It may be a wiser strategy to seek fewer hits and to make sure that each one projects the company in a positive light that also reinforces the firm's IMC theme.

Consequently, when a public relations firm is used, the agency's personnel must be familiar with the client's IMC plan. Then, members of the public relations firm are able to work on ideas that reinforce the plan. Special events, activities, and news releases can be developed to strengthen the one voice needed to build a successful IMC program. The following sections describe public relations functions that must be performed, including reaching all of the targets of various company communications.

PUBLIC RELATIONS FUNCTIONS

Many public relations activities are not considered typical marketing functions. This is because the marketing department concentrates on customers and the channel members en route to those customers, such as wholesalers and retail outlets. In contrast, the public relations department focuses on a variety of internal and external stakeholders, including employees, stockholders, public interest groups, the government, and society as a whole.

Five key public relations functions are displayed in Figure 13.1. Each represents the tasks given to public relations personnel, whether they are internal employees or members of a public relations company hired to perform those functions.

IDENTIFYING STAKEHOLDERS

All the recipients of company communications are important. Any constituent who makes contact with a company should receive a clear, unified message. In this section, the stakeholders who are targets of public relations efforts are described. A **stakeholder** is a person or group who has a vested interest in the organization's activities. A vested interest can be a variety of things, including:

- Profits paid as common stock dividends
- Loan repayments that a lending institution seeks to receive
- Sales to the company or purchases made from the company
- Wages paid to employees
- Community well-being
- A special-interest topic

In essence, a wide variety of items can cause people or other companies to believe they hold a stake in the firm's activities.

To understand the nature of public relations programs, it is helpful to begin by identifying the publics that make contact with various companies. Figure 13.2 identifies the primary internal and external stakeholders that the public relations department should monitor.

◆ Employees	◆ Media	
◆ Unions	◆ Local community	
◆ Shareholders	◆ Financial community	
◆ Channel members	◆ Government	
◆ Customers	◆ Special-interest groups	

FIGURE 13.2
Stakeholders

Communications to each of these stakeholder groups are crucial. To ensure consistency, the company should develop a clear communication strategy that fits well with the firm's IMC plan and corporate image that is to be conveyed. The overall message to each stakeholder should be the same. Then, each message will be tailored to meet the different expectations of the various audiences. By customizing the content, style, and channel of communication, each stakeholder group receives a message that best resonates with them, yet is consistent with other messages.

In addition to sending communications to each of the stakeholders, the public relations department closely monitors the actions and opinions of each group. When changes in attitudes, new views, or serious concerns develop, the public relations department should be ready to address the problem. Most importantly, it is the responsibility of the public relations department to be certain that all forms of communications to each of these publics remain consistent with the firm's message and image.

Internal Stakeholders

Company leaders should not underestimate the value of quality internal communications. Employees provide a powerful channel of communication to people outside of the organization. They can either enhance the firm's reputation or damage it. What employees say to those around them has a much higher level of credibility than what a company says about itself. Word-of-mouth communications, even informal statements by employees, impact decisions about purchasing and investing.[2]

Employees should receive a constant stream of information from the company. The same is true for other internal stakeholders, such as corporate shareholders and labor unions. Many of these individuals are quite distant from the marketing and public relations departments. They should be made aware of what the company is trying to achieve with its IMC program, even if this means only basic knowledge. Those closest to the marketing department, such as employees serving customers, are going to be more acutely aware of the nature of the IMC plan, including how the company's message theme is being sent to all other constituents.

The Motorola advertisement shown in this section states that the company's "Wireless Communications Centers help you stay connected." Employees who are aware of Motorola's theme can communicate the same message when dealing with customers, vendors, and other publics.

To work effectively in communicating with employees, the public relations department must work closely with the human resource (HR) department. Publications and communications aimed at employees must be consistent with the image and message that the firm is espousing to customers and other groups. For example, any firm that uses advertising to suggest that employees are always ready to assist customers should make sure those employees are aware of the message. Employee behaviors should then be consistent with the advertising theme that is being conveyed to customers. The HR department should hire the kind of worker who is attracted to such an approach and structure performance appraisals and rewards to favor those who "buy into" the company's overall IMC approach. The emphasis on providing information about company activities must logically extend to every public relations event and sponsorship program.

Motorola's theme is that the company's "Wireless Communications Centers help you stay connected." This theme should be used by employees in all communications.

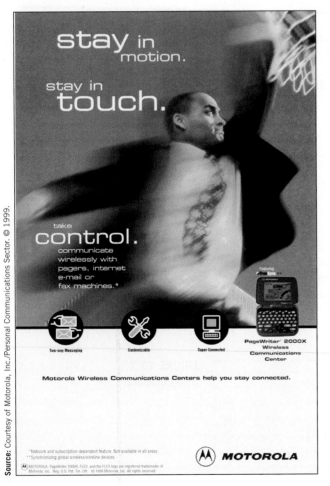

External Stakeholders

Overseeing external communications is a daunting task, because the company has little or no influence on how these publics perceive organizational activities. External stakeholders include groups such as the media, local community, financial community, government, and special-interest groups. The company usually has little power over what these groups say or how they interpret information about the company. It is important, therefore, for the company to disseminate positive information and quickly react to any negative publicity or views that are expressed.

In general, a totally integrated communications program accounts for all types of messages that an organization delivers to both internal and external stakeholders. Every contact point provides the opportunity for a message to be sent. The marketing department tends to create contact points with customers and potential customers. To complement this effort, the public relations department deals with the myriad of contact points that are not created or planned, yet are just as critical as those that are planned. An unplanned contact point such as a news story or an individual talking to an employee of the firm at a social gathering allows the firm to build a positive image or reduce any negative messages that are being passed along. Naturally, it is more difficult to deal with unplanned contact points, because they cannot always be anticipated. The key is to monitor constantly what is going on around the firm in order to keep constituents as happy and satisfied as possible.

ASSESSING CORPORATE REPUTATION

A corporation's reputation is fragile. It also is valuable. Well-received corporate and brand names can enhance businesses during the good times and protect them when a crisis or problem occurs. Consumer preferences about which brands to purchase are influenced by a company's reputation. People make decisions about where to invest based on corporate reputations. Potential employees decide where to apply and where to work based company on reputations.

A Wal-Mart advertisement directed at employees, the local community, and other stakeholders.

In one survey, two-thirds of those who responded believed that most businesses would take advantage of consumers if they thought they wouldn't get caught.[3] Corporate scandals, accounting fraud, and CEO greed have damaged more than just the few companies involved. Recent incidents, including the publicity regarding Home Depot CEO Bob Nardelli, who collected a $210 million exit check after being fired for poor performance, create long-lasting images that affect both employees and the general public.[4]

People are leery of big business, suspicious of business motives, and are unsure if any company should be trusted. Perceptions of corporate reputations by external publics are at an all-time low. As one homemaker stated, "I'm very disappointed in how money can rob the goodness in people." She went on to state that putting money under her mattress would be a safer place than investing in today's corporations.[5]

Assessing and managing a company's reputation is as important as promoting its products. Yet, with all that is at stake, less than half of the companies in the United States have someone assigned to monitor corporate reputation. This means company leaders have little idea what consumers, investors, employees, and the public think about the firm. A public relations program is impossible to pursue effectively if company leaders do not know what other people believe about the organization.

Assessment begins when company leaders take the time to conduct surveys and interviews to find out what people think of the organization. These efforts can be completed internally or be performed by an outside company, such as a public relations firm. The process of assessment should include internal views of the corporation's reputation as well as opinions held by those outside the company.

This General Mills advertisement thanks both customers and employees.

AUDITING CORPORATE SOCIAL RESPONSIBILITY

Social responsibility is the obligation an organization has to be ethical, accountable, and reactive to the needs of society. Figure 13.3 outlines some of the general areas in which firms can become more ethical and reactive to society's needs.

Business experts agree that socially responsible firms are more likely to thrive and survive in the long term. Companies engaged in positive activities generate quality publicity and customer loyalty that result in a positive image of the firm. Firms that work strongly toward reductions in unfair practices, pollution, harassment, and other negative activities are more likely to stay out of court, and the company will suffer fewer negative word-of-mouth comments by unhappy employees or consumers. By managing these activities properly, a firm can reduce damage to its public image and increase positive public perceptions of the organization.

A corporate social responsibility audit is usually undertaken by the organization's management team in conjunction with department managers. Often, external agencies provide guidelines. The purpose of a social responsibility audit is to make sure the organization has clear-cut ethical guidelines for employees to follow and that the company acts to serve the interests of all publics. Guidelines include use of a corporate or professional code of ethics, specifying activities that would be construed as being unethical, and statements about the positive activities a company will pursue. Many firms also have access to "ethics hotlines," where employees can call or e-mail to discuss specific ethical dilemmas.

If a firm is found to be deficient during a social responsibility audit, clear steps should be outlined to show how the issues will be resolved. Firms without codes of ethics should start by setting up committees or groups to develop them. Companies without other ethical guidelines should move quickly to establish them.

It is the task of the public relations department to make sure internal publics are aware of a corporation's social responsibility efforts. The department can then inform the general public about these activities to help enhance the firm's image.

CREATING POSITIVE IMAGE-BUILDING ACTIVITIES

In an effort to positively influence the views that consumers and other stakeholders have about a company, many firms have turned to cause-related marketing and green marketing. These *planned events* are designed to draw positive attention to the organization as a solid corporate citizen, one committed to social responsibility. The public relations

FIGURE 13.3
Examples of Activities that Affect a Company's Image

Image-Destroying Activities	Image-Building Activities
◆ Discrimination	◆ Empowerment of employees
◆ Harassment	◆ Charitable contributions
◆ Pollution	◆ Sponsoring local events
◆ Misleading communications	◆ Selling environmentally safe products
◆ Deceptive communications	◆ Outplacement programs
◆ Offensive communications	◆ Supporting community events

department can then send out messages in the form of press releases and hold press conferences to highlight these positive, image-building activities.

Cause-Related Marketing

Cause-related marketing is a program whereby a firm ties a marketing program to a charity in order to generate goodwill. American businesses pay over $600 million each year for the right to use a nonprofit organization's name or logo in company advertising and marketing programs. This type of partnership agreement between a nonprofit cause and a for-profit business is based on the idea that consumers are more likely to purchase from companies that are willing to help a good cause.

As noted previously, brand parity is the norm for many goods and services. Customers perceive that there are few notable differences between products and the companies that sell them. Many marketers use cause-related marketing to help develop stronger brand ties and to move consumers, as well as businesses, toward brand loyalty. A survey by Cone Communications and Roper Starch Worldwide revealed the following:[6]

- 78% of consumers are more likely to purchase a brand associated with a cause they care about.
- 54% would be willing to pay more for a brand that is associated with a cause they care about.
- 66% would switch brands to support a particular cause.
- 84% indicated that cause-related marketing creates a more positive image of a company.

The Peace Corps is a social cause supported by a number of companies.

A Wal-Mart advertisement highlighting a social cause.

One difficulty businesses can encounter is that what is a "good" cause to one customer may be disliked by another. Dayton Hudson found a large number of picketers outside company stores objecting to contributions the company made to Planned Parenthood, even as others praised Dayton Hudson's involvement.[7]

In the past, a number of companies donated to causes with little thought to the impact or benefit of such gifts. These philanthropic efforts were expected of big business. Today, most companies want to know what the benefit will be. Although company leaders believe a charity is worthwhile, supporting that charity must, in some way, result in a tangible benefit. Otherwise the company should not give support. Possible benefits include:

- Additional customers
- Increased profits
- Consumer goodwill for the future
- Better relations with governmental agencies
- Reduced negative public opinion

These benefits lead companies to get involved. Relationships that do not yield positive benefits to the business sponsor do not last long. Figure 13.4 highlights the top five areas consumers want businesses to consider as they seek causes to support.

In choosing a cause, the marketing team focuses on issues that relate to the company's business. Supporting these efforts makes the activity more credible to consumers. When the company supports an unrelated cause, consumers may feel that the business simply is trying to benefit from the nonprofit's reputation. This may lead some consumers to stop buying the company's products or to believe the company is trying to cover up unethical behavior. Consumers are becoming skeptical about the motives behind the increased emphasis given to various charities. Even though most people understand that a business must benefit from the relationship, they still tend to develop negative views when they believe that the business is exploiting a relationship with a nonprofit.

When a good fit exists, positive reactions emerge. For example, a cosmetic dentist established partnerships with a homeless shelter for battered women and a residential education center for former substance abusers and ex-convicts. The dentist offered free services to these centers. Several television and newspaper reporters showed up to observe him treating patients. Individuals who had been in pain for months were interviewed. When they stated that cosmetic dental work gave them relief, positive feelings in the community were the result. The publicity was extremely valuable. The dental services were something neither the centers nor individuals who were living in the centers could afford.[8]

Cause-related marketing is also important for nonprofit organizations. Competition has increased in both the business world and the nonprofit world. An increasing number of nonprofit organizations are competing for contributions and gifts. Strategic relationships with businesses can boost contributions for a nonprofit organization considerably. For instance, the General Mills Yoplait campaign raised over $10 million for the Susan G. Komen Breast Cancer Foundation. Using the slogan "Save Lids to Save Lives," General Mills donates 10 cents for each lid of Yoplait that is returned by consumers.[9] These relationships with businesses result not only in direct increases in revenues, but also in greater publicity for the nonprofit organization.

The public relations aspect of cause-related marketing is complicated. To benefit from cause-related marketing, company leaders want publicity about what is being done.

FIGURE 13.4
Causes Consumers Prefer

◆ Improve public schools	52%
◆ Dropout prevention	34%
◆ Scholarships	28%
◆ Cleanup of environment	27%
◆ Community health education	25%

Source: Bevolyn Williams-Harold and Eric L. Smith. "Spending with Heart," *Black Enterprise* 28, no. 12, (July 1998), p. 26.

Yet, if the company publicizes too much, people will think the cause is simply being used for commercial gain. In a survey of British consumers, the vast majority said a company should spend funds on communications about their cause-related efforts. The same survey indicated that two-thirds also said the amount that should be spent should not be significant. At the same time, the majority of those surveyed said their purchase decisions are influenced by the causes a company supports. This makes informing people about what a company is doing important; however, doing so involves walking a thin line between publicizing and what might be perceived as corporate self-aggrandizement.[10]

Green Marketing and Pro-Environmental Activities

Green marketing is the development and promotion of products that are environmentally safe. When asked, most consumers strongly favor the concept of green marketing. One recent survey indicated that 58 percent of Americans try to save electricity, 46 percent recycle newspapers, 45 percent return bottles or cans, and 23 percent buy products made from, or packaged in, recycled materials.[11]

Although consumers favor green marketing and environmentally safe products, actual purchases of such products only occur when all things are considered equal. Most consumers are not willing to sacrifice price, quality, convenience, availability, or performance for the sake of the environment. In fact, according to a recent study, about 40 percent of consumers say they do not purchase green products because they believe the products are inferior to regular goods.[12]

To benefit from green marketing, the company should identify market segments that are most attracted to environmentally friendly products. Figure 13.5 divides U.S. consumers into five segments based on their propensity to use green products and their attitudes about environmental issues. Notice that only 9 percent of American consumers are classified as "True Blue Greens," and another 6 percent are classified as "Greenback Greens." The True Blue Greens are active environmentalists who support environmentally safe products and shop for brands that utilize green marketing. The Greenback Greens purchase environmentally safe products, but are not politically active.

Company leaders must carefully choose a green marketing strategy that matches the target audience. In making the decision on how much emphasis to put on green marketing, managers should ask three questions. First, what percentage of the company's customer base fits into the green marketing segments? Second, can the brand or company be differentiated from the competition along green lines in such a way that it can become

This Peace Corps ad asks young adults to join the organization.

FIGURE 13.5
U.S. Consumers Segmented on Their Attitudes Toward and Support of Green Marketing

+ **True Blue Green (9%)**—Have strong environmental values and are politically active in environmental issues; heavy users of green products

+ **Greenback Greens (6%)**—Have strong environmental values, but are not politically active; heavy users of green products

+ **Sprouts (31%)**—Believe in green products in theory, but not in practice; will buy green products, but only if equal to or superior to nongreen products

+ **Grousers (19%)**—Are uneducated about environmental issues and cynical about their ability to affect change; believe green products are too expensive and inferior

+ **Basic Browns (33%)**—Do not care about environmental issues or social issues

Source: Jill Meredith Ginsberg and Paul N. Bloom, "Choosing the Right Green Marketing Strategy," *MIT Sloan Management Review* 46, no.1 (Fall 2004), pp. 79–84.

a competitive advantage? Third, will the company's current target audience be alienated by adopting a green marketing approach?

Almost all firms say they are pro-environment and provide information on company Web sites about their environmental activities. The amount of effort given to publicize these activities varies widely.[13] For example, Coca-Cola tries to protect the environment, but most people are unaware of the company's efforts. Coca-Cola has invested heavily in various recycling programs and recyclable package designs. The activities are not publicized, because there is some fear that it would reduce the product's appeal to some of the company's audience. Overemphasizing the green aspects of Coca-Cola's operation may actually hurt sales.

An alternative approach to being pro-environment is to promote the direct, tangible benefits of a product first, with the environmental benefits presented as a secondary factor. The Toyota Prius was launched with an emphasis on fuel efficiency. Consumers were told they would spend less on gas. The fact that the Prius was an environmentally advanced, fuel-efficient hybrid vehicle was mentioned, but not stressed. The idea was that strong environmentalists would believe a hybrid car is important. For those who were not strong environmentalists, it did not matter, because the car delivered fuel efficiency.

Starbucks is another example. Renewable energy now accounts for about 20 percent of the power used in its company-owned stores. For this initiative, Starbucks was named one of the Environmental Protection Agency's Top 25 Green Power Partners. The citation is posted on Starbucks' Web site, but it is buried deep in the social responsibility section.[14]

For a few companies, environmental activities are fully integrated into the business' design and marketing approach because the primary customer base is True Blue Greens and the Greenback Greens. Examples of these types of companies include The Body Shop, Patagonia, and Honest Tea of Bethesda, Maryland. For Honest Tea, social responsibility is embedded in every company activity, from the manufacturing process to the marketing of products. Honest Tea uses biodegradable tea bags, organic ingredients, and community partnerships. The focus of Honest Tea's marketing program is the company's concern for and support of both environmental and social issues.

In 2008, Nike released its Trash Talk brand of basketball shoe. The product is made from manufacturing waste. NBA player Steve Nash wore the shoes in the 2008 All Star Game. Nash has a longstanding interest in environmental causes. The free publicity was an excellent tie-in for the Trash Talk launch.

Most business leaders believe their companies should be involved in protecting the environment and creating green products; however, the marketing emphasis each one gives varies. If it thinks new customers will be gained or product sales will rise, the company will be more likely to aggressively promote its environmental stance. Other companies, such as Coca-Cola, may be less willing to make such bold statements. Each company's marketing team will decide whether green marketing should be a central part of the IMC message and how to position itself in terms of the environment.

PREVENTING OR REDUCING IMAGE DAMAGE

One of the most important public relations functions is damage control. **Damage control** is reacting to negative events caused by a company error, consumer grievances, or unjustified or exaggerated negative press. Corporate and brand images are quickly damaged by negative publicity and events. A strong company image, which took years to build, may be destroyed in just a few weeks or months. ExxonMobil still suffers from an event that occurred nearly 20 years ago. The 1989 *Exxon Valdez* accident, in which 11 million gallons of crude oil were spilled into the bay at Prince William Sound, Alaska, has resulted in a great deal of animosity toward the company. There are still consumers who will not buy Exxon gas. Many do not believe any messages from ExxonMobil about what the company is doing for the environment. ExxonMobil may not recover until a new generation of drivers grows up.

Bad news travels quickly and hits hard. Any time rats are found in a restaurant or some other disgusting event happens, the media report the story and it circulates widely. For example, in 2007, when Jet Blue experienced an incident in which passengers were essentially forced to sit in a plane on the ground for many hours due to bad weather, damage was done to the company's reputation for quality customer service that had taken many years to build. Company leaders tried to quickly respond in order to limit the harm to Jet Blue's image.

Not all negative publicity is generated by the media. Sometimes negative publicity comes from word-of-mouth communication from customers, employees, or other individuals connected with the company. With the Internet, bad experiences and negative talk can be posted and spread to thousands, even millions, within a very short time.

Damage control is used in two situations. The first occurs when the firm has made an error or caused legitimate consumer grievances. The second takes place when unjustified or exaggerated negative press appears. Defending an organization's image and handling damage control takes two forms: (1) proactive prevention strategies and (2) reactive damage-control strategies (see Figure 13.6).

Proactive Prevention Strategies

Proactive prevention means that rather than waiting for harmful publicity to appear and then reacting, many firms charge certain employees with minimizing the effects of any bad press. These approaches may prevent negative publicity from starting in the first place. Two proactive prevention techniques are entitlings and enhancements.[15] **Entitlings** are attempts to claim responsibility for positive outcomes of events. **Enhancements** are attempts to increase the desirable outcome of an event in the eyes of the public.

Entitling occurs when a firm associates its name with a positive event. For example, being the official sponsor of a U.S. Olympic team that wins a gold medal attaches the company's name to the athletic achievements of people who don't work for the firm, yet the firm can claim responsibility for some aspect of their successes.

Enhancements occur when a bigger deal is made out of something that is relatively small. For instance, many products now claim to be *fat free*, which makes it sound like they are diet foods. In fact, many fat-free products have just as many calories as do those that contain fat. At the same time, the fat-free label helps convince customers that the company is trying to help them to eat healthy food and watch their weight at the same time.

Reactive Damage-Control Strategies

Company leaders often must react to unforeseen events, because they cannot anticipate every possible contingency. In these instances, managers must work diligently to blunt the effects of unwanted bad publicity by every means possible. Crisis management and other techniques should be designed to help the firm cope with circumstances that threaten its image. Reactive damage-control strategies include:

- Internet interventions
- Crisis management programs
- Apology strategy
- Impression management techniques.

Proactive Strategies
  Entitlings
  Enhancements
Reactive Strategies
  Internet interventions
  Crisis management programs
  Apology strategy
  Impression management techniques

FIGURE 13.6
Damage-Control Strategies

Internet interventions are designed to combat negative word-of-mouth that is placed somewhere online. With the rise of the popularity of the Internet, new forums for sharing negative word-of-mouth and spreading bad experiences have arisen, including e-mail, chat rooms, rogue Web sites, and Internet blogs. All provide an environment in which consumers from every part of the world can share horror stories. Individuals can put any information they desire on the Internet, even when it unfairly portrays certain industries, companies, or brands.

The Internet has opened an entirely new venue for people to vent emotions, which can be devastating to a company's reputation. Unfortunately, some companies fail to monitor these communications and many do not respond to negative messages.

Vigilant public relations officers realize the power of the Internet and what it can do to an organization's reputation. These leaders make sure someone monitors what is being said. When they see messages criticizing a company unjustly or proclaiming untruths, company representatives take action. Some log into a chat room and immediately identify themselves as company representatives. They then attempt to explain the company's point of view and try to correct misconceptions. In other situations, the company's public relations department prepares public statements and press releases. Not every activity warrants a formal reaction. Still, monitoring the Internet keeps the company's leadership informed about what people are saying and what they are thinking.

When reports surfaced of hypodermic needles in Pepsi products, Pepsi quickly reacted by showing the public how cans and bottles were filled.

Crisis management involves either accepting the blame for an event and offering an apology or refuting those making the charges in a forceful manner. A crisis may be viewed as either a problem or an opportunity. Many times a crisis contains the potential to improve the firm's position and image. For example, when PepsiCo encountered claims that hypodermic needles were being found in its products, the management team quickly responded with photographs and video demonstrating that such an occurrence was impossible, because the bottles and cans turn upside down before being filled with any soft drink. Next, footage of a con artist slipping a needle into a can was shown. This fast and powerful answer eliminated the negative publicity, and Pepsi was able, at the same time, to make a strong statement about the safety of its products. Pepsi's reaction was quite effective in dealing with this particular crisis.

Unfortunately, some company leaders manage only to make matters worse, as was the reaction of Ford and Bridgestone to the faulty tires on the new Ford Explorers. Instead of immediately seeking to correct the problem, both denied a problem existed and tried to put the blame on others. Ford CEO Jacques Nasser blamed Bridgestone/Firestone, Inc., for the tire separation problems. Bridgestone blamed consumers, saying they did not inflate the tires to the correct pressure. This finger-pointing ended Ford's 100-year relationship with Firestone. Bitter words were exchanged and the public did not buy either excuse. The outcry was so strong that both companies lost sales, suffered image damage, and eventually Nasser lost his job at Ford.[16]

1. An expression of guilt, embarrassment, or regret	4. Approval of the appropriate behavior and a promise not to engage in inappropriate behavior
2. A statement recognizing the inappropriate behavior and acceptance of sanctions for wrong behavior	5. An offer of compensation or penance to correct the wrong
3. A rejection of the inappropriate behavior	

FIGURE 13.7
Elements of an Apology Strategy

An **apology strategy** is another reactive form of crisis management and damage control. If the end result of the investigation is the revelation that the firm is at fault, an apology should be offered quickly. A full apology contains five elements, as shown in Figure 13.7.[17]

Apologies are most often used either in situations in which the violation is minor or ones in which the firm or person cannot escape being found guilty. It is also a good strategy for creating a strong emotional bond with the public. It is more difficult to be angry with a company that admits a mistake was made. If people feel the apology is sincere and heartfelt, they not only will forgive the company, but they may also feel more positive about the company afterwards.

The tendency to protect one's self-image is called **impression management** or "the conscious or unconscious attempt to control images that are projected in real or imagined social interactions."[18] In order to maintain or enhance self-image, individuals and corporations attempt to influence the identities they display to others. The goal is to project themselves in such a manner as to maximize access to and the visibility of positive characteristics while minimizing any negative elements.

Any event that threatens a person's self-image or desired identity is viewed as a predicament. When faced with such predicaments, individuals make concerted efforts to reduce or minimize the negative consequences. If the predicament cannot be avoided or concealed, then an individual engages in any type of remedial activity that reduces the potentially harmful consequences. Remedial tactics include:[19]

- Expressions of innocence
- Excuses
- Justifications
- Other explanations

An *expression of innocence* approach means company leaders provide information designed to convince others (clients, the media, and the government) that they were not associated with the event that caused the predicament. In other words, they say, "We did not cause this to happen. Someone (or something) else did."

Excuses are explanations designed to convince the public that the firm and its leaders are not responsible for the predicament or that it could not have been foreseen. Thus, they should not be held accountable for the event that created the predicament, they say, "It was an act of God. It was totally unavoidable."

Justifications involve using logic designed to reduce the degree of negativity associated with the predicament. Making the event seem minor or trivial is one method. Making the argument that the firm had to proceed in the way it did ("We pollute because if we don't we'll be out of business, and our employees will lose their jobs") is another form of justification.

Other explanations may be created to persuade individuals that the cause of the predicament is not a fair representation of what the firm or individual is really like. In other words, the case was the exception rather than the rule, and customers should not judge the firm too harshly as a result. You will hear comments such as "This was a singular incident, and not indicative of the way we do business."

Each company's management team, marketing department, and public relations specialist should be acutely aware of the speed with which events can cause great damage to a firm's image. Both proactive and reactive measures should be taken to make sure the firm survives negative publicity without major damage.

SPONSORSHIPS

To build brand loyalty and other positive feelings toward a company, many marketing leaders utilize sponsorships and event marketing. These programs make it possible to meet with prospects, customers, vendors, and others in unique situations. People who attend sponsored activities or special events already have favorable feelings about the activity taking place. These positive attitudes are easily transferred to a company that has provided funding. In this section, sponsorship programs and event marketing are described in greater detail.

Sponsorship marketing means that the company pays money to sponsor someone, some group, or something that is part of an activity. A firm can sponsor a practically unending list of groups, individuals, activities, and events. For years, firms sponsored everything from local Little League baseball and soccer teams to national musical tours, NASCAR drivers, and placed corporate names on sports stadiums.

Forms of Sponsorships

In North America, approximately $14.4 billion a year is spent on sponsorships and events.[20] Figure 13.8 provides a breakdown of how the money is spent. Sports represent nearly 70 percent of all sponsorships. Sporting events are highly popular and often attract large crowds. In addition to the audience attending the game or competition, many more watch on television. Popular athletes can be effective spokespersons for various products. If possible, the firm should be the exclusive sponsor of the person or team. It is much easier to be remembered if the firm is the only sponsor rather than one of multiple sponsors.

Gillette's sponsorships are a major component of the company's marketing program. Gillette spends millions of dollars each year on various sponsorships, many of which are sports related. The company has an employee whose job description is to manage sponsorship activities. The Gillette Fusion razor was featured as part of a sponsorship for the *Apprentice* television show. Gillette consistently sponsors the FIFA World Cup, including a $50 million global promotion featuring soccer star David Beckham. An integrated marketing campaign featured a $20 million Gillette Young Guns Campaign musical concert tour tied with six NASCAR drivers and a sampling and couponing program at the concerts. In 2001, Gillette acquired the naming rights for the New England Patriots football stadium (Gillette Stadium) in Foxboro, Massachusetts. The team's two Super Bowl victories in 3 years added to Gillette's national following.[21]

FedEx uses sponsorships to build customer loyalty. The company sponsors many sporting events and makes sure key customers not only get to attend them, but also are allowed to go into places they could not get into on their own. This includes NFL locker rooms, trackside passes at the Daytona 500, and access to famous golf courses such as Pebble Beach. These unique experiences create strong bonds with FedEx.[22] In addition,

FIGURE 13.8
Marketing Expenditures on Sponsorships and Events

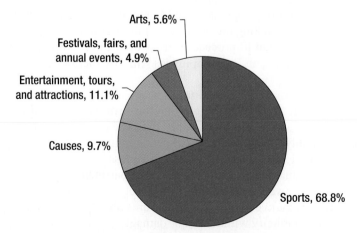

Arts, 5.6%

Festivals, fairs, and annual events, 4.9%

Entertainment, tours, and attractions, 11.1%

Causes, 9.7%

Sports, 68.8%

Source: Based on "Events & Sponsorships," *2007 Marketing Fact Book*, July 15, 2007, p. 31.

the marketing department tracks revenues from these customers before and after each event. Company figures indicate these activities generate positive revenues along with customer loyalty.

FedEx sponsors a college football bowl game (FedEx Orange Bowl), sports teams, sporting events, and sports stadiums. The company has relationships with the NFL, NBA, NASCAR, the PGA Tour, horse racing, and the NCAA. These programs create a great deal of company exposure. The FedEx Orange Bowl generates $32 million worth of TV exposure. The NASCAR sponsorship costs $16 million but generates nearly $50 million in TV exposure. More recently, FedEx became the transportation carrier for many of the company's sponsored events. FedEx ships equipment for the halftime shows for the Super Bowl and Pro Bowl. The company also ships game films to every professional football team on a weekly basis.

Some organizations have moved away from sports sponsorships toward more cultural events, such as classical music groups and jazz bands, visual art exhibits by noted painters, dance troupes, and actors for various theater performances. Cultural sponsorships are not the best match for every firm. They are most effective for products sold to affluent members of society. Consequently, financial institutions are the primary sponsors of these types of performers and performances. In the past, many institutions provided funds without receiving much recognition. Now these philanthropic efforts are being leveraged by having the name of the company strongly associated with the

In addition to milk, notice all of the corporate sponsors listed on Jeff Gordon's uniform.

cultural activity. This includes printing the name of the firm on programs and regularly mentioning the brand or corporate name as being responsible for arranging for the artist to be present at the cultural event. Also, sponsors usually receive choice seats at performances that can be given to key clients.

Rather than sports or the arts, Coca-Cola, Ford, and AT&T chose to sponsor the popular television show *American Idol*. Each company paid $35 million for the right to be part of one of the most watched TV shows, to post online content, and to run off-air co-branded marketing programs. Ford featured its vehicles in music videos sung by the final 12 contestants. Ford also gave away its Ford Escape Hybrid to the top two finalists. Coca-Cola made sure its branded cups were front and center on the judges' tables and that Coke graphics were visible behind the contestants when they were being interviewed. AT&T may have benefited the most from the sponsorship, because it was responsible for the text-message voting each week. The company also featured *Idol* downloads, ring tones, and videos of bad auditions and poor performances.[23]

Choosing Sponsorships

In choosing a sponsorship, it is important to match the audience profile with the company's target market. A firm sponsoring a participant at an event attended mainly by females is best when the company's primary customers are female. Marketing executives also consider the image of the individual participant or group and how it relates to the firm's image. For instance, a contestant in an "upscale" competition, such as a beauty contest, should be sponsored by a tuxedo or formal gown company.

To maximize the benefits of a sponsorship effort, it is important to define the primary goals of the program. As with the other marketing tools, the goals of the sponsorships should be integrated with the firm's overall IMC theme. The public should easily recognize the link

Matching the audience profile with the company's target market is important in selecting sponsors.

between the person or group being sponsored, the activity, and the company involved. To achieve the maximum impact for the sponsorship, the message should be combined with other advertising and promotional efforts, such as a sampling program or a giveaway (T-shirts, caps, etc.). Sampling is an effective method for encouraging people to try a product. Unless a sponsorship is surrounded by supporting marketing efforts, the money invested may not accomplish its objectives.

Sponsorship Objectives

It may be hard to measure the impact of a sponsorship program directly. Sponsorships are designed to accomplish many different objectives for organizations. Sponsorships can be used to:

- Enhance a company's image.
- Increase a firm's visibility.
- Differentiate a company from its competitors.
- Showcase specific goods and services.
- Help a firm develop closer relationships with current and prospective customers.
- Sell excess inventory.

One company that attempted to build visibility and image through the use of a sponsorship was the Great Florida Bank of Miami. After being open for just 11 months, Great Florida signed on as a sponsor of the NBA's Miami Heat for the 2005 playoffs. Great Florida marketed itself as the "Official playoff bank of the Heat." The bank's name appeared on the team's official "Red Zone" playoff logo, on billboards, game programs, print ads, and signs inside the American Airlines Arena, where the Heat play home games. The sponsorship program may have seemed like a dangerous approach, because it came with a hefty price tag. The marketing team at Great Florida Bank felt it was worth the money to gain such huge exposure in a short time period. When the team almost made the NBA finals, Great Florida Bank had received wide exposure for nearly a month, because the Heat played in numerous home playoff games.[24]

The best sponsorship programs include a method of assessment. The idea is to follow up to see if the goals that were set have been reached. In the case of Great Florida Bank, for example, market research could be undertaken to see how much brand awareness increased following the playoffs. In each sponsorship program, there should be an attempt to gather tangible evidence that the sponsorship is worthwhile.

EVENT MARKETING

Sponsoring the right event can provide a company with brand-name recognition and help develop closer ties with vendors and customers. Events can also help boost morale for the employees who participate in or attend them. Sponsoring local events such as the Special Olympics provides a company with the potential to generate free publicity. These events can also be used to enhance the company's image in the local community.

Event marketing is similar to sponsorship marketing. The major difference is that sponsorship marketing involves a person, group, or team. **Event marketing** occurs when the company supports a specific event. Event marketing is closely related to lifestyle marketing. Both often include setting up a booth or display and having some type of physical presence at an event.

As is the case with sponsorships, many event marketing programs feature sports. Other events are more related to lifestyles. A rodeo sponsored by Lee Jeans or a music concert put on by a radio station are marketing events. More segmented events can also be held. A Hispanic food festival funded by a food company is event marketing, as is a health fair conducted by a local hospital (e.g., "An Affair of the Heart" wellness program sponsored by Freeman Medical Hospital).

Several key steps are involved in preparing an event. Therefore, to ensure the maximum benefit from event sponsorships, companies should:

- Determine the objective(s) of the event.
- Match the event with the company's customers, vendors, and employees.
- Promote the event.
- Make sure the company is included in all event advertising and brochures.
- Track results.

Determining Objectives

The first step is to determine the communication objectives to be accomplished before becoming involved in a particular event. When the objective is to reward customers, it is crucial to find an event major customers would be interested in attending. Objectives that are more internally oriented, especially those designed to get employees involved and boost morale, should be met by finding events internal members will enjoy. Many times, the goals of sponsoring an event are to help the firm maintain its market share, to build a stronger brand presence in the marketplace, to enhance the product or firm's image, or to increase sales.

Matching the Event to Publics

To meet these goals means carefully selecting an event to sponsor. It should match the firm's customers, vendors, or employees. Different companies have customers who are more likely to attend certain events. Vendors and employees may also favor different events.

A number of companies could become involved in sponsoring events such as Boom Town Days.

BOOM TOWN DAYS

Friday – Sunday, the first weekend in June

You'll DiG iT!

You can take part in Joplin's Festival for the Four States!

- **Host a kids' booth**
- **Join the Arts & Crafts Show**
- **Enter the Car, Truck, and Cycle Show**
- **Promote your product or business**

It's not too late but space is filling fast!
Check out www.BoomtownDays.com or call 417.624.4150 today

Source: Courtesy of Joplin Globe.

Promoting the Event

Any event should be promoted using both advertisements and public relations releases. Special effort will be given to contacting interest groups that would benefit from an event. Thus, an event such as a local Special Olympics requires commercials, contacts with the press, and finding ways to reach parents and relatives of those who might participate.

Advertising at the Event

Event sponsors should insist on placement of the company's name and logo and other product information in every advertisement and brochure for the event. Many attendees of special events keep the program as a souvenir or as something to show others. Placing the sponsor's name and message on the program generates an ad with a long life span. The sponsoring business must work to maximize brand-name exposure by connecting the firm's name with the event's marketing program. Working closely with the event management team

The marketing team at Victoria's Secret tracked the results of the "Pink" event marketing program.

is vital to seeing that the sponsor's name receives prominent attention in all materials associated with the occasion.

Tracking Results

Some events turn out better than others for the sponsor. To determine the best events, the marketing team should *track results.* In addition to sales, employees can monitor how many pieces of literature were given to attendees, the number of samples distributed, and the number of visitors to the sponsor's display booth. Further, marketing research can be conducted to measure brand awareness before and after the event to find out if any new brand recall or brand awareness developed.

Tracking the results allows the business to evaluate the investment in the event. Company leaders and marketing managers then can decide if sponsoring a particular event was beneficial and whether to sponsor the event in coming years or similar events in the future. When Victoria's Secret launched its new brand "Pink," it was coupled with a unique event marketing promotion during spring break. The goal was to reach 18- to 24-year-old females. The event began when a three-story pink box was set up on a Miami beach. Advertisements, postings, street teams of employees giving out fliers, aerial signs, signs in nearby hotels, and public relations press releases built excitement during the 5-day countdown. On March 17, 2005, 5,000 spring breakers showed up at the pink box. They were treated to a fashion show and a live concert by No Mercy. After the concert, Victoria's Secret Pink gift cards were passed out and the company hosted nightclub parties. The unique marketing event spurred sales of both the new Pink brand and other Victoria's Secret brands. The Victoria's Secret marketing team completed the evaluation stage and discovered that the Pink brand sales increase in the Miami area was huge and that the other Victoria's Secret brand sales also rose dramatically.[25] The evaluation suggested that the event was a major success.

A study by the Advertising Research Foundation (ARF) found that purchase intentions in buying a particular branded product increased from 11 to 52 percent among consumers who attended a brand-sponsored event, such as a sporting event, walkathon, or themed event. Further research found that purchase intentions translated into sales about half the time. The ARF study involved events sponsored by companies such as Frito-Lay, State Farm, and Coca-Cola. As with sponsorships, sports-related events tended to have the best results.[26]

Cross-Promotions

Cross-promotions with the event sponsor or other companies involved are often used to boost the impact of an event marketing program. A **cross-promotion** is a marketing event that ties together companies and activities around a specific theme. Recently, eBay partnered with Sony and Baskin-Robbins to create a unique event called "Camp eBay." During the summer months, consumers are typically outdoors enjoying the warm weather and not logged onto the Internet, so eBay decided to go to consumers. Camp eBay was eBay's first attempt at event marketing. The aim was to create awareness in and to educate people who do not use eBay. The program was also designed to encourage existing buyers and sellers to be more active in the summertime.

The Camp e-Bay program began with the purchase of a refurbished school bus that was sent out on a mobile marketing tour to six high-traffic areas: the Indy 500, Country Music Fanfest, eBay Live, Taste of Chicago, the Ohio State Fair, and the Minnesota State Fair. The school bus classroom drew 52,000 people who attended 30-minute sessions on how to use eBay. Participants earned badges redeemable for prizes that were furnished by

Sony and Baskin-Robbins. The prizes were worth a total of $85,000. In addition, eBay pitched tents at 20 Clear Channel Entertainment venues that hosted nearly 400 concerts. The impact of the event marketing program was that 45 percent of existing users increased their purchases, leading to an overall increase in sales of 2 percent during the promotion and 9 percent after the event.[27]

Sponsorship programs and event marketing have increased in popularity during the past decade due to their potential to reach consumers on a one-to-one basis. In the future, sponsorships and event marketing tie-ins with other media, especially the Internet, will rise. Rock concerts, boat shows, music fairs, and a wide variety of other, more specialized programs are likely to be featured by various companies. Many marketing experts believe that making contact with customers in personalized ways that do not directly involve a sales call are valuable activities. Event marketing and sponsorship programs make these contacts much easier to create.

INTERNATIONAL IMPLICATIONS

The public relations function has become increasingly important in the international arena, for several reasons. First, the growing number of international firms creates the need to make sure the company is viewed in a positive light in every country in which it does business. Second, the impact of terrorism and war over the past decade has heightened sensitivities between many nations. Any company conducting business in a foreign land will have a public relations officer in charge of monitoring news stories and other events, so that the firm can react to negative press. Third, whenever there are differences among cultures, the potential exists to offend without intending to do so. In 2008, when Rocco Mediate was involved in a valiant effort to win a playoff in the U.S. Open golf tournament, sportscaster Johnny Miller made a joke that Mediate looked more like 'the guy that would clean your pool' than a professional golfer. Some citizens of Italy took offense, believing it was an ethnic slur. Miller apologized, stating he was referring to the "every man" quality Mediate possessed.

Corporate social responsibility also has no national boundaries. Many heated debates have taken place regarding outsourcing. Critics argue nations other than the United States have enjoyed the advantages of unfair wage rates and the ability to pollute freely, thereby cutting costs and attracting businesses to them. Any multinational corporation or company conducting business in foreign lands should be aware of these criticisms and find acceptable ways to respond to them.

Many sponsorships now contain an international flavor. Some of the more visible are found in sports, most notably automobile racing and soccer. The principles that guide the development of sponsorships domestically apply equally well to any international involvements. To fully prepare an effective sponsorship program in an international setting, the marketing team will employ a cultural assimilator to make sure any foreign language is being used correctly, that the sponsorship is legal, and that it does not violate any local cultural norms. As the world continues to become smaller, with increasing interactions between countries, companies, and individuals, the growth of multi-national

SUMMARY

The public relations department plays a major role in an integrated marketing communications program, whether the department is separate from marketing or combined as part of a communications division. Public relations efforts are primarily oriented to making sure that every possible contact point delivers a positive and unified message on behalf of the company. This includes assessing a corporation's reputation and involvement in socially responsible activities.

There are many stakeholders inside and surrounding a company. Any person or group with a vested interest in the organization's activities is a stakeholder. Internal stakeholders include employees, unions, and stockholders. External publics include members of the marketing channel, customers, the media, the local community, financial institutions, the government, and special-interest groups.

To reach all intended audiences, the public relations department has a series of tools available. These include company newsletters, internal messages, public relations releases, correspondence with stockholders, annual reports, and various special events. Even the bulletin board in the company's break room can be used to convey messages to internal stakeholders.

In the attempt to build a favorable image of the company, the public relations department develops special events such as altruistic activities and cause-related marketing programs. Due care must be given to making certain that these acts are not perceived with cynicism and skepticism. This means being certain that any good deed matches with company products and other marketing efforts. A natural fit between an altruistic event and the company's brand is more readily accepted by various members of the public.

The public relations team is also responsible for damage control when negative publicity arises. Both proactive and reactive tactics are available to maintain a positive image for the company. Damage control tactics include Internet interventions, crisis management programs, and impression management techniques.

Sponsorship programs enhance and build the company's image and brand loyalty. A sponsorship of an individual or group involved in some kind of activity—whether a sporting event, a contest, or a performance by an artistic group—can be used to link the company's name with the popularity of the player involved. Sponsorships should match with the firm's products and brands.

Event marketing occurs when a firm sponsors an event. A strong physical presence at the event is one of the keys to successfully linking an organization's name with a program. To do so, the firm must determine the major objective of the event sponsorship, match it with company customers and publics, and make sure the firm's name is prominently displayed on the literature accompanying the event.

Managing public relations, sponsorships, and event marketing programs requires company leaders to carefully assess both the goals and the outcomes of individual activities. A cost–benefit approach may not always be feasible, but the marketing team should be able to track some form of change, whether it is increased inquiries, the number of samples passed out at an event, or a shift in the tenor of news articles about the organization. The primary task of public relations is to be the organization's "watchdog," making sure those who come in contact with the company believe the firm is working to do things right and to do the right things.

KEY TERMS

public relations (PR) department A unit in the firm that manages items such as publicity and other communications with all of the groups that make contact with the company.

hit The mention of a company's name in a news story.

stakeholder A person or group with a vested interest in a firm's activities and well-being.

social responsibility An organization's obligation to be ethical, accountable, and reactive to the needs of society.

cause-related marketing Matching marketing efforts with some type of charity work or program.

green marketing The development and promotion of products that are environmentally safe.

damage control Reacting to negative events caused by a company error, consumer grievances, or unjustified or exaggerated negative press.

entitlings Attempts to claim responsibility for positive outcomes of events.

enhancements Attempts to increase the desirable outcome of an event in the eyes of the public.

Internet interventions Confronting negative publicity on the Internet, either in Web site news releases or by entering chat rooms, blogs, or social networks.

crisis management Either accepting the blame for an event and offering an apology or refuting those making the charges in a forceful manner.

apology strategy Presenting a full apology when the firm has made an error.

impression management The conscious or unconscious attempt to control images that are projected in real or imagined social situations.

sponsorship marketing When the company pays money to sponsor someone or some group that is participating in an activity.

event marketing When a company pays money to sponsor an event or program.

cross-promotion A marketing event that ties together companies and activities around a specific theme.

REVIEW QUESTIONS

1. Describe the role of the public relations department. How is it related to the marketing department? Should both departments be called the "department of communications"? Why or why not?

2. What is a stakeholder?

3. Name the major internal stakeholders in organizations. Describe their interests in the company.

4. Name the major external stakeholders in organizations. Describe the major interest in the company of each one.

5. What is social responsibility? How is it related to public relations activities?

6. What is cause-related marketing? How can company leaders create effective cause-related marketing programs?

7. What is green marketing? How do different companies promote environmentally friendly activities?

8. Name and briefly describe two proactive prevention strategies companies can use to create a positive image.

9. What reactive damage-control techniques are available to the public relations team?

10. What four forms of impression management are used to combat negative events?

11. What is sponsorship marketing? Name a pro athlete, a musician or musical group, or a performer of some other type who has been featured in a sponsorship program. Was the program effective or ineffective? Why?

12. Describe an event marketing program. What must accompany the event in order to make it a success?

13. What are cross-promotions? How are they related to event marketing programs?

CRITICAL THINKING EXERCISES

Discussion Questions

1. Watch the news on television or read your local paper for news about a local or national business. Was the report positive or negative toward the firm? Did the news report affect your attitude toward the company? Watch one of the many special investigative shows, such as *60 Minutes*. What companies did it investigate? If your firm was being featured, what would you do to counteract the bad press?

2. The public relations officer for a small but highly respected bank in a local community was charged with sexual harassment by a female employee. What type of communications should be prepared for each of the constituencies listed in Figure 13.2? Which of the constituencies would be the most important to contact?

3. How important is the local community for a manufacturing firm that sells 99 percent of its products outside the area? Does it really matter what the local people say or believe about the manufacturer as long as the firm's customers are happy?

4. What causes do you support or are special to you? Do you know which corporations sponsor or support the causes? If not, see if you can find literature or Web sites that contain that information. Why do you think the corporations choose a particular cause to support? What benefits do corporations receive from sponsorships?

5. When Starbucks opened its first coffee shop inside a public library, 10 percent of all proceeds from coffee sold there went to support the operation of the library. Do you think a public library should allow a for-profit organization such as Starbucks to sell products inside the building? Is this a conflict of interest for governmentally sponsored organizations such as libraries? What if the local doughnut shop wanted to sell doughnuts at the library? Should it be allowed to do so? How does a library manager decide?

6. Managers often are the most difficult group for the public relations department to reach. To entice employees to reach departmental goals, managers often communicate using memos or verbal messages. These messages may conflict with the IMC theme. For example, in an effort to trim costs, a manager may send a memo to all employees telling them to use only standard production procedures. Through verbal communications, employees learn that anyone caught violating or even bending the policy to satisfy a customer will be immediately reprimanded. The manager's action suggests that even though he wants employees to provide customer service, in actuality, they had better not do anything that is not authorized. Employees soon get the message that management cares only about costs, not the customer. Employees will perceive any advertising message about customer service as a big joke. Write a memo to employees that supports the IMC goal of high customer service, yet alerts them to the need to follow standard operating procedures. Is there anything else you would do to ensure that this is not a conflicting message being sent to employees?

7. Sponsorships are now a major component of professional sports. Football, basketball, baseball, and golf all have sponsors. Many stadiums are now named for companies. Why do you think companies spend millions on these sponsorships? What impact does it have on you? What sponsorships do you notice? Which ones do you not notice? Why?

INTEGRATED LEARNING EXERCISES

1. Although some firms handle public relations activities internally, many firms retain public relations firms to work on special projects and to handle unique situations. The Public Relations Society of America (PRSA) is one of the major associations for PR practitioners. In Canada, the primary association is the Canadian Public Relations Society. Access the Web sites of these two organizations at **www.prsa.org** and **www.cprs.ca**. What type of information is available? What types of services are offered? How would these organizations be beneficial to various companies?

2. *PRWeek* is an excellent publication. Access the online version at **www.prweek.com**. What type of information is available? How would this site be valuable to a PR practitioner? How could it be used by a firm seeking a public relations agency?

3. The American Institute of Philanthropy ranks the various charities. Access the Web site at **www.charitywatch.org**. How does the Institute rate the charities? How can this information be used by a company to determine which charities to support?

4. A number of companies offer services to help firms plan and develop sponsorships. One company is IEG. Access its Web site at **www.sponsorship.com**. Review the Web site. Identify the various services offered by IEG. If you were the marketing manager for a company that wanted to develop a sponsorship program, how could IEG help? Be specific.

5. Event marketing is used by many organizations to accomplish various objectives. Access the following companies that assist firms with event marketing. What type of services does each offer? What is your evaluation of each of the companies?

a. Advantage International, LLC (**www.advantage-intl.com**)

b. Pierce Promotions and Event Management, Inc. (**www.ppem.com**)

c. RPMC Event and Promotion Agency (**www.rpmc.com**)

6. Corporate sponsorships are very important to nonprofits. Without their financial assistance, many causes would not exist. Look up two organizations from the following list of nonprofits. Who are their corporate sponsors? What benefits do the profit-seeking companies receive from these sponsorships?

a. American Cancer Society (**www.cancer.org**)

b. Arthritis Foundation (**www.arthritis.org**)

c. Multiple Sclerosis Society (**www.mssociety.org.uk**)

d. United Cerebral Palsy (**www.ucp.org**)

e. Alliance for the Wild Rockies (**www.wildrockiesalliance.org**)

f. National Wildlife Federation (**www.nwf.org**)

g. Trout Unlimited (**www.tu.org**)

STUDENT PROJECT

Creative Corner

Circle K Ranch has been selling, training, and boarding horses for almost 20 years. With the recent downturn in the economy, however, Circle K has experienced a decline in all facets of its business. In talking with some marketing students at the local university, the owner of Circle K Ranch, Kathy Kroncke, wondered about using cause-related marketing, sponsorships, and even event marketing to boost the awareness and image of her business. She recently added horseback riding to her list of services and developed a 10-mile ride that went through a local state park. So far, business has not been what she expected, despite research that indicated a high level of interest in riding, especially by 15- to 40-year-old females. Design Kathy a cause-related marketing program, a sponsorship program, and an event marketing program. After you have designed each of the programs, choose the one you think would be the best for Circle K Ranch. Design a newspaper ad featuring the program. What other methods would you use, both traditional and nontraditional, to publicize the program you chose?

CASE 1

NEW DRUG FACES PUBLIC RELATIONS AND MARKETING CHALLENGES

It is unusual for a new product to create a vehement public response with both supporters and detractors. One such product, which was approved by the FDA in 2006 and made widely available in 2007, is Gardasil. The drug was developed by Merck and Company.

Gardasil is provided in the form of a vaccine. It was developed to prevent cervical cancer by blocking infection from human papillomavirus, which is spread through sexual contact. The Food and Drug Administration permits Gardasil to be used by females ages 9 through 26, with the goal of inoculating girls before they become sexually active. Although the vaccine does not prevent every form of papillomavirus, it does treat four of the most common, including 100% prevention of the most common type and 70% of the four most common types combined.

Nearly half a million women are diagnosed with cervical cancer each year. According to some experts, Gardasil might make it possible to eliminate cervical cancer within a generation. It is also a victory for Merck, the fourth-biggest U.S. drug maker, which has focused increasingly on vaccines and may generate $3 billion in annual sales from Gardasil alone. "It's important from a public health perspective because you're eliminating a cancer," said Les Funtleyder, an analyst in New York for Miller Tabak & Co. "The subtle point is these guys are creating new drugs for important health problems, which is what a pharma is supposed to do."

Gardasil requires three doses to be given over 6 months. In 2007, each dose cost around $120. Consequently, affordability may determine how effective the drug is in quelling cervical cancer. About 80 percent of cases are in poorer countries. "Critical to success will be ensuring that women in the world's poorest countries—where cervical cancer hits hardest—have rapid and affordable access to this lifesaving new tool," said Gabriel N. Hortobagyi, a physician at the University of Texas M.D. Anderson Cancer Center in Houston and president of the American Society of Clinical Oncology, in a statement. Human papillomavirus, or HPV, is one of the most common sexually transmitted viruses in the world, and it causes genital warts as well as cancer. About 20 million people in the United States are infected, according to the U.S. Centers for Disease Control and Prevention (CDC).

Why the controversy? Many social conservatives fear that providing the vaccine may provide subtle approval for young women to engage in sex, much in the same way as providing birth control information and condoms are sometimes condemned. Some of the response was in regard to the recommendations from a panel of experts assembled by the CDC. The panel issues widely followed guidelines, including recommendations for childhood vaccines that become the basis for vaccination requirements set by public schools. The panel recommended that the vaccine be required.

Merck company officials and others noted that research indicates the best age to vaccinate would be just before puberty to make sure children are protected before they become sexually active. The vaccine would probably be targeted primarily at girls, but could also be used on boys to limit the spread of the virus. "If you really want to have cervical cancer rates fall as much as possible as quickly as possible, then

Many young girls could benefit from the HPV virus vaccine Gardasil.

Source: Courtesy of Trish Gant © Dorling Kindersley.

you want as many people to get vaccinated as possible," said Mark Feinberg, Merck's vice president of medical affairs and policy, noting that "school mandates have been one of the most effective ways to increase immunization rates." That is the view being pushed by cervical cancer experts and women's health advocates.

Not surprisingly, a major clash emerged, mostly notably when the state of Texas made it a requirement to have the vaccine in order to be admitted to school. The battle lines were primarily drawn over girls being forced to take a medicine, with or without parental consent, along with the concerns expressed about sexual activity.

Company officials from Merck worked carefully with both governmental agencies and other groups to reduce concerns. In 2008, the company began advertising Gardasil in television commercials entitled "One Less" and "Guard Yourself." The powerful point is made that by taking the medicine, one less person will be infected.

Sources: Angela Zimm and Justin Blum, "FDA Approves Merck's Cervical Cancer Vaccine," *Boston Globe* and *Bloomberg News* (June 9, 2006) (**www.boston.com/business/healthcare/articles**, accessed January 28, 2008); Rob Stein, "Cervical Cancer Vaccine Gets Injected with a Social Issue," *Washington Post* (October 31, 2005) (**www.washingtonpost.com/wp-dyn**, accessed January 28, 2008).

1. Describe the stakeholders and the positions of each group involved in this controversy.

2. Outline the positive public relations opportunities available to promote Gardasil.

3. Describe how Merck should respond to negative publicity and complaints about the product.

4. Could Merck use cause-related marketing effectively or would it be construed as a means of marketing the drug?

5. What sponsorships and event marketing programs should be used to promote Gardasil?

CASE 2 CAN THIS RESTAURANT BE SAVED?

If there is any one industry in which word-of-mouth can do great damage in a hurry, that industry would be food service, especially restaurants. A single round of food poisoning can drive away customers for months. Any tale of contamination or unsanitary conditions that circulates in a local community creates a major crisis for a restaurant owner.

Juan and Bonita Gonzales knew the risks when they opened their new restaurant, The Mexican Villa, in a small shopping center in North Canton, Ohio. With the recent wave of Mexican immigrants to the area, two other successful Mexican restaurants had opened across town. The couple believed that if they provided high-quality food in a pleasant atmosphere, their restaurant could succeed.

The business opened in the fall of 2007. First-year sales were better than expected. A mixture of Hispanic and Caucasian customers regularly dined at The Mexican Villa. The restaurant had two distinct serving areas: the dining room and the cantina. In the dining room, authentic Mexican music played softly in the background. There was plenty of room between tables. The floors were carpeted and clean. Servers were dressed in bright colored clothing and were carefully trained to be pleasant, efficient, and helpful. In the cantina, the music was louder. The floors were tile. Smoking was permitted in a bar-type atmosphere. Television sets were tuned to sports programs. In both areas, customers were quickly greeted and served salsa and chips at no charge. The menu was the same for both areas.

Both the cantina and the dining room had regular customers who ate at the Villa as often as once a week. The Villa also had a strong lunch business, where a lighter menu with lower prices was featured. The restaurant was near a business district and shopping center, which provided access to many potential lunch guests.

The crisis occurred after The Mexican Villa had been open for 15 months. In the spring of 2009, one of the Villa food preparers contracted an infectious case of hepatitis. Hepatitis is highly contagious and dangerous. The local health authorities discovered the problem and forced the Villa to close for 7 days. Word was sent out in the newspaper, on the radio, and on the local television news that anyone who had eaten at the Villa in the past 2 weeks should contact the government health authorities to be tested. Word spread quickly through North Canton about the episode, both in the Spanish-speaking community and to other groups.

Fortunately, no one was infected. The employee had worn protective gloves while preparing food. The safety precautions used at the restaurant had kept the disease from spreading to others.

Juan and Bonita had a limited budget for advertising. Once the news stories had run, the media quickly lost interest. It was impossible for the couple to capture the same audience to tell people that the health crisis had passed. The number of customers who returned after the weeklong closure dropped dramatically. Sales had been down for more than a month. The couple began to wonder if people would ever come back.

1. What kinds of public relations tactics should be used to help The Mexican Villa?

2. Is there any kind of cause-related or event marketing program that might bring people back to the restaurant?

3. Do you believe The Mexican Villa can be saved, or is it a lost cause? Why?

ENDNOTES

1. "Harry Potter Sales Break Another Record," CNNMoney.com (**http://money.cnn.com/2007/08/02/news/companies/harry_potter/index.htm**, August 2, 2007); Bruce Weinstein, "So, Does Harry Potter Live?" *BusinessWeek* (**www.businessweek.com/careers/content/jul2007/ca20070718_121031.htm**, July 18 2007).

2. Jenny Dawkins, "Corporate Responsibility: The Communication Challenge," *Journal of Communication Management* 9, no. 2 (November 2004), pp. 106–17.

3. "Random Sample," *Marketing News* 38 (August 15, 2004), p. 3.

4. ABC News Exclusive: AFLAC CEO Dan Amos (**www.abcnews.go.com/Business/story/id=2899076**, February 23, 2007).

5. Ronald J. Alsop, "Corporate Reputation: Anything But Superficial—The Deep But Fragile Nature of Corporate Reputation," *Journal of Business Strategy* 25, no. 6 (2004), pp. 21–30.

6. Larry Chiagouris and Ipshita Ray, "Saving the World with Cause-Related Marketing," *Marketing Management* 16, no. 4 (July–August 2007), pp. 48–51.

7. Brad Edmondson, "New Keys to Customer Loyalty," *American Demographics* 16, no. 1 (January 1994), p. 2.

8. Steven Van Yoder, "Make It Mean Something," *Successful Meeting* 53, No. 2 (February 2004), pp. 27–29.

9. Nan Xiaoli and Heo Kwangiun, "Consumer Responses to Corporate Social Responsibility (CSR) Initiatives," *Journal of Advertising* 36, no. 2 (Summer 2007), pp. 63–74.

10. Dawkins, "Corporate Responsibility: The Communication Challenge."

11. Jill Meredith Ginsberg and Paul N. Bloom, "Choosing the Right Green Marketing Strategy," *MIT Sloan Management Review* 46, no. 1 (Fall 2004), pp. 79–84.

12. Ibid.

13. Examples based on Ginsberg and Bloom, "Choosing the Right Green Marketing Strategy."

14. Valerie Seckler, "Causes and Effect," *Women's Wear Daily* 194, no. 93 (October 31, 2007), p. 9.

15. Marvin E. Shaw and Philip R. Costanzo, *Theories of Social Psychology,* 2nd ed. (New York: McGraw-Hill, 1982), p. 334.

16. "Jac Nasser Out As Ford's CEO," *Tire Business* 19, no. 16 (November 15, 2001), p. 1.

17. Shaw and Costanzo, *Theories of Social Psychology,* 2d ed., p. 334.

18. Ibid, p. 329.

19. Ibid, p. 333.

20. "Events & Sponsorships," *2007 Marketing Fact Book, Marketing News* 41, no. 12 (July 15, 2007), p. 31.

21. Jack Neff, "Gillette Amps Up Sponsorships," *Advertising Age* 75, no. 36 (September 6, 2004), pp. 4–5.

22. Tom Weir, "When You Absolutely, Positively Need $$$$$," *USA Today* (December 29, 2004), p. 3C.

23. Gail Schiller, "Idol Sponsors Coke, Ford, AT&T Paying More," *Brandweek.com* (**http:// brandweek.com**, January 15, 2008).

24. Laura Thompson Osuri, "Little Bank, Very Big Guys," *American Banker* 170, no. 91 (May 12, 2005), p. 8.

25. Betsy Spethmann, "A Winning Season," *PROMO* 18, no. 1 (December 2004), pp. 32–41.

26. Kenneth Hein, "Study: Purchase Intent Grows with Each Event," *Brandweek* 49, no. 4 (January 28, 2008) p. 4.

27. Diane Anderson, "eBay's Campy Road Tour: One on One, No Mosquitoes," *Brandweek* 46, no. 10 (March 7, 2005), p. R6.

PART 5

IMC Ethics, Regulation, and Evaluation

14

Regulations and Ethical Concerns

Chapter Objectives

After reading this chapter, you should be able to answer the following questions:

- **What** legal restrictions apply to marketing communications?

- **Which** governmental agency is most responsible for enforcing laws regarding IMC programs?

- **What** enforcement tactics can be used to make companies comply with marketing communications laws?

- **Are** the major complaints about unethical marketing activities fair charges?

- **How** should the concepts of ethics, morals, and social responsibility apply to marketing communications programs?

A SALTY SITUATION

How much sodium should an adult consume per day? According to the National Research Council of the National Academy of Sciences, a daily dosage of 1,200 to 1,500 milligrams is sufficient. The body needs sodium for a number of key functions, including regulation of blood pressure and blood volume, as well as muscle and nerve functioning. A tablespoon of table salt, which is 40 percent sodium, contains 2,300 milligrams of sodium.

Many health care professionals are concerned with the amount of sodium in food products, especially processed foods. Overconsumption of sodium is related to numerous health problems, including high blood pressure, which can lead to strokes and heart attacks. Further, excess sodium is connected to fluid build-up, which aggravates cirrhosis and kidney problems, and can contribute to congestive heart failure.

These concerns have been well known for many years, yet the food industry has been slow to respond. Why? Essentially, there are two answers. First, salt gives food flavor. Everything from meats, such as bacon, sausage, and ham, to canned soups and vegetables use salt to add taste. A serving of Van Camp's Baked Beans contains over 390 milligrams of sodium (a 15 oz. can contains more than 3 servings). Products such as Worcestershire sauce, soy sauce, and bouillon cubes also contain high levels of salt. Typical diet food frozen dinners average between 510 and 590 milligrams per serving. Even cookies and cakes contain surprisingly large amounts of sodium.

The second reason for high sodium content is food preservation. Salt placed into food draws away moisture so that bacteria do not grow. Salt also kills existing bacteria that might cause spoilage. At one time, salting was one of the only methods available to preserve food. Currently, many other methods are available, which leads back to the taste issue.

Fast-food companies and other restaurants notoriously use high levels of sodium in the items sold. For example, a McDonald's Big Mac contains 1,040 milligrams of sodium (the number rises if a soda and fries are added). A Burger King Whopper contains nearly 1,500 milligrams of sodium.

The net result is that consumers, unless they are very careful, typically consume as much as 3,000 milligrams of sodium per day. The negative health effects of sodium overconsumption are well documented. Yet Congress and the Food and Drug Administration do little more than require the amount of sodium contained in products to be reported, with no attempts to limit amounts.

CHAPTER FOURTEEN

Source: Courtesy of Michal Heron; Pearson Education/PH College.

Some companies have begun to respond. In 2008, Lays launched a new line of products with the label "Pinch of Salt." A 1-ounce serving of these potato chips contains 75 milligrams of sodium (a bag is typically 12 ounces). In contrast, a 1-ounce serving of regular Lays chips contains 270 milligrams of sodium.

In 2006, Campbell's began selling soup flavored with sea salt, which reduces the sodium content. Campbell's is also looking for ways to reduce sodium in V8 drinks. Numerous companies specialize in low-sodium foods.

The sodium content of food products is an example of the intersection between what is legal and what is ethical. Time will tell if various organizations respond in ways that benefit profits or society, and whether the government will respond with legislation.[1]

OVERVIEW

The final level of an IMC program includes making certain the communications program meets ethical and legal requirements and is properly evaluated. In this section, these topics are examined. Figure 14.1 displays the completion of an IMC program.

The fields of marketing and marketing communications have long been the subject of scrutiny from the general public, special interest groups, and by the government. This is not surprising. In marketing and sales, money is involved as people make purchases. Also, however, there are concerns about the public trust and the well-being of the community. When goods and services are sold that can injure people or cause harm in some other way, criticisms and legal actions are likely to follow.

This chapter examines two interrelated topics. The first is a description of the legal environment surrounding marketing and marketing communications. The second part features views of ethics, morals, and social responsibility as they relate to marketing, advertising, and promotions.

FIGURE 14.1
Overview of Integrated Marketing Communications

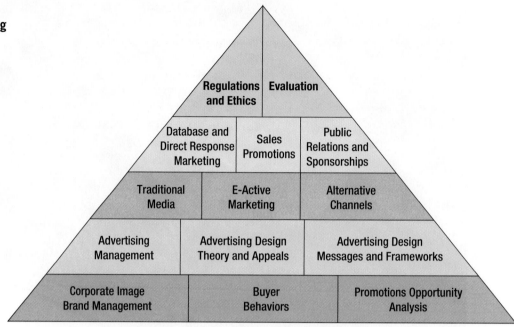

In essence, those who are involved in marketing programs should consider both the letter of the law—regulations and other legal limitations—as well as the spirit of the law. Guided by both personal principles and organizational guidelines, marketing professionals can try to ensure that their actions are both legal and ethical.

MARKETING COMMUNICATIONS REGULATIONS

The U.S. federal government has passed a considerable amount of legislation designed to keep companies from taking advantage of consumers. Various states also regulate for-profit companies and other organizations. Many of these federal and state laws are enforced by regulatory agencies. In this section, governmental actions are reviewed in the areas of legislation and regulation of company marketing practices.

Governmental Regulatory Agencies

Numerous governmental agencies serve as watchdogs to monitor for potential violations of the law, some of which are only partially related to marketing. For example, the Food and Drug Administration (FDA) regulates and oversees the packaging and labeling of products. The FDA also monitors advertising on food packages and advertisements for drugs, yet its primary responsibilities are ensuring food quality and drug safety.

The Federal Communications Commission (FCC) regulates television, radio, and the telephone industry. The primary responsibility of the FCC is to grant (and revoke) operating licenses for radio and television stations. The FCC also has jurisdiction over telephone companies. The FCC does not have jurisdiction over the content of advertisements transmitted by mass media. Further, the FCC does not control which products may be advertised. The organization is, however, responsible for monitoring advertising directed toward children. Under FCC rules, TV stations are limited to 12 minutes per hour of children's advertisements during weekdays and 10 minutes per hour on weekends. Recently, Viacom agreed to pay $1 million for programming on Nickelodeon that violated the time limitation 600 times in the span of 1 year. Under the same FCC investigation, Walt Disney Company agreed to pay $500,000 for children's commercials that aired beyond the time limit on its ABC Family Channel.[2]

The U.S. Postal Service (USPS) has jurisdiction over all mailed marketing materials. The USPS also investigates mail fraud schemes and other fraudulent marketing practices. The Bureau of Alcohol, Tobacco and Firearms (ATF) rules when the sale,

- Food and Drug Administration (FDA)
- Federal Communications Commission (FCC)
- U.S. Postal Service (USPS)
- Bureau of Alcohol, Tobacco and Firearms (ATF)
- Federal Trade Commission (FTC)

FIGURE 14.2
Government Regulatory Agencies

distribution, and advertising of alcohol and tobacco are at issue. Ordinarily, the governmental agency that examines incidents involving deceptive or misleading marketing tactics is the Federal Trade Commission (FTC). These agencies are listed in Figure 14.2. The next section examines the FTC in greater detail.

The Federal Trade Commission

The federal agency that presides over marketing communications is the **Federal Trade Commission**, or **FTC**, which was created in 1914 by the passage of the Federal Trade Commission Act. The act's original intent was to create an agency to enforce antitrust laws and protect businesses from one another. It had little authority over advertising and marketing communications except when an advertisement was considered to be unfair to the competition, therefore restricting free trade.

Unfair and Deceptive Marketing Practices

In 1938, Congress passed the Wheeler–Lea Amendment to Section 5 of the Federal Trade Commission Act to increase and expand the authority of the FTC and to prohibit false and misleading advertising. The agency was given the authority to stop unfair or deceptive advertising practices and to levy fines when necessary. The law also granted the FTC access to the courts to enforce the law and ensure that violators abide by FTC rulings.

Advertising professionals should remember that a firm can violate the act even when the company did not expressly intend to deceive. An advertisement or communication is deemed to be deceptive or misleading when:

1. A substantial number of people or the "typical person" is left with a false impression or misrepresentation that relates to the product.
2. The misrepresentation induces people or the "typical person" to make a purchase.

Consumers may be misled by advertisements, mailings, corporate literature, labels, packaging, Web site materials, and by oral and written statements made by salespeople. This gives the government a great deal of latitude in dealing with deceptive practices.

Deception Versus Puffery

Before going any farther, it is important to point out that advertising can include what is called *puffery* in advertisements and messages. **Puffery** exists when a firm makes an exaggerated statement about its goods or services. The key difference, in terms of the FTC and the courts, between puffery and a claim is that puffery is not considered to be a *factual statement*. In contrast, a *claim* is considered to be a factual statement

This Sunkist ad is an excellent example of using puffery by stating "you'll have them eating right out of your chopsticks!"

Source: Courtesy of Novartus Consumer Health Inc.

An example for Cruex using puffery.

that can be proven true or false. Firms are entitled to make puffery statements without proving them; claims must be substantiated or proven in some manner.

Terms normally associated with puffery include words such as *best, greatest,* and *finest.* Therefore, it is acceptable to state "our brand is the best" or "our signature dishes use only the finest ingredients." Courts and the regulatory agencies view these statements as puffery and believe that consumers expect firms to use them routinely in their advertisements. The Sunkist advertisement on the previous page states that "you'll have them eating right out of your chopsticks!," which is a form of puffery. It is not a statement of fact that can be proven true or false. The ad suggests that the product will help the consumer "master the yin and yang of Asian flavors," which is also an untestable claim.

Although the word *best* is normally accepted as puffery, the word *better* is somewhat vague and implies a comparison, which has recently been tested through the FTC, the National Advertising Division of the Better Business Bureau, and the courts. Papa John's use of the phrase "Better Ingredients, Better Pizza" was found to be puffery, as was the phrase "Only the best tomatoes grow up to be Hunt's."

In another situation, however, Progresso used the statement "Discover the Better Taste of Progresso" in company advertisements. The slogan was challenged by Campbell's Soup Company, which argued that Progresso's "better taste" phrase was not puffery. Campbell's representatives argued that it is possible to determine if one food does taste better than other brands through the use of taste tests. The courts agreed and forced Progresso to either modify the phrase or prove that Progresso soups do taste better.[3]

Substantiation of Marketing Claims

When a claim is made that is not deemed to be puffery, the concept of substantiation applies. **Substantiation** means that an advertising claim or promise must be proven with data, facts, or through competent and reliable evidence. Failure to do so can result in either a lawsuit or governmental action.

If the advertisement features an endorser, the statements must be truthful and represent the person's experiences or opinions. If the commercial uses an expert's endorsement, the statements must be based on legitimate tests performed by experts in the field.

All marketing claims must reflect the typical experience that a customer would expect to encounter from the use of a good or service, unless the advertisement clearly and prominently states otherwise. A few years ago a Kleenex ad made the claim that the product was softer. Kleenex used actual touch tests by consumers as evidence. The company then used engineering and lab tests to show that Kleenex tissue is made with 24 percent more cottony, soft fiber. Thus, Kleenex was able to substantiate the claim.

Substantiation is not always easy. To increase the probability the substantiation will be accepted by the FTC and courts, company leaders can use the following principles:[4]

1. The federal government assumes consumers read ads broadly and do not pay much attention to fine print and qualifying language. Thus, hiding a qualifier at the bottom of the ad or using words such as *usually, normally,* or *under typical situations* somewhere in the ad is not normally accepted as substantiation.

2. The evidence has to be for the exact product being tested, not for a similar product, regardless of the similarity.

An advertisement by Kleenex Cottonelle using a substantiation claim.

The FTC would expect substantiation by Miller Lite to support the phrase "Half the carbs of Bud Light."

3. Evidence should come from or be accepted by experts in the relevant area of the product and would be considered valid and reliable by the experts. Studies conducted by the company or something found on the Internet is not acceptable.

4. The FTC and courts will consider the totality of the evidence. If the company has one study that supports the claim but there are four studies by other independent organizations that indicate something different, then the evidence will not be accepted as valid substantiation.

Regardless of the type of communication, the FTC prohibits unfair or deceptive marketing communications. Marketers must be able to substantiate claims through competent and reliable evidence. Unfortunately, a great deal of gray area exists between puffery and a claim that must be substantiated. Consequently, lawsuits are filed and governmental agencies are forced to address complaints and suspected violations of the law. These agencies and their rulings strongly affect individual marketing practices as well as company actions.

How Investigations Begin

Many companies have been cited for illegal activities, including deception. In each case, various types of complaints triggered an FTC investigation. These include problems noticed by:

- Consumers
- Businesses
- Congress
- The media

Tree Top must be able to substantiate its claim that it puts two apples in every glass of juice.

Each can raise questions about what appears to be an unfair or deceptive practice. Most investigations by the FTC are confidential at first, which protects the agency and the company being investigated.

Consent Orders

When the FTC believes a law has been violated, a **consent order** is issued first. If company leaders sign the consent order, they agree to stop the disputed practice without admitting guilt.

Kentucky Fried Chicken (KFC) signed a consent agreement with the FTC concerning two ads the FTC investigated and believed were not adequately substantiated. In the first, the FTC held that KFC made false claims in an advertisement that stated eating two Original Recipe fried chicken breasts had less fat than the Burger King Whopper. It was true that the chicken did have slightly less total fat and saturated fat than the BK Whopper; however, the chicken had more than three times the trans fat and cholesterol, more than twice the sodium, and had more calories. Thus, to the FTC the claim was inadequately substantiated. In the second ad, Kentucky Fried Chicken claimed that one Original Recipe chicken breast had only 11 grams of carbohydrates and 40 grams of protein, compatible with a "low-carbohydrate" weight-loss program. The FTC found the ad misleading, because the "low-carbohydrate" weight-loss programs such as the Atkins Diet and the South Beach Diet specifically recommend against eating breaded, fried foods.[5]

Administrative Complaints

Most FTC investigations end with the signing of a consent order. If a consent agreement cannot be reached, the FTC issues an **administrative complaint**. At that point a formal proceeding similar to a court trial is held before an administrative law judge. Both sides submit evidence and render testimony. At the end of the administrative hearing, the judge makes a ruling. If the judge feels a violation of the law has occurred, a *cease and desist order* is prepared. The order requires the company to stop the disputed practice immediately and refrain from similar practices in the future. If the company is not satisfied with the decision of the administrative law judge, the case can be appealed to the full FTC commission.

The *full commission* holds hearings similar to those before administrative law judges. Rulings are made after hearing evidence and testimony. Companies not satisfied with the ruling of the full FTC commission can appeal the case to the U.S. Court of Appeals and further, to the highest level, the U.S. Supreme Court. The danger for companies that appeal cases is that consumer redress can be sought at that point. This means companies found guilty of violating laws can be ordered to pay civil penalties.

Courts and Legal Channels

Occasionally, the FTC uses the court system to stop unfair and deceptive advertising and communications practices. This occurs when a company violates previous FTC cease and desist orders or when the actions of a company are so severe that immediate action is needed. The latter situation was the case involving the National Consumer Council (NCC), a debt reduction and negotiation firm based in Santa Ann, California. The FTC investigation found that the National Consumer Council encouraged consumers to stop paying their debts once they signed up with NCC for debt reduction. At the same time, NCC did not normally start negotiation with debtors for 6 months. By then, the customer's debtors were irate and not willing to negotiate. In the meantime, the NCC customer had been making payments into a fund at NCC. Charges and monthly fees were being withdrawn for payment to NCC. Many customers did not know NCC was making the charges. Eventually, the customers discovered that not only did NCC ruin their credit ratings, but they were also deeper in debt than when they signed on. Almost all of them were forced to declare bankruptcy. Due to the severity of NCC's activities, the FTC obtained a restraining order from a federal court to immediately close NCC's operation. The FTC also obtained a restraining order against the London Financial Group, which provided telemarketing, accounting, and management services to NCC.[6]

The FTC also works with other legal entities, such as state and federal attorneys general. The FTC, Orange County (CA) district attorney, and the California State Attorney investigated Body Wise International, Inc., for false and deceptive advertising and for violating a consent agreement between Body Wise International and the FTC that was made in 1995. The complaint against Body Wise involved the alleged medical benefits of a product called "AI/E-10." Body Wise International advertised that AI/E-10 could prevent, treat, and cure diseases such as cancer, HIV/AIDS, and asthma. Body Wise supported these claims through the expert testimony of a physician, Dr. Stoff. The FTC investigation revealed that Stoff was receiving royalties from every bottle that was sold and that he did not have sound, medical substantiation for any of the claims being made. The FTC order not only banned Body Wise International from making such claims, but it also prohibited Stoff from misrepresenting the existence of tests and studies concerning AI/E-10. In the final settlement, Body Wise International agreed to pay $2 million to the FTC in civil penalties and $1.5 million in civil penalties to the State of California. Further, the final agreement contained a $358,000 monetary judgment against Dr. Stoff.[7]

Corrective Advertising

In the most severe instances of deceptive or misleading advertising, the FTC can order a firm to prepare **corrective advertisements**. These rare situations occur only when the members of the FTC believe that discontinuing a false advertisement is not a sufficient remedy. When the FTC concludes that consumers believed the false advertisement, it can require the firm to produce corrective ads to bring consumers back to a neutral state. The goal is for consumers to once again hold beliefs they had prior to the false or misleading advertisement.

A few years ago, the FTC ordered corrective advertising in a judgment against Novartis Corporation. The judgment was based on false and deceptive advertisements of a product called Doan's analgesic. During the investigation, members of the FTC concluded that Doan's claim of greater efficiency than competing products was not properly substantiated. The FTC ordered Novartis to immediately cease comparative advertising and to make the following statement in corrective ads: "Although Doan's is an effective pain reliever, there is no evidence that Doan's is more effective than other pain relievers for back pain." Novartis was ordered to spend $8 million advertising the statement and include it for 1 year in all advertisements, except for 15-second broadcast ads. Unhappy with the order, leaders at Novartis filed a lawsuit in federal court against the FTC, but the federal court upheld the FTC order.[8]

Trade Regulation Rulings

The final type of action the FTC takes is called a **trade regulation ruling**, which applies to an entire industry in a case of unfair or deceptive practices. Normally, the commission holds a public hearing and accepts both oral and written arguments. The commission then makes a ruling that applies to every firm within an industry. As with other FTC rulings, decisions can be challenged in the U.S. Court of Appeals.

In the jewelry industry, the FTC issued trade regulations that addressed gemstones that were treated. The FTC requires all jewelers to disclose to consumers if a gemstone is treated in a nonpermanent way (such as a coating), if the treatment requires special care, or if the treatment affects the value of the gemstone. The disclosure ruling does not mean the jeweler must provide a great deal of technical information. It does imply, however, that the jeweler must communicate with customers in an easily understood manner regarding any coating or treatment applied to gemstones or other pieces of jewelry.[9]

A similar industry trade ruling occurred with gift cards issued by retailers. Many retailers were charging dormancy fees if a card was not used immediately and many had expiration dates. Neither was conveyed to consumers at the time of purchase. The FTC issued a trade ruling that any merchant issuing a gift card must "boldly" display any fees or expiration dates concerning the card.[10]

INDUSTRY OVERSIGHT OF MARKETING PRACTICES

It is clear that federal regulatory agencies cannot handle all industry activity. Although industry regulatory agencies have no legal power, they can reduce the load on the FTC and the legal system. The three most common and well-known industry regulatory agencies are all a part of the Council of Better Business Bureaus: (1) the National Advertising Division, (2) the National Advertising Review Board, and (3) the Children's Advertising Review Unit (Figure 14.3).

Council of Better Business Bureaus

The Council of Better Business Bureaus is a resource available to both consumers and businesses. Consumers and firms can file complaints with the bureau about unethical business practices or unfair treatment. The bureau compiles a summary of all charges leveled against individual firms. Customers seeking information about the legitimacy of a company or its operations can contact the bureau. The bureau gives them a carefully worded report that will raise cautionary flags when a firm has received a great number of complaints and reveals the general nature of customer concerns. The Better Business Bureau is helpful to individuals and businesses that want to make sure they are dealing with a firm that has a low record of problems.

National Advertising Division

Complaints about advertising or some aspect of marketing communications are referred to the National Advertising Division (NAD) of the Better Business Bureau for review. The role of the NAD is to discover the real issue. The NAD collects information and evaluates data concerning the complaint to determine whether the advertiser's claim is substantiated. If it is not, the NAD negotiates with the business to modify or discontinue the advertisement. If the firm's marketing claim is substantiated, then the complaint is dismissed.

Individuals and companies both can file complaints about unfair ads. Recently, Alcon, Inc. filed a complaint with the NAD challenging claims Bausch & Lomb made in its advertisements and on the company's Web site. The NAD investigated two claims. First, Bausch & Lomb claimed that its ReNu MultiPlus was the "number one contact lens solution." After hearing evidence from both companies, the NAD ruled that Alcon's brand was the number one selling solution. Bausch & Lomb had combined its private-brand sales with the ReNu MultiPlus sales to arrive at higher figures. The NAD ruled that was an inappropriate method of calculating market share.

The second claim investigated was the Bausch & Lomb copy "trusted by over 20 million contact lens wearers and their eye-care professionals." Although estimates that 23.1 million consumers had tried the Bausch & Lomb product were true, the NAD said sales cannot be used to determine if the individuals actually trusted the product. That type of claim would have to come directly from interviews with consumers and eye-care professionals.[11]

FIGURE 14.3
Regulatory Agencies of the Council of Better Business Bureaus

- National Advertising Division (NAD)
- National Advertising Review Board (NARB)
- Children's Advertising Review Unit (CARU)

The Bausch & Lomb decision was a typical NAD recommendation. In the majority of cases, the NAD concludes that the advertisement being investigated is false or misleading and that it should either be modified or halted. In a typical year, the NAD hears about 225 to 250 cases. For 50 to 60 percent of the cases, the NAD will rule that the advertisement was not properly substantiated. In less than 5 percent of the cases will the NAD rule the ad has been fully substantiated.[12]

National Advertising Review Board

When a complaint is not resolved by the NAD or the advertiser appeals the NAD's decision, it goes to the National Advertising Review Board (NARB). The NARB is composed of advertising professionals and prominent civic individuals. If the NARB rules that the firm's advertisements are not substantiated, it then orders the firm to discontinue the advertisements. This is very similar to the consent order by the FTC, but is issued by this private advertising board. If the business firm being accused refuses to accept the NARB ruling, then the matter is turned over to the FTC or an appropriate federal regulatory agency.

An advertisement for Progresso Soups with a testable claim.

The NARB has been involved in numerous business-versus-business disputes. For instance, Minute Maid was ordered to modify its ads because the ad copy claimed that consumers preferred Minute Maid orange juice to Tropicana by a 2:1 margin. Tropicana originally lodged the complaint about the ad and won when it was heard by the NAD. Minute Maid disagreed with the NAD ruling and appealed to the NARB. Minute Maid complained that the decision by the NAD placed an unnecessary and unfair burden on comparative advertising, because all claims relative to a competitor must be substantiated. The NARB supported the NAD decision and issued an order for Minute Maid to comply with the ruling.[13]

The NARB seldom refers a case to the FTC. In fact, such an action has been taken only four times in the last 25 years. The last was a case dealing with Winn-Dixie, which made direct price comparisons with competitors. The NARB found that Winn-Dixie was using prices that were sometimes up to 90 days old. The NARB ruled that any price comparisons made in an advertisement by Winn-Dixie must use prices that are no more than 7 days old. The decision to forward the case to the FTC was made when Winn-Dixie refused to modify its ads and accept the NARB ruling.[14]

Children's Advertising Review Unit

The Children's Advertising Review Unit (CARU) investigates and monitors all forms of advertising in all media directed toward children younger than 12 years of age. It also monitors online privacy practices of Web sites that involve children younger than 13 years of age.

The CARU operates very similar to the NAD. For instance, Mattel, maker of Barbie dolls, filed a complaint against Bratz, which is owned by MGA Entertainment. Mattel alleged:

- The Bratz Catz Superstar Kendall doll was not plush and could not be "posed" before having its picture taken, as alleged in the Bratz advertisement.
- The Big Bratz Babyz did not move on its own, as depicted in the advertisement.
- The Bratz Babyz Ponyz was sold separately and could not hold things in its hands, as depicted in the ad.

After investigating the ads, the CARU ruled that the first complaint, involving Kendall, was unfounded and that MGA Entertainment could continue the Kendall ad as it was.

FIGURE 14.4
CARU Guidelines for Advertising to Children

- Ads for toys should not create unreasonable expectations. Toys shown in ads should look and act as they would if a child were playing with it.
- Ads should not blur the line between fantasy and reality.
- Ads should have clear and visible disclosures about what items come with a toy and what items do not.

- Items that require adult supervision must be shown with adults supervising the child.
- Products and ad content should be appropriate for children.

Source: Based on Wayne Keeley, "Toys and the Truth," *Playthings* 106, no. 2 (February 2008), p. 8.

In the other two cases, CARU agreed with Mattel and requested that MGA Entertainment modify the ads.[15]

In addition to handling complaints about advertising to children, CARU began prescreening ads directed to children in 2005. In 2007, CARU examined more than 300 ads. The prescreening allows CARU to highlight any potential problems with an advertisement before it goes into production. CARU has also issued a series of guidelines to help advertisers prepare ads for children that will be truthful. Figure 14.4 highlights these guidelines.[16]

Children younger than age 12 do not have the same reasoning abilities as adults. Consequently, the CARU stresses the importance of advertisers acting responsibly. Advertisements must show a toy as it would appear as if a child were playing with it. They must be sure the child sees the difference between any fantasy used in an ad and the reality when he or she plays with the toy. If accessories are shown in the ad, then the ads must clearly state that the accessories do not come with the original toy so the child is not disappointed. If an item such as a trampoline is advertised, then adult supervision must be shown in the ad also.

These industry-based actions are designed to control the marketing communications environment and prevent legal actions by either the courts or a governmental regulatory agency. As highlighted in Figure 14.5, these industry regulatory agencies provide several benefits over FTC and legal remedies. The cases are normally heard sooner and are less costly for the companies involved. Most important, complaints are heard by attorneys and business professionals who have experience in advertising. Although FTC judges may have knowledge of the advertising industry, it is not normally as extensive as the individuals involved in the CBBB's agencies.

Effective management, however, is proactive rather than reactive. Company leaders can work to create an image of a socially responsible firm. This is a far better approach than reacting to the constant scrutiny of angry consumers and regulatory agencies.

ETHICS AND SOCIAL RESPONSIBILITY

There are many instances in which an advertising or marketing practice may be deemed legal but be ethically suspect. In this section, various marketing and advertising tactics are considered. Then ethical frameworks and responses are described.

Ethics and morals are key principles that can be used to guide a person's activities in the world of commerce. **Morals** are beliefs or principles that individuals hold concerning what is right and what is wrong. **Ethics** are moral principles that serve as guidelines for both individuals and organizations. Marketing and marketing communications activities are affected by ethical and moral concerns. Ethical issues are present in advertising

FIGURE 14.5
Advantages of Using the CBBB's Industry Regulatory Agencies

- Lower cost
- Faster resolution
- Heard by attorneys and business professionals with experience in advertising

1. Advertisements cause people to buy more than they can afford.	5. Advertisements often make unsafe products, such as alcohol and tobacco, seem attractive.
2. Advertising overemphasizes materialism.	6. Advertisements often are offensive.
3. Advertising increases the costs of goods and services.	7. Advertising to children is unethical.
4. Advertising perpetuates stereotyping of males, females, and minority groups.	

FIGURE 14.6
Concerns and Criticisms Regarding Advertising

decisions and actions. At the most general level, several major ethical concerns and criticisms have arisen. They include the items shown in Figure 14.6.

Ethics and Advertising

One common complaint is that advertisements cause people to *buy more than they can afford.* It is closely connected to the comment that advertising *overemphasizes materialism.* A case can be made that many commercials do indeed stress luxury, social standing, and the prestige of being first to purchase an item. At the same time, the messages are still just commercials. Those who defend advertising point out that consumers should be responsible for spending money wisely.

Another criticism is that advertising *increases the costs of goods and services.* This debate has been waged for many years. Advertising professionals note that without consumer awareness, products would not be purchased, because consumers would not know of their existence. Further, advertising widens the base of potential customers and may increase repeat business. Additional sales lead to economies of scale and lower, rather than higher, prices.

Perpetuating Stereotypes

Many social commentators have suggested that advertising and other forms of media perpetuate stereotyping of males, females, and minority groups. This leads to several questions. For instance, is segmentation the same as stereotyping? In an era in which the term *political correctness* is routinely used, there is debate regarding what is acceptable. In marketing, some of the categories in which market segments are identified include age, race, gender, social status, and income. When marketing to or portraying individuals from these categories, do advertisers use clichés that are no longer appropriate?

Advertisements often depict teenagers in one-dimensional ways rather than reflecting the complexities of young adulthood. Teens are often depicted as rebellious, carefree, and sexually starved. For baby boomers, the image presented is of a white, well-educated, well-off person with a spacious home and expensive cars and toys instead of the complex makeup of multiple nationalities of all income levels. From a marketing perspective, it is much easier to group people into smaller subgroups with common interests. Is it unethical, bad business, or simply a practical matter to represent or misrepresent consumers in these ways?

Elderly people are often stereotyped in advertising.

Source: Courtesy of Patrick Watson; Pearson Education/PH College.

Advertising Unsafe Products

Marketing is often associated with unsafe products, such as alcohol, cigarettes, and other potentially harmful items. In 2002, NBC began accepting money to run advertisements for liquor products with alcohol contents that were stronger than beer or wine. Almost immediately, a host of critics argued that it would be unwise to subject minors to such ads. Eventually the network decided against running the ads even though such commercials are run on cable network programs. The practice raises questions about free speech and free enterprise and why the tobacco and alcohol industries are banned from advertising on specific media when other product categories do not face this media restriction.

Other concerns remain. For example, by the age of 18 the average American teen has viewed more than 100,000 beer commercials. Critics of the brewing industry and marketing agree: Too many beer commercials are designed to encourage underage drinking and build brand loyalty or brand switching in a population that is not even supposed to use the product. Occasional underage drinking can lead to an addiction in a few months, because underage drinkers are less developed mentally, physically, and emotionally.

Young males are often the targets of beer ads prepared for baseball, football, basketball, and auto racing telecasts. Use of sexuality and social acceptance are common themes, along with humor. Recent testimony in Congress suggests the brewing industry is walking a fine line.

The questions becomes: Do a few public relations ads, such as the "Know When to Say When" campaign authorized by Budweiser and the "21 Means 21" advertisement sponsored by Coors, represent a real attempt to reduce underage drinking, or are they designed to placate the government and critics?

Drunken driving, diminished performance in school, health problems, and even death by binge drinking are all part of the problem. In the alcohol industry, as in many other circumstances, the role of advertising should be under constant scrutiny.

The same is true for tobacco products. There are many charges that tobacco companies focus on reaching young people, through characters such as Joe Camel. Any marketing professional entering the field should consider his or her comfort level with such questionable tactics.

After television tobacco advertising was banned by the government, marketers have created a series of tactics to make certain company products are mentioned on the air. Sponsorships of the Virginia Slims Tennis Tournament and Marlboro Cup Racing have come under congressional scrutiny, because sportscasters must state the names of the products while reporting scores and results. Is this ethical?

Offensive Advertisements

Many adult products require tasteful advertising and marketing programs, even when they are free to be shown through any medium. Feminine hygiene products, condoms, and other personal adult products may be featured in practically any medium. It is the responsibility of the marketing professional to select media that are appropriate as well as create ads that will not be offensive.

In the international arena, this responsibility becomes even greater. In many Islamic countries, advertisements for personal hygiene or sexually related products would be highly offensive. It is important for company leaders to explore these cultural differences before undertaking any kind of marketing campaign.

Another ethical issue that has arisen concerns the use of nudity and sexuality featuring children. For many years, critics disparaged Calvin Klein for pushing the envelope. The original objections arose in the 1980s, when 14-year-old Brooke Shields appeared in an advertisement saying, "Nothing comes between me and my Calvins."

Later, in an attempt to sell children's underwear, the same company decided to prepare a large billboard in Times Square to accompany a series of magazine advertisements. The photo in the ads showed two 6-year-old boys arm wrestling while two girls about the same age were jumping on a sofa. All were only wearing underwear. The ads were pulled after strong objectives from numerous groups.

In recent years, there has been an increase in sensitivity to issues of child molestation, child pornography, and related sexual issues. Marketing professionals must carefully consider what the limits should be. Suggesting that sex sells is simply not enough, nor is making a defensive claim about freedom of speech or freedom of expression. Ethics, morals, and a clear conscience should serve as additional guides when a company pushes the limits of sexuality using young people as models.

Advertising to Children

A continuing controversy in the field of marketing is the ethical acceptability of advertising to children. Children represent a tremendous level of spending and buying power, over $20 billion annually. The question is in regard to the tactics used to reach them.

Mary Pipher, clinical psychologist and author of *The Shelter of Each Other*, suggests that "No one ad is bad, but the combination of 400 ads per day creates in children a combination of narcissism, entitlement, and dissatisfaction."[17] Ads targeted to children employ multiple tactics, including building brand awareness through images and logos, featuring toys and collectibles, and developing tie-ins with television programs and movies, including the recent *Hannah Montana* phenomenon. Characters such as Barney, Ronald McDonald, and Harry Potter vend everything from food to toys to clothes.

With so many potential venues to sell directly to children and to put pressure on their parents, many company leaders believe it is best to "get them while they're young." From a societal perspective, however, the question remains as to whether such impressionable young minds should be subjected to so many messages.

MARKETING AND ETHICS

Ethical dilemmas are present in places other than advertisements. Many times, however, there is a connection between a marketing program and what takes place in the marketing communications area. A review of some of these issues follows (see Figure 14.7).

Brand Infringement

There have always been ethical challenges associated with brand management. One continuing problem is brand infringement. **Brand infringement** occurs when a company creates a brand name that closely resembles a popular or successful brand, such as when the Korrs beer company was formed. In that case, the courts deemed the brand an intentional infringement, and the name was abandoned. Another brand-infringing company that was forced by the courts to give up its name was Victor's Secret.

The brand infringement issue becomes more complex when a brand is so well established that it may be considered a generic term, such as a Kleenex tissue or a Xerox copy. Band-Aid encountered the problem in the 1970s, forcing the marketing team to make sure the product was identified as "Band-Aid Brand Strips" rather than simply "band aids," to keep the competition from being able to use the name. The most vulnerable new brand name may be Google, as in "I Googled myself" or "I Googled it."

The newest form of unethical behavior, at least according to some sources, is called *domain squatting* or *cyber squatting* on the Internet. This is the controversial practice of buying domain names (barnesandnoble.com, kohls.com, labronjames.com, etc.) that are

◆ Brand infringement	◆ Gifts and bribery
◆ Medical marketing	◆ Spamming and cookies

FIGURE 14.7
Ethical Issues in Marketing

valuable to specific people or businesses in the hopes of making a profit by reselling the name. At the extreme, whitehouse.com was a pornographic Web site. Any new company trying to build a presence in the marketplace may find itself stifled by domain squatters. Names matter, and cyber squatters are willing to take advantage of these activities to make profits at some else's expense.[18]

Medical Marketing and Advertising

Is it ethical to advertise a physician's services or new drugs? For many years, attorneys, dentists, and physicians did not advertise for fear of being viewed as "ambulance chasers." Recently the trend has gone in the opposite direction. In some instances, a dermatologist will advertise a "skin rejuvenation" practice with only a bare mention that it is also part of a medical practice. Critics argue this takes medicine into the area of merchandising and suggest that it is deceptive to do so.

Pharmaceutical companies now spend millions advertising new drugs. A recent television news report noted that anti-inflammatory and nonsteroidal painkillers such as Celebrex have benefited from massive advertising campaigns, yet there is some medical evidence that they are no more effective than much cheaper alternatives, such as Advil or Aleve. One product, Vioxx, was removed from shelves because it created potential new medical risks for patients.

When consumers are in pain and simply want the best relief possible, should they be subjected to marketing programs that include free samples and gifts to physicians, along with extensive advertising programs, or should there be some way to know which medicine is clinically proven to be the most effective? Congress is now looking into this issue. In addition, individuals within the marketing field are debating the role of advertising in promoting medical practices and drugs, and whether the advertising profession should adopt guidelines. Other marketers, however, contend that medical practices and drug companies have the right to market services or goods as much as Nike or Wal-Mart has the right to promote their products. In the meantime, advertising companies and marketing teams are continually being asked to convince consumers to purchase new drugs.[19]

A great deal of discussion has taken place with regard to sexual dysfunction products. The unfortunate reality is that many young men are buying and using the drugs for recreational purposes. Some marketing critics complain that advertising and promotional tactics feed into this misuse.

The marketing of herbs, supplements, and other nontested products also is problematic. Claims are made regarding their contributions to energy level, sexual stamina, and mental acuity. Some marketers report unsubstantiated results related to weight loss.

Is it ethical, knowing that placebo effects exist, to claim a product will make a man better in bed, stronger, wiser, or more ambitious? After all, consumers are used to exaggerated claims. It is common for such products to offer a money-back guarantee in which the consumer may receive a full refund if not satisfied. Most people who buy these products are either willing to delude themselves into believing a benefit existed when it did not or are too embarrassed to ask for a refund.

Gifts and Bribery in Business-to-Business Marketing Programs

When marketing to other businesses, close personal contacts are often common, both in personal sales calls and in other venues such as trade shows. Among the more serious ethical issues are gifts and bribery.

To influence sales, purchasing agents and other members of the buying company are often the recipients of gifts, meals, entertainment, and even free trips. From a personal ethics standpoint, many concerned leaders question accepting personal gifts that are designed to influence business decisions. The International Olympics Committee wrestled with this problem when Salt Lake City was chosen to host the 2002 Winter Olympics. Exorbitant gifts may have swayed the selection process.

Closely tied with the issue of receiving gifts is that of offering or accepting bribes. These can be related to gaining governmental contracts or making business contacts. Without them, permits may not be granted or can be very difficult to obtain. In Germany and France, the government actually allows companies to write off bribes as tax deductions.

Internet Marketing: Spamming and Cookies

Technology is a two-edged sword in the area of marketing. On the one hand, it creates marvelous new ways to quickly reach a set of consumers with a key message and to keep in continuous contact with those customers. On the other hand, it can be invasive and intrusive and presents ethical dilemmas for those working on the Web.

There have been long and loud complaints about spamming. Even with anti-spam legislation, individuals continue to receive unwanted e-mails. Is this an ethical issue or simply a practical matter? Either way, the marketing team must assess the viability of spamming programs.

At a more dramatic level, cookie technology allows a Web site to track which sites a consumer has visited. Is this ethical? Should an Internet company be allowed to gather this information? Should the company be allowed to sell the information to other companies? Answers fall into two categories: (1) legal and (2) moral. Although it may still be legal to collect and transfer consumer information in this manner, the ethical issue remains. Marketing professionals will continue to face the need for quality information. They must balance this need with the ethical ramifications of invading privacy rights and customer sensibilities. Failure to do so may have long-term implications for both the company and those who use the Internet to shop for products.

Many complain about *interstitial advertising*, which interrupts a person on the Internet without warning. These types of ads have to be clicked off to remove them from the screen, and they are controversial. Although they have intrusion value, they also are annoying. Interstitial ads can come onto a person's computer even after logging off the Internet or come on the screen the next time the person logs on.

Some of these concerns have been lessened through technology. Anti-spam devices and programs that block cookies have been developed. Many businesses have created Internet firewalls that keep out such unwanted intrusions.

RESPONDING TO ETHICAL CHALLENGES

The foundation and frameworks for ethical guidelines are derived from several sources. These include philosophy, law, religion, and common sense.

One *philosophy of life* involves maximizing pleasure and minimizing pain. This idea represents **hedonism**. Critics note that life is often more than the simple pursuit of pleasure and avoidance of pain. **Homeostasis** is the natural craving for balance. People balance a variety of urges throughout life.

The **law** offers guidelines regarding right and wrong as well as what is acceptable and what is not within a geographic area. Legal systems are designed to tell people what they can and cannot do. Remember, however, that not all legal systems are the same.

Many **religions**, or belief systems, profess a version of the philosophy that is summarized by the *Golden Rule*: Do until others as you would have them do unto you. Acting in a morally acceptable manner starts with treating others well. Still, specific religious ideologies vary widely. Many disagreements about what is right or wrong exist. Respect, tolerance, discussion, compromise, and accommodation should become ethical guidelines when the religious views of others contradict your own.

At the end of the day, one overriding constant may be that ethical actions, moral correctness, and social responsibility all boil down to *common sense*. Two processes can be used to analyze an ethical concept. The first is logic and reasoning, which leads to common-sense conclusions. One's conscience may become muted over time if it is continually ignored; however, most people know when they are doing something right or wrong. The second element of common sense is gut instinct. Deep down inside, most people know when something is appropriate or inappropriate. A person's thoughts and gut reaction should never be ignored in an ethical reasoning process.

Ethical Frameworks

The building blocks and personal ethical systems noted in the previous sections help to define various approaches to ethical reasoning. As shown in Figure 14.8, there are several ideas about what constitutes the best framework for the analysis of ethic issues, including utilitarianism, individualism, the rights approach, and the justice approach.

Utilitarianism is a means of making decisions based on what is the greatest good for the greatest number of people. Utilitarianism is referred to as the "calculus of pain," because it tries to minimize pain and maximize pleasure for the greatest number of people, relying a great deal on the concept of homeostasis.

Unfortunately, utilitarianism perspectives may overlook the rights or needs of the minority. As an extreme example, the use of slaves may create greater well-being for a vast majority of slaveholders, but at the same time the rights of the few, the slaves, are being destroyed. It is impossible to argue that slavery is ethical.

Ethicists may conclude that utilitarianism involves a judgment call as to what is "good" as well as considering that "good" in light of its effects on both the majority and the minority. Care should be given in deciding how much "pain" to others is acceptable.

Individualism is the degree to which society values personal goals, personal autonomy, privacy over group loyalty, commitments to group norms, involvements in collective activities, social cohesiveness, and intense socialization. Therefore, ethical decisions are based on personal self-interests, so long as one's actions do not harm others.

The individualism approach may cause the weakest members of society to suffer the most. In health care, individualists favor systems in which those with money are able to retain the best medical professionals. The individualist position is consistently used to criticize programs such as socialized medicine. It suggests that those who do not contribute to society's well-being, by being employed and paying taxes, should not have equal access to those who work hard and pay the bills.

The **rights approach** is a means of making decisions based on the belief that each person has fundamental rights that should be respected and protected. These rights include freedom of speech, privacy, and access to due process, plus the right to a safe and healthy environment at work and at home. Rights to free speech include the rights of companies to advertise any kind of product, even those that make people uncomfortable or ones they object to.

The difficulty with the rights approach is that many times the rights of one group, or a certain type of right, may impede on others. For example, there is a conflict between rights to privacy versus freedom of speech, when the issue is a job reference. Someone who has been fired for being incompetent, unreliable, or unethical may wish to keep that information confidential. Freedom of speech, however, should protect the rights of a former employer who simply tells the truth about why the person was terminated. As an ethical framework, the balancing act is present in defining what rights apply to a situation, and which rights take precedent.

The **justice approach** is a method of decision making based on treating all people fairly and consistently. *Distributive justice* concentrates on the fairness of rewards, punishments, and outcomes. *Procedural justice* focuses on fair and consistent application of rules and protocols.

FIGURE 14.8
Ethical Frameworks

- Utilitarianism
- Individualism
- Rights approach
- Justice approach

The justice approach suggests that when someone is hurt by another's actions, as an individual or in a collective, there should be consequences. These consequences are supposed to punish the perpetrator for the misdeeds and serve as a deterrent to others. Also, when one's actions help others or lead to a greater good, the consequences should be in the form of a reward. In both circumstances (harm or good), the methods by which rewards are granted or negative sanctions are imposed should be based on an impartial, reasonable, and constant program of judgment and justice.

One problem with the justice approach is that what one person considers to be a proper reward or punishment may not seem fair to another. Many people believe capital punishment is a just outcome. Others believe it is never justified. The same is true regarding those who make the judgments. What may seem like a fair procedure to one could appear to be totally biased to another.

SOCIAL RESPONSIBILITY

Ethics can be observed at many levels, from what individuals do to what groups do to what companies do to the actions of entire countries. The ethical frameworks described in the last section can be applied to each level. Utilitarianism and individualism point to the conflict of personal interest and well-being versus the consideration of the good of the larger group. The utilitarian position favors the group; individualism favors the individual. These views are reflected in concepts regarding social responsibility, which considers the actions of companies combined with the actions of persons in those companies, especially individual leaders.

Social responsibility can be defined as "the obligation an organization (profit-seeking or nonprofit) has to be ethical, responsible, and responsive to the needs of members in the organization as well as the larger society." The first aspect includes *eliminating negatives*, or unethical and immoral company activities.

The second aspect of social responsibility is what may be called *doing positives*. A responsible company engages in actions that help both internal members and external constituents or stakeholders. Doing positives is more than simply engaging in *altruistic activities*. Although one motive is to benefit other human beings and the larger society, it is not the only motive. These actions may also inspire *goodwill* toward the organization, which in turn means that the company may enjoy the benefits of gaining quality applicants, as job-seekers in the community respond favorably to the organization.

Social responsibility is associated with better relationships with customers and the government. When a firm that has always acted in a socially responsible manner makes a legal misstep or somehow injures a consumer, the company may be less likely to end up in court or face legal action by the government. The same organization may fare more favorably in the court of public opinion. In the long term, many believe that socially responsible companies are the most likely to survive and thrive.

Social Responsibility Perspectives

Three classic models regarding who should be in charge of social responsibility are available (Figure 14.9). Each generates debate regarding the best approach.

The **invisible hand of the marketplace** argues that competition eliminates any product or corporate practice that is harmful and inappropriate. Free choices made by consumers without governmental restraint lead to the elimination of unworthy products and companies. Some evidence suggests that unethical companies do wither and die. Unfortunately, this can be of little solace to those injured by illegal or immoral actions. The marketplace does tend to reward socially responsible companies over time.

◆ Invisible hand of the marketplace
◆ Governmental duty perspective
◆ Ethical or enlightened management

FIGURE 14.9
Three Classic Models of Social Responsibility

The invisible hand approach essentially posits that the only duty management has is to make profits and enhance stockholder wealth in a legal and moral fashion. Without the presence of guardians, such a model may not yield the best results for individual consumers and investors, especially in the short term.

The **governmental duty perspective** states that government should write legislation and create regulatory agencies to emphasize ethics and social responsibility. This includes writing and enforcing liability laws and stridently following legal procedures against those individuals and companies who injure consumers.

Critics of this approach note that government can be, and often is, every bit as corrupt as private enterprise. As a result, the government is able to favor unethical companies while regulating others. The net result may be very little gain for the "little" man or woman who can't fight city hall.

The **ethical**, or **enlightened management** perspective states that managers can and should be trusted to create an ethical environment with an enlightened sense of employee and customer well-being. Managers act on internal convictions to seek the best path for themselves, the company, and those in the surrounding community. This leads to long-term success and survival of the firm.

Managers are in the unique position of being both consumers and producers. They should know, more than others, that an organization has both a short-term and long-term vested interest in behaving in an ethical and moral fashion. In the short term, eliminating negatives and doing positives creates favorable publicity for the company, generates customer loyalty, and helps keep the company out of court, both in terms of lawsuits and governmental interventions. In the long term, acting in an ethical and morally responsible manner helps the organization survive over time.

The ethical management perspective is one that favors training for those preparing to enter the world of business, counseling for those caught in ethical quandaries, and self-regulation by individual companies, industries, and professions. Organizations such as the Council of Better Business Bureaus can be formed to help businesspeople regulate themselves.

ETHICS PROGRAMS

Various individuals and groups have responded to the need for a more ethical environment by creating ethics training programs, codes of ethics, and ethics consulting systems. These attempts are designed to assist individual employees, managers or supervisors, and others within a company facing ethical challenges or dilemmas.

Ethics Training Programs

Ethics training can take place at several points. Early moral training occurs in many families as part growing up, both in secular settings and in religious organizations. Those attending college receive further instruction. The Association to Advance Collegiate Schools of Business (AACSB), which is a major accrediting body for schools of business, has placed a strong emphasis on ethics instruction for over a decade.

Many corporations now add ethics topics into new employee training programs as well as manager training systems. Some are self-created; others are developed in conjunction with professional organizations and nearby colleges and universities.

Codes of Ethics

Codes of ethics are created in two ways. The first is within professional organizations. In marketing, two key organizations are the American Marketing Association (AMA) and the American Academy of Advertising (AAA). The AMA code of ethics may be found on the organization's Web site, **www.marketingpower.com**.

The second way ethical codes are developed is within business organizations. Many firms have written and revised ethical codes. Some of the more common components of codes of ethics are displayed in Figure 14.10.

> * The purpose of the code, including (1) regulation of behavior and (2) inspiration to employees.
> * A statement of aspirations often included in a preamble that outlines the ideals a company aspires to for its employees. The statement should include the values and principles of the organization.
> * A list of principles.
> * A list of rules, if needed.
> * A statement regarding how the code was created.
> * How the code will be implemented.
> * How the code will be publicized internally to employees.
> * How the code will be publicized externally to constituents and publics.
> * How the code will be enforced.
> * A statement regarding how and when the code will be revised.
> * Most of the time, values, principles, and rules are listed in order of importance.

FIGURE 14.10
Components of Codes of Ethics

Ethics Consulting Systems

Numerous individuals and organizations are willing to provide counsel regarding ethical dilemmas. Some employ what are in essence "ethics hotlines" through which a concerned employee can make contact to discuss an ethics problem. The services offered by such organizations vary. Some provide additional instruction, whereas others offer ethical consultations designed to build in-house ethics advisors as well as formulate codes of ethics.

It is important to remember that ethics and social responsibility concerns all boil down to the actions and decisions made by individuals and groups. Any person entering the fields of marketing and advertising should carefully consider what he or she considers to be acceptable and unacceptable acts prior to taking a position as well as while working within any role. The term *whistle-blower* is used to describe an individual who is willing to go public with charges about an organization doing something that is illegal or unethical. Making the choice to be a whistle-blower is difficult; it can cause a career setback and make the individual vulnerable to lawsuits and other retaliatory actions. Failure to take action is also a choice. One's conscience and belief system provide the ultimate guides as to when and how to respond to moral issues.

INTERNATIONAL IMPLICATIONS

Each individual country has its own set of laws regarding what is legal and what is not in the areas of marketing, promotions, and advertising. The role of the marketing department is to make sure these laws and regulations are clearly understood. The company should make every effort to comply with them.

Remember that legal systems vary. In the United States and many Western countries, the form of law is known as common law. *Common law* is based on local customs, traditions, and precedents. Legal history, previous cases, and national customs serve as guides, and judges typically have more discretion in making legal decisions.

Civil law, which is present in many European countries, is based on a broad set of legal principles, and decisions are made based on legal codes that have been written over time. This gives judges less flexibility.

Theocratic law is based on religious teachings. The most common form of theocratic law is Islamic law, which is based on the *Koran* and *Sunnah*. In many Islamic countries, transactions are regulated in different ways. For instance, charging interest is not permitted in the Islamic system.

Moral reasoning follows a similar pattern in international marketing. One cannot assume that a given system of ethics and morals is completely acceptable in another country. For example, views of the roles of men and women in society vary widely. Any marketing program with an international outreach should employ a cultural assimilator to help individuals understand ethical principles present other nations.

SUMMARY

To enforce fair standards in the areas of advertising and marketing communications, a number of governmental agencies are ready to take action when needed. These include the Federal Trade Commission, the Food and Drug Administration, the Federal Communications Commission, and others. Each tries to keep unfair marketing activities from taking place.

The FTC is the primary agency regulating marketing communications, and it makes special efforts to stop instances of unfair or deceptive practices. In conjunction with the courts, the FTC and other governmental agencies regulate the majority of companies and industries in the United States. The FTC regulates cases of fraudulent practices targeted at individual consumers as well as conflicts between businesses. Through the use of consent orders, administrative complaints, cease and desist orders, and full commission hearings, the FTC is able to make its findings and rulings known to the parties concerned. Court actions and corrective advertising programs are utilized in more severe cases. Trade regulation rulings apply when an entire industry is guilty of an infraction.

Ethics and morals are key principles that can be used to guide a person's activities in the world of commerce. Morals are beliefs or principles that individuals hold concerning what is right and what is wrong. Ethics are moral principles that serve as guidelines for both individuals and organizations. Marketing and marketing communications activities are affected by ethical and moral concerns.

Some of the more common complaints about advertising include issues of materialism and overconsumption. Also, there are criticisms that advertising perpetuates stereotypes, features unsafe products, sends out offensive messages, is deceptive, and unfairly targets children. Each of these issues requires consideration by anyone entering the profession.

Marketing programs are also subject to ethical concerns. Brand infringement, questionable medical marketing and advertising programs, business-to-business tactics, and Internet marketing programs have all come under scrutiny. Responses to these criticisms are the responsibility of top management, the marketing department, and those associated with public relations.

A number of ethical frameworks and guidelines are available. Those in the field of marketing may be guided by concepts regarding social responsibility. Also, ethics programs consisting of ethics training, codes of ethics, and ethics consulting systems are available to those facing dilemmas or wishing to pose questions.

The issues of legality and morality are present in the international arena as well. Each is complicated by different bodies of law and views of ethics in various nations. Companies seeking to expand internationally should be aware of these differences in order to find ways to respond to them.

KEY TERMS

Federal Trade Commission (FTC)   A federal agency that regulates marketing communications.

puffery   When a firm makes an exaggerated claim about its products or services without making an overt attempt to deceive or mislead.

substantiation   Firms must be able to prove or back up any claims made in their marketing communications.

consent order   A directive issued when the FTC believes a violation has occurred.

administrative complaint   A formal proceeding similar to a court trial held before an administrative law judge regarding a charge filed by the FTC.

corrective advertisements   Ads that bring consumers back to a neutral state, so consumers once again hold beliefs they had prior to being exposed to a false or misleading advertisement.

trade regulation ruling   Findings that implicate an entire industry in a case of unfair or deceptive practices.

morals   Beliefs or principles that individuals hold concerning what is right and what is wrong.

ethics   Moral principles that serve as guidelines for both individuals and organizations.

brand infringement   Occurs when a company creates a brand name that closely resembles a popular or successful brand.

hedonism   Maximizing pleasure and minimizing pain.

homeostasis   The natural craving for balance.

law   Governmental guidelines for what is right and wrong as well as what is acceptable and what is not within a geographic area.

religions   Belief systems.

utilitarianism   A means of making decisions based on what is the greatest good for the greatest number of people.

individualism   The degree to which society values personal goals, personal autonomy, privacy over group loyalty, commitments to group norms, involvements in collective activities, social cohesiveness, and intense socialization.

rights approach   A means of making decisions based on the belief that each person has fundamental rights that should be respected and protected.

justice approach   A method of decision making based on treating all people fairly and consistently.

social responsibility   The obligation an organization has to be ethical, responsible, and responsive to the needs of members in the organization as well as the larger society.

invisible hand of the marketplace The argument that competition eliminates any product or corporate practice that is harmful and inappropriate.

governmental duty perspective The argument that government should write legislation and create regulatory agencies to emphasize ethics and social responsibility.

ethical (enlightened) management The argument that managers can and should be trusted to create an ethical environment with an enlightened sense of employee and customer well-being.

REVIEW QUESTIONS

1. Name the governmental agencies that oversee marketing programs.
2. What role did the Wheeler–Lea Amendment play in regulating advertising practices?
3. When does an ad or message become false or misleading?
4. What is puffery? Should a company use a great deal of puffery in its ads? Why or why not?
5. What does substantiation mean? How does a company know it has met the substantiation test in an advertisement?
6. What four groups can trigger an investigation by the Federal Trade Commission?
7. What are the steps of the process when the FTC investigates a claim of false or misleading advertising?
8. What is a consent order?
9. What is an administrative complaint?
10. What is the purpose of a corrective advertisement?
11. What is a trade regulation ruling? How is it different from other FTC rulings?

12. What is the relationship between the Council of Better Business Bureaus and the National Advertising Division?
13. What is the primary function of the National Advertising Review Board?
14. How does the Children's Advertising Review Unit operate?
15. Define ethics and morals.
16. Identify the types of ethical complaints that are raised regarding advertising.
17. What is brand infringement?
18. What types of ethical issues have been raised regarding medical marketing and advertising?
19. Describe the ethical issues associated with Internet marketing.
20. Describe four ethical frameworks noted in this chapter.
21. Define social responsibility. What three perspectives regarding social responsibility are described in this chapter?
22. Name the three types of ethics programs that can be used to help marketing professionals cope with moral challenges.

CRITICAL THINKING EXERCISES

Discussion Questions

1. In labeling of food products, companies walk a fine line between promoting the product and truth in content. Phrases such as "low sodium," "fat free," "no sugar added," and "light" may give the impression that a food is healthful, but not reveal the entire truth. How often do you read package labels and make purchases based on their content? On your next trip to the grocery store, examine various labels that have one of the words identified earlier in this question and compare it to other brands. Does it actually contain less than a competing brand?

2. Reread the section "Deception Versus Puffery." Find three advertisements that you think are examples of either deception or puffery. How difficult is it to differentiate between the two? When does an ad cease to be puffery and become deceptive?

3. One of the industries closely watched by the FTC is the weight-loss industry. Find three advertisements from magazines, newspapers, or television that deal with

weight loss. What claims were made? Do you believe the claims are truthful and legitimate? How do you, as a consumer, distinguish between what is truthful and what is deceptive?

4. Advertising directed toward children is always a hot topic among parents and educators. Many feel that advertising unfairly targets children and creates materialistic desires. By the time a child is 3 years old he or she already knows many brands of products, such as McDonald's. What is your opinion of advertising to children? Is the current regulation enough, or should it be more stringent?

5. One of the criticisms of advertising is that it causes people to buy more than they can afford. Each year a large number of people in United States declare bankruptcy, often because they have overspent. Do you agree that advertising causes people to buy more than they can afford, or is advertising just responding to the materialistic desire of individuals? Defend your response.

6. Advertising does increase the cost of goods and services, but a common defense is that advertising provides people with knowledge about availability of products, which allows consumers to make more intelligent decisions. Do you think this is a valid defense of advertising? Why or why not? What other defense could you offer to support why advertising is important?

7. Think about advertisements you have seen or heard recently and identify one that you believe is offensive. Why was it offensive? Why do you think the advertiser ran the ad if it is offensive? Do you think offensive ads can be effective? Why or why not?

8. What is your opinion of alcohol and tobacco advertising? Should alcohol and tobacco companies have the same freedom to advertise as other product manufacturers? Do you think it is a danger for children to see alcohol or tobacco ads, and does it influence their desire to use these products?

9. Using sex to sell products is another area that many consumers find offensive. Locate two print ads or television ads that are highly sexual in nature, one that you consider offensive and one that you consider is appropriate. What makes the difference? Are there too many ads that use sexual themes? Why or why not?

10. You undoubtedly have seen advertisements by attorneys and medical professionals. Discuss your opinion about these advertisements? Do you think ads by attorneys just increase the number of lawsuits and bankruptcies? Why do medical professionals such as doctors and dentists advertise? Does it affect your opinion of their professionalism? Why or why not?

11. Figure 14.8 identifies four ethical frameworks. Although each framework has its merits, which one do you lean toward or believe in the most? Why? Discuss the other three frameworks in terms of your own personal philosophical view of life.

12. In Figure 14.9, three classic models of social responsibility are listed. Which one do you believe is the best model? Discuss each as it relates to your understanding of the business environment in America today.

13. Do you believe ethics can be learned or is it something an individual has internally? What can companies do, if anything, to make their employees more ethical? Why has America seen so much corruption in the corporate world? What steps would you suggest to curb this corruption?

INTEGRATED LEARNING EXERCISES

1. The FTC is the primary federal agency that oversees advertising and other marketing-related communications. Access the Web site at **www.ftc.gov**. What type of information is available on the Web site for consumers? For businesses? Pick one of the headlines and write a brief report about the article's contents.

2. The FTC's Bureau of Consumer Protection works for the consumer to prevent fraud, deception, and unfair business practices in the marketplace. Access the FTC's Web site at **www.ftc.gov** and go to the Consumer Protection section of the site. What information is available? Find an article or recent event from the Web site and write a short report. How does the FTC's Bureau of Consumer Protection safeguard consumers?

3. Access the FTC's Web site at **www.ftc.gov**. Access each of the following components of the Web site. What type of information does each section contain? Why is it important?
   a. Competition
   b. Economics
   c. Policy

4. One of the primary functions of the FTC is to investigate possible false and deceptive advertising and marketing practices. Access the FTC at **www.ftc.gov**. Go to the "Actions" section of the site. Read through the list of recent actions. Find two that are interesting. Review the cases and write a brief report on each case. What were the results of the FTC investigation?

5. Access the FTC Web site at **www.ftc.gov**. Go to the "News" section of the Web site. Read through the list of recent actions. Find two that are interesting. Review the cases and write a brief report on each case. What were the results of the FTC investigation?

6. The Council of Better Business Bureaus is an important industry organization for businesses as well as consumers. Access the Web site at **www.cbbb.org**. What type of information is available on the Web site? How can the CBBB assist consumers? How can it be beneficial to businesses?

7. Access the Web site of the Council of Better Business Bureaus at **www.cbbb.org**. Go to the "Consumer" section of the site. What types of information are available? Briefly describe each component of the Consumer section of the Web site and how it is beneficial to consumers.

8. Access the Web site of the Council of Better Business Bureaus at **www.cbbb.org**. Go to the "Business" section of the Web site. What types of information are available? Briefly describe each component of the "Business" section of the Web site and how it is beneficial to businesses.

9. The National Advertising Division (NAD) of the Better Business Bureau can be found at **www.nadreview.org**. Access the site. Look through the recent cases the NAD has investigated. Find two of interest to you. Write a report about each case, discussing the issues and the findings of the NAD.

10. The Children's Advertising Review Unit (CARU) of the Better Business Bureau can be found at **www.caru.org**. Access the site. Look through the recent cases the CARU has investigated. Find two of interest to you. Write a report about each case discussing the issues and the findings of the CARU.

11. Protecting the privacy of children is an important function of the Children's Advertising Review Unit (CARU). Access the CARU Web site at **www.caru.org**. Go to the "Privacy Program" component of the site. Discuss the information that is available on the site. How does this protect children? How is it beneficial to parents?

STUDENT PROJECT

Creative Corner

Solidax ADX was developed in the United States in 2005 and was recently rated by the Weight Loss Institute to be the best weight-loss product on the market. Solidax ADX is based on Syneprhrine, Picolinate, and Pyrovate and is designed to suppress appetite and increase metabolism and calorie expenditure. It does not have negative central nervous effects as with comparable diet pills. The ingredients found in Solidax have been proven to be effective in controlled laboratory human weight loss studies.[20]

Concerned about recent FTC investigations of false and deceptive advertising of competing brands, the makers of Solidax ADX want a print ad that will be effective, yet not be subject to FTC investigation. Based on the information provided, design a print advertisement for Solidax ADX.

SAFETY IN THE SKY

CASE
1

Every marketing professional should be aware of the nature of warranties. Two varieties include express warranties and implied warranties. An *express warranty* spells out the conditions under which a good or service is guaranteed. For example, the standard "money back guarantee" states that if a customer is not satisfied, the item can be returned for a full refund. Others offer conditions, such as when a tire warranty offers protection only "under routine driving conditions."

The second form, an *implied warranty*, applies to all forms of commerce and means that every product sold works if used correctly and is safe. In 2008, Southwest Airlines, which had enjoyed a practically impeccable reputation, faced some devastating news: The Federal Aviation Administration (FAA) charged the company with "failing to follow rules that are designed to protect passengers and crew," according to Nicholas A. Sabatini, the FAA's associate administrator for aviation safety, in a written statement. Minnesota Congressman James Oberstar characterized the infraction in this way, "The result of inspection failures, and enforcement failure, has meant that aircraft have flown unsafe, unairworthy, and at risk of lives."

The complaint documents were prepared by two FAA safety inspectors who requested whistle-blower status from the House Transportation and Infrastructure Committee. The two inspectors were subpoenaed to testify. The inspectors say FAA managers knew about the lapse in safety at Southwest, but decided to allow the airline to conduct the safety checks on a slower schedule, because taking "aircraft out of service would have disrupted Southwest Airlines' flight schedule." One of the FAA inspectors seeking whistle-blower status charged that a manager at the FAA "permitted the operation of these unsafe aircraft in a matter that would provide relief" to the airline, even though customers were on board.

The report noted that the safety inspections that had been ignored or delayed by the airline were mandated after two fatal crashes and one fatal incident, all involving Boeing's 737, the only type of airplane Southwest flies. Documents revealed 70 Southwest jets were allowed to fly past the deadline for the mandatory rudder inspections. The complaint also stated that 47 more Southwest jets kept flying after missing deadlines for inspections for cracks in the planes' fuselage, or "skin."

In one case, an FAA inspector at a Southwest Airlines maintenance facility spotted a fuselage crack on one of the airline's 737s and notified the airline. The inspector began looking through safety records and discovered that dozens of planes had missed mandatory inspection deadlines. In a subsequent news release, the FAA reported that Southwest operated 46 Boeing 737s on nearly 60,000 flights between June 2006 and March 2007 while failing to comply with an FAA directive that requires repeated checks of fuselage areas to detect fatigue cracking.

The FAA also initiated an action to seek a $10.2 million civil penalty against Southwest. The complaint stated that the

Concerns about safety at Southwest expanded to other major carriers.

Source: Courtesy of © Dorling Kindersley.

company allegedly operated 46 airplanes without conducting mandatory checks for fuselage cracking. These same types of cracks had been associated with airline crashes and problems in several instances.

This type of legal action was likely to cause a great deal of concern within the leadership of Southwest. The company had a strong reputation for friendliness, customer care, and a devoted and loyal staff. News that both employees and customers had been put at risk undoubtedly created serious questions.

The airline's management team did prepare a statement saying that, "Southwest Airlines discovered the missed inspection area, disclosed it to the FAA, and promptly reinspected all potentially affected aircraft in March 2008. The FAA approved our actions and considered the matter closed as of April 2008." The company's leaders also promised full cooperation with the investigation.

Source: Drew Griffin and Scott Bronstein, "Records: Southwest Airlines Flew Unsafe Planes" (**CNN.com/2008/US/03/06/southwest.planes/ index.html,** accessed March 12, 2008).

1. What are the ethical and legal failures in this case?

2. Explain how the three viewpoints of social responsibility apply to this incident.

3. What should the leadership team at Southwest Airlines do to repair the damage to the company's reputation?

4. How should the marketing and public relations departments at Southwest respond to this incident?

CASE 2

CRAIG'S LIST: COMMUNITY AND CONTROVERSY

In 1995, Craig Newmark, an enterprising software engineer, created an e-mail list for friends and coworkers. At the time, he was employed by Schwab after stints with several other companies in IT departments. In 1999, Craig Newmark retired and began working full time on the Craig's List Web site.

The original intention of the page was to help people to locate jobs, housing, goods, services, romance, local activities, and advice—just about anything. Today, the site provides local classified ads and forums for over 450 cities worldwide. By 2008, Craig's List had over 9 billion visitors per month.

In 2000, the organization was headed by a new CEO, Jim Buckmaster. Buckmaster has been described as a communist, a socialistic anarchist, and an anti-establishment leader. He has been condemned by many, including now-deceased minister Jerry Falwell on a national Fox television broadcast.

Why such a high level of antipathy toward an organization linked with eBay (25 percent ownership)? Why the frustration with a forum for finding a house or getting a job? The answer may be with the community itself.

Although Craig's List is careful to avoid illegal activities, such as cyber-stalking, identity theft, and prostitution, it has been used

to facilitate some of these crimes. For example, one woman used Craig's List to find a contract killer to execute her husband.

Even after these events had been addressed, many complain that some of the content on Craig's List is explicitly sexual, scatological, offensive, graphic, tasteless, and/or not funny. The site acknowledges that this is the case.

At the same time, Craig's List is involved in community work, makes charitable contributions, and serves as a resource for nonprofit organizations. The company's mission includes a statement regarding "helping people help."

1. How might laws and regulations associated with marketing affect an organization such as Craig's List?

2. Should any additional laws be created to deal with social community Web sites such as Craig's List? If so, what type?

3. What are the moral implications of a Web site that hosts arrangements for ethically questionable activities, such as sexual encounters among married people with nonspouse partners?

4. How do the concepts regarding social responsibility apply to an organization such as Craig's List?

ENDNOTES

1. **www.nuitrition.about.com**, **www.conagra foods.com**, **www.mcdonalds.com/**, **www. foodproductdesign.com**, **www.fritolay.com**, and **www.nlm.nih.gov**, all accessed March 13, 2008.

2. "Broadcasters Breach Kids Rules," *Marketing Magazine* 109, no. 35 (November 1, 2004), p. 4.

3. Bart Lazar, "This Column Is the Best One You'll Ever Read," *Marketing News* 38, no. 13 (August 15, 2004), p. 8.

4. Gary D. Hailey and Jeffrey D. Knowles, "Claiming Sufficient Substantiation Is No Easy Task," *Response* 13, no. 4 (January 2005), p. 50.

5. "KFC's Claims That Fried Chicken Is a Way to 'Eat Better' Don't Fly," *Federal Trade Commission* (**www.ftc.gov/opa/2004/06/ kfccorp.htm**, accessed June 30, 2002).

6. "FTC Takes Aim at Another Credit Counseling Firm," *Mortgage Servicing News* 8, no. 7 (August 2004), p. 21.

7. "Body Wise International to Pay $3.5 Million to Settle Federal and State Deceptive Advertising Charges," *Federal Trade Commission* (**www. ftc.gov**, accessed September 20, 2005).

8. Debbi Mack, "FTC Use of Corrective Advertising Upheld," *Corporate Legal Times* 10, no. 108 (November 2000), p. 80.

9. Cecilia Gardner, "Industry Insight," *National Jeweler* 99, no. 17 (September 1, 2005), p. 20.

10. Loraine Debonis, "FTC Sends Issuers a Message: Adequately Disclose Card Fees," *Cards & Payments* 20, no. 5 (May 2007), pp. 16–17.

11. Jennifer Webb, "Bausch & Lomb Agrees to Alter Contact Lens Solution Ad Claims," *Ophthalmology* 32, no. 23 (December 1, 2007), p. 4.

12. Ibid.; Jim Edwards, "NAD a Not-So Challenging Forum for Ad Challengers," *Brandweek* 45, no. 45 (December 13, 2004), p. 5.

13. "Minute Maid Complains, But NARB Forces Change," *Advertising Age* 68, no. 15 (April 14, 1997), p. 51.

14. "NARB Sends Winn-Dixie Complaint to FTC," *Advertising Age* 67, no. 52 (December 23, 1996), p. 2.

15. Jim Edwards, "Barbie Reaches for Her Lawyers," *Brandweek* 47, no. 20 (May 15, 2006), p. 42.

16. Wayne Keeley, "Toys and the Truth," *Playthings* 106, no. 2 (February 2008), p. 8.

17. Mary Pipher, *The Shelter of Each Other*, (New York: Ballentine Books, 1996).

18. Internet Marketing Register (**www.marketing-register.com**, accessed February 28, 2005).

19. *ABC Nightly News*, May 30, 2002.

20. **www.weight-loss-institute.com/products/ solidax_adx.html**, accessed March 23, 2008.

Evaluating an Integrated Marketing Program

Chapter Objectives

After reading this chapter, you should be able to answer the following questions:

- **Which** items should be assessed when evaluating an IMC program?

- **When** are advertising messages evaluated?

- **How** are evaluations of messages different from measures of behavioral responses?

- **Why** is it important to examine the quality of public relations efforts?

- **What** types of long-term variables or issues should be evaluated when assessing an IMC program?

PRETESTING FOR EFFECTIVENESS

The New High-Tech World of Advertising Design

For many years, management and marketing specialists have known that the easiest way to fix many problems is to prevent them from occurring in the first place. The "rocket" analogy is the reasoning that is used. If a rocket is off course in the first few minutes after the launch, it will drift much farther off course as the trip proceeds. A correction early in the flight puts the rocket back on track, and the ride goes much more smoothly.

The same is true in advertising design. If the ad is off course at the beginning, the company spends money developing a campaign that is doomed from the start. One new approach to making ads more effective is to send them through a series of pretests before the actual campaign begins. A company known as Decision Analyst is one of the leading international marketing firms in the world of advertising testing.

One program the company uses is based on Internet research. It is called CopyScreen. To test an ad, a sample is drawn using 200 to 300 target audience consumers who are identified over the Internet. The subjects are shown preliminary versions of print ads and asked for opinions in four areas: (1) attention value, (2) Internet value, (3) purchase propensity, and (4) brand recognition. The responses are given mathematical scores, and a total is generated for the test ad. Ads that exceed a threshold score are deemed worthy of further development.

Those ads moving on to the next stage may be tested through a program called CopyCheck. This program provides more specific feedback concerning the ad's probable effectiveness. Questions CopyCheck attempts to answer include:

1. Will the ad capture the viewer's attention?
2. Will the brand name be noticed and remembered?
3. Does the ad increase the consumer's interest in buying the brand?

CHAPTER FIFTEEN

Source: Courtesy of Summer Bradley.

4. Does the ad trigger the intent to purchase?
5. How memorable is the brand name?
6. What are the key ideas in the ad?
7. What is missing from the ad (i.e., what would the viewers like to know)?
8. What did viewers like about the commercial?
9. What did viewers not like about the commercial?
10. How could the commercial be improved?

Decision Analyst provides ad feedback about a week after an advertiser purchases the CopyCheck program. This type of program gives the company preparing the ad two major advantages. First, money is not wasted on ineffective ads. Second, the final ads have a much greater chance of stimulating the desired response.

Decision Analyst also provides feedback regarding the potential for effectiveness of a completed ad as well as tests of recall for ads that have run. Even a rocket that is "in orbit" occasionally needs to have its course adjusted.

The use of computers, the Internet, and more sophisticated research techniques have made it possible for many companies to spend advertising dollars more wisely. In a world where marketing departments and advertising account executives are being asked to produce tangible results, the use of these types of programs is likely to increase.[1]

99

OVERVIEW

John Wanamaker, a well-known nineteenth-century department store owner, was one of the first to use advertising to attract customers to his store. He once remarked, "I know half the money I spend on advertising is wasted, but I can never find out which half." Evaluating the effectiveness of advertising has become increasingly difficult. In an environment in which company executives demand measurable results, the challenge for advertising account executives and others who prepare ads is to offer evidence that a campaign will be successful *before* it is even launched along with additional proof *after* the ads have run. This is understandable, because company leaders are trying to allocate marketing funds wisely. A single advertising campaign can cost millions of dollars.

To meet this growing insistence for accountability, research and media experts spend more time and energy seeking to develop new and more accurate measures of success. These measures, known as **metrics**, should accurately portray the effectiveness of a marketing communications plan, which is not an easy task.

This final chapter is devoted to the various methods available for evaluating components of an IMC program. At the most general level, two broad categories of evaluation tools can be used to evaluate IMC systems: message evaluations and respondent behavior evaluations.

Message evaluation techniques examine the message and the physical design of the advertisement, coupon, or direct marketing piece. Message evaluation procedures include the study of actors in advertisements as well as the individuals who speak in radio ads. A message evaluation program considers the cognitive components associated with an ad, such as recall and recognition, as well as emotional and attitudinal responses.

Respondent behavior evaluations address visible customer actions, including store visits, inquiries, or actual purchases. This category contains evaluation techniques that are measured using numbers, such as the number of coupons that are redeemed, the number of hits on a microsite, and changes in sales.

The emphasis on providing compelling proof that advertising actually works has led to a greater emphasis on respondent behaviors. Higher sales, increases in store traffic, a greater number of daily Internet hits on a Web site, and other numbers-based outcomes appeal to many managers. At the same time, both message evaluations and behavioral responses should be used to help the marketing manager and advertising team build short-term results and achieve long-term success.

This advertisement for the Lafayette House could be tested using either a message evaluation or a respondent behavior technique.

A SANCTUARY that nurtures, empowers and improves the quality of lives.

Lafayette House SINCE 1978

Working to end domestic violence and substance abuse in our communities.

A United Way/United Fund member agency

Supported by the Domestic Violence Shelter Tax Credit Program, through the Missouri Department of Public Safety

MATCHING METHODS WITH IMC OBJECTIVES

Methods of evaluation should be chosen that match the objectives being measured.[2] When the objective of an advertising campaign is to increase customer interest in and recall of a brand, then the level of customer awareness should be measured. Normally, this means the marketing team measures awareness before and after the ads are run. This procedure is commonly known as *pretest* and *posttest* analysis. At other times objectives vary. For instance, redemption rates measure the success of a campaign featuring coupons, which means the behavior (purchasing) rather than the cognitive process (recall) is being tested. Redemption rates can reveal how many items were purchased, both with and without coupons.

Several levels are used to analyze an advertising or IMC program. They include the following:

- Short-term outcomes (sales, redemption rates)
- Long-term results (brand awareness, brand loyalty, or brand equity)
- Product-specific awareness
- Awareness of the overall company
- Affective responses (liking the company and a positive brand image)

Keep in mind that the temptation is to overemphasize the first factor, short-term outcomes, without considering the long-term impact of a campaign or marketing program. The company must maintain a voice that carries across campaigns over time. For example, consider the advertising conducted by Budweiser. Many ads achieved short-term success because they were funny. Anheuser-Busch has maintained a strong and consistent voice by using humor to promote products, from the Budweiser frogs and lizards to the "Whazzup" team, the "True" campaign, and more recent radio ads glorifying odd habits and occupations.

In light of the overall marketing and advertising goals, then, the marketing manager considers the various options for evaluating advertising. It helps to think about evaluation procedures prior to launching a particular campaign. Then, an ad placed in a trade journal may contain a code number, a special telephone number, or a special Internet microsite that can be used to track responses to a particular campaign. For coupons, premiums, and other sales promotions, code numbers are printed on each item to identify the source.

When assessing the advertising effectiveness, the date or time the commercial appeared can be important. An Internet banner ad campaign should be reviewed by keeping a record of inquiries or hits associated with the banner. In the same way, the dates a magazine reaches the newsstands and when subscribers receive copies are important items used in evaluating magazine ads.

In general, careful planning prior to initiating an IMC program makes evaluation of the campaign easier and more accurate. At the same time, the evaluation of a specific advertisement or marketing piece is difficult, because many factors affect the outcome being measured. For instance, a retailer may run a series of newspaper and radio ads to boost store traffic. In order to measure the impact of the ads, the retailer keeps records of store traffic before, during, and after the ad campaign. Unfortunately, the traffic count may be affected by other factors, even something as simple as the weather. If it rains for 2 days, the traffic count will probably be lower. Further, the store's chief competitor may be running a special sale during the same time period. This would also affect traffic. A TV program, such as the season finale of a major series, or even a special program at the local high school (commencement, school play), could have an impact. In other words, many extraneous factors can affect results. When reviewing an advertising program, it is important to consider these factors.

Also remember that one specific analysis does not assess the influence of the impact of an ad on a company's image. Even though store traffic was low, the ad may have been stored in the buyer's long-term memory, which may make a difference later. Conversely, the same ad may have been awkward or in some way offensive, and the store owner may believe the weather affected the outcome instead of a poor advertising design. Consequently, company leaders should consider both short-term consequences and long-term implications when assessing an IMC program.

YOU CAN'T RIDE OFF INTO THE SUNSET IF YOUR NEST EGG WON'T CARRY YOU. We're big believers in a long-term retirement plan based on objective financial advice. And in having a financial consultant who can help you every step of the way. To see whether your nest egg could benefit from such Midwestern horse sense, visit agedwards. com or call 866-379-4243.

A.G. EDWARDS.
FULLY INVESTED IN OUR CLIENTS.

Careful planning prior to launching a campaign can help a company such as A.G. Edwards better evaluate the effectiveness of advertising.

MESSAGE EVALUATIONS

Evaluation or testing of advertising communications occurs at every stage of the development process. This includes the concept stage before an ad is produced in which testing normally involves soliciting the opinions of either a series of experts or from "regular" people.

Ads are tested after the design stage is complete but prior to development. Many television ads are produced using a **storyboard**, which is a series of still photographs or sketches outlining the structure of the commercial. After the commercial is produced, experiments can be used to evaluate the ad. At that point, a group of consumers is invited to watch the ad in a

FIGURE 15.1
Message Evaluation Techniques and When to Use Them

Message Evaluation Method	When the Test Is Normally Used
◆ Concept testing	◆ Prior to ad development
◆ Copytesting	◆ Final stages of development or finished ad
◆ Recall tests	◆ Primarily after ad has been launched
◆ Recognition tests	◆ After ad has been launched
◆ Attitude and opinion tests	◆ Anytime during or after ad development
◆ Emotional reaction tests	◆ Anytime during or after ad development
◆ Physiological tests	◆ Anytime during or after ad development
◆ Persuasion analysis	◆ Primarily after ad has been launched

theater-type setting. The test ad is placed in a group of ads to disguise it. Viewers are then asked to evaluate all of the ads (including the test ad) to see if the test ad had the desired effect.

Before launching a campaign, an agency may show the ad in a *test market* area. Several tools are used to measure the quality and impact of the ad. These instruments will be presented in detail later in this chapter. The final stage of evaluation takes place after the marketing communications have run. Information collected at this time helps the company's leaders and the advertising agency to assess what worked and what did not. These findings are then used in the development of future campaigns.

Company leaders employ several methods to investigate the message content of an advertisement or marketing communication piece. These methods are listed in Figure 15.1, along with when the technique tends to be used. Although most of the methods deal with the verbal or written components of the communication piece, peripheral cues are also important and should be part of the message evaluation.

The ideal message evaluation scheme depends on the objectives of the communication plan. Most market researchers employ more than one method to ensure that the findings are as accurate as possible. Although each evaluation tool is discussed separately in this section, in most instances more than one is used. Also, as mentioned earlier, pretests and posttests normally are used for the purposes of making comparisons before and after a series of ads have run.

Concept Testing

Concept testing examines the proposed content of an advertisement and the impact that content may have on potential customers. Many advertising agencies conduct concept tests when developing an advertisement or promotional piece. The average cost of producing a national 30-second television ad is around $350,000.[3] It is clearly more cost-effective to test a concept in the early stages of an ad's development rather than after taping the commercial. If changes must be made, it is less costly to complete them during the planning stage than after the marketing piece has been completed. Once the marketing communication item is finished, creatives and others who worked on the piece tend to feel a sense of ownership and become resistant to making changes.

The most common concept testing procedure is a focus group. *Focus groups* normally consist of 8 to 10 people who are representative of the target market. These individuals are paid money or given financial incentives, such as gift certificates, to entice them to participate. In most cases, it is wise to use independent marketing research firms to conduct focus groups. The goal is to prevent biased results. An independent company is more likely to report that a certain advertising approach did not work than is someone who developed the approach and has a vested interest in it.

As a result of concept tests, the Newcomer, Morris, & Young Agency created this advertisement.

Show Your True Colors.

Flair
J·E·W·E·L·E·R·S
Monroe • West Monroe

◆ Copy or verbal component of an advertisement	◆ Effectiveness of peripheral cues, such as product placement in the ad and props used
◆ Message and its meaning	◆ Value associated with an offer or prize in a contest
◆ Translation of copy in an international ad	

FIGURE 15.2
Examples of Components of a Marketing Plan that Can Be Evaluated with Concept Tests

The number of focus groups used to study an issue varies greatly. It can be as many as 50 or as few as one. Focus group reactions can be quite different. Results are affected by the makeup of the group and the ways the session is conducted. As a result, it is risky to base a decision on just a single focus group's opinion. A humorous ad may have a great deal of appeal to one group, yet another might disagree or even find it offensive. It is a good idea to study the responses of several groups to study the impact of the humor on a series of individuals. Even trained focus group leaders experience varying results due to the composition of the group, the question being asked, and the degree of formality in the session. Further, one person's opinions may strongly influence the rest of the group. Therefore, most agencies use more than one group in order to ensure more reliable results. When several different focus groups arrive at the same conclusion, the finding is more reliable.

As highlighted in Figure 15.2, several components of a marketing communications plan can be evaluated with concept tests. Evaluations are typically performed using either comprehension or reaction tests, or both. *Comprehension tests* are used when participants in a study are asked the meaning of a proposed marketing communication piece. The idea is to make sure viewers correctly understand the message. The moderator can also explore the reasons why the intended message was misinterpreted.

Reaction tests are used to determine overall feelings about a proposed marketing piece, most notably whether the response is negative or positive. If the focus group reacts negatively to an ad concept or proposed copy, the agency can make the changes before the ad is developed. It is possible for an advertising concept to be correctly comprehended but elicit negative emotions. Therefore, exploring any negative feelings provides creatives with inputs to modify the marketing piece.

Copytesting

The second form of message evaluation, copytests, is used when the marketing piece is finished or in its final stages of development. **Copytests** are designed to elicit responses to the main message of the ad as well as the format used to present the message. For many television ads, copytests are conducted using a storyboard format or a version that is filmed by agency members rather than professional actors.

Two common copytesting techniques are portfolio and theater tests. Both place the marketing piece with other ads. A **portfolio test** is a display of a set of print ads, one of which is the ad being evaluated. A **theater test** is a display of a set of television ads, including the one being evaluated. The individuals who participate do not know which piece is under scrutiny. Both techniques mimic reality in the sense that consumers normally are exposed to multiple messages, such as when a radio or television station plays a series of commercials in a row or when a set of newspaper ads appears on a single page. The tests also allow researchers the opportunity to compare the target piece with other marketing messages. For these approaches to yield the optimal findings, it is essential that all of the marketing pieces shown be in the same stage of development (e.g., a set of storyboards or a series of nearly completed coupon offers).

Copytesting can utilize focus groups as well as other measurement devices. An ad or coupon that is in the final stage of design can be tested with a **mall intercept technique**. The approach involves stopping shoppers. They are asked to evaluate the item. The mall intercept technique can incorporate a portfolio approach. To do so, subjects are asked to examine the marketing piece, which is mixed in with 6 to 10 other ads, coupons, or other marketing communications pieces. This is a better approach than showing an item by itself. The disadvantage of displaying only one item is that people tend to give it a more positive evaluation than when it is mixed with others. Comprehension and reaction tests are commonly utilized in a mall intercept setting.

Source: Courtesy of Bob Daemmrich; The Image Works.

A mall intercept technique is often used for copy testing advertisements and other communication pieces.

Theater tests are often used to evaluate television commercials. The test ad is placed among other ads within a television documentary or a new show, such as a pilot episode of a new comedy or drama. The advantage of using a new show is that it is better able to hold the subject's interest. At the end of the program, the individuals participating in the study are asked for reactions to the ads. For more valid results, those participating in the study should not know which ad is being tested.

There is some controversy regarding copytesting. First, a number of advertisers and marketers strongly believe that copytesting favors rational approaches over affective or even conative methods. Second, some individuals believe copytests stifle the creativity that is needed to produce ads that will stand out in the clutter. Recently, creatives working for brands such as Nike, Volkswagen, Budweiser, and Target have been allowed to skip the copytesting phase of advertising design and move straight into production. The last reason given is that some agency leaders believe that copytests are likely to lead to ad messages about product benefits that are believable and understandable to members of a focus group. Most consumers know little, if anything, about how to create an effective ad. It may not make sense to have them serving as final judges of an ad's quality.

Although, a number of marketing professionals do not favor using copytests, the majority believe they are necessary, primarily due to accountability issues. When it is time to make a decision to go forward on a high-dollar campaign, advertising agency and company executives want evidence that supports the decision. A creative's "gut feeling" is difficult to justify in a corporate boardroom when millions of dollars are at stake. The members of an advertising agency may feel an ad is good and that copytesting wastes time and money, but they still recognize that company clients seeking top management approval of an ad campaign need evidence the ad will succeed. As a result, the client will want the ads tested. The copytesting techniques that are currently available may not be perfect, but it seems likely they will continue to be used.[4]

Recall Tests

Another popular method used to evaluate advertising is a **recall test**, which involves asking an individual to recall what ads he or she viewed in a given setting or time period. Then, in progressive steps, the subject is asked to identify information about the ad. Figure 15.3 lists some of the parts of an advertisement that can be tested for recall.

The most common form of recall test is the **day-after recall (DAR)** test. The DAR method is often used to evaluate TV advertisements. Individuals participating in the study are contacted by phone the day after the advertisement first appears. Normally, they are tested using an approach called **unaided recall**, in which the subjects are asked to name, or recall, the ads they saw or heard the previous evening, without being given any prompts or memory jogs. For magazines and newspaper ads, there are two approaches. In the first,

FIGURE 15.3
Items Tested for Recall

◆ Product name or brand
◆ Firm name
◆ Company location
◆ Theme music
◆ Spokesperson

◆ Tagline
◆ Incentive being offered
◆ Product attributes
◆ Primary selling point of communication piece

consumers are contacted the day after the ad appeared or they received the magazine. The individuals name the ads they recall and then are asked a series of questions to discover the features of the advertisements they remember. In the second, an individual is given a magazine for a certain period of time (normally 1 week) and instructed to read it as he or she normally would during leisure time. Then, the researcher returns and asks a series of questions about which ads became memorable and what features the individual could remember. In the business-to-business sector, the second method is a popular way to test ads for trade journals.

The day-after recall method works best when the objective is to measure the extent to which consumers have learned or remembered the content of an ad. DAR is a valuable test, because advertisers know that increased recall enhances the probability that the brand is becoming a part of the consumer's evoked set, or the primary choices remembered when purchase alternatives are considered. An evoked-set brand is much more likely to be purchased.[5]

The second type of recall test is the **aided recall** method. With this method, consumers are prompted by being told the product category and, if necessary, names of specific brands in the category. The respondent does not know which brand or ad is being tested. When the consumer states that he or she does recall seeing a specific brand being advertised, the person then is asked to provide as many details as possible about the ad. At that point, no further clues are given regarding the ad's content.

Most researchers believe the unaided recall approach is superior to other evaluative tests because it indicates an advertisement has become lodged in the person's memory. Unaided recall is also better than aided recall because some people may respond to a prompt by saying they do indeed remember an ad, even when they are uncertain. Recall scores are almost always higher when the aided recall method is used. Some ad agencies use both methods. First, they use unaided recall to gather basic information. Then, the researcher follows up with prompts to delve deeper into the memories that are present, even if it takes a little help to dig them out.

In both aided and unaided recall tests, if incorrect information is provided, the researcher continues the questioning. Individuals are not told they have given inaccurate answers. Incorrect responses are important data to record. Memory is not always accurate in both aided and unaided recall situations. Consequently, people give incorrect answers. In other words, they may mention commercials that did not actually appear during the test period, but rather were viewed at some other time. Although this may seem strange, bear in mind that the average person sees between 50 and 100 ads on a typical night of television viewing. It is easy to become confused.

An incorrect response is often triggered by exposure to a similar ad. For example, a person may remember seeing a commercial for Firestone tires when it was actually presented by Uniroyal. Seeing the Uniroyal ad triggered the recall of the Firestone brand because the individual is more familiar with Firestone or holds the brand in higher esteem. This type of error is more common in aided recall tests. In that situation, the individual is being provided with clues from a particular product category, which increases the odds of remembering the wrong brand.

Recall tests are used primarily after ads and marketing materials have been launched. They can also be used in the early stages of communication development. In those

3M

Growth through education

Post-it® Products for Kids are creating new learning opportunities in classrooms everywhere. Post-it® Education Notes aid reading readiness and can be produced in literally any language. 3M's commitment to new products for education markets is helping develop young minds. One more reason why Post-it® and Scotch® are among the world's most recognized brands. Visit Post-it.com/kids.

Post-it **Scotch**

3M, Post-it and Scotch are trademarks of 3M. © 3M 2006

Source: Courtesy of 3M/SPD.

This 3M advertisement could be tested using either aided or unaided recall to see if viewers noticed the Spanish wording.

FIGURE 15.4
Factors Researchers Must Keep in Mind When Evaluating Recall Tests

- The respondent's attitude towards advertising in general
- Prominence of the brand name in the ad
- Use or familiarity of the brand to the respondent
- Age of the respondent

instances, participants in the study are recruited, and the test is a more standard experimental design. For example, an agency that has created a new business-to-business ad may wonder if the ad would work when aired with consumer ads. Using a theater lab setting, the new ad can be placed in a documentary with other ads. At the end, either the aided or unaided recall method can be used to measure ad and brand awareness.

Advertisers consider three factors when evaluating recall tests (see Figure 15.4). The first is a person's general attitude toward advertising. Individuals who regularly watch ads, believe advertising helps them stay informed, and have positive attitudes toward advertising will have higher recall scores. It is important, therefore, to measure a person's general attitude toward advertising in evaluating recall scores.[6]

A second factor that impacts recall scores is the prominence of the brand name in the ad. Recall scores are highly sensitive to the presence of a brand name and its visibility or prominence in the ad. Television ad copy that mentions the brand name 7 times during the 30 seconds is likely to receive higher recall scores than an ad that states the name only once. A third factor appears because an individual is more likely to remember a brand name that she uses regularly, especially if it is featured prominently in the ad. Institutional ads normally have lower recall scores because of the difficulty in remembering the company's name.[7]

The fourth factor is the age of the respondent used in the recall tests. Recall scores tend to decline with age. Older people do not remember things as well. Table 15.1 displays average recall scores for different age segments using both DAR and brand recall instruments.[8] There are several explanations for lower recall scores in older people:

- They have reduced short-term recall capacity.
- Older persons are more fixed in terms of brand choices, making them less easily influenced by advertisements.
- The TV ads used to develop Table 15.1 may have been targeted more toward younger people.

For whatever reason, age does affect recall scores. Still, recall tests are valuable instruments used in testing to see if the ad has the potential to move into a person's long-term memory and affect future purchase decisions.

Recognition Tests

A **recognition test** is a format in which individuals are given copies of an ad and asked if they recognize it or have seen it before. Those who say they have seen the ad are asked to provide additional details about when and where the ad was encountered (e.g., specific television program, the name of the magazine, the location of the billboard, etc.). This information is collected to validate that it was indeed seen. Next the individual is asked a

TABLE 15.1 Impact of Age on DAR and Brand Recall

Day-After Recall		Brand Recall	
Age Segment	Average Recall	Age Segment	Average Recall
12–17	34%	13–17	70%
18–34	29%	18–34	53%
35–49	24%	35+	36%
50–65	22%		

Source: Based on Joel S. Debow, "Advertising Recognition and Recall by Age—Including Teens," *Journal of Advertising Research* 35, no. 5 (September–October 1995), pp. 55–60.

series of questions about the ad itself. This helps the researcher gather information and insights into consumer attitudes and reactions to the ad. Recognition tests are best suited to testing for comprehension of and reactions to ads. In contrast, recall tests tend to work well when testing brand and ad awareness. Recognition tests help when the advertiser is more concerned about how the ad is received and what information is being comprehended. This is especially important for ads using a cognitive message strategy, in which some type of reasoning process is invoked in persuading the consumer about the value of a product.

Unlike a recall test, a recognition test is not a memory test. Recognition measure a person's interest in a particular advertisement.[9] Ads that are of no interest do not register and are not remembered. In a recognition test, it is as if the respondent is saying, "Yes, advertisements of that kind usually attract my attention, so I did pause and look at it when I went through the magazine." An ad that a person likes is about 75 percent more likely to be recognized than an ad the individual did not like. This is one reason celebrities are selected for ads, such as the milk ad featuring Spike Lee in this section. If an individual likes the celebrity in the advertisement, then he or she will be more likely to recognize the ad. For ads the respondent thought were interesting, the odds of recognition were about 50 percent higher than for ads that were deemed not interesting.[10]

Further, when the consumer uses the brand being displayed in the ad, the likelihood of recognizing the ad rises. A person who uses a brand is about 50 percent more likely to recognize the ad than an individual who does not.

Using celebrities such as Spike Lee increases recall and recognition through greater interest in and liking of the ad.

Source: Courtesy of Bozell Worldwide Inc.

Researchers look beyond the number of respondents who recognize a particular ad. Questions are asked about the brands subjects normally buy in the product category, if they liked the ad, and if they found the ad to be interesting.

A recognition score is also affected by factors such as the color and size of the ad. Larger ads are more easily noticed, as are color ads (as compared to black and white).[11] As a result, when studying ad recognition the research team should also account for the size of the print ad, whether the ad is in color, and the length of the broadcast ad.

One difference between recognition scores and recall scores is that recognition scores do not decline over time, primarily because consumer interests remain relatively stable. If a person liked the milk ad with Spike Lee when he or she first viewed the ad, it is likely he or she will like the ad and recognize it in the future, even months after it first appeared.

Recognition and recall tests measure different things. Consequently, many research teams perform both tests on the same subjects. First, recall measures are used at the start of the interview and then recognition tests are given later. A subject may have viewed an ad during a particular TV show but not mention the ad when undergoing a recall test. The respondent can then be given a recognition test to see if he or she remembers seeing the ad.

Recall and recognition do have things in common. For one, both help to establish the brand in the consumer's mind.[12] Loyalty and brand equity are more likely to result. Therefore, even though recall and recognition are more oriented toward the short-term impact of a given ad or campaign, the long-term consequences of a series of successful and memorable ads should be considered.

Attitude and Opinion Tests

Many of the tests used to study advertisements and other marketing pieces are designed to examine attitudinal components. These types of instruments may be used in conjunction with recall or recognition tests. Attitude tests deal with both the cognitive and affective reactions to an ad. They are also used to solicit consumer opinions. Opinions are gathered

Conducting attitude tests would be important for Family Circle to ensure this advertisement will accomplish its stated objective.

from surveys or focus groups. They can be obtained as part of a mall intercept plan or even in laboratory settings. They can be used anytime during the ad development process or after the ad has been launched.

Roper Starch Worldwide developed a testing system called ADD+IMPACT. The goal of the program is to study consumer reactions to advertisements before they are launched. As part of the testing process, Roper conducts one-on-one interviews with 60 or more consumers. Each participant responds to open-ended questions as well as more standardized closed-ended attitudinal questions. The results of the test, transcripts, and a quantitative analysis of the numbers-based responses are provided to clients within 2 weeks of the test. By testing the ad prior to a launch, advertisers are more likely to know what people think about the ad and what type of reaction to expect. Changing an ad at this point is less costly than after a campaign has been launched.[13]

There are many aspects to the buying decision-making process. Attitudes and opinions are connected to short-term behaviors and longer-term assessments of a company and its products. Therefore, in addition to simply remembering that a firm exists, advertisers and IMC planners try to understand how people feel about the company in the context of larger, more general feelings.

Emotional Reaction Tests

This Chic Shaque advertisement could be tested using one of the emotional reaction methods.

Many ads are designed to elicit emotional responses from consumers. Emotional ads are based on the concept that ads eliciting positive feelings are more likely to be remembered. Also, consumers who have positive attitudes toward ads develop more positive attitudes toward the product. This, in turn, should result in increased purchases.[14]

It is difficult to measure the emotional impact of an advertisement. The simplest method is to ask questions about an individual's feelings and emotions after viewing a marketing communication piece. This can be accomplished in a laboratory setting or as a theater test. Also, the ad can be shown to focus groups. In all of these circumstances the test ad should be placed with other ads rather than by itself.

A **warmth monitor** is an alternative method developed to measure emotions. The concept behind the warmth monitor is that feelings of warmth are positive when they are directed toward an ad or a product. To measure warmth, subjects are asked to manipulate a joystick while watching a commercial. The movements track reactions to a commercial by making marks on a sheet of paper containing four lines. The four lines are labeled:

1. Absence of warmth
2. Neutral
3. Warmhearted or tender
4. Emotional

The warmth meter was developed to evaluate TV ads. It can be adapted to radio ads.[15]

A more sophisticated warmth meter was developed at the University of Hawaii. Individuals view advertisements in a theater-type lab featuring a big-screen television. Those who feel negatively about what they are watching pull a joystick downward. Those who feel more positively push the joystick in the opposite direction. Thus, as they are watching the commercial, the subjects constantly move the joystick, thereby conveying their feelings during every moment of the ad. The results of the 20 participants are tallied into one graph and then placed over the commercial. This technology allows an advertiser to see which parts of the ad elicit positive emotions and which parts elicit negative emotions. After graphing the test results, the group can then be used as a focus group to discuss the ad and to explain why group members felt the way they did at various moments of the ad.[16] The same technique has been adapted to political debates on television.

A similar technology has been developed by Reactions & Opinions, Inc., for use on the Internet. Reactions & Opinions can poll 1,000 or more people who view an advertisement online. As they watch the ad on streaming video, participants use a mouse to move a tab on a sliding scale from 1 to 10. If they like what they see, they slide the scale toward the 10. Those who don't like what they see slide the scale toward the 1. After the data have been collected, a graph can be superimposed over the advertisement. This shows the advertiser the likable and dislikable parts of the commercial. A major advantage of using the Internet is that subjects selected for the study can provide ratings at their convenience. If the agency needs a focus group to discuss the ad, subjects can be selected from the participants. The focus group session can even be held online.[17]

Most of the time, emotions are associated with shorter-term events, such as the reaction toward a given advertisement. At the same time, emotions are strongly held in the memories of most people. An ad that made a viewer angry may be retrieved, along with the accompanying anger, every time the individual remembers either the ad or the company. It is wise to attempt to discover emotional responses to ads before they are released.

Emotional advertising based on a substantial amount of pretesting led to a highly successful antismoking campaign in Minnesota. Based on focus group information, ads were structured to show the devastating effects of smoking (lost vocal chords) and of secondhand smoke on children. The ads were shown to groups of smokers and nonsmokers before being released because they were so dramatic and graphic. The net result was much stronger attitudes favoring smoke-free environments and additional calls to the state's quit-smoking hotline.[18]

Physiological Arousal Tests

Emotional reaction tests are *self-report* instruments. In other words, individuals report their feelings as they see fit. Although this may not be a flawed instrument, many marketing researchers are interested in finding ways to measure emotions and feelings without relying on people to self-report how they feel.

Physiological arousal tests measure fluctuations in a person's body functions that are associated with changing emotions. The primary physiological arousal tests are shown in Figure 15.5.

A **psychogalvanometer** measures a person's perspiration levels. It works by evaluating the amount of perspiration in the palm and fingers. As an individual reacts emotionally to a situation (in this case, an advertisement), the amount of perspiration generated changes. Perhaps you have noticed that you sweat when watching an exciting movie or sports event. This arousal indicates interest and emotional involvement. An ad producing these effects may be more memorable and powerful than something boring.

Emotional reactions can be negative or positive. The psychogalvanometer simply measures the individual's physiological reaction. One benefit of the psychogalvanometer

---

◆ Psychogalvanometer

◆ Pupillometric meter

◆ Psychophysiology

FIGURE 15.5
The Primary Physiological Arousal Tests

Physiological arousal tests could be used to study the impact of this advertisement for Maidenform.

is that it can be used to assess emotional reactions to many different types of marketing communication pieces, including television commercials, consumer promotions, and trade promotions.

A **pupillometric meter** measures the dilation of a person's pupil. Dilation levels also change with emotional arousal. A person who is frightened has wider pupils, as does someone who is excited. Pupil dilation can be studied as the subject views a television or print advertisement. Pupils dilate more when the person reacts positively to the ad or marketing communication. Pupils become smaller when the subject reacts negatively.

When conducting a test, the subject's head can be set in a fixed position. The dilation of the pupil can then be measured while viewing the ad. In this way, each aspect of the message can be evaluated for positive or negative responses. A graph can be superimposed on the commercial to show evaluators how each person responded to the advertisement.

In recent years, significant advances have occurred in **psychophysiology,** which is a brain-image measurement process. It tracks the flow and movement of electrical currents in the brain. One study demonstrated that the currents in a subject's brain indicate a preference for Coke or Pepsi that is the same as the product the person chooses in a blind taste test. According to neuroscientist Justin Meaux, "Preference has measurable correlates in the brain; you can see it." Richard Siberstein, an Australian neuroscientist, used physiological measurements of the brain to show that successful ads tend to generate higher levels of emotional engagement and long-term memory coding.[19]

To demonstrate how physiological tests work, consider an advertisement that is sexually provocative. In a focus group, respondents may enjoy the ad but cover up these feelings, stating that the ad is sexist and inappropriate. These reactions may be due to social pressure; they may also occur because the subjects want to be accepted by those around them. The same individual may not move the joystick to report his or her true feelings when participating in a study using the warmth monitor. The stigma attached to sex in advertising often affects self-reported reactions. Thus, a physiological arousal test may be a better indicator of a person's true response.

The most recent research in this area has been by companies such as EmSense, Neuro-Focus, and OTX Research. These companies are experimenting with portable devices that measure both brain waves and biologic data. Coca-Cola used this methodology to evaluate which ads to use on the 2008 Super Bowl. Coke produced a dozen ads, which were evaluated by the EmSense device, which is shaped like a thin, plastic headband. The EmSense measures brain waves and monitors breathing, heart rate, blinking of the eyes, and skin temperature of consumers as they watch ads. Through these physiological measurements, Coca-Cola researchers were able to determine which ads to use during the Super Bowl. Some Super Bowl ads were modified to produce higher levels of emotions.[20]

Many advertising researchers believe physiological arousal tests are more accurate than emotional reaction tests, because physiological arousal cannot easily be faked. As scientists gain a better understanding of physiological responses, the brain, and the electrical currents that move through the brain, the use of these methods of evaluation is likely to increase.[21]

Persuasion Analysis

The final type of message evaluation tool is designed to appraise the persuasiveness of a marketing communication item. There are other measures of awareness, emotions, liking, and physical reactions; however, these do not measure the ability of the marketing piece to persuade the consumer. Persuasion techniques require pretest and posttest assessments.

A researcher analyzing the persuasiveness of a television ad may start by gathering a group of consumers in a theater. Measures of brand attitudes and purchase intentions are then gathered for the test brand and other brands put in the study. A series of commercials is shown as part of a program. Next, measures are taken to see if any changes in attitude or purchase intentions resulted from exposure to the ads. The amount of change indicates how well the persuasion in the ad worked.

One company that conducts persuasion analysis programs is ASI Market Research. Typically, a sample of 250 consumers is recruited to attend a new television program. Once they are in the theater, the consumers are informed that prizes will be given away through a drawing. These individuals are asked to identify the specific brand they prefer in each product category. The subjects are then shown two new TV programs complete with commercials. At the end, the subjects are told that a product was inadvertently left off the initial survey, and they are asked to fill the form out again in order to enter the drawing. ASI compares before and after responses to the same questions in order to see if there were any changes in attitudes; the subjects are not aware of the intention of the study.[22]

Knowing the ad actually has persuasive power is a major advantage for the advertiser. Attempts to assess the impact of such ads before they are released to a wider audience are solid investments of marketing dollars.

EVALUATION CRITERIA

For all of the programs mentioned thus far, it is important to establish quality evaluation criteria. One helpful program is **positioning advertising copytesting (PACT)**, which was created to evaluate television ads. It was formulated by 21 leading U.S. advertising agencies.[23] Even though PACT examines the issues involved in copytesting television ads, the principles can be applied to any type of message evaluation system and all types of media. Figure 15.6 lists the nine main principles. These should be followed when a written or verbal marketing communication piece is being tested.

First, no matter which procedure is used, it should be *relevant to the advertising objective being tested.* If the objective of a coupon promotion is to stimulate trial purchases, then the test should evaluate the coupon's copy in order to determine its ability to stimulate trial purchases. On the other hand, an evaluation of attitudes toward a brand would require a different instrument.

Researchers should agree on how the results are going to be used when selecting test instruments. They should also agree on the design of the test in order to obtain the desired results. This is especially true for the preparation stage in an advertisement's development, because many tests are used to determine whether the advertisement eventually will be created.

The research team should also decide on a *cutoff score* to be used following the test. This will prevent biases from entering into the findings about the ad's potential effectiveness. Many ad agencies use test markets for new advertisements before they are launched in a larger area. A recall method used to determine if people in the target market remember seeing the ad should have a prearranged cutoff score. In other words, the acceptable percentage may be established so that 25 percent of the sample should remember the ad in order to move forward with the campaign. If the percentage is not reached, the ad has failed the test.

FIGURE 15.6
Copytesting Principles of PACT

- Testing procedure should be relevant to the advertising objectives.
- In advance of each test, researchers should agree on how the results will be used.
- Multiple measures should be used.
- The test should be based on some theory or model of human response to communication.
- The testing procedure should allow for more than one exposure to the advertisement, if necessary.

- In selecting alternate advertisements to include in the test, each should be at the same stage in the process as the test ad.
- The test should provide controls to avoid biases.
- The sample used for the test should be representative of the target sample.
- The testing procedure should demonstrate reliability and validity.

Source: Based on PACT document published in the *Journal of Marketing* 11, no. 4 (1982), pp. 4–29.

Using multiple measures allows for more precise evaluations of ads and campaigns. It is possible for a well-designed ad to fail one particular testing procedure yet score higher on others. Consumers and business buyers who are the targets of marketing communications are complex human beings. Various people may perceive individual ads differently. As a result, advertisers usually try to develop more than one measure so that there is greater agreement on whether the ad or campaign will succeed and reach its desired goals.

The test to be used should be *based on some theory or model of human response to communication.* This makes it more likely that the test will be a predictive tool of human behavior. The objective is to enhance the odds that the communication will actually produce the desired results (going to the Web site, visiting the store, or making a purchase) when the ad is launched.

Many testing procedures are based on a single exposure. Although in many cases this is sufficient for research purposes, there are times that *multiple exposures* are necessary to obtain reliable test results. For complex ads, more than one exposure may be needed. The human mind can comprehend only so much information in one viewing. It is vital to make sure the person can and does comprehend the ad in order to determine whether the ad can achieve its desired effects.

Often ads are tested in combination with other ads to disguise the one being examined. Placing the test marketing piece in with others means the test subjects do not know which ad is being evaluated. This prevents personal biases from affecting judgments. To ensure valid results, *the alternative ads should be in the same stage of process development.* Thus, if ad copy is being tested prior to ad development, then the alternative ads should also be in the ad copy development stage rather than established ads.

Next, adequate controls must be in place to *prevent biases and external factors from affecting results.* To help control external factors, experimental designs are often used. When conducting experiments, researchers try to keep as many things as constant as possible and manipulate only one variable at a time. For instance, in a theater test the temperature, time of day, room lighting, television program, and ads shown can all be the same. Then, the researcher may display the program and ads to an all-male audience followed by an all-female audience. Changing only one variable (gender) makes it possible to see if the ad, in a controlled environment, is perceived differently by men as opposed to women.

This does not mean that field tests are ineffective. Testing marketing communications in real-world situations is extremely valuable because they approximate reality. Still, when conducting field tests, such as mall intercepts, those performing the testing must try to control as many variables as possible. Thus, the same mall, same questions, and same ads are shown. Then, age, gender, or other variables can be manipulated one at a time.

As with any research procedure, sampling procedures are important. It is crucial for the *sample being used to be representative of the target population.* For example, if a print ad designed for Spanish-speaking Hispanic Americans is to be tested, the sample used in the test normally will be in Spanish.

Finally, researchers must continually try to make tests *reliable and valid.* Reliable means "repeatable." In other words, if the same test is given five times to the same person, the individual should respond in the same way each time. If a respondent is "emotional" on one iteration of a warmth test and "neutral" when the ad is shown a second time, the research team will wonder if the test is reliable.

Valid means "generalizable." Valid research findings can be generalized to other groups. For instance, when a focus group of women finds an ad to be funny, and then

In evaluating this television storyboard, it is important that the sample used in the evaluation represent the target market for Maidenform.

Maidenform, Inc.
"PTA" :30
XMEI-4143

(MUSIC UNDER)

(FEMALE VO): This is the bra

that goes under the sweater

which is worn by the woman

who attends the school meeting

where she speaks her piece

which causes the vote

that throws the bums out

and makes way for a set of reforms so popular,

the school is renamed

in her honor.

Maidenform. What's your lingerie doing for you?

MAIDENFORM

a group of men reacts in the same way, the finding that the humor is effective is more valid. This would be an increasingly valuable outcome if the results were generalizable to people of various ages and races. Many times an ad may be reliable, or repeatable in the same group, but not valid or generalizable to other groups of consumers or business buyers.

The PACT principles are helpful when designing tests of short-term advertising effectiveness. They are also helpful when seeking to understand larger and more long-term issues such as brand loyalty and identification with the company. The goal is to generate data that document what a company is doing works. When this occurs, the company and its advertising team have access to invaluable information.

BEHAVIORAL EVALUATIONS

The first part of this chapter regarding message evaluations focuses on insights into what people think and feel. Some marketers contend that the only valid evaluation criterion is *actual sales*. It is less important for an ad to be enjoyed; if it does not increase sales it is ineffective. The same reasoning is applied to other marketing communication tools, such as consumer promotions, trade promotions, and direct marketing tactics.

It is reasonable to believe that tangible results should be the bottom line of any marketing program; however, not all communication objectives can be measured using sales figures. Leaders of companies with low brand awareness may be most interested in the visibility and memorability aspects of a communication plan, even though a marketing program designed to boost brand awareness does not result in immediate sales.

Measuring the results of a consumer promotion campaign featuring coupons using sales figures is easier to do than measuring the results of an advertising campaign on television. Consequently, effective promotions evaluations should involve the study of both message and behavioral elements. In this section, various behavioral measures are discussed. Figure 15.7 lists the common behavioral techniques.

Sales and Response Rates

Measuring changes in sales following a marketing campaign is relatively simple. Universal product codes and scanner data are available from many retail outlets. These data are available on a weekly and, in some situations, daily basis. It is available by store. Many retail outlets even have access to sales information on a real-time basis and the information can be accessed at any point during the day.

Scanner data make it possible for companies to monitor sales and help both the retailer and the manufacturer discover the impact of a particular marketing program. Remember that extraneous factors can affect sales. In a multimedia advertising program, it would be difficult to know which ad moved the customer to action. A company featuring a fall line of jackets may be affected by a cold snap. If so, what caused the customer to buy—the ad or the weather? Firms utilizing trade and consumer promotion programs must account for the impact of both the promotion and the advertising when studying sales figures. Sales are one indicator of effectiveness; however, they may be influenced by additional factors.

As highlighted in Figure 15.8, advertisements are probably the most difficult component of the IMC program to evaluate, for several reasons. First, as just discussed, it is difficult to distinguish *the effects of advertising from other factors*. This is because ads have short- and long-term effects, and consumers and businesses see ads in so many different contexts. Thus, the direct impact of one ad or one campaign on sales is difficult to decipher.

Second, *advertising often has a delayed impact*. Many times consumers encounter ads and are persuaded to purchase the product, but will not actually make the buy until later, when they actually need the item. A woman may be convinced that she wants to buy

◆ Sales	◆ Test markets
◆ Response rates	◆ Purchase simulation tests
◆ Redemption rates	

FIGURE 15.7
Behavioral Measures

- ◆ Influence of other factors
- ◆ Delayed impact of the ads
- ◆ Consumers changing their minds while in the store
- ◆ Whether the brand is in the consumer's evoked set
- ◆ Level of brand equity

a new pair of jeans in response to a sexy and effective advertisement by Calvin Klein. Still, rather than buying them herself, she leaves several well-placed hints for her husband before her next birthday, which could be several months later. The problem is that her husband may have purchased another brand or a different gift. So, she either waits for another special occasion for her husband to purchase the jeans or she makes the purchase herself at a later time.

Third, many times consumers may decide to make purchases based on an advertisement but *change their minds when they arrive at the retail store*. A competing brand may be on sale, the store could be out of the desired brand, or the salesperson could persuade the customer that another brand is better. In each case, the ad was successful on one level but another factor interfered before the purchase was made.

Fourth, *the brand being advertised may not be part of the consumer's evoked set.* Upon hearing or seeing the ad, however, the brand is moved into the evoked set. Thus, even when the brand is not considered at first, it will be in the future when the need arises or when the consumer becomes dissatisfied with a current brand.

Fifth, advertising is an essential component of building brand awareness and brand equity. Although sales may not be the result immediately, *the ad may build brand equity,* which in turn will influence future purchases.

It is easier to measure the effects of trade and consumer promotions, direct marketing programs, and personal selling on actual sales. Manufacturers can study the impact of trade promotions by observing changes in sales to the retailers at the time the promotions are being offered. The same is true for consumer promotions, such as coupons, contests, and point-of-purchase displays. Many manufacturers' representatives push hard to get retailers to use the company's POP displays. At the same time, the retailer is more interested in the effects of the display on sales. Using scanner data, both the retailer and the manufacturer can measure the impact of a POP display. Retailers normally use POPs that have demonstrated the ability to boost sales.

To track the impact of POP displays, Anheuser-Busch, Frito-Lay, Procter & Gamble, and Warner-Lambert joined together as initial sponsors of a program developed by Point-of-Purchase Advertising International (POPAI). In the initial study, POPAI tracked 25 different product categories in 250 supermarkets nationwide. Sponsors paid between $50,000 and $75,000 to receive customized data about the POP displays featuring particular brands. One advantage of using POPAI data is that each firm not only can see the impact of the POP for its brand, but also receive comparative data showing how well the display fared against other displays. The major advantage of the POPAI program is its low cost. Sponsors of the POPAI program attained valuable data at a much lower cost than if they had sought the information on their own.[24]

A wide variety of responses to marketing communications programs are available besides sales. Figure 15.9 lists some of the responses that can be tracked. These items are described in the remainder of this section.

One method of measuring the impact of an advertisement, direct mailing piece, TV direct offer, or price-off discount to a business customer is to assign a *toll-free number* to each marketing piece. A great deal of information can be collected during an inbound

- ◆ Changes in sales
- ◆ Telephone inquiries
- ◆ Response cards
- ◆ Internet responses
- ◆ Direct-marketing responses
- ◆ Redemption rate of sales promotion offers—Coupons, premiums, contests, sweepstakes

call. Sales data can be recorded and demographic information gathered. Psychographic information then can be added by contacting various commercial services.

In business-to-business situations, a toll-free number provides contact names to help the vendor discover who is performing the various functions in the buying center. As a result, a toll-free number provides sales data to determine which marketing program is the best and also can be used to generate valuable customer information that can be tied to the sales data. Knowing who is responding to each offer helps a firm better understand its customers and the approach that should be used for each target group.

Reduce the signs of aging

Introducing

COOLTOUCH
The new laser system designed to reduce wrinkles and rejuvenate your skin with no downtime

Schedule your complimentary CoolTouch consultation today!

Before

After

Frank W. Shagets, M.D.
417-623-5111

One measure of effectiveness of this advertisement is the increase in the number of phone calls to schedule a consultation.

Another method for measuring behaviors comes from *response cards*. These customer information forms are filled out at the time of an inquiry. The primary disadvantage of response cards is that less data are obtained. Consequently, commercial sources are needed to obtain additional demographic and psychographic information. This is because response cards solicited from current customers contain information the firm is already likely to have in its database.

Internet responses are excellent behavioral measures. By using cookies, a marketing team can obtain considerable information about the person or business making the inquiry. In addition, many times the person or business responding is willing to provide a great deal of helpful information voluntarily. It is also possible to track responses to direct advertising through Internet views. For instance, the Canadian Tourism Commission tested direct-response ads that were placed on television, radio, direct mail, and online. Each ad used a different URL for viewers to access for additional information. To the tourist, there was no perceivable difference, because each URL took the person to the designated Canadian Tourism site. The Tourism Commission could easily track which ad the person viewed and which URL the person used. This made it possible to count the number of visitors from each of the direct-response advertisements.[25] The next section goes into more detail about online evaluation methods.

Various kinds of redemption rates can be used as behavioral effectiveness measures. Coupons, premiums, contests, sweepstakes, and direct-mail pieces can be coded to record redemption rates. Comparing a current campaign with previous campaigns makes it possible for a firm to examine changes made in the design or execution of an ad. The results are reviewed in light of positive or negative changes in redemption rates.

Immediate changes in sales and redemptions are one form of behavioral evaluation. It is tempting for the advertiser and company to use them and fail to see "the forest for the trees." One campaign, advertisement, or promotions program should be viewed in the context of all other marketing efforts. Behavioral measures are best when the team sees them as part of the bigger picture.

Online Metrics

To evaluate interactive marketing communications from the Internet, a number of metrics are available that provide hard data as well as soft data. Figure 15.10 identifies methods of measuring interactive marketing and the percentage of companies using each method.

Clickthroughs are still the number one way companies measure the impact of online advertising. It provides companies an idea of how many people who see an online ad click on it and go to the new Web site. Once there, other metrics that are being used include length of engagement, redemption and response rates, and sales. Redemption rates and response rates occur when visitors to the site take some action and of course sales occur when the individual makes an actual purchase. A newer metric that is being used is length of engagement, which measures how long the person stays at the site. It is a surrogate measure of a person's interest in the product and site being visited.

FIGURE 15.10
Methods of Measuring the Effectiveness of Interactive Marketing

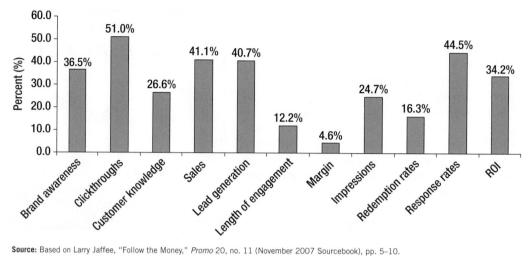

Source: Based on Larry Jaffee, "Follow the Money," *Promo* 20, no. 11 (November 2007 Sourcebook), pp. 5–10.

Online metrics examine many of the message and behavioral concepts discussed earlier in the chapter. Brand awareness and customer knowledge are message evaluations. Lead generation, margin, impressions, and ROI are considered to be behavioral-type responses, because they measure activities and are quantitative in nature.

AdKnowledge introduced an online management tool called MarketingMatch Planner to evaluate Internet advertising campaigns. MarketMatch Planner software includes two components: Campaign Manager and Administrator. Campaign Manager records traffic to a site and performs postbuy analysis. Administrator integrates Web ad-buy data and performance analysis with the firm's accounting and billing systems. In addition, MarketMatch Planner has the capability of integrating third-party data, including audience demographics, from the following sources:

- MediaMetrix for basic demographics
- NetRatings for GRP and other ratings instruments
- Psychographic data from SRI Consulting
- Web site ratings and descriptions from NetGuide
- Web traffic audit data from BPA Interactive

Interactive data should be evaluated carefully. Results should be viewed in light of the company's IMC objectives. An IMC objective of building brand awareness requires something other than Internet sales data to be assessed. An Internet ad can bring awareness to a brand but not lead to an online purchase. This might occur, for example, when a consumer or business uses the Internet to gather information but then makes the actual purchase at a retail store, by telephone, or by fax. When that happens, the impact of an Internet advertising campaign may not be able to reflect all of the brand awareness or sales that the campaign generated.

By using technology such as MarketingMatch Planner the McCormick company can track who goes to the Web site for recipes.

YOUR CLIENT CUT YOUR DEADLINE. AT LEAST DINNER CAN GO ON AS PLANNED.

CHICKEN DIJON

Delicious Dijon sauce. Savory chicken breasts. All the makings of a mouth-watering meal, in just 25 minutes. So no matter what they do at work, it won't hurt your dinner plans. Look for it in our color-coded Meal Idea Center. For more chicken ideas, look for the yellow packages or click to www.mccormick.com.

McCormick
The taste you trust

Test Markets

Another form of behavioral response is a test market. Test markets are used when company leaders examine the effects of a marketing effort on a small scale before launching a national or international campaign. The primary advantage of test markets is that an organization can examine several elements of a marketing communication program. If the test market is successful, then it is likely that the national campaign also will be effective. It is also an excellent method of testing a campaign in a new country before launching a full-scale international campaign. Test market programs can be used to assess:

- Advertisements
- Consumer and trade promotions
- Pricing tactics
- New products

Test markets are cost-effective methods to analyze and make changes in marketing efforts before millions of dollars are spent on something that will not accomplish the intended objectives. Ads can be modified, promotions revised, and pricing policies revisited before a more widespread program is undertaken. For example, McDonald's tested new ads that touted cleaner restaurants and friendlier service. The goal of the ads was to test a campaign emphasizing McDonald's effort to improve in-store and drive-through service. Two television spots and one radio spot were produced and aired in Tampa and Seattle. Reactions from the test markets provided McDonald's marketing team and the advertising agency information about the impact of ad campaign, the parts of the ad that should be modified, and whether the campaign should be launched nationally.[26]

One major advantage of a test market is that it resembles an actual situation more than any of the other tests discussed thus far. The key is to make sure that the site selected for the test market strongly resembles the target population. A product targeted toward senior citizens should be studied in an area with a high concentration of senior citizens.

It is also important to design the test marketing campaign as close to the national or full marketing plan as possible. A lengthy time lapse may cause a company to experience differing results. The goal is to make sure the test market is a mirror image of the actual marketing program.

A test market can be as short as a few days or as long as 2 to 3 years. The longer the test market program runs, the more accurate the results. A test that is too short may yield less reliable results. If the test market is too long, the national market situation may change and the test market may no longer be a representative sample. The greater fear, however, is that the competition is able to study what is going on. This gives competitors time to react to the proposed marketing campaign.

Competing companies can respond to a test market program in one of two ways. First, some firms may introduce a special promotion in the test market area in order to confound the results. This may reduce the sales for the product or campaign, making it appear less attractive than it actually is. The second approach is not to intervene in the test market, but to use the time to prepare a countermarketing campaign. Firms that use this tactic are ready when the national launch occurs, and the impact may be that the test market results are not as predictive of what will happen.

Scanner data make it possible for results from test market campaigns to be quickly available. The figures can be studied to determine if test market results are acceptable. A firm also can design several versions of a marketing campaign in different test markets. Through scanner data, the firm can compare the sales from each test market to determine which version is the best. For example, in one test market the firm may present an advertising campaign only. In the second test market coupons may be added to the ad program. In test market three, a premium can be combined with advertising. The results from each area help the marketing team understand which type of marketing campaign to use.

Other test markets can study different prices in different regions in order to determine the price to charge and the elasticity associated with that price. It is also possible to vary the size of the coupon or premium to discover the impact. Rather than making a change at the national level, company leaders can modify the consumer promotion in selected markets to see what happens.

Test marketing offers the opportunity to test communication ideas in more true-to-life settings. They can be used for trade and consumer promotions, direct marketing, and other marketing communication tools. They are not quite as accurate when assessing advertising because changes in sales take longer, and the test market program may not be long enough to measure the full impact. In any case, test markets are valuable instruments to use when examining specific marketing features and more general communications campaigns.

Purchase Simulation Tests

Instead of using test markets, marketing researchers can use purchase simulation tests. Consumers can be asked in several ways if they would be willing to buy products. For instance, they could be asked about purchase intentions at the end of a laboratory experiment. In this situation, however, intentions are self-reported and tend not to be an accurate predictor of future purchase behaviors.

A useful and cost-effective approach to examine purchase behaviors is called a *simulated purchase test*. Research Systems Corporation (RSC) is a leading marketing research firm that specializes in purchase simulation studies. RSC tests the impact of commercials by studying consumer behaviors in a controlled laboratory environment.

RSC does not ask consumers to render opinions, describe their attitudes, or even ask if they plan to purchase the product. Instead, RSC creates a simulated shopping experience. Subjects are able to choose from a variety of products they would see on a normal store shelf. After completing a simulated shopping exercise, the subjects are seated and watch a television preview containing various commercials. The participants are asked to watch the TV preview as they would watch any TV show at home. The test ad is placed in with other ads, and the subjects do not know which ad is being tested.

When the preview is completed, the subjects are asked to participate in a second shopping exercise. Researchers then compare the products chosen in the first shopping trip to those selected in the second. Shifts in brand choices are at least partly due to the effectiveness of the advertisement, because it is the only variable that has changed.

A major advantage of this methodology is that the test procedures do not rely on opinions and attitudes. Among other things, this means that RSC's procedure can be used in international markets as well as domestic markets.[27] In some cultures, subjects tend to seek to please the interviewer who asks questions about opinions and attitudes. As a result, the answers are polite and socially acceptable. The same subjects may also seek to provide answers they think the interviewer wants to hear. By studying purchases instead of soliciting opinions, subjects are free to respond in a more accurate fashion.

Any methodology designed to tap into behaviors rather than emotions and feelings has a built-in advantage. Opinions and attitudes change and can be quickly affected by other variables in a situation. Observing behaviors and changes in behaviors gets more quickly to the point of the experiment, which is whether the buyer can be influenced in a tangible way by a marketing communications tool.

In summary, the systems designed to examine respondent behaviors are response rates, online metrics, test markets, and purchase simulation tests. Many of these programs are used in conjunction with one another and also with the message evaluation techniques described earlier. None of these approaches is used in a vacuum. Instead, the data generated and findings revealed are tested across several instruments and with numerous groups of subjects. In that manner, the marketing department manager and the advertising agency can try to heighten the odds that both short- and long-term goals can be reached through the ads, premiums, coupons, and other marketing communications devices used. Even then, the job of evaluation is not complete.

EVALUATING PUBLIC RELATIONS ACTIVITIES

Most public relations can be studied using one or more of the evaluation techniques that have already been described. Many times, however, company leaders use four additional methods. These evaluation techniques are listed in Figure 15.11.

The first approach involves obtaining the number of clippings. The number of clippings can be obtained when a company subscribes to what is called a *clipping service.*

◆ Number of clippings   ◆ Advertising equivalence technique
◆ Number of impressions   ◆ Comparison to public relations objectives

FIGURE 15.11
Methods of Evaluating Public Relations

The service scours magazines, journals, and newspapers looking for a client company's name. The number of clippings found is then compared to the number of news releases that were sent out. A firm that sends out 400 news releases that results in 84 clippings would have a 21 percent return.

The second approach, which became popular in the 1990s, is to calculate impressions. *Impressions* are counted as the total number of subscribers and purchasers of a print medium or the number of viewers of a broadcast medium in which the client company's name has been mentioned. For example, when a company's name is mentioned in a newspaper article with a circulation of 800,000 and newsstand sales of 150,000, then the total number of impressions is 950,000.

Although clippings and impressions are the most frequently utilized measures of PR success, both ignore whether an article spoke positively or negatively about the company. Any clipping is counted when the company's name is mentioned, no matter the context. Unfortunately, this means an article criticizing the company counts as much as one praising the company. With impression counts, everyone who subscribes to or buys a magazine or newspaper is part of the total. No effort is made to see what percentage of those who bought the paper or magazine actually saw the company name or read the article.[28]

Firms that continue to use clippings and impressions can modify these techniques when possible. Clippings can be sorted into piles of positive and negative articles in order to see which occurs more frequently. Also, evaluators should summarize what was said in the article rather than simply noting that the company's name was mentioned. It is also helpful to note if the article, whether negative or positive, appeared in a setting that would reach the company's customers or if it is "buried" somewhere with less importance.

For impressions, surveys are conducted to indicate the percentage of the total audience that saw or heard the company's name. This can be accomplished by using recall or recognition tests, or both. In addition, attitude questions can be posed to see how people reacted to what was in the story. Again, merely counting impressions does not provide adequate feedback about a PR campaign.

The problems associated with clippings and impressions have led to a third method used to measure public relations effectiveness. The approach, called *advertising equivalence,* involves finding every place the company name was mentioned in print and broadcast media. Then, the market researcher calculates the cost of the time or space as if it were a paid advertisement. For example, if the company is discussed in an article that occupies one-half page of a magazine, the firm finds out the cost of a half-page ad. A similar approach is used for TV publicity. The cost of an ad running for the amount of time the company was discussed on the air is calculated. This method is only useful when positive publicity stories are counted.

The least used but best method involves examining the public relations piece in *comparison to the company's PR objectives.* Many times, the objective of a particular PR campaign is to increase awareness of the firm or product's name. Evaluation includes developing an index of awareness before a PR campaign begins. Then, after the PR event, awareness is measured a second time to see if it actually increased. This kind of information is valuable in the motion picture industry. When celebrities make personal appearances and visits to talk shows in the effort to generate publicity, awareness should increase.

In other situations, the goal of a PR campaign is to build a positive image for the company because of bad publicity or some other negative event. Again, the image should be measured before and after the PR campaign. The goal is to see if the image changed and, if so, to what degree. This approach is time-consuming and difficult. It may take time for a PR campaign to have a full impact. Still, many public relations teams are interested in knowing whether their efforts are working.

Each of these methods is based on the goal of discovering the impact of the PR program. When combined with assessments of the effectiveness of advertisements and behavioral responses, the company has a fairly solid grasp regarding what is going on in the current marketplace. Completion of a full IMC evaluation involves one more crucial process.

EVALUATING THE OVERALL IMC PROGRAM

As has been noted throughout this textbook, the huge expenditures companies make on marketing communications has led CEOs and other executives to continue to push for greater accountability. These individuals, as well as stockholders and boards of directors, want to know what type of return results when a firm spends a large sum of money on an advertising campaign or other marketing activity. The idea is to try to discover the *return on investment (ROI)* of an advertising and promotions program.

The problem is that there is no agreement about what the ROI means when it is applied to a marketing program. There is also no consensus on how to measure marketing ROI. In one study, more than 70 percent of marketers said it would be difficult to measure the impact of advertising and marketing on sales. The same number predicted that it would be extremely difficult for the marketing industry to reach any agreement on what constitutes ROI for marketing. Table 15.2 lists some of the potential definitions of marketing ROI. The most commonly used descriptions of ROI are behavioral responses, such as incremental sales, total sales, and market share. Notice that the measures used to set prices for advertising time and space, such as gross rating points delivered and reach/frequency achieved, are not often considered the best definition of ROI.[29]

This confusion is likely to continue, even as company executives try to justify advertising and marketing expenditures. This means those in the marketing profession should keep trying to identify some way to measure the impact of marketing communications, ultimately in dollars and cents.

Many years ago, Peter Drucker outlined a series of goal areas that are indicative of organizational health. These goals match very well with the objectives of an IMC program and are listed in Figure 15.12.[30] As marketers struggle to find a way to measure ROI of marketing communication expenditures, understanding the various measures of overall health of an organization can provide valuable insight on how marketing communications contributes.

Market share has long been linked to profitability. It demonstrates consumer acceptance, brand loyalty, and a strong competitive position. A promotions opportunity analysis should help the marketing team understand both market share and the relative strengths and weaknesses of the competition. IMC programs are designed to hold and build market share.

TABLE 15.2 Definitions of ROI for Marketing

Definition of ROI	Percent Using
Incremental sales from marketing	66%
Changes in brand awareness	57
Total sales revenue from marketing	55
Changes in purchase intentions	55
Changes in market share	49
Ratio of advertising costs to sales	34
Reach/frequency achieved	30
Gross rating points delivered	25
Post-buy analysis comparing the media plan to its delivery	21

Source: Paul J. Cough, "Study: Marketers Struggle to Measure Effectiveness," *Shoot* 45, no. 29 (August 20, 2004), pp. 7–8.

FIGURE 15.12
Measures of Overall Health of a Company

◆ Market share	◆ Profitability
◆ Level of innovation	◆ Manager performance and development
◆ Productivity	◆ Employee performance and attitudes
◆ Physical and financial resources	◆ Social responsibility

Source: Based on Peter Drucker, *Management: Tasks, Responsibilities, Practices* (New York: Harper and Row, 1974).

Innovation is finding new and different ways to achieve objectives. This applies to many marketing activities, including new and unusual trade and consumer promotions, public relations events and sponsorships, e-commerce and e-active programs, and the firm's advertising efforts.

Productivity is reflective of the industry's increasing emphasis on results. IMC experts are being asked to demonstrate tangible results from IMC campaigns. Both short- and long-term measures of the effects of advertisements and promotions demonstrate the "productivity" of the organization in terms of gaining new customers, building recognition in the marketplace, determining sales per customer, and through other measures.

Physical and financial resources are also important to an IMC program. Physical resources include the most up-to-date computer and Internet capabilities. The firm must provide sufficient financial resources to reach this goal. Scanner technologies and other devices that keep the firm in contact with consumers are vital elements in the long-term success of an IMC plan.

Profitability is vital for the marketing department and the overall organization. Many IMC managers know that more than sales are at issue when assessing success. Sales must generate profits in order for the company to survive and thrive.

Manager performance and development is possibly an overlooked part of an IMC program. Effective marketing departments and advertising agencies must develop pipelines of new, talented creatives, media buyers, promotions managers, database Webmasters, and others in order to succeed in the long term. Also, new people must be trained and prepared for promotion for more important roles.

Employee performance and attitudes reflect not only morale within the marketing department, but also relations with other departments and groups. An effective IMC plan consists of building bridges with other internal departments so that everyone is aware of the thrust and theme of the program. Satisfied and positive employees are more likely to help the firm promote its image.

Social responsibility is linked to the long-term well-being of an organization. Brand equity and loyalty are hurt when the firm is known for illegal or unethical actions. Therefore, marketing leaders should encourage all of the members of an organization to act in ethical and socially responsible ways.

When these goals are being reached, it is likely that the firm's IMC program is working well. Beyond these targets, IMC plans continually should emphasize the evolving nature of relationships with customers. Retail consumers and business-to-business buyers should be constantly contacted to find out how the company can best serve their needs.

Simply stated, every chapter in this book implies a series of key performance targets for IMC programs that should guide the actions of the marketing department and the advertising agency both in the short term and for the long haul. Firms that are able to maintain one clear voice in a cluttered marketplace stand the best chance of gaining customer interest and attention as well as developing long-term bonds with all key publics and stakeholders. An effective IMC program helps set the standards and measure performance and, in the end, becomes the model for marketing success for the entire organization.

INTERNATIONAL IMPLICATIONS

Many of the techniques described in this chapter are available worldwide. IMC programs should be assessed in several ways, including: (1) domestic results, (2) results in other countries, and (3) as an overall organization.

Individual advertisements and promotional programs are examined within the countries in which they appear. Due to differing standards regarding advertising content, they must be evaluated in light of local cultures and purchasing habits.

Many times, advertising and promotional programs must be assessed across national boundaries. For example, a campaign launched in Europe leads to evaluations in individual countries such as France, Spain, and Italy, but also as a collective, such as the European Union. Measures of attitudes are difficult to collect. Sales are easier to assess due to the use of the Euro in all of these nations; however, inflation rates and other statistics are affected by local conditions.

It may be advisable to contract with local advertising agencies to discover which techniques are most viable in other countries. In some nations the use of coupons is seen as a sign of poverty, and users are either secretive or embarrassed about redeeming them. In those situations it is helpful to study results in light of the cultural norms that are present.

Numerous multinational conglomerates assess advertising and promotional efforts through regional offices. Pacific Rim information will be combined with information from Europe, Africa, and other places. The goal is to make sure an overall image and theme is projected worldwide.

SUMMARY

Assessing an IMC program often involves examining the effects of individual advertisements. These efforts are conducted in two major ways: (1) message evaluations and (2) evaluating respondent behaviors. A wide variety of techniques can be used. Most of the time, marketing managers and advertisement agencies use several different methods in order to get the best picture of an ad's potential for success. Advertisements are studied before they are developed, while they are being developed, and after they have been released or launched.

The guiding principles for any marketing tool include agreement on how test results will be used, pre-establishing a cutoff score for a test's results, using multiple measures, basing studies on models of human behaviors, using multiple exposures, testing marketing instruments that are in the same stage of development, and preventing as many biases as possible while conducting the test. Many times it is difficult for certain members of the marketing team to be objective, especially when they had the idea for the

ad or campaign. In these instances, it is better to retain an outside research agency to study the project.

Public relations programs should be assessed in light of not only how many times a company is mentioned in the media but also what various ads and stories said about the company. Also, public relations efforts should be compared with the goals for the department in order to see if the company is achieving the desired effects with its publicity releases and sponsorship efforts.

IMC plans are general, overall plans for the entire company. Therefore, more general and long-term criteria should be included in any evaluation of an IMC program. When the IMC theme and voice are clear, the company is achieving its long-range objectives, the principles stated in this book are being applied efficiently and effectively, and the company is in the best position to succeed at all levels, including in all international operations.

KEY TERMS

metrics   Measures that are designed to accurately portray the effectiveness of a marketing communications plan.

message evaluation techniques   Methods used to examine the creative message and the physical design of an advertisement, coupon, or direct marketing piece.

respondent behavior evaluations   Methods used to examine visible customer actions including making store visits, inquiries, or actual purchases.

storyboard   A series of still photographs or sketches that outlines the structure of a television ad.

concept testing   An evaluation of the content or concept of the ad and the impact that concept will have on potential customers.

copytests   Tests that are used to evaluate a marketing piece that is finished or is in its final stages prior to production.

portfolio test   A test of an advertisement using a set of print ads, one of which is the ad being evaluated.

theater test   A test of an advertisement using a set of television ads, including the one being evaluated.

mall intercept technique   A test where people are stopped in a shopping mall and asked to evaluate a marketing item.

recall tests   An approach in which an individual is asked to recall ads he or she has viewed in a given time period or setting.

day-after recall (DAR)   Individuals participating in a study are contacted the day after an advertisement appears to see if they remember encountering the ad.

unaided recall   A test in which subjects are asked to name, or recall, the ads without any prompts or memory jogs.

aided recall   A test in which consumers are prompted by being told such information as the product category and, if necessary, names of specific brands to see if they recall an ad.

recognition tests   A test format in which individuals are given copies of an ad and asked if they recognize it.

warmth monitor   A method to measure emotional responses to advertisements.

psychogalvanometer   A device that measures perspiration levels.

pupillometric meter   A device that measures the dilation of a person's pupil.

psychophysiology   A brain-image measurement process.

positioning advertising copytesting (PACT)   Principles to use when assessing the effectiveness of various messages.

REVIEW QUESTIONS

1. What is the difference between a message evaluation and respondent behaviors when assessing the effectiveness of an advertisement?

2. What does a concept test evaluate? How are storyboards and focus groups used in concept tests?

3. Describe the use of portfolio tests and theater tests in copytesting programs.

4. What is DAR? How are aided and unaided recall tests used in conjunction with DAR evaluations? What problems are associated with both types of tests?

5. What is a recognition test? How does it differ from a recall test?

6. What is a warmth monitor? What does it measure?

7. Describe how psychogalvanometers, pupillometric meters, and psychophysiology analysis techniques are used in evaluating advertisements.

8. How do the positioning advertising copytesting principles help advertisers prepare quality ads and campaigns?

9. What are the three forms of behavioral evaluations that can be used to test advertisements and other marketing pieces?

10. Name the measures of behavioral responses described in this chapter.

11. What items can be evaluated using test markets?

12. Describe a purchase simulation test.

13. Describe counting clippings and calculating the number of impressions as methods for assessing public relations effectiveness. What problems are associated with these two techniques?

14. Describe the advertising equivalence approach to assessing public relations programs.

15. Name and describe the criteria that can be used to assess the impact of the overall IMC program, as noted in this chapter.

CRITICAL THINKING EXERCISES

Discussion Questions

1. Create an advertising approach for one of the following products. Put the idea down in three or four sentences. Organize a small focus group of four other students in your class. Ask them to evaluate your advertising concept. What did you learn from the exercise?
   a. Retail pet store
   b. Baseball caps
   c. Computers
   d. Sweaters
   e. Watches

2. A very popular form of recall testing is day-after recall (DAR). Write down five advertisements you remember seeing yesterday. In addition to writing down the product and brand, note whatever else you can remember. Form into groups of four students. Compare your lists. How many commercials were recalled? How much could each of you remember about the commercials?

3. Pick out five advertisements you like. Conduct an aided recall test of these five ads. Ask five individuals, independently, if they saw the commercial. Mention only the brand name. If so, ask them to recall, in an unaided fashion, as much about the ad as they can. If they do not remember the ad immediately, give them cues. Be sure to record how much each person remembers unaided and how much each person remembers with aided information. Report your results.

4. Form into a group of five students. Ask students to write down two advertisements they enjoyed and their reasons. Ask students to write down two advertisements they dislike and their reasons. Finally, ask students to write down an advertisement they believe is offensive and their reasons. Ask each student to read his or her list comparing ads that were liked, disliked, and offensive. What common elements did you find in each category? What were the differences?

5. How important are sales figures in the evaluation of integrated marketing communications? How should hard data such as redemption rates and store traffic be used in the

evaluation of marketing communications? In terms of accountability, how important are behavioral measures of IMC effectiveness?

6. From the viewpoint of a marketing manager of a large sporting goods manufacturer, what types of measures of effectiveness would you want from the $500,000 you pay to an advertising agency to develop an advertising campaign? Knowing that evaluation costs money, how much of the $500,000 would you be willing to spend to measure effectiveness? What type of report would you prepare for your boss?

7. A clothing manufacturer spends $600,000 on trade promotions and $300,000 on consumer promotions. How would you measure the impact of these expenditures? If an agency was hired to manage these expenditures, what type of measures would you insist the company utilize?

8. Look through a magazine. Make a record of how many advertisements include methods for measuring responses. How many list a code number, a toll-free number, or a Web site? Just listing a toll-free number or a Web site does not ensure the agency or firm will know where the customer obtained that information. How can the ad agency or firm track the responses from a specific advertisement in the magazine you examined?

9. In some Asian countries it is improper to talk about oneself. Therefore, questions about feelings and emotions would be too embarrassing for citizens to answer. Those who answer the questions tend to provide superficial answers. Explain the advantages of a simulated purchasing test methodology in this situation. What other methods of evaluating feelings and emotions could an agency use in Asian countries?

INTEGRATED LEARNING EXERCISES

1. Pick five print or television advertisements that provide Web site URLs. Visit each site. Was the Web site a natural extension of the advertisement? What connection or similarities did you see between the Web site and the advertisement? Do you think your response was tracked? How can you tell?

2. Decision Analysts, Inc., is a leading provider of advertising and marketing research. The company's Web site is **www.decisionanalyst.com**. Access the site and investigate the various services the company offers. Examine the advertising research services that are available. Write a short report about how advertising research services provided by Decision Analysts could be used.

3. Reactions & Opinions, Inc. offers ad testing through the warmth meter technology discussed in this chapter. Access the Web site at **www.reactionsopinions.com**. Review how Reactions & Opinions conducts advertising research and

write a report on when and how Reactions & Opinions, could be utilized for advertising research. What are the advantages and disadvantages of each research methodology offered?

4. Ipsos-ASI at **www.ipsos-asi.com** is an advertising research firm that has developed a high level of expertise in ad testing and measurements. Access the company's products and services. What services are offered? When would the various services be used? How would each be used?

5. AdKnowledge and comScore Networks are two firms that excel at measuring Internet traffic and Internet advertising. Access their Web sites at **www.adknowledge.com** and **www.comscore.com**. What services are offered by each company? Which companies do you like the best? Why? Describe a research project that you feel each company could do successfully to assist in advertising or Internet research.

CREATIVE CORNER

Student Project

After leaders at PepsiCo and Starbucks became concerned about the diminishing supply of fresh, clean water, they teamed together to sell Ethos Water. The product's distribution has expanded and is now sold in major grocery stores, convenience stores, and drug stores. The goal of Ethos Water is to ensure that children throughout the world have clean water.

Access the Ethos Water Web site at **www.ethoswater.com**. After reviewing the site, design a print ad for a magazine aimed at college students in your area. When you have finished designing the ad, trade your ad with another student or ask him or her to show it to 10 students not enrolled in a class that is using this textbook. Explain to the student how to conduct a copytest to gather attitudes and opinions about the ad. Before conducting the copytest, make a list of questions that you want to ask. Some suggestions are:

1. Have you ever heard of Ethos Water?

2. What do you think is the primary message of this advertisement?

3. Does the copy make sense? Is it understandable?

4. Does the visual attract your attention?

5. What types of feelings does the ad elicit?

6. How likely would you be to access the Ethos Water Web site for more information?

7. What is your overall evaluation of the advertisement?

It is important that someone else conduct the copytest for you to gain honest answers. Respondents are less likely to be honest, especially about any negative feedback, if you show them the ad and they know you designed it.

CRUISING FOR INCREASED PROFITS

Adventure Cruises owns a fleet of ships that tour the Caribbean and the Bahamas and make trips to Hawaii. The company has been in operation for more than 20 years. Recently, there has been a drop in passengers on each voyage. Adventure's leadership believes increasing competition in the cruise ship industry, combined with additional new leisure-time activities, have led to the decline. Some worry that cruise ship tours are viewed as something "old people" do and that Disney has taken away the family cruise business.

To combat these problems, the marketing team at Adventure Cruises has decided on two tactics. First, the department will present a new ad campaign highlighting the advantages the company has compared to other lines. Second, a new type of passenger will be recruited, a "working business vacationer."

Adventure Cruise rebuilt the staterooms on 10 of its ships to accommodate business travelers. These individuals can be members of a company or guests of the company. The idea is to get the customer alone on a ship to conduct business for a series of days, all the while being able to enjoy the many features of cruise travel, including fine dining, gambling, shows, and stops at various ports. The advantage to the company is that it essentially has a "captive audience" when a customer is given a free cruise in exchange for doing business with the company footing the bill. Adventure Cruise intends to take out ads in business magazines and journals, selling these new packages to various business buyers. Adventure Cruise president Henry Crouch points out, "Lots of companies pay really big bucks to rent luxury boxes in football stadiums. They get the customer for what, 4 or 5 hours? We can offer them a chance to keep a customer for 4 or 5 *days.*"

Henry hired a large international advertising agency to prepare ads for both regular passengers and the new business-to-business market. Lauren Patterson was the account executive who signed the deal, by emphasizing that she would follow the Roper Starch copytesting principles. For cruise ship passengers, the ads would pass muster only if they met the following criteria:

1. *The eyes have it.* The ads must be clear and easy to follow.
2. *Never place copy above an illustration.* People see the picture first, so if the copy is higher, it's ignored.
3. *Great visuals work.* The idea is to capture attention and interest.

4. *Make sure the headlines and visuals blend with the copy.* Don't confuse the reader.
5. *Don't use confusing visuals.*
6. *Don't use confusing headlines.*
7. *Testimonials increase believability and readership.*
8. *Size matters.* The ad must be big.
9. *Keep it simple.* Readers are not as interested in the product as you are, so make the ad easy to follow.
10. *Break the rules.* Be creative.

In the business-to-business marketplace, three problems routinely occur. Lauren is going to insist that the ads avoid these problems. She calls them the ABC sins in business-to-business marketing. The problems are:

a. Ads that are not visually appealing
b. Ads that are abstract rather than designed with a human appeal
c. Ads that fail to emphasize the benefit to the business buyer

Henry realizes that these two markets (regular passengers and business customers) are somewhat distinct. Still, he believes Adventure Cruises should speak with one voice. He believes his company has three major advantages: better food, unusual entertainment, and excellent service. He wants to be sure that Lauren incorporates these three elements into the ads that appear on television and in the trade journals that they select.

1. Design a print ad for Adventure Cruises' regular passengers.
2. Design a print ad for Adventure Cruises' business customers.
3. What type of testing should be done during the design phase of the advertisement?
4. What type of testing should be done after the ad is designed but prior to placing it in a magazine or other print media?
5. What type of testing should be done after the advertisement is launched? How can the effectiveness of the advertisement be measured?

THE MEETING

John Mulvaney waited impatiently for a key meeting to begin. As the accounting executive for a new advertising agency in the Los Angeles area, he knew his company was in competition with over 400 other local agencies. His first major client was the CEO of Action Bowling, Inc., a company that owned nearly 30 bowling alleys in the greater metropolitan area.

Bowling suffers from the same stigma associated with several other activities—the perception that it is a pastime for the

elderly. Television ratings for bowling have dropped to the point where they are now rarely featured. The average age of a regular bowler continues to rise. Enrollments in youth bowling leagues has been on the decline.

Action Bowling hired an agency to conduct research regarding perceptions of its locations. Many believe that bowling alleys are still places where people chain smoke, even though local ordinances have prohibited indoor smoking for several years. Also, many perceive alleys as places for hoodlums to gather and play pool and pinball. Some express fears that the locations are actually dangerous for young people.

John had been tasked with creating an integrated advertising and promotions program for Action Bowling. His team developed a theme that focuses on a "new age" for bowling, in which exciting, action-oriented ads feature young people enjoying themselves in a safe, lighted, energetic atmosphere.

Commercial spots were purchased on local radio stations with rock formats. Television spots were placed on cable shows on MTV and other youth-oriented channels and programs, including some on the Disney network. Billboard buys were made near grade schools and high schools across the city.

Several consumer and trade promotions were also developed. A coupon program for free bowling during a birthday party or some other event was established. The coupons were printed in local school papers and given out at teen hangouts near each alley. A contest had been set up in which bowlers were ranked into brackets based on past scores. Prizes were given to tournament winners in each bracket.

Businesses were contacted with incentives to hold company bowling parties at the alleys. Tie-ins with a local hot dog restaurant were created so that someone who bought a hot dog for lunch was also entitled to a discount at a local bowling alley. As reminders, a set of coffee cups had been given out to HR managers in firms across the city. Copy on the cups mentioned that bowling was a great family activity, as well as an ideal social event for an organization.

Susan Rogers was the new CEO of Action Bowling. As she was driving to the meeting with John, she kept wondering how well her advertising dollars had been spent. In their first meetings, John had stressed the roles that ratings and GRP play in advertising effectiveness. She was particularly interested in effective reach and effective frequency as concepts. Now, however, she was considering an entirely new set of ideas.

John had spent a great deal of time explaining the concepts of recall and recognition. He also focused on ideas such as persuasiveness and behavioral responses. Susan wondered why he had shifted terminology. Her bottom line was that she wanted to know if the ads did anything to change people's minds about the sport or activity of bowling. She was interested in finding out if the campaign moved anyone to actually give bowling a try or return to something the person had long since abandoned.

Susan was a realist. She knew that rejuvenating interest in bowling would take time. The first question she intended to ask John was "Did this work?" quickly followed by "How long will it take to make a noticeable difference?" John was bracing himself. He knew his answers would have a major impact on his client's perception of his work and referrals to other companies in the future.

Creating a new generation of bowlers is one of the challenges for Action Bowling.

Source: Courtesy of Getty Images, Inc.– Photodisc.

1. Prepare John's comments about the relationship between ratings, GRP, reach, and frequency with recall, recognition, attitudes, and behavioral responses.

2. Which media do you think are connected to the concepts of recall and recognition for Action Bowling? Which are best for persuasion and actual behavioral changes?

3. Can you think of any type of public relations program that might have been helpful in these marketing efforts? How could you assess the effectiveness of any PR campaign?

4. Are there any other marketing tactics that John should have developed for Action Bowling? If so, what are they and how should they be evaluated?

ENDNOTES

1. Decision Analyst (**www.decisionanalyst.com**, accessed September 25, 2005); Patricia Riedman, "DiscoverWhy Tests TV Commercials Online," *Advertising Age* 71, no. 13 (March 27, 2000), pp. 46–47.

2. Gordon A. Wyner, "Narrowing the Gap," *Marketing Research* 16, no. 1 (Spring 2004), pp. 6–7.

3. "AAAA Survey Finds 8 Percent Hike in Cost to Produce 30-Second TV Commercials," *Film & Video Production & Postproduction*

Magazine (ICOM) (**www.icommag.com/november-2002/november-page-1b.html**, accessed January 14, 2005).

4. Stefano Hatfield, "Testing on Trial," *Creativity* 11, no. 9 (October 2003), pp. 18–21.

5. David W. Stewart, "Measures, Methods, and Models in Advertising Research," *Journal of Advertising* 29, no. 3 (1989), pp. 54–60.

6. Abhilasha Mehta, "Advertising Attitudes and Advertising Effectiveness," *Journal of Advertising Research* 40, no. 3 (May–June 2000), pp. 67–72.

7. William D. Wells, "Recognition, Recall, and Rating Scales," *Journal of Advertising Research* 40, no. 6 (November–December 2000), pp. 14–20.

8. Joel S. Debow, "Advertising Recognition and Recall by Age—Including Teens," *Journal of Advertising Research* 35, no. 5 (September–October 1995), pp. 55–60.

9. William D. Wells, "Recognition, Recall, and Rating Scales," *Journal of Advertising Research* 40, no. 6 (November–December 2000), pp. 14–20.

10. Jan Stapel, "Recall and Recognition: A Very Close Relationship," *Journal of Advertising Research* 38, no. 4 (July–August 1998), pp. 41–45.

11. William D. Wells, "Recognition, Recall, and Rating Scales," *Journal of Advertising Research* 40, no. 6 (November–December 2000), pp. 14–20.

12. Stapel, "Recall and Recognition."

13. Christina Merrill, "Roper Expands Testing," *Adweek Eastern Edition* 37, no. 45 (November 4, 1996), p. 6.

14. Steven P. Brown and Douglas M. Stayman, "Antecedents and Consequences of Attitude Toward the Ad: A Meta-Analysis," *Journal of Consumer Research* 19 (June 1992), pp. 34–51.

15. Douglas M. Stayman and David A. Aaker, "Continuous Measurement of Self-Report or Emotional Response," *Psychology and Marketing* 10 (May–June 1993), pp. 199–214.

16. Freddie Campos, "UH Facility Test Ads for $500," *Pacific Business News* 35, no. 23 (August 18, 1997), pp. A1–A2.

17. Patricia Riedman, "DiscoverWhy Tests TV Commercials Online," *Advertising Age* 71, no. 13 (March 27, 2000), pp. 46–47.

18. Steve Jarvis, "Minnesota Campaign Grabs Smokers by Throat," *Marketing News* 36, no. 8 (April 15, 2002), pp. 5–6.

19. Bruce F. Hall, "On Measuring the Power of Communications," *Journal of Advertising Research* 44, no. 2 (June 2004), pp. 181–88.

20. Steve Mclellan, "Mind Over Matter: New Tools Put Brands in Touch with Feelings," *Adweek*, (**www.adweek.com**, February 18, 2008).

21. Hall, "On Measuring the Power of Communications."

22. David W. Stewart, David H. Furse, and Randall P. Kozak, "A Guide to Commercial Copytesting Services," *Current Issues and Research in Advertising,* James Leigh and Claude Martin, Jr., eds. (Ann Arbor: Division of Research, Graduate School of Business, University of Michigan, 1983), pp. 1–44.

23. Based on PACT document published in *Journal of Marketing* 11, no. 4 (1982), pp. 4–29.

24. Amanda Beeler, "POPAI Initiates Study Tracking Effectiveness of Displays," *Advertising Age* 71, no. 15 (April 10, 2000), p. 54.

25. Chris Dillabough, "Web Lets Canadian Tourism Test Media Effectiveness," *New Media Age* (October 31, 2002), p. 12.

26. Kate MacArthur, "McDonald's Tests Ads That Focus on Service," *Advertising Age* 74, no. 1 (January 6, 2003), p. 3.

27. Tim Triplett, "Researchers Probe Ad Effectiveness Globally," *Marketing News* 28, no. 18 (August 29, 1994), pp. 6–7.

28. Kay Bransford, "Just Measure," *Communication World* 22, no. 1 (January 1, 2005), pp. 16–20.

29. Paul J. Cough, "Study: Marketers Struggle to Measure Effectiveness," *Shoot* 45, no. 29 (August 20, 2004), pp. 7–8.

30. Peter Drucker, *Management: Tasks, Responsibilities, Practices* (New York: Harper & Row, 1974).

Name/Organization Index

Subject Index